Universal Horrors

WITZEL
HOLLYWOOD

Universal Horrors

The Studio's Classic Films, 1931–1946

by

Michael Brunas
John Brunas
Tom Weaver

McFarland & Company, Inc., Publishers
Jefferson, North Carolina, and London

Frontispiece: A characteristic "mad" pose of Dwight Frye as Renfield in *Dracula,* 1931. (Photo courtesy Steve Jochsberger.)

British Library Cataloguing-in-Publication data are available

Library of Congress Cataloguing-in-Publication Data

Brunas, Michael.
Universal horrors : the studio's classic films, 1931–1946 / by Michael Brunas, John Brunas, Tom Weaver.
p. cm.
[Includes index.]
ISBN 0-89950-369-1 (lib. bdg. : 50# alk. paper) ♾
1. Horror films—History and criticism. 2. Universal Pictures Corporation. I. Brunas, John. II. Weaver, Tom, 1958–
III. Title.
PN1995.9.H6B7 1990
791.43'616—dc20 89-42706
CIP

Manufactured in the United States of America

McFarland & Company, Inc., Publishers
Box 611, Jefferson, North Carolina 28640

This book is gratefully dedicated to . . .

Ruth (Mrs. John Brunas), for her boundless love, devotion, and support, and her unswerving belief that her husband would some day write a book.

Mario "Matt" Brunas, who unwittingly created a pair of monsters by allowing his two young sons to stay up late to watch "Shock Theater."

Steve Jochsberger, the most dedicated and generous collector/fan we ever knew.

And to Bela. Poor Bela.

Table of Contents

Introduction

Divergent Schools of Thought

To today's generation of jaded slasher movie fanatics, the horror film had its roots in Herschell Gordon Lewis' slice-and-dice epics of the early '60s. The more broadminded among them harken back to the halcyon days of the Technicolored Hammer shockers of the '50s. What both these camps fail to realize is that the horror movie, as a popular American entertainment, owes its most substantial debt to the vintage Universal classics of the early '30s. These timeless films, once revered by nearly all horror fans, have nowadays all too often been contemptuously dismissed as too temperate and too removed from today's morbid preoccupation with entrails and prosthetics. Consequently, those who appreciate the subtler, more artistic films of the past are becoming increasingly alienated by what passes for macabre film entertainment today.

This sorry situation can only become worse. The early classics have virtually disappeared from the television airwaves as the major markets dump their black-and-white inventories. The horror film scene has become splintered into two distinct subgenres, with the output of the past 25 years bearing little resemblance to the movies of old.

Reappraising the Classics

The aim of this book is to examine the Universal horror film not only as a body of work, but on a picture-by-picture basis. The times *have* changed and many of these movies are ready for a fresh evaluation. Classic reputations, once etched in stone, have fallen by the wayside, while some of the more creative, entertaining B's and other lesser titles have yet to receive their full due. Indeed, many of these pictures have not been appraised, individually or collectively, since they were written up in the trade papers upon their original release.

It's disenchanting that general film buffs often have more respect for the Universal classics than the so-called horror fans who tend to shun them today. While posters, lobby cards and other paper treasures are increasing astronomically in value, the movies themselves have begun to be taken for granted.

Although it's true that films such as *Dracula, Frankenstein* and *The Wolf Man* have lost their edge in their ability to frighten an audience, they still rank as vintage Hollywood classics while even the more mediocre titles have retained their ability to thrill and entertain audiences.

That Was Then, This Is Now

The history of Universal can be traced back to 1906, when Carl Laemmle, a 39-year-old German emigrant with high aspirations, returned to Chicago after holding down a bookkeeper's post in an Oshkosh clothier's store and opened up a chain of nickelodeons. Under the banner of the Laemmle Film Service, he set up a series of exchange offices in the western United States and Canada. In April, 1909, Laemmle pulled out of the Patents Company, organized Independent Motion Pictures and incorporated Yankee Films Company. Between 1909 and 1912, the industrious tycoon produced a variety of low-budget multireelers.

In 1912, Laemmle joined forces with Robert H. Cochrane, Charles Bauman, David Horsley, Pat Powers and W.H. Swanson to form Universal Film Manufacturing Company. Three years later, the company gave birth to Universal City, a 230-acre municipality in the San Fernando Valley that offered the motion picture producers an expansive area for the development of soundstages and a diverse terrain for exterior shooting.

Over the next 20 years, Universal grew into one of the major forces of the film industry. Under the guiding genius of *Wunderkind* Irving Thalberg, stars such as Rudolph Valentino, Wallace Reid and Lon Chaney, and a powerhouse of a director like Erich von Stroheim, carried the studio on a wave of prestige and profits through the early '20s. When Thalberg and Universal parted ways, the studio was left without a strong, creative influence in the production department, and suffered greatly.

Lewis Milestone's 1930 achievement *All Quiet on the Western Front* won Universal its first Academy Award for Best Picture of the Year and restored some of its prestige in the industry. With the advent of the talkies, major talents such as James Whale, John M. Stahl and a budding William Wyler were entrusted with the studio's most valuable story properties. First-class productions like *Back Street, Waterloo Bridge, Counsellor-at-Law, Only Yesterday,* and of course, the early horror classics *Dracula, Frankenstein* and *The Invisible Man,* made an impact at box offices across the nation.

Yet, despite this glowing track record, Universal Pictures was in dire trouble. The dynasty that "Uncle Carl" Laemmle built was slowly crumbling. The devastating effects of the Depression, an industry-wide strike that forced the studio to cease production for several months, and charges of gross nepotism (the beneficent "Uncle Carl" imported shiploads of relatives and friends from Germany and employed them in dozens of diverse positions) created turmoil and had a negative effect on the studio's profit margin. Net losses exceeded profits quarter after quarter. (The accounting department's report for the nine months ending October 31, 1932, showed a net loss of $759,646, a figure greater than the profit for the whole year of 1931.)

Wall Street sources predicted in January, 1934, that every company in the business with the exception of Universal would show a considerable profit for 1933. This grim forecast was not refuted by the ailing film factory.

Faced with financial ruin, Laemmle seriously considered offers from entertainment competitors to buy the studio from him. In October, 1935, he left for New York to talk turkey with one of several groups of enterprising businessmen which expressed an interest in acquiring the studio. He flatly refused to sell out to Warner Bros. Still clinging to the slim chance that he could salvage his company, Laemmle hoped to induce former Columbia manager Sam Briskin to take charge of the lot for him. The deal didn't come off.

On November 1, 1935, Laemmle was forced to enter a deal with J. Cheever Cowdin's Standard Capital Corporation and tycoon Charles R. Rogers to secure emergency funds to sustain his studio. The two businessmen lent Laemmle the sum of $750,000 with the stipulation that they be given the option to buy the studio within three months at a cost of $5.5 million.

Confident that the returns on his new slate of pictures would stave off financial ruin, Laemmle agreed to the terms of the loan. It was a fatal mistake. Cowdin and Rogers amassed enough capital to purchase 90 percent of Universal's stock. On March 14, 1936, the Laemmle empire toppled, and the Standard Capital Corporation assumed control of the sprawling studio.

From the ashes of the Laemmle empire rose the "New Universal." J. Cheever Cowdin was named chairman of the board; Robert H. Cochrane, one of the studio's original founders, became the new corporation's president, and Charles R. Rogers moved into Carl Laemmle, Jr.'s former position as vice president in charge of production.

Twenty-eight-year-old Junior Laemmle planned to make a comeback in pictures by starting his own production company. Instead, he ended up at MGM as an associate producer but resigned shortly after, without a single film to his credit. "Uncle Carl" Laemmle retired to his palatial home in Beverly Hills and died three years later at the age of 72.

Unlike Laemmle, Rogers ruled the lot with an iron fist. Joe Pasternak, a Universal production head in Central Europe, was brought to Hollywood. The "shining light" of the new Universal, Pasternak produced *Three Smart Girls* (1937), which brought immediate stardom to an unknown pubescent soprano named Deanna Durbin. The picture's success saved the shaky new corporation.

After the release of *Dracula's Daughter* in May, 1936, all horror film projects were dropped from the production schedules to make way for low-budget action subjects, innocuous musicals and comedies.

Less than two years after the Cowdin-Rogers takeover, Universal was once again courting bankruptcy. The 1937–38 season had been a financial disaster and a rift had developed between the company's business partners; in short, the immediate future of the revamped film studio seemed bleak indeed. On November 30, 1937, Nate Blumberg, who had been in charge of theater operations at RKO, was elected president, ousting Cochrane. Six months later, on May 20, 1938, Rogers resigned, and Cliff Work, also from RKO, succeeded him as vice president in charge of production.

The new production team pulled off a miracle. The savvy reissuing of *Frankenstein* and *Dracula* pumped some much-needed coin into the company's coffers, prompting the production of the costly *Son of Frankenstein,* which reaped similar rewards. Within three years, Blumberg turned a financially ailing film studio into a profit-making enterprise again.

Unlike the formidable Rogers, Blumberg was a genial, benign presence. Although he had no previous experience making films, he was an adept organizer, kept up the morale of his work force, and possessed a great sense of mass entertainment, all crucial ingredients in running a successful lot.

Universal's good fortunes started wearing down in the mid–40s, as the studio's main attractions began to suffer from overexposure. On November 28, 1945, Universal joined hands with J. Arthur Rank's United World Pictures and a new production company, International Pictures Corporation, was founded. A program of modernization and improvement of the Universal City studio and the construction of added soundstages was put into effect.

The merger of Universal and International Pictures on July 31, 1946, was the biggest amalgamation since 20th Century took over Fox in the '30s. Nate Blumberg was pushed up to the position of chairman of the board, while William Goetz (that rare breed, a sharp businessman with aesthetic values) and Leo Spitz took charge of production.

Goetz had no use for Abbott and Costello and even less for the menagerie of monsters he inherited, but was keenly aware of their box office power. So, between releasing such prestige fare as *A Double Life* (1947) and such J. Arthur Rank British imports as *Black Narcissus* and *Great Expectations* (both 1946), Goetz begrudgingly gave the go-ahead to such box office bonanzas as *The Egg and I* (1947) and the Abbott and Costello monster matches. This shotgun marriage of art and popular entertainment, an uneasy compromise that Goetz was forced to live with, saved Universal-International from a premature demise.

The next decade brought about greater dramatic changes in the film studio's hierarchy. In November, 1951, Decca Records acquired 28 percent of Universal-International's stock. Five months later, Goetz and Blumberg sold out their stock to Decca, thus giving the recording company controlling interest. Milton R. Rackmil, Decca's president, also took over the presidency of Universal-International, while Nate Blumberg remained chairman of the board. Edward Muhl became the new production vice president in July, 1953.

Glossy soap operas starring the likes of Lana Turner and Jeff Chandler, frothy Doris Day–Rock Hudson bedroom farces, Western shoot-'em-ups, and of course, science fiction pictures with strong horrific elements constituted the company's output in the '50s.

In June, 1962, the MCA talent agency was converted to a holding company for Universal and Decca. The talent agency and the International tag was gradually dropped. Four years later, Universal became the subsidiary of MCA, Inc., the feature film production division of Universal City Studios, Inc., Hollywood's busiest television series factory. MCA's Jules Stein and Lew Wasserman assumed control of the conglomerate.

In the early '70s, Universal reaffirmed its standing in the industry as a financial powerhouse with a flock of box office triumphs including such all-time moneymakers as *Airport* (1970), *The Sting* and *American Graffiti* (both 1973), and *Jaws* (1975), one of the highest grossing films of all time.

Universal City, a Disneyland-style complex, offers the visitor to Southern California a behind-the-scenes glimpse into movie, television and video production, as well as a variety of amusement park attractions built around the studio's past successes and forthcoming pictures. It ranks under the two Disney parks as one of America's busiest tourist traps.

The Thrill of It All

Only the devoted film fan can fully appreciate the experience of discovering and handling original papers and documents that pertained to the Universal heyday. Contracts, assistant directors' reports, budget sheets, scripts, memos—memorabilia such as these hold a special significance for the person who's spent countless hours in front of the television and in darkened screening halls enjoying these movies.

To such a fan, the experience, as we three authors had, of actually meeting and interviewing the survivors of this bygone age is a rare privilege and a delight. Lunching with Frances Drake at the Beverly Hilton Hotel, chatting about Karloff and Lorre and Colin Clive. Discussing Lugosi's earliest days in America with Arthur Lubin. Remembering Lon Chaney, Jr., with his old-time hunting and drinking buddy Peter Coe. Learning personal details about George Zucco from John Howard and Alex Gordon. Finding out what *really* went on at those polite English tea breaks from *Tower of London's* Rose Hobart. Talking with Gloria Stuart about doing the town with James Whale. Unearthing the Mummy memories of Peggy Moran and Virginia Christine. Enjoying the running commentary of our late friend Reginald LeBorg as he watches his own film *Destiny* for the first time in more than 40 years (and enjoying derisive yuks *with* the director as we all screen *Jungle Woman*). Swinging down memory lane with Vincent Price, Curt Siodmak, Acquanetta, Virginia Grey, Patric Knowles, Henry Brandon, Carroll Borland, the late Henry Koster, Victoria Horne, Grey Shadow, Moose and Peanuts, Susanna Foster, Anna Lee, Robert Clarke, the late Nell O'Day, Hillary Brooke, Richard Davies, Don Porter, Richard Gordon, Harry J. Essex, the late Edward Dein, Fritz Feld, Gil Perkins, Anthony Eisley, the late Jerry Warren, Beverly Garland, Gloria Talbott, Howard W. Koch, Jack Pollexfen, Harry Thomas, Gordon Hessler, Edward Bernds ... and a special person whom we are honored to call our friend, Martin Kosleck.

And may the wrath of Amon-Ra descend upon the handful of aging starlets, would-be actors and uppity directors who enjoyed and encouraged the gifts of video tapes, stills and other assorted goodies with no intention of consenting to the interviews they knew we were seeking.

A Thousand Thanks

In preparing this book, we had the pleasure of making new friends and taking every advantage of our old ones: Forry Ackerman, Bill and Roberta

Amazzini, Lou Antonicello, the Brunas "kids," Ernie Catucci, John Cocchi, Dave Domzal, William K. Everson, Robert Franklin, Donna Hope, Tom Johnson, Greg Luce, Greg Mank, Dave McDonnell, **our moms,** Niel Palmieri, Ed Robins, Mary Runser, Florence Seibold, John Skillin, Tony Timpone, Ed Watz and Jon Weaver.

To those who contributed above and beyond the call of duty, we owe special thanks. Ned Comstock of the University of Southern California film department library painstakingly excavated reams of invaluable Universal production records. Michael Fitzgerald, author of Arlington House's *The Universal Story* and probably the world's number one fan and authority on the subject, invited us to his annual reunions of Universal players and provided many of the anecdotes he's collected through the years. Once again, Mark Martucci came to the rescue with his staggering video collection and store of knowledge. The late Stephen Jochsberger gave us *carte blanche* to his fabulous archive of stills and other material. Jim Knusch furnished his professional photographic services. James LaBarre offered his technical expertise and invaluable support. And Donald Ybarra, a special friend, made us a gift of his computer equipment and came to the rescue when the complexities of high tech proved to be more than we could handle.

Final note: The most frustrating aspect of research is not the inability to come up with that elusive bit of data, but the difficulty in sorting out the correct information from the wrong. Release dates, running times, credits, character names, and all manner of facts are prone to all sorts of interpretations. Trade newspapers, theater source books, interoffice memoranda, cast sheets, assistant director's reports—even the main or end title credits on the prints themselves—are not always trustworthy sources of accurate information. (Often a main title will carry the names of actors not present in the final cut, or misspell a performer's or a character's name, or attribute a role to the wrong actor or actress.) It's a very frustrating endeavor, this business of writing a book about films and keeping it free of error. But you have our word that we've done our best.

Michael Brunas, John Brunas *and* Tom Weaver
December, 1989

Dracula (1931)

Released February 14, 1931. 75 minutes. *Associate Producer:* E.M. Asher. *Produced by* Carl Laemmle, Jr. *Directed by* Tod Browning. *Screenplay by* Garrett Fort. *Continuity by* Dudley Murphy. *Based on the novel by* Bram Stoker *and the 1927 stageplay by* Hamilton Deane & John L. Balderston. *Scenario Supervisor:* Charles A. Logue. *Cinematographer:* Karl Freund. *Art Director:* Charles D. Hall. *Film Editor:* Milton Carruth. *Supervising Film Editor:* Maurice Pivar. *Recording Supervisor:* C. Roy Hunter. *Set Designers:* Herman Rosse & John Hoffman. *Photographic Effects:* Frank J. Booth. *Musical Conductor:* Heinz Roemheld. *Makeup by* Jack P. Pierce. *Set Decorations:* Russell A. Gausman. *Costumes:* Ed Ware & Vera West. *Casting:* Phil M. Friedman. *Research:* Nan Grant. *Art Titles:* Max Cohen.

Bela Lugosi (Count Dracula), Helen Chandler (Mina Seward), David Manners (John Harker), Dwight Frye (Renfield), Edward Van Sloan (Professor Van Helsing), Herbert Bunston (Dr. Seward), Frances Dade (Lucy Weston), Joan Standing (Maid), Charles Gerrard (Martin), Moon Carroll (Briggs), Josephine Velez (Grace, English Nurse), Michael Visaroff (Innkeeper), Daisy Belmore (English Coach Passenger), Nicholas Bela, Donald Murphy (Coach Passengers), Carla Laemmle (Girl), Tod Browning (Harbor Master).

The vampiric vanguard of the first Universal horror cycle, *Dracula* was for years revered as perhaps the best-known of all vintage horror films, a sacred cow among buffs in general and Bela Lugosi fans in particular. Time, alas, has proved to be less kind to the film than to its ageless protagonist: *Dracula* is now widely regarded as the least satisfying of the Universal originals. The film remains rich in historical importance, and its inestimable influence is felt to this day: in the minds of most people, Bram Stoker's Count Dracula wears the face of Bela Lugosi. But while the film's reverberations are still being felt more than a half century later, *Dracula* is now recognized as a film of missed opportunities. After a highly-promising, much-talked-about opening, its macabre mood quickly dissipates, leaving its viewers immersed in a lot of stagebound boudoir intrigue.

Written in 1897, the novel *Dracula* was the work of Dublin-born Bram Stoker. Sickly as a child (he could not stand or walk until the age of seven), Stoker grew into a red-haired giant of a man with a keen interest in writing. His first novel, a romance titled *The Snake's Pass,* didn't create much of a stir, but *Dracula* was an instant and immense success. *Dracula* is written in epistolary style, with chapters comprised of a grab-bag of personal letters, diary musings, entries in a ship's log, newspaper accounts as well as a phonograph diary.

While popular in its own era, the novel *Dracula* is a crashing bore today, with people, places and repetitive episodes described down to the last exasperatingly minute and unnecessary detail. Writer C.K. Hillegass rightly calls the novel an example of a type of literature in which the kernel idea far transcends the execution. (Stoker's mother liked the book very much and felt it would bring Bram into immediate prominence, but, after all, that's what moms are for.) Stoker's later works included *The Mystery of the Sea* (1902) and *The Man* (1905) as well as horror/mystery novels like *The Jewel of Seven Stars* (1903), *The Lady of the Shroud* (1909) and *The Lair of the White Worm* (1911). (*The Jewel of Seven Stars* was filmed twice, in 1972 as *Blood from the Mummy's Tomb* and in 1980 as *The Awakening; The Lair of the White Worm* came out in 1988.) Stoker's biographers didn't know (or avoided mentioning) the cause of his death in 1912 until his own grandnephew cited it in his 1975 book *The Man Who Wrote Dracula* as locomotor ataxy—also known as general paralysis of the insane—implying that Stoker had contracted syphilis.

The first film version of Stoker's novel was the 1922 German film *Nosferatu,* from the famed Expressionist director F.W. Murnau. Since the filmmakers did not secure the literary rights to *Dracula,* they made plot alterations and changed character names to camouflage their otherwise baldfaced piracy, but the Stoker estate was not fooled: they sued, won, and (unsuccessfully) sought to have all prints of the film destroyed.

Two years later, British producer Hamilton Deane (once a friend to Stoker) presented a stage version of "Dracula" at the Grand Theatre in Derby, England. A modernized retelling of the Stoker story, it was a huge success which Deane was able to take on tour for the next three years.* The play finally opened at London's Little Theater on February 14, 1927, with a well-publicized trained nurse in attendance for the benefit of the weak-hearted; critics blasted the production, but Londoners packed the house. Horace Liveright, an American producer, bought it for Broadway, hiring John L. Balderston to streamline and further update the hoary plot. Forty-four-year-old Bela Lugosi, a stage star and screen matinee idol in his native Hungary, now an obscure political refugee scratching for work in a new country, took on the role of the thirsty count. The other leading roles were played by Dorothy Peterson (as Lucy Harker), Edward Van Sloan (Van Helsing), Herbert Bunston (Dr. Seward) and Bernard Jukes (Renfield). A hit, "Dracula" ran for 261 performances, finally closing in New York in May of 1928 and going on tour.

Universal had been keeping its corporate eye on "Dracula" ever since London theatergoers began queuing up outside the Little Theatre, but the difficulties of conveying the story in a silent version seemed insurmountable;

**Deane, who was also an actor, had initially intended to play the part of the Count in the production, but circumstances forced him to accept the larger role of vampire-hunter Van Helsing. Dracula was played by Raymond Huntley, who in his later film career was strangled by Christopher Lee in Hammer's* The Mummy *(1959).*

"I bid you . . . welcome." Bela Lugosi as *Dracula.*

interoffice communications from studio readers argued against the purchase of the property because of censorship problems. (One reader sternly reproved, "Were this story put on the screen, it would be an insult to every one of its audiences.") But both these barriers were lifted with the near-simultaneous birth of the talkies and a lessening of the censors' clout, and treatments and continuities of various lengths were solicited from such Universal scenarists as Fritz Stephani, Louis Stevens and Louis Bromfield. In August, 1930, the studio bought the rights to the book and play for $40,000, and less than a month later a completed script was turned in by Dudley Murphy. Johnny-come-lately Garrett Fort contributed some finishing touches and received sole screen credit.

The title page of a fourth draft final script dated September 26, 1930, splits the credit for adaptation and dialogue between Fort and Tod Browning, who was signed to direct the picture. Lon Chaney, Sr.'s "favorite" director, Browning had his reputation as a horror specialist etched in stone for many years until, one by one, his rarest and most promising-sounding silent horror and mystery films began coming to light; more often than not these eagerly awaited "rediscoveries" were revealed as turgid, plotty bores, each representing one more nail in the once-fabled director's critical coffin. Indisputably there are themes and other common threads running through Browning's work, which to many is the sign of an auteur and a stylist, but Browning's handling of these films is too often mechanical and aloof. His best-known silents are remembered because they star the still-popular Chaney, Sr., but they're not the best or most famous of Chaney's films; Browning's only notable sound films are again "carried" by their stars—Bela Lugosi in *Dracula* and *Mark of the Vampire,* and a gang of *Freaks.*

Carroll Borland, who played Luna in *Mark of the Vampire* (1935), can recall almost nothing about the noncommunicative Browning except that he dressed in loud sports coats and looked more than anything else like a racetrack character. "He seemed to simply stand around and puff on his cigarette, and I really didn't get much direction from him at all. He simply was not what you would expect a director of horror films to be like." Browning's apologists, whose numbers are a-dwindling, blame the sick and exploitative *Freaks* (1932) for his Hollywood decline (this "compassionate" look at the lives of circus grotesqueries created a storm of controversy and was widely banned), but the simpler truth probably was that his pedestrian, old-fashioned style and characteristically morbid film themes no longer had any place in the film capital. Browning made his last film (*Miracles for Sale*) in 1939, and *Variety* published—in error—his obituary in 1944. Career-wise they were right, but Browning lingered on this earth right up into the early 1960s.

Not surprisingly, the unknown Lugosi was not Universal's initial choice for the Dracula role. The senior Chaney was of course the natural, but the star character actor had been stricken with bronchial cancer. While the Chaney name would certainly have insured box office success for the movie, the legendary Man of a Thousand Faces seems a poor choice as the Transylvanian bloodsucker. Without his traditional gobs of facial makeup, the Colorado-born Chaney looked like a Midwestern trucker or a Detroit gangster; had he lived, it seems likely that he would have eventually drifted toward Wallace Beery-style roles. The idea of Chaney skulking around ruined castles with a cape and phony accent is almost ludicrous; there's no reason to suspect that he would have fared any better than his own son did playing a well-fed middle-American Count in 1943's *Son of Dracula.* (Chaney, Sr.'s last film, released after his death, was the 1930 sound version of *The Unholy Three,* in which the actor plays a snarling criminal mastermind; in the final scene he boards a prison train with a carton of cigarettes tucked under his arm!) Chaney died August 26, 1930, just four days after Universal secured the rights to *Dracula.*

Other candidates for the role included Paul Muni, Ian Keith, William Courtenay and Conrad Veidt. Of these four, only Veidt seems like a viable contender; Keith eventually got the chance to play a vampire-type in a 1946 Republic cheapie, *Valley of the Zombies,* and chewed the scenery unforgivably. Supposedly John Carradine also came under consideration; the actor later made a fine Count in *House of Frankenstein* and *House of Dracula,* but at age 24 Carradine would probably have been entirely wrong. Eventually the stage Dracula prevailed: Lugosi was brought in for a screen test and came away with the coveted role, the first in a $500-a-week, two-picture deal. A Universal A-picture budget of $355,050 was allotted to the film, and cinematographer Karl Freund's cameras began grinding on the morning of September 29 on the studio's backlot country inn set.

The film's credits unreel to the melifluous strains of Tchaikovsky's *Swan Lake,* a restful musical piece that Universal curiously chose to play behind the titles of several of their early horror thrillers. Renfield (Dwight Frye), a British real estate salesman, has traveled to Transylvania to finalize a sale of property in England to Count Dracula. The proprietor of a local inn (Michael Visaroff) gravely warns that Dracula is a vampire, but Renfield disregards what he knows can only be peasant superstition and politely states his intention to continue on to Castle Dracula. Boarding a coach, he journeys yet deeper into the mist and gloom of the Carpathian Mountains.

As night falls over the desolate countryside, the undead Count Dracula (Bela Lugosi) and his three undead brides rise from their coffins in the catacombs beneath his castle. "Disguised" as a coachman, the Count is waiting at midnight at a prearranged spot as the coach carrying Renfield arrives. Transferred to the vampire's coach, Renfield endures a rough ride which terminates at the door of Dracula's castle.

The vast interior hall of Castle Dracula remains the most imposing set from any of the vintage horror films, fully living up to the description in the script:

> . . . a huge, square affair, in the manner of ancient feudal castles, with a long, impressive-looking staircase at the back. There is no furniture of any sort. . . . Dust is piled thick on every side – cobwebs – mold – broken architraves – bits of crumbling masonry which has fallen from the roof. . . . Across the steps a little way up from the first landing is a giant, dust-covered spider-web. . . .

Descending the stairs, and passing (off-camera) through the still-unbroken web, comes Dracula, who welcomes Renfield to his ruined castle. Leading the solicitor into a "more inviting" upstairs chamber, Dracula finalizes the real estate deal before serving Renfield a goblet of wine.

But the drink has been drugged: after Dracula leaves, Renfield feels its effects and staggers to the nearby terrace windows, where he is accosted by a huge bat and faints. Dracula's brides appear, hovering hungrily over Renfield's prostrate body, until Dracula enters from outside and silently motions his brides away. Dracula now crouches over Renfield, moving in on his unprotected throat. (Poor continuity mars the finale of this classic vignette: a wall of fog not present in one shot appears in the next; "bat" Dracula exits to the left just before "human" Dracula enters from the right.)

The first two reels of *Dracula* are nearly perfect, packed with grim atmosphere and classic set pieces; unfortunately, from here on it's all downhill. The scene switches to a storm at sea, as the crew of the England-bound schooner *Vesta* battles to keep their boat from capsizing. In the cargo hold, a now-insane Renfield exhorts his "master" Dracula to rise from his coffin, and reminds the vampire of his promise to provide him with lives ("Not human

Helen Chandler, Bela Lugosi and Dwight Frye in an obviously posed shot, from *Dracula.* (Photo courtesy Steve Jochsberger.)

lives, but *small* ones—with *blood* in them!"). Dracula ascends to the deck and watches dispassionately as the crew fights the gale. In the film the ensuing carnage is not depicted, although the original script calls for Dracula to stalk and kill the crew members in an impressionistic montage. The derelict ship eventually drifts into England's Whitby Harbor, where the sailors' deaths are conveniently attributed to the storm. Lunatic Renfield, discovered in the hold, is committed to the private lunatic asylum of a Dr. Seward.

Now at large in London, Dracula proceeds to a concert hall where he makes the acquaintance of Dr. Seward (Herbert Bunston), his daughter Mina (Helen Chandler), her fiancé John Harker (David Manners) and the Sewards' weekend house-guest Lucy (Frances Dade). Dracula is attracted to the lovely Lucy, and puts the bite on her that night at the Seward home. Despite transfusions, Lucy later dies in a London hospital. Seward consults with the eminent Dutch scientist Professor Van Helsing (Edward Van Sloan), who perceives at once that they are dealing with the undead. Van Helsing also suspects that Seward's patient Renfield, who is obsessed with the idea that he must eat flies and spiders for their blood, is in league with the vampire.

Mina falls ill and complains of strange dreams; unbeknownst to her father and fiancé, she has become Dracula's newest unsuspecting victim. Van Helsing detects that the vampire is at work again and, when Dracula pays a somewhat ill-timed visit to the Seward home, the scientist deduces that the Transylvanian Count is their culprit.

All sorts of humdrum comings-and-goings ensue, with Renfield escaping from his cell at regular intervals, Dracula making an attempt on Van Helsing's life and a worsening Mina trying to put the bite on Harker. As dawn approaches, Dracula steals into the house once again and abducts the somnambulistic Mina. Renfield makes another of his periodic escapes, unknowingly leading Van Helsing and Harker to Dracula's lair at nearby Carfax Abbey.

Sensing (wrongly) that Renfield has betrayed him, Dracula kills his slave, tossing his body down a massive staircase (another jaw-dropping set with few equals in the early horror films). The sun is rising as Van Helsing and Harker burst into the Abbey and discover Dracula abed in his coffin. Van Helsing drives a wooden stake through the vampire's heart, releasing Mina from his unearthly spell.

Dracula was completed in mid–November, 1931, after 42 working days. A Spanish-language version was filmed on the *Dracula* sets at night for the foreign-language market. Carlos Villarias starred as Dracula in this version, although at least one exterior long shot of Lugosi turns up in the film.

The flaws inherent in *Dracula* are so self-evident that they are outlined in nearly every critique; only Lugosi freaks and the nostalgically inclined still go through the motions of praising and defending the film. The main problem is that it hews too closely to the play, abandoning many potentially exciting scenes delineated in the novel. Browning is slavish in his faithfulness to the stage production, indulging in wearisome long takes and filming scenes in long and medium shots as though the audience were viewing the proceedings through the proverbial proscenium arch. Any action not seen in the stage production remains off-screen here as well (Dracula's flight from the Seward home in wolf form, Mina's midnight confrontation with the vampire Lucy, Renfield and his army of rats); later descriptions of these events add to the verbiage of an already overly-conversational film.

Bela Lugosi's excruciatingly slow delivery seems to set the pace for the other players as well as for the film itself. It's a flawed, hammy, stagy performance and far from the best work that Lugosi did in films. Lugosi had an eerie magnetism and a sensually sinister presence which made him something of a screen idol for the short period when he was really in his prime. Time marches on, however, and the attributes which caused women to swoon and actresses like Carroll Borland to call him "probably the most sexually attractive male I have ever known in my life" are largely lost on modern movie-watchers. Lugosi's ashen face, slicked-back hair and beestung lips give him the look of a creep, not a Casanova; his accent and stiff, halting delivery add to that impression of weird decadence.

Undeniably Lugosi had just the right exotic "undead" look for a role like Dracula, but his broad, unnatural acting in this initial go-round leaves much to be desired. There's more humor than horror in those big screen-filling silent closeups of Lugosi looking alternately stunned, bemused, goony and stoned; the shot of Lugosi sizing up Dwight Frye with what can only be described as bedroom eyes seldom fails to get a laugh. And even the staunchest Lugosi devotees would probably be hard-pressed to defend their idol while he's mangling a fairly simple line like, "Vee vill be *le-e-e-eaving* . . . to-*morrow* . . . *e-e-e-e-e*-veningkk!"

Lugosi remains, however, the very incarnation of suave screen evil, and portrayed vampires to near-perfection in other films. Lugosi's is a truly frightening presence in *Mark of the Vampire,* possibly because he never speaks while in his vampire guise; whatever flaws the film may have, there's something ghoulishly gratifying about the way the horror scenes are overloaded with grim atmosphere. *The Return of the Vampire* (1943) was an obvious Universal clone with a somewhat juvenile plot, but Lugosi's performance as vindictive vampire Armand Tesla (who is Dracula in everything but name) is strong and effective.

Purists may howl, but Lugosi seems at or near his vampiric peak in the bastard child of the Universal horror series, *Abbott and Costello Meet Frankenstein* (1948). Smooth, articulate and at-ease despite the ravages of drugs and approaching old age, he gives one of his best '40s performances; it's one of the few comedies where Lugosi not only seems to finally be in on the jokes, but is actually enjoying himself.

Lugosi apparently had what amounts to a love/hate relationship with the Dracula character throughout his long career. Playing the role in the 1931 film eventually led to bitterness on the actor's part; Universal reaped millions from *Dracula* and its later reissues, and even from merchandising, but Lugosi never saw a nickel of it. He craved roles that were not in the Dracula/bogeyman mold, but Hollywood bigwigs (and movie audiences) could picture him as little else.

Lugosi obviously was his own worst enemy: he never bothered to completely master the English language, showed an amazing lack of judgment in his choice of film roles, and had a mulish, hard-headed streak which screwed up everything his other foibles didn't. He turned down the "undignified" role of the Monster in *Frankenstein* partly because he didn't care to be unrecognizable beneath heavy makeup, yet the following year he was caterwauling under artless clumps of facial hair in Paramount's *Island of Lost Souls;* two short years after *Dracula* he was already lampooning the role (and himself) in a *Hollywood Parade* opposite a flesh-and-blood Betty Boop.

In actuality Count Dracula was probably the best friend Lugosi ever had; it's tough to imagine him ending up as anything more than the Paul Lukas of Poverty Row had the film role of Dracula not come his way. And probably Lugosi knew this as well. Despite his lofty pretensions and his frequent coulda-been/shoulda-been sulks, his last wish was to be buried in his Dracula cape.

While Lugosi dominates the first two reels of *Dracula,* he turns up only occasionally thereafter; the presence and menace of Dracula are felt throughout the film, but Lugosi only has three major scenes ahead of him once he leaves his Carpathian digs. The task of carrying the film now falls onto the shoulders of Helen Chandler, David Manners, Dwight Frye and Edward Van Sloan.

Van Sloan, undeservedly fifth-billed, really becomes the star of the film after the first third, at least in terms of screen time; it's a shame that this is probably one of his least enjoyable performances. Van Sloan appears to be trying to match or outdo Lugosi's funereal delivery: he speaks too slowly and precisely, as though lecturing a backward child. The actor also has the annoying habit of talking with his hands, gesticulating at every character to whom he talks, then never putting his hands *down;* many shots end with Van Sloan silently standing in what almost looks like a boxer's stance. Van Sloan is one of the best-loved character actors from the old horror films, but his baby-talk and lugubrious rolling of r's in *Dracula* is atypically amateurish and irritating. (Surely it was Browning who elicited this performance; when Van Sloan reprised the Van Helsing role in *Dracula's Daughter,* he had the ratatat delivery of a Warners stock player!) Another curious *faux pas* in *Dracula* is that Van Sloan wears impossibly thick-lensed glasses throughout the film, and then discards them just before the finale.

Helen Chandler and David Manners are inadequate romantic leads. Chandler's much-persecuted Mina is a wistful, weak-willed heroine; one author recently wrote that the actress appears far too bloodless to attract any self-respecting vampire, a criticism well-taken. By all accounts, Chandler went through life with her head in the clouds, but her movie career certainly never got off the ground. Once touted as "the new Lillian Gish," as though we needed two of them, her career petered out around 1937; health and emotional problems, not to mention an inordinate fondness for the grape, had her in and out of sanitariums and hospitals for many years. She died forgotten in 1965.

David Manners holds the enviable distinction of starring in three of the best-known classic horror films—*Dracula, The Mummy* and *The Black Cat*—but his fey pretty-boy looks and the callow, lovesick characters that became his stock-in-trade have won him few fans among the horror crowd. Manners' John Harker is a particularly stuffy and petulant bore, always on the verge of bollixing up Van Helsing's meticulously-laid plans.

Bela Lugosi was typecast as a horror film star after *Dracula,* but he got off easy compared to poor Dwight Frye. Frye's unique, bizarre portrayal of Renfield remains one of the more striking performances in the movie, mostly for the wrong reasons; the one-time Broadway player was typecast as morons, ghouls and hunchbacks from that point on. "If God is good, I will be able to play comedy in which I was featured on Broadway for eight seasons and in which no producer of motion pictures will give me a chance!" Frye whined in the pressbook for *The Vampire Bat* (1933). "And please, God, may it be before I go screwy playing idiots, halfwits and lunatics on the talking screen!"

Apparently God never read the *Vampire Bat* pressbook, for Frye remained solidly entrenched in that ignominious little niche. Born in Kansas and raised in Colorado, Frye caught the acting bug early, worked in vaudeville and even sang and danced in something called "La La Lucille." After a few years doing stock he found himself on Broadway, where he generally got good notices for his work; he also owned and operated a 69th Street tearoom patronized by stage personalities of the era. While appearing in a play on the West Coast he was spotted by a Warner Bros. representative and hired for the small role of a machine-gun toting hood in the 1930 gangster picture *The Doorway to Hell.* This *Doorway* led to other Frye film roles as undersized tough guys, including the part of gunsel Wilmer in 1931's *The Maltese Falcon.* But *Dracula* abruptly and permanently changed the diminutive actor's screen image.

Like other performances in *Dracula,* Frye's is oft-praised even though it's mostly hammy and indulgent. Renfield seems a bit of a queen in early scenes with his effeminate look and prissy manner; he's less restrained and more effective in the later segments set in London. Unfortunately, the "mad" Renfield character serves little real purpose in the film: there's never any hint of what services he renders for Dracula, nor any indication why he takes such an intense interest in Mina's well-being. He often seems on the brink of spilling his guts to Van Helsing when an abrupt mood shift turns him back into the cagey, tight-lipped Renfield once again, rendering the whole damn scene pointless.

Frye is at his best in the brief scenes where his character's "normal" side gleams through; the vignette of Renfield hopelessly sobbing in his cell is actually rather moving, and more of a highlight than the protracted soliloquy ("Rats . . . rats-s-s . . . *rats-s-s-s-s!*") which he directs at the camera in an outdated stagebound rendition.

The remainder of the cast ranges from the competent (Herbert Bunston as Dr. Seward, Frances Dade as Lucy) to the completely inept (Charles Gerrard as a Cockney guard, Michael Visaroff as the innkeeper). Dade, whose screen time is unfortunately limited, is a strikingly pretty actress whose brief performance seems more realistic than those being given around her, and it's not surprising that Dracula passes over demure Mina and makes Dade's Lucy his first victim. Lucy returns from the dead in the film and goes off on her own modest vampiric spree; in the script there's a mood-crusted scene in which Van Helsing and Harker observe Lucy as she returns to the Weston family vault after one of her midnight jaunts.

A number of interesting scenes and minor visual touches are described in the *Dracula* script but do not appear in the film.* Obviously Universal executives had not forgotten the less-than-encouraging initial comments of the studio's readers, and sought to downplay the horror wherever they could. (The

**The script includes several scenes of Dracula with fangs bared and also depicts his victims' neck wounds. The description of Dracula's rampage on board the storm-swept* Vesta *makes for particularly exciting reading. The script calls for a sequence filled with flash-cuts of "furiously increasing tempo": a closeup of the captain at the wheel screaming; faces of sailors wild with fear; a large closeup of Dracula with fangs bared; a sailor plunging over the rail into the surging sea; and finally a huge and impressive shot of Dracula, "arms upraised, dark cloak billowing in the gale, about to close in upon a screaming, helpless wretch he has cornered." None of this is seen in the film (we dissolve from a shot of Lugosi in a ship's doorway to a large closeup of a wharf pile around which a ship's hawser has been looped; the* Vesta *has arrived in Whitby, and the voice of an off-camera harbor master played by Tod Browning describes the tragedy).*

Time has been kind to neither Bela Lugosi's performance nor to his classic vehicle, *Dracula*. (Note Bela's cigar on a door bolt at left.)

blame might rest with Browning, but considering the fact that the man gave poor taste a bad name the following year with *Freaks,* it isn't likely that the horrific touches in the *Dracula* script offended him.) The result, after those first two magnificent Transylvania-set reels of chills and atmosphere, is a talky, thin-blooded filmed play, a tepid melodramatic exercise with tame and timorous horror embellishments.

Universal was indecisive, too, in their marketing of the film: they debuted it on Valentine's Day, 1931 (four years to the day after the play's London opening), playing it up as a Gothic romance. Whereas the play had advertised itself as "The Ultimate in Horror," Universal dubbed its new macabre feature "The Story of the Strangest Passion the World Has Ever Known."

The judgment of time has sadly gone against *Dracula,* and most of the film's problems stem from Browning's unskilled direction. Perhaps Browning's idea was to fashion a deliberately paced, hypnotic film that would weave a spell over its audience; if so, the director was unable to sustain the required mood. Certainly it must be kept in mind that *Dracula* was made in 1930 while the motion picture industry was in a period of transition from silents to talkies; filmmakers were suddenly encumbered by the limitations of the microphone, and stagebound drawing room affairs became the order of the day.

Die-hard fans can see the *Dracula* that could have been in the film's Spanish-language incarnation. Directed by George Melford and photographed by George Robinson, it's a strikingly good film brimming with fine camerawork and inventive directorial touches. In a well-researched article on the Spanish *Dracula* in *Midnight Marquee,* writer Bill Littman asserts that "if Tod Browning's direction of the Lugosi version looks dull enough without comparison, it withers completely when viewed against Melford's work."

Like the novel and play before it, there's the germ of a great idea in Universal's *Dracula* but it's quickly sterilized by an unimaginative and impassive director. After the initial reels build up all sorts of expectations, the film becomes a creaky antique that not once budges the needle on the drama meter. Not surprisingly, even the men behind *Dracula* had their reservations. John L. Balderston wrote in a studio memo that the film's last third dropped badly; Bela Lugosi apparently saw it as a bungled opportunity, and harped on the idea of one day starring in a worthier remake. Even Tod Browning, when asked in 1936 which of his own films was his favorite, bypassed *Dracula* and named the silent *The Unholy Three.*

An already anemic film, *Dracula* was further emasculated prior to a mid–30s reissue. Renfield's screams (as he is being choked by Dracula) and the Count's own cries (as the stake is pounded into his heart) were removed from the soundtrack. A quaint closing curtain speech delivered by Van Helsing was also deleted.

Dracula was more or less remade just one year later by Universal: transposed to Egypt, the plot of *Dracula* was revamped into *The Mummy,* which is a carbon-copy of *Dracula* right down to individual scenes. Hollywood moviemakers had marched forward in seven-league boots since the production of *Dracula,* and the infinitely better *Mummy* is a film that looks ten years removed from Browning's stodgy piece.

A number of screen Draculas have come and gone in the decades since the Universal version: Lon Chaney, Jr., John Carradine, Christopher Lee, Francis Lederer, Jack Palance, Louis Jourdan, Klaus Kinski, Frank Langella and many more. For all its primitivism, crude special effects and sunlit scenes of midnight, it's still Murnau's *Nosferatu* that probably ranks as the best screen version of the Stoker tale.

Dracula's flaws are legion; its stately pace, stolid direction and overripe performances quickly betray it; the absence of a musical score is keenly felt during its many painfully protracted stretches of complete silence. But its importance in film history and its influence on later films is tremendous. It set forth all the conventions of the archetypal vampire film, laying groundwork that would be capitalized upon in scores of latter-day follow-ups. It sparked Lugosi's unique horror career and, most importantly, spawned the classic Universal horror series of the early '30s. Its status as a movie milestone is untarnished.

Frankenstein (1931)

Released November 21, 1931. 71 minutes. *Produced by* Carl Laemmle, Jr. *Directed by* James Whale. *Screenplay by* Garrett Fort, Francis Edwards Faragoh, John Russell (uncredited) & Robert Florey (uncredited). *Based on the composition by* John L. Balderston. *Adapted from the play by* Peggy Webling. *From the novel* ***Frankenstein; or, The Modern Prometheus*** *by* Mary Wollstonecraft Shelley. *Associate Producer:* E.M. Asher. *Scenario Editor:* Richard L. Schayer. *Continuity:* Thomas Reed. *Director of Photography:* Arthur Edeson. *Supervising Film Editor:* Maurice Pivar. *Film Editor:* Clarence Kolster. *Art Director:* Charles D. Hall. *Recording Supervisor:* C. Roy Hunter. *Set Designer:* Herman Rosse. *Makeup by* Jack P. Pierce. *Assistant Director:* Joseph A. McDonough. *Technician:* William Hedgcock. *Special Electrical Effects:* Kenneth Strickfaden, Frank Graves & Raymond Lindsay. *Technical Advisor:* Dr. Cecil Reynolds. *Music by* David Broekman. *Property Master:* Eddie Keys.

Colin Clive (Henry Frankenstein), Mae Clarke (Elizabeth), John Boles (Victor Moritz), Boris Karloff (The Monster), Edward Van Sloan (Dr. Waldman), Frederick Kerr (Baron Frankenstein), Dwight Frye (Fritz), Lionel Belmore (Herr Vogel, the Burgomaster), Marilyn Harris (Little Maria), Michael Mark (Ludwig), Arletta Duncan, Pauline Moore (Bridesmaids), Francis Ford (Extra at Lecture/Hans, the Wounded Villager on Hill), Mary Sherman.

In spite of the unparalleled box office performance of *Dracula,* Universal Studios remained a crippled giant. The studio heads desperately sought to get the company's finances in order, often resorting to laying off its employees. Carl Laemmle, Sr., fancied his company to be one of the bulwarks of the industry but, unlike the other majors, Universal did not own a vast chain of theaters hungry for a steady flow of new product. The studio's reliance on independently-owned theaters for most of its business placed it at a serious disadvantage. Less critical, but undeniably vexing, was the constant charge of nepotism leveled against the studio.

Director Henry Koster recalled working on the Universal lot in the early '30s:

> Carl Laemmle brought all of his relatives over from Germany. They used to say the European comes over here not to start as a producer, but to establish a beachhead. At Laemmle's studio, everybody was a Laemmle. I remember reporting for work on one of my first days at Universal. One of the reception

policemen said to me, "You're Mr. Koster?" I said, "Yes. And you're Mr. Laemmle, aren't you?" He said, "Oh, you know me?"

In those more imaginative days, talk of a sequel wasn't the instant reaction to a major hit. But the disreputable horror genre was looming as a necessary market if the studio was to remain solvent. Tod Browning's retreat to his home base, MGM, did little to deter the studio's ambition to follow *Dracula* up with another horror feature. Universal's real challenge was to find the right material.

Frankenstein: or, The Modern Prometheus, Mary Wollstonecraft Shelley's sprawling Gothic nightmare of a novel, quite unfilmable without considerable pruning, was an attractive possibility. The novel was well known and inspired at least one earlier film, Thomas Edison's 1908 short, though it was barely remembered by the early '30s.

Universal's classic movie version of *Frankenstein* is recognized as the brainchild of French-born writer-director Robert Florey with the picture's actual director, James Whale, a relative latecomer in the picture's genesis. Florey was invited to the studio by story department head Richard Schayer to work on a horror property. Edgar Allan Poe's "The Murders in the Rue Morgue" and H.G. Wells' *The Invisible Man* fit the bill but the director was pushing the idea of bringing *Frankenstein* to the screen. Stripping the novel down to its bare essentials, Florey delivered a treatment to meet Universal's rigid length and budget requirements. If Shelley's turgid plotting, meandering construction and philosophical diversions were drawbacks to the novel's appeal, Florey's streamlined, unadorned adaptation was, in contrast, simplicity itself. Florey compressed the novel's lumbering narrative into a modernistic horror mode, confining the action to a handful of sets while retaining the allegorical feel of the material. Shelley's novel was rendered all but unrecognizable, but it provided Universal with an ideal property. The go-ahead was given for a complete script.

Florey's first draft of the screenplay, written in collaboration with Garrett Fort, reveals the director's significant contribution to the finished film. Although most of the dialogue (reportedly written mainly by Fort) would be revised, the script outlines virtually every scene in the finished film, with some minor adjustments. That Florey did not receive official screen credit is a shameful injustice.

Florey's test reel of *Frankenstein,* virtually his audition for the studio brass who were still unsure of the director as well as the subject matter, remains one of the most sought-after of the lost Hollywood treasures. Photographed by Paul Ivano, the footage (which lasted only 20 minutes after editing) showed Bela Lugosi in Jack Pierce's early makeup design of the monster. The reel did not finalize the studio's choice as to who was to direct the film, and Florey was left in limbo until a decision was reached.

James Whale, in the meantime, was riding high at the studio, having just adapted Robert Emmett Sherwood's play "Waterloo Bridge" to the screen, greatly improving it in the process. It was one of the few prestige pictures the studio produced that year and Carl Laemmle, Jr., gave the director *carte*

blanche to select any property the studio owned for his next picture. The pickings were slim but *Frankenstein* offered Whale the opportunity to get away from the war subjects with which he was rapidly becoming identified. (Besides *Waterloo Bridge* [1931], Whale's most notable achievement was directing the film and stage versions of R.C. Sherriff's "Journey's End.")

Despite this early acclaim, Whale's now-famous flamboyance had yet to materialize on the screen. *Journey's End* (1930) and *Waterloo Bridge* (long suppressed to make way for MGM's glossy remakes; today it's practically a lost film) demonstrated more than anything Whale's sensitivity and intelligence as well as his gift for handling actors. Most notable was his direction of an inexperienced newcomer named Mae Clarke, who played the prostitute Myra in *Waterloo Bridge* with heart-rending persuasion.

Whale's entry into *Frankenstein* forced out a crestfallen Florey who, to his chagrin, discovered his one-picture contract did not stipulate a specific title. Having no other recourse, he assumed directorial duties on *Murders in the Rue Morgue,* a project which didn't nearly fire his imagination as *Frankenstein* had. Florey, at least, picked up Universal's leading horror player, Bela Lugosi, who was more than happy to forsake the nonspeaking role of the Monster.

Francis Edwards Faragoh was recruited to submit a rewrite of the *Frankenstein* script, adding at Whale's insistence some mild comic touches to the decidedly downbeat material. Unlike the somber, purposeful Florey, Whale had a whimiscal spirit and beefed up his cast with with eccentric, amusing supporting players. Seizing the opportunity to inject a bit of cantankerous humor into the dully written role of old Baron Frankenstein, Whale cast British comedy player Frederick Kerr, whom he directed in *Waterloo Bridge.* Bette Davis, an ingenue who had a featured role in *Waterloo Bridge,* was briefly considered for the part of Elizabeth, but Whale understandably favored Mae Clarke.

Discussing her casting in the role, Clarke said in an interview many years later, "When Jim was preparing *Frankenstein,* he chose me for the part of Elizabeth. Like John Ford, he had his own stock company. I was the reigning queen on the lot for a short spell and we were all treated like royalty. . . . I was supposed to do the part with an English accent to blend in with Colin Clive's. There was an English touch to the whole production."

The part of Victor Moritz, Henry Frankenstein's rival in love, went to Universal's up-and-coming leading man John Boles, a fittingly uninteresting role for a singularly uninteresting actor. There was no need to look beyond the cast of *Dracula* to fill the roles of Dr. Waldman and Fritz, Frankenstein's misshapen laboratory assistant. Edward Van Sloan and Dwight Frye, both holdovers from Florey's test footage with Lugosi, were born to the parts.

The casting of the lead role of Henry Frankenstein was a crucial decision. Leslie Howard was suggested, but Whale's first choice was Colin Clive, the neurotic young actor who had replaced Laurence Olivier in the original stage production of "Journey's End." Clive's bearing suggested learning and sensitivity, but his deep-rooted restlessness and insecurity marked him for high-

Colin Clive, Edward Van Sloan and Dwight Frye do their best to keep a good monster (Boris Karloff) down, in *Frankenstein*.

strung, slightly over-the-edge characterizations. He was, in short, perfect for the part.

Lugosi's rejection of the role of the Monster left a vacancy which could not be filled by any of the studio contract players, leaving Whale no choice but to look elsewhere. Among the half-dozen contenders was a lean, imposing Shakespearean actor/movie bit player by the name of John Carradine (he was usually billed as John Peter Richmond at this time). With a temperament that matched Lugosi's, the young actor announced with finality he was not available for nonspeaking roles and walked out on a test which might have catapulted him to stardom. "I have no regrets," Carradine said in a 1986 talk show appearance. "The fellow who did get it was a good actor and a very charming guy."

The "charming guy" was, of course, Boris Karloff, who steadfastly claimed in the ensuing decades that it was luck and a chance encounter with James Whale at the studio commissary which led him to be cast in the history-making role. But David Lewis, who was living with Whale at the time, insists he was the one who suggested to the director that Karloff would make an ideal Monster after spotting him as a killer in Howard Hawks' *The Criminal Code* (1931).

After several lean years, Karloff was beginning to establish his Hollywood career, usually playing small-time villains and crooks. He had already worked with an impressive array of directors such as Lewis Milestone, Mervyn LeRoy, Michael Curtiz and Raoul Walsh, but always in featured roles. Carl Laemmle told the press, "Karloff's eyes mirrored the suffering we needed." But the actor was never his first choice.

To Karloff, the role of the Monster was a gamble as well as a dramatic challenge. At one point in the production, he confided to Edward Van Sloan that he felt the picture would ruin his career. He had little fear of being recognized; the grueling makeup sessions with Jack Pierce have been reported to be as brief as three and a half hours and as long as eight. Karloff's slender six-foot body was propped up to over seven feet.

The idea of a square-shaped head for the Monster came to Pierce while he was watching a surgical operation on a man's head. The abnormal shape represented how the top of the head would look removed, with more gray matter piled in and a new cranium supplied to accommodate the oversized brain. An artificial skull was fitted over Karloff's head and he was covered with a thick layer of grey-green greasepaint. Artificial veins were actually strips of cotton soaked in collodion and the actor's hands were encased in plaster. Pierce worked slowly and meticulously; even the slightest bit of makeup caused unbearable pain when caught in the actor's eyes.

Of the $262,007 budget, $10,000 was spent on the electrical effects alone. Frank Graves, Kenneth Strickfaden and Raymond Lindsay were in charge of the picturesque electrical gadgetry installed in Frankenstein's mountaintop laboratory. The devices were given exotic names like a lightning bridge, bariton

Boris Karloff in *Frankenstein:* a splendid example of Charles D. Hall's Expressionistic sets. (Photo courtesy Steve Jochsberger.)

generator, vacuum electrolyzer and nucleus analyzer. The publicity department's claim that each device carried over a million and a half volts fooled no one, but the scene was designed to be the most spectacular in the movie.

Production started on August 24, 1931. The first scene shot, quite appropriately, was the first page of the script, on Charles D. Hall's hill and cemetery set, constructed especially for the film. The picture wrapped on October 3, five days over its allotted schedule.

For the uninitiated: *Frankenstein* is set on the outskirts of the Tyrolean Alps. Henry Frankenstein (Colin Clive), a brilliant if erratic medical student, works in secret, assembling a human body from parts of corpses stolen from graveyards. Needing only a brain to complete his artificial man, he sends his hunchback assistant Fritz (Dwight Frye) to his old medical school. There, Dr. Waldman (Edward Van Sloan) placed on exhibit two specimens of the human brain for his anatomy students. Dropping the jar containing a normal brain, Fritz grabs the other specimen, unaware that it has been removed from the body of a psychopathic killer.

Henry's fiancée Elizabeth (Mae Clarke), his friend Victor Moritz (John Boles) and Dr. Waldman set out for Henry's mountaintop laboratory one stormy night to try to persuade Henry to give up his experiments. They find the obsessed young scientist on the brink of madness. He sets his fabulous electrical apparatus in operation, sending the artificially conceived body to the rooftop where it is baptized by a powerful bolt of lightning. The body descends back into the lab, endowed with life, as Henry rejoices in triumph.

But Frankenstein's joy is short-lived. His creation (Boris Karloff) is more monster than man, the obvious result of the abnormal brain stolen from Waldman's lecture hall. Viciously intimidated by Fritz, the Monster slays the hunchback at his first opportunity. He is overpowered by a massive dose of tranquilizer administered by Henry and Waldman. Waldman urges Frankenstein to resume his wedding plans while he prepares to dispose of the Monster by dissection.

On the eve of Henry's wedding, Waldman is about to begin his grim task of dissecting when the Monster comes out of the anesthesia and strangles Waldman to death. While roaming the countryside, the Monster comes across a little peasant girl, Maria (Marilyn Harris), who innocently befriends the brute. The encounter ends in tragedy with the Monster accidentally drowning the child in a pond.

Frankenstein's wedding is rudely interrupted by the news of the murders. The Monster crashes into Elizabeth's bedroom, sending her into shock. Henry leads a search party after his creature as the bloodhounds track him into the mountains. Confronting the Monster, Henry is quickly overpowered and dragged to an abandoned windmill. The villagers arrive on the scene and set the decaying structure ablaze. The Monster throws Henry's body to the ground below and becomes trapped in the inferno. Pinned under the falling rafters, the pitiful creature is consumed by the flames.

The film's climax presented Whale with the vexing problem of what to do with Henry Frankenstein. As the results of his experiments culminated in several gruesome deaths, it seemed rather unfair to have him go unpunished.

Florey's intention was to have the father of the little girl take advantage of the confusion at the windmill and "accidentally" shoot Henry to death while presumably aiming for the Monster. Florey ended his script on a distinctly downbeat note, with Elizabeth, Victor and old Baron Frankenstein praying for Henry's soul in a funeral scene. Whale, too, opted for a tragic wrap-up with the deaths of the creator and his creation, but at the last moment settled on a conventional happy ending with Henry recovering from his wounds and Elizabeth sitting at his bedside. Ironically, the sequel revises the original ending, starting the story off with Henry being mistaken for dead by the villagers.

Frankenstein went on to its well known success but only by surveying Hollywood trade papers in those last three months of 1931 can one appreciate the furor it unleashed. The picture was phenomenal, smashing box office records and igniting a storm of controversy wherever it played. Far from being regarded as the artful, literate horror classic it is now considered, *Frankenstein,* in its day, was seen as a grisly, blood-soaked example of exploitative filmmaking. Its detractors were numerous and vocal.

The picture was literally mangled by censors in Kansas City, who ordered that 32 cuts be made on all prints screened in their district. The "approved" version cut the original running time in half, rendering the film incomprehensible. Incensed editorial writers responded so loudly to this butchery that the governor was forced to take a hand, resulting in the restoration of all the missing footage. Carl Laemmle, Jr., expressed his gratitude to the newspapers for championing free speech, but inwardly the young executive was probably snickering with delight. The uproar undoubtedly sent box office grosses even higher.

The Motion Picture Theatre Owners Association, feeling the pressure of civic groups, did an about-face. Urging its members to discourage producers from making horror movies, the organization knew the plea would fall on deaf ears. The exhibitors were making a bundle on *Frankenstein* as well as Paramount's latest horror release, *Dr. Jekyll and Mr. Hyde* (1931).

For years Universal continued to make a fortune off *Frankenstein,* but predictably very few of the spoils trickled down to the creative talents. Karloff and Whale soon found themselves clashing with the Laemmles over well-deserved pay hikes. Universal retained the rights to Jack Pierce's world famous makeup years after they canned the genius in 1947.

Playwright John L. Balderston successfully fought for a bigger piece of the action. Shortly before Florey penned his version of the screenplay, Balderston was commissioned to adapt a stage version of the Shelley novel by Peggy Webling for 1 percent of the film's profits. In 1951, Balderston filed a joint-suit with Webling's estate demanding 1 percent of the gross of the *entire eight film series.* A lavish out-of-court settlement was reached, but to suggest Webling's and Balderston's contribution extended to *Abbott and Costello Meet Frankenstein* (1948) is as laughable as the movie itself. Ironically, Florey has claimed he never bothered to read Balderston's adaptation in the first place!

Frankenstein, unlike *Dracula,* is a film that doesn't need apologies, and rightfully takes its place as Universal's first great all-talking horror movie. Yet it's easy to take the film for granted. Countless imitations have taken a bit of

***Frankenstein*'s Monster (Karloff) experiences joy for the first time.**

the gleam off its reputation and the picture stubbornly stands in the shadow of its first sequel. To be fair, *Bride of Frankenstein* was a self-conscious attempt to outdo the original and had the advantage of far greater resources. While *Bride* certainly rates as a better movie, there's a unique appeal in the original's simplicity and lack of pretense. And *understatement.*

The original is one of the few films without a score that actually *doesn't* need one (a credit to Whale's alert visual style). The scene of Frankenstein and Waldman breaking into the Monster's chamber to find Fritz's twisted body dangling from the ceiling in a long shot is just one moment that works very well without musical punctuation. Even minus orchestral accompaniment, the soundtrack is unusually rich. The climactic mountaintop pursuit of the Monster is accompanied by the mournful baying of bloodhounds and the jeers of the villagers. The windmill scene is played against the rhythmic creaking of the pump shaft. Considering that *Frankenstein* was made when film composing was a fledgling art and that most scores of this period were usually undistinguished or worse, the lack of music actually works in the movie's favor.

The grandiose, self-mocking style of the sequel is absent in the original. *Frankenstein*'s stylistic indebtedness to such silent classics as *The Cabinet of Dr. Caligari* (1921) and *The Golem* (1919) have been somewhat exaggerated through the years. Whale opted for a starker, more naturalistic realism here than in *Bride* (no one could ever mistake *Frankenstein* for a fairy tale). It's a horror movie played for shocks, although they have been greatly diluted by time and imitation. Like the film's humor, the undercurrent of sympathy for the Monster isn't strained.

Karloff himself preferred his nonspeaking but no less inventive performance in the original to his work in the sequel. After *Frankenstein*'s release, the actor was instantly hailed as "the new Lon Chaney," but the typically self-effacing Boris refuted the title. "He was the master," Karloff said in early 1932. "No one suffered as he did to bring a tragic, poignant quality to his roles." Karloff went so far as to suggest that almost *any* actor could have played the role. It *is* true that no other actor brought the dimension that Karloff brought to the character, but it is equally true that none of these actors enjoyed the benefit of Whale's direction.

Karloff's early performances were uneven and he tended to lay it on a bit thick in pictures like *The Unholy Night* (1929), *Five Star Final* (1931) and *Behind the Mask* (released in 1932, but actually shot before *Frankenstein*). He excelled in *The Criminal Code* (1931) as the homicidal plug-ugly, a virtual warm-up for his stint as the Monster. Later producers tended to cast the Monster role for name value (Chaney, Jr., and Lugosi) for physical prowess (Glenn Strange and virtually all of the Hammer players, including Christopher Lee), but Whale may have been the only director to cast the role with an eye on characterization. Whale brought out the best in Karloff, who displayed a gift for mime untapped in earlier roles.

Brian Taves, Robert Florey's biographer, makes an unconvincing case that *Frankenstein* would have been a much better film under Florey's direction. Florey's banishment from the official credits was unpardonable, obscuring his considerable input in the final cut. But to suggest that Florey is a better director than Whale merely exposes Taves as a writer with an axe to grind. Using Florey's *Murders in the Rue Morgue* as a basis of what could have been expected from his version of *Frankenstein,* one imagines an ingeniously designed but dramatically stilted movie, a dated classic that could be admired for its technical niceties but falling far short as entertainment. Whale lagged behind Florey visually but was far more at ease with the language, possessed a far sharper wit and was a far more discriminating judge of actors. Florey's operatic indulgences were exactly what Whale was burlesquing in *Bride of Frankenstein*; it simply wasn't the stuff to attract a mass audience. The final proof is that Florey never had a major Hollywood hit. Had he directed *Frankenstein* there might not have been a series at all.

The casting of Colin Clive was another unmistakable Whale contribution. Poor Clive: even star billing in a Hollywood classic failed to launch a major career. Karloff unexpectedly walked away with most of the attention, upstaging even Whale, much to the director's surprise and irritation. Even today, Clive is usually compared unfavorably to Peter Cushing in Hammer Studio's derivative series of the '50s and '60s. Cushing is almost always excellent but the roles are entirely different conceptions and are difficult to compare.

Clive's Henry Frankenstein is a tragic hero so driven by ambition he only sees when it is too late the horror he has spawned. His tortured inner conflict and guilt are mistaken for weakness and indecisiveness, especially by writers drum-beating the Hammer pictures. But Clive's less colorful character at least has a solid basis in Shelley's novel and his downfall underscores the novel's less-than-subtle quasireligious theme. Hammer retained Shelley's original name of "Victor" Frankenstein and little else. The Cushing character was more of a sinister, "Victorian" version of Brian Donlevy in the studio's Quatermass films of the mid-50s, an outlaw scientist who justifies his criminal acts to the bitter end.

He's a strong, compelling character, but it reduces the Shelley novel to a classy mad-scientist potboiler.

Except for the bland John Boles, Whale's cast selection is sound. Mae Clarke's Elizabeth is refreshingly real and unflowery. Frederick Kerr's comedy relief as the crotchety old Baron Frankenstein is genuinely funny and the reliable Edward Van Sloan is the perfect Waldman. Lionel Belmore as the much put-upon Burgomaster and Dwight Frye as Fritz are classic supporting contributions.

The inclusion by MCA of the rather tame missing footage of *Frankenstein* in the video release was welcome but a bit anticlimactic. These long unseen snippets of film, including the drowning of Maria, don't amount to much and only call attention to how little it took to shake up a 1931 audience. *Frankenstein* has long since lost its ability to frighten, but the film still exerts a hypnotic power. Technically, it's a marvel, from Arthur Edeson's atmospheric lensing to Charles D. Hall's sumptuous, Expressionistic sets. Whale's talents hadn't quite peaked, but he still towered over the average studio director and his excellent judgment is everpresent. Add Karloff's milestone performance and one realizes that *Frankenstein* is still a warhorse worth viewing and reviewing.

Murders in the Rue Morgue (1932)

Released February 21, 1932. 62 minutes. *Associate Producer:* E.M. Asher. *Produced by* Carl Laemmle, Jr. *Directed by* Robert Florey. *Screenplay by* Tom Reed & Dale van Every. *Based on the story "The Murders in the Rue Morgue" by* Edgar Allan Poe. *Adaptation by* Robert Florey. *Additional Dialogue:* John Huston. *Scenario Editor:* Richard Schayer. *Cinematographer:* Karl Freund. *Art Director:* Charles D. Hall. *Recording Supervisor:* C. Roy Hunter. *Film Editor:* Milton Carruth. *Supervising Film Editor:* Maurice Pivar. *Musical Director:* Heinz Roemheld. *Special Effects:* John P. Fulton. *Special Process:* Frank Williams. *Makeup by* Jack P. Pierce. *Set designer:* Herman Rosse. *Assistant Directors:* Scott Beal, Joseph McDonough & Charles S. Gould. *Technical Advisor:* Howard Salemson.

Sidney Fox (Mlle. Camille L'Espanaye), Bela Lugosi (Dr. Mirakle), Leon Waycoff [Ames] (Pierre Dupin), Bert Roach (Paul), Betsy Ross Clarke (Mme. L'Espanaye), Brandon Hurst (Prefect of Police), D'Arcy Corrigan (Morgue Keeper), Noble Johnson (Janos, the Black One), Arlene Francis (Woman of the Streets), Edna Marion (Mignette), Charlotte Henry, Polly Ann Young (Girls), Herman Bing (Franz Odenheimer), Agostino Borgato (Alberto Montani), Harry Holman (Landlord), Torben Meyer (The Dane), John T. Murray, Christian Frank (Gendarmes), D. Vernon (Tenant), Michael Visaroff, Ted Billings (Men), Charles T. Millsfield (Bearded Man at Sideshow), Monte Montague (Workman/Gendarme), Charles Gemora (Erik, the Ape), Joe Bonomo (Double for Gemora), Hamilton Green (Barker), Tempe Pigott (Crone).

> "You're like a song the girls of Provence sing on Mayday. And like the dancing in Normandy on Mayday. And like the wine in Burgundy on Mayday. Aw, Camille, I love you!" "And I love you, too, Pierre!" [Leon Ames and Sidney Fox, *Murders in the Rue Morgue*].

For both Robert Florey and Bela Lugosi, dissociation from *Frankenstein* signalled unfortunate career turning points: Florey never again had the opportunity to direct a film with that sort of potential, and Lugosi, in backing away from the project, allowed for the emergence of a horror screen rival (Boris Karloff) who would quickly eclipse him. In retrospect, the studio's consolation prize to the two men, *Murders in the Rue Morgue,* seems quite a poor crumb of comfort. A midibudgeted oddity, it features some of Lugosi's broadest acting, a lurid and silly script, and the sort of avant-garde directorial excesses which made it look like a curio even in its own day.

Arlene Francis never lived down her role as an ill-fated hooker in *Murders in the Rue Morgue,* with Bela Lugosi (left) and Noble Johnson.

The idea of adapting Poe's public domain tale to the screen occurred to Universal in the early part of 1931, while *Dracula* was in release and *Frankenstein* in preparation. A story treatment was ready by April, Lugosi was slated to star and George Melford, who had helmed the atmospheric and highly cinematic Spanish-language version of *Dracula,* was assigned to direct. But when Robert Florey suddenly found himself shooed off of *Frankenstein,* the French director wound up in charge of *Rue Morgue* instead. A severe slash in the film's planned budget (from $130,000 to $90,000) incensed Florey, who stalked off the picture, only to be coaxed back a short time later. The film was in production 23 days, commencing October 19, 1931, and wrapping November 13 (appropriately a Friday). Encouraged by *Frankenstein*'s grosses, Universal put the picture back into production in December, upping the budget to a total of $186,090 after seven days of retakes and added scenes.

Attending a carnival in 1845 Paris, medical student Paul Dupin (Leon

Ames) and his sweetheart Camille (Sidney Fox) are drawn to a unique sideshow. Dr. Mirakle (Bela Lugosi), a strange foreign type, expounds his theory of evolution, and displays a caged ape which Mirakle announces is the ancestor of present-day man. Mirakle tells the onlookers that his life is consecrated to one great experiment: to prove man's kinship with the apes. Paul and Camille move forward to examine Mirakle's ape, Erik, more closely; the simian is attracted to the lovely Camille. Mirakle, who clearly has some sinister plot in mind, orders his servant Janos (Noble Johnson) to trail Paul and Camille when they leave the carnival.

Later that night, after secretly following the lovers to Camille's home, Mirakle and Janos watch as two men fight over a prostitute (Arlene Francis) on a Seine embankment. The two men kill each other, and Mirakle gently guides the sobbing prostitute into his coach. The girl winds up at Mirakle's hovel of a home-cum-laboratory in the Rue Morgue, where she is bound to an ×-shaped cross while Mirakle injects her with Erik's blood. The girl is not the right specimen: she dies from the crude transfusion. Mirakle and Janos dispose of her body, dropping it through a trap door into the Seine River below. She is Mirakle's third victim that week.

Paul Dupin is determined to solve the riddle of the "drowned" girls who are dredged out of the river with no water in their lungs. Bribing the local morgue keeper (D'Arcy Corrigan), he is able to secure samples of the blood of the three women, and finds the same unidentifiable foreign substance (the ape blood) in each. When Paul learns that Mirakle has sent a present to Camille, he begins to sense a connection between the sideshow scientist and the Seine "suicides."

Mirakle pays a midnight call on the apartment that Camille shares with her mother (Betsy Ross Clarke); he insists on taking Camille to see Erik. ("He talks only of you. He can't forget you!" Mirakle explains.) Camille, understandably frightened, closes the door in his face but Mirakle, undeterred, sends Erik shimmying up the side of the building. The ape kills Camille's mother, shoving her broken body feet-first up a fireplace flume, and abducts Camille.

Paul excitedly explains to the Prefect of Police (Brandon Hurst) that Dr. Mirakle and his trained ape are responsible for the recent rash of mysterious deaths, and the magistrate finally agrees to investigate. Meanwhile, at Mirakle's, the madman has determined that the unconscious Camille is the perfect subject for his ultimate experiment, but the arrival of the Prefect and his squad of gendarmes sends the scientist into a quandary. Janos is shot and killed by a gendarme while Erik, for absolutely no good reason, suddenly turns on Mirakle, throttling him to death. The ape seizes Camille and carries her across the Paris rooftops, followed by Paul and an excited mob on the street below. Paul, armed with a revolver, confronts Erik on a riverfront rooftop and shoots the angry beast, who somersaults off the roof into the rushing Seine. In a nice bit of climactic irony, Mirakle joins his victims in the morgue.

Murders in the Rue Morgue has recently become the subject of some close scrutiny, with biographies of Bela Lugosi and of Robert Florey turning a critical spotlight on this oft-neglected melodrama. It's fun, and funny, to compare what the Florey-fancier (singular) and the Lugosiphiles (plural) have to say about the film. Brian Taves, Florey's biographer and the only person who's still making a fuss over the man, raves about Florey's contribution to *Rue Morgue,* extends to Lugosi none of the credit, and even allows Florey to take a mild swipe at the actor. Writer Arthur Lennig, Lugosi fan and booster, plays up Bela's performance and high-handedly dismisses Florey's "uninspired direction." The funny part is that these men are both right about what was wrong with the picture, and both wrong about what's right.

A stilted and pretentious triumph of style over substance, *Murders in the Rue Morgue* wallows in fancy camerawork, weird lighting, Caligarian set design and other, equally bizarre Germanic flourishes. Florey apparently decided that the visual style of his film would put it over, and goes all out (with the able assistance of Karl "Papa" Freund on camera) to create the same sort of weird world that he brought to the screen in such pioneering avant-garde silent shorts as *The Life and Death of 9413—A Hollywood Extra* and *Johann the Coffin Maker.* But these eccentric niceties of production don't compensate for the poor script and the poor acting: *Rue Morgue*'s bizarre look only calls attention to itself, and eventually adds to the off-putting aura of the film.

Taves has been spearheading a one-man campaign to elevate Florey, writing a well-researched but overly generous book (*Robert Florey, the French Expressionist*), and spilling his diatribes over onto the pages of magazines like *The American Cinematographer.* Taves' is the sort of book that will get many readers into bashing Florey, because Taves has skewed the critical pendulum; some good, hard knocks are now needed to restore the proper balance. Florey is a near-perfect auteur for "film students" with fetishes for cinematographic tomfoolery, tilted camera angles and all of the other pedantic delights that crop up in his forgettable films. Taves sees *Murders in the Rue Morgue* as Florey's finest hour (and two minutes), but this hokey, outdated stiff doesn't belong at the top of any self-respecting director's list. About the nicest thing that it can be called is an object of curiosity for the scholar; otherwise it shapes up (with *Dracula*) as one of the most unsatisfying horror films from this early Universal era.

The acting goes a long way toward sinking *Murders in the Rue Morgue*; it's easily the worst-acted Universal horror film. As the mad Dr. Mirakle, Bela Lugosi is his old dependable self: ranting and raving in that thick accent, running words and phrases together, leering, making sweeping gestures, indulging in double takes and all the other silly gyrations which make him some fans' favorite bogeyman. This is quintessential early Lugosi, a performance in a league with Count Dracula and Murder Legendre (*White Zombie,* 1932). There's no denying that it's fascinating, watching Lugosi strut his stuff in these early pictures; it's the same sort of pleasure that's derived from watching disaster footage, belly-whops and football bloopers. Poor Bela gives his all putting on a show, and what little fun there is in *Murders in the Rue Morgue* is due to Lugosi's work. Unfortunately, the actor was victimized by the makeup department (his curly hair, lipstick and single unbroken eyebrow give him a goony look) as well as by the front office, who allowed ingenue Sidney Fox top-billing in the film's credits.

Beast and beauty: Charles Gemora makes time with Sidney Fox in *Murders in the Rue Morgue.*

Fox is a lackluster leading lady, giggling and simpering coquettishly and having all the sex appeal expected from a girl named Sidney. A diminutive actress (under five feet and 100 pounds), her talent was commensurate with her physical stature; she made just over a dozen films during her five-year Hollywood career, retired from acting and died a mysterious death in 1942, at age 31. Leon Ames, who makes his film debut in *Rue Morgue* under his real Dutch name Leon Waycoff, gets saddled with a lot of the film's forced, unreal dialogue along with the cornball love speeches. Ames later proved that he was capable of far better work under saner conditions, and carved quite a respectable career for himself in movies. Reminiscing about *Murders in the Rue Morgue* in an old issue of *Famous Monsters of Filmland,* Ames held an unsurprising opinion, calling it "a perfectly awful film which still pops up on TV to haunt me!"

The comedy relief in *Rue Morgue* is exasperating, and cripples the picture yet further. Bert Roach, a fat, bug-eyed sissy of a buffoon, plays Leon Ames' roommate-friend, and spoils every scene he's in. (It's a good thing that the picture shows us that both of these characters have girlfriends, otherwise Roach's scaredy-cat antics and effeminism would have had audiences wondering about their *real* relationship.) The film reaches rock bottom in the one scene that's actually derived from the original Poe story, with three foreigners bickering over a strange "voice" (Erik's) they heard coming from the murder apartment. The three men get into a loud, excited argument, each of them yammering in his own language; the scene goes on so long that you almost expect them to start indulging in Stooge-style eye-pokes and nose-tweaks. The ridiculous scenes where Lugosi talks to the ape in his "native tongue" were not intended as comic relief, although they play that way. (Apparently the ape is bilingual, since Lugosi speaks to it in English half the time.)

Some of the supporting players are able to retain their dignity despite the foolishness going on around them. Noble Johnson, who wears white-face(!), is effective as Mirakle's sadistic manservant Janos, while long-faced actors like Brandon Hurst (as the Prefect) and D'Arcy Corrigan (as the runny-nosed morgue keeper) restore a small degree of sobriety to the film. Arlene Francis' acting is mostly confined to a series of screams as she hangs from Lugosi's rack. Charles Gemora, a Filipino "actor" who parlayed an ape costume into an undignified Hollywood career, plays Erik; strongman Joe Bonomo squeezed into the hairy suit for the more strenuous scenes. The closeups in the film are of a real orangutan whose frequent yawns become quite contagious.

Part of the problem with *Murders in the Rue Morgue* is that the film was restructured in the editing room after completion. In its intended form the film began with the scene of Lugosi watching the knife fight on the embankment and luring the prostitute to his home. This would segue into the scene on the wharf, the first scene at the morgue, and then the carnival sequence where renegade scientist Lugosi is seen in his other "identity," as the sideshow character. This original sequence of events is certainly preferable to the confusing jumble of scenes with which the film now kicks off. The hasty reshuffling of footage even creates some odd juxtapositions: a clear night inexplicably becomes a windy, foggy one; Erik disappears from Mirakle's coach between shots; and the character of Paul makes an unfathomable comment about morgues long before there's the hint of one in the picture. The harm done to *Rue Morgue,* though, is actually minimal. Had the scenes been projected in their proper order, it would be remembered as a dismal film with a promising opening (à la *Dracula*) rather than as a wholly dismal film. This seems a small distinction indeed.

Because Florey adapted Poe's story in haste, there are a number of minor parallels between this film and Florey's aborted assignment, *Frankenstein;* in interviews, Florey himself tries to give the impression that *Rue Morgue* and

Frankenstein share the same basic story. ("The Universal people, not being particularly bright, didn't realize that I again used the same plot," the director sniffishly told Taves.) Florey bases his claim on the fact that *Rue Morgue* uses an ape instead of the Monster, Dr. Mirakle instead of Dr. Frankenstein, and human blood rather than a human brain as the doctor's goal. It's Florey who isn't particularly bright if he actually thinks that these horror movie conventions originated with him; the *Rue Morgue* plotline comes not from *Frankenstein* but from the German silent classic *The Cabinet of Dr. Caligari* (1919), from which Florey steals his visual style as well.

"The Murders in the Rue Morgue" first reached the screen in the Danish short *Sherlock Holmes and the Great Murder Mystery* (1908), which pits Poe's mischievous monkey against Conan Doyle's dauntless detective. The 1912 short *The Raven,* in which Poe dreams of scenes from some of his own tales, uses a smidgen of the story; a 1928 borderline horror film called *The Leopard Lady,* while based on some obscure play, also supposedly bears more than a passing resemblance in its story of a gorilla committing murder. At the height of the 3-D craze, Warner Bros. filmed the color/stereoscopic *Phantom of the Rue Morgue* (1954) with Karl Malden using an ape (Charles Gemora again) as an instrument of murder in 19th century Paris. When American International Pictures got around to adding *Rue Morgue* to their Poe series in 1971, the resultant film owed more to Gaston Leroux's *The Phantom of the Opera* than to anything written by Poe. "The problem was that the original Poe story, which is a mystery where the *monkey* did it, was not the kind of story you could do any more," explains director Gordon Hessler. Instead of struggling to squeeze a workable screenplay out of Poe, the screenwriters developed a *Phantom*-type story of a killer terrorizing a French theater. "The Murders in the Rue Morgue" was the play within the movie.

The 1932 film *Murders in the Rue Morgue* remains the best known of the many versions of the Poe tale. It's got the Lugosi name going for it, which means a lot to many people, and it *is* a film from Universal's Golden Age, which also gives it some much-needed legitimacy. Bad as *Rue Morgue* is, and as much as most fans resent it, the "look" of the film is striking, and it's always enjoyable to see those old watchtower sets from *Frankenstein* turning up in picture after picture (here they're used as Mirakle's lab). There are also a few modest highlights, like the abduction of Arlene Francis, her "crucifixion" on Lugosi's rack and the climactic cross-rooftop chase.

Overall, however, the film is a major disappointment. Instead of diddling around with painted shadows, Expressionistic gobbledygook and cameras on swings, Florey's time would have been better spent rewriting dialogue, paring mindless comedy relief sequences, building atmosphere and pressing his actors for real performances. Neither Florey nor Freund, nor all their European influences, nor all the king's horses nor all the king's men could possibly have turned this sow's ear into a silk purse. *Rue Morgue* puts the lie to the statement that Robert Florey should have been allowed to direct *Frankenstein;* in fact, rather than having us pining for a Florey-directed *Frankenstein,* the film instead has us yearning for a George Melford–directed *Rue Morgue!*

The occasional show-offy camerawork in the film scarcely camouflages the fact that as a whole *Rue Morgue* looks like something left over from the '20s. It doesn't even stack up favorably against *Dracula.* Slow and static as *Dracula* is, it really never tries to be more than a filmed stageplay, and it succeeds or fails on that humble level. *Rue Morgue,* with its footloose camera, Continental ambience and look-at-me precociousness, is clearly the work of émigrés putting on airs, and the dismal little potboiler they have crafted is now doubly laughable.

Florey's horror "reputation" is built around three films (*Murders in the Rue Morgue, The Face Behind the Mask,* 1941, and *The Beast with Five Fingers,* 1946) but savvy fans realize that these pictures have followings only because they feature horror stars Lugosi and Peter Lorre; Florey's directorial whimsies are only frosting. (Where's the fuss, incidentally, over *The Florentine Dagger,* 1935, Florey's one horror film without a horror star?) If Bela Lugosi were not in *Murders in the Rue Morgue,* the film would have no appeal at all.

With its shabby, dashed-off look, a superabundance of foolish dialogue, inept acting and wrong-headed, self-indulgent direction, horror film fans have readily recognized the film for what it is: the low point of the first Universal horror cycle.

The Old Dark House (1932)

Released October 20, 1932. 71 minutes. *Produced by* Carl Laemmle, Jr. *Directed by* James Whale. *Screenplay by* Benn W. Levy. *Based on the novel Benighted by* J.B. Priestley. *Additional Dialogue:* R.C. Sherriff. *Director of Photography:* Arthur Edeson. *Film Editor:* Clarence Kolster. *Art Director:* Charles D. Hall. *Music by* Bernhard Kaun. *Assistant Director:* Joseph A. McDonough. *Sound Recorder:* William Hedgcock. *Makeup by* Jack P. Pierce.

Boris Karloff (Morgan), Melvyn Douglas (Roger Penderel), Charles Laughton (Sir William Porterhouse), Gloria Stuart (Margaret Waverton), Raymond Massey (Philip Waverton), Ernest Thesiger (Horace Femm), Lillian Bond (Gladys DuCane/Perkins), Eva Moore (Rebecca Femm), Brember Wills (Saul Femm), Elspeth Dudgeon [John Dudgeon] (Sir Roderick Femm).

January, 1932: The startling success of *Frankenstein* assured the Laemmles that their confidence in the studio's slightly pampered star director James Whale was justified. But Whale's next production was not a grand slam. *The Impatient Maiden* (1932) was a pedestrian affair concerning a mismatched couple, a naive intern (Lew Ayres) and a cynical secretary (Mae Clarke), who eventually fall in love. This entertaining but slight film is of interest today for what it reveals of Whale's technique with a somewhat atypical subject. Whale's gifts were obviously better suited to more flamboyant material. Hoping to strike box office lightning again, Universal steered him into another horror venture.

The suggestion of a film version of *Benighted,* a demure, curious thriller by the eclectic British writer J.B. Priestley, was probably Whale's. The story of a demented Welsh family under siege by a bevy of unwelcome outsiders had obvious appeal for Whale, with its roster of bizarre characters and ripe potential for black humor. The book's American title, *The Old Dark House,* happily was retained by the studio, which had profitable runs with such haunted house thrillers as *The Cat and the Canary* (1927) and its talkie remake *The Cat Creeps* (1930).

Whale chose playwright Benn W. Levy to write the screenplay and solicited the assistance of his long-time associate R.C. Sherriff. The pair added a touch of whimsy utterly lacking in the novel; the result was one of the wittiest scripts ever written for a horror movie. The finished screenplay followed the novel faithfully but jettisoned Priestley's long, recurring introspective passages which cropped up with irritating frequency, even in the climactic action scenes. Priestley may have been interested in man as a social animal, but Whale envisioned the story as a mild burlesque on the Gothic thriller. The screenplay completed, *The Old Dark House* was at last ready to be cast.

Finding a follow-up role for Boris Karloff, the new king of mayhem, was a priority, but his acting range had yet to be tested. He slid easily into the role of Morgan, the mute, brutish butler. It was a relatively small part, but Universal wasn't taking any chances with their new star. His first lead role after *Frankenstein* wasn't very encouraging. Miscast as a nightclub owner in *Night World* (1932), Karloff didn't win many favorable notices. Tacking a written foreword onto the opening credits of *The Old Dark House* assuring the audience that this was indeed the same actor who scared the wits out of them in *Frankenstein* was a canny move; the studio sheepishly added, "We explain this to settle any disputes in advance, even though such disputes are a tribute to his great versatility."

For the roles of the Mr. and Mrs. Waverton, the smart young English couple who needed only a shriek-filled night in a remote Victorian mansion to quell their constant bickering, there was no need to look beyond the studio's contract players. Raymond Massey, an old friend of Whale's during the director's brief acting career, had just signed with Universal, and Gloria Stuart, a theater-trained ingenue hailing from California, were selected for the roles. Whale used outside talent to fill out the cast, a craftily-chosen assemblage of seasoned stage actors. With the exception of Melvyn Douglas, a last-minute replacement for Russell Hopton, all of them were British: Charles Laughton (in his first American film), Lillian Bond, Eva Moore and Ernest Thesiger.

As usual, Whale oversaw every phase of the production, with little creative input from producer Carl Laemmle, Jr. Sets constructed from art director Charles D. Hall's specifications were erected on the soundstage, highlighted by an imposing Victorian staircase, a large fireplace and an adjoining parlor and dining room. The sets were modified for the studio's later horror movies, and even turned up in non-Universal thrillers such as Majestic's *The Vampire Bat* (also with Melvyn Douglas) and Chesterfield's *Strange People* (both 1933). The special effects crew built a miniature set for a heart-stopping trick scene in which Waverton's roadster narrowly avoids being crushed in a landslide. Huge wind machines and hoses were readied on the backlot for the spectacular nighttime storm which opens the show. By April, the cameras were ready to roll.

"It was wonderful. Every morning Whale would come on the set with all the camera layouts for his script," recalls Gloria Stuart. "He was also a brilliant cameraman besides being one of the most talented, meticulous directors I have ever worked for in films. Whale was also great with dialogue. He really knew what he was doing."

Whale followed his usual procedure of thoroughly rehearsing his cast and blocking out each scene carefully. The time-honored British tradition of tea-time was religiously observed, much to the irritation of Stuart, who felt slighted by her colleagues. She told *Films in Review:* "The British were very clannish on that picture. They felt they were a rather superior colony and they didn't pretend otherwise. They had tea at eleven and four, the whole English cast and Whale, and they never once asked me or Melvyn or any other American to join them. It put me off. No, they were not very polite."

Despite this minor friction, the production went smoothly, finally closing in mid-March.

Wanting to exploit Karloff's new career in horror films, Universal cast him as Morgan the butler in *The Old Dark House.* (Photo courtesy Steve Jochsberger.)

The Old Dark House characteristically begins in the midst of a raging thunderstorm as a lone automobile, lost in the Welsh mountains, tries to make its way through the primitive dirt roads. Inside are a bickering, nerve-wracked young couple, Philip and Margaret Waverton (Raymond Massey and Gloria Stuart) and their war-disillusioned friend, Roger Penderel (Melvyn Douglas). Deciding it is too dangerous to continue, the trio arrive at an imposing stone house, the only shelter in sight.

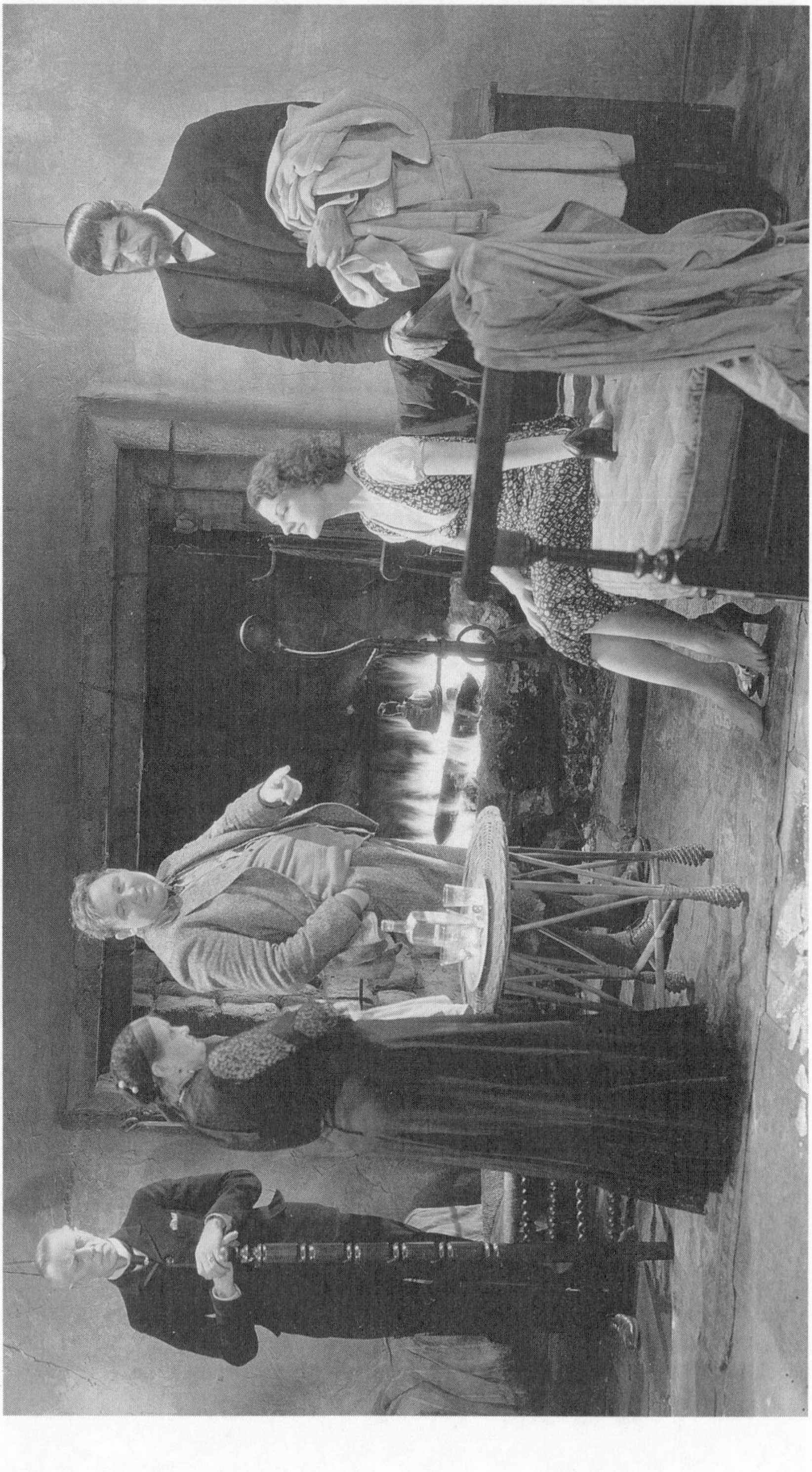

A Neanderthal-like manservant, Morgan (Boris Karloff), ushers them into a well-upholstered living room. They are met by the gaunt Horace Femm (Ernest Thesiger) who urges them to press on, and his sister, the cranky, half-deaf Rebecca (Eva Moore). The group is soon joined by another pair of lost travelers, the prosperous Sir William Porterhouse (Charles Laughton) and his unlikely companion, out-of-work chorus girl Gladys DuCane (Lillian Bond).

Rebecca Femm turns out to be a religious fanatic, while her brother Horace seems fearful of some terrible secret. A drunken Morgan gets into a brawl with Philip and is knocked unconscious. Investigating what sounds like a frail, child-like voice, Philip and Margaret come across the bedroom of the master of the house, 102-year-old Sir Roderick Femm (Elspeth Dudgeon). He warns the couple that his eldest son, Saul, who is locked away in the nursery, is a madman determined to set fire to the house.

The dazed Morgan awakens and frees the dreaded Saul (Brember Wills). Philip and Porterhouse manage to subdue the brutish butler but Saul torches the upper landing of the house. Penderel tries to stop him. During the struggle, a banister gives way, sending both men crashing to the floor below. Saul is killed but the injured Penderel slowly regains consciousness.

The storm finally subsides. The Wavertons wearily make their way to their car, Penderel and Gladys decide to get married and the Femms, hardly turning a hair after the night's melodramatics, carry on as if nothing has happened. It's a new day.

After its reissue in the late '40s, *The Old Dark House* dropped completely from sight and was considered a lost film. Its reappearance is largely due to the tireless efforts of director Curtis Harrington, a friend of Whale's in his last years, who made an intensive search for a print in 1968. Universal claimed to have destroyed the negative and all prints when the story rights reverted back to J.B. Priestley, who, in turn, optioned the property to Columbia. Playing a hunch, Harrington contacted William Castle. King of the gimmick horror movie in the late '50s, he directed a cloddish and unwatchable color remake of *The Old Dark House* in 1963. The charismatic filmmaker, as it turned out, not only denied owning a copy of the original film, but claimed Universal couldn't even provide him with a screening while he was preparing his remake.

Undaunted, Harrington returned to Universal, who steadfastly stuck to their story that the negative had been destroyed. At Harrington's insistence, a search of the studio vaults was made, turning up a single "lavender negative" (actually a fine grain print) still in printable condition despite shrinkage and years of neglect. The find was a real treasure, but Universal's reaction was one of indifference. Having lost the rights to the film and unable to market it commercially, the studio saw little reason to shell out the two or three thousand dollars it would cost for its restoration. Harrington came up with funding from Eastman House of Rochester, New York, for the printing of a new negative, and the film enjoyed a brief theatrical revival in the early '70s.

The limited accessibility of *The Old Dark House* invariably makes it the

Ernest Thesiger, Eva Moore, Charles Laughton, Lillian Bond and Boris Karloff in *The Old Dark House.*

last of the classic Universal horror titles buffs get around to seeing, which places it at an immediate disadvantage. Predictably, Whale's film was greeted with bewilderment by baby boomers seeing it for the first time when it finally resurfaced. Anticipation ran high, with good reason. All those enticing stills of Karloff menacing Gloria Stuart in dog-eared copies of *Famous Monsters* magazine, assurances of the film's classic status from the likes of Forrest J Ackerman and Robert Bloch, and, of course, the stalwart reputation of James Whale fueled fans' expectations for another *Bride of Frankenstein*. And what a cast! But no one ever mentioned that *The Old Dark House* was intended as a mild burlesque. (There wasn't much in the way of horror film scholarship at the time, so Forry Ackerman's word counted heavily.) Some of the reviewers who caught the film during its last reissue didn't get the joke either, and *The Old Dark House* accumulated more than its share of condescending notices.

The Old Dark House is perhaps an acquired taste, but it's a film that grows in stature with each viewing. It has been said that only a Frenchman can fully appreciate Jean Renoir's *The Rules of the Game* (1939); likewise, William K. Everson suggests that only an Englishman can fully understand *The Old Dark House*. Perhaps. The film's wit is so dry and so gently self-mocking, a casual viewer can easily laugh the dialogue off as being ridiculous ("Philip, this is an *awful* house." "It isn't very nice, is it?"). In one scene, Horace proudly shows off his sister's talent for floral arrangements and then casually tosses the bouquet in the fireplace.

Whale paces the film carefully, portioning small increments of humor as the story progresses and then unleashing a full onslaught of mayhem in the last reel. Often he deflates his own build-up of tension with a flip remark. Karloff's creepy introduction when he responds to the travelers' frantic knocks at the door is set up with Melvyn Douglas' ominous dialogue: "Supposing the people inside were dead. All stretched out with lights quietly burning about them." When Karloff finally appears, growling like a provoked dog, Douglas quips, "Even Welsh oughtn't sound like that." Later, an equally unruffled Charles Laughton puts the fearsome Karloff in his place with, "Looks to me he could do with a shave!"

The introduction of Saul, too, is deliberately anticlimactic. A threatening hand on the banister slowly gives way to a meek, frightened old man, then Whale unexpectedly cuts to a chilling close-up of his half-mad grin. There is no such scene in Priestley's novel, which depicts Saul as a mindless, homicidal animal without the cunning of his celluloid alter ego.

Whale counters the staginess of the material by digging deep into his bag of cinematic tricks. *The Old Dark House* is in fact the director's most stylized film to this date. Whale puckishly responds with his camera to Levy's funny lines. He cuts to snarling reaction shots of Eva Moore on appropriate occasions, and includes an unexpected shot of the sagging, frumpy hag quickly doing her hair after she menaces Gloria Stuart. The scene is one of Whale's boldest.

Whale photographs Moore with a distorted, funhouse mirror effect as she details the grisly death of her heathen sister. Fingering Stuart's chic evening dress, Moore's demented, evangelistic ravings take a sinister turn: "That's fine

The gang's all here! Gloria Stuart, Lillian Bond, Charles Laughton, Raymond Massey, Melvyn Douglas, Boris Karloff and Eva Moore in *The Old Dark House.*

stuff too, but it'll rot." Then placing her hand on Stuart's half-exposed bosom: "That's finer stuff still, but it'll rot too in time." Moore exits but Stuart's memory of her lingers as a twisted mirror image of the hag reprises her demented speech. The dialogue is Priestley's but the style is unmistakably Whale's.

Priestley's bleak but realistic dinner scene is turned into an elaborate and hilarious feast in the movie. Whale again focuses on the peculiarities of the incompatible diners: the ritual of passing sliced bread, Moore wolfing down gobs of pickled onions, Massey extracting an unsightly black spot from a boiled potato.

When asked what she remembers about this marvelous scene, Gloria Stuart offered,

> My dress. I told James, "I don't understand. Nobody else changed for dinner, but I'm in this pink, bias-cut silk velvet, practically strapless dinner dress. I just don't understand!" "Well," he said, "when Karloff chases you through the halls, I want you to be like a flame or a dancer and I want that light down the dark halls and so forth." Well, you know, you don't argue with Whale. It was pretty ridiculous but that's what he wanted and that's what he got.

Priestley's stray characters are neatly varied and play off one another well. The retiring Waverton, the tweed-and-pipe hero representing the thinking man, contrasts with the cynical but charming man-of-action Penderel. Likewise, Priestley carefully contrasts his female characters, from the elegant, upper-crust Margaret to the common chorus girl Gladys. The Femms are introduced with a careful eye on story progression, with each character slightly madder than the last. Whatever reservations one may have about Priestley's novel, it *is* a marvel of construction.

The Old Dark House boasts a gallery of memorable performances, although Charles Laughton is a bit overripe even by *his* standards. Karloff's surprisingly brief appearance as Morgan is almost a footnote to the film in spite of his star billing. Wisely, there was no attempt to beef up his rather uninteresting stock brute character, except for his last and most poignant scene, when he silently cradles the lifeless body of Saul (a moment which may have inspired a similar scene between the Monster and Ygor in *Son of Frankenstein*). The role lacked the depth of the Monster in *Frankenstein,* and Karloff does little to make the character memorable. Even Boris' grunts in his introductory scene were inexplicably looped-in by an unidentified actor during post-production.

Gloria Stuart provides a charming testimonial to the cultured Englishman: "He was brilliant, beautifully educated. For his role in *The Old Dark House,* he had to come to the set at three or four in the morning so they could do his makeup. So naturally he wasn't given to a lot of horsing around or light conversation during the day. But I thought he was a lovely man."

For the role of Sir Roderick, the ancient patriarch of the Femm clan, Whale gambled by casting Elspeth Dudgeon, a stage actress, in the part, passing her off as a man. The deception doesn't come off but Dudgeon (whose first name was changed to John in the credits) gives a fine account. Unbelievable as it may seem, she was still making films in the late '40s. One of her last credits is *Lust for Gold* (1949) with Glenn Ford and Ida Lupino. As the fanatical Rebecca Femm, Eva Moore is as cranky and crusty as one can hope.

The conventional characters come off well also. Gloria Stuart, who would later be saddled with too many weepy heroine roles (such as in *The Invisible Man* and, even more irritatingly, John Ford's *The Prisoner of Shark Island,* 1936), is alluring as Margaret, and Raymond Massey is competent as Waverton. The excellent Melvyn Douglas is fine as always as the acerbic, world-weary Roger Penderel. Almost a character out of Hemingway, his is one of the most interesting horror heroes of the '30s, if one overlooks his mawkish love scenes. (It's hard to believe that the hard-boiled Penderel is so easily swept away by so common a waif as Gladys, well played by Lillian Bond.)

But, of course, it's Ernest Thesiger who steals *The Old Dark House* as the sniffish, craven Horace Femm. He is nothing short of the ideal materialization of the Priestley character. ("A man so thin, with so little flesh and so much shining bone ought to be braver than that; he was almost a skeleton, and skeletons, jangling and defiant, are brave enough.") Jack Pierce completes the image, providing the actor with heavy eye makeup, achieving a wonderful, skull-like effect.

The Old Dark House was well-received by critics upon its initial release, but it was too eccentric to match the mass popularity of *Frankenstein.*

Raymond Massey, who fancied himself as going on to bigger and better things, later dismissed his role as "a long and colourless juvenile part that didn't permit much acting." He admitted in his autobiography that he never saw the movie. His co-star, Gloria Stuart, takes exception: "I think it's a wonderful film. I remember I did a seminar at Filmex on James Whale, and someone said to me, 'How did it feel, Miss Stuart, making classics?' Well, we didn't know we were making classics. All we were hoping for was to make a good movie. But *all* of James' films are classics."

The Mummy (1932)

Released December 22, 1932. 72 minutes. *Produced by* Carl Laemmle, Jr. *Directed by* Karl Freund. *Associate Producer:* Stanley Bergerman. *Screenplay by* John L. Balderston. *From a story by* Nina Wilcox Putnam & Richard Schayer. *Camera:* Charles Stumar. *Film Editor:* Milton Carruth. *Art Director:* Willy Pogany. *Music by* James Dietrich. *Special Effects:* John P. Fulton. *Makeup by* Jack P. Pierce.

Boris Karloff (Imhotep/Ardath Bey), Zita Johann (Helen Grosvenor/Princess Anck-es-en-Amon), David Manners (Frank Whemple), Edward Van Sloan (Dr. Muller), Arthur Byron (Sir Joseph Whemple), Bramwell Fletcher (Ralph Norton), Noble Johnson (The Nubian), Kathryn Byron (Frau Muller), Leonard Mudie (Professor Pearson), James Crane (King Amenophis), Henry Victor* (The Saxon Warrior), Arnold Grey* (Knight), Eddie Kane (Dr. LeBarron), Tony Marlow (Inspector), Pat Somerset (Dancing Partner), C. Montague Shaw, Leland [Leyland] Hodgson (Small Talkers), Gordon [Bill] Elliott (Dance Extra). [**Does not appear in the final print.*]

The setting: a rocky area just north of the Valley of the Kings in the Egyptian desert. The year: 1921. Sir Joseph Whemple (Arthur Byron), director of an archaeological expedition sponsored by the British Museum, has made a remarkable find—a condemned burial spot containing the mummy of Imhotep, high priest of the Temple of the Sun at Karnak, and an alabaster box which bears a forbidding inscription: "Death—Eternal punishment for anyone who opens this casket. In the name of Amon-Ra, the King of the Gods." Ralph Norton (Bramwell Fletcher), Whemple's young assistant, is eager to open the box despite the protests of Sir Joseph's friend Dr. Muller (Edward Van Sloan), a Viennese expert in the occult.

While Whemple and Muller are debating the issue, Norton blunders ahead and opens the forbidden box. Inside, he finds the sacred Scroll of Thoth, handed down from pharaoh to pharaoh, which contains the great spell by which Isis raised Osiris from the dead. As the Oxford lad reads the magic spell aloud, the Mummy (Boris Karloff) slowly, painfully comes to life. By the time Whemple returns to the hut, he finds the Mummy and the Scroll of Thoth gone, and Norton, laughing hysterically, half out of his mind.

The story advances 11 years. Sir Joseph's son Frank (David Manners) and his associate Professor Pearson (Leonard Mudie) are in the midst of breaking camp after a disappointing season in the desert when they are visited by Ardath Bey (also Boris Karloff), a dignified Egyptian scholar. ("His face is tanned like leather," wrote scenarist John L. Balderston, "it is the face of a mummy, but

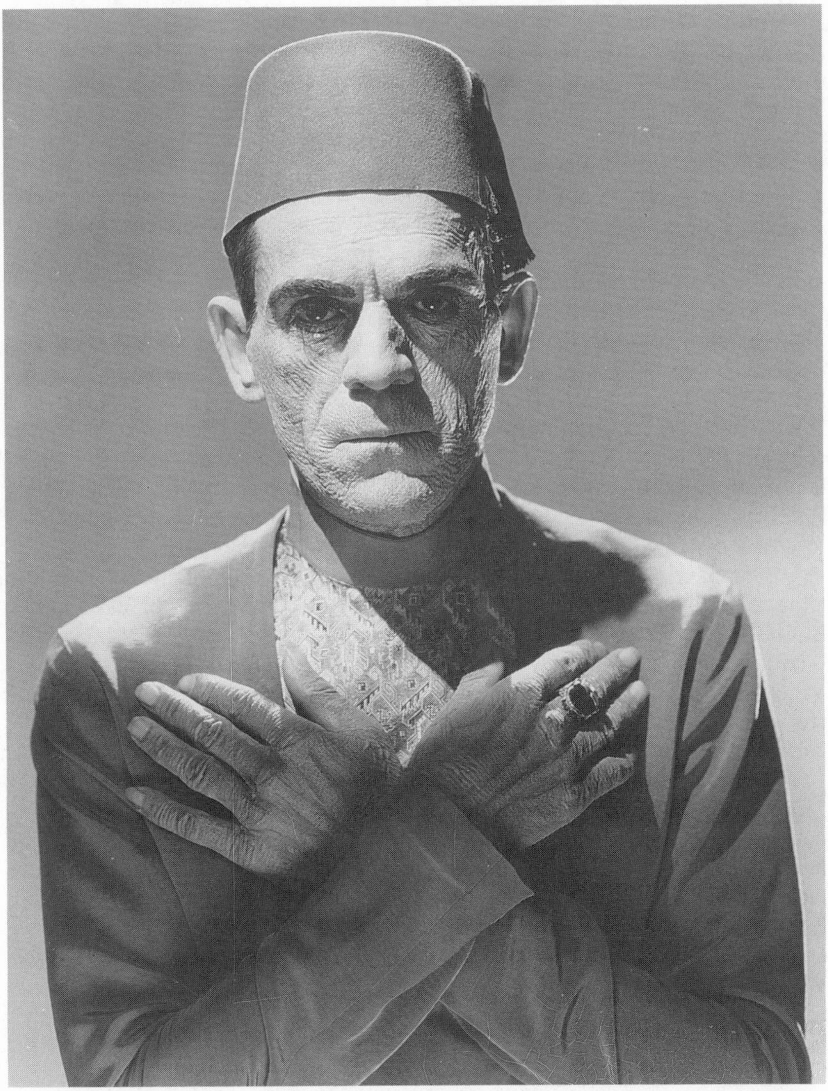

Boris Karloff (here in the guise of Ardath Bey) gave one of his most distinguished performances as *The Mummy*.

not unlike that of many Orientals who have lived in the tropical sun all their lives.") The stranger generously offers to lead the two Englishmen to the site of a find of incredible magnitude: the burial spot of the Princess Anck-es-en-Amon, the daughter of Amenophis, one-time ruler of all Egypt. A treasure-trove of priceless artifacts and the mummy of the Princess are recovered from the tomb and sent to the Cairo Museum.

Little do Frank and Sir Joseph realize, but Ardath Bey is, in actuality, the resuscitated high priest Imhotep. Centuries before, the Egyptian was put to death for trying to bring his beloved Anck-es-en-Amon back from the dead. With the Scroll of Thoth in his possession, he futilely attempts to raise the mummy of the Princess, but discovers her *ka* (spirit) has been reincarnated in the body of a 20th century woman, Helen Grosvenor (Zita Johann), a patient of Dr. Muller. By the time the two men learn of Bey's true identity, it is too late: the ancient Egyptian has already taken command of Helen's mind and soul. Realizing she is indeed the reincarnation of Anck-es-en-Amon, Helen is quite literally torn between two lives. Her blossoming love for Frank and instinct to survive are tested by the persistent influence of Ardath Bey.

Summoning forth his ancient powers, Bey strikes down Sir Joseph and makes an attempt on Frank's life. He lures Helen to the museum and prepares her for "the great night of terror and triumph," when he will release her soul from its present incarnation and, through the power of the Scroll of Thoth, resurrect the young woman in the form of a living mummy like himself. Speaking as Anck-es-en-Amon, Helen protests; she acknowledges the tremendous suffering Imhotep has endured in the name of love, but she cannot allow him to destroy the life of the modern-day woman she has become.

Surrendering to Bey's hypnotic influence, Helen voluntarily lies upon the altar of Anubis, the Guide of the Dead, and awaits the thrust of Bey's knife. But before Bey can administer the mortal wound, Frank and Muller intervene, bringing Helen back to her senses. She prays to the statue of Isis for salvation. Magically, the goddess lifts her hand bearing the *crux ansata* (or symbol of eternal life) and issues forth a blinding flash of light. The Scroll of Thoth is destroyed and with it the Mummy Imhotep.

One of Universal's most potent horror thrillers, *The Mummy* is an ingenious creation. From its first brilliantly-realized set piece, one of the most indelible of '30s horror (who could forget Bramwell Fletcher's maniacal peals of laughter?), to the final image of Imhotep's pitiful remains scattered across the marble floor, *The Mummy* evokes an aura of wonder, romance and mystery. Eschewing the lurid and the blatantly sensational, the picture modulates its chill elements with exquisite refinement. The atmosphere is almost palpable. We are ushered into a world where antiquity seamlessly melds with the modern, where ancient rituals, reincarnation of the spirit, and the all-powerful gods of Egypt are still as potent as they were centuries ago. Blessed with a director who knew the mechanics of the camera intimately, *The Mummy*'s visual richness was almost assured. This, plus splendid performances by Boris Karloff, Zita Johann, Edward Van Sloan and Bramwell Fletcher, a masterful script by John L. Balderston, impressive sets, and one of Jack Pierce's most accomplished makeup jobs elevate *The Mummy* to the status of an *undisputed* classic, relatively untarnished by the cruelties of time.

Junior Laemmle conceived the idea of making a film loosely based on the highly publicized discovery of the boy king Tutankhamen's tomb in 1922, and the alleged "curse" that struck down its plunderers. In early 1932, he assigned Nina Wilcox Putnam, author of novels, short stories and newspaper articles, and Richard Schayer, head of Universal's scenario department, to come up with a feasible story treatment. The pair put their imaginations to work and came up with "Cagliostro," a nine-page original story.

Cagliostro was an ancient Egyptian magician who discovered the secret of eternal life: by injecting himself with nitrates, he's managed to prolong his existence for 3,000 years. Not one to forgive easily, Cagliostro avenges himself on the woman who betrayed him centuries before by seeking out and murdering females who resemble her. Posing as the blind uncle of one Helen Dorrington, a San Francisco movie cashier, Cagliostro and his Nubian servant commit a series of robberies and murders using (of all things) radio and television waves. Professor Whemple, an eminent archaeologist, discovers the truth about the baleful magician and plots his destruction.

Evidently satisfied with Putnam and Schayer's efforts, Laemmle announced in March his plans to feature Karloff in the title role of his newest horror production, *Cagliostro*. It wasn't until summer, however, that John L. Balderston (of *Dracula* and *Frankenstein* fame) began working on the screenplay.

By the time the script was submitted to the studio on September 12, it had gone through no fewer than *three* title changes: from *Cagliostro* to *The King of the Dead* to *Im-Ho-Tep*. Balderston made some refinements in the story, abandoning the scientific explanation for Cagliostro's (now Imhotep's) resurrection in favor of a purely supernatural one. By setting the story in Egypt rather than San Francisco, he buoyed the mystical elements of the tale, thus doubling its effectiveness. (At an early stage of the script's development, actor Rollo Lloyd was credited with having provided additional dialogue; his contribution – proved that any of his material was retained – was also doomed to neglect in the picture's credit roster.)

Amply filling the director's chair on *Im-Ho-Tep* was blowzy, 360-pound Karl "Papa" Freund, the brilliant German cinematographer who lensed Lugosi's *Dracula*. Praised as "the Giotto of the screen," the boldly innovative cameraman was a pioneer in the development of subjective photography, devising unorthodox techniques (such as strapping the camera to his chest) to capture particular shots.

Born in Koeniginhof, Bohemia (now Czechoslovakia), in 1890, Freund began his career behind the camera as an apprentice projectionist in Berlin at the age of 15. Mastering photographic technique, he made on his own two low-budget features in 1907 and the following year signed a contract as a full-fledged cameraman at Pathé News in Berlin. By the '20s, Freund had made a name for himelf in the field of cinematography. Working at Ufa and Messter studios, he "freed" the camera from its static position on the soundstage, creating breathtaking shots for such early film classics as *The Golem* (1921), *The Last Laugh* (1924), *Variety* (1925) and Fritz Lang's *Metropolis* (1926). Freund introduced process shot techniques, pioneered dolly shots by placing the camera on a motorized wagon, and developed a steel tape which was to become today's magnetic film.

Freund signed his first Hollywood contract in 1928 and immediately immersed himself in the study of American technique. Freund told film columnist Marguerite Tazelaar:

> I think [being a cameraman] is one of the most interesting jobs in the whole industry. The most important thing is to catch the mood of the scene in a single shot. Perhaps it is only a close-up of the heroine's eyes, yet this instant can be the most significant in the entire film. Each separate scene, each setup, has a meaning to the artist. The mood of the scene is everything.

By coming to the rescue of Lewis Milestone, Freund earned himself a directing contract at Universal. Dissatisfied with the ending of *All Quiet on the Western Front* (1930), and with only three days left before the scheduled premiere, Milestone turned to Freund for suggestions. In a burst of inspiration, the cameraman came up with the deceptively simple, unforgettable "butterfly finale." (Soldier Lew Ayres, captivated by the sight of a beautiful butterfly, absentmindedly strays into the range of enemy gunfire and is shot down; moments later, we hear an announcement that all fighting has come to a halt on the Western front.) Milestone was delighted. Universal signed up Freund to direct two films a year, beginning with *Im-Ho-Tep* (the title was changed to *The Mummy* more than halfway through production).

Freund's reputation as a tireless taskmaster was certified by his industrious performance on this film. He received the script on a Saturday in late September, 1932, spent the next day casting and screen-testing, and was all ready to begin shooting on Monday. Seven long, hard weeks of intensive work followed; it wasn't unusual for the company to toil well past midnight.

Karloff, in particular, felt the strain of Freund's arduous work schedule, as did Zita Johann. After sitting in Jack Pierce's chair for eight grueling hours, undergoing the most torturous man-into-monster makeup transformation of his career, poor Boris had to endure several hours of shooting the acclaimed resurrection scene. At 2 a.m. the following morning, after numerous retakes, the scene was in the can. By the time Pierce removed the suffocating Mummy makeup and sent Karloff on his way, it was almost dawn.

Zita Johann painted a less-than rosy picture of Papa Karl in an interview she granted Gregory Mank for his superb retrospective piece on *The Mummy* in *Films in Review:* "Karl Freund made life very unpleasant. It was his first picture as a director, and he felt he needed a scapegoat in case he didn't come in on schedule (23 days, I believe). Well, *I* was cast as the scapegoat—and I saw through it right away!"

Two weeks before the production wrapped, Freund took his company on location in picturesque Red Rock Canyon in the Mojave Desert to film some exterior shots with Karloff, David Manners and Leonard Mudie. Extensive process shots (utilizing footage taken in Egypt by staff cameramen dispatched by Universal's Berlin office), coupled with internationally renowned illustrator and artist Willy Pogany's evocative set designs and props, lent the picture an air of authenticity.

On October 30, Freund put the wraps on his first directorial assignment, under schedule and under budget ($196,161 was the final cost).

In transforming the Putnam-Schayer story into a screenplay, John L. Balderston leaned heavily upon his (and Hamilton Deane's) play "Dracula." It wouldn't be an exaggeration to call *The Mummy* a disguised remake of the Lugosi picture. Both the Count and Imhotep are immortal souls who cannot be

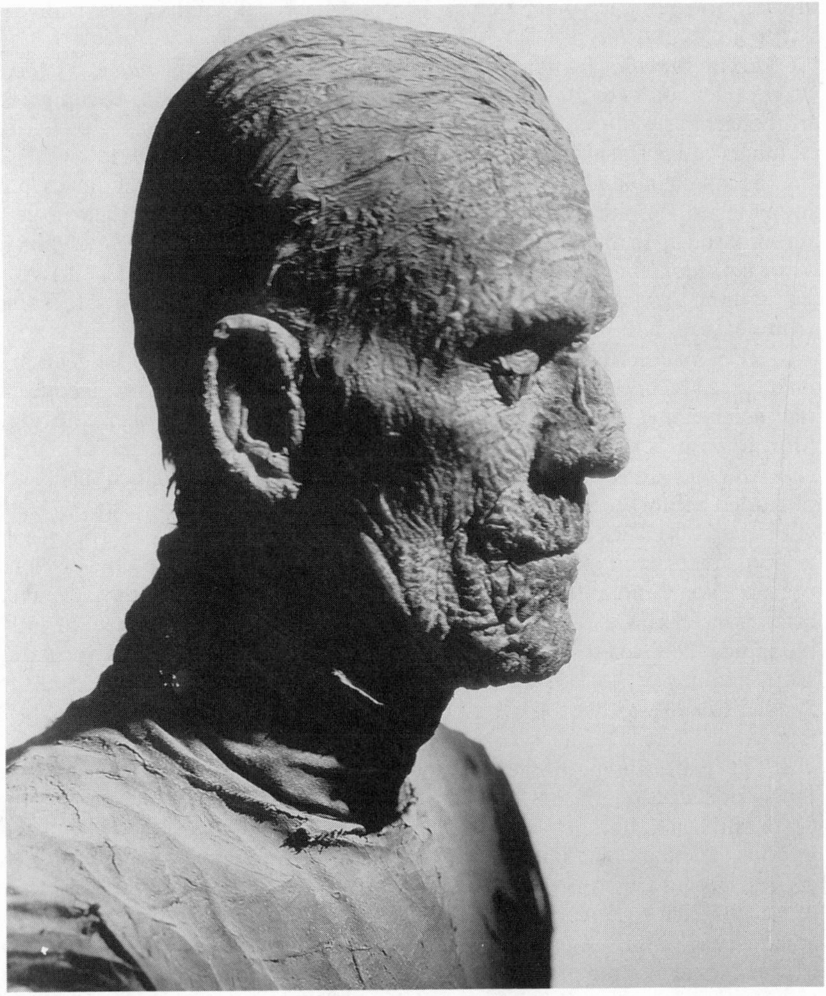

It took Jack Pierce eight hours to transform Boris Karloff into *The Mummy.*

destroyed by conventional means. They both possess hypnotic powers that can bend others to do their bidding. Dracula preys on the weak-minded Renfield to carry out his misdeeds; Imhotep enslaves the Nubian for similar purposes. Yet, in spite of their malevolent leanings and absolute powers, both are slaves to forces greater than themselves, thus arousing our pity and compassion.

Structurally, *The Mummy* follows *Dracula* very closely. Both films begin in the atmosphere-rich, ancestral homelands of the title protagonists, then shift to a cosmopolitan setting (despite this change of scene, both creatures inhabit abodes strikingly similar to those they left behind). At this point in both stories, a vulnerable young woman becomes the focal point in a struggle between good and evil.

As in *Dracula,* Edward Van Sloan, monster terminator *par excellence,* wages the good fight almost singlehandedly. In both films, he is encumbered by the victim's well-meaning but ineffective fiancé (both times played by David Manners). Like Helen Chandler's Mina, Zita Johann's Helen becomes a scheming, uncontrollable pill as Imhotep makes every attempt to lure her back into his clutches. Despite Van Sloan's safeguards, both women elude their protectors and end up in the arms of their seducers. But not for long. In *The Mummy,* as in *Dracula,* Van Sloan and Manners track the menace to his lair, arriving just in time to witness his destruction and save the heroine from a fate worse than death.

Rich in descriptive detail and fascinating Egyptian lore, Balderston's unabridged scenario makes good reading. The reincarnation motif (a concept that reached the height of fashion in the '50s with the highly publicized Bridey Murphy case) is emphasized in several scenes which went unfilmed, or, in the case of Zita Johann's trip-through-time, were produced, then foolishly discarded before the film went into general release. In one such episode, Helen visits the Cairo Museum and becomes immersed in the Anck-es-en-Amon collection. Balderston painstakingly described in glorious detail the various funerary items and toiletries that are on display. Suddenly, Ardath Bey makes his presence known. "I watched you admiring her jewels," he says. "She took the things she loved to the Kingdom of the West," Helen muses, as she stares at the mummy of Anck-es-en-Amon (which translates "Royal Daughter of the Sun"). "Her *ka* may live today, in a body as beautiful as hers was in Old Egypt," Bey says.

The exquisite pool scene is divided into two separate episodes in Balderston's script. In the first, Bey awakens images of Anck-es-en-Amon's death and her elaborate burial. Later, after the Mummy has lured Helen back into his sanctuary, she (and the audience) is taken on a trip through time as each of her past lives is revealed. First, we see Helen dressed in the costume of an 18th century French court lady, being romanced by a persistent young gallant in a setting suggesting the Garden of Versailles. Her preceding existence, set at the time of the Crusades in 13th century England, has Helen (again) enjoying romantic overtures, this time expressed by a handsome knight (Arnold Grey) as she stands on a dais in the hall of a medieval castle. In the midst of this time journey, the camera cuts occasionally to our heroine, lying opposite Bey's pool, writhing in mental torment.

Next, we are catapulted back to the 8th century. In the garb of a Saxon princess, Helen is seen hovering behind a blockade as a bloody battle is raging about her. With his last breath, a dying warrior (Henry Victor) reveals that all is lost. Helen picks up his dagger and stabs herself in the heart. A dungeon in the bowels of the Roman Coliseum is the grim setting of Helen's next rest stop. The valiant young woman stands amongst a band of Christian martyrs. She kisses a rough-hewn cross and fearlessly walks out into the arena with another doomed martyr. The film then cuts to a shot of hungry lions leaving their den.

Awakening from her troubled sleep, Helen, her soul now fully possessed by the spirit of Anck-es-en-Amon, looks around the room with understandable confusion. "Are we in the Kingdom of Set? Are we both dead?" she asks. "We *were* dead, we are alive again," Bey says passionately. At this point in the script, Balderston reveals (via flashbacks framed within the pool) the terrible fate Imhotep suffered for attempting to raise Anck-es-en-Amon with the aid of the Scroll of Thoth.

Freund's direction is succinct and to the point, with little time devoted to the kind of character eccentricities beloved by such stylists as Whale, Florey and Ulmer. (Unlike the other horror films of this period, *The Mummy* contains not an ounce of humor.) As in *Dracula,* the spell that his undead being casts over his victims extends to the audience as well, suggesting Freund probably picked up a few directing pointers from Tod Browning. Freund obviously influenced his cameraman, Charles Stumar (who might have felt a little intimidated working under this giant of the cinematography world). Under Freund's guidance, Stumar sets his focus on the paralyzing gaze of the Mummy and the transfixed reactions of his pawns, creating a disquieting mood. Pacing is sometimes sacrificed for this studious build-up of atmosphere and tone. Yet *The Mummy* escapes falling into the stagey, monotonous pattern of *Dracula:* imaginative camerawork and direction is the answer. (Stumar died in the 1935 crash of his private plane.)

The dual role of Imhotep/Ardath Bey was a radical departure from Karloff's other horror assignments at Universal up to this time. Unlike his inarticulate, childlike Monster in *Frankenstein* and his lumbering brute servant in *The Old Dark House,* Karloff's Mummy is a well-spoken, all-powerful menace. He has but one purpose in the strange new world into which he has been reborn: to find Anck-es-en-Amon's latest reincarnation and reawaken in her the sleeping spirit of his beloved.

It's difficult to despise a character with such richly romantic aspirations. Imhotep may be a cold-blooded murderer, but he doesn't belong in the same category as such blatantly evil Karloff characters as his Oriental sadist Fu Manchu (*The Mask of Fu Manchu,* 1932) or his Satan-worshipping Hjalmar Poelzig (*The Black Cat*). Having suffered the most hideous of deaths for the woman he loved, we commiserate with Imhotep when he is spurned and even *insulted* ("I loved you once, but now you belong with the dead!") by her alter ego.

Garbed in a silk Egyptian robe, his head topped with a red velvet fez, Ardath Bey's unassuming presence belies his destructive capabilities. (Freund modifies Whale's technique of heralding the first glimpse of his monsters with a series of quick-cut close-ups.) The combined effect of Jack Pierce's makeup and Karloff's acting totally convince the audience that Bey is as ancient and potentially crumbly as the mummy we know him to be. By optically illuminating Karloff's eyes in key close-ups, John P. Fulton achieves the illusion that the omnipresent Egyptian knows all and sees all. Quietly understated and free of theatrical affectation, *The Mummy* is among the handful of Karloff's finest performances.

Only an actress of Zita Johann's talent and training could convincingly

pull off the difficult role of Helen Grosvenor. (Balderston had suggested that Katharine Hepburn be screen tested for the part but she had already left the West Coast for New York.) No shrinking violet, the Hungarian-born actress was keenly aware of her capabilities and firmly stood her ground in a world of male power-trippers. Hollywood held little fascination for the diminutive, dark-eyed actress. She turned down a lucrative five-year contract with Universal and the opportunity to star in the studio's 1929 version of *Show Boat* so that she could appear in Arthur Hopkins' play "Machinal" (opposite a young Clark Gable).

Following a headlining role in D.W. Griffith's *The Struggle* (1931), Johann signed up with MGM and later RKO. Both engagements left the actress frustrated and professionally unfulfilled. Warners cast her opposite Edward G. Robinson in *Tiger Shark* (1932) and Universal planned to feature her in their production *Laughing Boy,* scripted by a budding John Huston. When this project failed to materialize, Johann consented to appear in *The Mummy* to fulfill her contractual obligation with the studio. Long working hours and Karl Freund's chicanery soured her on Tinsel Town; she made few films following this one (making it all the more unfortunate that Johann's multiperformance reincarnation flashbacks are lost to today's film buffs).

Back for another round of undead-chasing, David Manners and Edward Van Sloan virtually do a repeat of their performances in *Dracula.* Manners is stalwart enough in the film's early scenes in the Egyptian desert, but once he comes under Johann's spell, he once again reverts to a whiny schoolboy, begging her favors, and mouthing the most arcane love talk this side of Harlequin romances. Edward Van Sloan pursues the Mummy with the same dogged determination he did the vampire. The epitome of Old World sobriety and iron-fisted will, Van Sloan has the facility to make us *believe* the supernatural gibberish he spouts is gospel.

In supporting roles, Arthur Byron adequately fulfills the dictates of Balderston's directive ("The actor should be able to display nerves") while Noble Johnson, as the enslaved Nubian, exudes power without uttering a syllable. In his later years, Bramwell Fletcher balked about being remembered exclusively for *The Mummy* by film fans. He needn't have complained. Fletcher (who costarred with John Barrymore in 1931's *Svengali* and opposite Atwill in 1932's *The Silent Witness*) has gained cinematic immortality for his relatively brief role as The Man Who Laughed.

Jack Pierce's contribution to *The Mummy* is nothing less than extraordinary. Born in Greece in 1889, the slightly built former baseball player arrived in California in 1910. After obtaining work as a nickelodeon projectionist and later a theater manager, Pierce hooked up with Universal as a bit actor and assistant cameraman. But it was his early experiences in movie makeup work, and a striking ape guise for Fox's 1926 *The Monkey Talks,* that won Pierce the title of Universal's chief of studio makeup. (One report claims Pierce learned his trade by studying the techniques of his mentor Lon Chaney, Sr.)

Karl "Papa" Freund directs Boris Karloff in the flashback scenes from *The Mummy.*

Although Jack Pierce's talents as an artist have never been doubted, the man himself has gotten some bad publicity as of late. Veteran stuntman and actor Gil Perkins, whom Pierce transformed into a hairy imbecile for the 1957 Howco-International disaster *Teenage Monster,* described Jack Pierce as "a miserable old bastard" without a moment's hesitation. In her 1983 autobiography *Elsa Lanchester, Herself,* the late actress pictured Pierce as an arrogant, self-proclaimed monarch, "meting out wrath and intolerance by the bucketful." Lanchester continued, "He had his own *sanctum sanctorum,* and as you entered (you did not go in; you entered) *he* said good morning first. If I spoke first, he glared and slightly showed his upper teeth."

Virginia Christine, who underwent a particularly taxing makeup job for her role as the crumbling Princess Ananka in *The Mummy's Curse,* recently recalled the master in a slightly more favorable light. "He elevated himself to the position of top monster maker in the business. He was kind of an arrogant man, but we got along beautifully." Makeup man Harry Thomas, who inherited Pierce's reputation as a monster specialist in '50s horror cheapies, studied under him. "He was a little, feisty man that I enjoyed knowing; I respected his genius. I used to visit him over at Universal in the 1940s." Asked whether Pierce was bitter after the studio unceremoniously gave him the heave-ho in 1947, Thomas answered,

> Yes, he was kind of bitter. I believe his pride was hurt, and I don't know whether or not he resented the fact that Bud Westmore went in there and took his place. I believe that Universal mentioned that he was getting older, and they wanted somebody who would work faster, and do prosthetics; that was their excuse. I don't think anybody's ever compared with what he did. Universal was very, very ungrateful in doing this to a man whose pictures all made a lot of money.

Susanna Foster, on the other hand, saw only the positive side of the man. "How could anyone *not* get along with Jack Pierce?" she asks rhetorically. "He was cantankerous but as cute as hell. I loved him. He was sharp and to the point."

Karl Freund directed only a handful of pictures after *The Mummy,* including musical-comedies (*Moonlight and Pretzels,* 1933), dramas (*I Give My Love,* 1934) and all-star novelties (*The Gift of Gab,* also 1934). Shortly after *The Mummy's* release, Freund was assigned to direct Universal's elaborate and technically complex *Gulliver's Travels.* Slated for a Christmas, 1934, release, the production never made it to the soundstages. He left the studio when his contract expired in the fall of 1934. Freund's most noteworthy directorial accomplishment aside from *The Mummy* was MGM's *Mad Love* (1935), a kinky mix of sadism, madness and sexual aberration.

Directing held little intrigue for Freund the cameraman. "I gave up directing because of a dull routine of stories," he said in a 1950 interview. "The camera at least gives some latitude for special creativeness." In a later interview, he brusquely dismissed the director's role on a film with the comment, "Anyone can make a good cake if he has the right ingredients. It all depends on story, cast and circumstances."

Returning to his position behind the camera, Freund walked away with the Oscar for his work on 1937's *The Good Earth,* and was nominated four times afterward. When Lucille Ball wanted audience participation in the filming of her classic television series "I Love Lucy," Freund solved the problem with a multiple camera set-up which has since become standard procedure. As a result, Lucy made Freund chief cinematographer for Desilu.

At the time of his death (on May 3, 1969), Karl Freund had been enjoying a short-lived retirement from his multimillion dollar Photo Research Corporation, a firm which manufactured television and film equipment. Pooh-poohing the art of cinematography, Freund called candid camerawork "the only type of photography that is really art."

Secret of the Blue Room (1933)

Released July 20, 1933. 66 minutes. *Produced by* Carl Laemmle, Jr. *Directed by* Kurt Neumann. *Screenplay by* William Hurlbut. *Based on the story by* Erich Philippi. *Director of Photography:* Charles Stumar. *Art Director:* Stanley Fleischer. *Music by* Heinz Letton. *Film Editor:* Philip Cahn.

Lionel Atwill (Robert von Helldorf), Gloria Stuart (Irene von Helldorf), Paul Lukas (Capt. Walter Brink), Edward Arnold (Police Comr. Forster), Onslow Stevens (Frank Faber), William Janney (Thomas Brandt), Robert Barrat (Paul), Muriel Kirkland (Betty), Russell Hopton (Max), Elizabeth Patterson (Mary), Anders Van Haden (The Stranger), James Durkin (Kruger, the Commissioner's Assistant).

Probably one of the best of Universal's "nonhorror" horror films, *Secret of the Blue Room* is an engaging example of the early "spooky house" mystery at or near its best. It's a low budget film with few pretensions, but it has the advantages of a sturdy cast, a beguiling premise and a plot nicely filled with atmosphere. Most of the early Universal mysteries that masquerade as horror films are fairly dismal affairs, but *Secret of the Blue Room* remains a charming bit of spookery that still plays well today.

At the lonely, storm-swept Castle Helldorf, a birthday party is in progress. Present are Robert von Helldorf (Lionel Atwill), master of the castle; his daughter Irene (Gloria Stuart), who has just turned 21; and Irene's three suitors, Captain Walter Brink (Paul Lukas), a marine officer, Frank Faber (Onslow Stevens), a newspaper reporter, and Thomas Brandt (William Janney). Catching her alone, the boyish Tommy proposes to Irene but she doesn't take his offer seriously.

The subject of conversation turns to ghost stories and a reluctant von Helldorf is compelled by his weekend guests to tell the tragic story of the castle's "haunted" Blue Room. Twenty years before, Helldorf relates, his sister fell from the window of the blue salon and died in the castle moat. Four months later a houseguest was found shot to death in the room, an apparent suicide since the door was locked from the inside (although no gun was ever found). A detective seeking to unravel the riddle of the room spent a night there; there was a look of horror on his face when they found his body. All three of these mysterious deaths occurred at the stroke of one in the morning; the room has been locked up since. Tommy, determined to prove his courage to Irene, proposes to spend the night in the "haunted" guest chamber and Walter and Frank both agree to do the same on subsequent nights. Intercut throughout this early portion are short scenes of Paul (Robert Barrat), the butler, regretfully refusing to admit a shabby stranger (Anders Van Haden) out of the storm and into the house.

Come the dawn, the Blue Room is found to be vacant: the chamber had been locked from the inside, and a window overlooking the moat is wide open. It appears clear that Tommy has become a victim of the room, but von Helldorf will not notify the police until the body is found. Frank is insistent upon living up to his word and sleeping in the Blue Room that night. To ease the anxiety of Irene, who is downstairs, he loudly plays a piano as the hour of one approaches; just after a clock chimes, a shot rings out. The household members rush once again to the fatal room, where Frank's dead body is found.

Police Commissioner Forster (Edward Arnold) is summoned and immediately begins his inquiry. The stern, sharp-witted detective initially suspects that some of the servants may be involved in skullduggery but later sets his sights on von Helldorf, who has trouble keeping his story straight. Forster and his men apprehend the mystery stranger, and von Helldorf is forced into confessing that the man, his brother, is Irene's father. The brother had deserted his wife and baby daughter (Irene) years before; the wife died and von Helldorf raised Irene, posing as her father. Now a broken man, the brother has returned to beg for money, which von Helldorf planned to give him. Realizing that the brother and the Blue Room murder are unrelated, Forster drops the issue.

Hoping to help break the case, Walter announces his intention to stay in the Blue Room. At the stroke of one a secret wall panel opens and a shot is fired into the room, apparently striking Walter in the head. But the "victim" is only a dummy: the real Walter now springs forward, chasing the would-be assassin into the passage. A running gunfight ensues as Walter pursues the killer into the catacombs below the house; the two men brawl, with the killer about to gain the upper hand, when Forster and his men finally arrive on the scene and take the killer into custody. The culprit is young Tommy Brandt: hopelessly in love with Irene, Tommy had discovered the secret passage in the Blue Room and hatched this plan to take advantage of the room's tragic history and bump off his romantic rivals. Walter consoles Irene as Tommy, charged with Frank's murder, is led away by Forster's men.

Secret of the Blue Room has most of the recognizable elements of the classic Universal horror films, but never quite crosses the thin line that divides spooky mysteries from horror thrillers. There are gales blowing and thunder roaring, an old castle with a secret room, Lionel Atwill, a hidden passage, a shadowy stranger, lots of closeups on guilty-looking pusses and even the beloved *Swan Lake* playing behind the titles, but for all this atmosphere the picture unmistakably remains a whodunit at heart. It's become a sort of poor cousin to pictures like *The Old Dark House,* which kept their horror elements front-and-center and had the extra dividends of stars like Karloff. *Blue Room* is often dismissed by fans who are turned off by what the picture lacks and fail to appreciate the considerable charm it does exert.

There's a quaint once-upon-a-time quality about *Blue Room:* the castle setting, the Germanic feel of the picture, the way a ghost story told at midnight

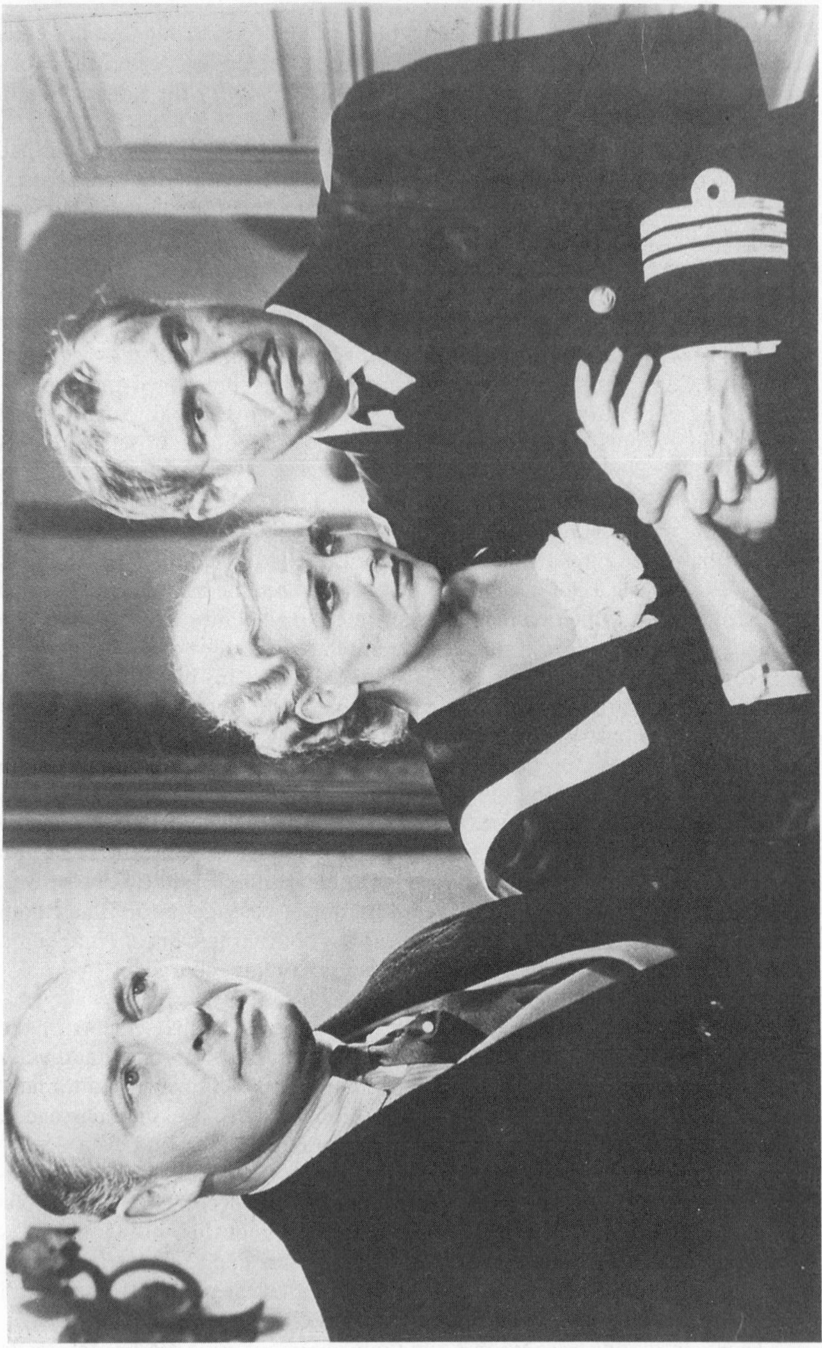

sparks the action of the film. It's the sort of picture that quietly draws a viewer into it, building steadily but without haste until its audience has been hooked. It has a great cast of character stars who have not yet reached their peaks and the added bonus of the *Old Dark House* set, brightly and luxuriantly appointed. The picture was made quickly and inexpensively ($69,000, the cheapest film made at Universal that year), and admittedly it never rises above second-feature status. But despite the economics involved *Blue Room* remains a strikingly good B.

As Robert von Helldorf, Lionel Atwill makes his first of 12 appearances in horror (and borderline-horror) Universal films. One of the most beloved of the oldtime chiller personalities, the distinguished British stage star got stuck with the "horror" tag early in his Hollywood career, when he starred in the Technicolored First National productions of *Doctor X* (1932) and *Mystery of the Wax Museum* (1933), and never quite shook it despite his fine work in many major pictures. Atwill generally tended to ham it up in his horror films, leaving no piece of scenery unchewed, but he's nicely reserved in *Blue Room*, giving a realistic performance rather than his usual too-exuberant exhibition.

Despite his star billing, Atwill is just a red herring in *Blue Room,* with the finger of suspicion pointing directly at him throughout most of the film's unspooling. The fact that he's Gloria Stuart's father tips off a savvy audience that he couldn't have done it (in mystery films, the heroine's father is never guilty), but he's fair game again after the midpoint revelation that in reality he's only her uncle (and maybe a "funny uncle" at that; twice in the picture he gives her lingering mouth kisses). But Atwill becomes too obvious a suspect, especially when the skulking killer dresses like him. (In early films like *Blue Room* Atwill is without the mustache we're all used to seeing, and it's curious how much older he looks in the earlier pictures than he does in later films where he sports that dashing little lip adornment.)

"Lionel was what we call 'an actor's ac-tor,' very much involved with one's self," Gloria Stuart reminisces. "He had been a fantastic matinee idol, but of course by the time he got to Universal he had a little potbelly, and he seemed old to me at the time although probably he was only in his late forties. He was a brilliant actor."

One of the most attractive and popular ingenues from the Golden Age of Universal horror films, Stuart began her stage career as an amateur in high school. While she was not a fan of motion pictures during her youth (she saw not more than a dozen pictures during her first 21 years), Stuart caught the acting bug while in college, played in various dramatic productions and ultimately ended up at the famed Pasadena Community Playhouse, where she appeared in such plays as "Twelfth Night" and "The Sea Gull."

Casting agents from Universal and Paramount caught her "Sea Gull" performance on opening night and both studios asked her to make a screen test. Stuart had little interest in working in films—her real ambition was to act on the New York stage—but she made the tests, both studios offered her contracts

Lionel Atwill, Gloria Stuart and Paul Lukas discover the identity of the mysterious murderer in *Secret of the Blue Room.*

and the whole mess ended up in arbitration with the MPAA, who suggested a coin toss to settle the dispute. Universal won, and Carl Laemmle, Jr.'s promise of a bright future at the studio convinced Stuart to sign with Universal.

In retrospect, she sees her decision as a "ghastly mistake": "I should never have gone to Universal, it was a second-rate studio and Paramount was first rate and I was very badly advised. I really didn't have to do it, and the more I think about it [*laughs*], the angrier I get." Regarding Junior Laemmle and his empty promise, she recalls, "No, he didn't have great plans for me because the studio was not making great films regularly. Once in a while they came up with an *Old Dark House* or a *Back Street* or something, but most of them were made by independent producers using Universal facilities. Junior Laemmle was very nice—I can't fault him—but Irving Thalberg he wasn't."

After making her movie debut as a loan-out player in Warner Bros. picture (1932's *Street of Women,* replacing a recalcitrant Marian Marsh), Stuart appeared in a baker's dozen Universal pictures, including *Air Mail* (1932), James Whale's *The Old Dark House* and *The Invisible Man, The Kiss Before the Mirror* (1933), *Beloved, I'll Tell the World* and *The Gift of Gab* (1934). Her dissatisfaction with Universal grew in 1934 when she went after roles in *Glamour* and *The Countess of Monte Cristo* only to see noncontract players like Constance Cummings and Fay Wray come in and play these parts.

Eventually Stuart got Universal to sell her contract to Fox, but when she ended up in the Sol Wurtzel B unit over there she knew that she was just spinning her wheels career-wise. When her Fox contract expired in 1939 she more or less quit Hollywood, returning to the stage, traveling and ultimately settling down to a normal life as wife and mother. After the death of her husband (writer Arthur Sheekman) in 1978, she decided once again to try her hand at acting, and has turned up in pictures like *Mass Appeal* (1984) and *Wildcats* (1986).

Contractually binding herself to Universal may have been a bad career move for Stuart, but for fans of such films as *The Old Dark House* and *Secret of the Blue Room* her presence goes a long way toward enhancing these vintage productions. While chic and classy, she also had an appealing girl-next-door quality and a realness that's missing from the performances of many of her acting contemporaries. It's sad that she considers her stint at Universal as an unfortunate blunder, but for most of us that MPAA coin-toss worked out just fine.

Other performances in *Blue Room* are equally professional. Paul Lukas is a smooth and likable hero, and his character clearly has the inside track with Irene throughout the film. A Hungarian with a background similar to Bela Lugosi's, Lukas is the sort of actor Lugosi might have become with a little more discipline and lot less pig-headedness; he parlayed his Continental suaveté into a lucrative Hollywood career.

Onslow Stevens, who was discovered at the Pasadena Playhouse the same night as Gloria Stuart, also gives his role color, and there's a nice feeling of easy camaraderie in the scenes he shares with rival suitor Lukas. Edward Arnold is an imposing presence as the detective and William Janney plays up his persuasive boyish qualities as Tommy. Early on Universal announced that Lillian

Bond would star with Atwill and Gloria Stuart in *Blue Room,* but she doesn't appear in the picture nor is there a role for a second leading actress *in* the picture.

Secret of the Blue Room was the Americanized version of a German (probably a Ufa) mystery film, and there's some murky looking stock footage in *Blue Room* that probably came from the earlier German production. The castle exteriors have an uncommonly authentic look to them (it's clearly not one of Universal's backlot "castles"); stock footage also looks to have been employed at other spots as well (von Helldorf's car leaving the castle grounds; a shot of the nearby forest). The film's locale is never specified but these clips, the castle setting, character names like von Helldorf and an all-around European flavor give the unmistakable impression that it's somewhere on the Continent (we'd guess Germany; Everson says Hungary). Unfortunately, unsuited players like Edward Arnold, Muriel Kirkland and Russell Hopton spoil the Continental ambience; they're too American in their looks, delivery and deportment, and don't fit into the picture at all. It's as though Castle Helldorf had somehow been transported from Europe to Upper Saddle River, New Jersey.

Universal tried an unusual publicity tack with *Secret of the Blue Room,* fashioning a pressbook that looked more like a daily newspaper. The front page told in bold headlines about the mysterious goings-on at Castle Helldorf, and various plot angles were described in the accompanying articles. The pressbook played up *Blue Room* as "The 10 Star Picture," and while the word "star" does apply to the first five or six players, the studio was on shaky ground bestowing this title on the others. Tenth-billed James Durkin, an unheard-of actor who briefly plays Edward Arnold's assistant, was probably pleased as punch to be listed as a star, but it was an obvious cheat.

Some writers feel that the mystery in *Blue Room* is embarrassingly transparent, with Janney clearly pinpointed as the killer right from the start. But critics of the day commended the picture for its surprise denouement, and none of the authors of this book pegged Janney as the killer the first time we saw *Secret of the Blue Room.* Janney's plans are flimsy and poorly thought-out, another debit that *Blue Room*'s detractors point out, but despite this forced finish the film plays nicely on its modest scale. The subplot of the mystery stranger only succeeds in muddling the plot slightly; this minor angle seems to have been lifted out of *The Hound of the Baskervilles* and adds little to the film. The footage involving von Helldorf's white-trash servants is also unrewarding, although (thankfully) these episodes never completely lapse into comedy relief. In another nice touch, the old Blue Room tragedies are never explained away: this may be simply an error of omission, but it enhances the picture that the eerie original mystery of the blue salon is not dispelled at the end.

Kurt Neumann's direction is just right for this type of no-frills melodrama. Neumann was brought to Hollywood from his native Germany by Junior Laemmle in the late 1920s. Among his first jobs at Universal was the directing of Spanish and German versions of Universal pictures; he later graduated(?) to Slim Summerville comedies. Neumann had a wooden leg and liked to tell people that he lost his real leg in World War I, fighting on the

German side, but Henry Koster more accurately remembers that Neumann got pegged by a bus. He never really made his mark in Hollywood, although today he's affectionately remembered for many of the science fiction films he made in the 1950s: *Rocketship X-M* (1950), *She Devil, Kronos* (1957) and *The Fly* (1958). Except for *Rocketship X-M,* a striking sci-fi noir, none of these films is really all that good, but these are the films that Neumann's reputation is built around and his fans say that he had a feel for the genre. Neumann's wife died while he was in the midst of shooting *Watusi* (*The Return to King Solomon's Mines*) in 1958 and Neumann himself, who was only in his early fifties, dropped dead ten days after wrapping up the picture. He's interred in a Jewish mausoleum in Hollywood, across from (but below!) third Stooge Shemp Howard.

A low-budget mystery item with the added spice of mild horror touches, *Secret of the Blue Room* remains an old-fashioned gem and a fine debut vehicle for Universal first-timer Lionel Atwill. It was remade twice by Universal (in 1938 as *The Missing Guest* and in 1944 as *Murder in the Blue Room*), and in both instances the quaint, almost indefinable charm of the original is replaced by lowbrow comedy hijinks. *Secret of the Blue Room* is Universal's best horror whodunit.

The Invisible Man (1933)

Released November 13, 1933. 70 minutes. *Produced by* Carl Laemmle, Jr. *Directed by* James Whale. *Screenplay by* R.C. Sherriff. *Based on the novel The Invisible Man by* H.G. Wells. *Director of Photography:* Arthur Edeson. *Art Director:* Charles D. Hall. *Film Editor:* Ted Kent. *Special Effects Photography:* John P. Fulton. *Retake Photography & Miniatures:* John J. Mescall. *Music by* W. Franke Harling. *Makeup by* Jack P. Pierce.

Claude Rains (Dr. Jack Griffin), Gloria Stuart (Flora Cranley), William Harrigan (Dr. Kemp), Henry Travers (Dr. Cranley), Una O'Connor (Jenny Hall), Forrester Harvey (Herbert Hall), Holmes Herbert (Chief of Police), E.E. Clive (Police Constable Jaffers), Dudley Digges (Chief of Detectives), Harry Stubbs (Police Inspector Bird), Donald Stuart (Inspector Lane), Merle Tottenham (Milly), Walter Brennan (Bicycle Owner), Dwight Frye (Reporter), Jameson Thomas, Craufurd Kent (Doctors), John Peter Richmond [John Carradine] (Informer), John Merivale (Newsboy), Violet Kemble Cooper (Woman), Robert Brower (Farmer), Bob Reeves, Jack Richardson, Robert Adair (Officials), Monte Montague (Policeman), Ted Billings, D'Arcy Corrigan (Villagers).

Deprive the average special effects film of its visual tricks and you rob it of its heart and soul. *The Invisible Man,* Universal's superb 1933 filmization of one of H.G. Wells' most enduring novels, is a firm exception to this rule. Its gripping narrative, masterful direction and believable performances elevate the film beyond mere novelty, and hold up alongside the unerring technical effects for the audience's attention. One of the handful of fantastic films unblemished by the ravages of time, *The Invisible Man* is a monument to the genius of four remarkable artists: director James Whale, screenwriter R.C. Sherriff, special effects ace John P. Fulton and star Claude Rains. So brilliant is this diverse combination of talents, it's difficult to image what the film would have been like minus the participation of any one of them. And yet, in *The Invisibile Man*'s earliest stages of development, three out of four of these artists weren't even considered for the project.

The phenomenal success of *Dracula* prompted Richard L. Schayer and Robert Florey to suggest the H.G. Wells novel as a suitable follow-up as early as 1931. Considering the cost and the complexities of such an undertaking, the Laemmles balked at the suggestion. *Frankenstein* followed the Tod Browning film, scoring an even greater success. The idea of translating the Wells novel to the screen came up again in December, 1931, in the mad scramble to furnish Universal's newly crowned King of Horror, Boris Karloff, with a fitting successor to *Frankenstein.* Along with *The Wolf Man, The Invisible Man* was earmarked as a Karloff starrer, with both productions to be developed by Robert Florey. Garrett Fort was elected to adapt the work for the screen.

But Universal, not willing to wait for Florey to iron out the project's considerable scriptwriting and technical difficulties, forged ahead and featured Karloff at the head of an illustrious cast in James Whale's *The Old Dark House.*

By June, 1932, the production took an unexpected turn. Producer Sam Bishoff left Universal to set up his own independent studio and invited Florey to accompany him. Florey, whose relations with the Front Office were often strained, decided to jump ship. Cyril Gardner was named as the new director, while John L. Balderston joined forces with Garrett Fort to write a viable script. (In the meantime, *The Wolf Man,* Florey's second proposed horror project, was abandoned.) Within three months, Gardner, Balderston and Fort joined the casualty list in the bumpy metamorphosis of *The Invisible Man* from printed page to silver screen.

German émigré E.A. Dupont came on the scene for what couldn't have amounted to more than a few weeks. The celebrated director of *Variety* (1925) had been brought to Hollywood by Carl Laemmle years before but returned to his native country following a disagreement over his first American picture. Like Florey, Dupont also lost out on his share of landmark fright films. Besides *The Invisible Man,* he was announced as director of *The Black Cat* the following year, only to be replaced by Edgar Ulmer. When Dupont finally made his directorial bow in horror films, it was the schlocky 1953 United Artists release *The Neanderthal Man,* a sad commentary on the career of this once-esteemed filmmaker.

At long last, the man who should have been Laemmle's first choice to direct the production, James Whale, took charge of *The Invisible Man* in September, 1932. No sooner did Universal sign on Paul Lukas (he had been at Universal for nine months and hadn't yet appeared in a picture), then the studio temporarily shelved Whale's new project, along with *The Road Back,* which was due to go before the cameras in early 1933. In their place, he was asked to direct *The Kiss Before the Mirror,* a romantic melodrama based on a Hungarian play, and starring Nancy Carroll, Frank Morgan and Lukas (whose name never came up again in conjunction with *The Invisible Man*).

Having fulfilled his obligation, Whale returned to work on *The Invisible Man,* making some immediate changes. He wasn't at all happy with Preston Sturges' free adaptation of the novel, which set the story in czarist Russia at the time of the Revolution, turning Wells' protagonist (in R.C. Sherriff's words) into "a sort of transparent Scarlet Pimpernel." As the film was being planned as a Karloff horror vehicle, Universal purchased the rights to the Philip Wylie novel *The Murderer Invisible,* published in 1931, with the intention of lifting a few of the more gruesome elements from that work and incorporating them into the adaptation of the Wells novel.

But Whale had ideas of his own. He respected Wells and insisted on a faithful translation. Most important of all, he wanted the character of Jack Griffin to be portrayed in such a way as to elicit the audience's sympathy, not just its fear. He entrusted the job of writing the script to his friend R.C.

Una O'Connor and Claude Rains in the perfect realization of the H.G. Wells novel, *The Invisible Man.*

Sherriff, who had labored long and hard on *The Road Back,* providing Whale with a screenplay faithful to the Erich Maria Remarque novel. (The film was eventually produced by the New Universal in 1937, and was all but ruined by the studio's concession to political pressures.)

Sherriff toiled on the script at his country home near London. Disregarding the studio's request that he draw his material from the Wylie book and the dozen or so failed scripts (one pictured Wells' hero as an alien who threatened to conquer the world with an invisible army of Martians!), Sherriff found his inspiration in the original source. His work completed, he returned to Hollywood in June, 1933, winning Whale's instant approval with his straightforward, unaffected adaptation. (Though some sources state that Philip Wylie revised Sherriff's final draft, there is no evidence to support this claim.)

Having won the first round in his battle to insure that *The Invisible Man* was true to his own vision, Whale next set about getting rid of Karloff, whom he always felt was wrong for the part and whose casting would further put the film in the horror category. Colin Clive's name came up as a possible alternative, but Whale had his heart set on Claude Rains, a 43-year-old fellow Briton whom Whale had befriended during the director's brief career as an actor on the stage. Rains had an admirable stage career in both London and New York, appearing on Broadway in a number of Theater Guild productions. But to motion picture audiences, he was an unknown, a fact that discouraged Junior Laemmle from following the advice of his star director. Besides, Rains had only recently tested at RKO, with disastrous results, for *A Bill of Divorcement* in the role eventually played by John Barrymore.

But Whale stuck to his guns and informed Rains' agent that he wanted the actor (who was then appearing in the Broadway play "Peace Palace") to give Hollywood another try. Rains was puzzled; after faring so poorly with his first screen test, why was he invited to make another one? "My agent said, 'I must admit there was a certain amount of laughter in your performance, but they were looking for a voice, not an actor,'" Rains later told an interviewer. The test called for the actor to enact the scene wherein Griffin boasts of his plans to rule the world to his associate Dr. Kemp.

Whale purposely kept Rains in the dark about the nature of his first Hollywood assignment and sent him over to the studio lab to have a cast made. "The laboratory had an odd look," Rains told a *New York Times* reporter. "There were all sorts of casts about, in papier-mâché, clay and plaster. Men in white coats walked around without noise. They made a cast and nailed me in it. Just my head stuck out. They smeared me with vaseline and then stood me off and threw plaster at my head. I thought I was going to die. Really, I'm afraid I behaved rather badly. I went back again the next day and saw masks and half-masks of my head all over the place."

Whale wanted the stage-trained actor to get a feel for film acting. In another chat with the press, Rains related, "James kept talking about this and that in pictures, about actors and pictures of whom I'd never heard. When he learned I'd only seen about six films in my life, he told me to go right out and see pictures—to see three a day until I knew something about them."

Sherriff wisely followed the author's example by beginning his script with the arrival of the mysterious stranger (Claude Rains) at the inn in Iping on a snowswept evening, at once evoking an aura of mystery and urgency. His entire head swathed in bandages, a pair of black goggles perched upon a jutting nose, he cuts a striking figure, arousing the curiosity of the townspeople. Is he the victim of some horrible accident, they wonder, or perhaps an escaped criminal? Setting up shop in one of Jenny Hall's (Una O'Connor) cozy parlors, the stranger immerses himself in scientific research.

We are briefed on the man's identity and the nature of his "problem" through the conversations of his fiancée Flora Cranley (Gloria Stuart), her father Dr. Cranley (Henry Travers), and his colleague Dr. Kemp (William Harrigan). The stranger is Jack Griffin. While in the midst of a crucial experiment he packed up his belongings and left town, without a word. Going through

Claude Rains (here with William Harrigan) soared to Hollywood stardom in the title role of *The Invisible Man*.

Griffin's effects, Cranley and Kemp discover a reference to a mysterious East Indian drug, monocane, which has the ability of bleaching the color out of living creatures, driving them mad in the process.

Unbeknownst to his friends, Griffin has rendered himself invisible, and is now struggling desperately to find the antidote to the drug. Out of his mind, he reveals his identity to the nosey villagers and makes a mad dash through the town, eluding the police, and terrorizing all in his path.

Seeking shelter at the home of Dr. Kemp, Griffin forces the astonished chemist to be his "partner" and intimidates him with his insane plans to rule the world. Kemp is forced to accompany the invisible Griffin back to Iping so that he may collect the journals he left behind at the inn. Before departing, the Invisible Man disrupts a police hearing and coldbloodedly murders an inspector (Harry Stubbs). A massive manhunt is mounted and search parties scour the countryside for the invisible killer.

At Kemp's entreaty, Flora makes a determined effort to placate Jack, but it is too late; the effects of the monocane have turned him into a power-hungry monster with a compulsion to kill. Learning Kemp has betrayed him, Griffin promises to murder him at ten o'clock the following evening. The Invisible

Man escapes from the house, making a mockery of the police's efforts to track him down, and disappears into the country.

Kemp is taken into protective custody as various traps are set to capture his would-be murderer. Meanwhile Griffin's reign of terror begins. A speeding train is derailed, its cars sent cascading down the side of a mountain; members of a search party are picked off one by one by the unseen fiend. Disguised as a policeman, Kemp drives deep into the country to elude Griffin, but to no avail: the Invisible Man has been alongside him all along. Bound with rope, Kemp is killed as Griffin sends his car hurtling of a cliff.

Forced to take shelter inside a barn during a blizzard, the Invisible Man's presence is detected by an old farmer (Robert Brower). He alerts the police to surround the barn and set it afire, drawing Griffin out into the open. Racing madly across the snow, Griffin is stopped by a policeman's bullet. He is taken to a hospital where he dies from his wound. In death, the power of the drug subsides and his body becomes visible once again.

Initial shooting on *The Invisible Man* began at the end of June, 1933, and concluded in late August. Whale worked closely with John P. Fulton on the complex special effects work, which consumed another two months. As Fulton had devised his own processes to pull off the feats described in the script, there was a hush-hush air about the closed set. John J. Mescall, who would later provide the wonderful camerawork for *The Black Cat* (1934) and *Bride of Frankenstein,* worked in unison with Fulton.

It was John P. Fulton who convinced Junior Laemmle that a method could be devised to bring an Invisible Man to life on the screen, thus encouraging Universal to purchase the screen rights to the property in the first place. Nicknamed "The Doctor" by his admiring colleagues and producers who required the services of a genie to pull off the miracles called for in their scripts, Fulton was a born innovator. He worked for the Frank Williams Laboratory in Hollywood, birthplace of the traveling matte system, and developed his talents in special photographic effects. Appointed by Universal as head of their effects department, Fulton contributed to virtually all their horror productions, from *Dracula* (he created those richly atmospheric glass shots of Castle Dracula and its environs) to *House of Dracula* (Carradine disintegrating into a skeleton, a wonderful, surrealistic dream sequence, etc.). Fulton left Universal in the fall of 1945 and joined up with Sam Goldwyn studios, which led to his winning his first Academy Award for the Danny Kaye vehicle *Wonder Man* (1945). (As head of Paramount's special effects department, he netted Oscars for *The Bridges at Toko-Ri,* 1954, and *The Ten Commandments,* 1956, and contributed interesting shoestring-budget effects for *I Married a Monster from Outer Space, The Space Children* and *The Colossus of New York,* all 1958.)

Fulton's greatest challenge on *The Invisible Man* was in those instances where a partially clad Invisible Man dominates the screen. In a fascinating interview Fulton granted *The American Cinematographer* (September, 1934), he divulged how this trick was accomplished:

> The wire technique could not be used, for the clothes would look empty, and would hardly move naturally. So we had recourse to multiple-printing—with variations. Most of these scenes involved other, normal characters, so we

> photographed these scenes in the normal manner, but without any trace of the invisible man. All of the action, of course, had to be carefully timed, as in any sort of double-exposure work. This negative was then developed in the normal manner.
>
> Then the special-process work began. We used a completely black set—walled and floored with black velvet, to be as nearly nonreflective as possible. Our actor was garbed from head to foot in black velvet tights, with black gloves, and a black headpiece rather like a driver's helmet. Over this, he wore whatever clothes might be required. This gave us a picture of the unsupported clothes moving around on a dead black field. From this negative, we made a print, and a duplicate negative which we intensified to serve as mattes for printing. Then, with an ordinary printer, we proceeded to make our composite: first we printed from the positive of the background and the normal action, using the intensified, negative matte to mask off the area where our invisible man's clothing was to move. Then we printed again, using the positive matte to shield the already printed area, and printing in the moving clothes from our "trick" negative. This printing operation made our duplicate, composite negative to be used in printing the final masterprints of the picture.
>
> The two principal difficulties, photographically speaking, were matching up the lighting on the visible parts of my shot with the general lighting used by Arthur Edeson, A.S.C., for the normal parts of the picture; and eliminating the various little imperfections—such as eye-holes, etc.—which were naturally picked up by the camera. This latter was done by retouching the film—frame by frame—with a brush and opaque dye. We photographed thousands of feet of film in the many 'takes' of the different scenes, and approximately 4,000 feet of film received individual hand-work treatment in some degree....

For the shot of the Invisible Man unwrapping the bandages around his head, the same system of combining multiple printing with traveling mattes was utilized. A stand-in was used for Rains for some of the more complicated shots that called for precisely-timed movements. Both the double and Rains endured stifling mid-summer's heat and the added ordeal of breathing through an air hose.

The whole experience had a humbling effect on the pompous Rains. He later told newswoman Eileen Creelman,

> And for five years, five years mind, I was prating to the Theater Guild about my artistic integrity. I was so cock-a-hoop about it. My artistic integrity. Then the first day at the studio James brought over some bandages. I asked about them; and he said, Oh, yes, I was to be bandaged during most of the picture. And there I had been fighting with the Theater Guild about my artistic integrity. Oh, it served me right.

As Whale had promised Junior Laemmle, *The Invisible Man* was a big success at the box office. The film broke house records at New York's immense Roxy Theater for the 1932–1933 season, shattering a three-year record. Eighty thousand patrons saw the film in four days; a whopping $42,000 was collected during the first week, prompting the theater to hold the film over for a second. *The Invisible Man* singlehandedly revived the fortunes of the financially ailing studio.

The Invisible Man was released at a time when the literary reputation of H.G. Wells was near its peak. Film reviewers, ever respectful of the distinguished man of latters, applauded Whale's good intentions with a shower of enthusiastic notices. (Actually, only the first third of the picture is truly faithful to Wells.) *The Invisible Man* instantly became one of the most acclaimed fantasy films of its day, and its reputation more than half a century later remains intact. Seldom studied today, Wells was once greatly admired for his lean prose style, dry wit and mastery of detail. He is remembered chiefly as a pioneer of early science fiction, a literary genre still widely regarded as pulp. Consequently, the internationally renowned author doesn't command the respect he once enjoyed. On the other hand, Whale, while rarely praised as a great director, is still ranked as one of the '30s most interesting stylists. In this age of reevaluation, it is no longer heresy to suggest that Whale's version of *The Invisible Man* is actually better than Wells'.

Wells' opening chapters are his best, and Whale and Sherriff wisely retained them. One literary critic described the first half of the novel as falling into the category of rural comedy; these early sequences capture the mystique of the heavily-bandaged stranger, as well as the quirky humor of the local rustics. Whale's casting of the secondary characters veered the film even more in the direction of comedy, particularly Irish stage performer Una O'Connor, whose beak-like nose and ear-splitting screeches became her trademark.

The Invisible Man is a typical James Whale production. Again, the director stubbornly avoids most of the formulaic, heavy-handed horror movie conventions. The best moments in *The Invisible Man* combine black comedy with a sense of awe (for example, the superb unmasking scene). The laughably pompous Constable Jaffers (E.E. Clive) struggles to keep his authoritative pose as Griffin whisks off his clothes. A madcap chase ensues as Jaffers and the villagers, literally tumbling over one another, try to handcuff the prancing shirt.

John Fulton's inventive technique was soon to become commonplace in pictures, but the effects here remain fresh and witty because Whale never allows *The Invisible Man* to become *just* a special effects picture. The director's splendid build-up in the expertly paced opening reels makes the film a dramatic as well as a technical tour de force. In another memorable confrontation with the law, Griffin pulls the trousers off a bobby. Moments later, we see a terrified woman charging down a country lane, pursued by the same pair of trousers merrily skipping along to a jaunty ditty. It's still a great scene, and one has to appreciate the shock value these episodes must have had on a 1933 audience experiencing them for the first time.

The Invisible Man is that rare case in which an obviously tacked-on romantic interest works. Wells devised wildly imaginative plots to hold his audience, but his characters are often insufficient and poorly developed. All that Wells really tells us about Griffin is that he is an albino (which presumably aided the invisibility process), as well as a sociopath. In fleshing out this slight, inadequate character, Sherriff and Whale expanded Wells' story (over the novelist's objections), and turned the invisibility formula into a mind-altering drug. This fresh twist provides Griffin with a badly needed motive for his misdeeds, thus elevating him from one-dimensional villain to tragic hero. In the bargain, he becomes a global, rather than a local menace. Griffin's love

Gloria Stuart consoles her dying transparent fiancé, in the climax of James Whale's *The Invisible Man.*

interest, alas, becomes a weepy bore, but at least she adds some much-needed poignancy to the story. Sherriff's superb dialogue, a vast improvement over Wells', is one of *The Invisible Man*'s greatest assets. The reunion of Griffin and Flora is, hands down, the best noneffects scene in the picture. Momentarily returning to his gentle, sensitive self, Griffin's mania slowly reasserts itself, culminating in his delivery of one of Sherriff's most colorful and impassioned speeches.

Whale employs Wells' detached, impersonal style in the fairly humorless last half, which focuses on the intense police investigation. Kemp's character, like Griffin's, is greatly embellished in the screenplay. Introduced late in the novel, Kemp is an old acquaintance of Griffin who meets up with the Invisible Man (not very convincingly) by chance. He is marked for death by Griffin at the earliest hint of betrayal; only in the movie is the threat carried out. The Invisible Man's casual little speech outlining his campaign of terror is still chilling in its dispassion. ("We'll start with a reign of terror. A few murders here and there. Murders of big men, murders of little men. Just to show we make no distinction. We might even wreck a train or two. . . .") Whale and Sherriff don't soft-pedal Griffin's atrocities, yet manage to keep him reasonably sympathetic. On the other hand, pains are taken to show Kemp as an unlikable weasel from the start. On screen for only a few moments, he is already trying to corral Griffin's fiancée.

Whale's supporting characters are a varied lot. The army of police officials are faceless and interchangeable; clearly, the director's heart is with the colorful country bumpkins who flock to the village inn. In Una O'Connor, Whale found the ideal comedienne to complement his black humor; loud, cantankerous and maddeningly officious, she is the perfect candidate to send the nerve-wracked Griffin teetering over the edge. (A minor detail, not in Sherriff's script, is a framed portrait of a coyly smiling Jenny hanging on the wall of the sitting room turned laboratory. At the height of his mad confrontation with the villagers, Griffin smashes a bottle of chemicals against the picture as though he were paying the landlady back for all those weeks he had spent under her thumb.)

The Invisible Man will long be remembered as the film that launched Claude Rains' long and distinguished American screen career. Whale needed an actor whose voice alone conveyed presence, and Rains fit the bill perfectly. As in most of his early films, Rains' performance is ripe and over-theatrical, but considering the role's limitations, his indulgences are forgivable. Within a few years, he adapted to screen acting brilliantly, refining his technique and mastering the fine art of underplaying.

Always a magnetic actor, Rains gave his most subtle performances in the '40s, keeping his flamboyance in check until the situation called for it (as in the powerful Senate scenes in 1939's *Mr. Smith Goes to Washington,* or the 1946 Bette Davis vehicle *Deception,* in which he was called upon to enact the role of an incorrigible ham). Trying to select a favorite among Rains' treasure-trove of performances isn't easy, but his Alex Sebastian, the debonair Nazi sympathizer in Alfred Hitchcock's 1946 *Notorious,* gets our vote.

Gloria Stuart, so sleek and capable in *The Old Dark House* and in a small role in Whale's *The Kiss Before the Mirror* (1933), does the best she can as the maudlin heroine. As Kemp, William Harrigan, who was chosen to replace the dull and stolid Chester Morris, is dull and stolid. Henry Travers, the British character actor who spent most of his movie career playing folksy Americans (he was Clarence the angel in Frank Capra's Christmas favorite, *It's a Wonderful Life,* 1946), is blandly efficient as Stuart's retiring scientist father. But it's Una O'Connor, Forrester Harvey and E.E. Clive who come off best in vividly etched featured roles. (Modern audiences get a kick out of spotting Walter Brennan, John Carradine and Dwight Frye in brief walk-ons.)

The Invisible Man is arguably the best H.G. Wells adaptation on film. Wells tried to top it with the British production of *Things to Come* (1936), but the passage of time has reduced this once state-of-the-art fantasy into a barely watchable bore. Admittedly a triumph of production design, not even the best efforts of Raymond Massey, Cedric Hardwicke and Ralph Richardson could find the dramatic core to the pompous, thesis-like oratory which posed as a plot.

The Invisible Man is one of the few of Universal horror classics that didn't enjoy a major remake. Hammer Pictures, not renowned for sophisticated special-effects films, passed up the opportunity to add the Wells character to its roster of Technicolored horrors. The two attempts at an "Invisible Man" television series, one produced in England in the late '50s, and the other made in the '70s by NBC with David McCallum in the title role, bore little if any resemblance to Wells.

Universal revived the Invisible Man character from time to time, but the attempt to continue a direct story line, as in the Frankenstein and Mummy pictures, proved awkward. The invisibility gimmick quickly became old hat as it found its way into increasingly inferior Hollywood movies that usually employed the same crude piano wire effects that Fulton rejected. *The Invisible Man* remains a definitive film of its kind. Wells and Whale captured the magic of their subject in two strokes of creativity that no one has yet been able to duplicate.

The Black Cat (1934)

Released May 7, 1934. Reissued by Realart as *The Vanishing Body*. 65 minutes. *Directed by* Edgar G. Ulmer. *Production Supervisor:* E.M. Asher. *Screenplay by* Peter Ruric. *Story by* Edgar G. Ulmer & Peter Ruric. *Suggested by the short story "The Black Cat" by* Edgar Allan Poe. *Continuity:* Tom Kilpatrick. *Assistant Directors:* W.J. Reiter & Sam Weisenthal. *Director of Photography:* John J. Mescall. *Film Editor:* Ray Curtiss. *Camera Operator:* King Gray. *Special Photographic Effects:* John P. Fulton. *Musical Director:* Heinz Roemheld. *Art Director:* Charles D. Hall. *Makeup by* Jack P. Pierce.

Boris Karloff (Hjalmar Poelzig), Bela Lugosi (Dr. Vitus Werdegast), David Manners (Peter Alison), Jacqueline Wells [Julie Bishop] (Joan Alison), Lucille Lund (Karen Werdegast Poelzig), Egon Brecher (The Majordomo), Harry Cording (Thamal), Albert Conti (The Lieutenant), Henry Armetta (The Sergeant), Anna Duncan (Maid), Andre Cheron (Train Conductor), Herman Bing* (Maitre d'Hotel), Luis Alberni (Train Steward), George Davis (Bus Driver), Alphonse Martell* (Porter), Tony Marlow (Border Patrolman), Paul Weigel (Station Master), Rodney Hildebrand* (Brakeman), Albert Polet* (Waiter), Peggy Terry, Lois January, Michael Mark, John George, Duskal Blane, King Baggott, John Peter Richmond [John Carradine], Harry Walker, Symona Boniface, Virginia Ainsworth, Paul Panzer (Cultists). [**Does not appear in the final print.*]

A work of great artistry and sinister beauty, *The Black Cat* occupies a very special niche in the history of macabre cinema. Ostensibly a showcase to exploit the mystiques of Universal's coveted Masters of Mayhem, Boris Karloff and Bela Lugosi, as well as the Edgar Allan Poe name, *The Black Cat* emerged as one of the decade's most disturbing exercises in the Grand Guignol. Boldly thumbing its nose at convention, the film is a veritable catalogue of human corruption. Sadism, shades of incest, revenge, murder, torture, voyeurism, Satan worship, ailurophobia, necrophilia, rape and (in an earlier phase) insanity are weaved into the nearly plotless story with remarkable precision. While this unsavory roll call of vice and obsession alienated many mainstream critics (who also took exception to the flagrant melodramatics and mugging of the two stars), *The Black Cat* provided the kind of sensationalism audiences craved. The picture quickly became Universal's top-grossing release of 1934.

Not only did *The Black Cat* come to symbolize the unalterable status of its star players (Lugosi would hereupon assume a subordinate position in terms of billing and salary to his professional rival, the mystically-billed KARLOFF), the production was an invaluable proving ground for its director, Edgar

Bela Lugosi gave a rare sympathetic performance in *The Black Cat*, but his old hamminess came out in the publicity pose. (Photo courtesy of Steve Jochsberger.)

George Ulmer. The Austrian-born filmmaker transformed a studio property into an intensely personal work. Keeping his adaptation faithful to the "spirit" if not the word of Poe, the psychologically-scarred Ulmer integrated into the work his personal quirks, including a childhood Oedipal complex and a fascination for such larger-than-life personalities as the notorious modern-day Satanist and all-purpose degenerate, Aleister Crowley.

The Black Cat begins in a crowded, smoke-congested train depot in Budapest. Aboard the Orient Express, en route to a Carpathian resort, American novelist Peter Alison (David Manners) and his new bride Joan (Julie Bishop) make the acquaintance of Dr. Vitus Werdegast (Bela Lugosi), a noted Hungarian psychiatrist. Werdegast, who bears the burden of a tragic past, reveals he is planning to visit an old "friend," whom he hasn't seen since the height of the war.

Sharing a bus, Werdegast, his giant servant Thamal (Harry Cording) and the Alisons are treated by the garrulous driver (George Davis) to a vivid account of the carnage that had taken place on that very spot during the Russian invasion of Hungary. The blinding storm causes the road to give way, sending the bus hurtling into a ravine. The driver is killed instantly while Joan sustains minor injuries. Gathering their belongings, the hardy band make their way up the side of the mountain to the cliff-top home of Werdegast's expectant host, renowned Austrian engineer Hjalmar Poelzig (Boris Karloff).

Werdegast and Poelzig clash almost immediately. The doctor accuses the enigmatic Poelzig of selling their side down the river while he was in command of Fort Marmaros (Poelzig's ultra-modern fortress stands atop the fort's foundation). Werdegast was taken prisoner and sent to Kurgaal, a dreadful military prison, "where the soul is killed, slowly." Upon his release, Werdegast learned that the unscrupulous Poelzig spirited away his (Werdegast's) wife and child after deceiving them into believing he had been killed in action. Now, 18 years later, the vengeful doctor has returned to reclaim his family.

After the Alisons have retired, Poelzig escorts Werdegast deep into the bowels of his dark kingdom. There, encased in glass cases, rest the perfectly preserved bodies of beautiful women. One of them is Werdegast's wife, Karen (Lucille Lund). Werdegast refuses to believe she died of natural causes, as Poelzig claims, and draws a revolver. But before he can pull the trigger, a black cat enters the room and terrifies him (Werdegast suffers from ailurophobia, a fear of cats). The two rivals agree to call a truce until the Alisons have departed. Unbeknownst to Werdegast, his daughter Karen (also Lucille Lund), now a grown woman, has succeeded her late mother as Poelzig's wife.

The following day, Peter and Joan attempt to leave Poelzig's house but find their efforts thwarted by their strange host. A chess match between Werdegast and Poelzig determines the fate of the newlyweds: the doctor's defeat puts the couple at the mercy of the crazed architect. Peter is imprisoned and Joan is locked away in an upstairs bedroom. Encountering Karen, Joan startles the confused girl with the news that her father is alive and has come to rescue her. Poelzig overhears the conversation and murders his wife in cold blood.

In the dark of the moon, Poelzig leads his cult of modern-day Satanists in a celebration of the Rites of Lucifer. Joan, who has been selected as the sacrificial maiden, is forced to witness the ceremony. Seconds before the sacrifice is to take place, Werdegast and Thamal take advantage of a commotion, snatching Joan from Poelzig's clutches and leading her to a secret passageway in the cellars. Finding his daughter's fresh corpse awaiting preparation in the embalming room, Werdegast goes berserk. He and Poelzig attack each other like wild animals. With the mortally-wounded Thamal's aid, Werdegast shackles Poelzig to a torture rack and slowly slices the skin from his body. Peter, who has escaped from the dungeon, misinterprets Werdegast's intentions and fires a shot into him. Igniting the dynamite that undermines the fortress, the dying Werdegast beseeches the couple to flee. Within minutes, a series of thunderous explosions reduces the house of horrors to rubble.

Many years before he earned the reputation as the Miracle Man of Poverty Row and was courted by the *auteurist* school of film critics, Edgar Ulmer cut his teeth as an assistant stage designer, art director and (for a brief time) an actor in Berlin. F.W. Murnau hired on the ambitious young man as his assistant and art director on such productions as *Faust*(1922) and *The Last Laugh* (1924). The following year, Ulmer came to America with Austrian director/producer Max Reinhardt and offered his services to Carl Laemmle as an art director. Not content with being restricted to a single craft, Ulmer went into training as a director and, between 1923 and 1929, directed or worked on a variety of two-reel Westerns and shorts. Occasionally, whenever his services were required, Ulmer returned to the art department. When production slackened at Universal, he would be loaned out to such studios as Fox where he toiled as a set designer and art director on Murnau's *Sunrise* (1927), *Tabu* (1931) and others. After a brief stay in Germany in 1929 (where he directed the documentarian *Menschen am Sonntag* for Ufa), Ulmer returned to Hollywood. MGM hired him for a position in the art department but found better use of his talents as a director of foreign language versions of such productions as *Anna Christie* (1930).

Back at Universal, Ulmer took a fancy to a project that had gone through several different treatments, without much success, a screen adaptation of the 1843 Edgar Allan Poe short story "The Black Cat." In December, 1932, Stanley Bergerman had co-authored a story treatment with Jack Cunningham which combined elements of Poe with a mad scientist/brain transplant plot, entitling it "The Brain Never Dies." It was rejected. Two months later, contract writer Tom Kilpatrick and producer/writer Dale Van Every (the team responsible for 1940's *Dr. Cyclops*) submitted a story draft which contained several elements used in the ultimately filmed Peter Ruric–Edgar Ulmer treatment: a young couple trapped in a castle ruled by two madmen, the dread of cats, torture on the rack and insanity. E.A. Dupont was scheduled to direct Boris Karloff in the impending production, but the Kilpatrick–Van Every draft was never scripted. Garrett Fort also worked on the project in its infancy, drafting a more or less faithful adaptation of the Poe story; his work wasn't used either.

With his friend Carl Laemmle, Jr., squarely in his corner (and Uncle Carl conveniently out of town), Edgar Ulmer set out to create the picture of his

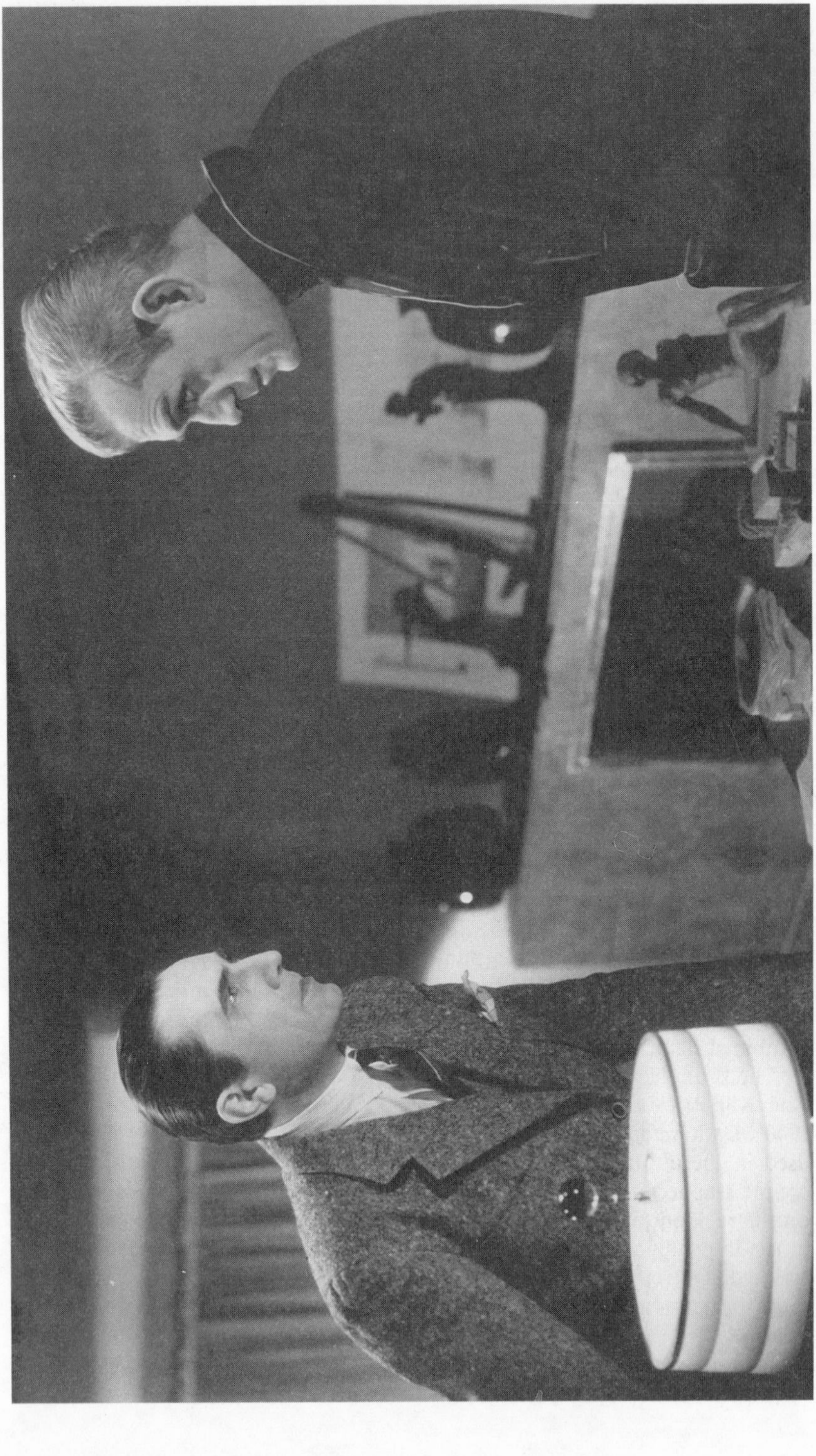

dreams, an Expressionistic horror tale utilizing the talents of both Karloff and Lugosi. Completing his story draft on February 6, 1934, Ulmer collaborated on a screenplay with Peter Ruric, a minor mystery story writer. On February 17 (two days before the finished script was submitted), *The Hollywood Reporter* made the announcement that shooting on *The Black Cat* would commence on the 24th of the month, and that actress Erin O'Brien-Moore had been tested for a principal role. But it wasn't until February 28 that John J. Mescall's cameras began recording the first scenes of the Ulmer production.

As was often the case with their horror film projects, Universal maintained that the production was draped in secrecy. Budgeted at a paltry $91,125, scheduled for a 15-day shoot, Edgar Ulmer's labor of love came in on March 17, one day over schedule.

And then, a bombshell was dropped over the director's head. The studio brass deemed that *The Black Cat* was too vile for public and censorial consumption.

On Sunday, March 25, Ulmer gathered together select members of his cast and technical crew for a hectic three-and-a-half days of retakes, and the filming of at least one entirely new sequence, a real beauty: Karloff's pre-dawn prowl through his private mausoleum. The tab for these alterations amounted to an additional $6,500. The final cost amounted to $95,745.31.

Wholesale changes were made in the portrayals of Werdegast and Karen. Ruric and Ulmer's original conception had the doctor losing his mind after seeing his wife's body in Poelzig's collection. Driven by vengeance and a lust for the nubile Joan Alison, Werdegast becomes a menace almost as dangerous as the satanist himself. Much to Lugosi's satisfaction, these dark glimpses into Werdegast's psyche were eliminated.

Lucille Lund's character was also given a complete overhaul. In a role that had been initially drawn as a human counterpart (à la Simone Simon in *Cat People*) Karen was now reduced to a child-like innocent with an almost celestial beauty.

Ulmer was also compelled to tone down the script's graphic depiction of Poelzig's torture and other suggestive/explicit moments. During editing, Ulmer discarded a lengthy preface which followed the main title, detailing the Alisons' wedding ceremony in Vienna, and a long-winded episode which featured the Orient Express' gregarious Maitre d'Hotel (Herman Bing) tempting the newlyweds with his culinary delights. A brief scene showing an uncharacteristically abrasive Peter Alison brow-beating Poelzig's Hungarian-speaking servants was also wisely shorn from the final print.

The critics were hardly impressed; the bashing that greeted *The Black Cat* was unprecedented even for a horror film. Reviewers found the picture revolting and incomprehensible; Karloff and Lugosi were cited for their endless mugging and the subject matter was branded unsavory. Even the trade papers, which tended to be kinder to the genre, pummelled the film mercilessly. The most frequent charge against *The Black Cat* is its major flaw—the lack of a

In their first teaming, *The Black Cat,* Bela Lugosi and Boris Karloff enjoyed equal footing.

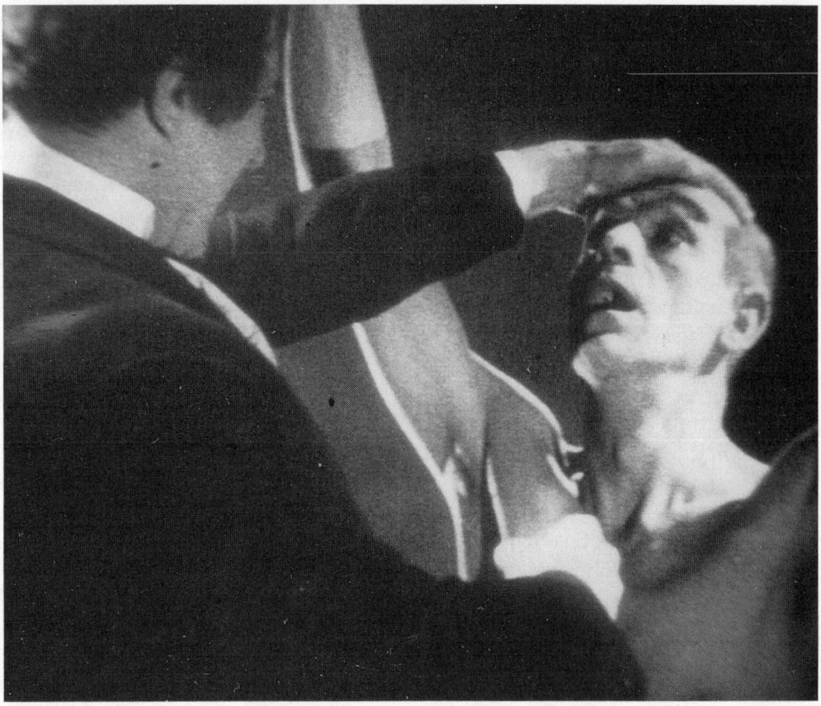

"How does it feel to hang on your own embalming rack, Hjalmar?" Lugosi and Karloff in Ulmer's *The Black Cat*.

clear-cut storyline. The latter-day canonization of Edgar Ulmer by the *auteurists* may have defused this charge to some degree. Today, the film is routinely praised, and praised lavishly, for its flamboyant technique. One cannot discuss *The Black Cat* without delving into the career of Edgar Ulmer but, the picture is hardly typical of the director. If anything, *The Black Cat* is an aberration in the highly erratic filmmaker's career.

The Black Cat not only towers over Ulmer's other horror/science fiction efforts, but a case can be made that it's his best film, including the laughably overrated *Detour* (1945). With the facilities of a major Hollywood studio at his disposal, Ulmer's imagination ran rampant. A fast shooter (he once bragged about completing 80 setups in one day), the director took full advantage of his three week shooting schedule and Charles D. Hall's extraordinary art deco sets to create a film visually as rich as anything Whale, Florey or Freund could have created. Whatever its dramatic weaknesses, *The Black Cat* displays Ulmer's talents as a designer and a stylist.

There wasn't much left of Poe in the final cut, but what little there remained is flavorful. In the original tale, Poe's typically dotty protagonist gouges out the eye of his pet black cat and later hangs the creature from a tree limb. Afterwards, he adopts another black cat as a substitute before regressing to his murderous ways. In the film, the black cat, too, serves as a recurring spectral figure. Werdegast spears the creature, but after a portentous discourse by Poelzig on the cat's proverbial nine lines, another black cat is seen in the satanist's arms. Whether the creature was resurrected or Poelzig has an endless supply is never revealed, but it's a nice, ambiguous touch.

The unrevised script contains yet another feline reference which did not make the final cut. In a postscript to the bus crash scene, a black cat suddenly materializes in the light of the moon to unnerve Werdegast as he is scrambling from the twisted wreckage. The black cat's frequent appearance serves to justify Universal's use of the Edgar Allan Poe story title, but Ulmer artfully weaves the creature's presence into the film as a lingering symbol of evil. Poelzig's black robes, evening jackets and even pajamas visually link him to his pet and they are often framed together in the same shot. The hypersensitive Werdegast isn't intent on slaying the animal in and of itself, but for what the cat stands for, adding to the supernatural aura of the picture.

The Black Cat has been hailed by such astute reviewers as William K. Everson for expertly evoking the somber spirit of Poe. Werdegast's longing for his lost love, his years of imprisonment, and his patient, well-plotted revenge, superficially at least, brand him as a typical Poe hero. But Ulmer himself downplayed the author's influence on his and Peter Ruric's screenplay. In a chatty, informative interview with Peter Bogdanovich, published in Todd McCarthy and Charles Flynn's *Kings of the Bs,* Ulmer admitted that the outline of the story evolved during discussions with Gustav Meyrinck, who novelized the story of "The Golem." Meyrinck's ambition was to write a play based on the French fortress Doumont (obviously the inspiration for Fort Marmaros in the film), which was shelled by the Germans during the Great War. The freed survivors, several of whom had gone mad, were faced with readjusting themselves after years of imprisonment. From this central idea, Ulmer added the two figures of Poelzig and Werdegast waging their sinister feud long after the war had ended.

Poe's original story was an uncompromised descent into madness, though little of this spills over into the Ulmer version. Werdegast, in fact, seems far more unhinged even in the revised, sympathetic version of his character than the principal heavy, Poelzig himself.

Poelzig is one of the most fascinating of the pre–Code horror characters. Beneath his otherworldly appearance and outward dispassion lurks a fertile if sadistic imagination. His collection of lovingly preserved, glass-encased corpses is an ingenious facet of his madness. The script is disturbingly casual in conveying how he murdered Werdegast's wife and courted her child, then finally killing her for mere disobedience. Poelzig is far more monstrous than any of Karloff's heavily grease-painted characters, and the actor plays him with subtlety and intelligence. (It's hard to believe John Ford's *The Lost Patrol,* which featured a hammy and uncontrolled Karloff, and *The Black Cat* were released within several months of each other.)

The picture is rife with excellent lines and Karloff, getting the lion's share, serves them up with chilling understatement. The most quotable is, "Did you hear that, Vitus? The phone is dead. Even the phone is dead." But Karloff is at his best in the longer passages, recalling the age-old myth of the black cat, or delivering a memorable monologue in a superb subjective shot as he and Lugosi ascend a spiral staircase. With the demonic second movement of Beethoven's *Symphony No. 7* tolling on the soundtrack, Poelzig wearily confesses how the War, too, has left him a burned-out shell. ("Are we any the less victims of the War than those whose bodies were torn asunder? Are we not both *the living dead*?")

The rewritten role of Werdegast (a major revision curiously unmentioned by Ulmer in his interview with Bogdanovich) could only have been a boon for Lugosi. Although it's an overripe and indulgent performance, the part of Werdegast ranks with Lugosi's Ygor as his best work. His and Karloff's characters ironically reflect their off-screen rivalry, with Poelzig somehow always getting the better of Werdegast, until Lugosi's ghastly retribution in the last reel. The recipient of far fewer juicy lines than Karloff, Lugosi still manages to be both sinister and poignant, finally coming off far more heroic than the prissy romantic lead, David Manners.

In one of his last Universal horror films, the boyish Manner is, as usual, beyond his depth. Having had little luck upstaging Karloff or Lugosi in separate pictures, he's quite up a creek pitted against the pair of them. Jacqueline Wells (later and better known as Julie Bishop) had a long career, appearing in such mainstream Hollywood fare as *Sands of Iwo Jima* (1949) and *The High and the Mighty* (1954). She was called upon to do little more than act demure, faint and occasionally shriek, all of which she handles capably. In the dual role of Lugosi's daughter and wife (in the person of one of Karloff's entombed beauties), Lucille Lund is an ethereal presence.

Ulmer had little affinity for humor; even the hardiest *auteurist* has a tough time sitting through Ulmer comedies such as *My Son, the Hero* (1943) and *St. Benny the Dip* (1951). Predictably, the comic banter between Albert Conti and Henry Armetta is the only poor scene in the movie. The scene, almost visibly stamped Comedy Relief, features the pair as bickering policemen boorishly debating the merits of their hometowns. But the film quickly rebounds, unreeling to a frantic and grotesque climax. The Black Mass episode alone qualifies *The Black Cat* as a masterpiece. A breathtaking succession of quick-takes framing Poelzig's clan in leering, atmospheric close-ups, the unsettling, low-keyed mood is shattered as the satanist braves his own torture rack.

Ulmer's horror career didn't pick up until 1944 when he revived his plans to bring *Bluebeard* to the screen. The production was originally slated by Universal as a vehicle for Karloff around the same time as *The Black Cat,* with Ulmer directing. By the time Ulmer resurrected the project, he had long been affiliated with grindhouse quickie factory PRC. Despite its bedraggled production values, *Bluebeard* remains a minor triumph. Buoyed by John Carradine's excellent performance and Ulmer's unerring eye for composition, the picture is everything that the highly-touted *Detour* isn't. But *Daughter of Dr. Jekyll* (1957), Ulmer's last horror entry, is a slipshod embarrassment. Unencumbered by style or imagination, this sleazy potboiler displays none of the ingenuity that marked *The Black Cat.* Even Ulmer's shoestring invasion-from-space mini-classic *The Man from Planet X* (1951) packed more atmosphere, although one suspects that its fog-shrouded landscape served to conceal the papier-mâché sets and crude studio backdrops.

If Edgar Ulmer's career isn't all that it's cracked up to be, *The Black Cat* at least proved him capable of producing a first-rate film under ideal conditions. The picture's all-classical background score perfectly captures the bizarre elegance of the director's striking visuals. Karloff and Lugosi are ideally matched, though it's fascinating to speculate how the pair would have fared had their roles been reversed. It's probably the only time in the stars' numerous couplings that such a swap might have been conceivable. Lugosi, always the more mystical of the two, could have easily filled the bill as Poelzig, while Karloff, quite adept at winning an audience's sympathy, would have made a splendid Werdegast.

In the current craze of plundering Hollywood's film vaults to piece together "restored" versions of classic movies, one hopes the original cut of *The Black Cat* will someday materialize. Though it's doubtful that anything could surpass the authorized release print, any new footage of what is perhaps the greatest Universal horror film would be a welcomed discovery.

Secret of the Chateau (1934)

Released December 3, 1934. 66 minutes. An L.L. Ostrow production. *Directed by* Richard Thorpe. *Screenplay by* Albert DeMond & Harry Behn. *Continuity by* Harry Behn. *Additional Dialogue by* Llewellyn Hughes. *Original Story by* Lawrence G. Blochman. *Director of Photography:* Robert Planck. *Film Editor:* Harry Marker. *Assistant Director:* Ralph Berger. *Sound Supervisor:* John A. Stransky, Jr.

Claire Dodd (Julie Verlaine), Alice White (Didi), Osgood Perkins (Martin), Jack La Rue (Lucien), George E. Stone (Armand), Clark Williams (Paul), William Faversham (Monsieur Fos/Professor Racque/Prahec), Ferdinand Gottschalk (Chief Inspector Marotte), DeWitt Jennings (Louis Bardou), Helen Ware (Madame Rombiere), Frank Reicher (Auctioneer), Alphonz Ethier (Commissioner), Paul Nicholson (Domme), Olaf Hytten (LaFarge), Cecil Elliott (Cook), Tony Merlo (Arthur), Frank Thornton (George).

Who is the infamous French book thief/murderer, Prahec? Will he (or she) succeed in nabbing a priceless first edition of the Gutenberg Bible? These are the questions that haunt Chief Inspector Marotte of the Paris Sûreté of Police in *Secret of the Chateau,* a creaky, dime-store whodunit that's all but forgotten today. It has little to distinguish it from the dozens of bottom-of-the-bill program mysteries that every Hollywood studio dumped out with depressing regularity in the 1930s.

Surprisingly, Universal took little advantage of the story's creepy country chateau setting and invested the film with precious few eerie effects. Chills and suspense are sacrificed for a succession of low-level gags. Judging from the film's advertising, however, one would have gotten the impression *Secret of the Chateau* was a bonafide horror film, or at least a mystery thriller with strong horrific elements. Ad lines, emblazoned above stock castle, bat and ghost artwork, cried "Shadows Come to Life!" "Traps Snare Women!" "Trunks Swallow Men!" and "Bells Toll Out Death!" Who would have thought, after reading these enticements, that the picture they were about to see was a lifeless hodgepodge about a stolen book? Those expecting the kind of florid melodrama so vividly displayed in *The Old Dark House* and *Secret of the Blue Room* were sorely disappointed.

Under the briskly efficient direction of Richard Thorpe, *Secret of the Chateau* went into production in late August, 1934, and wrapped in early September for a scheduled December theatrical release. Universal's sunny backlot European set was redressed to resemble the cafe and shop-dotted Montparnasse section of Paris. Rather than take advantage of Charles D. Hall's magnificent sets from the studio's past horror triumphs, the production's unbilled art director utilized prosaic library, dining room and bedroom sets.

Richard Thorpe earned a reputation in the film colony as a "one take director." He got his feet wet in vaudeville before coming to Hollywood in the late '20s. Graduating to the position of a Metro-Goldwyn-Mayer house director, Thorpe put his impersonal directorial stamp on pictures like *Night Must Fall* (1937), *Tarzan Finds a Son!* (1939) and the Joan Crawford vehicle *Above Suspicion* (1943). Evidently, someone at the Culver City superstudio felt Thorpe's talent lay in high-price costume epics. He directed, in rapid succession, *Ivanhoe, The Prisoner of Zenda* (both 1952), *Knights of the Round Table* (1954), *The Prodigal* (1955) and *Quentin Durward* (1956).

When the wealthy M. Le Duc de Poisse is mysteriously murdered, his collection of rare first editions is auctioned off by the respected Parisian dealer Monsieur Fos (William Faversham). Chief Inspector Marotte (Ferdinand Gottschalk) attends the event, believing it might attract Prahec, an infamous book thief and ruthless murderer whom he has been stalking for the past ten years.

Marotte spots Julie Verlaine (Claire Dodd) there and follows her. A convicted book thief who has just served six months in prison, Julie is attempting to go "straight," but is blackmailed into committing further thefts by her confederate Lucien (Jack La Rue). She befriends Paul (Clark Williams), nephew of the late Duc, who offers to sell Julie his uncle's rare first edition of the original Gutenberg Bible, which is reputed to be the most valuable book in existence. At Lucien's insistence, Julie accompanies the young artist to his chateau, Aubazines.

Julie gets a hostile reception from Louis Bardou (DeWitt Jennings), the village notary and executor of the Duc's estate. The blustery old man has the Bible safely hidden in a burglar-proof cabinet. Paul's announcement that he has promised to sell the book to Professor Racque of the Art Ministry irks both Bardou and Paul's aunt, Madame Rombiere (Helen Ware), who is entitled to half the book's worth. Fearing the Bible will be stolen, Bardou has had a counterfeit produced and has placed it in the cabinet above the concealed original.

Late that evening, the chateau's tranquility is disrupted by the sudden tolling of a bell in the old tower. "Its ringing is always followed by a death!" Madame Rombiere gasps. After all have retired, a shadowy figure steals into the library, shoots Bardou dead, and absconds with the tome.

Marotte and his men descend on the chateau and question the suspects. "A beautiful murder . . . a lovely murder," the little man beams with obvious relish as he examines Bardou's corpse. He questions Paul, his friend Armand (George E. Stone), Didi (Alice White), the butler Martin (Osgood Perkins) and Martin's wife, the cook (Cecil Elliott). Even the hunchbacked Professor Racque comes under Marotte's sharp scrutiny. Madame Rombiere startles the group by announcing it was the counterfeit Gutenberg, not the original, that was stolen. Her refusal to turn the book over to Marotte for safe-keeping seals her doom. Madame Rombiere's body is found the next morning following a second tolling of the bell.

His clues assembled, Marotte gathers the house guests in the library for the inevitable showdown. The secret hiding place of the real Gutenberg is discovered by Armand within the library's giant globe. Professor Racque suddenly draws a revolver. The chase is over . . . Marotte and his nemesis Prahec confront each other face to face. But before the master thief can fire, Marotte's men break in and overpower him. The "professor's" false beard falls to the floor, revealing Prahec's *true* identity—he is Monsieur Fos, the rare book dealer. Martin and his wife are arrested as Prahec's accomplices and Julie is pardoned for her past felonies by the magnanimous Marotte.

Like most films of its ilk, *Secret of the Chateau* doesn't stray far from familiar turf in fleshing out its slight story. All of the characters—from the wise-cracking blonde to the bull-headed administrator—are stock-bred. Potential victims can be spotted a mile away. Here again, we have a tolling bell warning of impending doom, quick reaction shots of each suspect as particularly incriminating bits of evidence are turned up, and most predictably of all, the round-up of the surviving suspects for the final reel's "surprise" denouement.

In this case, the revelation of the master criminal's real identity is less of surprise and more exasperation. Why pin the murders on a character who's been out of the story (and well forgotten) since the first reel? Observant audiences must have smelled a rat when William Faversham made his initial appearance at the chateau done up in a hoary wig and beard.

The Sûreté's Inspector Marotte is hardly a sleuth of the Sherlock Holmes school. For ten years he has been tracking down Prahec, yet he is still uncertain as to whether the criminal is male or female. Marotte's method of judging a person's innocence or guilt is by the amount of food left on the person's breakfast plate. ("A good appetite is a sign of a clear conscience.") Confronted with a collection of reasonably sound alibis, Marotte repeatedly grumbles, "Everyone has answers!" as though the suspects were purposely out to make his job difficult. The hiding place of the authentic Gutenberg is discovered not by Marotte or his men, but by the loutish Armand. To top it off, the detective can't be given credit even for discovering the identity of Prahec—Monsieur Fos tips his own hand when the Bible is found in the globe. British character actor Ferdinand Gottschalk imparts a certain impish charm to his portrayal of the smug but inefficient policeman.

The script by Albert DeMond and Harry Behn is loaded with witless gags, mostly insult humor between Alice White, DeWitt Jennings and Helen Ware. None of it is in the least bit funny. White, a shrill scatterbrained blonde who played more than her share of flappers and gun molls, gets her kicks snitching Jennings' floppy hairpiece, much to his irritation (and ours). George E. Stone, however, is the biggest offender in the "comic relief" department. As Armand, Stone swats flies with rare volumes, pours salad dressing over squeaky door hinges, and . . . well, you get the picture.

As Martin, the butler, Osgood Perkins (Tony's father) seems above the menial mentality of those upon whom he waits. He gets to deliver the film's

The tolling of a bell spells death in *Secret of the Chateau;* pictured here are Osgood Perkins, Clark Williams, Claire Dodd and Alice White.

single line of wry dialogue. When Alice White begs him to keep her company after DeWitt Jennings' murder, Perkins remarks in deadly serious fashion that he'd be glad to oblige but his wife wouldn't go for the idea. "She's funny that way," he says and takes his leave. Perkins was a familiar character player in early talkies; gangster Johnny Lovo in *Scarface* (1932) is probably his most remembered role. His real forte, however, was the American stage. Perkins "died with his boots on" at the age of 45 on September 21, 1937, after the final Broadway performance of "Susan and God" with Gertrude Lawrence.

Sixth-billed Clark Williams is the vanilla-bland leading man. *Secret of the Chateau* was his first film; an inconsequential role in *WereWolf of London* followed the next year. Former Ziegfeld Girl turned Warner Bros. contractee Claire Dodd does okay as the larcenous Julie. Jack La Rue trades on his Latin lover/gangster screen image as the swarthy Lucien, her partner-in-crime. Although she's not given an official credit, actress Binnie Barnes acted as the film's technical advisor. Her husband was renowned as one of London's best known dealers in rare books and manuscripts.

Secret of the Chateau is an ideal example of what reviewers of the day termed a "time killer." It's brief, somewhat lively, and totally predictable. Seldom revived, it richly deserves its status as a neglected Universal picture.

The Man Who Reclaimed His Head (1934)

Released December 24, 1934. 80 minutes. *Associate Producer:* Henry Henigson. *Produced by* Carl Laemmle, Jr. *Directed by* Edward Ludwig. *Screenplay by* Jean Bart [Marie Antoinette Sarlabous] & Samuel Ornitz. *From the play by* Jean Bart [Marie Antoinette Sarlabous]. *Director of Photography:* Merritt Gerstad. *Art Director:* Albert S. D'Agostino. *Musical Director:* Heinz Roemheld. *Film Editor:* Murray Seldeen. *Assistant Directors:* W.J. Reiter & Fred Frank.

Claude Rains (Paul Verin), Joan Bennett (Adele Verin), Lionel Atwill (Henri Dumont), Baby Jane [Juanita Quigley] (Linette Verin), Henry O'Neill (Fernand De Marnay), Henry Armetta (Laurent), Wallace Ford ("Curly"), Lawrence Grant (Marchand), William B. Davidson (Charlus), Gilbert Emery (His Excellency), Ferdinand Gottschalk (Baron), Hugh O'Connell (Danglas), Rollo Lloyd (Jean, De Marnay's Butler), Bessie Barriscale (Louise, the Verins' Maid), Valerie Hobson (Mimi, the Carnival Girl), G.P. Huntley, Jr. (Pierre), Doris Lloyd (Lulu), Noel Francis (Chon-Chon), Carol Coombe (Clerk), Phyllis Brooks (Secretary), Walter Walker, Edward Martindel, Craufurd Kent, Montague Shaw (Dignitaries), Purnell Pratt, Jameson Thomas, Edward Van Sloan (Munitions Board Directors), Judith Wood (Margot), James Donlan (Man in Theatre Box), Lloyd Hughes (Andre, a Secretary to Dumont), Bryant Washburn, Sr. (Antoine), Boyd Irwin (Petty Officer), Anderson Lawler (Jack), Will Stanton (Drunk Soldier), George Davis (Lorry Driver), Lionel Belmore (Train Conductor), Emerson Treacy (French Student/Attacked Pacifist), John Rutherford, Hyram A. Hoover, Lee Phelps (Soldiers), Rudy Cameron (Maitre D'Hotel), Norman Ainsley (Steward), Russ Powell (Station Master), Harry Cording (French Mechanic), Lilyan Irene (Woman Shopper), William Ruhl (Shopper's Husband), Rolfe Sedan (Waiter), Ben F. Hendricks (Chauffeur), Maurice Murphy (Leon), William Gould (Man), Carl Stockdale (Tradesman), Tom Ricketts, Jose Swickard, William West, Colin Kenny (Citizens), Ted Billings (Newsboy), William Worthington (Attendant), Nell Craig, Grace Cunard (Women), Wilfred North (Bit), Russ Clark (French Truck Driver), John Ince (Speaker), Margaret Mann (Granny).

Here we go with another picture that has no right being in this book, except through false advertising and perpetuated misconceptions. Despite the grisly promise of its title, *The Man Who Reclaimed His Head* is a straight melodrama indicting the war profiteers who made their fortunes through the slaughter of millions in World War I. It takes a little-explored theme and expands it into an effective message picture—but try and explain this to the average guy who's suffering through it on a Saturday afternoon "Creature Features."

The geniuses in the Universal publicity department obviously didn't quite know what to make of this thoughtful little exposé, so they took advantage of a gruesome sting in the picture's tail and promoted it as a horror thriller. The presence of actors like Claude Rains and Lionel Atwill made the deception even harder to see through. And like most all errors, it was perpetuated through the years, as *The Man Who Reclaimed His Head* got a horror movie buildup on local television stations, received coverage in monster magazines and remained permanently associated with horror films in the minds of too many fans. "This isn't a horror picture," begins Char's *Variety* review, but Char's small voice couldn't outshout the roar of the Universal publicity machine.

The film opens on a snowy winter's night in 1915, Paris, where a German air raid has just gotten underway. Drowned out by the booming of explosions are the sounds of a brawl and a woman's scream which come from the home of writer Paul Verin. A wild-eyed Verin (Claude Rains) leaves the house carrying his young daughter Linette (Baby Jane) and a large valise, walking to the home of eminent Paris lawyer De Marnay (Henry O'Neill). De Marnay, who knew Verin in his younger days, fears that the young intellectual has gone mad, and becomes convinced of this when Verin opens the valise to reveal its gruesome (unseen) contents. Verin, now slightly more lucid, begins to lay out his fantastic, tragic story....

Flashbacks show us a younger, happier Verin living a hand-to-mouth existence in prewar Paris with his wife Adele (Joan Bennett) and child Linette. Newspaper publisher Henri Dumont (Lionel Atwill), an old acquaintance of Verin's, appears at Verin's home and offers him a job ghost-writing pacifist editorials for him. Verin is reluctant because their last such association had ended with Dumont betraying him, but Adele is tired of the grind of poverty and convinces her husband to accept the high-paying job.

Verin begins to write heartfelt peace-mongering editorials under Dumont's name, and soon the publisher is the toast of Paris. But unbeknownst to Verin, the politically-ambitious Dumont is planning to betray the idealistic writer once again. Selling out to the munitions manufacturers, Dumont double-crosses Verin and uses his newfound influence to abruptly sway public opinion toward patriotism—and war. Archduke Ferdinand is assassinated, armies mobilize and munitions stocks boom on all exchanges while Dumont rides to yet-greater power on the wave of war hysteria. Verin is inducted into the French Army, sent to the front and finally transferred to Verdun, all through the behind-the-scenes manipulations of Dumont, who doesn't want Verin coming home. But when Verin overhears men discussing the false rumor that Dumont has taken up with Adele, the little egghead finally gets wise. Racing home from the front, he arrives just in time to find Dumont forcing himself upon the unwilling Adele. Verin's mind temporarily snaps as he pulls out his bayonet and stalks Dumont; this is the point at which the picture had begun. Obsessed with the odd notion that Dumont has stolen his mind, Verin struggles to hack off the publisher's head. Adele faints and screams (in the wrong order) as the blade finds its mark. Dumont's severed noggin winds up in Verin's knapsack.

Gendarmes arrive at the De Marnay home just as Verin finishes his story. De Marnay gladly agrees to act as Verin's defense at his trial, confident that no jury will convict the man. Verin, who has found peace again at last, leaves in the custody of the police with Adele at his side.

The Man Who Reclaimed His Head was based on a short-lived play that opened at New York's Broadhurst Theatre on September 8, 1932. Penned by Jean Bart (a pseudonym for Marie Antoinette Sarlabous), the pseudohistorical melodrama starred Claude Rains as Verin, Jean Arthur as his wife and Stuart Casey as the publisher. Had the play been transferred to film with more fidelity, *The Man Who Reclaimed His Head* might be at least partially deserving of its horror reputation: in the original play, Verin is deformed and (an added indignity) asthmatic. Herbert Biberman, husband of character star Gale Sondergaard, directed the play through its 28 performances.

Universal bought the Broadway play and put Bart to work on the screenplay. Early on Karl Freund was assigned to direct the film; another early plan called for

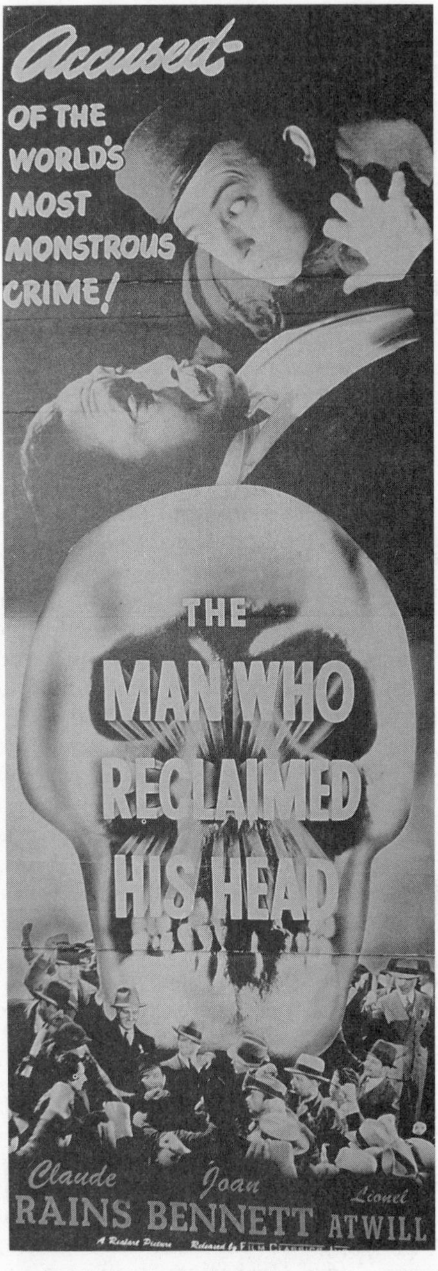

Claude Rains reprised his stage triumph in the 1935 film version of the Jean Bart play *The Man Who Reclaimed His Head.*

Lowell Sherman to direct as well as play the role of Dumont (eventually these chores were split up between Edward Ludwig and Lionel Atwill). *The Man Who Reclaimed His Head* was the first in a two-picture deal Claude Rains made with Universal; the studio initially lined up *The Return [Bride] of Frankenstein* as the second Rains film, but the actor instead made good his contractual obligation with *Mystery of Edwin Drood.* Coincidentally, actress Phyllis Brooks, who was briefly considered for the role of Frankenstein's Bride, has a bit part in *Reclaimed,* as a secretary.

Reviewers greeted *The Man Who Reclaimed His Head* coolly; *Variety*'s Char called it "arresting screen material," despite its fantastic story, in a mostly favorable writeup. More reviewers fell in line with *The New York Post*'s Thornton Delehanty, who branded it "a stilted harangue against war . . . made to seem even more stilted by pompous dialogue and an exhibition of artificial acting which probably is unique in recent screen history."

Fans who are partial to Rains and Atwill, and who have gotten over the disappointment that invariably follows the first screening, should find much to admire in the picture. Though the plot seems a bit long in unraveling, the picture does generate strong melodrama, and there's added interest in the fact that the story is based on then-recent disclosures about real-life munitions kings. The production is A-1, with opulent sets, impressive throngs of extras and an overall glossy look all combining to give the impression of a first-rate picture.

Performances are generally good, although there's room for improvement in Rains' interpretation. Rains' Verin is a doormat for the world, a mousy little recluse who's got VICTIM written all over him. Early on he appears tickled pink by his poorhouse lifestyle, and prefers to shower his wife with affection rather than to make an effort to improve their lot. A too-humble bookworm, Verin is the type of character with whom it's difficult to associate.

Rains is generally better in his scenes with Atwill, nicely conveying his near-rabid passion for peace in well-done and thought-provoking dialogue exchanges; the climactic scenes, where Rains finally gets his dander up, are genuinely effective, although diminutive Rains would clearly be no match for Atwill in their close-quarters struggle. Atwill's his dependable self: bluff and hearty, urbane and charming, sleek and dangerous, as the situations dictate. Joan Bennett, still a blonde, gives what was probably her best performance to date as Rains' wife, who becomes a triangle point as the picture builds toward its finish. (Bennett was also the highest-paid player in the cast, raking in $12,500 to Rains' $10,500 and Atwill's $8,000.)

All other roles are strictly subordinate: Henry O'Neill and Wallace Ford fare best in their supporting assignments. Baby Jane (Juanita Quigley), who plays the young daughter, is a squawking, unmodulated brat of a child actress whose scenes stop the picture dead in its tracks. Lots of easily-recognized faces turn up in unbilled bits: Gilbert Emery and Edward Van Sloan as munitions board directors, Valerie Hobson as a carnival girl, Doris Lloyd as an opera patron, Lloyd Hughes as Atwill's secretary and Lionel Belmore as a train conductor.

The picture tells its story in flashback, probably so that the minor horror angle (deranged Rains toting the disembodied head around) could be exploited

Altruistic Claude Rains is no match for the machiavellian treachery of Lionel Atwill, in *The Man Who Reclaimed His Head.*

as a takeoff point as well as in the finale. The framing sequences are far from the best scenes in the picture, although Rains is fairly convincing in his overwrought state. Director Ludwig deftly uses lighting and shadows in an effort to build suspense in the opening scene, but a few too many silent shots of Henry O'Neill casting apprehensive sidelong looks at the valise-in-question render the scene slightly comical; the eerie effect that the picture was going after here doesn't quite come off. A far more memorable scene is set aboard a giant yacht, with Atwill and munitions kings from the four corners of the world dispassionately hatching their plans to exploit the coming war. There's also a neat moment toward the end, when Rains decides to desert his post and return to Paris to settle his score with Atwill. Running recklessly across a crowded train platform, he collides with a nun who drops her cross while Rains drops his bayonet. Picking up both, Rains thoughtfully weighs the two symbolic objects in his hands before making his unalterable choice: he returns the cross, retaining the weapon. It's sledgehammer symbolism, but the scene gives us the satisfying foreknowledge that the picture is building to something other than a talk, talk, talk ending.

The Man Who Reclaimed His Head is a handsome dramatic picture which builds interest steadily and conceals its stage origins well. Bolstered by a good cast and some solid performances, it's a production for which Universal could and should have been proud. In promoting it as a horror film, the studio sought once again to rook audiences, but this time around they also rooked themselves. And this is unfortunate, since *The Man Who* is too sincere and well made a picture to be scoffed at by some bored kid who's catching it on a television double-bill with *The Incredible Two-Headed Transplant*.

Life Returns (1935)

Released January, 1935. Re-released by Scienart Pictures in 1938. 60 minutes. *Produced by* Lou Ostrow. *Directed by* Eugen [Eugene] Frenke. *Screenplay & Adaptation:* Arthur Horman & John F. Goodrich. *Dialogue by* Mary McCarthy & L. Wolfe Gilbert. *Original Story:* Eugen [Eugene] Frenke & James Hogan. *Photography:* Robert Planck. *Art Director:* Ralph Berger. *Musical Score:* Oliver Wallace & Clifford Vaughan. *Film Editor:* Harry Marker.

Onslow Stevens (Dr. John Kendrick), George Breakston (Danny Kendrick), Lois Wilson (Dr. Louise Stone), Valerie Hobson (Mrs. Kendrick), Stanley Fields (Dogcatcher). Frank Reicher (Dr. James). Richard Carle (A.K. Arnold), Dean Benton (Interne), Lois January (Nurse), Richard Quine (Mickey), Maidel Turner (Mrs. Vandergriff), George MacQuarrie (Judge), Otis Harlan (Dr. Henderson), Robert E. Cornish (himself), Mario Margutti, William Black, Ralph Celmar, Roderick Krida (Cornish's Staff).

Every fantasy film buff has experienced this situation countless times. There's a picture you've heard about for years but never seen. It's got a horror or science fiction angle, the plot sounds intriguing, there are players in it that you like, and so on. You get to the point where you're just *aching* to see this blasted picture. Finally good fortune smiles upon you and the opportunity presents itself.

Ten minutes into the picture and your enthusiasm is starting to go. Ten more minutes: your enthusiasm is gone and your interest is starting to go. You can't keep your mind from wandering, and the plot begins to get away from you. Long before the picture's over you're daydreaming like crazy and wishing you had never heard of the damned thing. For Universal fans, that picture is *Life Returns.*

One of the least-seen films covered in this book, *Life Returns* is a hopeless, exasperating conglomeration of events and images masquerading as a motion picture. The uninitiated know only that Universal released it and that the title and plotline suggest a borderline science fiction theme, and so expectations rise. But the cold light of rediscovery reveals a cheap and dismal production which builds a silly framework around a questionable scientific achievement.

On May 22, 1934, in reality, at the University of Southern California, a young scientist named Robert E. Cornish succeeded in surgically and chemically restoring "life" to a "dead" dog. Abetted by a team of assistants, Cornish coordinated and dominated the unusual experiment, which was captured for posterity by motion picture cameras. Dr. Eugene Frenke, a German producer-director, apparently latched onto Cornish and the filmed record of his operation, decided to make a film which would take advantage of this historical footage and struck a deal with Universal, contracting to split costs and profits on the production.

The film opens at Hoskins University, where three young eggheads have embarked on a noble mission. John Kendrick (Onslow Stevens), Louise Stone (Lois Wilson) and Robert Cornish (as himself) are striving to develop a life-giving fluid that can restore life to the dead. Upon their graduation Kendrick proudly announces to Louise and Cornish that he has secured positions for all three at the Arnold Research Laboratory. But Louise and Cornish, puzzled and dismayed by Kendrick's action, are convinced that a commercial laboratory is no place for this type of research: for one thing, the Arnold lab would take all the credit for the eventual discovery (so much for altruism!). Kendrick, undeterred, breaks off with Louise and Cornish and goes to work at the Arnold foundation.

A montage suggests the passage of time, and also alerts us to Kendrick's marriage to a socialite (Valerie Hobson) to whom the film doesn't even bother to give a name. A.K. Arnold (Richard Carle), head of the foundation, loses faith in Kendrick's experiment, which he has also decided is not commercial. "We want this foundation to help the living to live better—to give them better facial creams, better nail polish, better dandruff cures—all for a nominal sum!" the crotchety Arnold announces. Kendrick can't understand why his project is being dropped. Arnold tries to soften the blow by assigning him to create a hair-restoring brush out of pig's bristles. Kendrick resigns.

Already the picture is beginning to come apart. Obviously the audience was expected to perceive Arnold as an exploitation-minded meddler, interfering with the work of great men and true scientists. But Kendrick comes across as such a dazed, glassy-eyed dreamer that Arnold's misgivings seem well-founded. Kendrick had walked into the office annoyed at the interruption in his work, insisted on a new and expensive piece of lab equipment and became petulant and impatient at Arnold's delay in okaying the requisition. Apparently he's been there for years and hasn't made a bit of progress. He slipped into a world of his own while talking about his experiment, started whimpering when he didn't get his way, and staggered out like a zombie. Instead of resenting Arnold, the audience feels that he probably deserves a medal for putting up with Kendrick for as long as he did!

Kendrick has a private medical practice on the side, but he's in such a daze over the termination of this research work that he lets it go all to hell. Mrs. Kendrick tries to argue some sense into him—he has a wife and a little boy to support, yet all he does is mope and whine—but her pleas go unheeded. A few more years pass, and Mrs. Kendrick dies of some undisclosed ailment. Court officials want to send Kendrick's young son Danny (George Breakston) to Juvenile Hall; the irresponsible Kendrick shows up in court in his usual trance, looking like someone who sleeps in a cement mixer. To avoid being sent to Juvenile Hall, Danny and his dog Scooter run away.

A lot more footage unspools with nothing really happening. Danny finds a home with a gang of kids his own age, and brags about his genius father.

Kendrick lies around his house looking stoned while Louise and Cornish stand around the cheapest lab set in motion picture history and talk about him.

The local dogcatcher (Stanley Fields) nabs Scooter, and Danny is heartbroken. Danny's gang scales the dog pound wall in an attempt to spring the mutt, but everything goes wrong and one of the kids gets a leg fracture during the getaway. The dogcatcher gasses Scooter.

Danny begs his Dad to help the kid with the broken leg and to revive Scooter, but Kendrick moans that he can't do either. Finally fed up with his worthless dad, and rightfully so, Danny bawls him out and heads for Juvenile Hall to turn himself in. Kendrick finally snaps out of his slump, retrieves the dog's body and rushes it to a hospital. The U.S.C. film is cut into the picture at this point, with studio shots of Kendrick, Louise and other actor-doctors spliced in at intervals. Life returns to Scooter and Danny's faith in his father is restored.

Life Returns is a meandering, meaningless mess, one part unconvincing drama, one part boy-and-his-dog pabulum, and one part "science fact." The entire affair has a slapdash, slung-together quality reminiscent of the era's hopelessly cheap independent productions: it has the low-grade look and feel of a film consisting solely of first takes, good, bad and indifferent.

As Dr. Kendrick, actor Onslow Stevens is completely helpless to turn in anything other than a dreary, monotonous and humiliating performance. Stevens staggers through nearly the entire film in a fog, his hair mussed and clothes disheveled. Stevens' character loses our sympathy early on, in the scene at the research laboratory where his neurotic side first begins to show through. You feel as though the picture is expecting you to pull for Kendrick throughout, but when he allows his ailing wife to die and permits his son to live in the streets it becomes plain that Kendrick belongs not in a laboratory but in an institution. It's unclear what director Frenke hoped to achieve by allowing the character to sink so low and then building so much of the film around him anyway.

Kendrick probably does less than any other leading character in the history of motion pictures: he starts a project he can't finish, gets a job he can't hold and builds a family he can't support. He does not take part in the climactic experiment, merely standing off to one side, explaining the procedure and having the gall to take partial credit for the discovery. Throughout most of the film he dozes on an old couch.

The entire experience must surely have been an embarrassment for Onslow Stevens, a stage and screen actor capable of far better work. A native Californian, Stevens had begun acting with the Pasadena Community Playhouse in 1926 and appeared in his first film (Universal's serial *Heroes of the West*) in 1932. Bouncing back and forth between film and stage work, Stevens racked up a total of nearly 100 movie appearances between 1932 and 1962, including many films with horror or science fiction elements: *Secret of the Blue Room,* the serial *The Vanishing Shadow, The Monster and the Girl* (1941), *House of Dracula, The Creeper* (1948), *Them!* (1954), *The Couch* (1962) and others. He never had sufficient dash to gain popularity as a leading man nor the panache to establish himself as a memorable movie villain (he made numerous stabs at both), and soon settled into a niche as a reliable Hollywood supporting actor.

As Kendrick's son Danny, child actor George Breakston is slightly artificial and irritating. Breakston stuck with acting until the early '40s (he was in several of MGM's *Andy Hardy* films), remained overseas after serving in World War II and then later reappeared to try his hand as a producer of films like *The Manster* (1962) and *The Boy Who Cried Murder* (a 1966 rehash of the 1949 *noir* classic *The Window*). No one in the rest of the cast is in the picture long enough to make any real impression. Lois Wilson, who plays Louise, was a silent screen star on her way down, while 17-year-old British actress Valerie Hobson, who plays Kendrick's wife, was on her way up. Stanley Fields, Frank Reicher and Richard Carle are among the most recognizable faces in the supporting cast. Dr. Cornish, who appears as himself, hardly opens his mouth. Child actor Richard Quine, who plays a member of Danny's gang, later turned director and helmed films like *The Solid Gold Cadillac* (1956), *Operation Mad Ball* (1957), *Bell, Book and Candle* (1958), *The World of Suzie Wong* (1960) and *W* (a.k.a. *I Want Her Dead*) (1974). He killed himself in 1989. Scooter's portrayal of the dog is highly convincing and probably the best work in the film.

Life Returns is a prime example of a picture jerry-built around a single gimmick (the Cornish scenes). The footage of Cornish and his staff working to revive the dog are crudely filmed and uninteresting: shots of the various doctors at work and of Cornish coordinating things and doing a little skeevy mouth-to-mouth resuscitating. (These operation scenes are intercut with scenes of youngster Breakston tearfully hurrying toward the orphanage, with weepy violins on the soundtrack.)

Cornish and his scientific achievement appear to have slipped into near-total obscurity, which does not seem like it would be the case if Cornish had actually accomplished what the film purports he has done. The whole idea of a life-restoring serum on the real-life medical horizon is simply too far-out to accept and overlooks, for one thing, the brain's constant need for oxygenation.

James Hogan was responsible (along with Frenke) for the original story of *Life Returns,* which is interesting since Hogan later directed *The Mad Ghoul,* a somewhat similar but infinitely more satisfying Universal film. Frenke also engaged Reginald LeBorg as a writer on *Life Returns,* but the pair had disagreements over the handling of the story and LeBorg was dropped. Since LeBorg received no screen credit, his work may have been simply discarded.

Frenke himself has had only the spottiest of motion picture careers. He was, and still is, the husband of actress Anna Sten, the Edsel of '30s glamour girls, and most of his early pictures like *Exile Express* (1939), which he produced, and *Two Who Dared* (1937), which he produced and directed, were feeble attempts to "return life" to her moribund acting career. Frenke later took a small step-up in class, producing "better" pictures like *Let's Live a Little* (1948), in which the ubiquitous Sten was third-billed in support of Hedy Lamarr; *Heaven Knows, Mr. Allison* (1957), *The Barbarian and the Geisha* (1958) and *The Last Sunset* (1961). In 1962 he produced *The Nun and the*

Sergeant, a Korean War cheapie with (yawn) Sten again, and in '69 he coproduced what looks to be his last film to date, the U.S./British *The Royal Hunt of the Sun*.

Frenke apparently was happy with *Life Returns* (at least *some*body was!), and he even pressed Universal to allow him to make a follow-up picture in which a dead man was brought back to life. Universal couldn't quite see it, and Doc Cornish was demanding too much money for his participation and the use of his name anyway. In a funny postscript, Karl Freund contacted Frenke and asked to be allowed to view a print of *Life Returns.* Frenke had no idea why Freund wanted to see it but he probably assumed it had something to do with the proposed follow-up. Instead of using an available print, Frenke dipped into his own pocket and paid to have a new print struck, and showed the picture to Freund. After the screening was over, Frenke could not have been overly pleased to learn that Freund was just sniffing around for an idea or two to use in his upcoming Metro horror film *Mad Love* (1935)!

In 1937 Frenke brought a $145,424 lawsuit against Universal charging that the studio had not released *Life Returns* through regular channels with attendant publicity for his $48,000 investment. (The film was banned in England on the basis of "bad taste"; unlike *Island of Lost Souls, Freaks* and other early films that incurred the displeasure of the British censors, *Life Returns* has never been released there at all.) *Life Returns* was reissued in 1938 through an outfit called Scienart Pictures, at which point it garnered the bad reviews it *should* have gotten on the first go-round. *Life Returns* has since gone public domain, but even purveyors of p.d. video cassettes don't bother to peddle it. Poorly conceived, cheaply done and badly acted, *Life Returns* deserves its ongoing obscurity.

Mystery of Edwin Drood (1935)

Released February 4, 1935. 87 minutes. *Directed by* Stuart Walker. *Associate Producer:* Edmund Grainger. *Based on the unfinished novel* ***The Mystery of Edwin Drood*** *by* Charles Dickens. *Screenplay by* John L. Balderston & Gladys Unger. *Adapted by* Bradley King & Leopold Atlas. *Director of Photography:* George Robinson. *Special Effects:* John P. Fulton. *Film Editor:* Edward Curtiss. *Musical Score by* Edward Ward. *Assistant Directors:* Phil Karlstein [Karlson] & Harry Mancke. *Art Director:* Albert S. D'Agostino. *Technical Advisor:* Madame Hilda Grenier.

Claude Rains (John Jasper), Douglass Montgomery (Neville Landless/Mr. Datchery), Heather Angel (Rosa Bud), Valerie Hobson (Helena Landless), David Manners (Edwin "Ned" Drood), Francis L. Sullivan (Reverend Mr. Septimus Crisparkle), Zeffie Tilbury (Opium Den Hag), Ethel Griffies (Mrs. Twinkleton), E.E. Clive (Thomas Sapsea), Walter Kingsford (Hiram Grewgious), Forrester Harvey (Durdles), Vera Buckland (Mrs. Tope), Elsa Buchanan (Mrs. Tisher), George Ernest (Deputy), J.M. Kerrigan (Chief Verger Tope), Louise Carter (Mrs. Crisparkle), Harry Cording, D'Arcy Corrigan (Opium Addicts), Anne O'Neal (Crisparkle Maid), Will Geer (Villager).

When Charles Dickens died in 1870 while writing his novel *The Mystery of Edwin Drood,* he left behind a puzzle that has fired the imaginations of literary cognoscenti and armchair sleuths for many decades: what was the fate that befell the novel's protagonist, Edwin Drood? Did he take flight and disappear into the countryside during a torrential Christmas Eve storm? Did he perhaps go into hiding, only to reappear weeks later in the guise of the inquisitive Mr. Datchery? Or did he suffer a violent death at the hands of his demented uncle, John Jasper?

Not content to let the matter rest unresolved, 120 authors volunteered over 100 possible conclusions to the Dickens tale in the ensuing decades. Many of the books, plays and dissertations that evolved out of this investigation asserted that Jasper was indeed guilty of killing his nephew. The furor over this tempest in a tea cup peaked on the night of January 7, 1914, when John Jasper was literally put on trial in Kings Hall in Covent Garden, London. Jasper was represented by a Frederick T. Harry, the celebrated author/Dickensian Gilbert K. Chesterton presided over the hearing as judge, while the jury, composed mainly of writers, was headed by dramatist George Bernard Shaw. The result of this good-natured, entirely extemporaneous performance was that

Jasper was found guilty of manslaughter, a verdict, Chesterton sarcastically contended, the jury had arrived at during lunch. The mock trial attracted international attention and received front page coverage in the following morning's edition of *The New York Times.*

The idea of adapting a classic Gothic thriller by one of the giants of English literature was an attractive proposition to a status-conscious studio like Universal. Even more tempting was the potential for exploiting a property with an open-ended finale (a marvelous built-in gimmick that begged for publicity). Unaware of the disappointing box office response that their first Dickens adaptation, *Great Expectations* (1934), would receive, Universal pulled out all stops costwise and bolstered *Mystery of Edwin Drood* with a fine cast of popular players and lavish production values (the production was budgeted at $215,375). An aggressive advertising campaign was launched, capitalizing (naturally) on the novelty of the unresolved ending. Had the public's response to *Mystery of Edwin Drood* measured up to Universal's great expectations, the studio would have more than likely produced other features based on Dickens' works. (Imagine their ire when MGM released that same year successful adaptations of *David Copperfield* and *A Tale of Two Cities*!)

While it wasn't as faithful to Dickens as *Great Expectations, Mystery of Edwin Drood* won the approval of most film critics. Neither an all-out horror story nor a puzzling whodunit, this Edmund Grainger production stands up today as a quaintly charming and atmospheric Victorian melodrama, handsomely outfitted and authentically detailed, though lacking in genuine suspense. Stuart Walker directs with a steady hand and sustains a rich Dickensian flavor. The former Cincinnati playwright and producer formed a highly successful stock company in his home town and founded the famous Portmanteau Theatre there. After producing a series of one-act plays on Broadway, Walker became an assistant producer at Paramount, gaining valuable experience on their B unit. Moving to Universal, Walker was put in charge of his own production unit and made such films as *Romance in the Rain* and *Great Expectations* (both 1934).

Mystery of Edwin Drood is crisper and far better paced than Walker's follow-up thriller, *WereWolf of London,* which suffered from occasional staginess and a stagnant tempo. George Robinson's usual fine camerawork, Albert S. D'Agostino's evocative sets and a procession of accurately-drawn Dickens characters go the distance to impart the proper mood. *Mystery of Edwin Drood* avoids the pitfalls of the average staid Hollywood costumer and is consistently watchable.

Headlining the cast in a role that was originally considered for Boris Karloff, Claude Rains enacts the lonely, opium-addicted John Jasper with grim conviction and his customary flair for overindulgence. Rains' dedication to his craft led to personal injury during the making of *Mystery of Edwin Drood:* he twisted his right ankle leaping from an eight-foot rock while shooting the film's final scene. His character is portrayed as a victim of the strict conventions of the era. Jasper's fatal inability to come to grips with his unrequited passions lead him to commit murder and later resort to suicide.

The story is set in 1864 in the little English village of Cloisterham. Jasper, the distinguished choirmaster of Cloisterham cathedral, is hopelessly addicted to opium. His obsessive love for Rosa Bud (Heather Angel), a student whom he is teaching to sing, drives the restless churchman into deep despair. Rosa is betrothed to Jasper's cocky young nephew Edwin Drood (David Manners), an arrangement that pleases neither party. Although Jasper loves Edwin (whom he affectionately calls Ned) like a son, he subconsciously wishes the young man dead for taking Rosa away from him.

Enter Neville Landless (Douglass Montgomery), a quick-tempered youth from Ceylon who has come to Cloisterham with his sister Helena (Valerie Hobson) to live with the Reverend Mr. Crisparkle (Francis L. Sullivan). A feud immediately develops between the argumentative Neville and the arrogant Drood, creating an uncomfortable situation which Jasper is quick to seize upon. Unbeknownst to Jasper, Rosa and Edwin have broken off their engagement, leaving her free to enjoy Neville's affections.

Assuming the role of peacemaker, the scheming Jasper invites Edwin and Neville to dine with him on Christmas Eve. A furious storm erupts and causes considerable damange to the surrounding area. Before the night is through, the two young rivals join hands as friends.

The next morning, the village is shocked by the news that Edwin Drood has disappeared. A search of the countryside and the river turn up nothing conclusive. Jasper arouses the complacent constabulary to take action at once and as a result, Neville is placed under guard. Circumstantial evidence and his past history of violent behavior weigh heavily against the young man. He escapes from prison and takes off, destination unknown.

Weeks later, an inquisitive old man who calls himself Mr. Datchery (he's actually Neville in disguise) arrives in Cloisterham and begins making inquiries about the Drood case and John Jasper. Piecing together evidence he obtained from several townspeople, including the opium den hag (Zeffie Tilbury) and Durdles (Forrester Harvey) the stonemason, Neville concludes that Jasper murdered Edwin out of his insane love for Rosa. He then buried Drood's body in a coffin filled with quicklime in the crypt beneath the cathedral. Rosa's betrothal ring, which Drood was wearing at the time of his death, is all that remains of his former existence, but it's enough evidence to nail Jasper.

Revealing his true identity, Neville leads the authorities on a mad chase after Jasper through the upper reaches of the cathedral. Consumed with guilt, the tormented choirmaster throws himself from the parapet to his death on the steps below.

Banking on a winner from a critical as well as a commercial standpoint Universal made an effort to insure that *Mystery of Edwin Drood* bore the stamp of authenticity in every detail. In the summer of 1934, officials from the studio's London office shot thousands of feet of film and took numerous still shots of various Victorian-style structures in the town of Rochester in England. Albert S. D'Agostino, the production's art director, designed a replica of an English village of Dickens' time, which was erected at considerable cost on the backlot; it was the largest exterior set Universal had built since the days of the Chaney *Hunchback*. Madame Hilda Grenier, a former confidante of Queen Mary of England and an authority on the mid-Victorian period, was brought

Claude Rains (*right*) plays the tortured, opium-addicted choirmaster who needlessly murders his beloved nephew (David Manners above) in the handsomely mounted screen version of Dickens' unfinished *Mystery of Edwin Drood.*

to Southern California to act as technical advisor. Not only did Madame see to it that the furnishings and props were faithful to the era, she also painstakingly coached the performers in the proper rules of prissy Victorian deportment.

Delayed briefly on account of casting difficulties, shooting began on *Mystery of Edwin Drood* on November 18, 1934, and continued into January, 1935. The project was veiled in a shroud of secrecy (again). Supposedly, only a half-dozen people on the lot knew the solution to the mystery. Playwrights John L. Balderston, Gladys Unger and Leopold Atlas and Hollywood scenarist (Miss) Bradley King were all sworn not to reveal the ending. Grainger and Walker saw to it that none of the cast members knew until the final scenes were shot how the story was going to conclude (none of the scripts had the ending attached to them). Not even the censors' office was spared; only two men other than Joseph Breen himself were privvy to the picture's denouement. (Is it possible that the producers of television's "Dallas" picked up a cue from Universal when they concocted their "Who Shot J.R.?" mystery several years back?)

Many of the critics who reviewed *Mystery of Edwin Drood* when it was released in February, 1935, seemed satisfied (though certainly not overwhelmed) by the predictable solution arrived at by this quartet of writers. As Dickens had left behind voluminous notes indicating he was considering at least three possible alternatives, the scenarists simply chose the most logical one. A press release claimed that they drew up case histories of the major characters and charted their activities from the time of the story through old age. Using these "biographies" as a guide, each author wrote an original scenario without consulting the other three. From these different accounts a vote was taken and a decision was arrived at. As might be expected, murder won out.

For all the fuss and to-do generated by Universal to stir up interest in all of this business, it's a mite disappointing to learn how *obvious* is their solution to the mystery. Right from the start of the film (the camera eavesdrops on Jasper caught in the grip of opium-induced delirium tremens), we expect the worst from the frustrated churchman. "No wretched monk who ever groaned his life away in that gloomy cathedral could have been more tired of it!" he complains bitterly to his nephew. "He could take to carving demons for relief—and did! What shall *I* do? Must I take to carving them out of my heart?" Here is a man whose circumstances are suffocating him; Jasper is capable of the most heinous of crimes, including snuffing out the life of the man he loves most in the world.

By telegraphing Jasper's evil intentions so far in advance, Walker and his collaborators have done the audience a disservice. Precious little is left to our imaginations. Jasper's descent into the cathedral's ancient crypt and his inordinate curiosity about such esoteric matters as locating empty tombs and the effects of quicklime on a corpse most assuredly seals Edwin's fate. (Contrary to the claims fostered by this film and others such as 1958's *The Haunted Strangler,* quicklime doesn't destroy a corpse; it is more likely than not to act as a preservative!) By revealing the true identity of the stranger, Mr. Datchery, three-quarters of the way into the story, the suspense factor is further dissipated.

The stifling conventions of Charles Dickens' era are observed in several telling passages. Hemmed in by the rigid behavioral codes of the churchman ("The cramped monotony of my existence grinds me away"), Jasper dares not express his overwhelming feelings of desire for Rosa. When Neville is arrested for Edwin's murder, Jasper seizes it as an opportunity to claim the girl, and attempts to strike an odious bargain with her (Rosa's love for Neville's freedom). Jasper's pitiable declaration of love, passionately declared in the courtyard of Rosa's finishing school (where nary a word is whispered that isn't monitored by head mistress Miss Twinkleton [Ethel Griffies] and her network of spies), evokes our sympathies for Jasper if only for a moment. Racism and class structure rear their ugly heads in the tense confrontation between Neville and Edwin when Drood takes offense at the Ceylonese's affections toward Rosa ("We English don't encourage fellows with dark skins to admire our girls!").

Supporting Claude Rains are such attractive young players as Douglass Montgomery, Heather Angel, David Manners and Valerie Hobson. Twenty-five-year-old Montgomery (who began his picture career under the name Kent Douglass) had been wearying of the long procession of juvenile roles he was being assigned at Universal, and welcomed the chance to get into Jack Pierce's old age makeup. Montgomery's brooding, unconventional good looks made him an ideal romantic lead in such period dramas as *Edwin Drood* and *Little Man, What Now?* (1934). Heather Angel radiates girlhood innocence as the much-admired Rosa. Valerie Hobson has precious little to do as Helena, Neville's sister. The epitome of the decorative but bland and inefficient '30s horror leading man, David Manners fared better in roles such as Edwin Drood and the screenwriter in 1933's *The Death Kiss,* both of which were spiked with a dash of ginger.

Even better are the rich, fruity portraits etched by the minor players: Walter Kingsford's self-effacing Hiram Grewgious, Forrester Harvey's drunken stonemason, Zeffie Tilbury's crusty old opium den hag, and, as always, the superbly pompous E.E. Clive as magistrate Thomas Sapsea. (Actor John Howard, who costarred with Clive in a string of '30s Bulldog Drummond mysteries, recalls the British actor with affection, and says Clive claimed to be quite a rake in his younger days.)

Mystery of Edwin Drood made a comeback via television and several Manhattan revival houses in the mid-80s as a result of an immensely popular Broadway musical staged by the New York Shakespeare Festival. Capitalizing on Dickens' open-ended finis to the hilt, "Drood"'s canny producers left the solution of the mystery not to the discretion of the play's author, but to the audience itself. Which goes to show, as far as *The Mystery of Edwin Drood* is concerned, it isn't what Dickens wrote but what he *didn't* write that counts.

Night Life of the Gods (1935)

Released March 11, 1935. 73 minutes. A Lowell Sherman Production. *Produced by* Carl Laemmle, Jr. *Directed by* Lowell Sherman. *Screenplay by* Barry Trivers. *Based on the novel by* Thorne Smith. *Director of Photography:* John J. Mescall. *Film Editor:* Ted Kent. *Art Director:* Charles D. Hall. *Musical Director:* Edward Ward. *Special Effects:* John P. Fulton. *Makeup by* Jack P. Pierce.

Alan Mowbray (Hunter Hawk), Florine McKinney (Meg Turner), Peggy Shannon (Daphne Lambert), Richard Carle (Grandpa Lambert), Theresa Maxwell Conover (Alice Lambert), Phillips Smalley (Alfred Lambert), Wesley Barry (Alfred Lambert, Jr.), Gilbert Emery (Betts), Ferdinand Gottschalk (Ludwig Turner), Douglas Fowley (Cyril Sparks), William "Stage" Boyd (Detective Mulligan), Henry Armetta (Roigi), Arlene Carroll (Stella), Raymond Benard [Corrigan] (Apollo), George Hassell (Bacchus), Irene Ware (Diana), Geneva Mitchell (Hebe), Paul Kaye (Mercury), Robert Warwick (Neptune), Pat De Cicco (Perseus), Marda Deering (Venus), Bert Roach (Oscar), Fredric Santly (Drunk), Maidel Turner (Burly Woman); Maude Turner Gordon (Dowager), Tyler Brooke (Store Manager), G. Pat Collins (Times Square Policeman), Lee Moran (Bus Driver), James Burtis (Bit Man), May Beatty (Mrs. Betts), Wade Boteler (Policeman), Larry Wheat (Museum Guard), Don Douglas (Mr. Martin), Alan Davis (Hotel Manager), Leo McCabe (Assistant Hotel Manager), Harry Cornell (Roadhouse Manager), Joseph Young (Orchestra Leader), Lois January (Mulligan's Girl), Kenner G. Kemp (Dance Extra), King Baggott (Extra in Lobby), Dick Winslow (Student), Harold Nelson (Lecturer), Phyllis Crane, Lillian Castle (Bit Women), Beatrice Roberts, Claire Myers, Madlyn Talkot (The Three Graces), William L. Thorne (Detective), Velma Gresham (Sales Girl), Ruth Cherrington (Dowager), Al Hill, George Magrill (Masseurs), Anne Darling (Manicurist), Russ Clark, Jerry Frank (Lifeguards), Jean Fenwick, Ann Doran, Lu Ann Meredith, Ruth Page (Girls in Pool), Mabel Benard (Swimmer).

> "The Nuttiest Nightmare Man Ever Conceived
> And The Merriest, Sauciest, Funniest, Most
> Colossal Comedy Hollywood Has Ever Dared Produce!"
> —Universal publicity blurb

American farceur Thorne Smith's special brand of bubbly, madcap humor has been translated to the screen with varying degrees of success. Norman Z. McLeod's *Topper* (1937) and Rene Clair's *I Married a Witch* (1942) have retained much of their spunky charm while Hal Roach's absurd *Turnabout* (1940) remains a forgettable flop. Universal's adaptation of the Smith novel *Night Life of the Gods* falls somewhere in the middle. The humorist's sly supposition what would happen if the gods of Mount Olympus suddenly came to life and found themselves in the crazy world of 20th century Manhattan—sorely required the talents of an Ernst Lubitsch or a Preston Sturges to give it that needed air of bold irreverency and sheer abandon. Universal simply wasn't up to snuff for the work cut out of it. As a result, *Night Life of the Gods,* one of the studio's most promising projects on the 1934–1935 agenda, became (in the words of *Variety* reviewer Chic) merely an "acceptable version" of the Smith lark, not worthy of the exaltations of its admirers in the Universal publicity department.

We have only the word of critics like Chic and his colleagues, unfortunately, upon which to base an assessment of this entry. *Night Life of the Gods* has become virtually a lost film; 16mm prints, if they ever existed at all, have all but disappeared. Television and revival house screenings are similarly nonexistent. Reportedly, only a couple of 35mm prints remain. Some time ago, a collector advertised one of these for sale in the pages of *The Big Reel,* a monthly tabloid catering to film and video collectors. His ad ran for several months, apparently without success (evidently the movie's obscurity worked against it). Giving up all hope on making a buck off the print, our collector turned philanthropist and donated it to U.C.L.A.

On March 31, 1934, *The Universal Weekly* reported that Junior Laemmle purchased the Smith novel for motion picture adaptation. Lowell Sherman, a leading man in silents (*Way Down East,* 1920; *Monsieur Beaucaire,* 1924) and a character player in talkies (*Morning Glory,* 1933), had recently made his directorial bow and was put at the helm of *Night Life of the Gods.* Like Thorne Smith, Sherman didn't live long enough to take notice of the film's lukewarm critical reception. He became ill during shooting (possibly as a result of the rigorous schedule) and lost 21 pounds. Despite the protests of his physicians, Sherman next took on the direction of RKO's *Becky Sharp* (1935) and died several days into production, of double pneumonia.

Alan Mowbray portrays Thorne Smith's irrepressible hero Hunter Hawk. A brilliant but eccentric scientist, Hawk discovers a method of turning human beings into statues and vice versa. Hawk's first successful experiment is upon his dog, Blotto, whose tail he turns into stone through the rays emitted by a pair of rings. Confident of his newly acquired powers, Hawk turns the ray on his belligerent family, transforming his sister Alice (Theresa Maxwell Conover), her husband Alfred (Phillips Smalley) and their arrogant teenage son Alfred, Junior (Wesley Barry), into stone images. Only daughter Daphne (Peggy Shannon) is spared. Unfazed by her uncle's elimination of her family, "Daffy" takes her leave to keep a date with boyfriend Cyril Sparks (Douglas Fowley). (By now, you should have an inkling as to the off-the-wall nature of this film's humor.)

Traipsing through a cornfield, Hawk meets Ludwig Turner (Ferdinand Gottschalk). The strange little man introduces the inventor to his howling hellion of a daughter Meg (Florine McKinney). She claims to have been born

900 years ago; her name is short for Megaera, the most furious of the three Furies of ancient Greece.

Forming a partnership, the two misfits go on a wild spree, petrifying all who meet with their disfavor: half the occupants of a cafe, a traffic policeman who tries to stop their car and a detective (William "Stage" Boyd) who attempts to arrest Hawk for disturbing the peace.

Hawk and Meg head over to the Metropolitan Museum of Art. Musing about how wonderful it must have been to have lived one's life as a god or a goddess, Hawk and Meg try an experiment. Focusing his rings on the statues of five gods and three goddesses, Hawk imbues them with life. Their individual reactions are typical: Neptune (Robert Warwick) yearns for water and fish, Venus (Marda Deering) bemoans the loss of her arms, and so forth.

Dashing through the streets of the Big Apple, creating quite a stir, Hawk and Meg take their Olympian companions to a local department store and dress them up in modern-day fashions. A night on the town turns into a disaster. Neptune becomes embroiled in a heated dispute with a fish peddler (Henry Armetta). A riot ensues with fish flying through the air like arrows. Hawk demobilizes a squad of cops and heads back to his hotel suite with his charges in tow.

The whole party retires to the hotel pool room. Stationing himself at the bottom of the pool, Neptune playfully jabs the young women bathers with his trident. Another fracas develops before Hawk, tiring of all this excitement, hustles his friends onto a bus and transports them back to the museum where they resume their complacent existence as marble statues. Left alone in the museum, Hawk and Meg exchange understanding glances before he turns the power of the rings on himself and his companion.

The film ends with a cliche: Hawk awakens in an ambulance, suffering from a head injury that he sustained in a lab explosion. The whole crazy experience was nothing more than a dream.

According to the attendant publicity surrounding the release of *Night Life of the Gods,* Universal spared no expense in bringing Thorne Smith's lunacy to the screen. The bathing pool was built at a cost exceeding that of any soundstage set at the studio. Fifty plaster statues were created by 20 artists at a cost of $35,000. Supposedly, each weighed in excess of 600 pounds. Mounted on wheels for easy mobility, these life-size images were wheeled in by studio technicians three or four at a time on the tail of a motor dolly.

Universal's team of horticulturists had a formidable task ahead of them as well. A whole field of corn was grown by electric light for one scene. Several months before shooting began, a section of Soundstage 14 was heaped with earth and cultivated with seed, fertilizer and castor oil. The "field" was subjected to constant artificial sunshine, produced by violet lamps and huge arc lights. The studio's sprinkler system provided the necessary "rainfall." Under these intensive methods of cultivation, the corn crop came up in a fraction of the time it would take to grow the vegetable outdoors.

Judging from the reactions of *Variety* and the movie critics staffing the New York City dailies, *Night Life of the Gods* failed to capture the spirited cuckoo quality of Smith's prose. "Being the perfect medium for a crazy-fantasy about gods and men, the cinema, with characteristic nonchalance, loafs on the job and ends with a futile and heavy-footed attempt at gay madness," beefed Richard Watts, Jr., of *The New York Herald Tribune*. Watts took the opportunity to toss in a dig aimed at current horror pictures in his discussion of Alan Mowbray's feat of transforming his relatives into stone: "[It] has a way of seeming even less hilarious than Lionel Atwill's sinister determination to do the same thing to his foes used to be in the serious-minded melodramas."

The New York World Telegram's erudite critic William Boehnel sadly mused, "It's a pity that when the cinema . . . stumbles upon such a beguilingly original idea . . . it is unable to rise to the heroic stature of the theme in its possession. For *Night Life of the Gods* possesses not only a new and welcome series of situations, but its material is the very stuff on which the cinema should thrive. But the screen version, though frequently side-splitting, is, on the whole, so muddled and sluggish and has failed so wantonly to make the most of its opportunities that it must be classed among the saddest of the cinema might-have-beens." Boehnel went on to say that the industry's rigid censorship code put a lid on Smith's bawdy humor, thus weakening the screen narrative.

Movie reviewer Irene Thirer gave the film a "good" rating on the *New York Evening Post*'s moviemeter, and commented that "You've either got to go for this sort of screen stuff passionately . . . or else you're thoroughly cold on it. We giggled all the way through—from start to final fadeout."

The New York Times described *Night Life of the Gods* as "only moderately entertaining," adding that "somehow the petrified humans and revivified gods and goddesses are not as devastatingly mirthful as they seemed under the hypnosis of Mr. Smith's antic prose." *Variety*'s Chic reacted in kind: "There are moments when the mob direction gets beyond the director's control . . . and it's noisy instead of funny, but in the main there's plenty to laugh at, and humor that should be classed as for the family trade in spite of its occasional piquancy."

All of the critics we read were unanimous in their praise of the picture's technical effects (*Variety* called them "excellent"); most were in favorable agreement regarding the performances, particularly those of Alan Mowbray ("droll and quixotic," sayeth *The New York Times*) and the all-but-forgotten Florine McKinney ("grand work," praised *The New York World Telegram*). The dryly British Gilbert Emery also received accolades for his performance as Mowbray's typically imperturbable butler. As for the gods and goddesses: "all work toward the common end and help to create an excellent ensemble" (*Variety*). (Lowell Sherman had hoped to play the lead himself, but when his voice went bad he was confined to the director's chair. Second-choice Edward Everett Horton was tied up with Metro's *Biography of a Bachelor Girl,* 1935, and Alan Mowbray was ultimately signed.)

Considering the material we have at our disposal upon which to base an assessment of *Night Life of the Gods,* we're inclined to agree with Watts' remark that "unless such a picture is brilliant it is nothing at all."

Bride of Frankenstein (1935)

Released May 6, 1935. 75 minutes. *Produced by* Carl Laemmle, Jr. *Directed by* James Whale. *Screenplay by* William Hurlbut. *From an adaptation by* William Hurlbut & John L. Balderston. *Suggested by the novel* ***Frankenstein; or, The Modern Prometheus*** *by* Mary Wollstonecraft Shelley. *Director of Photography:* John J. Mescall. *Music by* Franz Waxman. *Music Director:* Mischa Bakaleinikoff. *Editorial Supervisor:* Maurice Pivar. *Film Editor:* Ted Kent. *Art Director:* Charles D. Hall. *Special Photographic Effects:* John P. Fulton & David Horsley. *Sound Supervisor:* Gilbert Kurland. *Assistant Directors:* Harry Menke & Joseph McDonough. *Electrical Effects:* Kenneth Strickfaden. *Makeup:* Jack P. Pierce.

Boris Karloff (The Monster), Colin Clive (Baron Henry Frankenstein), Valerie Hobson (Baroness Elizabeth Frankenstein), Ernest Thesiger (Dr. Septimus Pretorius), Elsa Lanchester (Mary Wollstonecraft Shelley/The Monster's Mate), Una O'Connor (Minnie), E.E. Clive (The Burgomaster), O.P. Heggie (The Hermit), Gavin Gordon (Lord Byron), Douglas Walton (Percy Bysshe Shelley), Dwight Frye (Karl), Lucien Prival (Albert), Reginald Barlow (Hans), Mary Gordon (Hans' Wife), Anne Darling (Shepherdess), Ted Billings (Ludwig), Gunnis Davis* (Uncle Glutz), Tempe Pigott* (Auntie Glutz), Neil Fitzgerald (Rudy), John Carradine, Robert Adair, John Curtis, Frank Terry (Hunters), Walter Brennan, Rollo Lloyd, Mary Stewart (Neighbors), Helen Parrish (Communion Girl), Edwin Mordant* (The Coroner), Lucio Villegas* (Priest), Brenda Fowler (A Mother), Sarah Schwartz (Marta), Arthur S. Byron (Little King), Joan Woodbury (Little Queen), Norman Ainsley (Little Archbishop), Peter Shaw (Little Devil), Kansas DeForrest (Little Ballerina), Josephine McKim (Little Mermaid), Billy Barty (Little Baby), Frank Benson, Ed Piel, Sr., Anders Van Haden, John George, D'Arcy Corrigan, Grace Cunard, Maurice Black, Peter Shaw (Villagers), Helen Gibson (Woman), Murdock MacQuarrie (Sympathetic Villager), Elspeth Dudgeon (Old Gypsy Woman), Monty Montague, Peter Shaw (Doubles for Ernest Thesiger), George DeNormand (Double for Reginald Barlow), Harry Northrup, Joseph North. [**Does not appear in the final print.*]

On January 12, 1935, Hollywood trade papers reported that Junior Laemmle was heading up his own production unit at the studio. Itching to leave his post as general manager in charge of all production, which he held since 1929, the newly-appointed "associate producer" was scheduled to bring in six titles a year. His old job would go to an unlikely candidate: Carl, Sr. In making the announcement to the press, the elder Laemmle declared that for some time his son "has been eager to pass on the duties and details of complete studio direction to others that he might concentrate on an independent production unit."

The simple reason for the change was that Junior Laemmle was bored in a job he wasn't very good at in the first place. In May, 1988, actress Rose Hobart recalled her days as a Universal contract player in the early '30s, and her long-standing feud with the "boy wonder."

"The trouble with Junior was that he had no real talent and was a lousy administrator," the feisty Miss Hobart says with disarming candor. "His father was pretty good. His father had some idea what he wanted. But Junior didn't know his ass from a shotgun! He really didn't care. He was a good Jewish boy and when Father hands you the business, you run the business. He couldn't have cared less about it."

Producer Carl, Jr. could boast that the films made under his wing were the most elaborate and prestigious the studio could afford. The first two of his planned six "specials" were a movie version of the Kern and Hammerstein musical *Show Boat* and *The Return of Frankenstein,* the long-awaited sequel to the horror hit which had been in the works for some time. A major obstacle was finding the right director, since James Whale, the most logical contender, disappointingly had no interest in repeating his past success. The assignment fell into the hands of Kurt Neumann. The competent but undistinguished director of *Secret of the Blue Room* was hardly in the same class as Whale, but at least he had some experience with Gothic subjects. An original story was written by Tom Read, who was also selected to supervise the production; Philip McDonald was commissioned to write a treatment.

It's ironic that James Whale, who directed *Frankenstein* partially to break away from the rut of war subjects, was now finding it a bit difficult to escape his identification with horror movies. A change of pace was sorely needed for the director who, since the technical rigors of *The Invisible Man,* was bemoaning his weariness of fantasy subjects to interviewers. Anxious to diversify his output, he took on the direction of *By Candlelight* (1934) when the original director, Robert Wyler (brother of William and *another* Laemmle!), left the film. A charming and underrated comedy of manners, *By Candlelight* starred Paul Lukas as a valet who poses as an aristocrat so that he may woo prospective paramours. It was an engaging trifle but it was dwarfed by a far more personal film for the director, *One More River* (1934), a straightforward, accomplished adaptation of John Galsworthy's novel. Surprisingly, after tackling such high-brow fare, Whale had a change of heart and returned to the realm of fantasy.

In February 1934, he came back from a two-month holiday in London with a script by R.C. Sherriff entitled *A Trip to Mars.* It was a fanciful, H.G. Wells-type confection about Earth people abducted by the leader of an underground Martian civilization. Whale plunged ahead with the details of the project, which was tentatively scheduled to go into production in March, 1934, as soon as its proposed star Boris Karloff completed his duties on *The Black Cat. A Trip to Mars* would never be made. According to Whale's biographer James Curtis, Senior Laemmle didn't like the script and refused to finance it. Whale grudgingly accepted the Frankenstein sequel.

Starting from scratch, Whale drew his inspiration from the original Mary Shelley novel, focusing his attention on the episode detailing Frankenstein's aborted attempt to create a mate for the Monster. It has also been suggested that Whale cribbed a few ideas from an early draft of Robert Florey's *Frankenstein* script. The original intention was to reunite the cast, except for John Boles, whose role of Victor Moritz was to be written out of the script.

By September, 1934, Whale pressed R.C. Sherriff, who was then teaching at Oxford, into service. The writer promised to have a complete script prepared by the next semester, but he soon wearied of his new assignment and backed out of the film. By January, the reliable John L. Balderston was commissioned to write an original treatment with a finished script by William Hurlbut (who penned *The Cat Creeps,* 1930) and mystery writer Edmund Pearson. (The latter's contribution appears to be negligible; his name doesn't even appear on the official credits.)

As the production evolved, major changes were made in the cast. The services of the irreplaceable Boris Karloff and Colin Clive were secured. Valerie Hobson, whom the studio was working heavily, was selected to replace Mae Clarke, whose brief fling at stardom had already peaked. For a time Brigitte Helm, so mesmerizing as Maria the Robot Girl in Fritz Lang's *Metropolis* (1926), was under serious consideration for the role of the Monster's mate. The statuesque Phyllis Brooks, a well-known New York illustrator's model, was announced as the most likely candidate for the part. The final choice of Elsa Lanchester, an old friend of Whale, was probably made when the director decided to have one actress play the roles of both the Bride and Mary Wollstonecraft Shelley in the film's prologue.

In her biography, *Elsa Lanchester, By Herself,* the actress wrote, "I think James Whale felt that if this beautiful and innocent Mary Shelley could write a horror story such as *Frankenstein,* then somewhere she must have had a *fiend* within." The twin casting proved to be another inspired Whalesian touch.

Amazingly, the role of Dr. Pretorius was originally slated for Claude Rains, who owed Universal a film on his two-picture contract. However, Rains was bumped from the picture and reassigned the lead in *Mystery of Edwin Drood.* Whale prevailed upon Ernest Thesiger, who stole the show as Horace Femm in *The Old Dark House,* to serve as a replacement.

Another key role, although a considerably smaller one, was the unnamed blind hermit who befriends and humanizes the Monster. Whale was so insistent that the Scottish stage actor O.P. Heggie play the part that he delayed production for ten days until Heggie finished another assignment *Chasing Yesterday* at RKO.

The projected budget of $293,750 exceeded the cost of the original film by over $30,000. But even this figure was optimistic and the final cost of the production approached $400,000. Whale was paid a princely $15,000, earning even more than star Boris Karloff, who received $12,500. Colin Clive still wasn't a big name by Hollywood standards and had a $6,000 check to prove it, while Thesiger received exactly half that.

The sum of $26,000 was targeted for set construction, with art director Charles D. Hall's magnificent tower laboratory amounting to $3,600, with

The Bride herself – Elsa Lanchester in the James Whale classic, *Bride of Frankenstein.*

another $2,000 spent on various electrical props. But the biggest-ticketed item on the art director's budget was the Castle Frankenstein set, which totalled $4,700, including the entrance way and the Great Hall.

Jack Pierce received $450 for his unique services, which not only included the makeup for the Bride, but a modified design for Karloff. As usual, the actor was weighed down with 62 pounds of makeup and costuming, including a pair of 11½-pound boots which propped him up to a height of just over 7½ feet. The worse for wear after his ordeal in the burning windmill, the Monster looked properly charred and disheveled. The mangy, newly-designed wig

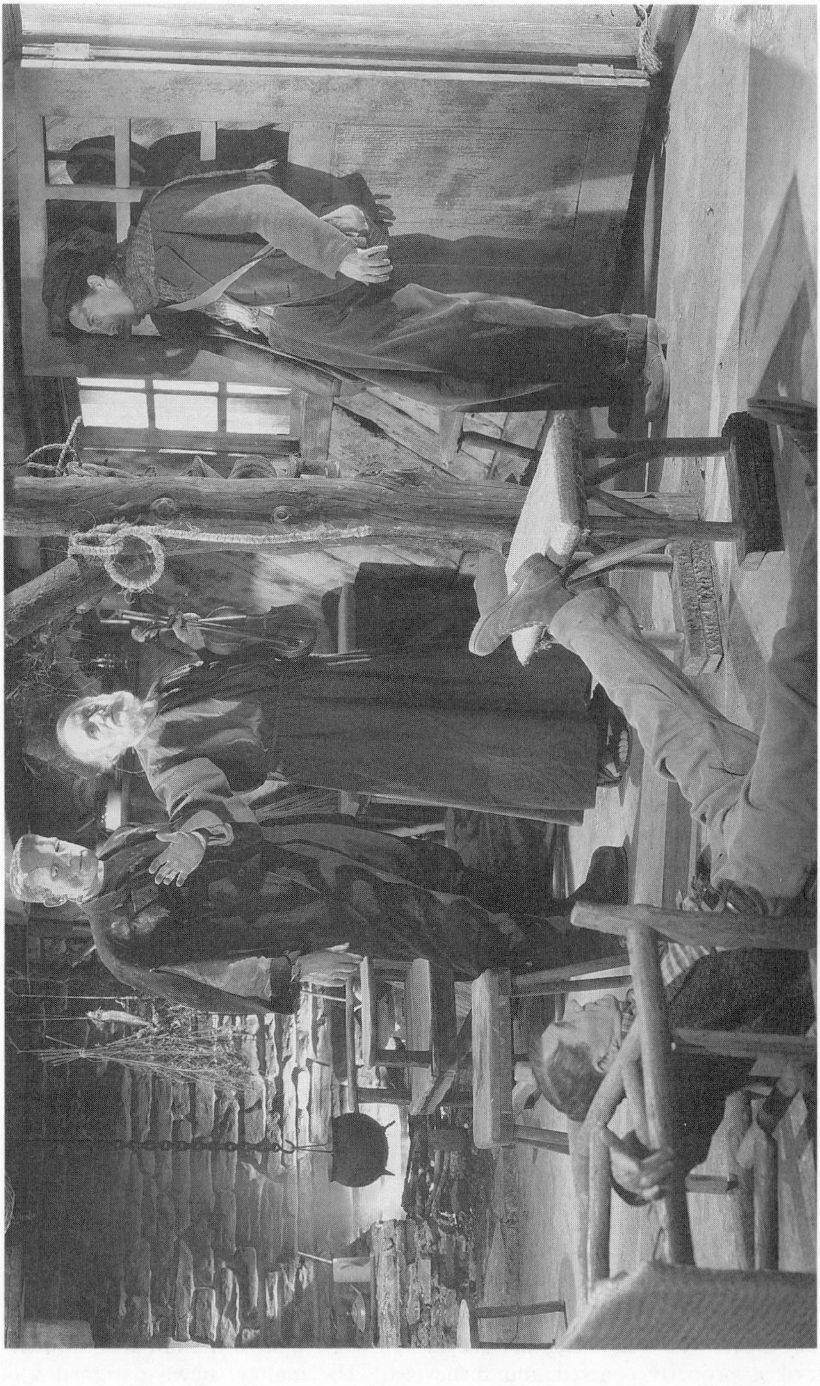

revealed the 11 metal clamps holding the sections of the head together, a detail not seen in the original makeup.

Choosing a title for the picture proved to be a vexing problem. It was alternately announced as *The Return of Frankenstein* and *Bride of Frankenstein* in the trade papers. *The Universal Weekly* of January 5, 1935, stated with finality that the title would be *Return* "since the Monster was not named Frankenstein," but by the January 19 edition, the title was changed back to *Bride.* Whale commenced shooting on January 2, 1935, and wrapped on March 7, ten days over schedule. To this day, pedants stubbornly insist that the Bride was *not* played by Elsa Lanchester, but by Valerie Hobson, based on the assumption that the title refers to the marriage of the doctor and not the Monster. (Ernest Thesiger triumphantly dubs Lanchester "The Bride of Frankenstein!" at the end of the creation sequence.)

The tone of the film is established with a blast of thunder and lightning as the camera prowls the rain-swept grounds of a medieval castle. But these obvious horror trappings prove to be a tease as the camera cuts to three elegant figures luxuriating before a hearth. The company is most distinguished: Percy Bysshe Shelley (Douglas Walton), his common-law wife, Mary Wollstonecraft (Elsa Lanchester), and their friend, poet Lord Byron (Gavin Gordon). The storm prompts Lord Byron to recap the plot of Mary's new novel *Frankenstein,* inspiring the authoress to contrive a follow-up.

The story picks up at the site of the burning windmill. The Burgomaster (E.E. Clive) orders the villagers to transport the body of Henry Frankenstein (Colin Clive) to his father's castle. As the crowd disperses, Hans (Reginald Barlow), father of the drowned child Maria, pokes through the charred remains of the structure and plunges into the cistern. The Monster (Boris Karloff), alive but badly burned, emerges from the ruins and drowns the terrified villager. Making his way to the surface, he sends Hans' wife (Mary Gordon) falling to her death and disappears into the countryside.

In the meantime, Henry regains consciousness and is reunited with Elizabeth (Valerie Hobson). Their few hours of peace are interrupted when Dr. Septimus Pretorius (Ernest Thesiger), Henry's former teacher, pays them an unexpected call. Luring the young Baron to his flat, Pretorius exhibits his collection of doll-like people housed in glass containers, a product of his strange experiments in the creation of life. Pretorius suggests they join forces to create a mate for the Monster in hopes of spawning a race of man-made beings.

Meanwhile, the Monster terrorizes the populace and then disappears back into the woods. A blind hermit (O.P. Heggie) befriends the creature and even teaches him to speak a few simple words before a pair of hunters, stumbling upon the unlikely companions, sends the Monster scurrying off. Seeking refuge in an underground tomb, the Monster comes upon Pretorius who's in the midst of snatching a body for his great experiment. The two form an alliance and confront Henry who has reneged on his promise to work with the deranged

The end of a beautiful friendship: hunters John Carradine (*at door*) and Robert Adair (*on floor*) stumble upon the idyllic lair of the blind hermit (O.P. Heggie) and the Monster (Boris Karloff), in *Bride of Frankenstein.*

professor. The Monster kidnaps Elizabeth, now Henry's wife, leaving Frankenstein no choice but to assist in the experiment.

Stitched together from body parts stolen from graveyards and a heart taken from a freshly murdered village girl, the Bride is ready to be endowed with life. In the spectacular, two-minute creation sequence, consisting of over 80 shots, she comes to life amid the blazing electrical apparatus of Frankenstein's mountaintop laboratory. Bound completely in bandages except for her head, the newly-created female (Elsa Lanchester), the very image of Queen Nefertiti, expresses horror at the sight of her intended suitor. The rejection of his mate is too much for the Monster to bear. Allowing Henry and the now freed Elizabeth to escape, the Monster throws the power lever. The laboratory is blown asunder by several massive explosions, burying the Monster, the Bride and Pretorius under tons of rubble.

Bride of Frankenstein is one of the best and least typical of the Universal horror films. In terms of acting, direction, photography, set design, editing and overall presentation, the film is close to flawless. It is another example of James Whale's back-door approach to horror. The introduction of the Monster, cruelly and pointlessly killing the parents of the drowned child, and the shock close-ups of the screeching Bride, are genuinely frightening. Otherwise, Whale seems hardly interested in inducing as much as a shudder from the audience. The sophisticated director was clearly bored with Universal's horror assignments and *Bride of Frankenstein* presented him with a good opportunity to poke fun at the genre with a hearty dose of parody.

The precautionary theme that man should not meddle with the laws of God received its solemn due in the original film. Whale was determined to use a fresh approach in what would be his last horror movie, spinning his yarn as if it were a macabre fairy tale. Evidence of Whale's restlessness is everywhere. He frequently avoids even a token attempt at realism. Screening *Bride of Frankenstein* back-to-back with the original is a bit jarring. In *Frankenstein,* Whale took pains in creating a reasonably authentic Middle European setting. In the sequel, the director thumbs his nose at such details, bringing a particularly English brand of eccentricity to the pseudo-Tyrolean settings.

Several key characters from the first film are changed radically in the sequel, or eliminated altogether. It is difficult to imagine such sensible, understated types as Mae Clarke and John Boles in the stylized surroundings of *Bride of Frankenstein.* The new Elizabeth, as played by Valerie Hobson, is reduced to operatic fits of hysteria at the drop of a hat. As per *The Old Dark House,* most of the cast were carefully chosen for their theatrical styles and then Whale pressed them to the limit; even the bit part of the grimacing gypsy grandmother in the campfire scene seems to be modeled after Eva Moore's Rebecca Femm.

Whale's attempts at religious symbolism, on the other hand, are strained and out-of-place. Trussing the Monster up in a Christ-like pose by a mob of jeering villagers is a heavyhanded conceit. The religious overtones are in full force in the hermit sequence. The Monster feasts on bread and wine, the Holy Sacrament, and the scene fades to black with the camera lingering on the luminous after-image of the crucifix.

Ernest Thesiger and fellow countryman James Whale "take five" while shooting *Bride of Frankenstein.* (Photo courtesy Steve Jochsberger.)

The director seems far more at ease working as much gallows humor as possible into the script. This was an easy task in the scenes with Dr. Pretorius, as played by Ernest Thesiger, whose immutable scowl is only relieved with a nip of gin ("My only weakness," he confesses, an in-joke directed to fans of *The Old Dark House*). Unlike the earnest, trailblazing Henry Frankenstein, Pretorius' fascination with the dead takes on an unwholesome air. When Pretorius and his party of body snatchers complete their grim duties in a dank crypt, the scientist dawdles behind, uncorks a choice magnum of wine and toasts the remains taken from an excavated coffin. When the Monster dejectedly voices his preference for the company of the dead, the necrophilic scientist glumly agrees. Thesiger delivers the goods in a rich, fruity performance that is at once pompous and slyly perverse; one wonders to what degree Pretorius' character is modeled on the actor himself.

James Whale only used Thesiger twice in his film career, but he remains the quintessential Whale actor. Born in 1879, Thesiger had early ambitions to become a painter, but gave it up when he felt that greatness eluded him. He tried his luck in the theater but his success was interrupted by military service at the outbreak of World War I. He returned to acting after being wounded at the front, landing a part in an unpromising play, "A Little Bit of Fluff." To Thesiger's amazement, the play lasted over 1200 performances, typecasting him as a comedy actor. Eventually he graduated to dramatic roles, scoring a triumph as Dauphin in Sir George Bernard Shaw's "St. Joan."

Offstage, Thesiger continued to paint and was an expert at needlework, authoring a book, *Adventures in Embroidery.* He was also quite skilled at female impersonation. Thesiger once asked Somerset Maugham, then the toast of the British stage, why he never wrote a part for him. The quick-witted Maugham snapped, "I do, but Gladys Cooper always plays them."

The accomplished actor appeared in over 50 films, and played everything from Greek drama to musical comedy on stage. But his Horace Femm in *The Old Dark House* and, most especially, his Dr. Pretorius in *Bride of Frankenstein* remain his best-remembered roles.

Colin Clive is at a disadvantage in the sketchily-written role of Henry Frankenstein. Despite an excellent performance in *Frankenstein,* Clive was overshadowed by the phenomenal popularity of Karloff's Monster. (The reaction was completely the opposite in the later Hammer series. How could Hammer's hulking brutes with their overdone, pie-in-the-face makeups compete with the suave villainy of Peter Cushing's Dr. Frankenstein?) Henry Frankenstein is understandably indecisive and on-edge after his harrowing encounter with his own creation, but the character's infirmities detract a good deal from his appeal. Clive, as highstrung as ever, has his hands full vying for attention when up against such grandstanding gargoyles as Karloff, Lanchester and Thesiger.

Inexperience weighs heavily on Valerie Hobson's strained, highflown hysterics. Usually an ingratiating actress in undemanding heroine roles, her modest talents are taxed by the florid dialogue in her initial scenes. She's clearly in over her head during her big breakdown scene in Henry's bed chamber. Happily, Hobson redeemed herself in her maturity in later British films like *Blanche Fury* (1948) and *The Rocking Horse Winner* (1950). She wasn't bad in *WereWolf of London,* either.

Understandably, it is Karloff who dominates *Bride of Frankenstein.* Promotional trailers boldly exclaimed "The Monster *Talks*!" but Karloff insisted that humanizing the character only detracted from his uniqueness. He steadfastly maintained this belief until his death.

Several months after the release of *Bride of Frankenstein, New York Sun* reporter Eileen Creelman (who had nothing but the most lavish praise for the film) was sent out to interview Karloff. But the reporter found the star, though gracious as always, surprisingly cool about his new movie.

"I don't know but that that was a mistake, that build-up of so much sympathy for the Monster," Karloff opined. "I think maybe they lost the excitement of the picture." Few people are in agreement with Karloff's assessment, and *Bride* is usually ranked as one of his triumphs. Karloff again proves he is a physical actor *par excellence,* wringing a full range of emotions from the subtlest of gestures or facial expressions.

Franz Waxman's score is lush and motif-laden, although the meager 22-man studio orchestra used is hardly the last word in sonic splendor. It is one of the most discussed of all horror film scores, encompassing as it does a remarkable variety of moods and styles. It easily ranks as Waxman's best for the genre; his other contributions, *The Invisible Ray* and Metro's *Dr. Jekyll and Mr. Hyde* (1941), are comparative letdowns. Universal, unfortunately, saw fit to cannibalize the *Bride* score, as well as those of *Dracula's Daughter, WereWolf of London* and others, for use as background filler in their juvenile Flash Gordon serials.

The MCA video cassette release of the "restored" *Frankenstein* might mean the original 90-minute release print of its initial sequel is on the horizon. The deleted scenes, which include the Monster's slaying of the Burgomaster, as well as Dwight Frye's murder of his rich uncle, may reveal a bit more of the dark side of Whale's humor. As in the uncut version of *King Kong* (1933), the audience's sympathy for the Monster may diminish the more we see of his carnage. On the other hand it may provide the Monster with greater motive when he hurls Frye to his death from atop the tower laboratory in the last reel (Frye conveniently pinned the murders of his relatives on the Monster).

It was widely anticipated that the box office grosses on *Bride of Frankenstein* would match those of the original, making the film a hot property for theater owners. Long before the days when "saturation bookings" were commonplace, a legal battle erupted between two New York City theaters to decide which of them held the legal right to screen the movie. A settlement was reached before the case went to Federal Court, with the Roxy Theater winning the rights to exhibit the attraction. Its rival, the Rialto, picked up *WereWolf of London* as a consolation prize. Despite excellent notices, *Bride of Frankenstein* didn't earn quite the bonanza reaped by its predecessor.

There have been few attempts to duplicate the fragile charm of *Bride of Frankenstein.* Hammer's rather nasty *Frankenstein Created Woman* (1967) doesn't remotely qualify as a remake and Franc Roddam's 1985 misfire, simply titled *The Bride,* was actually something of a sequel, although it did come a tad closer to the mark. Highlighted by splendid sets and a flashy laboratory sequence, the film courted disaster by casting the vapid Jennifer Beals and British rock star Sting in the leads. Even worse was a sappy and absurd upbeat ending which finds the Monster and his mate, romantically reunited, blissfully sailing down a Venetian waterway on a gondola. Unsurprisingly, the picture was savaged by the critics and quickly sold to television.

Despite James Whale's richly deserved reputation as one of the all-time great horror directors, he remains a curiously uninfluential figure. The Gothic look of his films has been slavishly duplicated, but Whale's sophisticated melding of humor and horror quickly became passé. His style was lightly mimicked in *Son of Frankenstein,* but not to the extent that has been suggested in numerous film books. The later Frankenstein movies were made by directors who appear as though they've never even seen a Whale film. Whale's elegance and wit were perfectly in tune with the glamourous '30s and his downfall was inevitable. William K. Everson, a tireless champion of Whale, laments that Universal-International didn't recruit the director during the horror–science fiction boom of the '50s. This is a bit unrealistic as his painstaking, handcrafted style was out of step with Hollywood's mechanized filmmaking techniques. The thought of Whale competing for the drive-in trade with Herman Cohen, for example, is downright depressing. More than archaic museum pieces, Whale's quartet of horror classics have comfortably withstood the test of time. *Bride of Frankenstein* is probably his finest.

WereWolf of London (1935)

Released June 3, 1935. 75 minutes. A Carl Laemmle Production. *Directed by* Stuart Walker. *Associate Producer:* Robert Harris. *Executive Producer:* Stanley Bergerman. *Screenplay by* John Colton. *Original Story by* Robert Harris. *Adapted by* Harvey Gates & Robert Harris. *Director of Photography:* Charles Stumar. *Special Photographic Effects:* John P. Fulton. *Assistant Directors:* Phil Karlstein [Karlson] & Charles S. Gould. *Film Editors:* Russell Schoengarth & Milton Carruth. *Art Director:* Albert S. D'Agostino. *Musical Score:* Karl Hajos. *Sound Supervisor:* Gilbert Kurland. *Makeup by* Jack P. Pierce.

Henry Hull (Dr. Wilfred Glendon), Warner Oland (Dr. Yogami), Valerie Hobson (Lisa Glendon), Lester Matthews (Paul Ames), Spring Byington (Miss Ettie Coombes), Lawrence Grant (Colonel Thomas Forsythe), Clark Williams (Hugh Renwick), J.M. Kerrigan (Hawkins), Charlotte Granville (Lady Alice Forsythe), Ethel Griffies (Mrs. Whack), Zeffie Tilbury (Mrs. Moncaster), Jeanne Bartlett (Daisy), Harry Stubbs (Jenkins), Louis Vincenot (Head Cooley), Reginald Barlow (Timothy), Eole Galli (The Prima Donna), Joseph North (Plimpton), Egon Brecher (Priest), Boyd Irwin, Sr. (Hotel Manager), Helena Grant (Mother), Noel Kennedy (Boy), William Millman (John Bull), Tempe Pigott (Drunk Woman), Maude Leslie (Mrs. Charteris), Herbert Evans (Jenkins' Aide), David Thursby (Photographer), Gunnis Davis, George Kirby (Detectives), Jeffrey Hassel (Alf), Amber Norman (Beggarwoman), James May (Bar-Man), Vera Buckland (Yogami's Housekeeper), Connie Leon (Yogami's Housemaid), Wong Chung (Cooley), Alex Chivra (Stand-in for Oland), Roseollo Navello (Maid), George DeNormand (Double for Hull), Edwin Parker (Double for Matthews).

WereWolf of London has gotten more than its share of hard knocks over the years. It's a film that's usually discussed in suppositions: "What if Karloff had played the Henry Hull part?" or "What if Lugosi had played the role essayed by Warner Oland?" or "Wouldn't the picture have turned out better if James Whale or Robert Florey had directed it?" These ponderings are not unjustified. Stuart Walker, the film's director, had neither the ingenuity nor the affinity for an all-out horror subject. Hull, despite his impressive theatrical track record, lacked Karloff's passion as much as Oland lacked Lugosi's mystery.

Compared with the satanic eroticism of *The Black Cat* and the cold-blooded brutality of *Murders in the Rue Morgue, WereWolf of London* is genteel indeed. It's poky, quaint and self-consciously theatrical; these restraints dim the gut-wrenching human drama at the heart of the story and take the edge off its honest chills and suspense. Still, *WereWolf of London* has enough atmosphere and flavor to warrant its status as a qualified classic.

Although the legend of the werewolf is as deeply seated in the history of mankind as the vampire, its cinematic treatment up to this time was, by comparison, negligible. Several short films (1913's *The Werewolf* and 1914's *The White Wolf*) featured lycanthropes of American Indian origin; there were also a number of domestic and foreign productions which bore the namesake of the supernatural creature, but whose protagonists were strictly human in nature (e.g., Reliance-Mutual's 1915 *The Wolf Man,* Fox's 1924 John Gilbert film *The Wolfman, Le Loup Garou [The Werewolf],* a 1932 German production).

Guy Endore's novel "The WereWolf of Paris," published in 1933, brought the mythic manimal the belated recognition it deserved. Curiously, when Universal decided to introduce the werewolf in its current horror cycle in late 1934, it ignored the Endore novel and opted for an original treatment instead. The French writer had taken up residence in Hollywood by this time, but was not invited to participate in the project. (MGM obtained his services to co-author the screenplays for *Mark of the Vampire* and *Mad Love,* both 1935.)

Of the scores of projects announced for Karloff and Lugosi by Universal during this hectic period, one of the most interesting proposals was to star Boris as a lycanthrope in *The Wolf Man.* A script was prepared in early 1932, Robert Florey was slated to direct, but the production never got off the ground.

Uncle Carl's son-in-law Stanley Bergerman was chosen to serve as the executive producer on *WereWolf of London* and Stuart Walker (riding high after his engagements on the studio's two Dickens transcriptions, *Great Expectations* and *Mystery of Edwin Drood*) was elected to direct, "bumping" Kurt Neumann. John Colton, a world-weary homosexual playwright/scenarist whose claim to fame was adapting Somerset Maugham's short story "Miss Sadie Thompson" into the Broadway smash "Rain," submitted a finished screenplay to Bergerman in late January, 1935. Bela Lugosi appears to have been an early contender for the Yogami role.

On January 19, 1935, Universal announced that *WereWolf of London* would be Henry Hull's first starring vehicle for the studio. The Louisville, Kentucky–born Hull was considered one of Broadway's most accomplished actors, racking up an extraordinary number of successes in long-running productions. David Belasco had given him his first stage break in his 1911 production "The Nigger." (Hull portrayed both a runaway slave and the county sheriff who pursued him.) Following a three-year stint in Margaret Anglin's Greek repertory company, the actor scored his first great Broadway success as the lead in the 1916 stageplay "The Man Who Came Back." While appearing in a Huntington, Long Island, production of "The Little Minister," producer-director Anthony Brown chose Hull to play the part of Jeeter Lester, tobacco-chewing patriarch of a dirt-poor Southern farm family, in a theatrical adaptation of Erskine Caldwell's novel *Tobacco Road.* The 1933 Broadway show was an instant hit and ran for over 3,000 performances.

Acting in motion pictures kept the stage star busy between theater engagements. Hull's silent film debut came in 1917's *The Volunteer,* shot in America's first film capital, Fort Lee, New Jersey. Scores of others followed, including a screen version of *The Man Who Came Back* for Fox in 1924. Hull's resonant speaking voice made him a natural in talkies.

"You can't hypnotize the camera," the actor said in a newspaper interview. "You *can* hypnotize a [theater] audience to the point where they forget your art and react to voice and gesture. You must fall back on sheer technique, and pray to the gods that your scene is effective...."

On March 24, 1934, Carl Laemmle signed Hull to a five-year contract while he was appearing in "Tobacco Road." His first assignment for Universal was of classic proportions; he made a strong impression as the escaped criminal Magwitch in Stuart Walker's first Charles Dickens adaptation *Great Expectations.* In July, 1934, Universal announced that it was planning to feature the distinguished actor as the lead in their forthcoming adaptation of Daniel Defoe's *Robinson Crusoe,* but the picture never materialized. Instead, Hull was given a supporting part in *Transient Lady* opposite Gene Raymond and Frances Drake.

In *WereWolf of London,* Hull portrays eminent British botanist Dr. Wilfred Glendon, whose quest for the only known specimens of the phosphorescent moon flower, the Mariphasa lupino lumino, takes him deep into a forbidden region of Tibet. Abandoned by his native bearers and shrugging off the prophetic warnings of a holy man (Egon Brecher), Glendon and his travelling companion Hugh Renwick (Clark Williams) enter a forbidden valley.

Suddenly, both men are overcome by unearthly sensations. Glendon reacts as though he has been struck down by a "ghostly fist" (Colton's own words). Catching sight of the elusive Mariphasa, Glendon rushes towards it, but stops dead in his tracks. Cast against the rocks above is the shadow of a lurching figure, paused, ready to strike. Within moments, the creature—a human being with animalistic tendencies—is upon him. The botanist wounds the beast with his knife, but not before it has inflicted a deep bite wound in his arm.

Returning to England with his specimens, Glendon is visited by the inscrutable Dr. Yogami (Warner Oland). Like Glendon, he too has searched Tibet for specimens of the phenomenal plant. Sensing a vague familiarity about the stranger, Glendon asks Yogami if they have ever met before. "In Tibet, once, but only for a moment ... in the dark," is his disturbing reply. Yogami informs an incredulous Glendon that the Mariphasa is the only known antidote for lycanthrophobia, a strange malady in which the victim becomes a werewolf when the moon is full. Asked how these unfortunate individuals contracted "this medieval unpleasantness," Yogami replies, "From the bite of another werewolf." He rests his hand on Glendon's scarred arm.

Although Glendon hasn't yet made the connection, the audience realizes it was Yogami who attacked the scientist in Tibet. The blood-and-lust conflict between two desperate men struggling to save their souls from the grip of a satanic power had the potential for great theater that is never fully realized in the film. Colton's overly restrained screenplay offers the two rivals no impassioned confrontation scenes until the climax, at which point severe deletions in the scenarist's dialogue lessens the dramatic impact to a considerable degree.

A rare, blood-curdling close-up of Henry Hull as the *WereWolf of London*. (Photo courtesy Steve Jochsberger.)

A giddy, behind-the-scenes shot from *WereWolf of London,* with Henry Hull, Valerie Hobson and Lester Matthews.

Haunted by Yogami's warning that a werewolf "instinctively seeks to kill the thing it loves best," Glendon spends every waking hour coaxing the buds of the Mariphasa open with the aid of a miraculous apparatus which creates artificial moonlight. He fears for the safety of his beloved wife Lisa (Valerie Hobson), whose loneliness and despair are driving her into the arms of her dear friend and former suitor Paul Ames (Lester Matthews).

The complicated process of shooting the man-into-werewolf transformations was accomplished with deceptive grace. Cameraman Charles Stumar, who died only a few months after the completion of this film, admitted at the time that he was scornful of shots whose beauty or power left audiences breathless; he felt they distracted the viewer's attention away from the story. Be that as it may, one cannot disregard the beauty *and* power of Hull's first full-fledged changeover, the finest sequence in the film. As the actor passes by a series of pillars, a different stage of the transformation is revealed. It was the job of John P. Fulton and his assistant David "Stan" Horsley to accomplish this feat of cinematic magic.

"John and I pondered a lot on how this shot was actually going to get done in the pre-production stages of the film," Horsley told *Photon*'s Paul Mandell. "It was obvious to us from the outset that a series of cuts would be a bit too obvious as it would entail breaks in an otherwise smooth piece of camera movement. It was decided to photograph Hull against a black velvet background and matte his figure onto the normal background scene. The pillars were separately photographed and further matted onto this composite, making the precise instant where the alteration in make-up occurred, so that in its final stage there appeared to be no break in camera movement."

Hull's werewolf differs from Chaney, Jr.'s later portrayal in that he's capable of reason, whereas the latter operated by pure animal instinct. Glendon hurries to the lab with the express purpose of anointing himself with the Mariphasa but discovers the blossoms have been stolen. Donning his cap and scarf (an eccentric touch), the lycanthrope seeks out Lisa, who's attending a social bash given by her flighty aunt, Ettie Coombes (Spring Byington in another of her dotty society matron roles). Lurking about Ettie's apartment building, Glendon climbs up a balcony and finds a tipsy Ettie sleeping off a drunk. In an eerily lit close-up, the werewolf approaches the socialite. Her full-throated scream frightens him off. On the street below, the lycanthrope snatches away the life of a streetwalker.

Colton's script becomes annoyingly episodic at this point. Ever desperate for the birth of the life-saving Mariphasa blooms, Glendon keeps dashing off to secret destinations to wait out his next transformation, and then returns home to check on the flower's painfully slow progress. In one of his finest moments, Hull, holed up in a seedy Whitechapel rooming house, prays to God that He intervene and prevent the botanist's awful transformation. "Dear Father in Heaven," he cries, "don't let this happen to me again! But if it must, keep me away from Lisa. Keep me away from the thing I love!"

Glendon's emotional entreaty doesn't postpone the inevitable and in a gloriously executed sequence, he becomes a werewolf in full view of Stumar's camera. Lisa almost falls victim to her husband's bestiality when she and Paul are attacked by the werewolf while on a sentimental evening outing.

Yogami, meanwhile, has his own problems. The Mariphasa blossoms he has stolen from Glendon have been used up. Unable to convince Scotland Yard that the recent rash of murders plaguing London is the work of a werewolf, and that they must secure Wilfred Glendon's specimens of the Mariphasa for mass cultivation, Yogami retires to his hotel. That night, Yogami himself becomes a werewolf and slays a chambermaid.

Finally, in Glendon's lab, the two rivals confront one another. Yogami greedily snatches the barely bloomed Mariphasa blossom right from under Glendon's nose. "You brought this on me!" the botanist cries. "That night . . . in Tibet!" Yogami tries to take flight but Glendon seizes him and the pair struggle violently. Ironically, Yogami dies in the claws of the monster he himself had inadvertently created.

The werewolf "instinctively" seeks out his beloved Lisa. Overcoming Paul, Glendon corners Lisa on a staircase and stalks her like a hungry cat. This time there can be no doubt in Lisa's mind who this strange creature really is. A policeman's bullet pierces the night air and the wolf man falls to the floor, mortally wounded. Before he expires, Glendon (still in werewolf form) bids his grieving wife a moving farewell.

By the time Stuart Walker gathered together his cast and crew for the first day's shooting of *WereWolf of London* (January 18, 1935), significant changes had already been made in Colton's talky, overwritten scenario. To the film's benefit, a plethora of superfluous chatter was excised and several of the major horror scenes were fine-tuned. The production's *pièce de résistance*—Hull's first transformation into a werewolf as he rushes through the column-lined corridor—doesn't even appear in the script. (Colton's version had an irate Glendon pursuing his panic-stricken cat across the estate grounds and into the laboratory, emerging moments later as a werewolf.)

In Colton's script dated January 26, 1935, greater emphasis is placed on the love triangle between Glendon, Lisa and Paul. Lisa is a lot more disenchanted with her marriage to the stuffy, preoccupied Dr. Glendon than the film indicates. Colton also introduced a character by the name of Dr. Phillips. (Reginald Barlow, originally cast in this part [the main and end titles still credit him for it], was recast as Timothy, the groundskeeper.) This family physician is summoned by the distressed botanist after he discovers coarse hair creeping down his forehead and a permanent five o'clock shadow. Stymied, Phillips promises to confer with an authority on hirsutism(!) before venturing a diagnosis. (The decision to discard Colton's suggestion that Hull play out the remainder of his straight scenes in this ludicrous transitional stage was a sound one.)

Other script deviations include the substitution of a streetwalker instead of a little beggar as the werewolf's first victim, and a sequence (which was probably shot, then later discarded) wherein a little boy is grasped by the octopus-like tentacles of the giant Madagascar Carnalia while attending Glendon's botanical garden party.

As the nosy old Mrs. Moncaster and her equally gin-sodden friend Mrs. Whack, Zeffie Tilbury and Ethel Griffies provide *WereWolf of London* with some flavorsome Cockney humor. But Colton would have had these crones wear out their welcome in a silly little scene which was evidently written for the purpose of giving the film an "upbeat" finis: Mrs. Moncaster, hailed by her fellow Whitechapelians as "the lady that lodged the werewolf," has her photo session ruined by the cantankerous Mrs. Whack, who claims she lodged Glendon first, and therefore deserves all the adoration *and* the six complimentary bottles of gin donated by the local pub!

Glendon's plea for salvation as he awaits the rising of the full moon in his rooming house apartment is decidedly more verbose (and consequently not as affecting) in Colton's script. However, there is one instance where a little *less* editing would have proven beneficial: the climactic confrontation scene between Glendon and Yogami (pared down to two lines of dialogue for the final shoot).

Colton sets up the intense exchange with the two men waiting breathlessly for the Mariphasa bud to bloom:

> Glendon: "We meet again, Yogami...for the last time..."
> Yogami: "Between us both and doom...there is only that..."
> Glendon: "The doom is yours, not mine, Yogami...one of us must go..."
> Yogami: "There is enough blood in that flower to save us both if it blooms in time—"
> Glendon: "No, Yogami. There isn't room on all the planet for both of us. *You* brought this thing on me."

The dialogue continues until, finally, the little flower begins to bloom. Both men rush to secure it. Glendon tears the blossom off its stem and tries to pierce his wrist with the thorn but Yogami bites him, causing the flower to fall to the floor. Glendon attacks him; Yogami, realizing he cannot secure the flower, stamps on it. The flower "dies" with an agonized cry. A ray of moonlight shoots from the dead blossom to the moon, "the soul of the flower returned to its final resting place."

Charles Stumar photographed the furious struggle between the two men in a continuous action, according to a studio interview with the artist. It was rehearsed like a dance, step by step, from a floor map of the huge greenhouse set. Though the final cut doesn't bear this out, Stumar claimed the scene consisted of 147 separate two minute "takes," with rest and makeup intervals. (The preview trailer for *WereWolf of London* contains a single shot, not seen in the final cut, of the werewolf inflicting deep claw marks on Oland's face.)

The atmospheric, otherworldly Tibetan sequences were shot on a tract of rugged terrain known as Vasquez Rocks. Stumar claimed that since the natural shadows of the rocks were too light for the required eerie effects of the night scenes, he manufactured his own moonlight and shadows. Sheet iron was scalloped by shears into jagged edges and set along rocks. Powerful blue-white lamps playing behind these screens threw the necessary jet black shadows and created a silvery-blue-green glow, much richer than natural moonlight.

While *WereWolf of London* was in production, Carl Laemmle decided to perk up interest in his latest horror outing by offering a $50 reward to any studio employee who could come up with a catchy title based on the film's plot synopsis. Hundreds of suggestions were submitted, some of them reasonable, others hilariously outlandish. Here are a few of our favorites: *Moon Doom, The Relief of Death, What Price Curiosity, The Whelp from Tibet, Dr. Yogami of London, Werewolf Yogami, Beyond the Ken of Man; Kismet, The Loose Wolf,* and, "best" of all, *Bloom, Flower, Bloom!* Only one submission was seriously considered, *The Unholy Hour*. But, by the time the picture was well into its final stages of post-production, the original title was reinstated. (The cryptic-sounding *The Unholy Hour* was retained for the film's Canadian distribution.)

Completed on February 23, at a cost exceeding $195,000 (more than $36,000 overbudget), *WereWolf of London* came in four days over schedule. With a tighter script, concise continuity and sharper direction, Walker's film would have done greater justice to its fascinating subject matter. The passion and sheer cinematic artistry of a Whale or an Ulmer are lacking in the director's placid staging, and there are only a few scenes which can be truthfully termed inspired. Colton's approach to lycanthropy is more scientific than supernatural. While the scenarist makes passing references to the werewolf's mythological origins, very little of the creature's mythic elements are incorporated into the script. Glendon is slain by an ordinary bullet, not a silver one. The whole business concerning the Mariphasa and its ability to thwart lycanthropic seizures is purely the invention of Colton and Robert Harris, who authored the original story. *WereWolf of London* shrugs off many of the Middle European influences which Curt Siodmak so dearly embraced in his later werewolf outings.

Unanimously praised by critics of the day, Henry Hull's studious performance has come under increasing attack. Many argue that Wilfred Glendon is an arrogant, unsympathetic stuffed shirt, quite the opposite of Lon Chaney's naive and child-like Larry Talbot. Glendon's unjustified jealousy of his neglected wife alienates us further. Paradoxically, the deeper the scientist descends into despair, the more human he becomes. Jack Pierce's marvelous makeup design, a subtly feline, almost satanic look, is marvelous and quite a contrast from his more bestial guise for Chaney. Pierce had originally designed the classic Chaney/Wolf Man makeup for Hull, but (according to reports) the actor protested about the prolonged application sessions, so a more modified look was created.

Hull enjoyed a long and prosperous career playing a variety of character parts in over 40 movies including *Jesse James, Miracles for Sale* (both 1939), *Lifeboat* (1944), *The Fountainhead* (1949) and *Master of the World* (1961) before he died on March 8, 1977, at the age of 88. While in retirement on his Lyme, Connecticut, farm in 1964, Hull admitted in a newspaper interview that (as of that date) he had never seen *WereWolf of London* in its entirety.

"I saw snatches of the film shortly after we shot it almost thirty years ago, and I saw perhaps the first ten or fifteen minutes of it on television Saturday night. Then I went to bed. Sleep means more to me than any movie, even my own. It was a pretty good get-up, wasn't it? Jack [Pierce] had a special talent for turning men into freaks. I got out of the monster mold while the getting was good. The studio liked the job I had done. . .and they wanted me for similar roles, but I declined because I didn't want to be limited to work in horror films. I'm glad I did, too. . ." (Hull conveniently "forgot" that Tod Browning began grooming him as a successor to Chaney, Sr., in 1939. A series of Browning/Hull horror/mysteries was planned, although only *Miracles for Sale* eventuated.)

Most of *WereWolf of London*'s supporting cast came from the London theater. Valerie Hobson's ingratiating performance is a distinct improvement over her wide-eyed, weepy Elizabeth in *Bride of Frankenstein* (the teenage actress reportedly filmed her first two scenes in *WereWolf* while finishing up the Whale picture, working up to 15 hours a day for 11 days straight). Often compared to Herbert Marshall by English theater critics, Lester Matthews is smooth and amiable as Paul Ames, Lisa's old flame. Matthews hailed from a celebrated theatrical family and, before signing a contract with Universal, played leading man parts on the London stage and in a variety of touring companies. Only Swedish-born Warner Oland, Hollywood's favorite Charlie Chan, seems ill-at-ease in his role as the sympathetic yet sinister Dr. Yogami. Plagued with a serious drinking problem, Oland was destined to die in two short years, after making Hollywood headlines for disappearing from a soundstage in the midst of a production.

Compared to George Waggner's dramatically superior study in lycanthropia *The Wolf Man, WereWolf of London* seems dated indeed. Most fans find it easier to criticize the film for its weaknesses than to champion it for its merits. With a more suitable director, stronger names in the cast and a zippier screenplay, *WereWolf of London* might not be regarded today as the "black sheep" of the Universal horror classics.

The Raven (1935)

Released July 22, 1935. 61 minutes. *Directed by* Louis Friedlander [Lew Landers]. *Associate Producer:* David Diamond. *Screenplay by* David Boehm. *Suggested by the poem "The Raven" and the short story "The Pit and the Pendulum" by* Edgar Allan Poe. *Director of Photography:* Charles Stumar. *Film Editor:* Albert Akst. *Editorial Supervision:* Maurice Pivar. *Dialogue Director:* Florence Enright. *Art Director:* Albert S. D'Agostino. *Assistant Directors:* Scott Beal & Victor Noerdlinger. *Sound Supervisor:* Gilbert Kurland. *Musical Score:* Clifford Vaughan, Heinz Roemheld & Y. Franke Harling. *Dance Staged by* Theodore Kosloff. *Makeup by* Jack P. Pierce.

Boris Karloff (Edmond Bateman), Bela Lugosi (Dr. Richard Vollin), Lester Matthews (Dr. Jerry Halden), Irene Ware (Jean Thatcher), Samuel S. Hinds (Judge Thatcher), Spencer Charters (Colonel Bertram Grant), Inez Courtney (Mary Burns), Ian Wolfe (Geoffrey "Pinky" Burns), Maidel Turner (Harriet Grant), Arthur Hoyt (Chapman), Jonathan Hale (Dr. Cook), Walter Miller (Dr. Hemingway), Cyril Thornton (Servant), Nina Golden (The Dancer), Raine Bennett (Poe), Joe Haworth* (Drug Clerk), Anne Darling,* Mary Wallace,* June Gittleson* (Autograph Hunters), Bud Osborne (Cop), Al Ferguson (Cook), Madeline Talcott (Nurse), Monte Montague (Double for Karloff), George DeNormand (Double for Lugosi). [**Does not appear in final print.*]

Edgar Allan Poe may have been a supremely gifted writer, literary critic and all-around scholar, but as a person, he wasn't the kind of guy you'd want as your bosom pal. In the course of his 40 years (and long after his death), he was depicted as a dypsomaniac, manic depressive, sadomasochist, sex pervert, obsessive neurotic and egomaniac. Driven to the brink of madness by private demons, unable to maintain a decent standard of living, and ridiculed by an intolerant world which couldn't appreciate his genius, Poe expressed his agonies in a body of work that reflected his inner torment. At least one scholar debunks the Poe myth and insists the dark side of the writer's personality was exaggerated by certain biased parties (he even claimed that Poe loved cats!). While there may be some truth to this claim, one cannot deny that the man was preoccupied with the grotesque.

A scandalously unflattering caricature of Poe, embodying many of his time-honored obsessions (plus an additional element of sadistic cruelty), emerged in the character of Dr. Richard Vollin, brilliant surgeon and proprietor of a modern-day chamber of horrors, in *The Raven,* Universal's final entry in their '30s Poe trilogy. Hoping to duplicate the success of *The Black*

Cat, the studio rigorously exploited the Poe name and the reunion of costars Karloff and Lugosi. Borrowing a reference or two from the poem of the same name and the short story "The Pit and the Pendulum," a bevy of writers developed a storyline which, in its final form, was charged with exciting possibilities. Regrettably, the screenplay that emerged from this fusion of ideas didn't measure up to its potential. Neither did the no-frills direction of Louis Friedlander (who later changed his name to Lew Landers), a specialist in serials and Westerns, capture the poetry and mystique of the tale's dark, brooding melodrama.

Right from the outset, it had to have been apparent to everyone concerned that *The Raven* couldn't compete with *The Black Cat* in terms of style and technique. Over the decades, few of the vintage Universal shock classics (with the exception of *Dracula*) have sustained as many brickbats as this ill-conceived film. Lugosi's passionate but unbridled performance, Karloff's miscasting in a secondary role beneath his abilities, and the generally slapdash quality of the writing and direction, are just a few of the common gripes leveled against *The Raven.* Of significance, too, was the effect that *The Raven* had on the British Board of Film Censors. By indulging in excessive, Poe-inspired sadism (this was a code-regulated feature!), the shocker hastened the ban on horror pictures in the British Isles, leading to a discontinuation of Hollywood production for two years. ("Just how horrible has a film to be before it is rejected?" groused one uptight British reviewer after *The Raven*—cut to 57 minutes—was passed for distribution by the skin of its beak.)

Admittedly, it's difficult to sit through a screening of *The Raven* and *not* come down hard on it. In spite of its many faults, however, true *aficionados* (particularly Bela fans) find great pleasure in the movie's uninhibited madness. David Boehm's dialogue is, by and large, fruity and eminently quotable, the pulse-quickening pace seldom falters, and the high-camp, serial-style climax (replete with swinging pendulums and bone-crushing death chambers) quaintly recreates the spirit and abandon of those old-fashioned Pearl White chapterplays. Best of all, there's LUGOSI (billed only by surname [as is KARLOFF] for the first and only time in his screen career at Universal), outshining his rival and pulling all stops in one of his most colorful portrayals.

Although Boehm's screenplay for *The Raven* starts off with dancer Jean Thatcher (Irene Ware) signing autographs for fans as she leaves a theater after a performance, the release print begins with the girl's car racing down a rain-slick highway. Encountering a detour, Jean's car spins out of control and plunges into a gully. Critically injured, the dancer is rushed to the hospital where a team of doctors, including her fiancé, Dr. Jerry Halden (Lester Matthews), can't rouse her from a coma. Jean's only hope for survival rests with Dr. Richard Vollin (Bela Lugosi), a gifted surgeon, now in retirement. Judge Thatcher (Samuel S. Hinds), Jean's father, desperately implores the callous surgeon to save his daughter's life. At first reluctant, Vollin finally agrees to take on the case. Jean makes a miraculous recovery.

Vollin's unique abilities as a doctor are but a facet of the man's accomplishments. He is also a scholar who has devoted his life to the study of the works of Edgar Allan Poe. Vollin's devotion to Poe borders on obsession:

he has furnished his home with a collection of torture devices used in the Spanish Inquisition, and has designed for his own edification several of the deadly implements Poe described in his stories.

Vollin's concern for Jean develops into a compulsive passion which she refuses to acknowledge. Not about to take this rebuff lightly, he plots to vent his frustration at the expense of Jean, her father and Halden.

The crazed surgeon finds a reluctant accomplice in the person of Edmond Bateman (Boris Karloff), a San Quentin escapee who seeks out the surgeon for a change of appearance. Bateman has a persecution complex: "Maybe if a man looks ugly, he does ugly things," he reasons. "You are saying something profound," Vollin says, obviously inspired. "A man with a face so *hideously ugly*...." Pretending to perform an advanced medical procedure on the fugitive's face, Vollin purposely mutilates him. To gain his cooperation, the mad doctor promises to restore his features after he has done a job for him.

That weekend, Vollin invites Jean, Jerry, Judge Thatcher, and their friends Geoffrey and Mary Burns (Ian Wolfe and Inez Courtney) and Colonel and Mrs. Bertram Grant (Spencer Charters and Maidel Turner) to spend a few days at his home. After his guests have retired for the night, Vollin orders Bateman to abduct Judge Thatcher and secure him to a slab in his torture chamber. Above the magistrate's body, a swinging pendulum mounted with a razor-edged blade is set in motion. In precisely 15 minutes, the blade will cut a fatal swath across Thatcher's body.

Holding the couple at gunpoint, Vollin orders Jean and Jerry into a chamber with walls designed to crush its occupants to death. As the pendulum descends and the moving walls close in on the couple, Vollin breaks into a fit of hysterical laughter. "Poe!" he cries. *"You are avenged!"* Bateman, who has developed a fondness for Jean, orders Vollin to release her from the death trap. When he refuses, Bateman frees the couple himself. Vollin promptly fires a bullet into his disobedient henchman. Summoning all his strength, the mortally wounded Bateman overpowers Vollin and seals him in the death chamber. Jerry and Geoffrey rush to Judge Thatcher's aid, ignoring Vollin's cries as the walls close in on him.

In transferring any of Poe's tales to the screen, scenarists are generally left to their own devices to come up with a workable plotline. No two film versions of the same story or poem are ever the same. In 1912, Eclair Studios produced a two-reeler in which scenes from the author's most famous tales are conjured up by Poe (Guy Oliver) in a dream. An inaccurate depiction of Poe's tragic life, based on George C. Hazleton's novel and play, was depicted in the 1915 Essanay six-reeler *The Raven* (described by *Variety* as "a most pretentious effort at something artistic"). As Poe, Henry B. Walthall is confronted by the ominous raven, revealed to be his tortured mind. Another early version, filmed at Poe's cottage in the Bronx, featured star Muriel Ostriche in a role that required her to be buried in a casket. Aside from the Universal film, the most popular version of *The Raven* is the 1963 American International Roger Corman/Richard Matheson collaboration which had that aging triumvirate of terror, Vincent Price, Peter Lorre and Boris Karloff, trying to outwit (and out-mug) each other against a medieval background of ghosts, potions and magic spells.

The road to the final realization of Universal's *The Raven* was a long and bumpy one. Probably the earliest mention of the production came in June, 1934, when *The Universal Weekly* announced that Lugosi had just signed a three-picture deal which included a screen adaptation of *The Raven.* The time was ripe for another fling with Poe. *The Black Cat,* in release for just one month, was already amassing tremendous box office grosses, while the studio's other recent horror releases, *Bride of Frankenstein* and *WereWolf of London,* were fattening up the company's coffers.

At the height of their popularity, Karloff and Lugosi's names popped up in the trade papers regularly (usually in regard to roles in pictures that never materialized). Universal shuffled the pair into the cast of *The Gift of Gab,* an all-star potpourri, produced in the summer of 1934. Billed as the Apache (Lugosi) and the Phantom (Karloff), the stars did walk-ons in a burlesque murder sketch staged by lead Edmund Lowe for a live radio broadcast.

Between August, 1934, and March, 1935, no less than *seven* writers toiled on the shooting script of *The Raven.* On August 31, novelist Guy Endore submitted a 19-page treatment based on the poem, with elements of Poe's "The Gold-Bug" included for good measure. A week later, Universal announced that it had signed rugged leading man Chester Morris for a key role. Both Morris and Guy Endore's treatment fell by the wayside.

In October, Michael Simmons and Clarence Marks collaborated on a fuller story treatment and wrote a screenplay based upon it. After careful consideration, it too was judged unsuitable. (John Lynch and Dore Schary had their hands in the stew, too; whether or not their contributions were used in part remains to be seen.)

Finally, David Boehm was pressed into service to come up with a reasonable script. The former Warner Bros. dialogue writer (*Gold Diggers of 1933, The Life of Jimmy Dolan, Easy to Love*) turned in not one but *three* complete screenplays. One was deemed satisfactory and the film was scheduled for production.

Once again, Bela Lugosi was slighted in matters of finance and billing by the shrewd Laemmles. As thanks for essaying the movie's dominant role, Lugosi was given second billing and paid $5,000. Karloff, on the other hand, was awarded first billing and paid a kingly $10,000 for his subordinate assignment. For the remainder of their professional association, Lugosi would be forced to accept second banana status to Karloff, a situation that only increased his bitterness.

Louis Friedlander took charge of directing *The Raven,* which began shooting on March 20, 1935, on a 16-day schedule. The picture wrapped on April 5, right on schedule, but over $5,000 over-budget (the final cost was $115,209.91). *The Raven* was a decided change-of-pace for Friedlander, whose last few assignments for Universal had all been serials (Buck Jones' *The Red Rider, Tailspin Tommy* and the science fiction actioner *The Vanishing Shadow*). The New York native began his Hollywood career in 1922 as an assistant director. By the late '20s, he worked himself up to the rank of a full-fledged director. Before his death in 1962, Friedlander directed some 150 films. He changed his name to Lew Landers after joining up with RKO in the late '30s.

Landers was destined to cross paths with his *Raven* stars again the following decade, directing Karloff in Columbia's screwball horror comedy *The Boogie Man Will Get You* (1942) and Lugosi in the same studio's *The Return of the Vampire* (1943).

Universal's resident art director Albert S. D'Agostino followed the example of Edgar Ulmer on *The Black Cat* by adopting the axiom "less is more" in designing Vollin's torture chamber. A standing set from *Bride of Frankenstein* (the prison cell where the Monster is briefly incarcerated) serves as the entranceway leading into the stone-walled dungeon. Illuminated by candlelight, the rooms are furnished with a modest-sized collection of ancient and *outré* devices, the *pièce de résistance* a life-size replica of Poe's deadly pendulum. Taking Universal's publicity department at its word (a risky business at best), several weeks before *The Raven* began filming, D'Agostino and his crew of technicians painstakingly developed this impressive prop. (Friedlander had originally planned on shooting the sequence with the aid of trick lighting or movable prams.) A real stone room was constructed and a steel table placed in the center of it. A pendulum mounted with a 50-pound knife was created and erected above the slab. Early attempts to operate the pendulum by means of an electrical switchboard proved unsuccessful: the current caused the crescent to descend in uneven arcs. To achieve a steady swing, a huge clock with wooden innerworks was built above the set and the pendulum attached. This set-up did the trick.

Boris Karloff himself cast doubt about a story released by Universal's publicity mavens at the time of *The Raven*'s release. While making the rounds of theaters, radio and television shows to promote AIP's *Raven* in the winter of 1963, Boris and Peter Lorre did a guest shot on "The Hy Gardner Show." Gardner, having done his homework, furnished Karloff with a newspaper clipping dated July 7, 1935, which reported a curious incident that allegedly happened during the filming of the 1935 Universal film. According to this article, Karloff was required to wear a 50-pound bullet-proof vest for the shooting of the climax. For some strange reason, blanks were out of the question for the scene in which Lugosi fires a fatal shot into Karloff. The plot required that the bullet go straight through his body. A studio firearms expert named Hugh Ames, using an infield rifle, stationed himself 150 feet away from the soundstage and aimed the real bullet between Karloff's left arm and his left side. Instead of hitting the designated target, the bullet grazed the actor's left side, cut through his coat and picked a chip out of the stone wall background.

Boris couldn't recall the incident. "If it happened," he laughed, "I'm sure I would have died of fright. With my experience with the chaps at the studio, they would never make mistakes and are very careful."

You'd think that after spending seven months picking the brains of a half-dozen writers, Universal would have come up with a script far superior to the one David Boehm had written. His scenario is the most taxing piece of writing since *Murders in the Rue Morgue*. Most of the characters are etched in such ludicrously broad strokes, it's hard to believe they were meant to be taken seriously. While Vollin's fixation with Poe, his fascination for pain and torture and his "longing for the lost Lenore" (personified by Jean Thatcher) account for his bizarre behavior throughout, Boehm's screenplay would have had a less theatrical hue had he put the brakes on the doctor's ravings. An actor with a far subtler style than Lugosi might also have toned down these excesses with an understated performance, but not Bela. He forges full speed ahead, milking every line for all it's worth. (We are grateful to be spared the spectacle of Lugosi's sing-song delivery of the line, "Nevermore. . . Nevermore. . . The lost Lenore! The lost Lenore!" at the height of his frenzy.) Yet despite these shortcomings, Richard Vollin is one of Lugosi's most memorable screen roles, taking its place beside Dracula, Ygor and *White Zombie*'s Murder Legendre.

As for Karloff, his performance as San Quentin escapee Edmond Bateman is ample proof that the actor was at a loss portraying American hoodlums. ("I want you should fix my face" is a line more suited to Jimmy Cagney or George Raft.) The transformation of Karloff from bewhiskered thug to a pitiful, mutilated slave is the picture's highlight. Using a nonsurgical procedure (twisting the nerve endings in Bateman's face), Vollin creates a mask of horror. "Do I look—*different*?" the fugitive asks in anticipation as Charles Stumar's camera savors the results of Vollin's handiwork. "Y-e-s-s," Vollin sardonically replies, relishing the moment.

David Boehm's text aptly describes the gory makeup design:

> Bateman turns so that his face is toward us. His face is a horror. Certain muscles have been paralyzed through cutting of the nerve ends. Certain others have been permitted to remain—giving life to the part of the face they control, so that here is a face—a crazy-quilt of death and life. One part of his face remains fixed in a horrible dead grimace, while the other remains alive—side by side with the corpse. One eye remains open, unblinking—staring straight ahead.

To create this ghoulish effect, Jack Pierce laid applications of cotton soaked in collodion over the right side of Karloff's face, then covered the actor's right eye with a false one made of beeswax and cellophane.

The Raven earns high marks in the cinematography and music departments. Charles Stumar (who died soon after the film's completion) captures some startling close-ups of his stars; a striking profile shot of Lugosi is particulary effective. Music supervisor Gilbert Kurland included a liberal number of Heinz Roemheld's wonderful classical music cues from *The Black Cat* which heighten the tension of the climax and complement the overall mood of the film. Ballet master Theodore Kosloff conceived a surreal interpretive dance evoking the alienation of Poe. Dancer Nina Golden doubled for Irene Ware in this brief but telling set piece.

It seems hardly likely that a man plotting a murder would stick out his neck and invite over a house full of witnesses to get in his way, but that's exactly what Lugosi does in *The Raven*. Of course, the real reason these partygoers are there is to provide some comic relief to lighten the gloom. It doesn't work. Strait-laced Ian Wolfe, his unlikely wife Inez Courtney (her character is described in the script as "a Gracie Allenish or Una Merkelish sort"), hefty Maidel Turner and irritatingly intrusive Spencer Charters provide the limpest "humor" this side of the three would-be linguists in *Murders in the Rue Morgue*. A sample exchange: "You know, I *like* horses! I grew up with

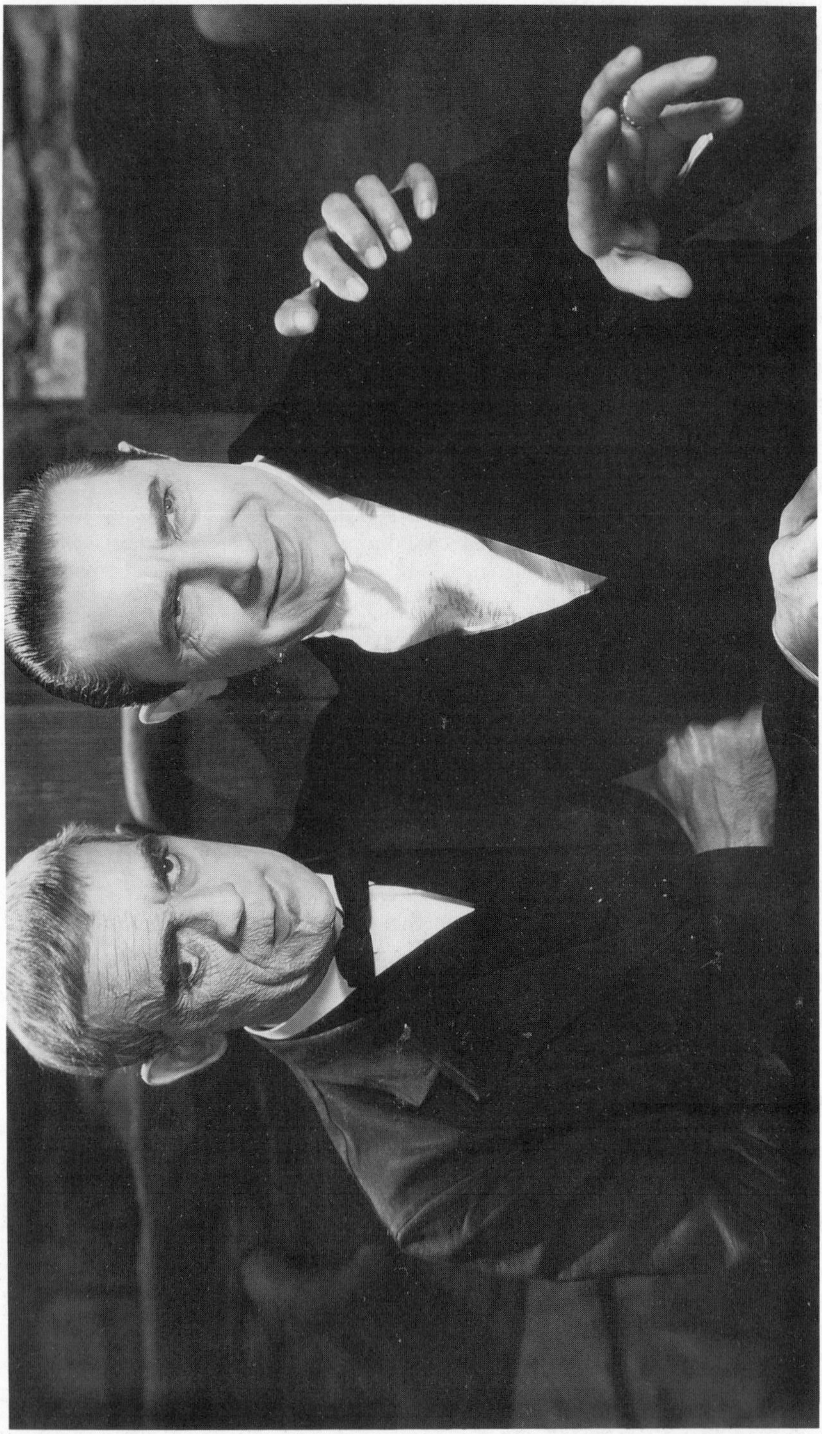

them says Ian Wolfe enthusiastically. "Yes," Maidel Turner quips. "I can see that when I look at you." Case closed.

Lester Matthews, who provided Valerie Hobson with an extramarital love interest and proved thoroughly ingratiating in *WereWolf of London,* isn't quite as believable in *The Raven* (he resorts to comical facial expressions when the going gets tough). In one amusing moment, Matthews pooh-poohs future father-in-law Samuel S. Hinds' apprehensions about spending the night under the same roof with self-professed sadist Lugosi ("There's nothing to be afraid of"), then starts at the sound of a door-knock.

Irene Ware is less ethereal and more down-to-earth than the average '30s lady-in-distress and performs her part capably. The Pelham Bay, New York, native became a showgirl in Earl Carroll's "Sketch Book" after she had won the title of Miss America in the International Beauty Contest held in 1929 in Galveston, Texas. She replaced Lillian Roth in Carroll's ninth edition of his "Vanities" and then made a talking picture test before the show closed. Arriving in Hollywood, Irene signed a two-year contract with Fox Films: it was there she first made the acquaintance of Bela Lugosi, playing Princess Najdi to his Roxor in the 1932 *Chandu the Magician.* In 1934, Ware obtained her release from Fox and signed a contract with Universal. Her first assignment was to play the goddess Diana in Lowell Sherman's fanciful *Night Life of the Gods.* Irene Ware's motion picture career was relatively brief. Following featured parts in such films as *Rendezvous at Midnight* (1935), *Outside the 3-Mile Limit* (1940) and a handful of British productions, she dropped out of pictures.

Giving what is probably the best performance in *The Raven* is Samuel S. Hinds, soon to become a pleasantly familiar fixture in '30s and '40s horror movies. Born to a well-to-do New York family (his father was president of the United States Playing Card Company), Samuel Southey Hinds enjoyed the fruits of the privileged class for the first 58 years of his life. The stock market crash of 1929 wiped out the fortune Hinds amassed as a top Los Angeles corporation lawyer. Undaunted, Hinds turned a lifelong interest in acting into a new career and enrolled at the Pasadena Community Playhouse (which he helped found in 1916) for dramatic training. Ironically, Hinds' professional break came when a casting director offered him a $20-a-day job as a bit player in the 1932 Paramount comedy, *If I Had a Million.* From that time on, the actor was seldom without a film assignment and kept active until his death at age 73 in 1948.

Not content with one screen version of "The Raven" to his credit, producer David Diamond launched plans to make a second movie adaptation of the poem, starring Vincent Price, in the fall of 1953. Diamond's ambition was to shoot the film in England in widescreen, Technicolor and 3-D, which was at the height of popularity at this time. Once again, David Boehm was commissioned to pen the screenplay, an entirely different story than the 1935 version, set in England in 1845. But, like so many proposed film projects, the 1953 *Raven* never made it past the planning stage. Quoth the Raven, "Nevermore."

Boris Karloff and Bela Lugosi share a light moment on the set of *The Raven.* (Photo courtesy Steve Jochsberger.)

The Great Impersonation (1935)

Released December 9, 1935. 64 minutes. An Edmund Grainger Production. *Directed by* Alan Crosland. *Screenplay by* Frank Wead & Eve Greene. *Based on the novel by* E. Phillips Oppenheim. *Cinematography:* Milton Krasner. *Art Director:* Charles D. Hall. *Special Cinematography:* John P. Fulton. *Film Editor:* Philip Cahn. *Sound Supervisor:* Gilbert Kurland. *Gowns by* Brymer.

Edmund Lowe (Sir Everard Dominey/Baron Leopold von Ragastein), Valerie Hobson (Lady Eleanor Dominey), Wera Engels (Princess Stephanie), Murray Kinnell (Seaman), Henry Mollison (Eddie Pelham), Esther Dale (Mrs. Unthank), Brandon Hurst (Middleton), Ivan Simpson (Dr. Harrison), Spring Byington (Duchess Caroline), Lumsden Hare (Duke Henry), Charles Waldron (Sir Ivan Brunn), Leonard Mudie (Mangan), Claude King (Sir Gerald Hume), Frank Reicher (Dr. Trenk), Harry Allen (Parkins), Nan Grey (Middleton's Daughter, the Maid), Willy Castello (Duval), Priscilla Lawson (Maid), Pat O'Hara (Chauffeur), Virginia Hammond (Lady Hume), Thomas R. Mills (Bartender), Tom Ricketts, Frank Terry, Robert Bolder (Villagers), Lowden Adams (Waiter), Violet Seaton (Nurse), Dwight Frye (Roger Unthank), David Dunbar, Frank Benson (English Farmers), John Powers (English Policeman), Leonid Snegoff (Wolff), Harry Worth (Hugo), Adolph Milar (German Bit), Larry Steers (Army Officer), Douglas Wood (Nobleman).

It's often difficult, looking back over more than 50 years, to figure out exactly what was going on inside Universal's corporate head at times. Horror films were at the height of their popularity in the early to mid '30s and Universal, which had the rights to Dracula, Frankenstein's Monster, the Invisible Man and various other bogeymen all sewed up, was top dog in the horror field. So it's a little surprising to realize that the studio only made one horror film per year in 1933 and in 1934 (*The Invisible Man* and *The Black Cat,* respectively). By 1935 things were starting to pick up again (*Bride of Frankenstein, WereWolf of London* and *The Raven* were all released within a three-month period), but one has to wonder whether the studio's confidence in the future of horror films had somehow been shaken.

What makes this minor riddle even more curious is the fact that many Universal films of this period were promoted as full-fledged horror thrillers while in fact they were simply mysteries or melodramas with slight, even negligible horror embellishments. If Universal feared that horror was "out," where was the sense in misleading audiences into believing that ordinary pictures like *Secret of the Blue Room* and *The Man Who Reclaimed His Head* were red-blooded chillers? Surely the hapless horror fan who strutted into a screening of a cheap, dreary programmer like *Secret of the Chateau* could only have exited the theater in something of a bad humor, with grave reservations about ever again taking a Universal poster at its printed word.

The Great Impersonation has more going for it than most of the phony Universal horror films of this period, although its blend of espionage and horror is a queasy one at best. At heart it's a spy story set in the pre–World War I (1914) era, but slipped into the film is an incongruous horror subplot lifted right out of Arthur Conan Doyle's *The Hound of the Baskervilles.* This curious melding of genres is as bizarre and distracting as it sounds; the result is a fanciful and offbeat little melodrama, oddly satisfying although it cannot possibly be taken seriously.

Everard Dominey (Edmund Lowe), once an English baronet, now a self-pitying drunkard, is found unconscious in the East African jungle and brought to a nearby encampment. The camp, by the sheerest of coincidences, is that of Dominey's Oxford schoolmate Leopold von Ragastein, who happens to be Dominey's exact twin (and is also played by Lowe). Both men are in Africa because of sordid events in their past lives: von Ragastein, an Austrian, killed a man in a duel over the affections of a princess, while Dominey is suspected of having killed a one-time rival for his wife's love. Von Ragastein devises a plan to send Dominey on a safari from which he shall not come back, then to take his place and return to England. Dominey's boss, unscrupulous munitions baron Sir Ivan Brunn (Charles Waldron), endorses this scheme, as it will allow for the use of Dominey Hall as their English headquarters; war clouds are gathering over Europe, and Sir Ivan needs an agent who can move in official circles.

The great impersonation seems a great success: in England, Dominey's solicitor (Leonard Mudie) and even his own cousin (Spring Byington) accept the newly-arrived adventurer as the baronet. In yet another impossible coincidence, "Dominey" runs into Princess Stephanie (Wera Engels), the femme fatale who caused the duel that ruined him, in a London hotel. To prevent her from exposing him as von Ragastein and ruining their intricate plot, Seaman (Murray Kinnell), another of Sir Ivan's operatives, brings the Princess in on their plans.

"Dominey" returns home to ancestral Dominey Hall, now a rundown pile occupied only by Dominey's wife Eleanor (Valerie Hobson) and servants. "Dominey" quickly learns that his home life is not going to be a happy one: Eleanor has gone slightly bats over the whole messy suspected-murder affair and Mrs. Unthank (Esther Dale), a servant and the mother of Roger Unthank (the man "Dominey" supposedly killed), spitefully warns him that the ghost of her son haunts nearby Black Bog. The screams of Roger's "ghost" fill the air that night as Eleanor reaches through a secret panel with knife in hand to kill the sleeping "Dominey," who awakens and disarms her in the nick of time.

Princess Stephanie shows up at Dominey Hall to help out with the spying, although she's clearly more of a hindrance than a help. Between secret conclaves and the construction of a radio transmitting room in an unused tower, "Dominey" finds time to gently woo his woozy wife; he's eventually able to get her out from under the influence of the hateful Mrs. Unthank and restore her to some degree of normalcy. To settle the question of the "ghost," "Dominey" orders the Black Bog set ablaze; Roger (Dwight Frye), very much alive, bolts screaming from the burning bog and bursts into Dominey Hall. The wild man attacks Eleanor and is throttling the girl when Mrs. Unthank appears, shooting and killing her own mad son rather than to see him institutionalized.

Stephanie becomes suspicious when "Dominey" continues to resist her romantic advances, and realizes that "Dominey" might indeed be Dominey after all. To identify him one way or the other she sends for von Ragastein's old associate Dr. Trenk (Frank Reicher), who arrives at the Hall just as Seaman is preparing a list of Sir Ivan's paid spies and saboteurs in England. Dominey's Dominey all right; he had overheard von Ragastein discussing his plan at the African camp, killed him, and has been impersonating von Ragastein impersonating him ever since. Seaman bolts toward the radio room to transmit the go-ahead order to Sir Ivan's English-based saboteurs, but despite a bullet in the shoulder Dominey remains on Seaman's heels in a chase up to the tower and puts the radio out of commission at the last possible instant. The authorities round up the spies and saboteurs, Sir Ivan is exposed, Dominey is hailed as a hero and England is safe to plunge ahead into the Great War.

The Great Impersonation has the look of a 1935 film but the feel of an older picture: the plot is a hoary affair and the broad acting puts one in mind of pictures from the earliest days of talkies. For fans who are partial to this kind of creaky entertainment, this is what "makes" the picture; for the uninitiated, this spoils it. The horror scenes, intrusive as they are, are handled with old-fashioned flair and the climactic revelation that "Dominey" really *is* Dominey comes as a genuinely surprising twist. Stilted and outmoded, pictures like *The Great Impersonation* can best be described as an acquired taste.

Edmund Lowe does a credible job in the leading dual role. Early in the proceedings both characters are irritating: Dominey is an unsympathetic drunk and von Ragastein, with his monocle, phony accent and immaculate white suit in the heart of the jungle, is the kind of character found nowhere else but in outdated movies. But as the plot begins to unfold and the locale shifts to England, Lowe becomes the sort of smooth charmer he played to perfection in any number of early films. He's most fondly remembered today for his portrayal of the boisterous Sgt. Quirt in the celebrated silent *What Price Glory?* (1926), but Lowe was basically from the Waxed Mustache school of acting, and was at his best in roles that called for a cool, impeccable suaveness. Lowe was paid a kingly $16,800 for his seven weeks' work in *The Great Impersonation,* a whopping sum which hardly seems commensurate with his box office worth.

Over the years it's become fashionable among fantasy film fans to seize every opportunity to take swipes at Lowe, who had played the title role in *Chandu the Magician* opposite Bela Lugosi in 1932. Critics carp that Lowe was unsuited for the Chandu role and that he gives a hopelessly bland performance; Lugosi fans always come down on him extra hard and rhapsodize over what

Edmund Lowe and Brandon Hurst schmooze conspiratorially in *The Great Impersonation.*

wonders their boy would have worked in that part. (Two years later, Lugosi *did* get a chance at the role in a fatiguing 12-chapter endurance test of a serial called *The Return of Chandu.* He gives the same blah performance Lowe gave, maybe not as good, with the professional apologists among the Lugosi fans now explaining that the actor was being faithful to the character of the *radio* Chandu—an "out" they refused to extend to Lowe.) Lowe made his last picture, *Heller in Pink Tights,* in 1960 and died in 1971.

Valerie Hobson does what can be done with the badly conceived and badly written part of Lowe's unbalanced wife. In her "mad" scenes she gives a breathy, faraway performance that never fails to get a laugh; she often seems on the verge of lapsing into her "Angel of Death" dialogue from *Bride of Frankenstein.* Although "cured" by Lowe's romantic solicitude, Hobson remains a weak-headed wisp, always guided by the last voice she hears. Wera Engels fares no better as Princess Stephanie, the hot-to-trot little man-eater who inflicts herself upon "Dominey" and Co. Despite her promises to distance herself from "Dominey" and to cooperate in Sir Ivan's plan, she's constantly hounding the hapless baronet and creating scenes; at one point she stupidly yells "Leopold!" at the poor man! Stephanie becomes such an exasperating presence that you find yourself sympathizing with the spies and saboteurs she's harassing, and become impatient for one of the other characters to knock her off or at least hose her down. Murray Kinnell, seedy second-string baddie of countless '30s films, is effective as "Dominey"'s second-in-command.

The rest of the leading players have insignificant roles. Spring Byington as Lowe's cousin plays the same tiresome flibbertigibbet she did in *WereWolf of London* (it might have been a nice in-joke to give her the same character name) and Lumsden Hare comes across as a pompous, silly ass. But no character is more insignificant than that played by Henry Mollison. Mollison's Eddie Pelham hangs around the edges of scenes with his arm in a sling: you're never quite sure who he is or why he's around, why the character has a broken arm or why Mollison himself is fifth-billed over players with bigger and better parts. Mollison simply appears to have crashed the movie.

While *The Great Impersonation* is set in 1914, the makers of the film seem to have completely forgotten that it did not have a contemporary setting. Characters wear then-modern clothes and drive around in nearly-new cars like a 1929 Ford and a 1931 Cadillac; one character sports a tobacco pouch with a zipper. In one of the picture's most curious juxtapositions, Edmund Lowe uses a candle to find his way to his bedroom, but after Valerie Hobson's secret-panel attempt on his life he climbs out of bed and flips on an electric light switch.

The film also has more than its share of clunker lines, plot holes and unintentionally funny moments. Early on, Dr. Trenk expresses disbelief that von Ragastein and Dominey should be exact twins who bump into each other first at Oxford and later in the middle of the African jungle; von Ragastein responds with a phlegmatic, "Lawngk odds, eh, *Tr-r-renk*?" Moments later Dominey greets the regal Baron with the exuberant, "Leopold von Ragastein—'Rags'!" During a meeting with von Ragastein and Seaman, a straight-faced Sir Ivan makes the profound comment, "No one likes tragedy." The spies always seem quite pleased with the progress they've made at Dominey Hall, but all they really accomplish there is the construction of a radio room that could have been built anywhere; "Dominey" spends all his time cozing with his nutty wife, fixing up the house and going off on giddy little carriage jaunts.

The best moment for Universal buffs comes at Dominey Hall, as Middleton the butler (sepulchral Brandon Hurst) escorts "Dominey" and lawyer Mangan (the equally sepulchral Leonard Mudie) to their bedrooms. "Dominey" asks where Mangan will be sleeping and Middleton solemnly responds, "The *Blue* Room, sir"—a pronouncement that causes an apprehensive over-the-shoulder reaction in the suddenly anxious solicitor!

Horror fans who gravitate to *The Great Impersonation* will find the spooky "ghost" subplot the highlight of the movie. There's never any doubt in the minds of the audience that the Roger Unthank ghost myth will eventually be debunked; *The Great Impersonation* is a spy story rooted in reality, and despite this bizarre detour the film basically has both feet on the ground. The entire Unthank angle has been lifted shamelessly from a subplot in the Sherlock Holmes novel *The Hound of the Baskervilles,* in which a butler and his wife are surrepticious accomplices to an escaped convict (the wife's brother) hiding out on the nearby moors. *The Great Impersonation* bounces back and forth between its two stories, and never is there any hint of one in the other: no one talks about the Unthank affair during any of the spy scenes, no one mentions the espionage angles during the "spooky" scenes.

The mad Roger is played by a hairy, bearded Dwight Frye, seen here in what is undoubtedly his most undignified role. Uncredited and unrecognizable, he scuttles across the courtyard a couple of times for the benefit of Edmund Lowe, who watches from various windows; does a lot of off-camera caterwauling; and finally flees from the fiery bog and into the house, where he's shot and does a Renfield-style stair-fall into the midst of the posse which had pursued him. The onetime Broadway actor is seen only in long shots, and for years even diehard Frye fans failed to realize that it was him under all that hair and grime. *The Great Impersonation* represented one day's work for the actor, who was paid $100 for appearing in the film.

The Great Impersonation is also interesting for giving audiences a look at sets from earlier Universal horror films, here brightly-lit rather than steeped in their customary gloom. *The Old Dark House* living room is seen as the foyer of Dominey Hall, and there are some great, eye-opening shots of the winding watchtower staircase from *Frankenstein* during *The Great Impersonation*'s climactic chase. About $2,225 of the film's budget went into special effects, including trick double exposures for shots featuring both von Ragastein and Dominey, the construction and photographing of the Black Bog miniature, and matte shots of Black Bog and the exterior of Dominey Hall. Director Alan Crosland replaced the originally signed Lloyd Corrigan.

The screenplay of *The Great Impersonation* was cowritten by Lt. Comdr. Frank "Spig" Wead, the famed naval hero turned screenwriter whose more typical credits include *Air Mail* (1932), *West Point of the Air, Ceiling Zero* (1935), *Dive Bomber* (1941) and *They Were Expendable* (1945). (Wead's life story formed the basis for a sorry, self-indulgent John Ford burlesque, *The Wings of Eagles,* 1957, with John Wayne as Wead; Edmund Lowe had a supporting role.)

The film was based upon a novel by E(dward) Phillips Oppenheim, internationally popular writer of more than 150 novels, volumes of short stories and plays. Most of Oppenheim's works dealt with espionage and intrigue, and several of his tales reached the screen during the silent and early sound period. *The Great Impersonation,* written in 1920, was first made into a movie only a year later, with silent screen actor/director James Kirkwood as Dominey and von Ragastein. (In *Variety*'s write-up of the 1921 *The Great Impersonation,* reviewer Fred questioned whether audiences would still buy such an old-hat spy plot!) Universal purchased the property and filmed the spy story twice, first in 1935 and then again in 1942, this time with Ralph Bellamy in the dual role and the action updated to the World War II era. The horror subplot, which does appear in Oppenheim's book, is not included in either the '21 or the '42 renditions. Oppenheim died in 1946.

For all its flaws and lapses it's tough to come down on a harmless picture like *The Great Impersonation.* The cast is an attractive one, it's a good-looking picture, you get two stories for the price of one and it never has a chance, at a scant 64 minutes, to wear out its welcome. The picture's old-fashioned appeal manages to elude most viewers, however; it's generally held in low esteem by vintage horror film fanciers, or at least by those who have even bothered to track it down. But when viewed with indulgence and with a nostalgia for its oldtime charm and acting styles, *The Great Impersonation* holds its own with many of the other quaint but largely indefensible relics from the same era.

The Invisible Ray (1936)

Released January 20, 1936. 79 minutes. An Edmund Grainger Production. *Directed by* Lambert Hillyer. *Screenplay by* John Colton. *Original Story by* Howard Higgin & Douglas Hodges. *Director of Photography:* George Robinson. *Art Director:* Albert S. D'Agostino. *Special Photography:* John P. Fulton. *Music by* Franz Waxman. *Film Editor:* Bernard Burton. *Sound Supervisor:* Gilbert Kurland. *Assistant Director:* Alfred Stern. *Technical Advisor:* Ted Behr. *Gowns by* Brymer.

Boris Karloff (Dr. Janos Rukh), Bela Lugosi (Dr. Felix Benet), Frances Drake (Diana Rukh), Frank Lawton (Ronald Drake), Walter Kingsford (Sir Francis Stevens), Beulah Bondi (Lady Arabella Stevens), Violet Kemble Cooper (Mother Rukh), Nydia Westman (Briggs), Daniel Haines (Headman), Georges Renavent (Chief of the Surete), Paul Weigel (Monsieur Noyer), Adele St. Maur (Madame Noyer), Frank Reicher (Professor Meiklejohn), Lawrence Stewart (Number One Native Boy), Etta McDaniel (Zulu Woman), Inez Seabury (Celeste), Winter Hall (Minister), Fred Toones [Snowflake] (Safari Boy), Hans Schumm (Attendant at Clinic), Lloyd Whitlock, Edwards Davis, Edward Reinach (Scientists), Clarence Gordon (Boy), Daisy Bufford (Mother), Jean De Briac, Francisco Moran, Robert Graves (Gendarmes), Ricca Allen, Isabella LaMal (Bystanders), Alex Chivar (Cook), Lucio Villegas (Butler), Mae Beatty (Mrs. Legendre), Paul McAllister (Papa LaCosta), Helen Brown (Mother), Ann Marie Conte (Blind Girl), Walter Miller (Derelict), Charles Fallon (Gentleman), Ernest Bowern, Charles Bastin (French Newsboys), Andre Cheron, Alphonse Martell (Surete Officials), Dudley Dickerson (Native), Ernie Adams, Raymond Turner, Jules Raucourt (Bit Men).

Producer David Diamond, who reunited Karloff and Lugosi in *The Raven,* hoped to find Bela a place in the upcoming Karloff film *Bluebeard.* However, the script by Bayard Veiller, which had Karloff playing a notorious strangler in a decidedly sympathetic light, had run into problems. Anxious to have another Karloff-Lugosi shocker in release before the end of 1935, impatient studio executives put *Bluebeard* on hold, and turned their attentions to an altogether different property.

In August, Universal announced that *The Invisible Ray* would commence production under the auspices of producer Edmund Grainger. The premise of the film was exciting, an all-out effort to break away from the Old World folklore that had been the mainstay of the studio's previous horror ventures. Instead of vampires, werewolves and Poe-inspired mayhem, the new Karloff-Lugosi vehicle would give full rein to special effects genius John P. Fulton, whose contribution to *The Invisible Man* made it a landmark trick film. *The Invisible Ray* further explored one of the genre's most overused themes: man's inability to cope with his own devices, and the corruption of science. Predictably, fragments of *Frankenstein* and most especially *The Invisible Man* crept into the script. The property wasn't based on a tested literary source, but Universal hoped to lure an audience with pseudoscientific gimmickry masquerading as "fact."

The Invisible Ray is usually cited as an example of early science fiction with its emphasis on death rays, futuristic gadgetry and a plot that broadly hints at space travel. Not quite ready to totally abandon its formulaic Gothic trappings, Universal kicked off the action in an imposing Carpathian fortress, cloaked in enough shadows to please a vampire.

Not only did *The Invisible Ray* unite Universal's reigning horror stars, it also brought together director Stuart Walker and scenarist John Colton, who had collaborated on *WereWolf of London* only a season back. Colton's latest work bore a marked resemblance to the earlier film. Having adapted Somerset Maugham's "Miss Sadie Thompson" into the Broadway hit "Rain," Colton knew full well the dramatic value of injecting an undercurrent of sexual tension, even in his horror scripts. Both *WereWolf of London* and *The Invisible Ray* have as their protagonists a scientist-turned-monster who comes to a bitter end while attempting to slay his young, sexually-repressed wife, whom he has forced into the arms of his rival.

The preproduction stage of *The Invisible Ray* was played out amid daily trade paper reports that the sale of the studio (possibly to Warner Bros.) was imminent. As news of Universal's desperate economic plight spread, there was increased pressure to get the project off the ground. Another obstacle loomed on the horizon: Stuart Walker, the director.

Not entirely satisfied with Colton's script (even after the writer returned to the lot to do some revisions), Walker requested a three-day delay in the start of production to iron out the deficiencies. The top brass refused to grant Walker the extension, and the director felt he had no other choice but to resign from the project.

"I am very enthusiastic about the story and the cast but I did not feel that I could do the studio or myself justice under the conditions that came up suddenly," Walker reported to the trades. "So far as I was concerned I needed more time and, as this could not be arranged, I suggested that some other director would be better for the assignment. It was not a matter of 'walking out'...."

Lambert Hillyer, rather surprisingly, ended up as Walker's replacement. A veteran director of action subjects and Westerns (he directed William S. Hart in 25 B oaters), Hillyer was already on the lot preparing a script (which was never finished) called *Killers on Parole.* Hillyer became quickly known as one of Hollywood's dependable "fill in" directors: he would eventually replace A. Edward Sutherland on Universal's final horror outing before the studio changed hands, *Dracula's Daughter.*

Categorizing *The Invisible Ray* as an upperclass B, the studio allotted a fairly lavish budget of $166,875. Producer Grainger took pains to create a big picture look, camouflaging old sets, utilizing glass shots to create an illusion of spaciousness, and even resurrecting Kenneth Strickfaden's electrical hardware. The cameras began rolling on Tuesday, September 17; and on October 25, 1935, the production wrapped, $68,000 over-budget *and* over-schedule. Walker, who was refused a paltry three days starting time, cattily remarked, "The director who did the picture started nine or ten days after I was ordered to start and finished twenty-five or more days *after* I was ordered to finish."

The Invisible Ray begins with a classic Universal bromide: the camera focuses on an imposing Carpathian castle on a stormy night. It is here that Dr. Janos Rukh (Boris Karloff) summons a small group of skeptical colleagues, ever impatient with his fantastic theories, to unveil his greatest discovery. Rukh has constructed a fabulous astronomical projector that can isolate light waves from outer space and reproduce images tracing the evolutionary stages of our planet. After years of work, he has uncovered evidence that a gigantic meteor crashed on the African continent eons ago, bearing a mysterious element more powerful than radium.

Convinced Rukh has made a major discovery, a scientific expedition headed by Sir Francis Stevens (Walter Kingsford) and the eminent Belgian astrochemist Dr. Felix Benet (Bela Lugosi) sets out for an uncharted region of Nigeria. Accompanying the scientists are Rukh's wife Diana (Frances Drake), Lady Arabella Stevens (Beulah Bondi) and her nephew Ronald Drake (Frank Lawton).

Insanely possessive of his discovery, Rukh separates from the rest and finds the site of the fallen meteor, still a raging inferno ages after it crash-landed on Earth. Donning a protective suit, the scientist descends into the blazing pit to secure a sample of the element. In his zeal, Rukh carelessly exposes himself to its powers and becomes contaminated. His body shines in the dark with a bright, unearthly glow and his touch means instant death.

Rukh confides his condition to Dr. Benet, who devises a counteractive which the doomed scientist must inject into himself all the days of his life if he is to survive. With the antidote comes a grim condition: the violent surcharge of poison and antidote may have a devastating effect on Rukh's brain.

Harnessing the powers of Radium X, Rukh returns to his Carpathian home and pulls off a miracle: restoring his blind mother's sight. Predicting tragedy, Mother Rukh (Violet Kemble Cooper) implores her son to remain and perfect his discovery, but Rukh has other ideas. His brain afire and his reason gone, he heads for Paris and wages a campaign of terror against those whom he believes cheated him: the Stevenses and Dr. Benet for bringing Radium X to the attention of the scientific community, and Diana for leaving him for Drake.

Rukh murders Sir Francis and Lady Arabella, and destroys two of the stone figures of the saints that adorn the cathedral where Diana and Drake were wed. Benet sets a trap for Rukh but his plan backfires and he himself falls victim to his insane colleague. Reaching out for his wife and her new husband, Rukh is accosted by his mother who destroys the counteractive before he can administer a life-saving injection. His body going up in flames, Rukh leaps from a window and disintegrates into a cloud of ash on the pavement below.

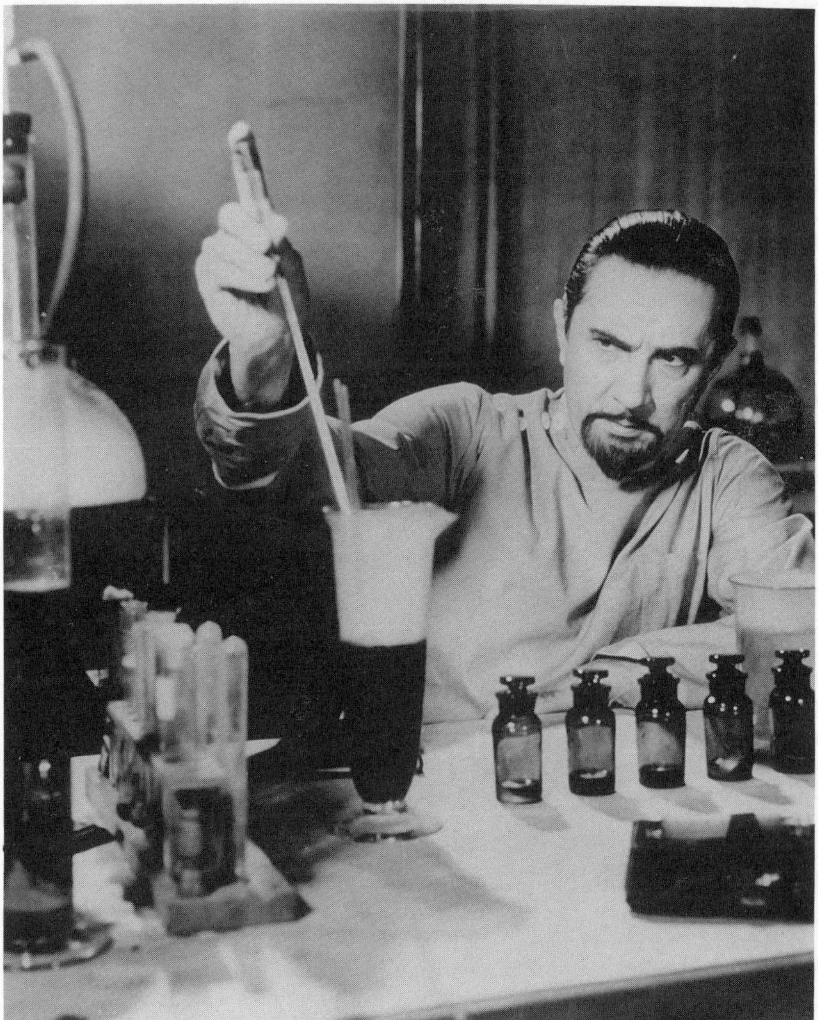

Bela Lugosi amidst an array of test tubes in *The Invisible Ray*.

Despite its status as one of the most intriguing thrillers of the period, *The Invisible Ray* belongs in the second tier of Universal's vintage horror films. Its chief asset is John Colton's intelligent, well-constructed screenplay which scrupulously avoids the excessive comedic interludes that marred *WereWolf of London*. The story is leisurely paced and is remarkable in its tasteful understatement; in fact, no other horror film since *Dracula* contains quite as much offscreen mayhem. Sir Francis' murder takes place offscreen, and Lady Arabella's death is described to us in a quick newspaper montage.

An examination of the shooting script discloses the pruning, padding and subtle alterations that took place during production. Scenes are occasionally rearranged and dialogue is often added or deleted, not always to the advantage of the film. In one particularly inventive turn, as Rukh spies on the wedding ceremony of Diana and Drake, he casually catches sight of the six marble representations of the saints standing on the church's facade. His mind envisages the religious figures as symbols of the six members of the African expedition. Eliminating his prey, he methodically applies his disintegrator ray on the corresponding statue. In the finished film, the frustrated viewer must read of the desecrations in yet *another* newspaper account; the original script depicts a statue melting before the horrified gaze of spectators (a gendarme raises his sword only to have it vaporize in his hand).

Colton never intended *The Invisible Ray* to contain quite as much unseen carnage. Rukh fakes his own death (in order to elude detection) by killing a Parisian derelict (Walter Miller), and then planting his identification papers on the cindered corpse. As originally intended, Colton had the derelict feted in Rukh's hotel room, only to be dispatched by the deadly touch of the scientist's luminous hand. Other cuts were more judicious. In Africa, Drake saves Diana's life by bagging a charging rhino. Colton specified in his script that animal footage from the studio's library be utilized, but the use of such obvious stock shots would have only cheapened the overall look of the film. Also eliminated, presumably for reasons of pacing, were one or two romantic episodes as well as a prolonged conversation between Rukh's rivals en route to the Carpathian observatory. The dialogue in Colton's script occasionally takes an embarrassingly racist tone directed towards the safari boys ("Come back here, you skulking black!" Rukh orders a hapless extra). Virtually all of this was cut before shooting.

Significantly changed was an elaborate special effects scene in the first act at Rukh's observatory. Rukh's guests are treated to a spectacular "battle of the suns" scene as part of his demonstration. As described in the screenplay, a gigantic sun emerges from the nebula "seeming to revolve in the blackness of universal ether." Another sun looms into view: "As the other star draws near, the surface of the sun becomes greatly agitated. Great fiery tides are raised.... It shoots forth great fingers of fiery atmosphere as though to tear the enemy apart and the intruder responds in kind.... For a moment, it looks as though the sun were about to be absorbed but already the pull of the second sun is lessening. It is passing on its way and our sun...begins to resume its natural spherical shape."

This sequence, which would have taxed the resources of the special effects department, was completely eliminated, to be replaced by Rukh's far less elaborate "tour of the universe" set piece. Though obviously employing miniatures, this footage, buoyed by Hillyer's direction and Bernard Burton's astute editing, conveys a much greater sense of awe and grandeur than any of Universal's Flash Gordon vulgarities.

Rukh's character in the unabridged text is pictured as a loving, affectionate husband at the outset, making his mental decline even more startling as the narrative progresses. (In the original script, after Benet cures a child of her blindness with a measured treatment of Radium X, Rukh cackles with delirious laughter.) The filmed version depicts the scientist as an embittered recluse from the beginning; his mental processes are glumly questioned by his own mother. He is close to raving in his introductory scene, vindictive toward his rivals, and so uncongenial that one sympathizes with his long-suffering wife. The dialogue halfheartedly blames Benet's antidote for Rukh's madness, but he was obviously a few cards short of a full deck to begin with.

Karloff truly inherited Chaney, Sr.'s title of "The Man of a Thousand Faces"; his physical appearance changed radically from one film to the next, even in straight roles. Jack Pierce capped him with a wig of curly, jet-black hair and gave him a Continental mustache for an overall Poe-like look. Though he contributes a solid performance, an appreciable detachment began to creep into Karloff's work, the monotony of horror tales evidently taking its toll.

Still relatively in his prime, Bela Lugosi is uniquely mesmerizing. Unceremoniously saddled with most of the clunker lines, his sinister, heavily-accented delivery inserts some unintentional humor into the proceedings. During an African dinner scene, Frank Lawton flippantly inquires if the good doctor uncovered any great secrets that day. Lugosi, helping himself to a plate of antelope stew, responds matter-of-factly, "Proof that the sun is the *mudder* of us all." Commenting on the marriage of Drake and Diana, he offers, "I hope they *will* be happy," but Lugosi imbues the line with so much deadpan foreboding, even this innocuous remark elicits chuckles.

A standout in the commendable supporting cast is Frances Drake. A dark, stately beauty, the New York–born, British-trained actress had a promising career in the '30s playing opposite the likes of Cary Grant and Clark Gable. A Paramount contract player, she was on loan much of the time and was chosen as a last-minute substitute for Virginia Bruce in MGM's *Mad Love* (1935). She and costar Frank Lawton were bumped from the cast of James Whale's *Remember Last Night?* (1935) and reassigned to *The Invisible Ray*. (Gloria Stuart was originally slated to play Diana.)

Her career cut short by her marriage to a British diplomat who hated show business, Miss Drake never fulfilled her early promise. She now lives lah-de-dah in Beverly Hills, and has nothing but pleasant memories of her participation in *The Invisible Ray*.

"Boris Karloff was charming," she recently recalled. "He was such a good sport because they played a trick on him when we were on location. He went up some sort of a pole. Lunch was announced and they *left* him there! I hate those horrible tricks, they're not funny to me, but he was a darling. Bela Lugosi was an awfully nice man, too, but a dreadful thing happened. I was walking to the set one day and this young woman said, 'Do you know where Mr. Lugosi is?' I said, 'I suppose he's on the set.' She said, 'I came to drive him home,' and I said, 'I'll tell him if I see him.' So I said to him, 'Your daughter has come to drive you home.' He said, 'That's my *wife*!' But he was charming, very quiet."

Star treatment must also be accorded John P. Fulton, whose special effects became the center of the publicity department's advertising campaign. (*The Universal Weekly* published garish, full-page ads with the tag "The Luminous Man" in such bold type one might have mistaken it for the title of the movie.)

Not averse to distorting the facts, or inventing new ones, the tabloid reported that Fulton's effects process was such a closely guarded secret that the set was completely closed off, the cast and crew were compelled to maintain a vigilant silence, and that daily production reports had been discontinued.

Immodestly extolling the studio's roster of new releases like an overbearingly proud parent, Carl Laemmle wrote in his *Universal Weekly* column, "Watch out for the technical effects, especially in a certain scene which will be discussed all over the world." Exactly *which* scene Laemmle had in mind was never revealed, though there are several that might qualify. The mesmerizing effect of Karloff's face and hands glowing from his overexposure to Radium X, according to *The Universal Weekly,* took six weeks to perfect, and entailed a system of light filters. David Horsley provided *Photon*'s Paul Mandell with a more accurate account of how this effect was achieved:

> Mr. Fulton had plenty of time to think this one over, and he discussed the problem with Frank Williams, who had the patents on the traveling matte processes and at the time was operating his laboratory in Hollywood. Frank suggested that John use a bi-pack film in photographing Karloff, using a suitable make-up, so that the hands and face would sort of separate out of the rest of the

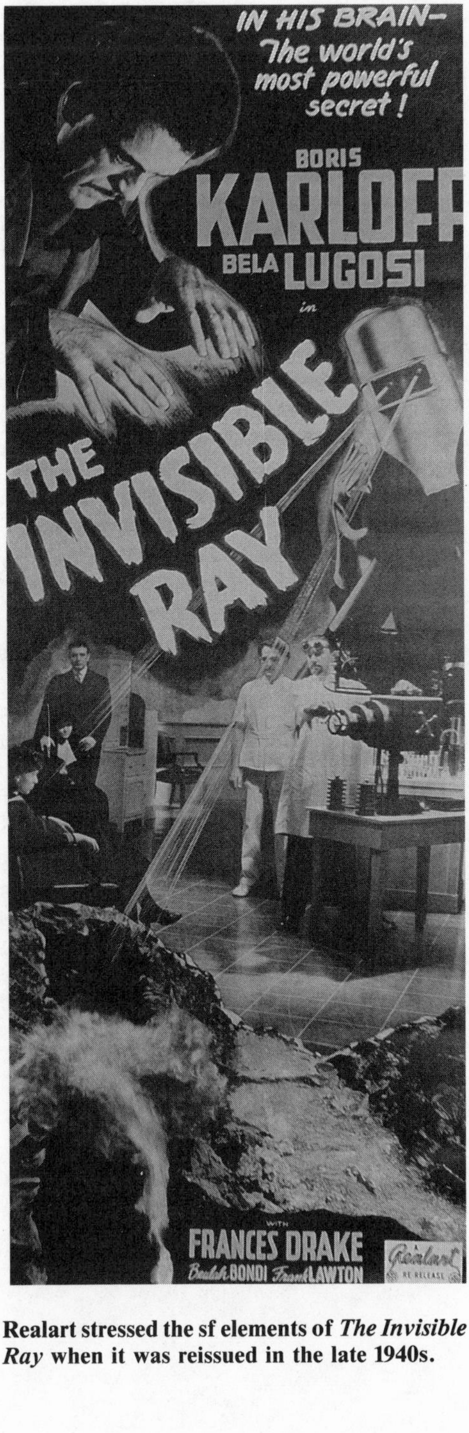

Realart stressed the sf elements of *The Invisible Ray* when it was reissued in the late 1940s.

> scene. One part of the bi-pack record would be used to print the regular scene, and the other half would be used to take-off the mattes for the glowing effect. John agreed to do this, we made some tests, and they looked pretty good.... We shot two days with (the bi-pack stock) before the lab discovered they could not get enough exposure and develop enough image on the pieces to make the system work (this was *old* film, quite old) ... so we had to go ahead and photograph the film, and Fulton had to figure out a way to ink the mattes after it was finished. And that was what was done. I actually had the task of compositing all of those shots of Karloff glowing.... We had a crew of girls working around the clock, three eight-hour shifts. We had three stands, these were overhead cameras projecting down onto animation boards. The girls would pencil-in the hands and face, one frame at a time, and these would be painted onto cells so that the hands and face were black. There was well over a thousand feet of these mattes, so this involved more than sixteen thousand of these drawings. I was there every four hours, day and night, from the time the job started until the time all the mattes were inked and painted.

None of the production stills nor the promotional trailer of *The Invisible Ray* reveal Karloff's glowing face and hands. According to the studio budget sheets, this particular effect cost a mere $250, a measly sum considering the manpower required to pull it off. Slightly more expensive were the effects scenes of Karloff frightening his native bearers by disintegrating a boulder with his Radium X projector, and the climactic shot of the actor's body vanishing in a burst of flame. These tricks set the budget back a total of $700.

The Invisible Ray is an ingratiating addition to the Universal canon with its lively interplay between the two stars, a respectable script and journeyman direction, but it falls just short of classic status. Director Hillyer and writer Colton are talented dabblers in the genre, but are not first-rate stylists. *The Invisible Ray* is too dated to be really effective science fiction, and not quite Gothic enough to rank as a serious horror film. Colton's globe-trotting script changes settings too frequently: the story opens in Transylvania, switches to Africa, then back to Transylvania, and finally to Paris. The plot has a rambling, slightly disjointed structure that is at odds with the hemmed-in, claustrophobic intensity of the best horror movies. Rukh lacks the pathos of a Jack Griffin or a Henry Frankenstein. Hillyer gets bogged down in the details of the plot and can't quite personalize the science-gone-made element that James Whale did so well. But all things considered, *The Invisible Ray* is of more than passing interest, and essential viewing for connoisseurs of fantastic cinema.

Dracula's Daughter (1936)

Released May 11, 1936. 70 minutes. *Directed by* Lambert Hillyer. *Associate Producer:* E.M. Asher. *Screenplay by* Garrett Fort. *Suggested by* Oliver Jeffries. *Based on the story "Dracula's Guest" by* Bram Stoker. *Director of Photography:* George Robinson. *Art Director:* Albert S. D'Agostino. *Special Photography:* John P. Fulton. *Film Editor:* Milton Carruth. *Supervising Editor:* Maurice Pivar. *Music by* Edward Ward (*or* Heinz Roemheld). *Sound Supervisor:* Gilbert Kurland. *Makeup by* Jack P. Pierce. *Gowns by* Brymer.

Otto Kruger (Dr. Jeffrey Garth), Gloria Holden (Countess Marya Zaleska/Countess Dracula), Marguerite Churchill (Janet Blake), Edward Van Sloan (Dr. Von Helsing), Irving Pichel (Sandor), Nan Grey (Lili), Gilbert Emery (Sir Basil Humphrey), Hedda Hopper (Lady Esme Hammond), E.E. Clive (Sergeant Wilkes), Billy Bevan (Albert), Halliwell Hobbes (Constable Hawkins), Claude Allister (Sir Aubrey Bedford), Edgar Norton (Hobbs), Eily Malyon (Miss Peabody), George Kirby (Bookstore Owner), Christian Rub (Coachman), Guy Kingsford (Radio Announcer), David Dunbar (Motor Bobby), Gordon Hart (Host), Joseph E. Tozer (Dr. Angus Graham), Douglas Wood (Dr. Townsend), Fred Walton (Dr. Bemish), Paul Weigel (The Innkeeper), George Sorel, William von Brincken (Police Officers), Douglas Gordon (Attendant), Eric Wilton (Butler), Agnes Anderson (Bride), William Schramm (Groom), Owen Gorin (Friend), Else Janssen, Bert Sprotte (Guests), John Blood (Bobby), Clive Morgan (Desk Sergeant), Hedwigg Reicher (Wife), John Power (Police Official), Fred Keck (Stand-in for Otto Kruger), Kathleen Deek (Stand-in for Gloria Holden), Katherine Stanley (Stand-in for Marguerite Churchill), Pietro [Peter] Sosso* (Minister), Paul Mitchell* (Messenger in Transylvania). [**Does not appear in the final print.*]

For a studio as economically imperiled as Universal, the sequel to the mega-hit *Dracula* endured a remarkably long gestation period. As with their follow-up to *Frankenstein,* Universal nursed the film along meticulously, developing different ideas and contracting for several versions of the screenplay until a workable final draft was hammered out.

Despite these lofty efforts, *Dracula's Daughter* developed into a costly, blundering production, typifying the inept and inefficient management that had turned Universal into a den of destitution. Whatever profits were reaped from the venture came too late to reverse the Laemmles' dwindling fortunes. The film was released two months after the studio was sold to a new outfit.

John L. Balderston, who was first tapped to develop the property, delivered a 20-page treatment in January, 1934. An obviously disgruntled Balderston prefaced his draft with a spate of complaints. He noted that his previous horror assignments (*Dracula* and *The Mummy* in particular) "dropped badly" in their last thirds due to scheduling and financial pressures, and insisted that this did not occur in *Dracula's Daughter*. Reasoning that an audience might more readily accept a female vampire seducing a young man than vice versa, Balderston suggested that Universal pull all stops to create a truly *horrible* horror movie.

"Why should Cecil B. DeMille have a monopoly on the great box office values of torture and cruelty in pictures about ancient Rome?" queried the writer. "I want to see her [Dracula's daughter's] loathsome deaf mute servants carry into her boudoir savage-looking whips, chains, straps, etc. and hear the cries of the tortured victims without seeing exactly what happens.... I feel sure that so long as it is a *woman* torturing *men,* the thing is not *too* unendurable as it would have been had the man Dracula so treated his female victims." (The italics are Balderston's.)

With this provocative introduction, Balderston opened his latest frolic with the final scene from *Dracula:* Van Helsing stakes the vampire in the cellars of Carfax Abbey. Realizing his work isn't quite complete, he journeys to Transylvania and destroys the remaining brides of Dracula. But Van Helsing misses the well-concealed body of Dracula's offspring. Under the assumed name Countess Szkekeley, the vampiress descends on London, setting her eyes on a young aristocrat, Edward "Ned" Wadhurst, who promptly falls under her spell. Van Helsing and Dr. Seward, aware of Ned's plight, ally themselves with the young man's friends and fiancée and confront Szkekeley on her own turf. Ned, nearly a vampire himself, finds the strength to end his ordeal by driving a stake into Dracula's daughter's heart.

Balderston's treatment, rejected by Universal, is an interesting blueprint for what might have been a grim shocker. As promised, Balderston loaded his outline with gruesome details. Before the introduction of Szkekeley, a throng of Transylvanians mutter about the disappearance of a baby and a village man. In the next scene, Szkekeley tosses a small sack, presumably containing the infant, into the ravenous clutches of one of Dracula's brides while she (Szkekeley) descends on the manacled villager. The horror highpoint comes later when Van Helsing and his colleagues trek through the mountain trails of Transylvania in search of Dracula's castle. Creating a circle of protection, Van Helsing uses the Host (the holy wafer) to combat the supernatural forces that surround them. When one of the party carelessly steps out of the protective circle, he is promptly savaged by a giant wolf.

Balderston's proposed sequel was in obvious need of a strong director and a bit of rewriting; the rambling plot construction is apparent even in outline form. Not given to employing extraneous humor in his writings, Balderston's treatment is a mite on the heavyhanded side. It is also strikingly unoriginal. Once again, we basically have another redressing of the *Dracula* script from which Balderston had already liberally borrowed in penning *The Mummy*. Except for the gimmick of a female vampire, the characters and the situations are basically stock. Again we have a determined Van Helsing summoning up godly powers to aid a young victim menaced by an unholy adversary. Balderston's grisly touches were a bit of a novelty for Universal, but were unlikely to survive the rigorous Production Code that had gone into effect some time before.

With the Balderston treatment shelved, *Dracula's Daughter* remained in limbo for over a year. By the fall of 1935, the project was revived when the studio announced that R.C. Sherriff and Finlay Peter Dunne were commissioned to work on a new script. (Sherriff was also mentioned around this time for the studio's proposed remake of *The Hunchback of Notre Dame.*) Having second thoughts about keeping Count Dracula out of the action, Bela Lugosi was signed for the lead with Edward Van Sloan set to reprise his Van Helsing role (inexplicably, his name was changed to *Von* Helsing). Jane Wyatt, the gifted, intelligent actress who made a strong impression in a featured role in James Whale's *One More River* (1934), was slated for a top role and A. Edward Sutherland was assigned to direct. Best known for his comedies at Paramount, Sutherland proved to be a surprisingly deft purveyor of screen terror with the gruesome Lionel Atwill vehicle *Murders in the Zoo* (1933).

Once again, the project underwent a major overhaul with a complete change in personnel. Jane Wyatt was dropped from the cast and replaced by Marguerite Churchill, borrowed from Warners; Otto Kruger replaced Cesar Romero. Although Count Dracula was cruelly ejected from the character roster, the studio was contractually bound to keep Bela Lugosi on the payroll. Lugosi pocketed $4,000 in the deal but his sole contribution to the film was to appear in a few publicity photos. The reliable Lambert Hillyer of *The Invisible Ray* undertook the directorial duties when Sutherland, miffed by delays and cuts in the proposed budget, moved on to other assignments.

The much-delayed production finally got underway February 4, 1936, on a 29-day shooting schedule. By this time, *Dracula's Daughter* was shaping up as one of Universal's most expensive projects. The constant reshuffling of personnel and various production setbacks due to script problems pushed the final budget up to $278,000, one of the highest for a Universal horror picture. Sutherland, who didn't shoot a frame of film, was paid $17,500 including "retained time"—about three times the salary received by Hillyer, who helmed the production over its 29-day shooting schedule! For all its cost overruns, *Dracula's Daughter* has the look of a low- to moderately-budgeted film at best.

The last horror film produced at Universal while the studio was still run by the Laemmles, *Dracula's Daughter* was a bad-luck penny. Nine days after the cameras began to roll, Hillyer was rushed to the Universal City hospital for two hours after a huge lamp toppled on his head during shooting. The publicity department was quick to note the date of the accident . . . Friday the 13th. The production wrapped on March 10, 1936, seven days over schedule.

Allegedly based on Bram Stoker's posthumously published story "Dracula's Guest," the final script by Garrett Fort bore little resemblance to its source material. (The Stoker story, about a lost traveller trekking through the Transylvanian hills on All Souls Night [when "the dead travel fast"], is closer to John Balderston's original treatment.) Picking up the action immediately after the last reel of *Dracula,* the film opens as two comic English bobbies

The first Universal horror cycle ended where it began – with vampires.

(Halliwell Hobbes and Billy Bevan) investigate the strange goings-on at Carfax Abbey. After first discovering the broken body of Renfield sprawled at the foot of a stone staircase, the constables happen upon Count Dracula lying in his coffin, a stake driven through his heart. Dr. Von Helsing (Edward Van Sloan), who presumably loitered behind after Mina and Harker took off, confesses to the strange crime and is immediately packed off to Scotland Yard headquarters where is booked on a charge of murder.

Sir Basil Humphrey (Gilbert Emery), the investigating official, is understandably skeptical of Von Helsing's claim that Dracula was a vampire. He summons the man's former pupil, psychiatrist Jeffrey Garth (Otto Kruger), who reluctantly agrees to act as the professor's advocate even though he's convinced that his mentor is mad.

Dracula's body disappears from the police station at Whitby and the guard is found drained of blood. The corpse has been stolen by the daughter of Dracula, using the pseudonym Countess Marya Zaleska (Gloria Holden). She cremates her father's remains with the assistance of her ghoulish henchman Sandor (Irving Pichel). Confident that the curse has been been broken, Zaleska hopes to lead a normal life. She finds herself unable to resist her vampiric cravings and attacks a male passerby.

Zaleska, who has gained a reputation among the London social set for her

Broadway actress Gloria Holden landed the juiciest role of her screen career in *Dracula's Daughter*.

macabre paintings, meets Garth at a dinner party. She discreetly enlists his aid in combating her affliction without actually revealing its gruesome nature. At Garth's urging, she decides to put her willpower to the test. Combing the streets of Chelsea, Sandor picks up Lili (Nan Grey), a starving waif on the brink of suicide, and induces her to pose for Zaleska. The vampiress makes a staunch effort to combat her overwhelming desires, but to no avail. Lili becomes her second London victim. Hours later, Lili is found wandering the streets in a state of shock and suffering from an extreme loss of blood. Taken to a hospital, she is put under Garth's care. He uses hypnosis in a vain effort to bring her back to consciousness, but, the strain proves too much for the frail girl and she expires. Before she dies, however, Lili provides Garth with a valuable clue as to the identity of her murderer.

Faced with the grim facts, Garth seeks out Zaleska but finds she and Sandor have left the city and flown to Transylvania with his kidnapped fiancée Janet Blake (Marguerite Churchill). Garth follows in a private plane and confronts Zaleska at Dracula's castle. Zaleska threatens to kill Janet, now in a trace, unless Garth joins her in the ranks of the undead. With Janet near death, Garth reluctantly agrees. As Zaleska begins weaving her spell, the jilted Sandor shoots a wooden arrow through her heart. He then takes deadly aim at Garth but is shot down by Sir Basil, who has followed the psychiatrist to Transylvania with Von Helsing. Zaleska's spell is broken and Garth and Janet are reunited.

After years of being dismissed as an unworthy follow-up to *Dracula, Dracula's Daughter* is gaining a reputation as being among the best vampire films of the '30s. This isn't too surprising considering the current reevaluation of Tod Browning, who also directed the only other film which has reasonable claim to this title, *Mark of the Vampire* (1935). The fraternity of Browning-bashers (our numbers are mounting impressively) may find satisfaction in the fact that the legendary director was upstaged not by a veteran horror director likes James Whale, but by the lowly Lambert Hillyer, a specialist in cheap oaters. The long-standing gripe that *Dracula's Daughter* denied Bela Lugosi the chance to reprise his role doesn't seem to carry much weight these days. Lugosi's slow, theatrical style long ago became passé and he doesn't attract the swarm of defenders he once did. Add up these points and the reputation of *Dracula's Daughter* has nowhere to go but up. It is surely a slicker and faster paced picture than the talky, stage-bound original, although there isn't a single scene in the sequel that can match the arresting, malignant atmosphere etched by Browning and his cameraman Karl Freund in the first reel of *Dracula.*

If John L. Balderston's original treatment seems like a rather humorless affair, Garrett Fort's final script takes on the other extreme. As in such '30s classics as *Doctor X, Mystery of the Wax Museum, Murders in the Zoo* and *Mad Love,* the prolonged stretches of comedy relief are a distracting nuisance. Billy Bevan's antics as a faint-hearted bobby, replete with Chaplinesque double-takes, are mild enough, but the rest of the film's humor is more suited to drawing room comedy. The likable romantic leads come dangerously close to wearing out their welcome with their playful bickering. And Claude Allister's epicene party host is a maddening bore.

These lapses are fortunately balanced out by Hillyer's workmanlike handling of the horror episodes. An especially noteworthy scene has Zaleska consigning Dracula's body to the flames on a desolate, fog-shrouded moor, accompanied by a chorus of howling wolves. It is beautifully rendered by George Robinson with his typically masterful eye for lighting and atmosphere. This is followed by another fine scene with the Countess at the piano. Convinced that her days as a vampire are numbered (and conveniently forgetting that she's just drained the blood of the meddlesome bobby), Zaleska rhapsodizes about her new life. In a scene later imitated in *House of Dracula,* Zaleska's piano serenade segues into a satanic dirge at Sandor's prompting. The dialogue is particularly rich here; each of Zaleska's idyllic childhood remembrances is counterpointed by Sandor's ghoulish rebuttals.

Fort's premise of a sympathetic vampire was something of a novelty at the time; he likens the curse of the undead to an addiction. The ploy not only gave dimension to Zaleska's character but weaved considerable suspense into the screenplay. In *Dracula's Daughter*'s most famous scene, Zaleska lures the penniless Lili to her art studio on the pretense of a modeling assignment. Irresistibly drawn to the girl's throat, Zaleska tenderly descends upon her victim as the camera darts up to the mocking, approving smile of a demonic stone mask. This episode, which rarely goes unmentioned in any self-respecting treatise on implied lesbianism in the movies, has given the film a measure of notoriety outside the usual circles. It's an obvious interpretation of the scene, but one that would probably have amused or embarrassed a no-nonsense, rough-and-tumble director like Hillyer.

Dracula's Daughter is well-served by a top technical crew. The anonymous music score, variously credited to Edward Ward or Heinz Roemheld, is one of the best for a horror film of this vintage. Albert S. D'Agostino, the officially billed art director, makes excellent use of Charles D. Hall's superb Castle Dracula set (he even recreated the monstrously oversized spider web on the staircase). One set would be later used in the Flash Gordon serials as Ming's lab.

The climax is unfortunately marred by a few ludicrously staged scenes of the Transylvanian populace reacting in horror to Dracula's apparent return. These ill-chosen extras with their cornball garb and mannerisms can be counted on to bring down the house as they partake in the festivities of a Hollywood-style Teutonic wedding. The scene is mercifully brief, and the film resumes its firm footing until the wrap-up at Dracula's castle.

The cast was sensibly chosen. In the plum title role, Gloria Holden is equally adept at enlisting the audience's sympathy as she is at conveying the full menace of her celebrated parent. Born in London but reared in the United States, Holden was trained as an interpretive dancer and an operetta singer. The most notable items on her résumé at the time of her casting was a few bit parts and a 26-week stint on the Eddie Cantor radio program. Subsequently, Holden's career was an unspectacular one. Many of her later roles were so brief that compiling a complete filmography is difficult. *Wife vs. Secretary* (1936), *The Life of Emile Zola* (1937), *Test Pilot* (1938), *Dodge City* (1939) and *The Hucksters* (1947) are among her best known films, although she was buried deep in the supporting ranks. Holden's role in *Dracula's Daughter* was undoubtedly responsible for landing her a spooky part in Tod Browning's *Miracles for Sale* (1939) in which she played psychic.

With his granite jaw and patrician nose, 50-year-old Otto Kruger seemed an unlikely choice as a romantic lead but he proves to be a refreshing change of pace from the ineffectual pretty boy types like David Manners and Lester Matthews. In marked contrast to their endless swooning, cooing and cuddling, the mature Kruger cuts an authoritative figure as Garth, at least when he isn't the foil for Marguerite Churchill's infantile pranks. Although she could never be mistaken for the daughter of a baroness, Churchill is engaging and shows a flair for light comedy. Edward Van Sloan's performance as Von Helsing is crisp and convincing; he is far better here than he was under Tod Browning's direction.

Irving Pichel, quite cadaverous in Jack Pierce's greasepaint, uses his rich baritone voice with effectively menacing results. (Unaccountably, Universal at first sought *Herbert Marshall* for the ghoulish role!) Pichel was a prolific but rather undistinguished Hollywood director who occasionally took time off to play minor heavies. (His sepulchral tones were heard in an off-screen appearance as a grown-up Roddy McDowall in 1941's *How Green Was My Valley.*) Pichel received codirector's credits for *The Most Dangerous Game* (1932) and *She* (1935), and in 1950 teamed up with George Pal for *The Great Rupert* and *Destination Moon.* Pichel had no shortage of opportunities yet most of his films are near-misses.

Nan Grey, a former Warner Bros. contract player who signed with Universal in 1933, went on to bigger roles but she was never as affecting as she is here as the doomed Lili. A distinctly English ambience is well-conveyed by such familiar Britons as Gilbert Emery, E.E. Clive, Halliwell Hobbes and Edgar Norton. Hedda Hopper, who gave up acting to become one of the film capital's most despised gossip columnists, is seen as a slightly asinine society matron early in the film.

While Tod Browning tried to stamp a stately Victorian look on *Dracula,* Hillyer and Fort firmly entrench *Dracula's Daughter* in the 20th century. The pace of the film is one of a bustling modern city in which characters use telephones and radios and drive about in motorcars, unlike the original film in which there is nary a modern device in sight. The updated approach was sorely needed to spruce up the creaky Dracula formula which was becoming old-hat by the mid–30s. Although a crisp realism is brought to the material, the picture still scores impressively when the rich Gothic trappings of a familiar vampire tale are finally trotted out. Pitting the Old World superstitions of Von Helsing against Garth (the modern, skeptical hero) not only provides the film with its share of lively dialogue exchanges but perfectly encapsulates the picture's style. In spite of its excess comedy, *Dracula's Daughter* is a well-conceived and unfailingly intelligent sequel.

Night Key (1937)

Released May 2, 1937. 67 minutes. *Directed by* Lloyd Corrigan. *Associate Producer:* Robert Presnell. *Screenplay by* Tristram Tupper & John C. Moffitt. *Original Story by* William Pierce. *Director of Photography:* George Robinson. *Art Director:* Jack Otterson. *Associate Art Director:* Loren Patrick. *Film Editor:* Otis Garrett. *Musical Director:* Lou Forbes. *Sound:* Jess Moulin & Jesse T. Bastian. *Special Photographic Effects:* John P. Fulton.

Boris Karloff (Dr. David Mallory), Jean Rogers (Joan Mallory), J. Warren Hull (Jimmy Travers), Hobart Cavanaugh ("Petty Louie"), Samuel S. Hinds (Stephen Ranger), Edwin Maxwell (Kruger), Alan Baxter (The Kid), David Oliver (Mike), Ward Bond ("Fingers"), Frank Reicher (Carl), George Humbert (Spinelli), Charles Wilson (Chief of Police), Michael Fitzmaurice (Ranger's Secretary), George Cleveland (Adams), Emmett Vogan, Charlie Sherlock (Reporters), Ethan Laidlaw, Monte Montague, Jack Cheatham, George Magrill, Frank Hagney, Ralph Dunn (Henchmen), Henry Rocquemore (Boarder), Roy Barcroft (Office Worker), Ruth Fallows (Waitress), Hal Cooke (Manager), Tom Hanlon (Radio Announcer), Nina Campana (Mrs. Spinelli), Charlie Sullivan (Taxi Driver), Johnnie Morris (Tailor).

After months of denying that a sale of the studio was underway, the Laemmles found it increasingly difficult to maintain their optimistic facade before the public gaze. Financial reports detailing devastating losses made headlines in the Hollywood trade papers. Literally in its death throes, the end of the Laemmle regime came on March 14, 1936, when Carl Laemmle, Sr., announced the sale of the studio to Standard Capital Corporation.

There was little left for Laemmle to do except retire gracefully. Taking advantage of his place in the spotlight, "Uncle Carl" drummed up a bit of publicity for one of the last major Universal films bearing his name, *Show Boat* (1936), directed by James Whale.

The new owners had their work cut out for them. Bravely facing up to the grim balance sheets inherited from the Laemmles, the studio sought a fresh identity. With the words "A *New* Universal Picture" emblazoned on all advertising, the new regime scuttled the proud, familiar trademark of the luminous plane encircling a spinning model of the globe. In its place, a rotating, art-deco style glass globe bearing the Universal name amid a cluster of shimmering stars introduced each new presentation. (The original glass model used to launch the resurrected studio's latest releases was last seen collecting dust in a Hollywood warehouse where it was unceremoniously dumped years ago.)

If the first year's releases had anything in common, it was overwhelming mediocrity. Strapped more than ever for revenue, production values dropped appreciably with even fewer bankable stars than before. Adding to the problem, the audience's appetite for horror movies (once the studio's most reliable source of profits) had fallen off sharply. With an outright ban on horror movies imposed by the British Commonwealth, Hollywood turned its back on the genre altogether.

Surprisingly, this crisis had little impact on the horror market's top star Boris Karloff, who had signed a contract with Warner Bros. long before the genre bottomed out. Playing it safe, the British actor swallowed his pride and picked up some easy money by signing a multipicture deal with Monogram, where he soon found himself in a rut starring in a string of look-alike Mr. Wong features. Warner Bros., who made good use of Karloff in Michael Curtiz's excellent *The Walking Dead* (1936), was at a loss as to what to do with their new contractee. After giving him star billing in *West of Shanghai* (1937), *The Invisible Menace* (1938) and *Devil's Island* (1940), it was painfully clear that Karloff's box office appeal was limited to shockers. When horror pictures made a comeback in the late '30s, Warners was quick to place Karloff in a legitimate horror meller, *The Return of Doctor X* (1939), but the picture turned into a casting director's nightmare. Karloff backed out of the film when caught in a scheduling conflict. Bela Lugosi was also an early contender. British actor James Stephenson was then chosen to star but was dropped in favor of an extremely uncomfortable-looking Humphrey Bogart, so wretchedly miscast he almost sunk the show. Unable to come up with another good horror vehicle, Karloff fulfilled his Warner Bros. contract with another turkey, *British Intelligence* (1940).

In 1937, Universal had found itself in a similar bind. Karloff was still under contract but the studio was unwilling to take a box office risk with a new horror attraction. *Night Key* at least gave Karloff another chance to escape from his horror image; otherwise, it did little to bolster his career. The film was nothing more than a standard melodrama with marginal science fiction gadgetry thrown in.

Karloff plays the myopic David Mallory, an aging inventor of burglar alarms and security devices. After putting the finishing touches on a revolutionary new system, he approaches his former friend and associate Steve Ranger (Samuel S. Hinds), now president of a security firm, for backing. Years before, Ranger had stolen the patent rights to Mallory's old alarm system, making a fortune and leaving the inventor near penniless. Ever the scoundrel, Ranger hoodwinks Mallory into signing an exclusive contract, then, after the deal is sealed, reveals that he has no intention of installing the new system. Realizing he has been duped into keeping his new invention out of the hands of Ranger's competitors, Mallory leaves the executive with the bitter warning, "What I create, I can destroy!"

Mallory devises a portable device he calls the Key, which has the ability to electronically override Ranger's alarm system. Hoping to discredit Ranger's company to the point that he will be forced to install Mallory's new system, the inventor hooks up with a small-time crook named "Petty Louie" (Hobart Cavanaugh). Together they execute a number of prankish break-ins targeting

Inventor Boris Karloff (right) uses the *Night Key* to spring two-bit crook Hobart Cavanaugh from the lock-up.

Ranger's clients. Mindful not to steal anything, the mischievous pair leave behind Mallory's calling card, a cryptic note reading, "What I create, I can destroy," and signed "Night Key." Mallory's break-ins are harmless. In a jewelry store, he sets all of the clocks to go off just as Ranger's security team arrives on the scene. Mallory's next hit is a parasol shop where he and Louie have fun opening up all of the umbrellas (yawn).

The inventor's "crimes" attract the attention of an underworld kingpin who calls himself The Kid (Alan Baxter). Hoping to use the Key for more profitable ends, he lures Mallory to his hideout. Mallory sabotages a bank robbery staged by The Kid by destroying the Key.

The gangsters kidnap the inventor's daughter Joan (Jean Rogers) in order to gain his cooperation in tinkering together a new Night Key from scratch. Armed with a new transmitter, The Kid pulls off another heist. Mallory escapes from the gang by wiring together an electric booby trap; Louie is shot dead in the melee.

Alerting the police as to The Kid's activities, Mallory joins them in an effort to net the hood. Using the power of the Night Key, Mallory electronically sabotages The Kid's car. The Kid and his gang are taken into custody by the cops. Mallory and Ranger rather unconvincingly bury the hatchet for the inevitable happy ending.

A comfortable 21-day shooting schedule and a $175,000 budget did not assure a trouble-free production for *Night Key*. A seemingly small-scale and inauspicious undertaking, the picture was wracked with problems. The script was poorly prepared and halfway through shooting the picture an entirely different ending was devised, threatening to put the film over budget. Lloyd Corrigan proved to be an inexperienced and slow director. Karloff, one of the founders of the Screen Actors Guild, insisted that union rules be followed to the letter and refused to work more than eight hours a day. Much to the aggravation of the front office, the militant actor wouldn't report to work during the day if he was required for night shooting. The production crawled along, finally wrapping on February 20, 1937, a full six days behind schedule and over $17,000 over budget.

Night Key failed to make much of an impression with the critics and is even less fondly remembered today. This mild-mannered, inconsequential little B has long been an object of derision among horror buffs and even Karloff fans. Indeed, more than a few individuals claim to *hate* the movie (one of them a collaborator on this book). While one is hard-pressed to defend the film on artistic grounds, it's difficult to imagine how such an innocuous, good-natured programmer could stir up so much passion pro *or* con.

Horror aficionados' resentment of *Night Key* goes back to the time the film was first showcased in the original "Shock" television package. The Karloff name alone was enough to lull unsuspecting viewers into thinking what they were getting was a full-fledged horror thriller. Instead what they *got* was Grandpa Boris on the right side of the law (well, almost), battling it out with a gang of thugs. Sandwiching the picture in between the '30s classics and the meat-and-potatoes horror fare of the '40s only made this decidedly lightweight film seem even more tame. As *Night Key* turns up on "Creature Feature"-type shows to this very day, the number of detractors are undoubtedly swelling in rank. This is rather unfair; unlike deceptively advertised Universal "chillers" like *Secret of the Chateau* and *The Man Who Reclaimed His Head, Night Key* was never promoted as a horror movie in the first place.

Night Key gives the audience the chance to see a side of Karloff which keeps cropping up in various biographies: the kindly, cultured English gent who liked nothing better than to tend his garden and read children fairy tales. Karloff again proves adept at eliciting an audience's sympathy. His Dave Mallory is about as sweet and cuddly as old men get. If he is to be accused of any faults, it's his awesome stupidity: the inventor turns over his life's work to the same man who swindled him 20 years before. Karloff doesn't miss a trick trying to convince us that his doddering character is a bowl of mush; he even resorts to playing his "blind" scenes with his eyelids closed after one of the heavies yanks off his spectacles. This mildest of characters is something of a tribute to Karloff's range as an actor considering the fact that in the months ahead he would be back to playing brutes in *Son of Frankenstein* and *Tower of London.*

Karloff's cuteness manages to spill over into the rest of the picture; in fact, *Night Key* fairly overflows with it. Most seriously affected are J. Warren Hull as the silly romantic lead and Hobart Cavanaugh as "Petty Louie," the ragamuffin two-bit thief who only seems to be along for the ride. Jean Rogers is a pert addition to Karloff's endless line of screen daughters and Alan Baxter brings an understated but chilling psychopathic touch to his performance as The Kid. His delivery, mannerisms and physical resemblance to Jack Nicholson are uncanny. Samuel S. Hinds is afforded the opportunity to indulge in a bit of white collar villainy himself, but as a heavy he's strictly in the minor leagues.

Veteran supporting player Lloyd Corrigan directed *Night Key* with the same easy-going congeniality that typecast him in jovial and buffoonish roles. (Corrigan replaced Sidney Salkow, who replaced Arthur Lubin, who replaced Ralph Murphy.) Except for Baxter's oily presence and a surprisingly nasty booby trap rigged by Karloff (thug Ward Bond is slowly and painfully electrocuted), the movie is pure fudge. *Night Key* has an "everything-but-the-kitchen-sink" approach to filmmaking with Hollywood's top horror man in the lead, but somehow it all comes out bland and sterile. Small wonder Universal films were having a tough time trying to find an audience. While *Night Key* is a must-see for Karloff completists, unsuspecting horror fans are bound to feel left in the lurch.

The Black Doll (1938)

Released January 30, 1938. 66 minutes. A Crime Club Mystery. A Walter Futter Production. *Produced by* Irving Starr. *Directed by* Otis Garrett. *Screenplay by* Harold Buckley. *Based on the novel by* William Edward Hayes. *Directors of Photography:* Stanley Cortez & Ira Morgan. *Film Editor:* Maurice Wright. *Assistant Director:* Phil Karlstein [Karlson]. *Art Director:* Ralph Berger. *Settings:* Emile Kurl. *Musical Director:* Charles Previn. *Production Manager:* Ben Hersh. *Sound Director:* Charles Carroll. *Gowns by* Vera West.

Donald Woods (Nick Halstead), Nan Grey (Marian Rood), Edgar Kennedy (Sheriff Renick), C. Henry Gordon (Nelson Rood), Doris Lloyd (Laura Leland), John Wray (Walling), Addison Richards (Mallison), Holmes Herbert (Dr. Giddings), William Lundigan (Rex Leland), Fred Malatesta (Esteban), Inez Palange (Rosita), Syd Saylor (Red), Arthur Hoyt (Coroner), John Harmon (Cabbie).

The detective mystery, a Hollywood staple as popular as the horse opera, had its heyday in the '30s. Every studio, from the lofty MGM to the penny-pinching Monogram, catered to fans of this genre. Gumshoes of every persuasion made the transition from page to silver screen. A few—Charlie Chan, Sherlock Holmes, Bulldog Drummond, Philo Vance, Ellery Queen, even a shrewd lawyer with a detective's instincts named Perry Mason—walked off with a series of their own.

In 1937, Universal struck a deal with the Crime Club, publishers of pulpy whodunits by such prolific writers as Jonathan Latimer. The studio was granted the right to select four of the 52 annually published novels for adaptation. Producer Irving Starr was made head-man of this unit, while former film cutter Otis Garrett frequently handled the directing chores.

Over the next couple of years, Universal released no less than seven Crime Club mysteries. According to the studio publicity mill (always a dubious source of information), the Club's legion of fans had a hand in selecting which novels/stories would be translated to celluloid. (Unlike the Inner Sanctum series of the '40s, Universal got its material straight from the source rather than just borrowing the Crime Club banner to promote their own properties.)

Evidently, the capers of dapper Inspector Bill Crane and his comic sidekick Doc Williams were favorites of readers, as they were the only regularly featured team of sleuths in the Universal series, appearing in three mystery thrillers. The first, *The Westland Case,* is a formularized B with all the standard ingredients: red herrings, brassy dames (Barbara Pepper doing a shameless

Mae West ripoff), valuable witnesses dropping like flies, and the inevitable eleventh hour round-up of all the suspects. Preston Foster and Frank Jenks were cast as the wise-cracking New York City investigators summoned to Chicago to save an innocent man (Theodore Von Eltz) from the chair. Foster's Crane seems patterned after William Powell's Nick Charles, always agreeably tipsy but right on the money when it came time to charm the ladies or come up with clues that everyone else involved in solving the case overlooked. (Whoever first fostered the notion that inebriation is synonomous with suavity should have been locked up for a month with Lee Tracy and Ted Healy!) Released on October 31, 1937, *The Westland Case* was directed by Christy Cabanne and based on the Jonathan Latimer novel, *Headed for a Hearse.*

While the Inner Sanctum pictures are basically straight murder melodramas masquerading as shockers, the Crime Club mysteries made no such pretense. But, occasionally, as in the second entry, *The Black Doll,* elements of horror creep into the corners of the plot.

Based on the novel of the same name by William Edward Hayes, *The Black Doll* begins as a taut little thriller, but quickly loses its effectiveness through the irritatingly intrusive comedy relief of Edgar Kennedy as a bull-headed country sheriff. Young Donald Woods does the sleuthing this time around. A quiet country estate, where all of the suspects are conveniently housed under one roof, provides a contrast from the big city background of *The Westland Case.*

Otis Garrett, making his series directorial debut, sustains an aura of apprehension in the early reels. Suspects are introduced (and motives revealed) in a slow, deliberate fashion. An element of the supernatural is introduced early on but it is quickly dismissed.

The victim-to-be is the misanthropic Nelson Rood, a ruthless businessman who gained his fortune by plundering an ore-rich Mexican mine. Rood eliminated one of his partners, Knox Barrows, and double-crossed the other two. Rood is played with silken menace by C. Henry Gordon, who achieved cinematic immortality two years earlier as the barbaric Surat Khan in Warners' *The Charge of the Light Brigade.*

Every member of Rood's household has good reason to hate him. He dominates his sister, Laura Leland (Doris Lloyd), and was instrumental in ruining her chance for happiness with the man she loves, Dr. Giddings (Holmes Herbert). Her son, Rex (William Lundigan), fears that his spiteful uncle will press charges against him for forging his signature on a check to cover gambling losses. Rood's Latin servants, Esteban (Fred Malatesta) and Rosita (Inez Palange), fear and despise him. His estranged business partners, Wallings (John Wray) and Mallison (Addison Richards), who are staying at the house overnight, don't trust him. Only Rood's daughter Marian (Nan Grey) loves him, but even she is miffed when he forbids her boyfriend Nick Halstead (Donald Woods) from visiting the house again.

Rood is shaken when he finds a crudely made Mexican black doll lying across the top of his desk. The last time Rood laid eyes on the doll (which is a portent of doom), he flung it into a ravine after disposing of Knox Barrows' body. Has Barrows come back from the dead 15 years later to avenge himself on his murderer? In a well-staged scene, Rood is knifed in the back as he stands in the doorway of Marian's bedroom (the murder is reflected in her vanity mirror). The killer's calling card, the black doll, is found opposite Rood's corpse.

Conveniently enough, Nick reveals he was once a private eye and begins collecting alibis. He is always two steps ahead of the local sheriff, Renick (Edgar Kennedy), who couldn't recognize a clue if he fell over one.

Humor has its place in mystery and horror films when it alleviates tension and suspense momentarily and then retreats into the background. When comedy oversteps these bounds and disturbs the flow of the plot, it does a film irreparable harm. *The Black Doll* is a case in point. The witless antics of Edgar Kennedy's sheriff shatter the film's somber mood and destroy its credibility. When Renick isn't putting his foot in his mouth, he's stumbling into furniture and upsetting any evidence Nick turns up.

Mallison, labeled a prime suspect, is found stuffed in a closet, strangled to death; the black doll is tucked in his pocket. An attempt is made on Marian's life, but Esteban intervenes and is shot through the heart for his trouble.

Halstead concludes that the murderer sent Nelson Rood the doll to frighten him into thinking his two partners were planning to kill him. Both of them knew he murdered Barrows so he could marry the man's wife. When Rood later came down with jungle fever, he spilled the beans to his attending physician, whose identity heretofore remains unknown.

The last reel gathering of the suspects scene is a real hoot. As Nick serves up his breakfast specialty, scrambled eggs and hash browns, he fits together the last pieces of the puzzle. Rood was *not* Marian's father after all, Knox Barrows was. Rood raised her as his own after marrying the dead man's widow. Nick unmasks Giddings as the mystery doctor, and the killer. Giddings murdered Rood to clear the way for his marrying Laura. That act would have put the family fortune within his grasp. Only Marian stood in his way. Giddings pulls out a revolver from under the tablecloth (how the others missed it is a mystery in itself). He fires a couple of shots, but is apprehended by Renick's men. Laura thanks Halstead profusely for getting her son off the hook, but she doesn't seem the least bit disturbed that Giddings was unmasked as a murderer and a fortune hunter.

Musical director Charles Previn borrows liberally from previous scores written by Karl Hajos, Edward Ward and Franz Waxman, with satisfying results. The main title is a swipe from *Bride of Frankenstein,* while themes from *WereWolf of London, Dracula's Daughter, The Raven* and *The Invisible Man* are sprinkled throughout.

Donald Woods and Nan Grey are pleasant juvenile leads, while the supporting cast is bolstered by such pros as Addison Richards, Doris Lloyd and Holmes Herbert. A young Bill Lundigan does an adequate job as Lloyd's irresponsible son.

Preston Foster and Frank Jenks returned as Crane and Doc in the third Crime Club mystery, *The Lady in the Morgue,* released on April 22, 1938. Taking its cue from the Jonathan Latimer novel of the same name, this confusing yarn had the intrepid pair trying to establish the identity of a luscious blond suicide whose body disappears from the city morgue. All the ingredients for a crackerjack mystery thriller are here, but somewhere along the line, the picture misses the mark.

Donald Woods, Nan Grey and William Lundigan were reunited in the July 1, 1938, release, *Danger on the Air.* Woods portrays Benjamin Botts, a clever radio sound engineer who launches his own investigation when a soft drink magnate with a roving eye (Berton Churchill) is found dead in the office of a major broadcast company. Deadly cyanogen gas is discovered to be the murder weapon. Otis Garrett directed this average but enjoyable mystery, based on the novel *Death Catches Up with Mr. Kluck* by Xantippe (a pseudonym). Look for Lee J. Cobb in a small role.

A mysterious blackmailer known as The Eye keeps Crane and Doc guessing in *The Last Warning,* the pair's last Crime Club outing. Released on January 6, 1938, it was adapted by Edmund L. Hartmann from Jonathan Latimer's grimly titled novel *The Dead Don't Care.* Albert S. Rogell put Preston Foster, Frank Jenks, Kay Linaker and a young Albert Dekker through his directorial paces. "A pleasant enough little mystery melodrama," wrote *The New York Times* movie critic, Thomas M. Pryor (December 8, 1938), ". . . intended for the not-too discriminating among armchair sleuths."

Murder in a metropolitan hospital is the theme of *Mystery of the White Room,* released on March 17, 1939. Head surgeon Addison Richards is stabbed to death when the lights go out during an operation. Once again, a nonprofessional (a doctor, played by Bruce Cabot) solves the crime, while the police fumble around foolishly. *Kong* alumni Cabot, Helen Mack and Frank Reicher are featured in the cast of this obvious but agreeable whodunit. In a scene prefiguring 1944's *Dead Man's Eyes,* an acid-blinded hospital attendant (Frank Puglia) has his sight restored via the transplanted corneas of the murder victim so that he might identify the person who assaulted him. The film was based on the novel *Murder in the Surgery,* written by real life medico Dr. James G. Edwards.

Universal wrapped up the Crime Club series with *The Witness Vanishes,* released on September 22, 1939. The trite though potentially suspenseful story concerned a series of revenge murders, evidently committed by wacky old Lucius Marplay (Barlowe Borland), who has escaped from an institution after being railroaded there by his unscrupulous business associates years before. All of Marplay's alleged victims die mysteriously *after* their obits have appeared in print. The real culprit turns out to be Mark Peters (Edmund Lowe), who took advantage of the old man's notoriety to eliminate his partners. Wendy Barrie, Bruce Lester and Forrester Harvey rounded out the cast. Inspired by James Ronald's magazine serial "They Can't Hang Me!" (the film's original title), *The Witness Vanishes* is dull and uninspired, and an inauspicious conclusion to a tepid series.

The Missing Guest (1938)

Released August 12, 1938. 68 minutes. *Associate Producer:* Barney A. Sarecky. *Directed by* John Rawlins. *Screenplay by* Charles Martin & Paul Perez. *Based on the story "Secret of the Blue Room" by* Erich Philippi. *Director of Photography:* Milton Krasner. *Art Director:* Jack Otterson. *Film Editor:* Frank Gross. *Musical Director:* Charles Previn. *Sound Supervisor:* Bernard B. Brown. *Technician:* Robert Pritchard. *Assistant Directors:* Charles Gould & Jack Bernhard. *Camera Operator:* Maury Gertsman. *Sound Mixer:* Joe Lapis.

Paul Kelly ("Scoop" Hanlon), Constance Moore (Stephanie "Steve" Kirkland), William Lundigan (Larry Dearden), Edwin Stanley (Dr. Carroll), Selmer Jackson (Frank Baldrich), Billy Wayne ("Vic"), George Cooper ("Jake"), Patrick J. Kelly (Edwards), Florence Wix (Linda Baldrich), Harlan Briggs (Frank Kendall), Pat C. Flick (Inventor), Guy Usher (Police Insp. McDonald), Margo Yoder (Maid), Hooper Atchley (Business Manager), Michael Slade (Kendall's Assistant), John Harmon, George Ovey (Gatekeepers), Thomas Carr (Man), Myrtis Crinley (Woman), Allen Fox (Man), Frank McCarroll (Oscar), Leonard Sues (Office Boy), Ray Parker (Wolf), Billy Engle (Bit Man).

Mile-a-minute wisecracks and inane humor take the place of atmosphere and chills in *The Missing Guest,* a dismal mystery/comedy that serves up none of either. It's one of those particularly awful little films that almost seems to work in reverse: the "scary" scenes are so poorly done that they're almost funny while the comedy relief interludes are so forced and appalling that the thought of someone's actually committing this dialogue to paper is almost scary. A film with nothing for everybody, *The Missing Guest* is among the worst Universal mysteries of the '30s.

The Missing Guest was the first of two remakes of Universal's 1933 *Secret of the Blue Room*. Revamped, updated and Americanized, *Guest* discards the elements which made the Erich Philippi story work the first time around. Gone are the atmosphere of mystery, the quaint Germanic charm and the attractive roster of players; replacing them are low-brow jokes, an offensive hero named "Scoop," goofy comics and a dispiriting sense of *déjà vu. The Missing Guest* is the kind of picture you watch with a growing detachment. You view dialogue scenes, comedy relief passages, "scary" parts and action scenes with the same low level of interest and the same bored, gloomy puss; you start counting the minutes, and wanting them back. When the hero finally begins to unravel the mystery, your spirits rise, not because the killer is about to be exposed or because of the promise of a climactic burst of action, but only because you know the damn thing's almost over and you can start living your life again.

Reporter "Scoop" Hanlon (Paul Kelly) has been demoted to writing a column of beauty hints for *The Daily Blade* because of his unreliability and his penchant for mixing women with newsprint. When his boss Mr. Kendall (Harlan Briggs) learns that the old Baldrich mansion on the South Shore of Long Island is being reopened, he assigns "Scoop" to inveigle his way into the house and spend a night in the haunted Blue Room where Sam Kirkland died under mysterious circumstances 20 years before. "Scoop" is reluctant since the room has a long history of mysterious deaths, but finally accepts the job.

At the Baldrich mansion, a masquerade party is in full swing. Hosting the event are Sam Kirkland's widow Linda (Florence Wix), her daughter Stephanie (Constance Moore) and her new husband Frank Baldrich (Selmer Jackson). Costumed as a ghost, Larry Dearden (William Lundigan), a would-be suitor of Stephanie's, disrupts the festivities with a ghoulishly staged entrance. During a dance, Larry proposes to Stephanie for the umpteenth time but she has no romantic interest in him and politely turns him down once again. The party is disrupted a second time when the lights go out and a piano inexplicably plays by itself.

To gain entry to the house, "Scoop" pretends to lose control of his car, crashing it into the gates. Feigning an ankle injury, he presents himself to the occupants of the house as a psychic researcher, figuring that this may get him into the Blue Room. Frank Baldrich quickly sees through the deception and "Scoop" is ejected from the house. Later, Larry insists on spending the night in the Blue Room, and despite the objections of Baldrich and of longtime family physician Dr. Carroll (Edwin Stanley), the young man gets his way.

In the morning, it's discovered that Larry has vanished from the room; an open window overlooking a sheer drop into the rocky ocean surf suggests an accident or suicide. "Scoop," who sneaked back into the house during the night, is found and detained by Baldrich, who sends for private investigators to look into the mystery.

The private eyes, "Vic" (Billy Wayne) and "Jake" (George Cooper) are a pair of moronic exjailbirds who search (and rob) the house looking for clues. Dr. Carroll surprises Stephanie with the news that Larry was her half-brother; her father Sam Kirkland had fallen in love with the woman who became Larry's mother years before. Stephanie takes the news hard (too hard, considering she never knew her father and didn't love Larry anyway), but "Scoop" shows up to console the weeping girl.

"Vic" and "Jake" leave orders that no one is to sleep in the Blue Room that night, but in the morning the shot-dead body of Dr. Carroll is found on the Blue Room floor. Tiring of the bungling of "Vic" and "Jake," Baldrich sends for the police, and soon Insp. McDonald (Guy Usher) arrives to take charge of the investigation. "Scoop" discovers that most of the spooky stuff that's been going on (including the self-playing piano) was engineered by Edwards, the butler (Patrick J. Kelly); Edwards confesses that it was the late Dr. Carroll who paid him to pull the eerie pranks.

"Scoop" finds a secret entranceway that leads from the garden into a hidden passage in the house. A shadowy figure stalks "Scoop" in the passage and gunshots are exchanged. The mystery figure is Larry Dearden, who confesses as he lays dying from "Scoop"'s bullet. Larry explains that he found the secret passage the night he slept in the Blue Room, and hoped to use it to trap his father's murderer. Dr. Carroll, who had been a suspect in Sam Kirkland's slaying, fell into Larry's trap and confessed at gunpoint; Larry killed him. (Dr. Carroll paid the butler to "haunt" the house so that no one would find the passageway which pointed to his guilt.) Larry himself now expires, with the ghoulish legend of a "haunted" Blue Room dying with him.

In the original *Secret of the Blue Room,* the menace and the mystery were largely confined to the blue salon; there was an eerie quality to the scenes set in that small, quiet little room as well as a suspicion early on that perhaps supernatural forces really were in operation. The film also benefited from its lonely and unspecified foreign locale, the only milieu in which the story could truly work. This is all dispensed with in *The Missing Guest:* the entire Baldrich mansion becomes a conventional "haunted house," with pianos and organs playing themselves, sheet-clad ghosts peeking through windows at bored occupants and spectral Halloween voices *oo-oooo-oooo*-ing in the night. These are not the elements for an effective mystery chiller but the trite trappings of a cheap funhouse.

The most annoying thing about *The Missing Guest* is the comedy. Unfunny and nonstop, it pervades the picture from one end to the other; we are never safe from it. "Scoop"'s editor is a smug wiseacre whose office is open to every loony inventor and his crackpot contraptions. Most of the major characters are introduced while they are in their masquerade costumes (Stephanie as Bo-Peep, Larry as a ghost, Dr. Carroll as the tail end of a horse); at one point there's even a big closeup of Dr. Carroll's horse's ass. "Scoop," who dominates the picture, is a cocky, self-satisfied jerk, the perfect hero for the kind of obnoxious picture where a pushy manner and a smart motor-mouth are equated with brains and initiative. But all of these misfits pale to insignificance beside "Vic" and "Jake," the excons who invade the house in the guise of private eyes. Loud, homely and irritating, these two bunglers are the final indignity. Ritz Brothers clones, they barge in and out of rooms, boss people around and stay even after the real police have ordered them off the premises.

This type of comic burlesque, oddly common to Universal pictures of that era, is often described as low-brow, but it's probably several notches below even that. The oldtime school of comedy that tried to wring laughs out of bug-eyed nitwits, zany foreign types, men with birdcages on their heads and closeups on asses is as dead as any dinosaur. The awful old movies—like *The Missing Guest*—that brim with this type of passé humor no longer serve any purpose.

The one thing the film has going for it is a good-looking "haunted" house. There's something persuasive about the look of the place: the bleak shadows, the narrow staircases and cramped hallways, the musty basement and the cobwebby secret passageway. Although we never get the impression of a large house (a must for any effective spook show), the combined efforts of photographer

Milton Krasner and art director Jack Otterson have furnished a fine backdrop for a goose-bumpy B. Now enter director John Rawlins, the Charles Martin-Paul Perez screenplay and the drab cast, and this neat spookhouse setting becomes the stamping grounds for a gang of smart alecks, grouches and nincompoops.

Nothing impressive goes on in the acting department; there's an affectedness about many of the performances that never lets you forget that you're watching a movie (and a B movie, at that). Paul Kelly, who plays "Scoop," was a gawky actor who brought a smarmy touch to most of his films; he treats everything like a big joke, his wiseguy antics quickly become tiring and he wears out his welcome even before the action begins. Constance Moore is pretty but unconvincing, and never gives the impression that she's much concerned about what's going on. Up-and-coming William Lundigan, who plays Larry, is only briefly seen. Selmer Jackson, usually an avuncular actor, plays an uncharacteristic hothead with a nasty disposition and an unnecessary fetish for keeping Paul Kelly at gunpoint throughout too much of the picture. Billy Wayne, George Cooper, Patrick J. Kelly, Harlan Briggs and Pat C. Flick are the film's resident idiots, saps, smartmouths and goons.

Hollywood moviemaking is, after all, an industry, and when a 68-minute piece of merchandise is needed to fill the bottom half of a cheap double bill it's unrealistic to expect an Oscar-winner. But a picture like *The Missing Guest* rankles a viewer to the point where even this rationalization no longer carries weight. It's inconceivable that the people who made the film could have felt that the ghost scenes could frighten anyone, that the mystery angle would interest anyone, or that the comedy scenes could possibly amuse anyone.

Universal was no doubt happy with *The Missing Guest:* it was made on a quickie schedule and budgeted at a paltry $80,400. Production went smoothly, it wrapped up on time and, thanks to director Rawlins' strict shooting and some script changes, it came in more than 10 percent under budget, at $72,000. John Rawlins, from all accounts, was a nice fellow and an easygoing guy, but it's clear after watching several of his pictures that the man was more interested in impressing studio executives than in impressing movie audiences. Rapidly and cheaply done, *The Missing Guest* probably did find favor at the Universal front office, but for the unwary viewer who comes upon it today it's just another lemon off the Hollywood assembly line.

Son of Frankenstein (1939)

Released January 13, 1939. 94 minutes. A Rowland V. Lee Production. *Produced & Directed by* Rowland V. Lee. *Original Screenplay by* Willis Cooper. *Suggested by the novel* ***Frankenstein; or the Modern Prometheus*** *by Mary Wollstonecraft Shelley. Director of Photography:* George Robinson. *Film Editor:* Ted Kent. *Assistant Director:* Fred Frank. *Art Director:* Jack Otterson. *Associate Art Director:* Richard H. Riedel. *Musical Score by* Frank Skinner. *Musical Director:* Charles Previn. *Music Arranged by* Hans J. Salter. *Special Photographic Effects:* John P. Fulton. *Set Decorator:* Russell A. Gausman. *Sound Director:* Bernard B. Brown. *Technician:* William Hedgcock. *Makeup by* Jack P. Pierce. *Costumes by* Vera West.

Basil Rathbone (Baron Wolf von Frankenstein), Boris Karloff (The Monster), Bela Lugosi (Ygor), Lionel Atwill (Inspector Krogh), Josephine Hutchinson (Baroness Elsa von Frankenstein), Donnie Dunagan (Peter von Frankenstein), Emma Dunn (Amelia), Edgar Norton (Thomas Benson), Perry Ivins (Fritz), Lawrence Grant (The Burgomaster), Michael Mark (Ewald Neumüller), Lionel Belmore (Emil Lang), Gustav von Seyffertitz, Lorimer Johnson, Tom Ricketts (Burghers), Caroline Cooke (Frau Neumüller), Clarence Wilson (Dr. Berger), Ward Bond, Harry Cording (Gendarmes at Gate), Dwight Frye* (Angry Villager), Bud Wolfe (Double for Karloff), Betty Chay, Jack Harris. [**Does not appear in the final print.*]

Horror film lovers couldn't have wished for a sweeter gift to usher in the 1939 new year than *Son of Frankenstein*. Not only did this long-awaited second sequel to the 1931 James Whale classic boast a top flight cast, sterling production values, and mounting on the same lavish scale as its predecessors; more importantly, *Son of Frankenstein* heralded the end of Hollywood's self-imposed ban on horror pictures. All it had taken to lift the two-year prohibition was the promise of big bucks (the only catalyst that ever moved Tinsel Town to do *any*thing). The tremendous public response to a limited run, triple horror bill comprised of *Dracula, Frankenstein* and RKO's *The Son of Kong* at a Los Angeles grindhouse prompted Universal to reissue the Lugosi and Karloff classics.

The gamble paid off. The Dynamic Duo cleaned up at wickets across the country, and horror films were *in* again. Soon after the release of *Son of Frankenstein,* Columbia, Warner Bros. and Paramount beefed up their production schedules with an assortment of penny dreadfuls.

Son of Frankenstein is the last of the great Frankenstein films. Grandiose in scope, magnificent in design, it supplanted the quaint romanticism and delicate fantasy flavoring of *Bride of Frankenstein* with a stark, grimly expressionistic approach to horror. Whale's influence is felt, however, in the screenplay's rich vein of black humor. The performances complement the material beautifully, from Basil Rathbone's floridly theatric Baron to the skillful portrayals of Bela Lugosi and Lionel Atwill, ranking amongst the finest of their careers. Only Karloff's Monster comes up short of expectations, not through any fault of the actor, but in the way the role was written. With *Son of Frankenstein,* Mary Wollstonecraft Shelley's creation began to assume the status of a supporting player whose activities took an increasingly secondary role to his human confederates.

James Whale's successor was Rowland V. Lee. Active in the movie business since he was 19, the 45-year-old producer-director had been enjoying the royal treatment at Universal for his expeditious handling of the frothy Constance Bennett comedy *Service de Luxe* (the film which introduced Vincent Price to movie audiences). A native of Ohio, Lee was destined for a career in Wall Street (as per his family's wishes), but his love of theater and acting lured him back to Broadway and summer stock. Lee then appeared in a few Hollywood pictures, but it was his association with Thomas Ince that turned the tide of his career. The veteran picturemaker offered the ambitious Lee a choice between acting and directing. "I decided I wanted to get on the other side, and give those directions instead of taking them," Lee remarked in an interview.

Ranking up an impressive list of silent film credits (*A Thousand to One, The Man Without a Country,* etc.), Lee made the transition to talking pictures without any difficulty. He directed Warner Oland in his most famous non–Charlie Chan Oriental role in Paramount's *The Mysterious Dr. Fu Manchu* (1929) and its follow-up, *The Return of Dr Fu Manchu* (1930). *Zoo in Budapest* (1933), considered one of Lee's finest films, made many of the year's Top Ten lists. With *The Count of Monte Cristo* (1934), Lee found his niche in motion pictures: producing and directing lavish costume pictures. He followed this highly popular film adaptation of the Dumas story with screen versions of *The Three Musketeers* and *Cardinal Richelieu* in 1935, and continued making extravagant period films well into the '40s.

Son of Frankenstein, Rowland V. Lee's second film for Universal, picks up the continuing saga of the Frankenstein family years after the deaths of the Monster and his Bride in the ruins of the old watchtower. Baron Heinrich von Frankenstein has died, leaving behind a legacy of hatred and contempt in the hearts of his fellow countrymen. His eldest son, Wolf (Basil Rathbone), an American college professor, becomes the victim of this hatred when he returns to the village of Frankenstein with wife Elsa (Josephine Hutchinson) and young son Peter (Donnie Dunagan) to claim his inheritance.

Settling into the sprawling medieval castle, Wolf is visited by Inspector Krogh (Lionel Atwill) of the district police. Krogh intimates that the evidence gathered from a recent spate of hideous murders points towards the Monster. "But he was destroyed years ago," Wolf insists. "Perhaps," the policeman responds cryptically. Wolf learns the reason for Krogh's hostile attitude: as a boy, he had his arm torn from his body by the marauding creature. A curious-looking prosthesis now takes its place.

"He could have *crushed* me, as I would have crushed an eggshell." Basil Rathbone and Boris Karloff in *Son of Frankenstein.*

While exploring the ruins of his father's lab (a separate structure situated on the grounds of the estate), Wolf is almost crushed to death by a boulder dislodged by a bearded hermit. The shaggy stranger identifies himself as Ygor (Bela Lugosi), a village blacksmith who was hanged for bodysnatching years before but survived the ordeal. A twisted neck punctuated by a protruding bone is mute evidence of Ygor's fantastic story.

Learning that Wolf is a doctor, Ygor leads him to the Frankenstein family crypt. There, lying on a slab in a death-like coma, rests the Frankenstein Monster (Boris Karloff). Only he isn't quite dead. Ygor tearfully explains that his "friend" was struck down by lightning while "hunting." Seizing the opportunity to continue his father's great work, and perhaps vindicate his good name, Wolf attempts to revive the Monster via electricity, but fails. The Monster slips back into a coma again.

It isn't long before another rash of brutal murders stuns the community of Frankenstein. When little Peter claims he was visited in his room by a "giant," Wolf realizes the Monster has returned to life. The panic-stricken scientist decides that brain surgery is needed to civilize the brute that his father made, but Ygor will hear none of this. He has been using the Monster to murder off the town burghers who had sentenced him to die.

To quell the fury of the villagers, Krogh promises to arrest Wolf and charge him with murder. He arrives at the castle minutes after the agitated Baron has shot Ygor to death for attempting to kill him. Unfazed by Krogh's threats to extract a confession from him, Wolf defiantly challenges the policeman to a game of darts.

The Monster, meanwhile, has discovered Ygor's corpse. He goes berserk, wrecks the lab, and charges through a secret passageway into the castle, hell-bent on vengeance. He abducts Peter and leads the child into the lab, with Wolf and Krogh hot on his heels. The policeman confronts his lifelong adversary for the first time since their initial meeting. Almost instinctively, the Monster grabs the inspector by his false arm and tears it from the shoulder harness, waving it madly like a club. Swinging from a ceiling chain, Wolfe topples the roaring Monster into a pit of flaming sulphur.

Hailed as a hero by the villagers, Wolf and his family return to America, deeding the castle and properties to the good people of Frankenstein.

The creator of the spooky radio show "Lights Out," Willis Cooper submitted an original *Son of Frankenstein* script which was rejected in its initial form. Dated October 20, 1938, the screenplay began with Wolf, together with wife Else and young son Erwin, arriving at Castle Frankenstein to claim his inheritance. The document contains a bizarre clause which stipulates that the Monster must have remained out of commission for at least 25 years following his death in the watchtower explosion before the inheritance may be claimed.

Cooper makes frequent reference to *Bride of Frankenstein* in this treatment. While searching through the ruins of the lab, Wolf happens upon the skeletal remains of Dr. Pretorius, the Bride and the tiny homunculi, but not the Monster. An excerpt Wolf reads from his father's diary on the temperament of his creation is especially telling: "We are certain that much of the Monster's evil-doing is the result of loneliness; it must be a terrible thing to be the only one of one's kind in the world."

Having survived the explosion and seeming none the worse for it, the Monster emerges from the ruins and kills a gendarme on a forest path during a violent storm. His lust for blood unfulfilled, he breaks into a peasant hut and murders its inhabitants. (Apparently the Monster's romantic rejection and despicable treatment in *Bride of Frankenstein* has vanquished any vestige of humanity left in him.)

A diabolic plan forms in his mind. He desecrates the tomb of his creator and steals the scientific records that were buried with him. Confronting Wolf in the lab, he grunts, "Now—you—make—friend—for—me." (Cooper has given the Monster ample dialogue in this draft.) He threatens to kill Else and Erwin if Wolf doesn't obey his orders.

Wolf's antagonist in this version is Inspector Neumüller, not Krogh (the name was later swiped for Michael Mark's burgher). Neumüller didn't suffer the loss of an arm in his childhood encounter with the Monster, but he did lose a father. He understandably bears the Frankenstein family a deep-seated grudge. Learning that Wolf has been aiding the Monster, Neumüller vows, "I will pursue this Monster of the Frankensteins to the ends of the earth. I will crush it, destroy it utterly. I will have no mercy. And you, Wolf Frankenstein, listen to me. If you hinder me in any way whatsoever, if you fail for one minute to aid me when I shall call on you . . . then you are a murderer yourself, and I shall see you die for it!"

The Monster attacks a military outpost, kills a gendarme, and brings the body to Wolf. "It's useless! Worthless! You've spoiled the brain!" Wolf scolds the creature. Learning of Wolf's intentions, Neumüller mutters in disgust, "Like father, like son."

In a fit of desperation, the Monster steals Erwin and takes him to the lab. Just as the Monster is about to perform brain surgery on the child, Wolf storms in. Neumüller and his forces polish the creature off with a round of bullets. He falls into a watery pit and drowns. For good measure, Neumüller tosses a hand-grenade into the pit after him.

Cooper (or allegedly Lee himself) salvaged the principal characters from this draft and built a new plot around them. All of the alterations were for the better. Neumüller became the false-armed Krogh. His antagonism towards Wolf was toned down. Wolf is every bit as dedicated to vindicating his father's memory in the final script while Elsa's (formerly Else) displeasure towards her husband's work isn't as emphatic as the first version demonstrated. ("Would you be willing to have *my* weary body brought back from the grave to walk with you again?" she counters in response to Wolf's enthusiasm.)

A writer who came from radio, Willis Cooper flooded his first draft with superfluous talk—between the servants, between the soldiers staking out the Monster, and, most irritating of all, between little Erwin and everyone else. Happily, the writer's revision kept the child (now called Peter) in the background. (We are spared a scene in which the little boy mimics the gendarmes marching before the castle, and another in which his nanny is dressed down for allowing her ward to vent his vivid imagination.) But the most important changes were eliminating the Monster's ability to speak and providing him with a comrade, Ygor, one of the most colorful characters in the series. (The broken-necked blacksmith comes "back from the dead" only to suffer an ignominious end in the third sequel, *The Ghost of Frankenstein*.)

Determined that *Son of Frankenstein* have the same lavish mounting as many of his earlier productions, Lee took advantage of his good standing with the studio brass and beefed up the $250,000 budget to $300,000. At one point, he considered shooting the picture in color, but this idea was ditched on

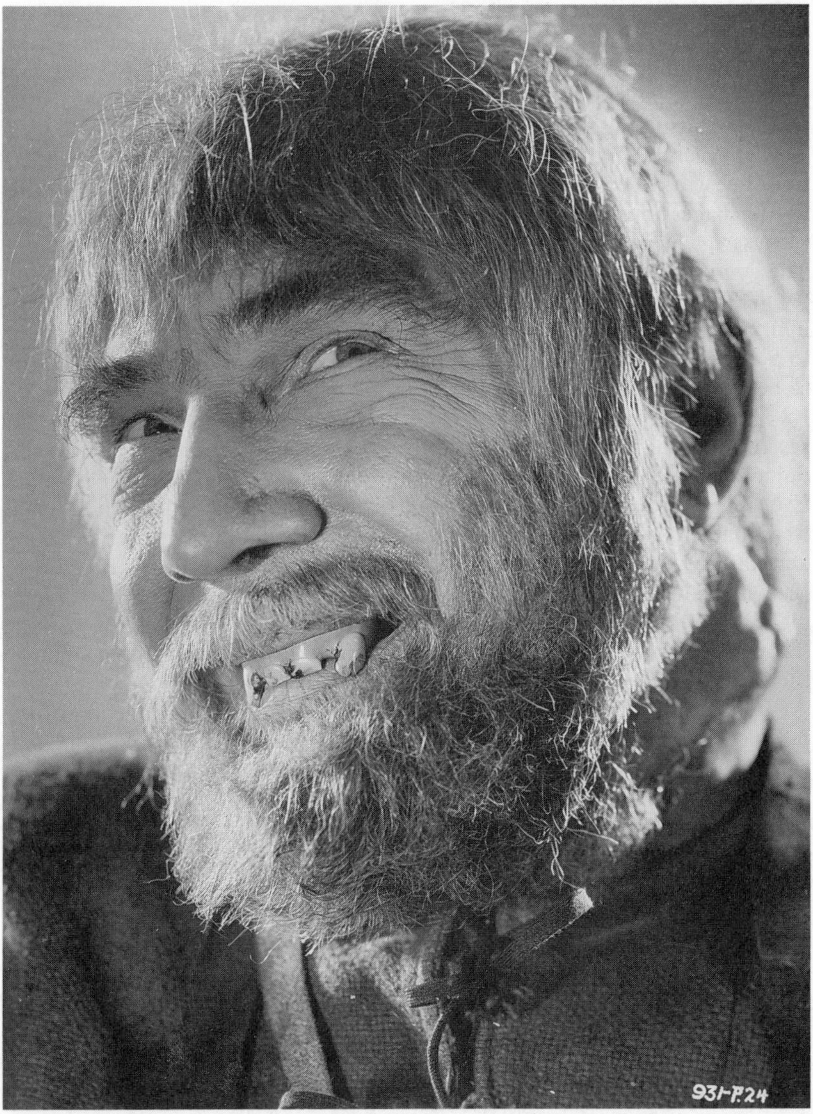

Bela Lugosi gave the performance of his career despite the dental appliance, in *Son of Frankenstein.*

account of the negative effect of Karloff's makeup in George Robinson's color tests.

No one foresaw the monumental difficulties Lee would have getting the film completed in time for the preview. Though *Son of Frankenstein* officially began production on October 17, 1938, shooting was delayed until November 9 due to Lee's dissatisfaction with Cooper's screenplay. As the cast was already on salary, the studio gave orders for Lee to forge ahead, script or no script. They had full confidence, based on his performance on *Service de Luxe,* that Lee would complete the production within the 27-day schedule. Their hopes were unrealistic.

The picture's intricate special effects only slowed down the pace of production. Lee worked continuously on the revised script. The actors received freshly written pages only minutes before scenes were set up to be shot. Without a complete script, it was impossible to plan a schedule and figure a realistic budget. The completion date was changed to December 15.

Despite the pressures on the cast and crew, Lee kept everyone's spirits high. Pranks and practical jokes were the order of the day. Karloff was treated to a surprise party on the occasion of his 51st birthday. He had double reason to be joyous. His wife gave birth to his only child, Sara Jane, that same day.

Problems persisted as the production neared the Christmas holiday season. Rainfall interfered with exterior shooting and a cold forced Lee to curtail his activities. Undaunted, he vowed to get the picture finished by Christmas Eve. The dubious brass gave him the benefit of the doubt. Meanwhile, plans were made to expedite the handling of the production in the editorial, sound and music departments. The heads of these units, Maurice Pivar, Bernard B. Brown and Charles Previn, respectively, alerted their personnel of the day-and-night grind that would lie ahead of them, including the possibility of working through the New Year's holiday in order to meet the required shipping date on the first 20 prints.

Christmas Eve arrived and Lee was still nowhere near completion of the production. The cast and crew toiled on the soundstages till 6:15 p.m. that evening (an unusual procedure in Hollywood as work customarily finished at noon on this day). Rathbone and several other principals had their engagements extended through December 29 at considerable cost to the studio. The production *finally* wrapped, circa 1:15 a.m., on January 5, 1939, culminating a feverish 47-day shooting schedule.

But the biggest challenge in completing *Son of Frankenstein* was met by the post-production units. Only a few days before the January preview date, Pivar, Brown, Previn and their various artists and craftsmen were still working industriously to prepare a finished print and rush additional prints to showcase theaters. The first cut ran over 100 minutes and had to be pruned down to a more acceptable length. The final cost of the production tallied a whopping $420,000, almost *double* the original estimate.

Son of Frankenstein taught Universal a good lesson: never embark on a production without a finished script. As Rowland V. Lee proved, it could be a costly proposition. His halo tarnished in the eyes of the studio brass, Lee undauntedly forged ahead with his next two productions, *The Sun Never Sets,* a dated, silly glorification of the British realm which reteamed Rathbone and Atwill, and the handsomely mounted historic spectacle, *Tower of London.* Both productions went through the ceiling in regard to budget and scheduling. Lee's excesses, as well as Joe May's poky (and costly) performances on *The House of Fear* (1939), *The Invisible Man Returns* and *The House of the Seven Gables,* are what probably convinced Nate Blumberg and production chief Cliff Work to scale down future shockers. With few exceptions, most of the studio's subsequent horror romps were given the B treatment and were assigned to competent craftsmen who could grind 'em out on schedule within the limits of the budget. Elaborately produced, high cost thrillers such as *Son of Frankenstein* were out, and modest programmers such as *The Mummy's Hand* and *Man Made Monster* were in.

Actually, Universal had little reason to grouse. *Son of Frankenstein* turned a tidy profit and certainly contributed towards the studio's financial turnabout in 1939. It was to be the last Frankenstein film the critical establishment treated with respect, and for good reason. Every aspect of the picture, from the acting to the technical departments, is first-rate.

There wasn't a dollar spent on the production that doesn't show on the screen. Art director Jack Otterson and his associate Richard H. Riedel fulfilled the considerable demands of the screenplay with uncanny perception.

"The sets were rather an orderly array of planes and mazes which, at first glance, resembled a castle interior," Otterson commented in a press release. "But the angles and marks were calculated to force an impression of a weird locale and without intruding too strongly into the consciousness of the spectator." Otterson went on to say that the sets departed from any known style of architecture without indulging in over-stressed cubist or surreal designs.

With the exception of *Bride of Frankenstein,* no other film in the series contains as many striking, bizarre sets. The train transporting the Frankensteins to their new home crosses through a barren, fog-blanketed land populated by twisted, leafless trees and strange rock formations. A massive stone edifice encircled by a foreboding wooden gate (within which Ygor torments the townspeople with the mournful wailing of his shepherd's horn), Castle Frankenstein contains cavernous foyers and living room, a dining room bedecked by two wild boar heads, bedchambers with oddly-positioned beds (presumably to ward off evil sendings) and a gloomy library dominated by the Baron's life-size portrait. These are all masterpieces of concept and design and add immeasurably in creating an atmosphere of shock and surprise.

But the most imaginative set of all is the ruined laboratory. A far cry from the old watchtower lab of the previous film, it is built on two levels and is sparsely decorated with Kenneth Strickfaden's marvelous electrical whirligigs. The central attraction is the fume-spewing, gurgling sulphur pit. (It doesn't take much foresight to predict the pit will play an important role in the plot's action.) Studio set technicians toiled for two weeks creating this "lava pit." First, a layer of plaster was smeared on the walls, followed by an application of strained mud to simulate a boiling mass. Pipes, attached to a garden hose, were run under the mud in the pit. Air and steam were pumped through, making huge bubbles and heavy vapors arise from the "sulphur." Pulleys and ropes were attached to the workmen preparing the set so they could be fished out promptly if they skidded into the mud. It was feared the pool was so thick with mud that Bud Wolfe (Karloff's stunt double who takes the plunge) might fracture an arm or leg.

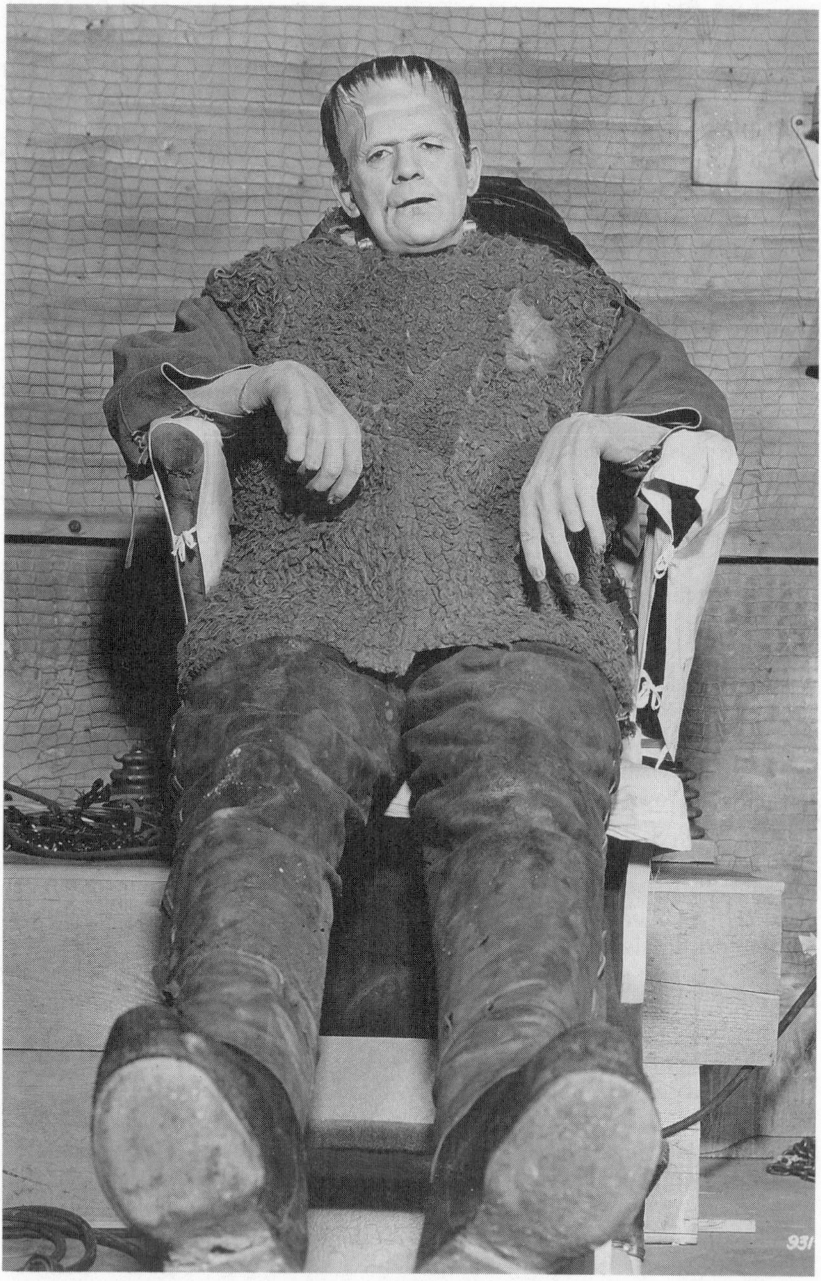

Boris Karloff has reason to look exhausted: he and the cast and crew of *Son of Frankenstein* put in long, hard hours to finish the picture before the scheduled preview date. (Photo courtesy Steve Jochsberger.)

On the day the climactic scene was shot, rescue parties were stationed near at hand in case of an emergency. A stunt man doubling for Rathbone swung across the lab set on a chain and struck Bud Wolfe head-on, pushing him into the pit. He was yanked to safety within a few seconds as he would have been unable to save himself from suffocation. First aid squads threw ropes to Wolfe and a trapeze was lowered into the pit for him to grab onto. Studio workers hoisted him out of the dangerous predicament. Luckily, Lee got the action on film in a single take.

Like its predecessors, *Son of Frankenstein* is a reflection of the man who made it. While Whale's Frankenstein pictures inherited the erudite Englishman's poetry, grace, and artistic sensibilities, Lee's film is as unaffected as the director himself. It bears the stamp of a sure-footed craftsman who, unlike the tragic Whale, was in step with the dictates of the New Universal.

Son of Frankenstein's narrative is crisp, direct and unobscured by the esoteric, stylistic little touches on which directors such as Whale and Robert Florey thrived. Despite his subordinate role, Karloff's Monster elicits genuine chills. (Whale's films have always made the god-forsaken creature more an object of curiosity and pity than of fear.) Never before has the Monster been photographed so imposingly. From our first glimpse of him lying in repose on the slab (George Robinson pulls his camera back so that we may appreciate the Monster's great size), to his destruction of the lab after discovering Ygor's bullet-riddled body, we are reminded of Wolf's scientific deduction that the creature is "completely superhuman."

The haphazard way the film was shot, with new pages of the script arriving on the set each day, probably accounts for the uneven, episodic pacing of its second half. Once the resuscitated Monster renews his campaign to wipe out the last remaining jurors, the action falters, and the beautifully sustained atmosphere of dramatic tension crumbles under the weight of repetitive incidents. It's almost as though Rathbone were on a merry-go-round. He dashes madly between castle and lab, trying vainly to assuage his mounting terror (and his wife's) while avoiding the suspicious eye of Inspector Krogh. Atwill also does his share of dizzying galavanting. Between meal courses, he's running hither and yon, collecting evidence against the Monster and Wolf at inquests, trying to keep a semblance of order in the village, and badgering the inhabitants of Castle Frankenstein for new clues. All of this rushing around dilutes suspense and creates an air of comedic chaos (quite the opposite effect Lee was hoping to achieve).

The dialogue is as rich and fruity as we've come to expect from these '30s classics. Since some of the best lines don't appear in Cooper's original draft (including all of Ygor's exchanges with Wolf), it is safe to assume that Lee, who worked on reconstructing the script, deserves the credit. The war of nerves waged between Rathbone and Atwill is a delight, and their skirmishes are among the film's brightest moments. Krogh never lets his guard down for a moment. Forever probing, he studies Wolf with the hypnotic intensity of a cobra about to strike. Reduced to a bundle of raw nerves, Wolf responds to Krogh's suggestion that he show him around the lab with the sardonic comment, "I'll have you come there sometime—and *parboil* you." Momentarily stunned, Atwill counters Rathbone's remark with one of his patented mad scientist titters.

For a third generation contender, *Son of Frankenstein* contains more than its share of great set pieces. Even Whale couldn't have improved on such bravura bits as Wolf's stirring reading of his father's letter between thunder-and-lightning claps, as an unobserved Ygor peers through the window; Wolf's memorable first meeting with the broken-necked blacksmith; the descent into the underground family crypt, climaxed by the discovery of the unconscious Monster; Wolf, burning with the desire to vindicate his sire, amending the graffito scratched upon his crypt to read *Maker of Men;* the Monster's medical examination, substantiating his indestructibility ("Two bullets in his heart—and he still lives!"); the Monster comparing his grotesque features with Wolf's in the mirror, then turning away in disgust; Ygor's demonstration of his power over the Monster, who obeys him like a trained dog; and the Monster's discovery of Ygor's dead body, his mournful sobs turning to a cry of rage and horror after his fingers are stained with blood.

Underlining the dramatic impact of these moments is the brilliant musical score, written by Frank Skinner, orchestrated by Hans J. Salter and directed by Charles Previn. These arrangements, ranging from pensive dirges to violent movements suggesting the Monster's outrage, are all the more admirable considering the great haste with which they were composed and orchestrated. Sliced, diced and rehashed for numerous B thrillers, this score (along with Skinner and Salter's themes for *The Wolf Man*) became as familiar to '40s audiences as *Swan Lake* was to '30s moviegoers.

Reconciled to the fact that his beloved Monster had outlived his dramatic potential, Karloff vowed never again to don the cumbersome makeup. (Except for the 1962 Halloween special "Lizard's Leg and Owlet's Wing" on television's "Route 66," he kept that promise.) Inexplicably deprived of speech, the Monster had become a mindless pawn in Ygor's campaign of terror against his persecutors, and lost most of the sympathy he earned in *Bride of Frankenstein.*

Son of Frankenstein furnished Lugosi with a role that enabled him to upstage his costar, Karloff. It was an opportunity he would never have again. Ygor is one of Lugosi's most vividly etched characterizations. Unlike *Dracula,* it hasn't aged a bit. Sacrificing his noble features to a shaggy mane, contorting his posture, and altering his melodious speaking voice to a rasp, Lugosi proved he had the resources to do fine work as a character actor.

In Ygor, the Monster finds the ideal soulmate. Both are social outcasts and, by all accounts, both are "dead." ("I *love* dead! Hate living," the Monster declared in *Bride of Frankenstein.*) This mutual affection stumps Wolf, who even suggests the Monster may be under the blacksmith's hypnotic control, "or something more elemental, perhaps." Contrary to Wolf's theory, it's love, pure and simple, that motivates the Monster to do his friend's bidding. Those inclined to read deeper into these things may find elements of necrophilia or homosexuality in this relationship. (In *The Ghost of Frankenstein,* Ygor is afraid of losing the Monster's affections to Ludwig, and even suggests that Heinrich von Frankenstein's second son unite their bodies via an operation so they'd be "together always.")

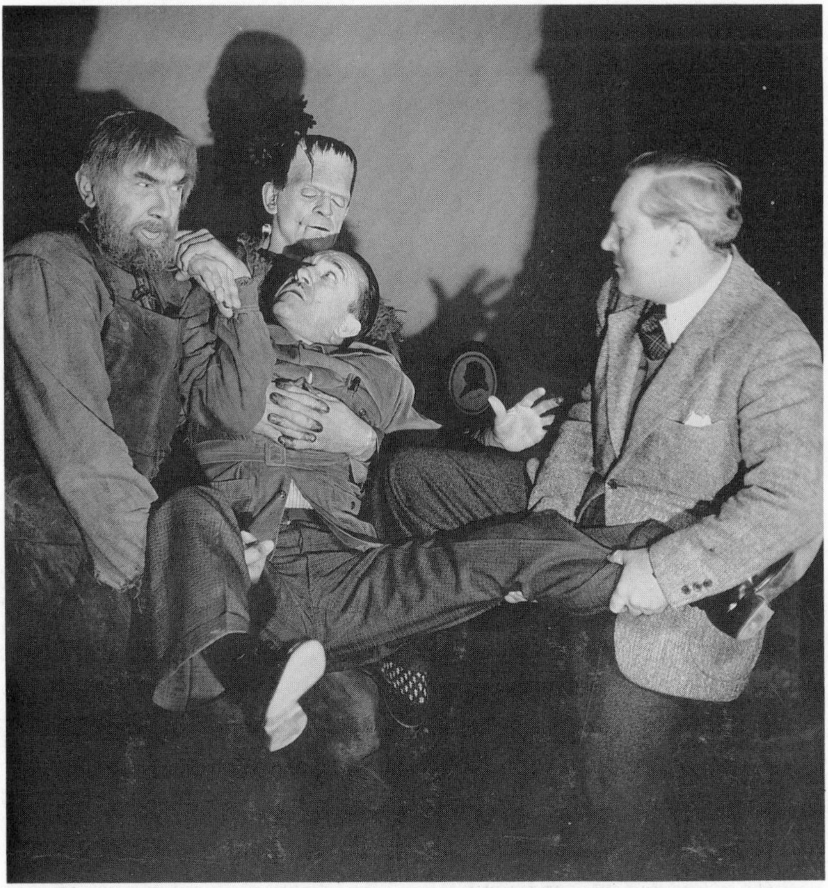

Boris Karloff, Bela Lugosi and producer-director Rowland V. Lee horse around with makeup man Jack Pierce, during the shooting of *Son of Frankenstein.* (Photo courtesy Steve Jochsberger.)

Basil Rathbone's high-strung performance, undeservedly lambasted by historians over the years, is in perfect harmony with the picture's larger-than-life melodramatics. (Compare it to Sir Cedric Hardwicke's laid-back, aloof portrayal of Ludwig Frankenstein in *The Ghost of Frankenstein* and see what a difference some good old-fashioned scene-chewing can make.) Rathbone was directed by Lee in the 1937 British thriller *Love from a Stranger,* an Agatha Christie adaptation, which featured Basil as an elegant Bluebeard-style murderer who seduces *nouveau riche* Ann Harding into marrying him. Rathbone's portrayal of Wolf von Frankenstein so closely approximates his acting style in *Love from a Stranger* (which begins on a fittingly reserved note, then rises steadily to a fever pitch), one can safely assume Lee encouraged the British star to "duplicate" his performance in the Frankenstein film.

Universal originally planned to work out a deal with 20th Century–Fox to obtain the services of Peter Lorre to play Wolf, but the actor wasn't interested. A more unlikely candidate cannot be imagined. It's far easier to visualize Lorre in cahoots with Ygor and the Monster than to picture him as a dedicated scientist, husband and father.

Making his Frankenstein film debut (he was destined to appear in all of the remaining sequels, usually as an authority figure), Lionel Atwill is peerless as Inspector Krogh. Like Lugosi, he realized the potential for stylistic expression and milked the role for all its worth. Not averse to spreading the ham on thick in such films as *Doctor X* (1932), *The Vampire Bat* and *Mystery of the Wax Museum* (both 1933), Atwill is the epitome of restraint here. There isn't a false note in his entire performance.

Josephine Hutchinson has the unenviable position of supporting the screen's Titans of Terror, and holds her own admirably. Emma Dunn and Edgar Norton head up the supporting cast which is peppered with such colorful Germanic types as Lionel Belmore, Michael Mark and Gustav von Seyffertitz. Ward Bond is scarcely noticeable in a bit part as a gendarme, and Dwight Frye's performance ended up in the cutting room's wastebasket. Little Donnie Dunagan, a San Antonio, Texas native, so delighted Rowland V. Lee that he cast him in three of his pictures, the RKO family comedy *Mother Carey's Chickens, Son of Frankenstein* of course, and *Tower of London*. The curly-haired urchin's charms undoubtedly outweighed his talents. As Peter, Donnie is amateurish and camera-conscious.

"Movie making isn't fun anymore," beefed Rowland V. Lee after making the decision to retire from the picture business in 1945. The day-to-day dealings with short-sighted executives and business majors who didn't know one end of a camera from the other finally got Lee's goat. It wasn't long, however, before the producer-director returned to the business he loved. Converting part of his San Fernando Valley ranch into a motion picture location, Lee played host to such long-time colleagues as Frank Borzage and Alfred Hitchcock (the climactic runaway carousel scene from Hitch's 1951 *Strangers on a Train* was shot at Lee's). It was Borzage who agreed to direct a project Lee had long dreamed of producing, a filmization of the inspirational Lloyd C. Douglas novel *The Big Fisherman* (1959).

On December 21, 1975, Rowland V. Lee died after suffering an apparent heart attack. The 84-year-old filmmaker had just completed writing a screenplay, a mystery thriller entitled *The Belt*.

The House of Fear (1939)

Released June 30, 1939. 65 minutes. *Associate Producer:* Edmund Grainger. *Directed by* Joe May. *Screenplay by* Peter Milne. *Based on a story and play "The Last Warning" by* Thomas F. Fallon. *Adapted from the novel* ***Backstage Phantom*** *by* Wadsworth Camp. *Director of Photography:* Milton Krasner. *Art Directors:* Jack Otterson & John Ewing. *Film Editor:* Frank Gross. *Musical Director:* Charles Previn. *Sound Supervisor:* Bernard B. Brown. *Technician:* Joseph Lapis. *Gowns by* Vera West. *Set Decorations:* Russell A. Gausman.

William Gargan (Arthur McHugh), Irene Hervey (Alice Tabor), Dorothy Arnold (Gloria DeVere), Alan Dinehart (Joseph Morton), Harvey Stephens (Richard Pierce), Walter Woolf King (Carleton), Robert Coote (Robert Morton), El Brendel (Jeff), Tom Dugan (Mike), Jan Duggan (Sarah Henderson), Donald Douglas (John Woodford), Harry Hayden (Coroner), Emory Parnell, William Gould (Policemen), Charles C. Wilson (Police Chief), Milton Kibbee (Telephone Repair Man), Ben Lewis (Tommy), Stanley Hughes (Cameraman), Eddie Parker (Watson), Donald Kerr (Cab Driver), Tom Steele (Stagehand), Raymond Parker (Bit Man).

The House of Fear is the kind of modest-sounding Universal flick that you put off seeing for years because it has no horror stars or monster characters—only to find out that it's a neat little whodunit which is better than some of the Universals you've seen repeatedly in the meantime. Breezy and compact, it's a good example of what can be done with a mildewed premise when a competent screenwriter and a spirited cast put forth their best efforts.

During a performance of the play "Dangerous Currents" at Broadway's Woodford Theatre, star John Woodford (Donald Douglas) collapses and dies on stage. His body is carried to a dressing room which is guarded from the outside. When detectives arrive, the dressing room is found to be empty. The theatre shuts down, and remains closed once rumors about Woodford's restless ghost begin to circulate on the Great White Way.

A year passes before Arthur McHugh (William Gargan) leases the theatre from owner Joseph Morton (Alan Dinehart). McHugh's audacious plan is to reopen the theatre with a production of "Dangerous Currents," and he hopes to reassemble the original cast. Just after McHugh signs the lease, he receives a telephone call from an unearthly voice which identifies itself as John Woodford and warns him not to reopen the theatre. After "Woodford" has rung off, McHugh discovers that the call had come in on a dead phone.

McHugh rehires many of the original players as well as the play's director,

Richard Pierce (Harvey Stephens). Carleton (Walter Woolf King), a supporting player in the old production, is promoted to Woodford's role while the sole newcomer, sexy Gloria DeVere (Dorothy Arnold), is assigned to the part of a secretary. Reunited for the first time since the night of Woodford's death, the assembled company begins to bicker and point accusing fingers. Handwritten warnings from "Woodford" are found inserted between the pages of the scripts. Leading lady Alice Tabor (Irene Hervey) becomes edgy over the coming production. Carleton receives more threatening notes. Comedy relief stagehands Jeff and Mike (El Brendel and Tom Dugan) observe all the standard Broadway superstitions. McHugh is nearly killed by falling scenery.

McHugh decides to spend the entire night at the theatre and catch a glimpse of Woodford's ghost. He convinces Pierce to share his all-night vigil and the two men wait in separate corners of the darkened theatre. In the dead of night weird lights appear and coalesce into the glowing, mask-like visage of Woodford. McHugh fires a gun into the spectral face, which disappears in a swirl of dust. McHugh finds Pierce, bloodied from a blow on the head (or perhaps grazed by a bullet?), unconscious nearby. The two hear a crash and find a broken death mask of Woodford in the star dressing room. Investigating further, McHugh finds a secret passageway that leads to a dressing room where Alice mysteriously appears. McHugh admits that he's a police detective posing as a producer in hopes of finally cracking the Woodford case. He extracts from Alice and Pierce a promise to keep his secret, and allows them to leave. In the secret passageway he finds Woodford's corpse plastered up in a wall.

On the eve of the first dress rehearsal, Joseph Morton argues with his brother Robert (Robert Coote) over Robert's romantic involvement with Gloria. During a mysterious blackout Carleton vanishes, and his dead body is later found by the bumbling Jeff. Despite another handwritten "Woodford" death threat, McHugh compels Pierce to replace Carleton in the jinxed leading role and determines to open on time. New evidence presents itself as opening night nears. A forged check against Woodford's account comes to light; McHugh conjectures that Woodford confronted the embezzler and was killed. It's also learned that Woodford was killed by a poisoned dart.

An army of cops, uniformed and plainclothes, attends the premiere. During a scene set at a broadcasting studio, McHugh notices a cable extending from a prop microphone down through a small hole in the stage floor; below the stage the masked killer is waiting to fire a dart from the mike into Pierce with a tug on the cable. McHugh saves Pierce's life by disrupting the performance, then orders a search of the theatre. The masked killer climbs up into the theatre rafters and a frantic chase ensues before he is trapped and unmasked as Mike, the stagehand. Mike, an ex-convict, stammers that he was blackmailed into committing the murders and "haunting" the theatre, and points out the real mastermind: Robert Morton. It was Morton who forged the Woodford check, and who hoped to eventually make a real-estate fortune on the theatre by keeping it closed for the present. The mystery at an end, Alice and Pierce announce their engagement, Gloria admits that she is Mrs. McHugh, an undercover policewoman, and McHugh announces that he is resigning from the force to try his hand in the theatre business.

Going into production as *Backstage Phantom, The House of Fear* "rolled" March 16, 1939, scheduled for a 15-day shoot and budgeted at just over $100,000. At the helm was director Joe May, a pioneer of German cinema who had fled to the United States when Hitler came to power. Curiously, May seems to have been unwilling or unable to master the English language; possibly it was for this reason that Universal had little faith that the veteran May could bring *The House of Fear* in on time. To help him meet his deadline, studio chiefs assigned one of their most efficient crews to the production, but problems arose and the cast and crew found themselves working until 10 o'clock every night and later. *The House of Fear* became a constant day-and-night grind, with production extending beyond the 15-day schedule into the early part of April; an April 5 memo described the picture as a terrific siege of hard work that had consumed 17 days and 13 nights. The film finally "wrapped" on April 6, considerably over schedule and $8,000 over budget. To studio insiders the film must have seemed as much a problem child as the jinxed stageplay around which its story pivoted.

Little of this production chaos spills over into the picture itself. Despite the behind-the-scenes hubbub, *The House of Fear* emerges as an efficient and thoroughly enjoyable B. The film is fun and generally fast-moving, much of the dialogue is genuinely amusing and the cast contributes the kind of high-energy performances too often missing from the mystery/horror films of this period.

William Gargan plays his role of the undercover detective/theatrical producer like a rat-a-tat Warners stock player. The gregarious Gargan (who was only a year away from his Oscar-nominated emoting in RKO's *They Knew What They Wanted*) turns in a bright, glib performance, and his vigorous playing keeps our interest on high even through some repetitive sequences. Irene Hervey is sober and reserved as the agitated Broadway star who reluctantly returns to the unlucky play, somber Alan Dinehart gets some of the best and funniest throwaway lines as the theatre owner, Harvey Stephens is a personable second lead and Robert Coote does a good job of diverting suspicion as the silly ne'er-do-well/killer. Although his acting scenes are restricted to the play-within-the-film, Donald Douglas has RAT written all over him as the disreputable Woodford. On the flip side of the coin, Dorothy Arnold as the golddigging Gloria primps and poses and sashays in the worst Mae West tradition and El Brendel falls back on his usual submoronic bag of tricks as the painfully unfunny comedy-relief stagehand.

The House of Fear is surprisingly well-paced considering the fact that nearly the entire film is confined to the Woodford Theatre: the stage and the audience, a cellar, the dressing room area and an office above. The film also benefits from the absence of a musical score: although Charles Previn receives a musical director's credit, there's nary a note of music heard during *The House of Fear*'s 65 minutes of running time (except during the main and closing credits). The lack of music enhances several scenes, especially the genuinely spooky scene when the glowing face of the murdered actor appears in the blackened theatre and floats menacingly toward Gargan.

Apparently the *House of Fear* screenplay was submitted to the Breen

Office while the blue-noses were napping, as there are a few surprising lines of dialogue and situations in the film. It's startling (and not entirely plausible) to learn at the end that Dorothy Arnold is Gargan's policewoman-wife, as this trollop of a character has been carrying on a heavy-duty romance with suspect Coote throughout the entire picture. Earlier in the film, when Arnold complains that her new hat is now minus a feather, an exasperated Gargan barks that he'd like to give her the bird. A gruesome image comes to mind when a police detective says of the local autopsy surgeon, "He's taken Woodford's body apart so many times now, he knows it like a book!" There's also some unintentionally ghoulish "retrospect" humor in a scene where Gargan's boss Charles C. Wilson chides Gargan for buying cigars with police money to perpetuate his impersonation of a Broadway producer. "Eighty-five bucks for fifty cent cigars?! That makes me sick!" growls Wilson. "Oh, not half as sick as they're makin' me!" Gargan groans. "Honest, Chief, they're *killing* me!" (Later in his life, Gargan lost his voice box to cancer of the larynx and began to campaign against smoking by speaking through an artificial voice box.)

Vienna-born Joe May, son of a wealthy Austrian merchant, was a racing driver, a businessman and a director of operettas before becoming a director of German films in 1911. May was a highly successful film pioneer in Germany, and became well-known for developing stars such as Conrad Veidt (whose first prominent role was in May's *Das Indische Grabmal,* 1922) and Emil Jannings (who first starred in May's 1922 *Tragödie der Liebe*). May fled to the United States in 1934, singing the praises of American films ("Hollywood makes far better pictures than all of Europe combined!") and making his U.S. directorial debut on Fox's *Music in the Air.* His reluctance or inability to learn English probably explains why this once-distinguished director had a spotty Hollywood career that finally petered to a halt in the mid-1940s.

Director Henry Koster and his wife, one-time Universal contract actress Peggy Moran, paint a fascinating and amusing portrait of the late Joe May. According to the Kosters, May came to the United States with a big-shot attitude and was never able to humble himself. May probably would not have seemed out of place in the Universal of the Laemmles, but by 1939 Universal was well on its way to becoming apple-pie American, and May, with his fancy European manners, his penchant for pointing with a cane and his swell-headed delusions, must have seemed something of an anachronism at the studio. (It's a sad sidenote that May not only had trouble with English, but also stuttered!) Peggy Moran was present at the Universal commissary the day that May walked in and high-handedly tossed his coat to the waitress—only to have the garment heaved back at him together with the cry, "Hang it up yourself!"

"He was such a temperamental man, he would lose his temper and go crazy," Peggy Moran Koster laughs. "The story went around that he had done a picture in Germany that involved Christians and lions. The crew was all in a cage so that the lions couldn't get at them. This one lion walked out, right in front of the camera, and sat down. Joe yelled, 'Get that lion out of there! Let's do it again, and don't let that lion sit down!' Well, they did it a couple more times, and the lion kept sitting down in front of the camera. Joe got so mad that he walked out of the cage, grabbed that lion by the tail and yelled,

'Now, get up and behave!' Then he got back in the cage, realized what he had done, and fainted!"

The House of Fear was a remake of a 1929 Universal called *The Last Warning,* a Paul Leni-directed mystery melodrama starring Montagu Love (usually seen as a screen villain) as McHugh. Laura La Plante, Roy D'Arcy, John Boles and dour D'Arcy Corrigan (as Woodford) played supporting roles in this part-talkie production. Both films were based upon the story and play "The Last Warning" by Thomas F. Fallon and the 1916 novel *Backstage Phantom* by Wadsworth Camp.

The House of Fear is no classic by any stretch of the imagination, but it's deft in its balancing of mystery, chiller and comedic elements, innovative in its frequent use of overlapping dialogue, and appealing in its choice of setting (the old *Phantom of the Opera* stage). Largely overlooked by fans of the Universal monster thrillers, it's a lively and likable little programmer that deserves better than it's gotten.

Tower of London (1939)

Released November 17, 1939. 92 minutes. A Rowland V. Lee Production. *Produced & Directed by* Rowland V. Lee. *Original Screenplay by* Robert N. Lee. *Director of Photography:* George Robinson. *Film Editor:* Edward Curtiss. *Art Director:* Jack Otterson. *Associate Art Director:* Richard H. Riedel. *Musical Director:* Charles Previn. *Orchestrations:* Frank Skinner. *Assistant Director:* Fred Frank. *Set Decorator:* Russell A. Gausman. *Technical Advisors:* Major G.O.T. Bagley & Sir Gerald Grove. *Sound Supervisor:* Bernard B. Brown. *Technician:* William Hedgcock. *Makeup by* Jack P. Pierce. *Gowns by* Vera West.

Basil Rathbone (Richard, Duke of Gloucester/King Richard III), Boris Karloff (Mord), Barbara O'Neil (Queen Elyzabeth), Ian Hunter (King Edward IV), Vincent Price (Duke of Clarence), Nan Grey (Lady Alice Barton), Ernest Cossart (Tom Clink), John Sutton (John Wyatt), Rose Hobart (Anne Neville), Leo G. Carroll (Lord Hastings), Miles Mander (King Henry VI), Lionel Belmore (Beacon Chiruegeon), Ronald Sinclair (Boy King Edward), Ralph Forbes (Henry Tudor), Frances Robinson (Duchess Isobel), G.P. Huntley (Prince of Wales), John Rodion (Lord DeVere), Donnie Dunagan (Baby Prince Richard), John Herbert-Bond (Young Prince Richard), Walter Tetley (Chimney Sweep), Georgia Caine (Dowager Duchess), C. Montague Shaw (Major Domo), Ernie Adams (Prisoner Begging for Water), Ivan Simpson (Retainer), Nigel de Brulier (Archbishop of St. John's Chapel), Holmes Herbert, Charles Miller (Councilmen), Venecia Severn, Yvonne Severn (Princesses), Louise Brian, Jean Fenwick (Ladies in Waiting), Michael Mark (Servant to Henry VI), Donald Stuart (Bunch), Reginald Barlow (Sheriff at Execution), Robert Greig (Father Olmstead), Ivo Henderson (Haberdeer), Charles Peck (Page Boy), Harry Cording (Tyrell), Jack C. Smith (Forrest), Colin Kenny, Arthur Stenning (Soldiers), Evelyn Selbie (Beggar Woman), Denis Tankard, Dave Thursby (Beggars), Claire Whitney (Civilian Woman), Russ Powell (Sexton/Bell Ringer), Ann Todd (Queen Elyzabeth's Daughter), Francis Powers, Edgar Sherrod, Caroline Cooke, Joan Carroll, Ed Brady, Schuyler Standish, Harry Bailey, Murdock MacQuarrie, Claude Payton, Arthur Mulliner, Marty Faust, Jean Fenwick, Howard Brooks, Margaret Fealy, Richard Alexander, Stanley Blystone (Bits).

Essentially a historical melodrama with cleverly exploited Grand Guignol accents, *Tower of London* is the product of a profit-minded studio hedging its bets. Never very proficient at producing epics, but exceedingly well-versed in making shuddery entertainment, Universal attempted to cover both bases at the same time. *Tower of London* had lofty ambitions but was marketed with the horror trade in mind. One critic described it as "'Richard III' with all of the gore and none of the art."

MGM or Warner Bros. would have most certainly forged an entirely different film out of the raw historic facts, but Universal felt comfortable doing it their way.

Tower of London was conceived several years earlier when producer-director Rowland V. Lee journeyed to England to research an epic with a background in British history. It was then that his brother Robert N. Lee hit upon the idea of bringing the story of the notorious English monarch to the screen. "We agreed that we wanted to use the roughest, hard-boiled period of all time," Robert explained in an interview. "Row was for the Stuart era but I held out for the time of Richard."

With typical zeal, Rowland pitched the idea to Universal. Lee had recently completed *The Sun Never Sets* (1939), an uneasy combination of comic book plotting and unabashed British flag-waving which, like *Son of Frankenstein,* overshot its budget and shooting schedule. For *Tower of London,* the studio staked the producer to a hefty $500,000 budget and gave him 36 days to complete shooting. The production got underway on August 11, 1939.

Universal and Lee were both optimistic that the schedule would be met. Getting the picture in within the budget was a different matter. The salaries of the cast as well as construction and costuming costs made economizing practically impossible. Art director Jack Otterson went to work on partially reproducing the magnificent Tower on the studio backlot, consulting historical records as well as the original blueprints of the 13th century edifice. The completed structure (now a major attraction on the Universal City tour) stands 75 feet high and would be used on occasion in forthcoming Universal horror and adventure pictures. With an eye for authenticity, the prop department recreated the various torture devices showcased in the script including racks, gauntlets, Spanish collars, bilboes, brakes and an iron maiden.

Caught in a scheduling squeeze, Basil Rathbone was forced during the first week of shooting to divide his time between two leading parts (*Rio,* which featured him as a prisoner on Devil's Island, was finishing up production). Pandro S. Berman enticed him with a principal role in his lavish remake of *The Hunchback of Notre Dame* at RKO, but Universal, who had legal claim to the actor's services, refused to release him. The studio, which had the foresight to extend Boris Karloff's contract for an additional two features after *Son of Frankenstein,* promptly cast him in *Tower of London.*

Jack Pierce went to work creating a makeup for the actor, who was slated to play Mord, the Tower executioner. The disguise required Karloff's head to be shaved as well as his hands and wrists every other day during the production. (The original design which had Karloff wearing a full black beard was shelved.) Karloff's naturally dark and bushy eyebrows, which provided the only contrast, were curled and waxed. His nose was built up and hooked to throw his head out of proportion and his ears were taped back flat. The character's club foot was created with a huge shoe similar to the one the actor wore in his Frankenstein days, with his right leg built up with leather padding.

The staging of the historic battles at Bosworth and Tewkesbury proved to be a disaster, dashing any hopes of keeping the production on schedule. On August 19, a 4 a.m. call was issued to over 300 extras, requiring them to travel 20 miles north of Hollywood to a ranch located in Tarzana. Hoping to recreate the actual climatic conditions in which the Battle of Bosworth was waged, the crew assembled fog-producing machines in the open terrain. But the early morning winds played such havoc with the fog effects, it was impossible to continue. Lee ordered the crew to switch over to the Battle of Tewkesbury scenes, requiring the rigging up of rain machines to simulate the exact weather conditions at the time the real battle was fought. This time the pump broke, leaving more than 300 people to swelter in 100+° summer heat. When the hoses were finally turned on, the cardboard helmets worn by the "troops" quickly fell apart. The assistant director noted in his daily report that "a group of unruly, uncooperative and destructive extras dressed in helmets and armor made this one of the most unsuccessful days the studio had with a large crowd of people in many years."

Lee's once-proud track record with the studio was quickly eroding. His last two films at Universal exceeded their original budgets and schedules considerably and *Tower of London* was shaping up poorly. Increasing pressure was placed on the producer to cut costs; the studio insisted on eliminating the child marriage scene at St. John's Chapel between Baby Prince Richard and Lady Mobray. Lee fought against this decision, insisting that the scene would add immeasurably to the pageantry and color of the production. The producer finally won out, agreeing to compensate for the $10,000 expenditure by finishing all the scenes with the higher-salaried players, starting with Boris Karloff.

On August 22, Lee again tried shooting additional battle footage, but once more the extreme California heat forced the production to a halt. Undeterred, Lee decided to get around the problem by filming small groups of players against process plates of previously shot battle scenes. On September 4, *Tower of London* officially wrapped, a full ten days over schedule, exceeding its budget by almost $80,000. Serial producer Ford Beebe, moonlighting as a second unit director, was assigned to complete a few remaining shots. One of his chief problems was rounding up cast members, many of whom had gone on to other films at other studios.

By early November, the finished film was screened to preview audiences. To the annoyance of the studio heads, who expected a conventional music score, authentic period compositions were recorded on the soundtrack. The studio demanded a new score be written, but the pressures of time necessitated cribbing selections from *Son of Frankenstein*. Frank Skinner's lumbering horror motifs provided a fitting backdrop to the grisly tale and only a few snippets of the original period score survived the final cut.

The film opens with a post-main title crawl which fills the audience in on the historical background of the story. Edward IV (Ian Hunter) usurps the throne of England from King Henry VI (Miles Mander), banishing the fallen monarch's son Henry Tudor (Ralph Forbes) to France. Poor Henry VI, degenerating into senility, is doomed to imprisonment in the Tower of London

Basil Rathbone at the peak of his dramatic powers in Rowland V. Lee's historic spectacle *Tower of London*. (Photo courtesy Steve Jochsberger.)

for the rest of his days. Richard, the Duke of Gloucester (Basil Rathbone) and brother of Edward, exposes Lord DeVere (John Rodion) as a traitor and has him beheaded on Tower Hill. Nursing a lifelong ambition to seize the crown, the humpbacked conniver uses the Tower's executioner, the monstrous, club-footed Mord (Boris Karloff), as his private henchman.

The Prince of Wales (G.P. Huntley) sends his troops to meet Edward's army at Tewkesbury. Richard slays Wales in combat and takes the opportunity to have Mord eliminate the enfeebled Henry VI. Wales' death rekindles Richard's love for the dead Prince's wife Anne Neville (Rose Hobart). Now a pawn in Richard's struggle for power, she consents to be his bride. Their union prompts Edward to divide the considerable land holdings of the much-despised Duke of Clarence (Vincent Price). Goaded into treason, Clarence is arrested

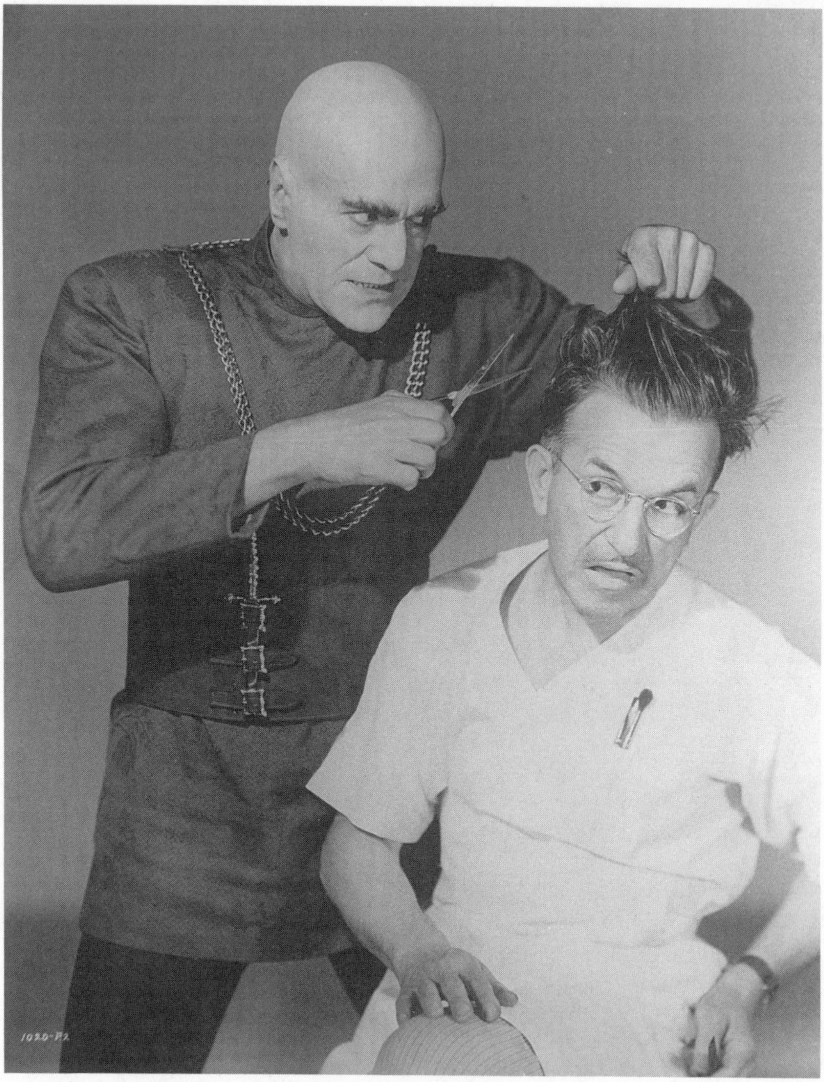

In this gag shot, during the production of *Tower of London,* Boris Karloff is about to even the score with makeup genius Jack Pierce.

and is drawn into a drinking match with Richard, with the winner claiming all of the lands of the other. The cunning Richard waits until Clarence collapses in a drunken stupor, then has Mord drown him in a butt of malmsey.

Several years later, Edward, on his deathbed, names Richard as Protector of the Crown till his young son Prince Edward (Ronald Sinclair) comes of age. Behind Edward's back, Richard stirs up popular support among the people to install him as King of England. Seizing power, he imprisons his two young nephews and has them both assassinated by Mord and his cohorts.

Queen Elyzabeth (Barbara O'Neil), widow of Edward, prevails upon John Wyatt (John Sutton), recently returned from his exile in France, to steal the King's treasure so Henry Tudor can finance an army to defeat Richard. Wyatt is arrested and imprisoned in the Tower, but even Mord's most agonizing tortures won't force him to reveal the hiding place of the stolen treasure. Escaping from the Tower, Wyatt joins Henry Tudor's army at Bosworth and soundly defeats Richard's troops. Wyatt kills Mord on the field of battle and Richard is slain by Tudor's sword. The battle scene fades to a quick shot of the wedding of Wyatt and Lady Alice Barton (Nan Grey) and the picture ends with Henry Tudor named King of England.

The star-studded gala premiere of *Tower of London* was held at the Warfield Theater in San Francisco on December 15, 1939. Screwball comedy actor Mischa Auer emceed the festivities with personal appearances by cast members Karloff, Nan Grey and John Sutton. Determined to lure the horror trade, Universal engaged Bela Lugosi to join the celebrity line-up. To emphasize the point further, large fearsome head shots of Karloff were displayed on all advertisements.

Tower of London garnered its share of respectable reviews, though some of the high-brow critics disparaged what they considered Universal's tasteless approach to a valid historical subject. Today, the picture is routinely classified as a horror film, much to the bewilderment of first-time viewers. There's certainly plenty for fans of the genre to enjoy—a strong cast, wonderful sets, lots of gruesome highlights, and elaborate production values. But it's borderline horror, at best.

Rowland V. Lee was, by all accounts, a producer with a lot of savvy (Vincent Price remembers him as being "fun and adventurous"), but no one ever accused him of being a first-class director. Lee's early output was eclectic. He drifted into costume pictures, a *milieu* for which he displayed little flair. Lee simply couldn't hack it as an action director; most of his period pieces are verbose and heavy-handed. His leaden, slightly impersonal style somehow suited *Tower of London,* and it certainly ranks as one of his best efforts.

Though he stubbornly keeps his camera immobile much of the time, Lee does display a sharp eye for composition. One of the best shots in *Tower of London* is Mord's introduction: his head shaved clean, a hawk picturesquely perched on his shoulder, he sharpens his executioner's axe with the pride of an artist. The director's slow, deliberate staging gives the torture chamber scenes bite as the camera savors each agonizing detail. The gratuitous gore is shoehorned into the picture to buttress the slender horror elements of the plot, but Karloff's dispassionate business-like air as he superintends his torture room adds an unexpected element of black humor.

The battle scenes, in contrast, are completely botched and are among the feeblest ever staged. Indeed, a friendly fencing bout between Richard and Edward in the first reel packs more excitement than the battles of Bosworth and Tewkesbury combined. As the Bosworth episode takes place at the climax of the picture, it makes for an abrupt and most unsatisfying conclusion. Lee's method of shooting the lead players against rear projected footage of the troops in action is cheap and obvious. The fully armored extras mill around and jab at each other in the fog and rain with barely concealed indifference.

Lee stages the deaths of his villains with similar detachment. After several dazzling displays of swordsmanship, Richard finally puts his skills to the test, only to be cut down by one of Tudor's lazily executed sword thrusts. The invincible Mord, too, is finished off by Wyatt with about as much effort as an old woman swatting a fly.

Far from being a creative, take-charge director, Lee preferred to sit on the sidelines, allowing his players to carry the ball. Basil Rathbone's Richard, encumbered by a barely noticeable hump, is considerably less deformed than Shakespeare's misshapen rendition of the character. (Surviving portraits of the monarch show no sign of any deformity, and most scholars agree his physical imperfections were a myth.) Rathbone's extensive Shakespearean experience (he portrayed 47 roles in 22 of the Bard's plays) made him an excellent choice to play Richard.

Admittedly a triumph of technique, Laurence Olivier's interpretation of Richard in *Richard III* (1956) so underlined the character's monstrousness, one couldn't imagine anyone being fooled by his empty gestures of good will. In contrast, Rathbone's more subtly concealed treachery made his Richard even more insidious as he plots the elimination of all who stand in his way. *Tower of London* shows off Rathbone at the peak of his talents and ranks amongst his most commanding performances. (As unsuited an actor as can be imagined, Brian Donlevy tested for this role a few weeks prior to production.)

Boris Karloff plays Mord with a sure hand on his executioner's axe and a sadistic gleam in his eye. The character is cleverly conceived, having inherited the club foot found in popular descriptions of Richard, so that the pair have a physical bond as well as a spiritual one. Karloff has some wonderful moments, such as begging Rathbone to take him into battle so that he may experience the joy of killing in "hot blood" as a change of pace from his tedious chores as the Tower's chief torturer. In another highlight, Karloff threatens to "tear the tongues out" of a singularly defenseless old couple if they spill the beans about Rose Hobart's abduction.

Karloff's off-screen gentleness did not go unnoticed by colleague Hobart, whose acquaintance with the actor had gone back to the Laemmle years at Universal. "He was a lovely and true gentleman," Hobart recently recalled. "Why he and Vinnie Price should end up as monsters when they're two of the gentlest people I've ever known is incredible."

Price turns the Duke of Clarence into a repulsive sop and seems to have a grand time doing so. Price hams up a storm; as bad performances go, it's a hoot. His drinking "duel" with Rathbone is the most arresting scene in the picture. Preparing a few comments about *Tower of London* for this book, Mr. Price offers: "I saw it again only recently and found it ponderous but interesting. The drinking match was all ad-libbed and had to be done in very few shots to heighten credibility. We shot it in one day."

Price was the victim of an oft-told practical joke during the shooting of his death scene. Left to drown in a sealed butt of malmsey (water was actually

Basil Rathbone's real-life son John Rodion is about to feel the bite of Boris Karloff's axe, in *Tower of London.*

used), Price eagerly waited for Lee to call "Cut!" But when the call finally came, Karloff and Rathbone continued to hold the lid down, leaving Price immersed in his bath for a few panic-filled moments.

Ian Hunter, borrowed from MGM, is a hearty, robust King Edward. Miles Mander, in his Universal horror debut, is perfect as the doddering "Paper Crown" King Henry. Those upholding the cause of peace and justice are disadvantaged by blandly written roles, but Barbara O'Neil brings stature to the role of the Queen Mother. Nan Grey is the token juvenile lead and John Sutton handles the heroics with little distinction.

Rose Hobart, a star in her own right who was drifting into character parts by the time this picture was made, has the truncated role of Anne Neville. Inexplicably dropping from sight after her betrothal to Richard, Hobart suggests, "Some of my scenes must have been cut. I worked on *Tower of London* for almost six weeks. When I see it now I think, 'They could have shot that in three days!'"

Hobart vividly recalls her colorful and frequently naughty costars on the film:

> All of those English actors were terrible womanizers and they were always telling stories about their conquests. I remember Rathbone telling me one story about Marlene which really made me kind of sick. We always stopped for tea and I was the only one of the women invited to join the four guys [Rathbone, Karloff, Price and Hunter]. And their conversation was getting dirtier every day. It was really getting *obscene!* One day when they had just finished one really bad one and they were laughing and having a ball, I asked, "What are the three most insulting words that a woman could say to a man?" And the answer was, "*Is it in?*" The reaction was fantastic because I knew exactly who had been asked this question and who had not. And they were so shocked that all conversation ceased on the subject for the rest of the time I was invited back. They were trying to outdo each other, of course. The boys were showing off. They were lying through their teeth!

Tower of London inspired a remake in 1962 when United Artists tried to compete with Roger Corman's Poe cycle at American International with a series of literary shockers of their own. Corman himself was signed to direct *Tower of London* but became disenchanted with the project when executive producer Edward Small balked at shooting the film in color. Vincent Price graduated to the role of Richard but his shrieking, superficial performance failed to enliven even this slapdash production. The film was a box office dud and is almost forgotten today.

In terms of acting and production values, *Tower of London* boasts the best that Universal had to offer by the dawn of the '40s. There's a great movie lurking within the confines of *Tower of London* but the Lee Brothers simply fail to bring it to light. Apart from the poor battle scenes and turgid scripting, the movie seems curiously unfinished and unsatisfying. The subject matter was quite a departure from the usual Universal fare and nothing quite like it was attempted again, even though *Tower of London* made a profit. Outclassed by the glossy costume extravaganzas of the major studios, Universal went back to releasing more conventional (and affordable) thrillers.

Black Friday (1940)

Released April 12, 1940. 70 minutes. *Associate Producer:* Burt Kelly. *Directed by* Arthur Lubin. *Original Screenplay by* Kurt [Curt] Siodmak & Eric Taylor. *Director of Photography:* Elwood Bredell. *Art Director:* Jack Otterson. *Associate Art Director:* Harold MacArthur. *Film Editor:* Philip Cahn. *Musical Director:* Hans J. Salter. *Gowns by* Vera West. *Set Decorator:* Russell A. Gausman. *Sound Supervisor:* Bernard B. Brown. *Technician:* Charles Carroll. *Special Effects:* John P. Fulton. *Makeup by* Jack P. Pierce.

Boris Karloff (Dr. Ernest Sovac), Bela Lugosi (Eric Marnay), Stanley Ridges (Prof. George Kingsley/Red Cannon), Anne Nagel (Sunny Rogers), Anne Gwynne (Jean Sovac), Virginia Brissac (Margaret Kingsley), Edmund MacDonald (Frank Miller), Paul Fix (William Kane), Murray Alper (Bellhop), Jack Mulhall (Bartender), Joe King (Chief of Police), John Kelly (Taxi Driver), James Craig (Reporter), Jerry Marlowe (Clerk), Edward McWade (Newspaper File Attendant), Eddie Dunn (Detective Farnow), Emmett Vogan (Detective Carpenter), Edward Earle, Kernan Cripps (Detectives), Edwin Stanley (Dr. Warner), Frank Sheridan (Chaplain), Harry Hayden (Prison Doctor), Dave Oliver, Harry Tenbrook (Cab Drivers), Ray Bailey (Louis Devore), Ellen Lowe (Maid), Franco Corsaro (Headwaiter), Frank Jaquet (Fat Man at Bar), Dave Willock, Tommy Conlon, Wallace Reid, Jr. (Students), William Ruhl (Man), Victor Zimmerman (G-Man), Jessie Arnold, Doris Borodin (Nurses).

A unique blend of science fiction, horror and gangster elements, *Black Friday* marked the fifth and final teaming of genre giants Boris Karloff and Bela Lugosi in a Universal horror vehicle. Unhappily, it's a film that fails to take proper advantage of its lead players, the horror equivalent of an Astaire-Rogers musical in which the two stars do not dance together or even meet. This, coupled with the fact that Lugosi plays a demeaningly minor role, has soured many fans, while still others complain that the juiciest role in the film is squandered on a character actor that no one cared to see. The fact that this character actor, Stanley Ridges, does a superb job that neither Karloff nor Lugosi could have matched is rarely mentioned, nor the fact that *Black Friday* is one of the slicker and more imaginative thrillers of Universal's second horror cycle.

Black Friday was at least partly the brainchild of Curt Siodmak, the talented German-born screenwriter whose efforts went a long way toward shaping the '40s horror film scene. The film's theme of brain-switching apparently became an *idée fixe* with Siodmak, who fell back on the device many times during his long career. Aside from cowriting *Black Friday,* the single-minded Siodmak also wrote the novel *Donovan's Brain,* its sequel *Hauser's Memory,* the screen stories for *House of Frankenstein, Creature with the Atom Brain* and *Earth vs. the Flying Saucers* (multiple brain transplants, remote-controlled brains and brain-draining, respectively), and the teleplay for the failed 1958 TV pilot "Tales of Frankenstein" (more brain juggling).

December 28, 1939, marked the first day of shooting for *Black Friday,* with work progressing more than two weeks into the New Year. Director Arthur Lubin was forced to contend with an extremely tight schedule and the added onus of frequent stage moves (to take advantage of standing sets). Production was further hampered by rain delays and by union-happy Karloff, who steadfastly refused to work more than eight hours a day. By January 12, *Black Friday* had been branded a problem picture in a studio memo which cited Karloff's hard-line attitude and director Lubin's "erratic pacing." Despite the delays, Lubin wrapped *Black Friday* on January 18, right on schedule and nearly $5,000 under the $130,750 budget originally earmarked for the film.

Dr. Ernest Sovac (Boris Karloff), sentenced to die in the electric chair, walks the last mile, pausing to hand his medical diary to a report who has come to witness the execution. Sovac is led away as the reporter thumbs through the journal....

In flashbacks we visit the university town of Newcastle, where George Kingsley (Stanley Ridges), a professor at the local university, is preparing to take the train east. Driving Kingsley to the depot is Kingsley's friend Sovac, accompanied by his daughter Jean (Anne Gwynne). Kingsley is just stepping out of the car when the sound of gunfire is heard and two cars appear from around a bend in the road: gangster Red Cannon (also Ridges, in a different makeup), driving one of the cars, is embroiled in a high-speed gun battle with the occupants of the second car. Cannon's car runs down Kingsley and crashes while the other car, occupied by rival gangsters Marnay (Bela Lugosi), Miller (Edmund MacDonald), Kane (Paul Fix) and Devore (Ray Bailey), makes a fast getaway.

Kingsley suffers head injuries and slips into a coma, Cannon sustains a broken spine. Sovac performs an illegal operation, transplanting part of Cannon's brain into the crushed cranium of his dying friend. Cannon dies while Kingsley rallies.

When Sovac learns that Cannon had hidden $500,000 in stolen cash shortly before his death, he becomes obsessed with the idea of reactivating the Cannon brain and locating the loot. Sovac invites Kingsley to accompany him on a trip to New York City: he tells the unsuspecting scholar that the trip will hasten his recovery while in reality he hopes that a visit to Cannon's stamping grounds will rouse the dormant Cannon brain.

Sovac and Kingsley check into the New York hotel where Cannon hid out from police. That night the schemy Sovac takes Kingsley to a club where Cannon's old sweetheart Sunny Rogers (Anne Nagel) is employed as a singer. When Kane—one of Cannon's killers—passes near their table, Kingsley spots him and instantly develops a blinding headache. Sovac rushes him back to the hotel where, as Kingsley sleeps, Sovac taunts him with Cannon's name; Kingsley writhes in agony as the music rises and images of Cannon's killers dance in his tortured noggin. When Kingsley raises his head, we see that his face has taken on a slightly different image. The Cannon brain has been awakened!

Sovac explains the situation to "Cannon," who catches on quickly. When Sovac is distracted by the arrival of a telegram, "Cannon" seizes the opportunity to vanish from the hotel. In a montage-style series of nighttime shots, we see "Cannon" at large in Manhattan, stealing into a vacant building where he throttles Louis Devore.

By morning, "Cannon" has reverted to Kingsley, who has no memory of the previous night's dirty work, but that night the sound of a siren triggers a second transformation. "Cannon" catches up with Kane and strangles him, then pays a visit to Sunny Rogers. Sunny is initially angry with the stranger who claims to be Cannon, but as he moves confidently around her apartment, opening secret panels that only Cannon knew about, the girl is dumbfounded.

Sunny betrays "Cannon," setting him up to be killed by Marnay and Miller. The two gangsters trail "Cannon" as he drives to the city reservoir and descends into the underground control room where his $500,000 is hidden in a metal box. Returning to the surface, he is confronted by Marnay and Miller, who hold him at gunpoint and demand the box. In the brawl that ensues, "Cannon" chokes Miller to death while Marnay escapes with the money. "Cannon" later catches up with Marnay at Sunny's apartment and seals him in a broom closet by blocking the door with a heavy freezer. Amidst the frantic cries of the suffocating Marnay, "Cannon" strangles Sunny and leaves.

"Cannon" falls asleep during a taxi ride to the airport, reawakens as Kingsley and asks the frustrated cabby to take him to this hotel. Absent-mindedly carrying "Cannon"'s metal box, Kingsley retires to his room and collapses into bed. Sovac finds and keeps the money.

Sovac and Kingsley return to Newcastle, Kingsley resumes his university post and the Cannon brain is dormant. Kingsley is addressing his students one day when the wail of a siren fills the air. Kingsley becomes frantic as the transformation begins; in a nice macabre touch, he envisions the ghosts of Marnay, Miller, Kane, Devore and Sunny rising up from between the rows of seated students and menacingly moving closer. "Cannon" bolts from the classroom and hurries to the Sovac home, bursts in and attacks Jean. Responding to his daughter's screams, Sovac appears with gun in hand and opens fire. "Cannon" slumps to the floor where, in death, he reverts for the last time to Kingsley.

With the flashbacks at an end, we return to the death house where the reporter (evidently a speed reader) has just finished perusing Sovac's diary. Sovac dies in the electric chair at the appointed hour, the tenth casualty of this 70-minute movie. On the last page of his diary he expresses the hope that, in better hands than his, these notes can be used for the benefit of mankind.

Of the five Karloff/Lugosi Universal pairings, *Black Friday* is the one which least resembles a horror or science fiction film. The opening sequence, with Karloff walking the last mile, gets the picture off to an appropriately weird and downbeat start, and the early flashback scenes efficiently establish every major character and create a strong interest in the unusual story that is building.

Stanley Ridges (sitting) transforms into Red Cannon for the benefit of two unenthusiastic bit players, in *Black Friday.*

But once the film shifts to New York the mood is somewhat dispelled: the urban milieu, tough New York gangsters, night club scenes and comedy-relief bellhops and cabbies combine to create the feel of a crime drama. Karloff's Dr. Sovac recedes into the background as Stanley Ridges' character(s) come to dominate the story. Lugosi, who finally gets to strut his stuff at this point, is just an oily, ineffectual thug, completely out of character and out of place.

Black Friday creates neither atmosphere nor chills, but clever writing, a high death rate, staccato Warners-style pacing and an outstanding performance from Stanley Ridges add up to a fast, lively and rather impressive B thriller. Yet it continues to hold a somewhat inferior reputation in the eyes of fans who know what Universal's initial plans for the film were, and who continue to complain over the studio's change of heart.

In *Black Friday*'s preproduction stage it was planned that Lugosi would play the surgeon Sovac and that Karloff would play the dual role of the professor/gangster. As the first day of production neared, however, the cast of *Black Friday* underwent a hasty reshuffling: Karloff became Sovac, character actor Ridges was signed on to play the dual role and Lugosi landed with a crash in the film's supporting cast, as the rival gangster. Some script modifications were made in the face of all this role-swapping, although the veddy British Karloff was still hung with a Slavic character name (one reference to Sovac's European roots, and his Jewishness, was deleted from the script; a second implication remained).

In a *Fangoria* interview, Curt Siodmak told us that it was Karloff himself who had prompted Universal to recast the picture. "Karloff didn't want to play the dual role in *Black Friday.* He was afraid of it; there was too much acting in it, it was too intricate. So they took Stanley Ridges, who was a stage actor, and he filled the part. Karloff was smart enough to know that he might not come off too well in the role." Still on the subject of *Black Friday,* Siodmak suddenly jumped on poor Bela Lugosi's case: "Bela Lugosi ended up playing a gangster in *Black Friday,* and that didn't turn out well at all. Bela never could act his way out of a paper bag. He could only be *Mee-ster Drac-u-la,* with that accent and those Hungarian movements of his."

Fangoria's mailbox was quickly filled with letters from offended fans who argued and debated over Siodmak's comments in the magazine's letter column. Englishman Richard Gordon, the New York-based producer of such '50s favorites as *The Haunted Strangler, Corridors of Blood* (both with Karloff) and *Fiend Without a Face,* got in the best shots at Siodmak. He dismissed the man's comments about Karloff as "rubbish," bringing up several interesting and valid points, and also rose to the defense of Lugosi. Of Siodmak himself Gordon wrote, "Regrettably he proves that he can no longer be taken seriously, and belongs inside the paper bag out of which Bela Lugosi had acted his way when Curt Siodmak was still a child."

Gordon's points are well taken, but his inference that Karloff would have done full justice to the gangster role in *Black Friday* is arguable. In the early '30s Karloff played gangland characters in a number of Hollywood films, with mixed results. With his British accent and lisp, Karloff was not suited to play American gangsters; the bogeyman screen persona he later cultivated now works against him in these pictures as well. It's quaint and enjoyable to see Karloff as a mug or a racketeer in pictures like *Smart Money* (1931), *Scarface* (1932) and others, but his presence effectively robs them of what versimilitude they had. That may sound like a slight, but it isn't; nor would it be a slight to say that Edward G. Robinson would have made a lousy Mummy. If *Black Friday* had been filmed as planned, there's little doubt that Karloff's Red Cannon would have held his own in nose-to-nose encounters with Lugosi's Dr. Sovac, and probably at other points as well. But it's embarrassing and ridiculous trying to picture a 1940 Karloff using gangland slang, jumping around urban rooftops, playing kissy-face with Anne Nagel or brawling in the waterfront dirt with burly Edmund MacDonald.

Although the slightly demented Dr. Sovac is a character right out of stock, Karloff was correct in opting for this more standard role, and leaving Cannon to a less British, younger and more energetic-looking actor. Like Kingsley/

Cannon, Sovac undergoes a change during the course of the picture as well. In early scenes in Newcastle Sovac is an affable and rather decent character, but once he learns about the Cannon cache the dark side of his personality manifests itself. He conspires to lay his hands on Cannon's $500,000, drags Kingsley along to New York on a pretext, and badgers the already sick Kingsley almost mercilessly. Finally achieving his goal of restoring Cannon to "life," he coyly belittles Kingsley's station in life as "a professor of English literature" to the amusement of "Cannon"; he does not seem overly concerned when the newly-reborn killer goes off on his revenge kick, even though Kingsley's life is at stake as well. Even when "Cannon" comes back from one of his forays with a bullet in his arm, Sovac allows the situation to continue. Karloff is ice-cold in the role, all sidelong looks, avaricious leers and sly innuendo, but it's still probably an improvement over the performance he would have given as a snarling, two-fisted Cannon.

Sovac is a somewhat different character in an earlier draft of the script. He does not learn about the hidden half-million until after his arrival in New York, so it's scientific curiosity and not the stolen money which prompts his trip. There's also a bizarre-sounding scene where Sovac rants at his daughter about his ultimate goal. He explains that the human brain requires 300 years of life to reach full development; if the brain of an old man is transplanted into the head of a child, time and again over the space of those centuries, it will eventually solve the riddles of the cosmos and bring happiness to all mankind.

While Karloff benefited from the switch, Lugosi, as usual, found himself holding the short end of the stick. The role of Eric Marnay is a minor, thankless one, and Lugosi is completely wrong for the part. Some rewriting was required to expand the role for Lugosi: in the first draft of the script, the head of the gang is killed in the fight at the reservoir, and a lesser gangster is smothered to death in Sunny Rogers' broom closet. By having Lugosi's Marnay survive the reservoir fight to become the closet victim, Lugosi's screen time is wisely extended.

But Lugosi is a complete washout: he's silly rather than sinister, and the gang members he bosses around look as though they could chew him up and spit him out. Lugosi also muffs several lines during the course of the picture ("He's leading us to half million dollars"; "Red's been dead since two month"), and on *Black Friday*'s super-tight schedule there was little time for retakes that were not entirely necessary. Lugosi should have turned down the assignment when he learned about the cast shake-up, but the actor, a forgotten man during the horror ban, was probably just glad to be working.

In casting Lugosi as Marnay, Universal gypped audiences out to Karloff-Lugosi encounters that first-time viewers of *Black Friday* naturally anticipate. Although behind-the-scenes still photographs depict Karloff and Lugosi on the set together, in the film itself the actors' paths never once cross. Expectedly, horror film fans felt cheated by a Karloff-Lugosi film in which the two premier bogeymen shared no scenes. Probably the most disappointed fans were the folks from Richmond, Virginia, who attended the movie after reading in their local paper *The News Leader* that Lugosi played the dual role of Kingsley/Cannon "with artful makeup"!

Despite the petty squabbles of close-minded horror fans, Stanley Ridges does a superb job of acting in the dual role. Ridges' Kingsley is a gentle and instantly likable sort, much beloved by his students and a staunch friend to the Sovacs; Ridges builds a rapport with the audience so quickly that his opening-reel "death" comes as a startling and unpleasant shock to first-time viewers. Ridges is equally fine in his other personality as Cannon, convincingly projecting a frighteningly evil and vengeful nature.

As is the case with most far-out films, there are some curious holes in the plot. There's no explanation for why Kingsley's face takes on a different image when he becomes "Cannon." His hair color also changes, and he can see without his glasses. It's difficult, too, to believe that Kingsley has the strength or endurance to do the things that "Cannon" does, like strangling the toughest of New York gangsters or outrunning police across rooftops. When "Cannon" snarls, "You never saw the day I couldn't break you apart!" at the height of his fight with Frank Miller at the reservoir landing, it's a sad commentary on Miller that he apparently never saw the day that George Kingsley couldn't break him in two, either!

It's unclear at the end why Sovac is going to the electric chair. Prof. Kingsley suffered a strange attack in full view of his students, barged into the Sovac home and viciously choked Jean (events to which the students and Jean would all have truthfully testified); Sovac could never have been convicted under these circumstances. Evidently conscience over Kingsley's death drove Sovac to confess to the entire affair, although this seems out-of-character for him and certainly was not in his best interests nor in Jean's. It's a cop-out ending that doesn't bear scrutiny, but it ties together all the loose ends and adds a little punch to the picture's finale.

The earlier draft of the script outlines an entirely different set of framing scenes. It opens at the State Hospital for the Criminal [*sic*] Insane, where Sovac has been sent for observation. Dr. Small, head of the institute, reads Sovac's diary aloud to three other alienists, and the film tells its main story in flashbacks. When the flashbacks end with Cannon/Kingsley's death, we cut back to the mental hospital where Small has just stopped reading from the journal; none of the doctors believe Sovac's incredible account. Sovac is waiting outside with Jean; "his whole bearing radiates the egotistic superiority of the insane." He goes in to hear the panel's verdict while Jean, bleak and hopeless, rightly convinced that her father has gone mad and will be permanently confined, leaves without hearing the official decision.

The original script underwent several other alterations, mostly minor. In the first draft Sovac outlines his brain-transplanting plan to Dr. Warner in the hospital where Kingsley lies dying. Despite Sovac's impassioned plea, Warner high-handedly reminds him that he (Sovac) is only an interne and not a surgeon, and has no right to operate in the United States. (In the finished film Dr. Warner, played by Edwin Stanley, is on screen only long enough to wearily describe the extent of Kingsley's injuries, and does not clash with Sovac.) The name of the gangster in this early draft is Red Banning, and we learn that he used a two-by-four to smash Devore's spine.

Universal evidently felt that *Black Friday* had come up somewhat short in

Bela Lugosi puts the touch on an unprepared Anne Nagel, in this publicity pose for *Black Friday*.

the horror department and in the Lugosi department, and sought to rectify these shortcomings in their marketing of the film. An imaginative publicity stunt, staged to promote *Black Friday,* centered on Lugosi and a hypnotist engaged to put the actor in a trance for the filming of his death scene. The hypnotist, Dr. Manley Hall, was a student of the stars who had provided the screen story for the 1938 Warner Bros. mystery *When Were You Born?* Warners publicists for that earlier film had announced that all phases of the film's production were to be governed by astral calculations: each player had to be born under the sign of the zodiac which governed their particular character, and Hall would read the horoscope of each player to insure scientific casting. Hall went so far as to determine that 11:26 on the morning of February 9, 1938, would be the most propitious time to start cameras grinding on the film.

Evidently the planets were in conflict or someone's watch was fast: *When Were You Born?* came and went quickly, and little was heard of this type of nonsense again.

Douglas W. Churchill, a columnist who apparently viewed the *Black Friday* publicity stunt in its proper light, described the event in an article in *The New York Times.* Lugosi, "looking like a benign Irish cop," was seated in a chair and placed under a spell by Hall. "Hypnotized," Lugosi was directed to the nearby two-sided set which represented the fatal broom closet in the film. Hall went over the script one last time with Lugosi before "action" was called. The hypnotist whispered, "Now you're suffocating," and Lugosi began sniffing the cracks in the door. Lugosi's voice became shrill as the scene progressed; he finally began to put his shoulder to the door, the set started to give and the actor slumped to the floor. (Karloff, who was also on hand, said he was positive that Lugosi had been hypnotized because he had never seen his fellow-actor keep his back to the camera for so long!)

After a doctor had stepped in and determined that Lugosi's pulse rate had increased from normal to 160, Lugosi was carried to a chair and Hall awakened him from the trance. Director Lubin stepped forward and claimed that the scene was 100 percent better than it had been in the afternoon, when it was enacted without benefit of hypnosis. "The one flaw in the experiment," Churchill concluded, "was revealed when the cameraman said that he had run out of film when the thing was half over." (The stunt gets a big play in the *Black Friday* trailer, where we get to see far more of this closet footage than the few split-second snippets that are in the actual film.)

Today, not surprisingly, Arthur Lubin dismisses the whole silly stunt. "There was no truth to that at all, that was only publicity," he asserts. The veteran director had known Lugosi since the actor first came to America: Lubin was assistant stage manager on Lugosi's first American play, and helped him with his English between rehearsals and at night. "I was very, very close to both Boris and Bela. They were charming, wonderful people to work with," Lubin reminisces.

Comedy, which would prove to be Lubin's forte, is well-handled in *Black Friday.* Early on there's some gentle humor in the absent-minded antics of Kingsley which helps to endear him to the audience. Later, in New York, there are several clever and effective comedic touches, like a bellhop (Murray Alper) completely flustered by alternate encounters with Kingsley and "Cannon," a blustery cab driver (John Kelly) who riles "Cannon" by complaining about his home life and a bartender (Jack Mulhall) who claims he'd be able to spot the killer—while pouring a drink for "Cannon." These minor, inobtrusive touches do not detract from *Black Friday,* but instead help to keep the film—which averages a death every seven minutes—from becoming overly cold or morbid.

Black Friday's theme of brain switching was not new to films, nor even to Boris Karloff films. In one of Karloff's best B productions, the Gaumont-British *The Man Who Lived Again* (1936), Karloff plays an eccentric brain specialist who has perfected a method of electronically transferring the consciousness from one human brain to another. When Karloff's financial benefactor (Frank Cellier) turns against him, Karloff swaps Cellier's mind with that of a bitter cripple (Donald Calthrop), and allows Calthrop to die. Karloff's former lab assistant (Anna Lee) figures out his mad plan and turns the tables on the aging doctor when he attempts to switch his own mind with that of virile leading man John Loder. *The Man Who Lived Again* was a witty and striking melodramatic thriller benefitting from a clever script, good performances and capable direction by Robert Stevenson. Seldom-seen today, it's a cut above most of Karloff's better-known "mad doctor" excursions, including the similar *Black Friday.* It's interesting to note that Curt Siodmak was working for Gaumont-British around the time of this film's production, and may possibly have been inspired or influenced by this earlier Karloffilm.

Elements of *Black Friday* turned up in several subsequent horror films. In 1941's *The Monster and the Girl,* the brain of an executed man (Phillip Terry) is transplanted into the head of a gorilla which begins knocking off the gangsters who had framed him. *The Phantom Speaks* (1945), a Republic thriller, had Stanley Ridges (!) as a scientist whose mind is taken over by a ghost out for revenge on his former partners-in-crime. The 1956 indie *Indestructible Man* had nothing to do with brain transplants, but it centered on a criminal (Lon Chaney, Jr.) who returns from the dead to wreak vengeance on three gangsters who had double-crossed him and to retrieve a stash of stolen money, not from a reservoir but from a storm drain. Of course *Donovan's Brain* and all the other above-listed Curt Siodmak efforts expand on the ideas he first laid out in *Black Friday* as well.

Karloff and Lugosi had other pairings ahead of them at RKO (1940's *You'll Find Out* and '45's *The Body Snatcher*), but *Black Friday* represented the last time the two men would work together at the studio which established them. In 1941 Universal announced the upcoming horror production *The Monster of Zombor,* which was to star Karloff and Lugosi, but it was never made. In all probability it never got past the wishful-planning stage.

Despite the grousings of horror fans who want what they can't have, *Black Friday* remains a brisk, polished and innovative B thriller. It's one of the best and cleverest entries in the crime/horror subgenre, despite a lopsided tendency toward the former, and boasts a remarkable performance by Stanley Ridges that none of our much-vaunted horror actors could have topped. But it's not a good showcase for Karloff, and it's an embarrassment to the frequently-embarrassed Lugosi clique, and so the film's reputation has little chance of improving.

The House of the Seven Gables (1940)

Released April 12, 1940. 89 minutes. *Associate Producer:* Burt Kelly. *Directed by* Joe May. *Screenplay by* Lester Cole. *Based on the novel by* Nathaniel Hawthorne. *Adaptation by* Harold Greene. *Director of Photography:* Milton Krasner. *Art Director:* Jack Otterson. *Associate Art Director:* Richard H. Riedel. *Film Editor:* Frank Gross. *Set Decorator:* Russell A. Gausman. *Gowns by* Vera West. *Dialogue Director:* Lester Cole. *Musical Director:* Charles Previn. *Musical Score:* Frank Skinner. *Sound Supervisor:* Bernard B. Brown. *Technician:* William Hedgcock.

George Sanders (Jaffrey Pyncheon), Margaret Lindsay (Hepzibah Pyncheon), Vincent Price (Clifford Pyncheon), Dick Foran (Matthew Maule), Nan Grey (Phoebe Pyncheon), Cecil Kellaway (Philip Barton), Alan Napier (Mr. Fuller), Gilbert Emery (Gerald Pyncheon), Miles Mander (Deacon Arnold Foster), Charles Trowbridge (Judge), Harry Woods (Wainwright), Margaret Fealy, Caroline Cooke, John K. Loofbourrow, Marty Faust, Murdock MacQuarrie (Town Gossips), Hugh Sothern (Rev. Smith), Edgar Norton (Phineas Weed), Mira McKinney (Mrs. Reynold), Ellis Irving (Man), Harry Stubbs (Jeremiah), Harry Cording (Mr. Hawkins), Kernan Cripps (Workman), Colin Kenny (Foreman), Robert Dudley (Bailiff), Etta McDaniel (Black Woman), Nelson McDowell (Courtroom Spectator), Hal Budlong (Driver), Ed Brady (Man with Blacksmith), Russ Powell (Grocer), Leigh De Lacy (Laundress), Claire Whitney (Woman), Michael Mark (Man), Ruth Rickaby, P.J. Kelly, Lois Ransom, Jack C. Smith (Bits).

Nathaniel Hawthorne (1804–1864), one of the greatest names from New England's Golden Age of Literature, dipped into his own family history for the plot of *The House of the Seven Gables* (1851), a relatively early work. According to a family legend (probably apocryphal), Hawthorne's great-great-grandfather was John Hathorne (no *w*), one of the judges at the 1692 Salem witchcraft trials, and the judge's family was cursed by two of his victims, Rebecka Nourse and Philip English. Later, supposedly, the daughter of English married a son of Hathorne, mingling the blood of accuser and accused, and the fortunes of the Hathorne family declined for nearly a century. Hawthorne's story elements of romance, intrigue and horror are reworked and interwoven in first-rate fashion in Universal's *The House of the Seven Gables,* a well-mounted period melodrama. It's a slow but meticulous and intriguing film marked by strong acting, a compelling story and fine period atmosphere.

On a side street in a quaint New England town stands a forboding seven-gabled mansion with a dark past. In the mid-seventeenth century, Colonel Pyncheon falsely accused carpenter Matthew Maule of practicing witchcraft; Maule was condemned to hang and Pyncheon claimed the man's land. From the scaffold Maule hurled out the curse, "God hath given him blood to drink!" Pyncheon built Seven Gables on the dead man's land, but on the day the house was completed he was found dead in the library. The strange seizure which killed Pyncheon became known as Maule's Curse, and the legend that the spirit of Maule dwells in the house was born.

The film opens (in 1828) with Boston lawyer Jaffrey Pyncheon (George Sanders) returning home to Seven Gables in response to an urgent summons from his father Gerald (Gilbert Emery). A series of bad investments has left the Pyncheon family penniless, and Gerald is preparing to sell the house before it falls in the hands of creditors. Jaffrey's older brother Clifford (Vincent Price) and distant cousin Hepzibah (Margaret Lindsay) are eagerly looking forward to the sale; using Clifford's share of the proceeds they will marry and live in New York, where Clifford will pursue a living as a musician. Both Gerald and Jaffrey are appalled at the idea of losing their centuried home, but Clifford, bright and forward-thinking, has no love for the decaying house nor respect for his scurrilous and disreputable ancestors. Clifford catches the money-grubbing Jaffrey searching the house in the middle of the night and realizes that he still clings to his belief in a persisting rumor that a valuable land grant has been well hidden somewhere in the house.

Gerald and Jaffrey maneuver desperately to find a way to retain the house while Clifford continues to plan on a sale. In private, Clifford gets into a vehement argument with his father, who suffers a sudden seizure and strikes his head as he falls. Jaffrey realizes that Gerald has succumbed to Maule's Curse but he grasps the opportunity to charge Clifford with murder. Clifford's day in court is a travesty reminiscent of the old Salem witch trials; the jury decides on a verdict of guilty without leaving the box. He is sentenced to life imprisonment.

The dead father's insurance money pays off the debt on the house but, unbeknownst to Jaffrey, Gerald had signed the deed over to Hepzibah, to prevent creditors from seizing Seven Gables. Ordering Jaffrey to leave the house forever, Hepzibah seals up the place and begins to lead a dismal, solitary existence pining for her lost Clifford. Many years pass, the house falls to near ruin and Hepzibah becomes a drawn, middle-aged spinster. In the State Prison, a brash young abolitionist who briefly shares a cell with Clifford turns out to be Matthew Maule (Dick Foran), descendant of the original landowner.

Living in poverty, Hepzibah is forced to take in a boarder and to turn her front parlor into a one-cent shop which is tended by Phoebe Pyncheon (Nan Grey), a distant relative newly-arrived. (The boarder is Maule, who lives there under the assumed name of Matthew Holgrave.) Clifford's sentence is commuted and he returns home to Seven Gables, but he has been stripped of his civil rights: he cannot leave the property or marry Hepzibah until he is able to prove his innocence. Romance blooms between Phoebe and Matthew.

The legend of the hidden land grant resurfaces and Matthew spreads the word that Clifford has lost his reason and is searching the house for the document. This news greatly intrigues Jaffrey, who becomes determined to take possession of Seven Gables and find the document himself. On the side, the sly Jaffrey has also duped the local Deacon (Miles Mander), who is treasurer for the local Anti-Slave Society, into investing $5,000 of Society money in an illegal venture.

Jaffrey shows up at Seven Gables, unaware that he is being played for a sucker: this revival of the land grant rumor has been cooked up by Clifford and Matthew. Clifford will allow Jaffrey to search the house only if he (Jaffrey) signs a paper exonerating Clifford. The frantic Deacon arrives on the scene with the abolitionists he has cheated practically on his heels; Jaffrey coldly turns him away and the Deacon shoots himself. Realizing that Clifford is in a perfect position to frame him, Jaffrey becomes understandably apoplectic. He signs the confession but then suffers one of the hereditary Pyncheon attacks, collapsing and dying before witnesses. Clifford is now cleared and the "curse" at an end. Clifford and Hepzibah as well as Matthew and Phoebe are joined in a double wedding.

As is invariably the case when Hollywood undertakes to film a classic story, certain changes were required for the sake of greater dramatic interest. The Hawthorne novel is set up quite differently from the Universal film: most of the action seen in this film transpired before the novel even began.

After laying out the story of Matthew Maule and his curse, the book begins with Hepzibah already a scowling, sixtyish spinster living at Seven Gables with Holgrave inhabiting a remote gable upstairs. Phoebe arrives early on, and Hepzibah's brother Clifford comes back to Seven Gables a broken man with the intellect of a child; there's no explanation (that is, his years in prison) for his partly demented condition until late in the story. Clifford dislikes Hepzibah's ugliness, and the task of caring for him falls to Phoebe. Judge Jaffrey Pyncheon, a wealthy cousin, shows up and warns that unless Clifford reveals to him the location of hidden land grant documents, he will have Clifford institutionalized. But the Judge has a seizure and dies quietly in the parlor. After a lot more comings and goings, everything is resolved with the late Judge revealed as the murderer of a rich uncle (for whose death Clifford has been jailed). The land grants, now useless, are found in a recess behind a portrait. Holgrave, pledged to wed Phoebe, reveals that he is a Maule just before the entire family packs up and leaves for Judge Jaffrey's country place.

Many of Universal's changes were for the better, making for a tidy, streamlined drama with more incident and less wordy detours than in Hawthorne's original. Working from an adaptation by Harold Greene, Lester Cole (of Hollywood Ten fame) does a good job of adding conflict and romantic flourishes, and fashions a workable screen story from Hawthorne's hard-bitten narrative.

The flaws in Cole's screenplay are its inclination toward talk and an over-reliance on coincidence. The film benefits from its deliberate pacing, but occasionally mistakes "pokey" for "stately." Most of the highlights are featured in the opening reels, and the let-up in dramatic tension is keenly felt during some plotty and uninteresting midpoint scenes. *Seven Gables* drops badly in the final

Sibling rivalry takes a violent turn in Joe May's *The House of the Seven Gables,* featuring George Sanders, Vincent Price and Margaret Lindsay.

third; these climactic passages have an entirely different "feel" than the dramatic scenes that kicked off the film. The plan that Clifford and Matthew concoct to entrap Jaffrey is silly and transparent, and the two men carry out their scheme with a mischievous twinkle that's not in keeping with the seriousness of the situation or the overall tone of the picture. The ending, too, is a disappointing copout, with the frazzled Deacon forcing his way into Seven Gables, committing a discreet off-screen suicide and inducing a too-convenient seizure in Jaffrey. It's a forced, *deus ex machina* wrap-up to an otherwise intelligent and respectable film.

The acting in *The House of the Seven Gables* is first-rate and adds materially to the texture of the film. George Sanders does a typically fine job as the blackguard whose false accusation of his brother sparks the film's action. (Curiously, and for no apparent reason, Sanders' Jaffrey is referred to in dialogue as the younger brother of Price's Clifford, even though Sanders looks, acts and in reality *is* five years older than Price; a minor script modification should have been made once the roles were cast.) "I always felt he was embarrassed playing that part," suggests Vincent Price, but Sanders' reported unease never shows through; Sanders' Jaffrey is a dark, brooding cloud that hangs portentously over the heads of the other characters.

Margaret Lindsay, one of the loveliest and most talented of '30s leading ladies, contributes a fine, mature performance that's probably the best, certainly the most striking, in the picture. In early scenes as young Hepzibah, she's ingenuous, intelligent and appealing; later disguised in artful middle-age makeup, she skillfully conveys the inner suffering of her staunch, scowling character in some masterful little bits of acting. Lindsay was another one of the many highly talented actresses who never got the breaks she deserved in the picture business: leads in Bs and secondary roles in major pictures would be her lot until her apparent retirement in '63. *The House of the Seven Gables* might well be the closest thing to a major picture in which Lindsay enjoyed a meaty part; she meets with flying colors the challenge of what practically amounts to a dual role. Had a Bette Davis played Hepzibah, this same performance would be hailed as a classic, but it's Margaret Lindsay and so-what? as far as snob appeal critics are concerned. "Margaret Lindsay was a delight to work with and a very good actress," Price adds.

Price himself is also effective as Clifford, the tragic victim of Jaffrey's evil machinations. Exuberant and impulsive—but with more than a trace of repressed bitterness seething beneath the surface—Price is also at his best in early scenes: wooing Hepzibah, tinkering away at his harpsichord, matching wits with his sardonic brother, and challenging his father's authority in a crackling dialogue exchange. Price's rendition of the song "The Color of Your Eyes" (music by Frank Skinner, lyrics by Ralph Freed) is a highpoint of the film, as is his emotional condemnation of perjuror Jaffrey in the courtroom. Most of Price's best acting opportunities are already behind him by the time his greatly-aged character has returned from prison, but there's still the touching, near-brilliant scene of Clifford's middle-of-the-night reappearance at Seven Gables: catching sight of himself in a mirror for the first time in years, finding that the clothes he wore as a young man have been ruined by moths, quietly playing the harpsichord to draw Hepzibah into the blackened room.

There's another good scene for Price in the opening reel, rattling off the crimes of his ancestors as he stands beneath their various portraits. It's a good, fervently acted, appropriately hammy monologue and a forerunner to many similar Price scenes in the Roger Corman Poe films of the '60s, particularly *House of Usher*. (In the original Hawthorne novel, the character of Clifford Pyncheon is often reminiscent of Poe's Roderick Usher, although few of these similarities are carried over into the filmed *The House of the Seven Gables*.) For Price it was a substantial, sympathetic part, the type of role that would later be denied him once Hollywood typecasters stuck their labels on him. Robert Cummings was originally pencilled in for the part of Clifford, although it seems unlikely that light leading man Cummings would have been effective in the role.

Supporting roles are also capably handled. Dick Foran seems altogether the wrong type of actor for this kind of film, but after a boisterous opening scene he's more modulated and in tune, and gives an okay performance. The book's depiction of Maule as a part-time mesmerist is wisely dropped; instead, the screenwriters (probably Lester Cole, whose politics landed him in the slammer) make him an abolitionist. Nan Grey is a lovely Phoebe, and her sunny presence is just what the picture needs to keep it from becoming morbid. Cecil Kellaway, Alan Napier, Gilbert Emery, Miles Mander and Charles Trowbridge, in more minor roles, add to the color and period flavor.

According to the film's publicity, initial preparations for the production of *Seven Gables* were made long before the film was officially announced, as Universal feared that other studios might try to beat them to the screen with the classic Hawthorne tale. (One previous version had been made, by Edison's company in 1910; Republic had planned to make one in 1935.) Jack Otterson was sent to the actual House of the Seven Gables on Turner Street in Salem, Massachusetts, where the art director inspected, photographed and drew plans which were used by Universal in their reconstruction of the famous edifice. Three stages were crowded with sets representing the Seven Gables interiors, including replicas of the main living rooms and of the upper and lower hallways. More than 500 pieces of authentic early American kitchenware and tableware were used to dress the sets.

Being a Joe May production, *The House of the Seven Gables* hit more than its share of production delays, snags and snafus. In a December 29, 1939, memo came the announcement that the start of production was being delayed due to casting difficulties. At this point the film's sets were still under construction, although the lower floor of the house had been completely finished. Production got underway on the third day of the new year, with 21 days' shooting and a budget of $161,625 allotted to the film. But by January 5 a studio memo was already describing the film as a difficult production, with time-consuming elements like aging characters, period costumes, special lighting effects, etc., making progress slow. Rain plagued the picturemakers, prompting a rearrangement of the scheduling in order to keep everyone working.

By January 19 the memo-writers were complaining that May was working too slowly. More difficulties, like airplane noises ruining exterior takes, caused additional delays. Pressure was put on May to speed up production, and by January 26 it had begun to pay off. *Seven Gables* finally wrapped two days over schedule with a final budget of $178,000; the company had worked ten nights until 10 o'clock or later.

Henry and Peggy Moran Koster, who were friendly with May and his wife Mia, remember him best for his impulsiveness and temper. "I remember that he and his wife used to come over at night and we'd play a game," recalls Peggy Koster. "It was a game they played in Germany, it's like parchesi, when you move the game pieces around and if you land on somebody else's, he has to go home again. Joe would play, and if you'd send his piece home, sometimes he'd get so mad he'd take the whole board and throw it across the room!"

The House of the Seven Gables was one of the last Universal films for May, whose once-great career, sadly, was already on its last legs. After May's Hollywood career went kaput, he and his wife opened a restaurant called the Blue Danube. But May was never one to leave well enough alone: whenever customers would come in, he would sit down at the table with them, read from the menu and then tell them what they wanted. Which apparently was the kiss of death for the Blue Danube. May died in 1954, his wife Mia in 1980. In its obituary for Mia May, *Variety* wrote that her husband "died in Hollywood more than twenty years ago after making *one or two films* in this country" (italics added), which suggests rather plainly that Joe May was already a forgotten figure.

In 1963 Price starred in the anthology *Twice-Told Tales,* a schlocky Hawthorne-inspired UA horror film "cashing in" on Price's popularity in the Poe pictures. The third and final sequence was a loosely adapted version of *The House of the Seven Gables* with Price as a money-grubbing Pyncheon who returns home to Seven Gables and his devil-worshipping sister (Jacqueline de Wit) to search for the missing land grant. Beverly Garland and Richard Denning costarred in this lurid, garishly colored exploitation item.

Universal's *The House of the Seven Gables* seems like the sort of "Shaky A" that the studio could and should have made a big deal out of, but instead they stuck it on the bottom rung of a double bill with the cheaper, shorter *Black Friday* and let it go at that. Is the film an effective treatment of Hawthorne's novel? Vincent Price says no, although he allows that it was an interesting picture to make. But the cinema isn't the place for a dry, heavy and intricately symbolic work like *Seven Gables*; this commercialized film version is an impressive, well-spun and largely faithful yarn that often seems to capture the spirit of Hawthorne, which is about as much as any viewer could realistically hope for. *Seven Gables* and *Black Friday* were world premiered at Chicago's Palace Theatre, with Vincent Price and Bela Lugosi in attendance.

Curious as it might sound, *The House of the Seven Gables* benefits from having been made by a second-string outfit like Universal rather than at a studio like Metro or Warners; there, a film version of this literary classic would probably have gotten puffed-up A treatment and glisteny production values that would have worked against its effectiveness. Universal gave *Seven Gables* exactly the look it needed: dark, stark and mood-crusted, as befits a brooding tale of Colonial America. (Frank Skinner's musical score was Oscar-nominated.) An impressive collaborative effort of director, stars, camera and set design, *The House of the Seven Gables* is a well-carpentered period piece endowed with good pictorial values. Despite its contrived finale, it's a strong drama flavored with dashes of spookery and stands as one of Universal's most respectable semihorror films.

The Invisible Man Returns (1940)

Released January 12, 1940. 81 minutes. *Directed by* Joe May. *Associate Producer:* Ken Goldsmith. *Screenplay by* Lester K. Cole & Kurt [Curt] Siodmak. *Original Story by* Joe May, Kurt [Curt] Siodmak & Cedric Belfrage (uncredited). *Suggested by the novel **The Invisible Man** by* H.G. Wells. *Director of Photography:* Milton Krasner. *Art Director:* Jack Otterson. *Associate Art Director:* Martin Obzina. *Special Photographic Effects:* John P. Fulton. *Film Editor:* Frank Gross. *Assistant Director:* Phil Karlstein [Karlson]. *Set Decorator:* Russell A. Gausman. *Music Score:* Hans J. Salter & Frank Skinner. *Musical Director:* Charles Previn. *Sound Supervisor:* Bernard B. Brown. *Technician:* William Hedgcock. *Gowns by* Vera West.

Sir Cedric Hardwicke (Richard Cobb), Vincent Price (Sir Geoffrey Radcliffe), Nan Grey (Helen Manson), John Sutton (Dr. Frank Griffin), Cecil Kellaway (Inspector Sampson), Alan Napier (Willie Spears), Forrester Harvey (Ben Jenkins), Harry Stubbs (Constable Tukesberry), Frances Robinson (Nurse), Ivan Simpson (Cotton), Edward Fielding (Prison Governor), Leland [Leyland] Hodgson (Chauffeur), Mary Gordon (Cook), Billy Bevan (A Warden), Dave Thursby (Bob), Matthew Boulton (Policeman), Bruce Lester (Chaplain), Ernie Adams (Man), Paul England (Detective), Ellis Irving, Dennis Tankard, George Lloyd, George Kirby, Harry Cording, George Hyde, Edmund MacDonald (Miners), Louise Brien (Griffin's Secretary), Frank Hagney (Bill), Frank O'Connor (Policeman at Colliery), Frank Hill (Policeman Attending Cobb), Rex Evans (Officer Briggs), Cyril Thornton, Ed Brady (Policemen), Clara Blore (Woman), Hugh Huntley (Secretary), Colin Kenny (Plainclothesman), Mary Field (Neighbor), Eric Wilton, Stanley Blystone, Berry Hays, William Newell, Charles Brokaw, Frank Colleti, Sidney Grayler, Boyd Irwin, Clem Willenchick, Jeanne Kelly [Jean Brooks].

Critically, *The Invisible Man* was possibly the best received of the studio's horror films of the '30s, and the New Universal had high hopes of duplicating the Laemmle success six years later. With a multipicture contract with H.G. Wells for the screen rights to the Invisible Man character under its belt, the studio contrived to make another first-class horror sequel on the same high plane as *Son of Frankenstein. The Invisible Man Returns* courted a certain respectability, and the reviewers responded with generally good notices. Yet the film has never been a great favorite among horror fans. It's a sober, conventional melodrama that takes few chances.

Sir Geoffrey Radcliffe (Vincent Price), wrongly accused of the slaying of his brother Sir Michael, is condemned to die on the gallows. When the hour of execution strikes, he vanishes from his prison cell. Scotland Yard Inspector Sampson (Cecil Kellaway) correctly deduces that the fugitive's friend Dr Frank Griffin (John Sutton), brother of the late Jack Griffin, the Invisible Man, injected the prisoner with the invisibility serum. Reunited with his fiancée, Helen Manson (Nan Grey), the now invisible Radcliffe realizes his only hope is to find the real murderer before the mind-altering effect of the drug overtakes him.

Radcliffe's suspicions are aroused with Willie Spears (Alan Napier), an oily, perennially inebriated night watchman, is promoted to a ranking position in the family mining operation. Geoffrey forces Spears' car off the road and confronts the terrified man. Spears confesses that Radcliffe's cousin, Richard Cobb (Sir Cedric Hardwicke), is the murderer, and has been buying the night watchman's silence ever since. Radcliffe binds and gags Spears, and then sets off to find Cobb.

Despite a heavy police guard, Geoffrey gets to Cobb and brings him face-to-face with Spears, who quickly incriminates him. Cobb kills Spears and escapes, but Radcliffe chases him through the teeming village streets. Making his way to the collieries, the Invisible Man pins Cobb to a coal wagon. A lucky shot, fired by Sampson, strikes Radcliffe seconds before the coal wagon releases its burden, sending Cobb hurtling to the ground below. With his dying breath, Cobb confesses to the murder of Sir Michael.

Near death from exposure and loss of blood, Geoffrey, wearing a ragged suit stolen from a scarecrow, makes his way to Griffin's clinic. Frank administers an emergency transfusion to save his friend's life. To Griffin's amazement, the new blood brings Geoffrey back to visibility, making it possible for the doctor to perform a life-saving operation on him.

Associate producer Ken Goldsmith filled three top roles of *The Invisible Man Returns* with principals of the recently completed *Tower of London*. Sir Cedric Hardwicke, the distinguished British actor who slummed his way through many a Hollywood potboiler, was given star billing in what amounts to a supporting role. Ostensibly, the star was Price, appearing in his third film under a long-term contract. The young actor showed a distinct flair for comedy in his first film, 1938's *Service de Luxe*. Price's slightly aristocratic bearing eliminated him for the usual run of leading man roles, and he soon drifted into character parts. His rich, theatrical voice made him an ideal choice to follow in the footsteps of Claude Rains in *The Invisible Man Returns*. Price had another unique qualification to fill the role: his ability to communicate with the film's director, Joe May.

"May was difficult to understand, as he spoke no English," Price recalls. "I had something of a rapport with him because of my knowledge of German."

Joe May unwittingly made an important contribution to the genre by hiring a writer friend he knew in Germany. His name was Curt Siodmak, and he would soon become one of the leading figures in Universal's new horror cycle.

The brother of Robert Siodmak, Curt got a start (of sorts) in the motion picture business while working as a reporter for a German newspaper in the mid-20s, when he and his wife were hired as extras on Fritz Lang's *Metropolis*

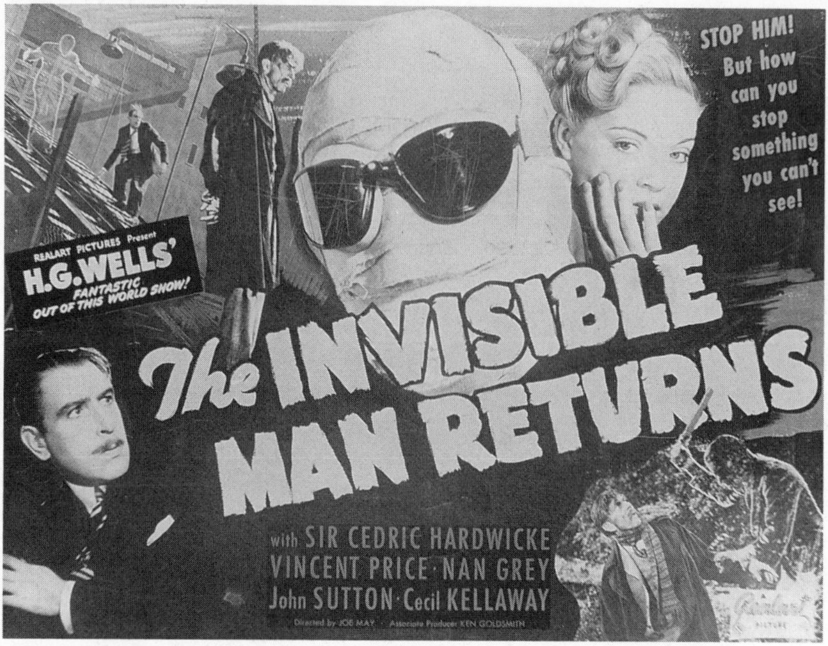

The first and best of the sequels, *The Invisible Man Returns.*

(1926) while on assignment to write a story on the director and his newest production. Siodmak's initial sf screenwriting job was the scenario for the 1932 German picture, *F.P.1 Antwortet Nicht (Floating Platform 1 Does Not Answer),* based on his own novel. Compelled to leave Germany when Hitler came to power, Siodmak emigrated first to England and then to Hollywood, where he met up with Joe May.

Asside from his work at Universal, Siodmak also contributed to the screenplays of shockers released at Monogram (*The Ape,* 1940), RKO (*I Walked with a Zombie,* 1943) and Warners (*The Beast with Five Fingers,* 1946). Earlier in their careers, Curt and brother Robert had an agreement that Curt would write, Robert would direct, and neither would become identified with the other's specialty. Curt broke this agreement in the early '50s when he entered the adventuresome arena of low-budget production/direction. Unhappily, his best screenwriting days were already behind him, and the films he directed from his own scripts, *Bride of the Gorilla* (1951), *Curucu, Beast of the Amazon* (1956), *Love-Slaves of the Amazons* (1957) and the smutty sex comedy *Ski Fever* (1969), were uninspired and eminently forgettable potboilers.

Now in his late eighties, Siodmak continues to write, lecture about horror films and travel extensively. "Today, nobody lives better than I do," he declares. "I have an estate, fifty acres overlooking the mountains, and every night I say 'Heil Hitler!' because without the son of a bitch I wouldn't be in Three Rivers, California, I'd still be in Berlin!"

Like most Universal thrillers of this period, *The Invisible Man Returns* was plagued with production problems. A $253,750 budget and a 27-day schedule proved barely adequate for the sophisticated special effects involved and a director with May's slow, meticulous work habits. Shooting began on October 13, 1939, but within a week, trouble was brewing. Despite favorable weather conditions, exterior shooting was time-consuming and difficult. To comply with the setting of the story, the studio backlot was transformed into a northern England mining town with a full-scale reproduction of a colliery. The elaborate sets included a huge coal pile and a coal escalator, 75 feet long, running to a platform 40 feet high.

By the end of the second week of shooting, production on *The Invisible Man Returns* was slipping precariously behind schedule, even before the filming of painstaking special effects sequences; these were rescheduled for the final weeks of shooting. As was becoming the norm on a Joe May picture, the tired company worked late into the night. By early November, the cast and crew were toiling past midnight with little hope of making the deadline. A long dinner scene alone consumed three days of shooting.

May's methodical ways didn't endear him to the front office, nor did his temperament. According to Henry Koster, when a studio executive arrived on the soundstage one day, the blustery May snapped, "I will not work as long as you are on the set!" When the astonished executive pressed for an explanation, May presented the classic ultimatim: "Either you leave or I leave." Sticking to his guns, the executive shot back, "Well, *you* leave. It's okay with me." Learning a bitter lesson, the proud director found himself crawling to the studio bigwigs to get his job back!

Vincent Price, who appears in the "flesh" for less than a minute, spent most of his days on the set being groomed as a "special effect." Says the actor,

> All of the effects scenes were done with my involvement. It was terribly tedious as I had to be dressed from top to toe in black velvet and I had to work against a set draped in black velvet. John Fulton, whose ingenuity contrived it all, was the leading special effects man at that time. I enjoyed it. The tedium was ultimately more than worthwhile, and I love special effects. . . . Sir Cedric Hardwicke was a delightful man. He ended up being one of my best friends. He didn't like doing this film; he was facing home problems at the time. We became very close.

On November 11, 1939, the production finally wrapped. Still left to be shot were three or four days of effects footage under Fulton's supervision. In all, the crew worked 15 nights until ten or later. On the last day of shooting, May worked his exhausted company until 4:45 a.m. the following morning. The final cost, including special effects and laboratory overruns, came to $270,000, more than $15,000 over the allotted budget.

For a film that has been in almost constant circulation on television for 30 years, *The Invisible Man Returns* is practically forgotten. Along with *Tower of London,* this film established a horror film career for Vincent Price, although the actor didn't return to the genre until 1953. *The Invisible Man Returns* is too well-intentioned to be dismissed as another cut-rate sequel, even though it falls short of capturing the sense of outrageousness and fun that

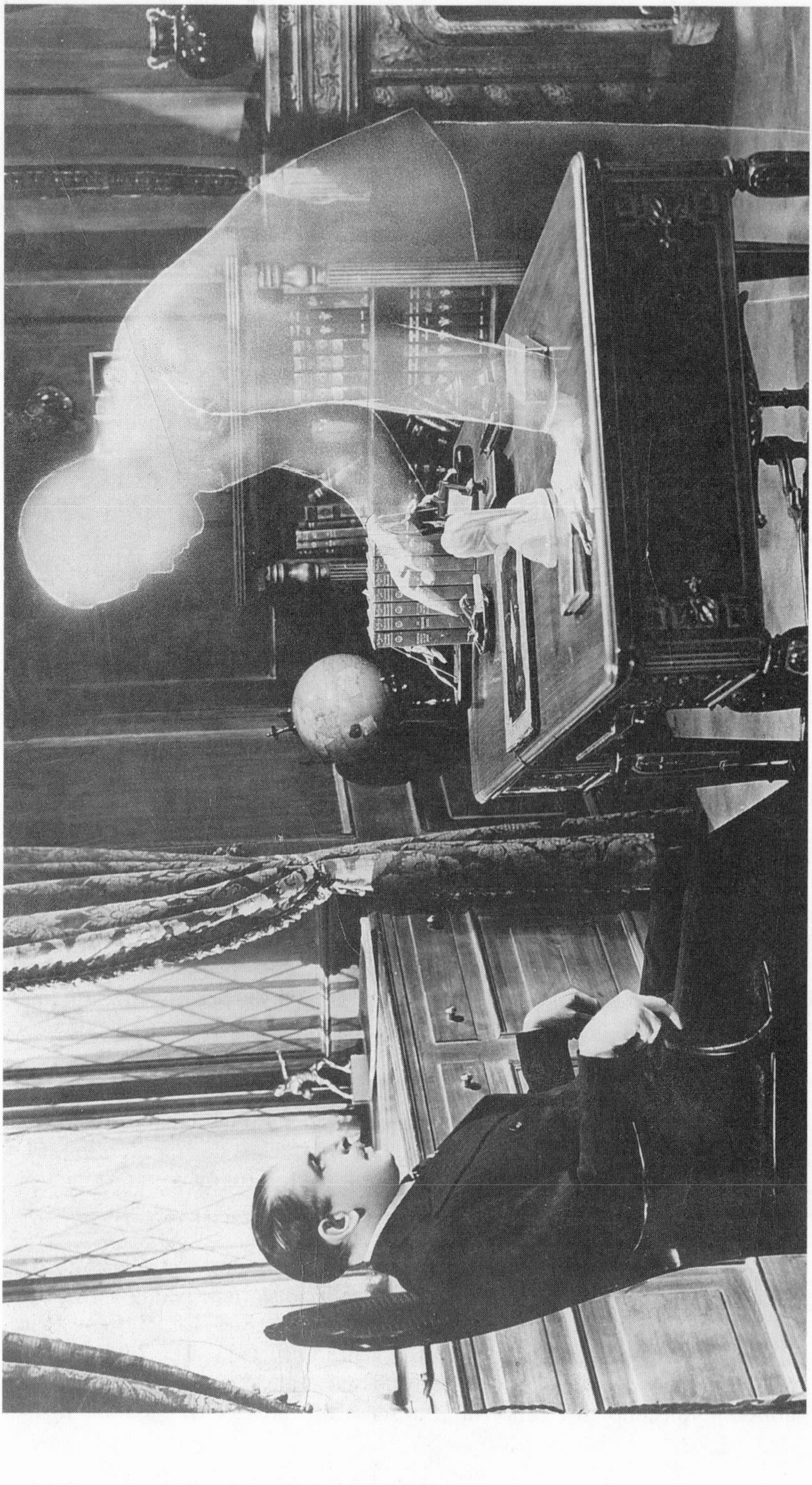

James Whale brought to the original. There *is* a grudging attempt to duplicate Whale's eccentric humor. Forrester Harvey, Una O'Connor's henpecked husband in *The Invisible Man,* is back as a scruffy, gout-stricken hermit, and the English bobbies, ever ripe for lampooning, are again put through the hoop. Otherwise, May and Siodmak, with a little help from Lester Cole, cloak the movie in a typically Germanic air of futility that one can't shake off even after the inevitable happy ending. Lacking Whale's freshness and wit, *The Invisible Man Returns* seems more dated than the original.

Joe May's direction is workmanlike, but rather literary and not particularly stylish. Whale used Fulton's special effects dynamically for shock effect or humor, often simultaneously. (Who could forget Rains unwrapping his bandages for the first time?) The far less inventive May utilizes the effects impersonally, as though they're a curiosity, with little awareness or interest in their dramatic value. Even less compelling is May's inability to rise above long, dialogue-heavy passages. (Two back-to-back scenes of Sutton getting unwelcome visits from Hardwicke and later Kellaway seem interminable.)

The Invisible Man was apparently closely studied by May and his writers as the same or similar plot points turn up in both pictures. The ingenuity of the police is no match for the Invisible Man, who effortlessly foils every attempt to capture him, even when his intended target is used as bait. Hardwicke even bears a superficial physical resemblance to William Harrigan in the original. Price's materialization, like Rains', is put off until the final scene. Both actors were comparative unknowns when these pictures were made, and their concealment was an inventive tease. It's still an effective ploy in Price's case; he looks so *impossibly* young, most audiences gasp at this revelation.

The Invisible Man Returns' inability to land a following probably has a lot to do with its insistence on keeping the melodramatics in check. A traditional happy ending precluded this Invisible Man from indulging in the murderous mayhem of his predecessor. Radcliffe's character is so virtuous, a hint of blandness occasionally comes through. His dream of power never gets beyond the gab stage as the drug monocane (inexplicably called duocane in this film) pushes him over the brink of madness. Price's dinner-table ravings about ruling the world are ambiguous enough to be written off as the vaunts of a tipsy party guest (he's back on track for the rest of the film). There's a decided emphasis on character, and the touching, understated romantic interludes are skillfully handled. Those broad, juvenile *Topper*-like antics, the kind that plagued the rest of the series, are happily kept to a minimum.

The Invisible Man Returns is rather slowly paced; a fuller background score would have done much to galvanize the sluggish passages. Hans J. Salter's wistfully melodic main title (one of his best) would turn up in other films *(Man Made Monster, The Strange Case of Doctor Rx)* in a slightly speeded-up version. Yet it was never as appropriate or as well-rendered as it is here. The theme works so beautifully in Price's materialization scene, it was later reprised for the haunting finale of *Son of Dracula.*

The Invisible Man (Vincent Price) has a captive audience in Sir Cedric Hardwicke, the villain of *The Invisible Man Returns.*

John P. Fulton's Oscar-nominated special effects surpass his work in the original. Shots of the transparent protagonist glimpsed through rain, fog and even the wisps of smoke from a burning cigar are cunningly executed. The matte shots of Price slowly becoming visible are more detailed than in the Whale film, as layers of muscle, sinew and blood vessels appear until the transformation is complete.

Considering that he's a disembodied voice most of the time, Vincent Price gives an entertaining performance in a role offering plenty of range. He's fine in the subdued passages, but Price, even in his younger days, just didn't know when to apply the brakes. Whether he is ranting like a madman, badgering the heavies, or even just plain enthused, Price indulges in his usual brio.

As in *Tower of London,* Nan Grey is far too American in these Anglo-Saxon settings, but she is appealing and dramatically right. Sir Cedric Hardwicke is believable in what is essentially a walk-through performance. Solid support, that overworked phrase, is entirely fitting for Cecil Kellaway and John Sutton. But the real surprise is Alan Napier as Willie Spears. Not yet typecast in professorial and high society roles, Napier stumbles down the social ladder as the grimy, underhanded night watchman and seems to be having a grand time doing so.

Fueled by receptive reviews, box office grosses for *The Invisible Man Returns* were healthy. New York's Rialto Theater reported that ticket sales equaled that of *Tower of London,* their all-time record breaker of the previous season. The least humorous of the Invisible Man pictures, *The Invisible Man Returns* ironically spurred an aftermath of comedic opuses. The studio promptly followed it up with *The Invisible Woman.* In 1951, the film was semi-remade (with obvious alterations) as *Abbott and Costello Meet the Invisible Man.* With the title character rewritten as a boxer framed for murder, lengthy passages of Siodmak and Cole's dialogue were lifted almost verbatim, as well as a couple of Fulton's trick shots. Well past their prime, Bud and Lou's antics were growing tiresome and Arthur Franz, a limited, unappealing actor to begin with, made a glum and obnoxious protagonist. The 1940 *Invisible Man Returns* never looked better.

The Mummy's Hand (1940)

Released September 20, 1940. 67 minutes. *Directed by* Christy Cabanne. *Produced by* Ben Pivar. *Screenplay by* Griffin Jay & Maxwell Shane. *Original Story by* Griffin Jay. *Director of Photography:* Elwood Bredell. *Film Editor:* Philip Cahn. *Art Director:* Jack Otterson. *Associate Art Director:* Ralph M. DeLacy. *Music by* Frank Skinner & Hans J. Salter. *Musical Director:* Charles Previn. *Assistant Director:* Vaughn Paul. *Set Decorator:* Russell A. Gausman. *Sound Supervisor:* Bernard B. Brown. *Technician:* Charles Carroll. *Makeup by* Jack P. Pierce. *Gowns by* Vera West.

Dick Foran (Steve Banning), Peggy Moran (Marta Solvani), Wallace Ford (Babe Jenson), Eduardo Ciannelli (High Priest), George Zucco (Professor Andoheb), Cecil Kellaway (Tim Sullivan, a.k.a. The Great Solvani), Charles Trowbridge (Dr. Petrie), Tom Tyler (Kharis), Siegfried Arno (The Beggar), Eddie Foster (Egyptian), Harry Stubbs (Bartender), Michael Mark (Bazaar Owner), Mara Tartar (Girl), Leon Belasco (Ali), Frank Lackteen, Murdock MacQuarrie (Priests), Jerry Frank, Kenneth Terrell (Egyptian Thugs).

Eight years had passed since the Egyptian goddess Isis issued forth the lightning bolt that transformed Imhotep into a pile of dust and dried bones. The star-crossed romance between him and the Princess Anck-es-en-Amon, a love that bridged the centuries, had come to a bitter end. But it would take a whole lot more than the fury of the ancient gods to squelch a formula as potent as this one.

Having recently revived (with glowing results) two icons of the Laemmle era, Frankenstein's Monster and the Invisible Man, the top brass at the New Universal felt the time was ripe to resurrect the Egyptian heartthrobs, furnish them with new identities, and retread the Karl Freund classic as a streamlined B, geared less for connoisseurs of pure cinematic horror and more for the action and thrill seekers.

The result was *The Mummy's Hand,* a slick, competently produced chiller, tailor-made for the kiddie matinee trade. Its title menace, the withered Kharis, supplanted Karloff's urbane Imhotep as *the* Hollywood personification of the killer mummy, and the series of films in which he starred made tana leaves and the Curse of Amon-Ra a part of our American culture (and fodder for nightclub and television comics).

With a budget set at a tight $80,000, *The Mummy's Hand* went before "Woody" Bredell's cameras at the end of May, 1940. (*Man Made Monster,* which began production seven months later, also felt the bite of the accounting office.) Rampant cost-cutting is evidenced by the film's utilization of stock shots (chiefly from *The Mummy*), hand-me-down sets (most notably the extravagant temple set left over from James Whale's *Green Hell*), a musical score lifted almost entirely from *Son of Frankenstein,* a cast boasting no horror names (fifth-billed George Zucco hadn't yet become firmly established in the genre), and a Rush! Rush! shooting schedule that left little time for aesthetic nuance. Many lines of dialogue are very obviously redubbed and the whir of the camera can be heard in several scenes.

A former film editor turned producer, Ben Pivar was put in charge of production on *The Mummy's Hand.* The British moviemaker piloted more B chillers for Universal during this period that any of his peers. According to director Reginald LeBorg, Pivar was the epitome of the artless, noncreative studio executive: he holed himself up in his office, was often crude, and displayed occasional flashes of illiteracy.

A former associate of D.W. Griffith and Douglas Fairbanks whose reputable career soured with the advent of talkies, Christy Cabanne handled the directing chores on *The Mummy's Hand.* Cabanne's credits dated back to 1910 and included various engagements at RKO, Columbia, Goldwyn Studios, MGM, and such defunct outfits as FBO and Tiffany-Stahl. Undistinguished programmers such as *Mutiny on the Blackhawk* (1939) and *Scattergood Baines* (1941) kept the director active until his death in 1950. Cabanne's only other fantastic film credit is a dismal one: the atrocious 1947 Lugosi-Zucco starrer *Scared to Death.*

Production on *The Mummy's Hand* continued through mid-June. In order to maintain the picture's (approximate) two-week shooting schedule, Cabanne and Company had no choice but to put in plenty of overtime. Though her memory of the film is a bit fuzzy, Peggy Moran recalls the arduous shooting schedule:

> I had to be there at six to do hair and make-up, and we started shooting at eight. We had to do those late-night shots in the caves. They were all done on the backlot at Universal, and we would work sometimes from eight in the morning until four the next morning. They could do that with people like me because we were under contract. The law requires that outside talent only work for X-number of hours, but me they could work all the time!

Despite everyone's efforts, *The Mummy's Hand* ran slightly over schedule and $4,000 over the allotted budget. Universal's editorial department, which had been working to capacity on a full schedule of features, made a final cut of the film before the end of June.

Answering a sacred summons, Andoheb (George Zucco), noted Egyptologist and member of the secret religious sect of Karnak, arrives at the Temple of Karnak on the Hill of the Seven Jackals. The resident High Priest (Eduardo Ciannelli), his life slowly ebbing away, passes onto his successor a secret guarded for centuries by their royal den.

Three thousand years ago, the Princess Ananka, daughter of King Amenophis, sickened and died. She was worshipped by Kharis (Tom Tyler), a prince of the Royal House. Daring the anger of the ancient guards, Kharis stole a quantity of forbidden tana leaves. With a brew distilled from the leaves, Kharis knew he could bring his beloved Ananka back to life. But before the

George Zucco, the High Priest in *The Mummy's Hand*. (Photo courtesy Steve Jochsberger.)

sacrilegious act could be done, Kharis was seized by palace guards. For the sin he had committed, the prince was condemned to be buried alive. First, his tongue was cut out so his words wouldn't assail the ears of the gods. Then, he was wrapped in gauze and buried in an unmarked grave. Later, his coffin was unearthed by disciples of Ananka and sealed in a secret location on the other side of the mountain.

To Andoheb's amazement, the High Priest reveals that Kharis never really died, that he still rests in his tomb waiting to bring death to any who would defile Ananka's resting place. Turning over a supply of the ancient tana leaves to Andoheb, the High Priest instructs him that he must brew three tana leaves during the cycle of the full moon and feed the fluid to Kharis. But under no circumstances is Andoheb to feed Kharis more than *nine* leaves. "Should Kharis obtain a large amount of the fluid, he will become an uncontrollable monster, a soulless demon with the desire to kill and kill." His mission completed, the High Priest dies.

Back in bustling Cairo, Steve Banning (Dick Foran), an accomplished young archaeologist who has recently fallen on hard times, discovers a piece of pottery which bears a clue to the location of Ananka's tomb. He and his doubting sidekick Babe Jenson (Wallace Ford) take the find to Dr. Petrie (Charles Trowbridge) of the Cairo Museum. The exuberant professor verifies the pottery's authenticity but insists on conferring with his colleague for a third opinion. Petrie's associate is none other than Andoheb. The saturnine scientist dismisses the relic as a worthless imitation. According to Andoheb, two expeditions had already penetrated that region; they were never heard from again.

Steve isn't discouraged. With the financial backing of a Brooklyn magician named Solvani (Cecil Kellaway), Banning organizes an expedition. Accompanying him on the quest are Babe, Solvani, Solvani's cautiously cynical daughter Marta (Peggy Moran) and Petrie. Unbeknownst to them, Andoheb and his underling (Siegfried Arno) are several steps ahead of them, anticipating their every move.

A freak explosion uncovers a sealed entranceway in the side of the mountain which, Steve believes, may lead to the sarcophagus of the Princess. Instead, the party discovers the mummy of Kharis in a remarkable state of preservation.

Garbed in priestly robes, Andoheb drops in on Petrie while his colleague is making a minute examination of the Mummy. With a dosage of tana brew, Andoheb brings Kharis back to life. The resuscitated ancient Egyptian promptly strangles the horror-stricken professor to death.

Plotting to do away with the rest of the unbelievers, Andoheb orders his henchmen to place vials of tana brew in each of their tents. Solvani is nearly killed by the roving Kharis, who carries Marta away, disappearing with her through a hidden passageway in the mountain.

Splitting up in two different directions, Steve and Babe search for the Mummy. With Marta as his captive, Andoheb prepares an injection of the immortalizing tana fluid for himself and the girl. Babe arrives in the nick of time and engages in a gun battle with the High Priest. Mortally wounded, Andoheb is sent hurtling down the temple's stone steps.

Discovering the entranceway into the temple through a tunnel, Steve frees Marta and attempts to escape with her but finds his path blocked by Kharis. A flaming brazier destroys Kharis before he can obtain an overdose of the mind-bending tana brew. With the mummy out of the way, the Banning expedition tracks down the tomb of Ananka and returns to America with a treasure-trove of riches.

Lacking the brooding atmosphere and poetic beauty of the 1932 Karloff classic, *The Mummy's Hand* subs old-fashioned thrills and serial-flavored action, making for 67 minutes of brisk entertainment. Its conviviality and boisterous spirit (there's even a gratuitous *Seven Sinners*–style barroom brawl to keep the proceedings moving at a lively clip) reminds one of Universal's B action-adventure programmers of the period, starring the likes of Richard Arlen and Charles Bickford. Despite the somber, pseudomystical opening

Doing what a Universal leading lady does best, Peggy Moran swoons in the clutches of Kharis (Tom Tyler) in *The Mummy's Hand.*

scenes and the eerie Mummy passages, Griffin Jay and Maxwell Shane have kept the tone of their script light. The so-called scientific expedition into the forbidden Egyptian hills comes off as little more than an adventuresome treasure hunt. (*Variety*'s Hobe is right on the money when he describes Dick Foran and Wallace Ford as "a couple of Rover Boy archaeologists.")

While many horror buffs begrudgingly concede that *The Mummy's Hand* is the best of the Kharis films, they're quick to admit that this lightheartedness seriously damages the film's versimilitude. Luckily, Foran, Ford, Moran and Kellaway are such immensely likable players, we're inclined to overlook this misplaced joviality in a picture about ancient curses and an avenging mummy. The actors *appear* to be having a good time, and this carries over to the viewer. Peggy Moran found her three costars a pleasure to work with, describing Foran as "very nice and friendly" and Ford as "very funny always."

Kellaway's ham magician and Ford's Brooklynite buddy notwithstanding, the funniest bit in the picture is strictly unintentional. Dick Foran's burly archaeologist, credited with having played an important role in the discovery of such wonders as the Temple of the Sun in the Gobi Desert, the ancient Mayan cities, and the Inca ruins in Mexico, is so down on his luck he can't even land a halfway-decent staff job at the Scripps Museum!

All of the elements of the Mummy films that had become stale by the time *The Mummy's Curse* rolled around in 1945 were fresh and exciting in 1940. The extended flashback sequence from *The Mummy* depicting Imhotep's sacrilege was cleverly re-edited by Philip Cahn, who inserted new close-ups of Tom Tyler in place of Karloff's. (Boris can still be seen in the long shots.) This handsome montage has become so ingrained in the minds of horror fans, one immediately assumes it was revived in every sequel, when in fact it made just one more appearance (in *The Mummy's Curse*).

The Mummy's key to eternal life, tana leaves, was the invention of screenwriters Jay and Shane (who claimed the ancient Egyptians used them for embalming purposes). With the indoctrination of the leaves into the series came a whole set of ludicrous laws governing their use. For some unfathomable reason, the leaves must be brewed during the cycle of the full moon. Three leaves keep Kharis' heart beating; additional dosages sustain his strength and correct such physical malformations as a paralyzed arm and a lame leg (neither of which was ever healed despite ample slugs of the stuff over the course of three sequels). *The Mummy's Hand* toys with the threat of the Mummy's becoming an uncontrollable and indestructible monster should he obtain a dosage exceeding nine brewed tana leaves. This state of sublime menace never came to pass in the Kharis pictures, nor did it need to. Nourished with the recommended serving of tana fluid, the Mummy is nasty enough. Any further enhancement of his homicidal disposition would be akin to adding sweetener to an ice cream soda.

Christy Cabanne draws more eerie chills out of the Mummy than any of the directors that followed in his footsteps. Slipping in and out of shadowy passageways, stalking through moonlit forests, the 3,000-year-old walking dead man assumes the form of an ancient Grim Reaper meting out eternal punishment to trespassers. In the film's most satisfying moment, Zucco demonstrates the power of tana fluid by dribbling a small amount on the dormant Mummy's lips, and then asks Charles Trowbridge to check his pulse. The rhythmic beating of the Mummy's heart increases in intensity on the soundtrack; it culminates as Kharis opens his eyes. Locked in the Mummy's powerful grip, Trowbridge is choked (and frightened) to death as the camera catches the monster's sphinx-like stare.

Rugged B Western star Tom Tyler was a fine choice to play Kharis. (Tyler was the first of two cowboy stars—the other was Glenn Strange—to portray Universal monsters.) One of Republic's popular Three Mesquiteers and the star of the 1941 serial *Adventures of Captain Marvel,* the darkly handsome actor surpassed the portly Chaney in the role. Tyler's expressive eyes do wonders in bringing life to the part. Jack Pierce made up Tyler only for the close-ups, which were shot in one day. The rest of the time he wore a rubber mask.

In real life, Tom Tyler, despite his athletic build, was a large, clumsy individual, later plagued by the ravages of arthritis. Kharis was probably the only role where his extreme awkwardness benefitted his performance. Recalls Peggy Moran,

> I never met Tom Tyler without his make-up. I think he had to be at the studio at four in the morning. I never did meet Tyler otherwise, and he couldn't talk with that make-up on, so I never heard his voice. So as far as I was concerned, he really *was* the Mummy! And I was really a little afraid of him, especially at night, on the backlot, when he'd creep up on us. When he picked me up and started carrying me around, I had the eeriest feeling.

Iowa-born Peggy Moran was one of Universal's brightest (and busiest) ingenues, appearing in no less than 22 productions over a period of just four years. Her wholesome good looks and sprightly charm were an asset to a variety of pictures including lively comedies (*One Night in the Tropics; Hello, Sucker*), B Westerns (*West of Carson City, Trail of the Vigilantes*) and homespun musicals (the Deanna Durbin vehicles *First Love* and *Spring Parade,* both of which were directed by Peggy's future husband, Henry Koster). Their marriage in October, 1942, signalled the end of the actress' brief screen career.

Peggy Moran delivers a worthy performance in *The Mummy's Hand:* her worldly-wise, no-nonsense attitude is in sharp contrast to that of her gullible father, well-played by the always delightful Cecil Kellaway. But it was George Zucco who plays the most interesting character in the film. Andoheb is introduced to the audience with almost the same aura of mystery as Kharis himself. Bespectacled, dark complexioned, and wearing a native fez, the aloof, professorial-looking gentleman is first glimpsed disembarking from a train in a bustling Cairo depot, seemingly oblivious to the throngs milling about him. Riding camelback through the desert and back country, Andoheb arrives at the imposing Temple of Karnak in the Valley of the Seven Jackals to lay claim to his holy position. It isn't until later that we learn Andoheb is affiliated with the Cairo Museum, for the chief purpose, it seems, of dissuading expeditions from entering the forbidden valley. From all indications, Andoheb is the first Karnakian disciple to unleash the Mummy on the heads of unbelievers. (Less than a week before *The Mummy's Hand* went into production, Universal was seeking to cast Peter Lorre in the film, presumably in the Andoheb role.)

Though for every *Dead Men Walk* and *The Flying Serpent,* there are three or four movies in the *Joan of Arc* and *Arise, My Love* class, it's George Zucco's B horrors that have earned the polished actor cinematic immortality. Following an appearance in 20th Century–Fox's *David and Bathsheba* in 1951, Zucco's career came to an abrupt halt. He fell ill and was committed to a sanitorium

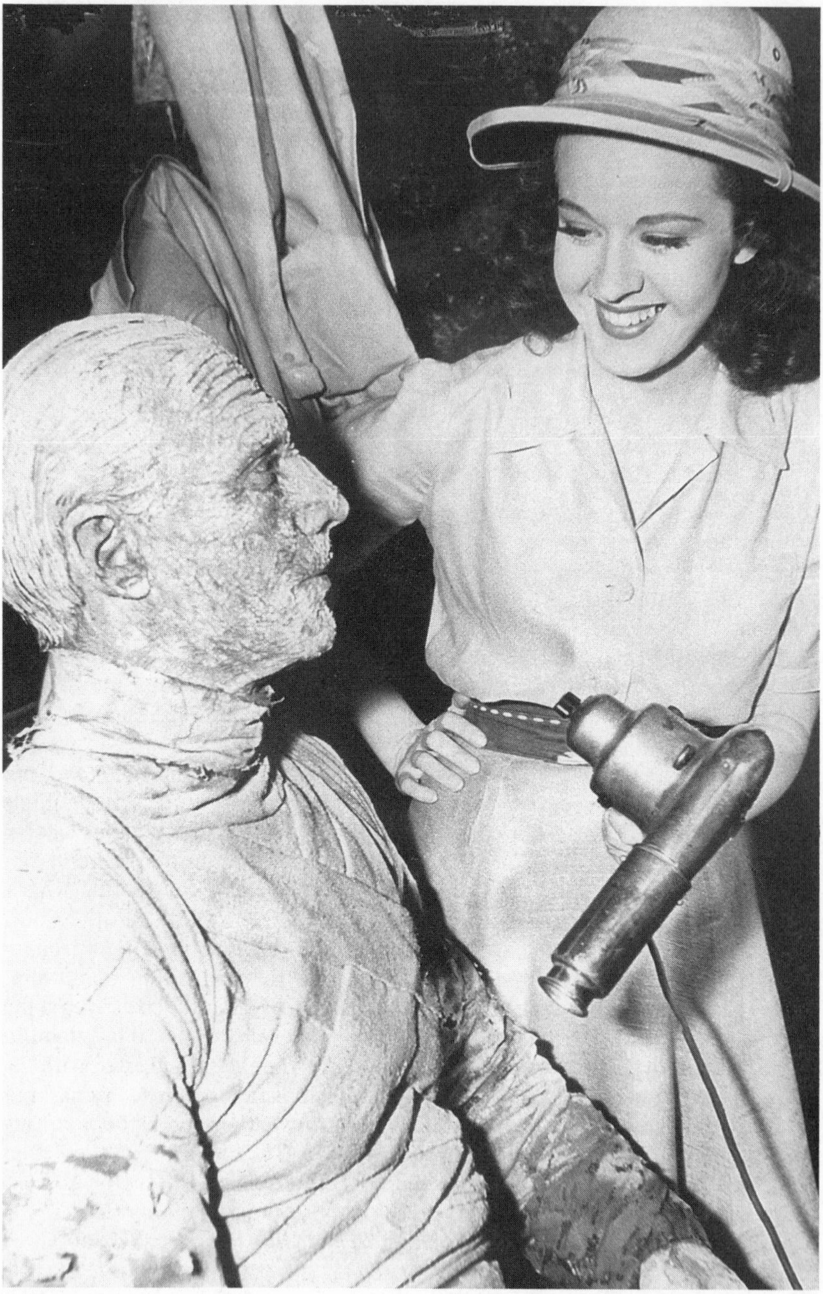

Peggy Moran, toting a portable drier, offers Tom Tyler a bit of relief between takes on *The Mummy's Hand*.

in South San Gabriel, California, where he died at age 74 on May 28, 1960. Kenneth Anger's highly speculative account of the actor's illness in *Hollywood Babylon II* claims Zucco had become a raving lunatic and spent his last days in the proverbial padded cell. Tragically, his 29-year-old daughter Frances died 20 months to the day after her father. (She had a short run in pictures, appearing in *Never Wave at a WAC* [1952] and one or two others.)

Actors like Zucco, Lionel Atwill, Dwight Frye and Conrad Veidt have a certain mystique. They all passed on before the galvanized forces of fantastic fandom had the chance to interview them firsthand. Consequently, we must content ourselves with the reminiscences of survivors of the Golden Age of Hollywood to ascertain what these people were like off-camera. As Bulldog Drummond, John Howard waged an on-screen battle with an especially dastardly George Zucco in Paramount's *Arrest Bulldog Drummond* (1939). Almost half a century later, Howard has this to say about his costar:

> George Zucco was a strange fellow but awfully nice. Completely different from the characters he always played. He wasn't the slightest bit menacing at all. He was a pussycat. It was as though he had a dark secret he didn't want anyone to know about.

Howard also revealed a little-known fact about Zucco. Like Harold Lloyd, he lost two fingers off his right hand and always wore a glove to conceal the disfigurement.

Fifties exploitation film producer/author Alex Gordon recalled the day he visited Zucco in his room at the sanitorium and offered the ailing actor the mad scientist role (eventually played by Tom Conway) in American International's *Voodoo Woman* (1957). Gordon had previously been told by Zucco's agent that the old trouper's career was through, but an offer to go back to work might cheer him up. Zucco graciously declined Gordon's offer, explaining that he didn't wish to appear in any more horror pictures. Perhaps old George was hoping for a vehicle worthier of his talents than the tawdry AIP film.

When Universal got around to producing the second Kharis film, *The Mummy's Tomb,* it not only carried over the storyline and two of the key characters from *The Mummy's Hand,* but a sizable percentage of that film's footage for flashback purposes. By spicing up *The Mummy's Tomb* with some of the best moments from the 1940 film, horror buffs of the postwar decade got a taste of a movie deprived them. For some unaccountable reason (a bookkeeping oversight or a legal problem), *The Mummy's Hand* was passed up when Universal sold its package of vintage shockers to Film Classics and Realart for theatrical reissue in the late '40s/early '50s.

The Invisible Woman (1940)

Released December 27, 1940. 70 minutes. *Directed by* A. Edward Sutherland. *Associate Producer:* Burt Kelly. *Screenplay by* Robert Lees, Frederic I. Rinaldo & Gertrude Purcell. *Original Story by* Kurt [Curt] Siodmak & Joe May. *Suggested by the character created by* H.G. Wells. *Director of Photography:* Elwood Bredell. *Special Photographic Effects:* John P. Fulton. *Art Director:* Jack Otterson. *Associate Art Director:* Richard H. Riedel. *Film Editor:* Frank Gross. *Musical Director:* Charles Previn. *Sound Supervisor:* Bernard B. Brown. *Technician:* Joe Lapis. *Set Decorator:* Russell A. Gausman. *Assistant Director:* Joseph McDonough. *Gowns by* Vera West.

Virginia Bruce (Kitty Carroll), John Barrymore (Professor Gibbs), John Howard (Dick Russell), Charlie Ruggles (George), Oscar Homolka (Blackie Cole), Edward Brophy (Bill), Donald MacBride (Foghorn), Charles Lane (Growley), Thurston Hall (John Hudson), Margaret Hamilton (Mrs. Jackson), Mary Gordon (Mrs. Bates), Anne Nagel (Jean), Maria Montez (Marie), Shemp Howard (Hammerhead/Frankie), Kathryn Adams (Peggy), Kitty O'Neill (Mrs. Patton), Eddie Conrad (Hernandez), Kay Leslie (Model), Kay Linaker, Sarah Edwards (Fashion Show Buyers), Harry C. Bradley (Want Ad Man), Kernan Cripps (Postman).

The success of *The Invisible Man Returns* encouraged Universal to take further advantage of their screen rights to the H.G. Wells novel. James Whale flirted with the comic possibilities of the Invisible Man; Hal Roach pushed his invisibility gags to the limit in the 1937 *Topper.* After the humorless *The Invisible Man Returns,* the time seemed ripe for an all-out farce, especially since the studio seemed most at home with lightweight fare at this time. With the added titillation of a sex role reversal thrown in, *The Invisible Woman* was eagerly announced.

Curt Siodmak was signed to develop the idea in March, 1940, but by May, veteran comedy writers Fred Rinaldo and Robert Lees were brought in to write a more conventional, slapstick-heavy script. After being burned by the costly budget overruns of the last sequel, a more realistic budget of $300,000 was allotted for the production. By Universal's standards, *The Invisible Woman* was a major attraction calling for a top cast of outside talent.

An exception was Margaret Sullavan who was earmarked for the title role. Sullavan never made the front ranks of box office stars despite being one of the subtlest, most intelligent Hollywood actresses. She still owed Universal a picture under her contract stemming back to the Laemmle days when she was directed by the likes of William Wyler and Frank Borzage. *The Invisible*

Woman might have been the new management's idea of a major release, but Sullavan saw little glory in appearing in a baggy-pants burlesque, especially with more enticing roles in the offing.

When Sullavan failed to report to Universal for *The Invisible Woman,* she was slapped with a restraining order preventing her from working elsewhere. The squabble was resolved after tempers cooled: Sullavan ended up fulfilling her contract with a remake of the Fannie Hurst sudser *Back Street* (1941). Universal tapped Virginia Bruce as her replacement on *The Invisible Woman,* signing the former Metro contractee on September 12.

John Barrymore, selected for the role of Professor Gibbs, a batty old geezer of a genius who tinkers together an invisibility machine, couldn't afford to be choosy. The once-legendary actor, now a sad parody of himself, had become *persona non grata* at most Hollywood studios and was exploited by B picture-makers to give their product a touch of respectability.

Adding to Barrymore's predicament was his worsening inability to memorize dialogue. John Howard, the romantic lead of *The Invisible Woman* and Barrymore's costar in Paramount's Bulldog Drummond series, remembers a few tricks the actor used to remedy his problem:

> He developed, with my help, a system of cutting up the script and putting it down on the set: behind vases, behind phones, on the *backs* of other actors, whatever. This way he could just look around and find the lines. And of course he was such a superlative actor it looked as though this was an inspirational way to *say* the lines! It worked very well, but it must have driven him nuts—he must have realized what was happening to him and I felt terribly sorry about that.
>
> Barrymore was an ordinary fellow. He wasn't stuffy and he had no pretense whatsoever. Even in pictures that you felt weren't up to snuff, I don't think he showed any disdain. We knew perfectly well *The Invisible Woman* wasn't going to be an award-winning picture, but it was fun to do. No one took it seriously; we took it seriously as a *picture,* but it was obviously designed to entertain rather than to make people think.

The Looney Tunes mood of the film is set from the first scene as an elegantly-attired butler (Charlie Ruggles), for no discernible reason, takes a pratfall down a flight of stairs. With this easy laugh out of the way, *The Invisible Woman* embarks on its dubious way.

Professor Gibbs (John Barrymore) is a dotty old inventor who perfects an invisibility machine, financed by millionaire lawyer Dick Russell (John Howard). He selects fashion model Kitty Carroll (Virginia Bruce) to be the first guinea pig. The experiment is an unqualified success but Kitty has plans of her own. Wasting no time, she gives her miserly, slave-driving boss Mr. Growley (Charles Lane) his well-deserved comeuppance.

While Professor Gibbs and the invisible Kitty pay a visit to Dick's lodge, Blackie Cole (Oscar Homolka), a gangster on the lam in Mexico, sends his battery of dimwitted thugs after the scientist's invisibility machine. Reassembling the apparatus at the hideaway, the fumbling fools can't get it to work. The gang kidnaps the now-visible Kitty and Gibbs, with Dick hot on their trail. Kitty,

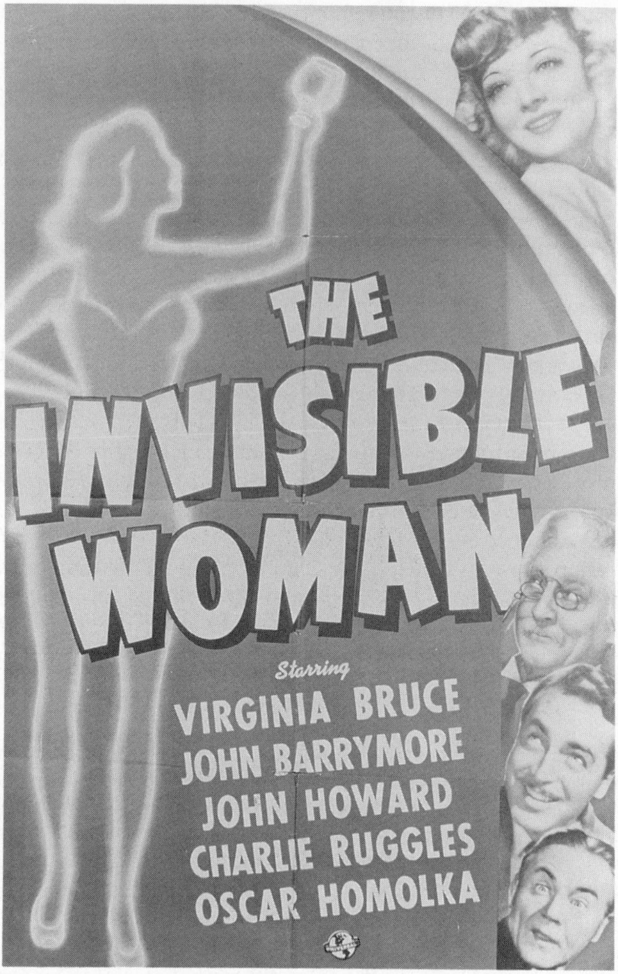

Would you believe Margaret Sullavan was Universal's first choice to play the vivacious *Invisible Woman*?

has learned that alcohol will revert her back to invisibility again, manages to sneak a drink and, with Dick's aid, overpowers her abductors.

A clever postscript brings the characters up to date a few years later. Now married, Dick and Kitty are fawning over their newborn son when the tot begins to fade. Gibbs suspiciously eyes the kid's rubbing alcohol and knowingly concludes, "Hereditary!"

The Invisible Woman is a typical low-brow comedy of the period. What it lacks in wit and sophistication, it makes up for in spirit, a galloping, madcap pace, a game cast, and an occasional funny line. The film was obviously geared for the mass consumption of a working-class audience—who got their money's worth.

The Invisible Woman plays out the middle class fantasies of a rags-to-riches Cinderella of a heroine who uses her newfound invisibility to exact a playful vengeance on snobs and bullies. Snooty butlers, petty crooks and a monstrous caricature of a sadistic boss fall victim to her pranks. Times have changed, but it's hard to believe that this trifle was considered mildly risqué when it was released. *The Invisible Woman* now seems more cartoonish than anything else.

Virginia Bruce is a pretty package of charm and energy in the title role. Although rarely materializing on the screen, her wonderfully melodious diction marks well her presence. John Howard smoothly plays millionaire playboy Dick Russell, a role he found particularly challenging:

> The thing that was difficult for me was that I had to work opposite *nobody,* to talk to a non-existent person. The first time I mentioned this to a reporter, he said, "Well, that's no different from just doing a scene with anybody who's not there and *that* happens all the time in pictures." But it's *not* the same, it really isn't. There's a kind of funny transition that you have to make, and I think it's a different technique in a sense.
>
> For instance, how can I kiss an invisible hand if it isn't there? Am I going to look as though I'm *pretending* to kiss an invisible hand? That would throw the whole picture out of kilter. I have no experience in life that deals with this sort of thing. Of course, the director is no help with it 'cuz *he* doesn't know, either!

John Barrymore was near the end of his life and at the nadir of his career, though Universal's publicity mill continued to play him up as the Great Matinee Idol and his hamming was reverently cited as "a notable acting triumph." Once America's most distinguished actor, Barrymore overplays like mad, but one can guiltily enjoy the audaciousness of his performance.

A studio press release insisted that Barrymore was delighted with his role and quotes him as telling the director, "It's a relief to play a straight role for a change" after playing so many madcap comedy parts. Obviously, the author of this publicity quip never bothered to see the film.

The supporting cast abounds with familiar faces. Charlie Ruggles, playing the much put-upon butler, comes off as the funniest. Only the sharpest eye will be able to spot Maria Montez (on her way up) and Anne Nagel (on her way down) in bit parts. Crack stunt work adds to the fun and includes some skillfully executed pratfalls and tumbles off ladders and down staircases.

More than 45 years after *The Invisible Woman* was released, John Howard recalled a particularly hazardous feat during the climactic rescue scene: "One stunt that blew my mind was when the stunt man dove into the fish pond which actually *was* a fish pond. That thing was only about three feet deep! I used to do a lot of shallow diving but I wouldn't have done that one for the love of money." (The stunt man looks like he might be Dave Sharpe.)

Technically, *The Invisible Woman* is expertly handled with John P. Fulton's now-familiar special effects again taking the spotlight, though there are not enough to carry the film. (Fulton's effects were once again Oscar-nominated.) Today the film's appeal is decidedly limited but the *Hollywood Babylon* crowd will take a snickering, gleefully sadistic delight in Barrymore's near-senile playing. It's a good bet for *aficionados* of vintage comedies (Leonard Maltin rates the film quite favorably) who'll appreciate the roster of veteran laugh-getters going through their paces. Horror and science fiction fans, on the other hand, will be laughing least.

For those who cherish the memory of the James Whale classic, *The Invisible Woman* is a minor desecration. As a lampoon, it's harmless enough and stands up better than the over-the-hill *Abbott and Costello Meet the Invisible Man,* released a decade later. H.G. Wells, who was generously paid, again receives screen credit for being the inspiration of this confection. His sole contribution was to sit back and watch one of his most renowned novels being shoved through the meat grinder.

Not quite ready to take the Invisible Man theme out of the province of clowns, comedians and aging vaudevillians, Universal used it as a throw-away gag in Olsen and Johnson's relentlessly overstuffed *Hellzapoppin',* released in 1941.

Man Made Monster (1941)

Released March 28, 1941. Rereleased by Realart as *Atomic Monster.* 59 minutes. *Directed by* George Waggner. *Associate Producer:* Jack Bernhard. *Screenplay by* Joseph West (George Waggner). *Based on the story "The Electric Man" by* Harry J. Essex, Sid Schwartz and Len Golos. *Director of Photography:* Elwood Bredell. *Art Director:* Jack Otterson. *Associate Art Director:* Harold H. MacArthur. *Film Editor:* Arthur Hilton. *Music by* Hans J. Salter. *Musical Director:* Charles Previn. *Special Photography:* John P. Fulton. *Set Decorator:* Russell A. Gausman. *Sound Supervisor:* Bernard B. Brown. *Technician:* Charles Carroll. *Makeup by* Jack P. Pierce. *Gowns by* Vera West.

Lionel Atwill (Dr. Paul Rigas), Lon Chaney, Jr. ("Dynamo" Dan McCormick), Anne Nagel (June Lawrence), Frank Albertson (Mark Adams), Samuel S. Hinds (Dr. John Lawrence), William B. Davidson (District Attorney Ralph B. Stanley), John Dilson (Medical Examiner), Frank O'Connor (Detective), Ben Taggart (Detective Sergeant Regan), Russell Hicks (Warden Harris), Connie Bergen (Nurse), George Meader (Dr. Bruno), Chester Gan (Wong), Ivan Miller (Doctor), Douglas Evans (Police Radio Announcer), Byron Foulger (Second Alienist), William Hall (Mike), Victor Zimmerman (Dynamo Operator), Gary Breckner (Radio Announcer), John Ellis (Assistant D.A.), Wright Kramer (Judge), Mel Ruick (Defense Attorney), Paul Scott (Minister), David Sharpe (Stunts), Francis Sayles (Frank Davis), Jessie Arnold (Mrs. Davis), Jack Gardner (Reporter), James Blaine (Charlie), Lowell Drew (Foreman of Jury), Bob Reeves (Guard).

Man Made Monster is a pivotal Universal horror film. It's not especially well-produced; in fact, it's far from the best that the studio was capable of making. But it introduced two of the most important figures to emerge from Universal in the '40s—Lon Chaney, Jr., and George Waggner.

A former pre-med student, George Waggner came to Hollywood in 1920 as an actor and writer. He landed a role in *The Sheik* (1921) starring Rudolph Valentino and played Buffalo Bill in John Ford's *The Iron Horse* (1924). His acting career floundered but he plugged away at various writing assignments and tried his hand at songwriting when the talkies came in. Frequently using the name Joseph West, he penned several long-forgotten potboilers at Monogram with titles like *Laughing at Danger, Son of the Navy* and *Phantom of Chinatown* (all 1940). He turned to directing in the late '30s and amassed over two dozen credits (mostly cheap Westerns), six of which were made for Universal in 1938.

Shooting to stardom with his performance as Lennie Small, the ironically named gentle giant in John Steinbeck's *Of Mice and Men* (1939), Lon Chaney, Jr.'s arrival at Universal was impeccably timed. The studio was in need of a marketable horror name as Boris Karloff was forsaking Hollywood for the allure of Broadway. Chaney seemed to fit the bill perfectly. A conspicuous, heart-wrenching role, Lennie almost couldn't be played badly and was an ideal showcase for any young actor. Although cynics insist that Lennie was Chaney's *only* good performance, one can't ignore the fact that the searing climax in which the hulking dimwit is shot by his friend George (Burgess Meredith) before the lynch mob arrives was immeasurably aided by Lewis Milestone's sensitive direction and Aaron Copland's rapturous music.

Despite the exploitable Chaney name, young Lon proved to be better suited for rough-and-tumble Westerns and action pictures than for Gothic roles. Then there were problems with Lon himself. The strapping six-foot, three-inch actor was no milquetoast and openly flaunted the spikey side of his personality. His drinking both on and off the set became well known (and in a few years, his once-handsome features quickly dissipated).

The flabby, gin-soaked character actor of the '50s to the '70s contrasted sharply with the trim, athletic Chaney who walked onto the Universal soundstage on the first day of shooting Universal's newest shocker (December 9, 1940). Chaney was about to embark on a major horror career and yet the studio hardly gave him a suitable build-up. On the contrary, *The Mysterious Dr. R* (*Man Made Monster*'s shooting title) was strictly a low-budget affair. With an estimated budget of $86,000, it was one of the most cheaply made films on the lot in spite of a generous three week shooting schedule and some complex trick shots.

Man Made Monster arose from the ashes of the unmade Karloff/Lugosi starrer *The Man in the Cab,* based on the story "The Electric Man" which Universal bought on August 1, 1935. The studio had lost interest in that project; it was possibly shelved in favor of the somewhat similar *The Invisible Ray.* The original yarn was cowritten by Harry J. Essex who intended it as a movie treatment while he was still a reporter on *The New York Daily Mirror.* Essex recently remarked,

> Sidney Schwartz, who also wrote for the paper, and Len Golos, a press agent, and I were bouncing story ideas around, and I came up with the notion to do a thing called "The Electric Man." It was based on a true story I read about: a government organization was performing tests on electricity and the human body, how much we use up throughout the day and how we "recharge the batteries" by sleep at night. Out of that was born the idea of "The Electric Man"—if there *was* some way to recharge the body's electricity, we wouldn't have to eat or sleep. The story was submitted to an agency, and sold to Universal. We didn't get much money for it at the time, I think we got something like $3,300, but it was my first big sale.

When Universal revived the project in 1940, it assigned George Waggner to direct the film and rewrite the script. Using his pseudonym Joseph West, Waggner changed the title to *The Human Robot,* polished up the rough edges, and submitted the finished screenplay for approval. On November 27, 1941, he was signed to direct the film.

Lionel Atwill was a natural choice for what was essentially the lead role as the loony Dr. Rigas. The portly actor had just left 20th Century–Fox and was about to enter the field of independent production, having bought the rights to the novel *The Dark River*. Atwill was eager to sign up his old friend and neighbor James Whale to direct. In the meantime, he picked up whatever fast money he could by appearing in Universal's penny-dreadfuls, unaware that this type of fare would soon be his main source of income. Atwill's infamous Christmas Eve orgy took place at his Pacific Palisades home just as *Man Made Monster* was wrapping up production. The scandal that erupted permanently short-circuited his acting career and cancelled his aspirations of becoming an independent producer.

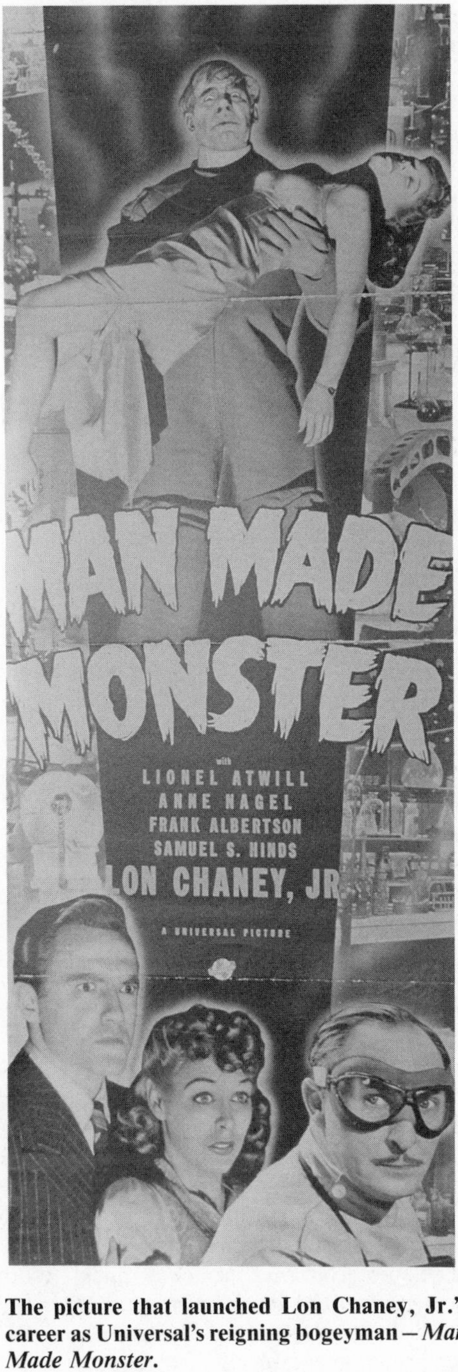

The picture that launched Lon Chaney, Jr.'s career as Universal's reigning bogeyman—*Man Made Monster*.

Man Made Monster benefits from a well-constructed plot that wastes little time in getting underway. A bus speeding across a rain-swept highway veers out of control and crashes into a high-voltage tower. The accident leaves five people electrocuted. The lone survivor, Dan McCormick (Lon Chaney, Jr.), escapes uninjured. Dr. John Lawrence (Samuel S. Hinds), a noted electrobiologist, suggests that Dan, who had exploited his "immunity" to electrical shock in a phony carnival act, may in fact be impervious to high voltage current. The scientist invites Dan to his country estate for observation. There Dan meets Lawrence's pretty niece June (Anne Nagel), and his obsessive associate, Dr. Rigas (Lionel Atwill).

Rigas sees Dan as the perfect guinea pig in his efforts to spawn a race of electrically-automated supermen, a pet project that has been a source of derision to his colleagues, including Lawrence. Secretly, Rigas experiments on Dan, sending tremendous surges of current into his body until he becomes dependent on electricity for strength. Soon Dan becomes a super-charged monster completely subject to Rigas' will. Lawrence learns of what has been going on in the lab and threatens to call the police. On Rigas' order, Dan pounces upon the scientist, breaking his neck in the struggle. Dan, returning back to normal, is convicted of the crime and condemned to die.

Strapped in the electric chair, Dan is "recharged" by the high voltage and once again becomes a human dynamo. He kills the warden (Russell Hicks) during his flight and heads for Rigas' lab. Finding the crazed scientist about to try out his electrical apparatus on June, Dan kills Rigas with his deadly grasp and, donning an insulating rubber suit, disappears into the moors with June unconscious in his arms. The electrical man tries to tear through a fence, but the razor-sharp barbs rip through his protective suit. As the power races out of his body, Dan's life slowly ebbs away and he collapses dead.

Man Made Monster is about as basic a horror film as one can get. Perhaps that's why it's such a hard film to dislike. It's fast-moving, unpretentious and entirely predictable. There isn't a single character that isn't a cliche, from the smart-ass newspaper reporter/hero to the lunatic scientist. It's the kind of shocker that Monogram and PRC regularly churned out, yet the style is distinctly Universal. *Man Made Monster* has a drive and crispness sorely lacking in the drab, flea-bag Poverty Row quickies. In fact, it has the cocky charm of a '30s Warner Bros. programmer with its slam-bang opening scene of the bus crash and the instant introduction of all the main characters within the first few minutes.

Man Made Monster has a few surface similarities to *The Invisible Ray:* both pictures showcase a man/monster who strikes his victims down with a mere touch, and both utilize John P. Fulton's eerily effective glowing man effects. *Man Made Monster* fits neatly into the streamlined, modernist mode of the '40s. The Gothic look of the old Frankenstein lab has been replaced by Eric Wybrow's state-of-the-art equipment which would become a fixture in many of the studio's forthcoming horror movies.

Clocking in at just under an hour, *Man Made Monster* is an extremely well-structured little picture. The opening scenes are lightweight and amiable; not even the electrocution deaths of the anonymous bus crash victims dampen the high spirits of our jovial players. The audience's identification with "Dynamo" Dan McCormick is quickly established with his easy-going, teddy bear charm. The vaguely European Dr. Rigas, voicing withering contempt for the little people, and his Master Race dream of creating electrically-powered supermen, telegraphs the tragic outcome of the plot. The groundwork of the

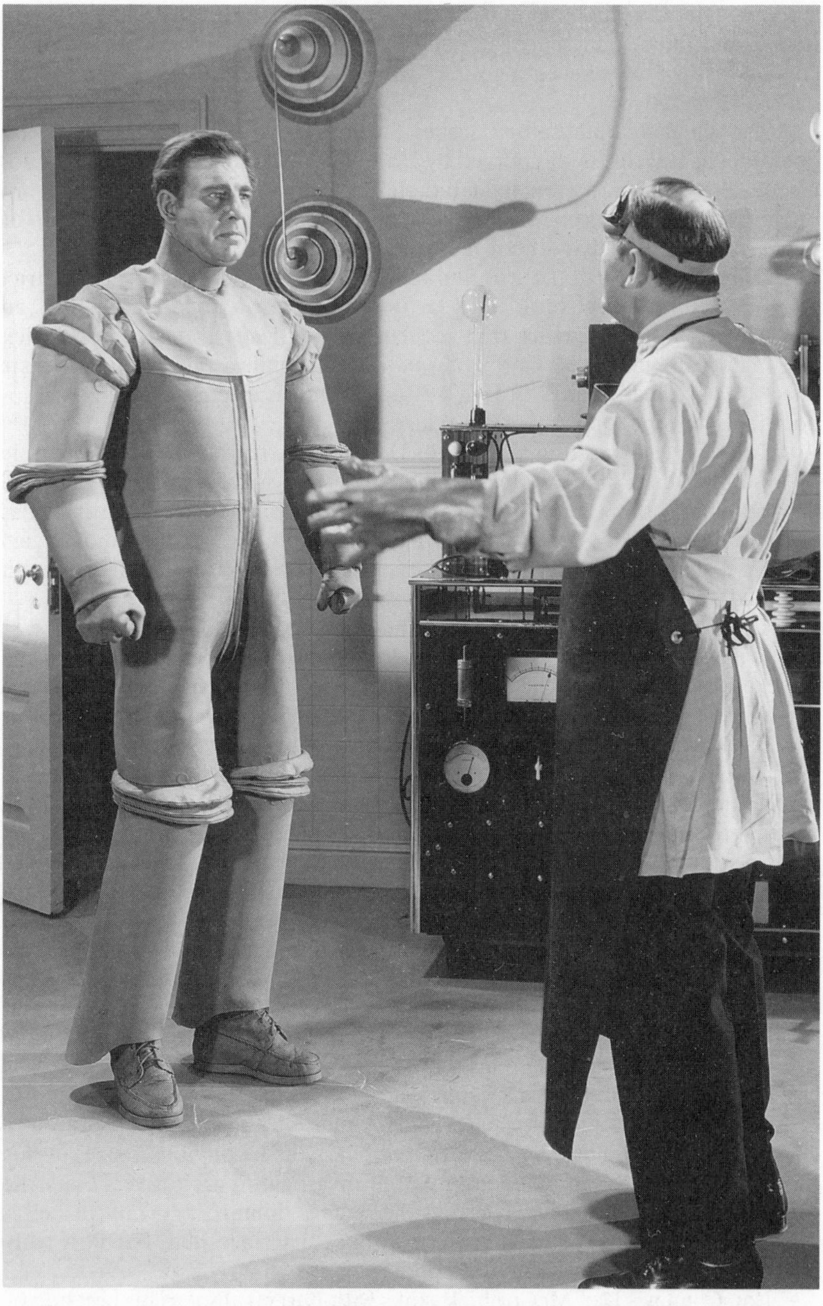

"The worker of the future! Electrically alive! Every impulse controlled by me!" Lon Chaney, Jr., and Lionel Atwill in *Man Made Monster*.

story is carefully laid out in a deliberately-paced first half. Dan's gradual transformation is punctuated visually by photographer Elwood Bredell's increased use of low-keyed lighting, which complements the script's ever-darkening mood.

The climactic laboratory scenes, with Rigas' high voltage hardware operating at full tilt, is well served by Hans J. Salter's unrelenting, crescendo-laden score. As Rigas raises the lab table, the camera closes in on a tight shot of Dan in full transformation, his neon head and arms throbbing in a halo of light. It's a beautifully-realized moment.

Only the mid-section of the film falters, with a stolidly-performed district attorney and his detective sidekick lazily conducting an investigation, and an awkwardly slapped-together trial sequence. *Man Made Monster* shifts back into high gear again as McCormick walks the "last mile." But, alas, good taste raises its ugly head, reducing Dan's escape from the electric chair to a disappointingly abrupt, off-camera episode.

There is compensating mayhem as Dan brings a festive moonlight hayride to a sudden halt; the walking dynamo's electric surge passes through the driver's whip, killing him on the spot. Fulton's special effects wizardry is, at times, *too* generous: all of Dan's victims (with the curious exception of Rigas) light up like fireflies the instant they are struck. It's a good shock effect (no pun intended), but an unnecessary one.

The cast was chosen along predictable lines. Frank Albertson, usually cast as the high-hearted second lead, is true-to-form as the newspaper man. Anne Nagel, the gun moll in *Black Friday,* is back to playing the good girl again. Samuel S. Hinds as Dr. Lawrence is kindly, silver-haired and professorial.

The dark side of science is again represented with crackling authority by Lionel Atwill as Dr. Rigas. The actor's well-calculated horror film performances in pictures like *Doctor X* (1932), *Mystery of the Wax Museum* and *The Vampire Bat* (both 1933), though restrained at the outset, slowly revealed the actor's inner demons as his characters unfurled. By the last reel, his ravings carried an unspoken sexual charge that was uniquely Atwill's. His presence gave pictures like *Man Made Monster* and the upcoming *The Mad Doctor of Market Street* an edgy intensity lacking in, for instance, a comparable George Zucco vehicle like *The Mad Ghoul.* He would have made the ideal Count Zaroff in *The Most Dangerous Game* (1932), lasciviously eying Fay Wray, and mouthing the classic line, "Hunt first the animal, and then the woman!" In the '40s, Atwill threw himself into his horror roles with even greater abandon. His Dr. Rigas ranks as the actor's hammiest.

Even in his "straight" scenes, Atwill overacts outrageously. Introduced to Chaney, Atwill's handshake is a little *too* hearty as he obviously sizes up his future guinea pig. One wonders how the investigating detective misses the demented gleam in Atwill's eye as he invites him to try out his electrophotostatic table. As Forry Ackerman once described him, Atwill is truly "the maddest doctor of them all."

Lon Chaney's Dan McCormick ranks with Larry Talbot as his best horror performance (at least we're not asked to believe he's the son of a titled Englishman). Perhaps because it was his first horror role, Chaney tried a little harder to convey pathos through Jack Pierce's greasepaint. In his early scenes, Chaney gets to the heart of Dan: he's a big, good-natured, decent guy, exactly the sort we'd like to think Lon actually was in real life. He's a bit forced going "cold turkey" off Atwill's high voltage treatments, and in a sudden, climactic outburst during a battering psychiatric cross-examination. Otherwise, Chaney is near-perfect.

Lon's performance prompted Universal to reward him with an exclusive, long-term contract upon completion of the film. For his services, Chaney was paid a modest $500 per week for a one year period; however, it wasn't long before his salary escalated. Director-writer Waggner didn't fare badly with Universal, either. On the basis of *Man Made Monster* and its companion feature *Horror Island,* Waggner secured a seven-year contract with the studio and went on to produce some of their most lavish pictures.

In his unflinching admiration for Lionel Atwill, the reliable William K. Everson accorded *Man Made Monster* an entire chapter in his landmark volume, *Classics of the Horror Film.* Actually, the picture isn't much better than *Black Friday* or *The Ghost of Frankenstein.* Universal's miserly production values are often infuriating. Hans J. Salter wrote a good deal of original music and a particularly arresting theme, only to pilfer the main title from *The Invisible Man Returns* for the opening credits. In spite of its penny-pinching demeanor, *Man Made Monster* delivers the goods as a modest, well-paced thriller.

Horror Island (1941)

Released March 28, 1941. 60 minutes. A Ben Pivar Production. *Directed by* George Waggner. *Associate Producer:* Jack Bernhard. *Screenplay by* Maurice Tombragel & Victor McLeod. *Based on the story "Terror of the South Seas" by* Alex Gottlieb. *Director of Photography:* Elwood Bredell. *Camera Operator:* Walter Strenge. *Assistant Director:* Seward Webb. *Film Editor:* Otto Ludwig. *Art Director:* Jack Otterson. *Associate Art Director:* Ralph M. DeLacy. *Musical Director:* Hans J. Salter. *Set Decorator:* Russell A. Gausman. *Sound Supervisor:* Bernard B. Brown. *Technician:* Jess Moulin. *Gowns by* Vera West.

Dick Foran (Bill Martin), Leo Carrillo (Tobias Clump), Peggy Moran (Wendy Creighton), Fuzzy Knight (Stuff Oliver), John Eldredge (George Martin), Lewis Howard (Thurman Coldwater), Hobart Cavanaugh (Professor Jasper Quinley), Walter Catlett (Sergeant McGoon), Ralf Harolde (Rod "Killer" Grady), Iris Adrian (Arlene Grady), Foy Van Dolsen (Panama Pete/The Phantom), Emmett Vogan (The Stranger), Walter Tetley (Delivery Boy), Eddy Chandler (Cop), Ed Parker, Dale Van Sickel, John Burton (Stunts).

Devised to support *Man Made Monster* on the second half of a double bill, *Horror Island* is the quintessential kiddie matinee crowd pleaser, concocted according to a fool-proof formula. Combine in equal measure one part chills-and-mystery and one part adventure; add a dash of romance; season it with humor, and simmer for about an hour. It's guaranteed to go down easy and not leave any aftertaste.

Made on a meager $93,000 budget, *Horror Island* is a modest entertainment that just misses the mark. We're inclined to reserve our critical sensibilities and play along with this good-natured romp for half of its length before the whole affair wears thin and becomes too silly for its own good. Most of the daily news critics and industry film reviewers shrugged off *Horror Island* as a mere trifle, no more, no less. *Variety,* however, came down on the film quite harshly, calling it "fourth rate" and "ridiculous."

Starring in his second horror picture in less than a year, Dick Foran plays Bill Martin, a Princeton grad who can't seem to pass muster in the business world. (Foran seems a little too old to be playing an out-of-work college grad, but his easy-going, affable personality compensates for this miscasting.) Searching for the perfect get-rich-quick scheme, Bill and his partner Stuff Oliver (Fuzzy Knight) join forces with peg-legged Spanish seaman Tobias Clump (Leo Carrillo), affectionately nicknamed the Skipper. The salty mariner

The ghostly visage of the Phantom hovers over Morgan's Castle in this spirited poster for *Horror Island*.

owns one half of an ancient map which, he claims, pinpoints the location of a treasure valued at $20,000,000 in Spanish gold and royal jewels. The other half of the map was stolen by a black-caped figure whom the Skipper refers to as the Phantom (Foy Van Dolsen).

Although Bill doesn't believe in the existence of the treasure, he sees gold dust on the horizon anyway. Why not arrange touristy treasure hunts on Morgan's Island off the Florida coast? (The property was left to Bill by his grandfather.) Gearing up the island's 400-year-old pirate castle with a variety of spook trappings, Bill leaves port with his first boatload of eager weekenders. The guest list includes heiress Wendy Creighton (Peggy Moran), her fortune-hunting suitor, Thurman Coldwater (Lewis Howard), escaped con Rod "Killer" Grady (Ralf Harolde) and his wife Arleen (Iris Adrian), Sergeant McGoon (Walter Catlett), timid map expert Professor Jasper Quinley (Hobart Cavanaugh) and Bill's shifty cousin George (John Eldredge).

Mayhem erupts almost immediately after the party settles into the castle. The Skipper is nearly skewered by an arrow fired off by an ancient suit of armor while Wendy has a nasty experience with a similar medieval adornment. Later, she is visited in her room by the Phantom himself. "This castle belongs to the spirits of the past!" the black-caped stranger bellows. "Death waits for those who *dare* spend the night here!" Ace photographer Elwood "Woody" Bredell has a field day capturing actor Foy Van Dolsen's angular, deeply shadowed face and bat-like figure darting across staircases and ship's hulls or peering through lattices and window panes.

When Rod is shot dead while attempting to leave the island, the party realizes the Phantom means business. Tracing the alleged location of the treasure to an old torture chamber, Bill and his partners discover an old jewel box with a gold coin inside. The Phantom, hidden behind a drape, is about to strike again when yet *another* suit of armor discharges an arrow, piercing the mystery man's heart. The Skipper identifies him as Panama Pete, a former shipmate who was there when he first discovered the map.

With the complete map in their possession, Bill, Stuff and the Skipper resume the search, but are interrupted in their progress when Wendy disappears. George is found shot to death, his body stuffed inside (guess what?) a suit of armor! Bill gets wise to Quinley, whom he has discovered "sleepwalking" through the castle corridors (real sleepwalkers don't wear slippers). Quinley admits he killed the Phantom and later George. Holding the group at bay, the professor slips the coin into the axe handle mounted above the treasure chamber. "Now you're going to see *my* treasure," he gloats. His triumph is short-lived. The axe dislodges and deals him a fatal blow to the head. As might be expected, the treasure turns out to be a fraud. But all ends well when the Coast Guard shows up unexpectedly and offers to buy the island from Bill for a naval defense base.

Horror Island had an incredibly hectic production schedule. It was originally slated to begin shooting on February 20, 1941, but was delayed until March 3. Faced with a previously set preview date, George Waggner had just three weeks to get his picture shot, scored and edited.

Although Peggy Moran's memories are dim concerning the particulars of *Horror Island,* she does recall that making the film was an exhausting experience. "Most of my pictures I felt they raced through! They were two-week pictures, but this was really two weeks day and night. I remember going home and being so exhausted I couldn't eat dinner. My mother would rub my back and I would start crying just from being so exhausted."

To trim expenses and save time, art directors Jack Otterson and Ralph M. DeLacy dusted off old *Tower of London* sets and pressed into service the elaborate Carfax Abbey stone staircase used in *Dracula.* A fine miniature of Morgan's Castle was devised. Atmospheric, misty night scenes were shot along briny Waterfront Street and in the studio tank.

Poor weather conditions hampered exterior shooting and only increased the pressure on the company. As an emergency measure, tarpaulins were erected to shield the cameras and sets from rain, but this did little or no good. Waggner worked his cast and crew until midnight on some nights in an effort

The Phantom (Foy Van Dolsen) strikes a Dracula-like pose in this publicity still for *Horror Island.*

to stay within the 12-day shooting schedule. Film editor Otto Ludwig screened and edited the dailies *during production* to save time. Dick Foran came down with a cold and had to miss a day's work. Consequently, his last scene was cut out of the script altogether in order to bring the film in—on schedule—at 11 o'clock on the night of March 15. Hans J. Salter swiped the rousing main title theme from *Seven Sinners* (1940) and borrowed musical cues from *The Invisible Man Returns, Man Made Monster, Black Friday,* etc., to round out the score.

Everyone's hard work paid off. *Horror Island* was ready for trade previews just 23 days after the start of production.

This frenetic shooting schedule didn't appreciably damage the quality of *Horror Island* from a technical standpoint. Despite a reliance on stock music and standing sets, it's a slick, good-looking picture with especially fine camerawork. Where greater attention should have been paid was in the writing of the screenplay. Once the basic situation is set up, the adventurers are nestled in the castle, and the treasure hunt begins in earnest, the plot flounders in its own devices. Maurice Tombragel and Victor McLeod dusted off their catalog of trite haunted house and pirate lore gimmicks with predictable, uninspired results. Sliding panels, torture chambers, cryptic treasure map messages and chalked-up victim countdowns are but a few of the half-baked elements they stirred into the potpourri.

Befitting the material, the characters are mostly cartoonish caricatures brought to life by an amiable cast. Foran and Moran are as ingratiating here as they had been in *The Mummy's Hand.* In his first film for Universal under a new term contract, Leo Carrillo gives a flavorsome account as the Skipper, looking as though he just stepped out of the pages of Robert Louis Stevenson. Considered (in the eyes of the studio publicity boys) a master dialectician, Carrillo lent an appealing Latin piquancy to his roles. Saucy Iris Adrian, as always, gets off a few well-timed cracks and Foy Van Dolsen (in a role originally given to Philip Sleeman) is physically imposing as the Phantom. The poorest written role in the movie is Hobart Cavanaugh's Jasper Quinley. He's so unbelievably timorous throughout most of the film that his last reel unmasking as the film's *second* villain shouldn't have provoked any cries of disbelief. Whether he's passing out on cue, or doing a burlesque comic's imitation of a sleepwalker, Cavanaugh strikes a false note. (Surprisingly, the meek little man gets the best of burly Dick Foran in a climactic donnybrook!)

Horror Island bears a passing resemblance to another Ben Pivar production released the same year, *A Dangerous Game.* One of several action-mystery thrillers costarring the screen team of Richard Arlen and Andy Devine (what a match!), this raucous film features a treasure hunt of another kind. Andrew Tombes portrays a wacky insurance beneficiary who conceals his loot somewhere on the premises of a shady sanitarium, prompting a wacky assortment of cops, gangsters and lunatics to mount a merry hunt after the hidden cache. Never before has a movie tried so hard for laughs and failed so miserably. As in *Horror Island,* murder is mixed with merriment, but with far less obliging results.

The Black Cat (1941)

Released May 2, 1941. 70 minutes. *Directed by* Albert S. Rogell. *Associate Producer:* Burt Kelly. *Screenplay by* Robert Lees, Frederic I. Rinaldo, Eric Taylor & Robert Neville. *Suggested by the short story "The Black Cat" by* Edgar Allan Poe. *Director of Photography:* Stanley Cortez. *Art Director:* Jack Otterson. *Associate Art Director:* Ralph M. DeLacy. *Film Editor:* Ted Kent. *Musical Director:* Hans J. Salter. *Special Photographic Effects:* John P. Fulton. *Assistant Director:* Howard Christie. *Set Decorator:* Russell A. Gausman. *Sound Supervisor:* Bernard B. Brown. *Technician:* Hal Bumbaugh. *Gowns by* Vera West.

Basil Rathbone (Montague Hartley), Hugh Herbert (Mr. Penny), Broderick Crawford (Gilbert Smith), Bela Lugosi (Eduardo Vitos), Gale Sondergaard (Abigail Doone), Anne Gwynne (Elaine Winslow), Gladys Cooper (Myrna Hartley), Cecilia Loftus (Henrietta Winslow), Claire Dodd (Margaret Gordon), John Eldredge (Stanley Grable), Alan Ladd (Richard Hartley).

James Whale's *The Old Dark House* prematurely sounded the death knell for the creaky old mansion thriller, a Hollywood staple since the '20s. But in 1939, Paramount proved the subgenre was only in repose. Adding a jarring note of brash American humor, as supplied by Bob Hope, the sleeper-remake of *The Cat and the Canary* spruced up the tired formula with a fresh vitality. Hope's follow-up, *The Ghost Breakers* (1940), again proved that glib parody was the order of the day and that the "haunted house" chiller was due for revival—one which would never quite come off. Graced with excellent sets and photography, and enough spooky atmosphere to give many a straight-faced shocker a run for its money, both Bob Hope pictures attained a respectability rare among horror spoofs.

Hoping to duplicate the formula, Universal readied two competitive offerings to be shot almost simultaneously for associate producer Burt Kelly: *Oh, Charlie,* a vehicle for their hot new contractees, Abbott and Costello (soon to be retitled *Hold That Ghost*), and an original script which cavalierly cribbed the title of a previously filmed Edgar Allan Poe short story, *The Black Cat.*

The screenplay by Eric Taylor and Robert Neville needed a bit more refinishing as it became apparent that neither writer had a flair for comedy. As he did on *The Invisible Woman,* Kelly brought in *Hold That Ghost* writers Robert Lees and Frederic I. Rinaldo to punch up the material with the sort of broad, fast-clipped humor that was the hallmark of Universal comedies of the period. The "new and improved" script easily won approval and Kelly was given a $176,000 budget to bring in the film.

Albert S. Rogell was signed to direct *The Black Cat* on January 22, 1941, five days before the scheduled shooting date, but production delays demanded a postponement to February 24. Casting proved to be a problem, necessitating the usual last-minute substitutions. Richard Carlson, who was maturing as a smooth, romantic lead, was dropped from the cast and was replaced by the burly, street-wise Broderick Crawford. Kelly negotiated with urbane British character player Paul Cavanagh for a leading role, but eventually signed the much higher-salaried Basil Rathbone, who was promptly given star billing. Claire Dodd, returning from a short-lived retirement, was pegged for a supporting part in her was her first assignment under a newly negotiated long-term contract. Tying up the loose ends in short order, the starting date was pushed ahead to February 17 with production wrapping on March 10.

The curtains open to the ominous strains of Frank Skinner's main title of *Tower of London* followed by an appropriate shot of a black cat slinking down a tree; its electronically distorted "meows" add a spooky touch. (This brief clip turned up several years later in the 1948 indie *The Creeper*.) The cat is only one of the dozens of felines who occupy the sprawling Gothic mansion of Henrietta Winslow (Cecilia Loftus), an eccentric spinster whose considerable fortune is constantly on the minds of her restless devisees. Henrietta's latest infirmity sends them flocking to her bedside, but when the old woman springs back to health, the greedy family can hardly conceal their disappointment. Henrietta assembles the group and relieves them of their anxieties by reading her last will and testament. Her granddaughter Elaine (Anne Gwynne) is heavily favored. But Henrietta fails to mention a strange stipulation in her will: no monies are to be dispersed until after the death of her housekeeper Abigail Doone (Gale Sondergaard), to whom Henrietta leaves the responsibility of caring for her beloved cats.

Antique dealers Gil Smith (Broderick Crawford) and Mr. Penny (Hugh Herbert) arrive at the estate at the request of Henrietta's son-in-law Montague Hartley (Basil Rathbone) to appraise the furnishings. Gil discovers in the nick of time that someone has poisoned the dowager's milk. Soon after, Henrietta is found murdered in the estate's private crematorium, stabbed to death with a knitting needle.

Much to their dismay, the family learns of Henrietta's provision for Abigail and the cats, and Monty moves to have the will contested. A storm strands the entire group in the house. An attempt is made on Abigail's life; later, her body is found dangling from the end of a rope, an apparent suicide. But Gil proves she was murdered.

A cloaked figure is seen prowling through the corridors of the estate, leaving a trail of ashes, apparently from one of the crematorium urns. Henrietta's daughter Myrna (Gladys Cooper) is nearly hanged in her room but is rescued by Gil. When she regains consciousness, she accuses the gardener, Eduardo Vitos (Bela Lugosi), of being the assailant. As the others search the grounds for the culprit, Eduardo enters Myrna's room and insists she accused him unjustly. Myrna pulls out a gun and shoots the gardener dead.

Doing a bit of detective work, Elaine realizes that Myrna is the real killer and that she faked her own attack in order to avoid suspicion. Hoping to put

A deadly mixture of merriment and mayhem: Brod Crawford, Bela Lugosi and Hugh Herbert in *The Black Cat*.

an end to husband Monty's affair with her cousin Margaret (Claire Dodd), she murdered Henrietta and Abigail in order to get her inheritance. Myrna overpowers Elaine and drags her to the crematorium. As she's about to ignite the gas, Gil intervenes. In the melee, Myrna brushes against a candle and her nightgown catches fire. Screaming, she flees across the grounds engulfed in flames.

Even allowing that *The Black Cat* is played for laughs, horror fans have legitimate reason to grouse. Its dismal reputation is well enough deserved so that the picture can't be called a disappointment. However, there was no reason for it to be as ineffectual as it is. *The Black Cat* is obviously a slick show, beautifully lit and crisply photographed, replete with Jack Otterson's redressed but excellent sets. But we're not far into the movie before discovering its proficiencies don't venture beyond the technical level. The plot is a shameless retread of *The Cat and the Canary* as a bevy of fortune-hunting relatives descend on a lonely old house for the traditional reading of a will and then get bumped off one by one. Granted, this is old stuff, ripe for parody, but even on the level of farce, the picture fails miserably.

Universal had an unfortunate bent toward low-brow humor and routinely engaged second-rate comedy stars, mostly pulled from the ranks of vaudeville. Among the studio regulars were Shemp Howard, Olsen and Johnson, Leon Errol, and the costar of *The Black Cat,* Hugh Herbert. Playing the archetypical scatter-brained friend of the hero, Herbert looks as if he were thrown in the film at the last minute to bolster the feeble comedy. His hijinks as an antique dealer whose *ideé fixe* is to batter every furnishing in sight to make them look more like antiques is repetitious and relentlessly unfunny. His character is so dense, obnoxious and outlandishly stupid that it's painful to watch him in action.

On a whole, the horror stars fare better than Herbert (it doesn't say much for the vaudevillian that Bela Lugosi is funnier than he is). Gale Sondergaard is delightful as the frozen-faced housekeeper and there's a good in-joke as Rathbone haplessly tries to clear up the mystery ("Who does he think he is, Sherlock Holmes?" quips Brod Crawford). But the biggest hoot comes late in the film when Crawford nabs Lugosi as he is apparently heaving a corpse into a wagon. The load turns out to be a large canvas sack filled with cats that poor Bela was bringing in out of the rain. Lurching about on all fours, crying "Here, kitty, kitty" in his typically s-l-o-w Lugosian delivery as the cats scatter like mad, Bela gets the biggest laugh in the picture.

Of course, that's not saying much for this witless film which has no shortage of talent, though little of it is visible on the screen. Lees and Rinaldo have done better work on any of their Abbott and Costello pictures; even *The Invisible Woman* is funnier. Coscripter Eric Taylor, no slouch himself, was evidently responsible for most of the melodrama, but falls far below the standards of his fine *Son of Dracula* screenplay penned a couple of years later.

Except for its old dark house setting, the supernatural/horror elements are slight to practically nonexistent, as the picture settles into the conventional whodunit mode. *The Black Cat*'s hectic pace proves deceiving. Excluding a couple of murders, the story is short on incident and the characters' motivations are fuzzy at best. Broderick Crawford spends most of his time heroically charging through the house at the slightest sign of trouble only to discover that there is nothing actually wrong in the first place. A scream in the night is nothing more than a whistling tea kettle; Anne Gwynne's disappearance is a false alarm (she was downstairs looking for a book). The phantom killer leaves behind a trail of crematory ash for no apparent reason and risks exposure in order to indulge in meaningless mischief, such as sneaking into the heroine's room to place a black cat on her bed while she sleeps. The old bromide of a bookcase concealing a secret passageway provides Herbert with an even more tiresome variety of antics.

The script doesn't entirely neglect Poe (remember him?). The tip-off of a wailing cat sealed in the crematorium (alerting Crawford to Gwynne's peril) in the closing act is a direct lift from the original story in which the cries of an imprisoned cat reveal the secret location of the entombed victim. Director

Rogell hasn't the wit to underscore the point as he plunges headlong into his climax, which admittedly packs a wallop. After over an hour of fluff, Gladys Cooper's well-staged, fiery death is an unexpected and shockingly gruesome wind-up. Rogell was a typical contract director who measured success by meeting deadlines and staying within the allotted budget. He never drew an all-out horror assignment, which is no loss to the genre. Rogell is stronger on pace that he is on atmosphere, leaving it up to photographer Stanley Cortez to create a properly eerie mood. *The Black Cat* was just a contractual assignment for the gifted cinematographer but he lenses some striking images of the cloaked murderer skulking through dimly-lit secret passageways.

The exceptional cast is wasted. A scruffy, unrecognizable Bela Lugosi, in another brief and humiliating role, is reduced to peering through windows and lurking around corners in silent close-ups. Basil Rathbone is only aboard to pick up some fast money and looks it. Broderick Crawford displays a gruff, amiable charm as the token hero and a bleached-blond Anne Gwynne is adequate in the female lead. Receiving eleventh billing, a young Alan Ladd, just on the brink of stardom, was still honing his hard-boiled persona. But minus his famous shoelifts, he comes off more as a diminutive sorehead than a charismatic tough guy. With the exception of the buffoonish Herbert, everyone else is just another red herring, although Gladys Cooper occasionally manages to rise above the material, nicely capturing the sullen desperation of her character.

Even sharp-eyed viewers are bound to miss Marlene Dietrich, who appears in at least one scene. According to Universal expert Michael Fitzgerald, Dietrich, who was on the Universal lot shooting *The Flame of New Orleans* at the time, frequently dropped by the *Black Cat* set to visit her current paramour, Broderick Crawford. One afternoon, the crew was about to shoot a non-dialogue scene with Claire Dodd when it was discovered the actress had already left for the day. Dietrich, her back to the camera, took Dodd's place in the shot.

The Black Cat has long been a sore point for horror fans not only for its rash squandering of a fine cast, but because of careless television broadcasters who routinely confuse the picture with the classic 1934 version. Universal typically downplayed the horror ingredients during production only to do a complete turnabout and sell the picture as a straight shocker in its trailers and advertising. The overnight fame of Alan Ladd in *This Gun for Hire* (1942) prompted the studio to re-release *The Black Cat* with the Paramount star given prominent billing even though he has but a few minutes of screen time.

A veil of deception still hovers over *The Black Cat*. An uninspired burlesque masquerading as a horror movie, it remains one of Universal's most misrepresented thrillers.

Hold That Ghost (1941)

Released August 8, 1941. 86 minutes. *Directed by* Arthur Lubin. *Produced by* Alex Gottlieb. *Associate Producers:* Burt Kelly & Glenn Tryon. *Screenplay by* Robert Lees, Frederic I. Rinaldo & John Grant. *Original Story by* Robert Lees & Frederic I. Rinaldo. *Assistant Director:* Gilbert J. Valle. *Director of Photography:* Elwood Bredell. *Film Editor:* Philip Cahn. *Art Director:* Jack Otterson. *Associate Art Director:* Harold H. MacArthur. *Musical Director:* Hans J. Salter. *Musical Numbers Staged by* Nick Castle. *Set Decorator:* Russell A. Gausman. *Dialogue Director:* Joan Hathaway. *Sound Supervisor:* Bernard B. Brown. *Technician:* William Fox. *Gowns by* Vera West.

Bud Abbott (Chuck Murray), Lou Costello (Ferdinand Jones), Richard Carlson (Dr. Jackson), Joan Davis (Camille Brewster), Mischa Auer (Gregory), Evelyn Ankers (Norma Lind), Marc Lawrence (Charlie Smith), The Andrews Sisters (Themselves), Ted Lewis and his Orchestra (Themselves), Milton Parsons (Harry Hoskins), Russell Hicks (Bannister), William Davidson (Sidney "Moose" Matson), Frank Penny (Snake-Eyes), Edgar Dearing (Irondome), Don Terry (Strangler), Edward Pawley (High Collar), Nestor Paiva (Glum), Thurston Hall (Alderman), Janet Shaw (Alderman's Girl), Paul Fix (Lefty), Howard Hickman (Judge), Harry Hayden (Mr. Jenkins), Shemp Howard (Soda Jerk), Frank Richards (Gunman), William Forrest (State Trooper), Paul Newlan (Big Fink), Joe LaCava (Little Fink), Bobby Barber (Bit Waiter), Mrs. Gardner Crane (Mrs. Giltedge), Harry Wilson (Harry), Jeanne Blanche (Pretty Thing), Kay, Kay & Katya (Dancers).

In January, 1941, that lean, fast-talking, double-dealing, comic straight man Bud Abbott and his partner Lou Costello, baby-faced, roly-poly top banana from Paterson, New Jersey, entered the fifth year of their show business association riding on the crest of a tremendous box office success, *Buck Privates* (1941), Universal's biggest money-maker to that date. Both men gained their reputations as first-class clowns on the burlesque circuit, teaming for the first time in a road show entitled "Life Begins at Minsky's" in 1936, just months before the risqué art form was outlawed in the Big Apple. Most of the team's great routines were devised for this showcase. Their astounding success in vaudeville theatres and nightclubs led to Kate Smith's offering them a regular spot on her immensely popular radio show. Bud and Lou added Broadway to their growing list of conquests with the extravagant musical revue "The Streets of Paris," which ran over a year.

Hollywood was the last frontier. Universal signed up the sizzling comics to a one-picture deal, but instead of providing them with their own vehicle, the studio awarded the burlesque kings supporting slots in the musical comedy *One Night in the Tropics* (1940) costarring Allan Jones and Robert Cummings. Widely considered a flop, the picture nevertheless garnered Abbott and Costello the attention of movie audiences and paved the way for *Buck Privates* and the Hollywood success that followed.

A creepy ghost-haunted house, the playground of a good many comics since the advent of pictures, provided the perfect setting for Abbott and Costello's next vehicle, *Oh, Charlie* (the title was eventually changed to the more salable *Hold That Ghost*). Hoping to duplicate the success of *Buck Privates,* Universal assigned that film's director, Arthur Lubin, to helm the team's new comedy, which began shooting on January 21, 1941, with a budget that escalated to $190,000 after all was said and done. (Up-and-coming director John Rawlins was put in charge of shooting second unit material.) An efficient no-frills craftsman with a long list of B's to his credit, Lubin developed a good rapport with "the boys" and ended up directing a total of four of their pictures. Lubin recently reminisced,

> I was the first director that Charlie Rogers signed up. I had finished *Where Did You Get That Girl?* [1941] and *Buck Privates* was the only thing that was open. They didn't think it would amount to anything. The minute it was previewed, they called me in and said, "We're going to give you $5,000 if you don't mind starting tomorrow on another picture." And that was *Oh, Charlie.*

As work progressed steadily on *Hold That Ghost,* the box office revenues from *Buck Privates* increased daily; it soon became *the* motion picture hit of the country. Universal's top brass rushed Lubin and Abbott and Costello into another service comedy, *In the Navy,* which they rightly felt would be a more appropriate follow-up to *Buck Privates,* and booked it into theatres across the nation.

In June (four months after production was halted), *Hold That Ghost* went back before the cameras. Pumping more greenbacks into the budget, Universal added to the script several lengthy production numbers, taking advantage of the talents of the Andrews Sisters and showman Ted Lewis and his Orchestra. This practice of sprucing up the team's comedies with glitzy, gratuitous musical numbers became a tradition (as it had in the Marx Brothers movies). One could never predict when the zany antics of the comics would come to a screeching halt to make way for a kitschy production number featuring the likes of the Merry Macs or the Saronga Dancing Girls.

Like every other Abbott and Costello vehicle, the plot of *Hold That Ghost* is a mere framework upon which the comics hang their routines. Chuck Murray (Bud Abbott) and Ferdinand Jones (Lou Costello), two virtually unemployable jacks-of-all-trades, inherit the fortune of big-time gangster Sidney "Moose" Matson (William Davidson), a total stranger, who's gunned down by the police in the presence of the two men. Bannister (Russell Hicks), the late gangster's mouthpiece, informs Chuck and Ferdy that the whereabouts of Matson's loot is a mystery; "Moose" always boasted that he kept his money "in his head." The best Bannister can do for them is turn over the keys to the Forester's Club, an abandoned tavern off the highway which was a speakeasy during Prohibition.

Bannister's associate, Charlie Smith (Marc Lawrence; the "Charlie" of the original title) arranges to have Chuck and Ferdy driven to the club by bus operator Harry Hoskins (Milton Parsons). Hoskins picks up a few extra passengers: the bookwormish Dr. Jackson (Richard Carlson), lovely Norma Lind (Evelyn Ankers) and radio actress/"sound effect" Camille Brewster (Joan Davis). No sooner do the passengers disembark than Hoskins drives off, leaving them stranded at the dilapidated watering hole.

From this point on, every predictable weird situation that could possibly occur within the confines of a haunted old house takes place. Charlie Smith is strangled by a mysterious figure (Don Terry) as he ransacks the cellar looking for Matson's loot. Later, the gangster's corpse keeps turning up in the least likely places, sending Ferdy into fits of hysterics. Camille encounters a "ghost" which later raids Ferdy's bedroom. A pair of men, identifying themselves as detectives, show up at the tavern and soon disappear, leaving no trace.

After much cavorting, Chuck and Ferdy stumble across Matson's bankroll, stuffed inside the mounted head of a moose! But before the boys can take stock of their fortune, the tavern is besieged by gangsters. Grabbing the bag containing the money, Ferdy leads the hoods on a frantic chase through the hotel, finally scaring them off by emitting a loud wailing cry which they foolishly mistake for a police siren.

Heartened by Jackson's discovery that the water in the area is a health tonic, Chuck and Ferdy raze the tavern and erect a glamourous resort, complete with (you guessed it) live musical entertainment.

As trite and hackneyed as the old dark house gags were at the time of *Hold That Ghost*'s release, it didn't make a bit of difference to audiences back then or today, almost a half-century later. *Hold That Ghost* has so much comic vitality and spirit, any attempt to criticize its considerable excesses pales in light of the picture's uninhibited joys. Bluntly put, it's one of the best horror farces ever made and, arguably, A & C's funniest film. Though *Abbott and Costello Meet Frankenstein* (1948) surpasses the film in terms of novelty, star names and production values, *Hold That Ghost* has the edge in several respects: the boys were younger and more agile in 1941 and their old burlesque routines (which were constantly revitalized by chief writer John Grant, an ex-vaudevillian himself) hadn't yet grown stale from overuse.

Hold That Ghost is essentially a one-joke picture: the old scare-'em gag wherein the comic is menaced by a variety of spooks, monsters or evil presences yet can't convince anyone he's on the level. As stale as it is, this old routine dominates Abbott and Costello's series of dismal monster farces released between 1949 and 1955. In *Hold That Ghost,* the exasperated Costello is always a second or two short of proving to others that the candle *did* move, or that his bedroom *did* change into a casino. The pudgy comedian's repertoire of wails, stammers and convulsive reactions to the strange phenomena he encounters qualifies him as the screen's most outrageously entertaining patsy.

Although he freely admits that working with the two was often a trying

Funnymen Lou Costello and Bud Abbott joined comedienne Joan Davis in the uproarious *Hold That Ghost.*

experience, Arthur Lubin's memories of them are, nevertheless, warm and affectionate:

> They were both generous men. When they first arrived, Bud gave the first party for me. What astonished me was they brought out pictures of their wives, who were strippers, completely nude. Bud was the brighter of the two. Lou hated to memorize his lines. Whenever we had any of their tricks to do, John Grant usually came on the set. If Lou went off the script, Bud would bring him back. They took direction and always added a little more.

In *Hold That Ghost,* the pair got plenty of competition in the laughs department from Joan Davis. Active in show biz since infancy, the klutzy comedienne's broad antics provided a welcome respite from the moonlight and roses schmaltz of the Sonja Henie vehicles *Thin Ice* (1937), *My Lucky Star* (1938) and *Sun Valley Serenade* (1941). Complementing each other's uninhibited zaniness, Davis and Costello share some great moments. The couple perform a fractured rendition of the "Blue Danube" waltz; Joan also contributes to the amusement of the famous floating candle routine (used again in *Abbott and Costello Meet Frankenstein* and on their television show). Although Joan Davis' character is conspicuously absent from the picture's wrap-up, she was written into the original ending. (Chuck and Ferdy hire her on as staff dietician of their deluxe spa.) This sequence was ditched in favor of a tuneful finale which had the Andrews Sisters performing a campy Latin number, "Aurora."

There are enough mysterious goings-on in *Hold That Ghost* (sliding panels, clutching hands, falling bodies, shrouded figures dashing in and out of rooms, etc.) for two straight melodramas. The queasy haunted house atmosphere, sustained by Elwood Bredell's fine camerawork and Hans J. Salter's kinetic scoring (many of the cues were lifted from *Black Friday*), effectively offsets the film's humorous situations. Of course, the whole set-up is a sham: it's gangsters, not goblins, that are driving the boys mad.

Two of fantastic filmdom's all-time favorites, Richard Carlson and Evelyn Ankers, do an admirable job in the romance department (a thankless task in this kind of film). Carlson gets in a few laughs himself as the stereotypical absent-minded professor, Dr. Jackson. As the writers neglected to provide Carlson with a first name, even Evelyn Ankers, who has fallen in love with him, calls him "Doctor."

Hold That Ghost was Ankers' first exposure to a genre with which she'd have more than just a passing acquaintance over the next three years. Born to British parents in Valparaíso, Chile, Evelyn spent most of her childhood in South America. It was there she developed her interest in acting. She studied theatre at the Royal Academy of Dramatic Art in England and eventually won small roles in such British films as *Belles of St. Mary's, Rembrandt* (both 1936), *Fire Over England* and *Knight Without Armour* (both 1937).

Arriving in the States in 1940, Evelyn's talents (and some canny connections) got her the plum role of the maid in the 1940 Broadway hit "Ladies in Retirement" with Flora Robson. While on tour with the play in Los Angeles, Ankers was offered long-term contracts at 20th Century–Fox, Warner Bros. and Universal. She signed with Fox and was scheduled to appear in the film

Scotland Yard, but the deal fell through. Universal stepped in and cast Evelyn in *Hold That Ghost.* On January 8, 1941, she entered into a seven-year contract with the studio. The rest is horror film history. Although she only worked at Universal for three of those seven years (she left the studio in 1944 after giving birth to a daughter by husband Richard Denning, himself no slouch in cinefantastique). Evelyn Ankers brightened the casts of no fewer than 27 of their B horror films, comedies, musicals and wartime propaganda efforts.

Rating a high seismograph reading in riotous entertainment, *Hold That Ghost* is Abbott and Costello at the height of hilarity. With Joan Davis on hand to buoy the merriment, the Andrews Sisters providing a touch of camp, and a better-than-average number of well-wrought thrills, it remains one of the best films of that rarely successful subgenre, the horror farce.

The Wolf Man (1941)

Released December 12, 1941. 70 minutes. *Produced & Directed by* George Waggner. *Original Screenplay by* Curt Siodmak. *Director of Photography:* Joseph Valentine. *Special Effects:* John P. Fulton. *Art Director:* Jack Otterson. *Associate Art Director:* Robert Boyle. *Film Editor:* Ted Kent. *Musical Director:* Charles Previn. *Music by* Hans J. Salter & Frank Skinner. *Assistant Director:* Vernon Keays. *Set Decorator:* Russell A. Gausman. *Director of Sound:* Bernard B. Brown. *Technician:* Joe Lapis. *Makeup by* Jack P. Pierce. *Gowns by* Vera West.

Claude Rains (Sir John Talbot), Lon Chaney, Jr. (Lawrence Stewart Talbot, The Wolf Man), Warren William (Dr. Lloyd), Ralph Bellamy (Captain Paul Montford), Patric Knowles (Frank Andrews), Maria Ouspenskaya (Maleva), Bela Lugosi (Bela), Evelyn Ankers (Gwen Conliffe), Fay Helm (Jenny Williams), Leland [Leyland] Hodgson (Kendall), Forrester Harvey (Victor Twiddle), J.M. Kerrigan (Charles Conliffe), Doris Lloyd (Mrs. Williams), Olaf Hytten (Villager), Harry Stubbs (Reverend Norman), Tom Stevenson (Richardson), Eric Wilton (Chauffeur), Harry Cording (Wykes), Ernie Stanton (Phillips), Ottola Nesmith (Mrs. Bally), Connie Leon (Mrs. Wykes), La Riana (Gypsy Dancer), Kurt Katch* (Gypsy with Bear), Caroline Cooke, Margaret Fealy (Women), Jessie Arnold (Gypsy Woman), Eddie Polo (Churchgoer), Gibson Gowland (Villager). [**Does not appear in the final print.*]

The last of the great Universal horror films, *The Wolf Man* proved that the new management could produce a first-rate shocker without a first-rate director on the payroll. A rather shrewd strategy was concocted. Lon Chaney, Jr.'s early promise was confirmed by the fine notices he received on the ultra-cheap *Man Made Monster.* All that Chaney now needed was a four-star vehicle to establish him as a major horror star, enabling the studio to exploit his name in lower-budgeted programmers. As far as Universal was concerned, the Chaney name was a potential gold mine.

There wasn't much else the studio could do with Lon. Chaney was kept busy in the months following the release of *Man Made Monster,* but his roles were uninspired. The burly actor was a natural at playing thugs and dimwits and drifted to supporting roles. He appeared in *San Antonio Rose* with Robert Paige and Jane Frazee and a Rudy Vallee vehicle, *Too Many Blondes* (both 1941). Universal showed little interest in grooming him as a Western star (they already had several) so he was again low-billed in *Badlands of Dakota* and in the serial *Riders of Death Valley* (both 1941). Apparently forgetting that

Chaney's greatest success was playing a *sympathetic* giant in *Of Mice and Men* (1939), Universal insisted on casting him as a one-dimensional heavy.

That would all change with *The Wolf Man* and Chaney's enduring portrayal of one of horror films' most tragic figures, the doomed Larry Talbot. Universal tailored the role to Chaney's talents with unprecedented success. The studio made millions off the picture and Chaney reportedly received more fan mail than any other star on the lot.

Universal entrusted the picture to George Waggner, whose stock with the studio was climbing quickly. Now a producer, Waggner's hectic days as a down-to-the wire fast-buck director on pictures like *Horror Island* were drawing to a close. Making sure all of Hollywood knew Universal was back in the horror market in grand style, Waggner assembled a name cast. Top-salaried stars were out of the question, so the producer courted a covy of well-regarded but reasonably-priced players to command the public's attention. Waggner undertook the direction himself but, having less confidence in his own writing abilities, recruited the dependable Curt Siodmak to author the original screenplay. Unlike *WereWolf of London,* which combined the werewolf legend with modern science, Siodmak temporarily forsook his science fiction proclivities and firmly rooted his story in European folklore.

According to Siodmak, he wrote the film from scratch without being influenced by the 1935 picture or the unfilmed werewolf script prepared for Boris Karloff in the '30s. Producer Waggner proved to be of little inspiration.

> I never talked to George, except on Thursdays. I'd go into his office and give him all the honey I could think of—I told him how big a man he was—and I figured, "This guy *must* know I'm kidding." He never found out. I couldn't sit down and talk about these pictures because he'd say, "I don't want *my* ideas, I want *your* ideas!" So, he never talked to me. But he was a nice man, and we had a good relationship.
>
> They told me who would be in the pictures before I would even start to write them. On *The Wolf Man,* for instance, I was told, "We have $180,000, we have Lon Chaney, Jr., Claude Rains, Ralph Bellamy, Warren William, Maria Ouspenskaya, Bela Lugosi, a title called *The Wolf Man* and we shoot in ten weeks. Get going!"

Unforeseen delays pushed the original starting date from September 8, 1941, to October 27. Dick Foran was being announced as one of the film's stars right up until a week from the start of shooting, but did not work on the film. The studio also had a change of heart about the title and redubbed the film *Destiny* for a brief period. (*Destiny* became the studio's standard label for untitled films in production in the early '40s, including *Son of Dracula.*)

As with *Son of Frankenstein,* much of the credit for the film's visual style belongs to art director Jack Otterson. His major contribution was a splendidly spooky forest set, all built indoors, composed of grotesquely knotted trees and decayed boughs. A topping of artificial fog not only heightened the atmosphere but enabled Waggner to shoot continuously on the same confined set without the audience catching on. Even so, photographer Joseph Valentine used a wide-angle lens when shooting on this set, capturing even more background than he otherwise would. A conventional lens was used for close-ups and long shots.

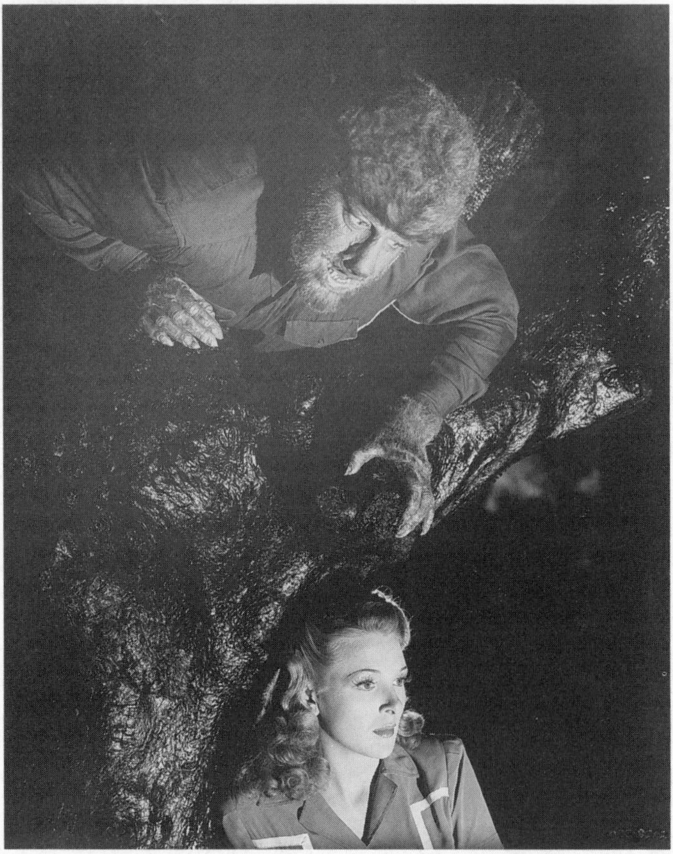

Although wolves aren't known for their ability to climb trees, Lon Chaney, Jr., as *The Wolf Man,* has a go at it, unbeknownst to Evelyn Ankers.

It had to have been a proud day for young Lon when the production unit shot a scene on the Notre Dame set from his father's classic *The Hunchback of Notre Dame* (1923). Sensing that the edifice appeared a bit too imposing a structure for a small country church in Wales, film editor Ted Kent cunningly eliminated all long shots of the exteriors in *The Wolf Man*'s final cut. Also quite recognizable are the stone pillars of Carfax Abbey as pallbearers carry Bela the gypsy's casket into the church crypt, as well as the famous European Street set which represented the country village.

Reportedly, Jack Pierce's famous Wolf Man makeup was originally created for Henry Hull and *WereWolf of London.* The publicity department laid it on a bit thick, claiming that Pierce traveled to Europe and spent five years combing countless histories of England to come up with a description or illustration of a werewolf. Baring his soul to a visiting reporter on the set, Pierce described how tough it is when a producer tells you to create a monster.

> Or when he tells you to come up with a *couple* of werewolves. So you try to do some research. And all you learn about werewolves is that they're supposed to howl in the light of the moon in the deserted castles of Scotland. Only nobody's ever seen one. So, you sit down and try to figure out how a werewolf ought to look. And then you go to work with hair and putty and glue and paint.

Pierce's creation, made from hard-to-find yak hair and a set of sharp, jutting teeth, took four hours to apply; that includes making up Chaney's hands and feet. The script called for two full transformations. Chaney was forced to lie prostrate on the ground while the makeup was removed, changing him from a wolf back to a man. Chaney griped that taking the makeup off was even worse than putting it on. "What gets me is after work when I'm all hot and itchy and tired, and I've got to sit in that chair for forty-five minutes while Pierce just about kills me, ripping off the stuff he put on me in the morning."

The same on-the-set reporter suggested that Chaney sleep with the makeup on; the actor testily replied that he had thought of that, but was afraid his eyes would glue shut during the night.

In her chatty and oft-quoted introduction to Doug McClelland's *The Golden Age of "B" Movies,* Evelyn Ankers admitted there was little love lost between her and Chaney, who delighted in creeping up behind the actress in his full makeup and scaring the wits out of her. Even more harrowing was the time a huge bear (appearing in the famous deleted wrestling match scene) broke loose from its chains and chased the actress straight up into the rafters of the soundstage.

Another delay in the less-than-harmonious production came during the shooting of the finale. Claude Rains, getting a bit carried away bludgeoning his werewolf son to death, whacked Chaney full force with the prop ten-pound silver-headed cane. Chaney, suffering from a black eye and considerable swelling, was sent home when an ice-pack treatment proved useless. As a result, his afternoon scenes, sans makeup, were postponed.

Falling just short of a one-month shooting schedule, *The Wolf Man* wrapped on November 25, followed by a hasty post-production period. By early December, the first prints were being screened for an unenthusiastic press while the studio readied the picture for its national release, topping a double bill with *The Mad Doctor of Market Street.* But Universal's confidence in its new gala horror show would soon be badly shaken. The attack on Pearl Harbor sent shock waves across the country, and it was feared that the public's appetite for Hollywood's manufactured horrors would suffer. Taking the hard line, *Variety* branded *The Wolf Man* a dubious entertainment in light of grim world events. Happily for the studio, their reservations proved unfounded as *The Wolf Man* became a top-grosser despite the critics' middling reception.

The opening scenes are routinely handled. Lawrence Talbot (Lon Chaney, Jr.), the second son of a titled European family, returns to his ancestral estate nestled on the outskirts of a small Welsh village. With the death of an elder brother, young Talbot stands to claim his rightful place in the family hierarchy. This sad state of affairs does not go unnoticed by his father Sir John (Claude Rains), who nevertheless greets his son warmly after his 18-year absence.

1195-6AD

Larry takes a liking to a village girl, Gwen Conliffe (Evelyn Ankers). Despite her engagement to Frank Andrews (Patric Knowles), Gwen keeps a date with Talbot. Taking along her friend Jenny Williams (Fay Helm), Gwen accompanies Larry to a nearby gypsy camp. Jenny volunteers to have her fortune told by Bela the gypsy (Bela Lugosi), who reacts violently to the girl's bouquet of wolfbane. Peering into the palm of Jenny's right hand, Bela sees the pentagram, the five-pointed star, marking her for death at the hands of a werewolf. Scaring Jenny out of his tent, Bela's transformation from man into werewolf takes place (off-camera) in the light of the full moon.

Jenny's screams fill the air as Larry, charging to her rescue, desperately tries to pull away the huge wolf hovering hungrily over her body. Using his newly purchased silver-tipped walking stick, Larry clubs the beast to death but is bitten in the struggle.

Investigating officer Captain Paul Montford (Ralph Bellamy) fails to turn up the carcass of the wolf, finding instead Bela's bludgeoned body at the scene. Paul questions Larry but his wounds from the animal have strangely disappeared. Soon, word that Larry has killed Bela sweeps through the village; his relationship with Gwen, too, raises eyebrows.

In keeping with gypsy tradition, Bela's funeral is a festive one, attracting crowds to the gypsy campgrounds. Larry confronts the dead gypsy's mother, Maleva (Maria Ouspenskaya). She warns him that the curse of the werewolf has been passed on to him. Disturbed, Larry flees as the power of the full moon exerts its terrible effect. Venturing out into the forest, Larry, now a werewolf, kills a gravedigger (Tom Stevenson).

He awakens the next morning dimly aware of his ordeal. The villagers set traps to ensnare what they believe to be a murderous wolf. That night, Larry transforms again into the werewolf and blindly blunders into one of the traps. With Maleva's aid, he sets himself free and returns to Talbot Castle.

In a determined effort to prove to his son that his childish beliefs are a figment of his overworked imagination, Sir John binds him to a chair facing a window before dutifully joining in the hunt to slay the wolf. Meanwhile Gwen, hopelessly in love with Larry, combs the woods to find him. A werewolf once more, Larry tears himself free and picks up Gwen's trail. He attacks Gwen, whose screams alert Sir John. Armed with his son's cane, Sir John beats the creature mercilessly, finally killing it. Maleva happens upon the grim scene and recites an ancient gypsy prayer over the monster's body. Larry slowly returns to human form. Montford and the other hunters, seeking Gwen, find Sir John, dumbstruck, leaning over the body of his son.

In spite of the popularity of *The Wolf Man,* it still hasn't received its due in certain critical quarters. To many, the '40s was the decade of Val Lewton and, compared to his highly imaginative thrillers wherein the focus was on the unseen presence of terror, *The Wolf Man* seems extremely conventional. It's

Top: **Maria Ouspenskaya and Claude Rains exchange barbs on Jack Otterson's excellent set in *The Wolf Man. Bottom:* Lon Chaney, Jr., armed with his silver-handled walking stick, confronts a smirking Bela Lugosi. This overlit publicity still does little to convey the film's rich atmosphere.**

a rather unfair assessment, considering the fact that RKO (Lewton's home studio) didn't jump on the horror bandwagon until *The Wolf Man* drew record crowds. It's worth noting, too, that Lewton's first horror movie, *Cat People* (1942), while excellent, smacks of imitation. In fact, Curt Siodmak's unrevised original script clearly anticipated Lewton's subtle approach, keeping the monster out of camera range throughout most of the movie. But concealed horrors just didn't fit in with Universal's formula. As a result, the werewolf bared his hair, fangs and claws in loving close-ups in the final cut. It's not the most sophisticated approach, but *The Wolf Man* remains an intelligent film that works on almost every level.

Nearly all of the werewolf scenes were added after Siodmak turned in his first draft of the screenplay, as well as the hallucinatory sequence at the end of the gypsy festival episode. Special effects ace John P. Fulton provided this dizzying, somewhat pretentious montage, representing Chaney's nightmarish visions before his physical change. The transformation scenes were also added as well as the scene of the werewolf stalking the gravedigger. Unseen, suggested horrors have their place but it's tough to make a case that these added scenes *don't* improve the film.

Not counting *I Walked with a Zombie* (1943), cowritten by Ardel Wray and undoubtedly touched up by Val Lewton, *The Wolf Man* is Curt Siodmak's finest script; his then upcoming *Frankenstein Meets the Wolf Man* is hackwork in comparison. Siodmak's intriguing ditty ("Even a man who is pure at heart. . .") is so apt and original that it's routinely ascribed to folklore. One may complain about the skimpily-drawn characters and the uneven dialogue, but Siodmak's screenplay is beautifully constructed and a model of simplicity. In later years, Siodmak admitted that he unconsciously duplicated the structure of Greek drama in his script by featuring a hero who cannot escape his fate; the Sir John character classically represents the ever-dominant Greek gods.

And then there's Larry's dual personality to consider. Claiming his legacy under somber circumstances, Talbot bears the pain of estrangement. Neglected by his aristocratic family as a child, Larry's uneasy reconciliation with his father soon splinters. ("Does the prestige of your family name mean more to you than your son's life?" family physician Dr. Lloyd [Warren William] pointedly asks Sir John.) A true outcast, there's nary one among the suspicious townfolk who doesn't brand him a murderer; their cold stares even freeze him out of church. Larry's boyhood friend Montford eyes him icily and cruelly ridicules him after Talbot, obviously in a frazzled state, suggests that a werewolf is responsible for the killings. The festering resentment of the outwardly kindly Larry comes out in his wolf-self, a marauding "id" terrorizing the populace. Siodmak spells this out in Sir John's thumbnail definition of lycanthropy: "It's the technical term for something very simple, the good and evil in every man's soul."

George Waggner's direction isn't particularly imaginative, but it's one of his most satisfying jobs. Like Rowland V. Lee, he wasn't much of a stylist and his real talents were in producing. Waggner's direction is usually brisk and perfunctory on a programmer level (*Man Made Monster, Horror Island*) and stiff and self-conscious in upscale pictures (*The Climax*). *The Wolf Man* has him standing on middle ground; the movie is dramatically sound and boasts good visuals (cinematographer Joseph Valentine shares much of the credit here). But of all of the great horror films, *The Wolf Man* may have the least memorable direction.

Top-billed Claude Rains made great strides since his debut in *The Invisible Man.* At age 51, he was the top character man at Warner Bros. and at the peak of his talents. There isn't a false moment in Rains' sturdy portrayal of the proud Sir John Talbot, whose determination to cure his son of his obsession tragically backfires.

Shortly after the film was released, an interviewer, reading off a list of Rains' recent credits, finished off with *The Wolf Man.* A bit embarrassed by the horror title listed among his prestigious credits, Rains sheepishly responded, "That's varying quality, of course, but it's the *role* that counts!" Perhaps the suave actor forgot that it was a Universal shocker that launched his Hollywood career. Rains' crisp performance is one of *The Wolf Man*'s major assets.

Larry Talbot remains Lon Chaney's most famous role following Lennie in *Of Mice and Men,* and is among his handful of first-rate performances. His brash, easygoing charm in the first reel and his dramatic intensity in the later scenes sharply contrasts with his dreary work in the Inner Sanctum pictures, making one wonder what became of Chaney's talents in a few short years. Unlike his Mummy performances, the Wolf Man was so uniquely Chaney, no one ever doubted it really was him under the yak hair and not a stunt man. Leering through the twisted timbers of Jack Otterson's misty forest set, Chaney's werewolf, now a familiar sight, must have been a real jaw-dropper to first-time viewers back in 1941. Chaney's most affecting scenes with Evelyn Ankers (never more beautiful or vulnerable as Gwen Conliffe) contain not a hint of their off-camera friction. The couple's mutual attraction is believable and unencumbered by the presence of Patric Knowles as Ankers' humorless suitor. The romantic triangle adds tension to *The Wolf Man,* though Knowles' character was probably added to the plot simply to furnish Ankers with a marriageable alternative to the ill-starred Chaney in the downbeat ending.

Maria Ouspenskaya's Maleva is a classic portrayal. In what might have been a stock role or a showy, high-camp performance, Ouspenskaya, with obvious respect for her character, lends the part intensity and dignity. The typically-luckless Bela Lugosi, who is well cast for a change, barely has enough lines to create much of an impression, but he makes the most of the opportunity. The role was something of a consolation prize for Lugosi, who unrealistically sought the Larry Talbot role even before the script was written.

Ralph Bellamy and Warren William, both rather poor, provided exhibitors with bankable names but very little else. The usually smooth, dependable Bellamy delivers an especially forced, hard-edged performance. William had a respectable career in the '30s when he was hailed as the new John Barrymore, a claim that seems mystifying today. Far lower-billed but altogether superior is Fay Helm as the ill-fated Jenny Williams. Adding a bit of dimension to a standard best-friend-of-the-leading-lady part, Helm proves, as she would

Lon Chaney, Jr., as *The Wolf Man* in a standard studio publicity pose. One critic complained that Chaney looked more like an ape than a wolf.

again and again, to be one of Universal's most reliable character players. Silent film buffs might have difficulty spotting Gibson Gowland among the villagers; the star of Erich von Stroheim's masterwork *Greed* (1923) was reduced to playing bits by this time.

Also contributing to the effectiveness of the film is its exciting score by Hans J. Salter and Frank Skinner. Rich in evocative gypsy melodies, melancholy processions and searing action cues, it's a benchmark horror movie score, fated to be recycled dozens of times in upcoming films. (Actually, the score is not a wholly original composition; at least one cue was cribbed from

Skinner's *The House of the Seven Gables*.) Siodmak had his own ideas on how the film should be scored, suggesting in his script that the Welsh folksong "Men of Halleck" be played over the titles. Thankfully, the suggestion was ignored.

The early draft of Siodmak's script is filled with curious and interesting deviations from the film that was to be. The protagonist here is Larry Gill, an American engineer who travels to Wales to install a telescope at Talbot Castle for amateur astronomer Sir John Talbot. The name of the chief constable (Colonel Montford in the finished film) is Inspector Kendall and his assistant (Mr. Twiddle in the film) is Mr. Cotton. Larry proposes to Gwen the morning after he is attacked by the wolf (and even offers to take her old man along on the honeymoon!); Gwen declines.

Bela is seen in his coffin with head bandaged, eyes open, the dark imprint of the pentagram on his forehead and a malevolent grin on his lips; as pallbearers carry his coffin from the church to the crypt, there's the description of a trucking shot (from Bela's point of view) to give the impression that Bela is alive but unable to move. The murder of the gravedigger is heard but not seen. The script has an abundance of religious references, crosses, hymn music, church bells and stained-glass tableaux; the Reverend Norman has a beefed-up role; there's even a prominent picture of Christ in a hunting lodge.

The tension between Larry and Frank Andrews is thicker, and Frank even threatens to "shoot [Larry] down like a dog"; later, Larry gives wolf-hunting Frank the silver bullet which he himself has forged from Maleva's charm. The script's one transformation scene (Larry turning into the Wolf Man) is seen in a reflection in a dark pool, through Larry's eyes, so that the audience will get the impression that perhaps Larry only imagines himself to be a monster. A four-legged wolf attacks Gwen, but Frank arrives in time to shoot it with a silver bullet; wounded, the beast runs off. Moments later, Larry, shot, his face unseen by the camera, staggers once again to the edge of the pool and sees a monstrous wolf's face in the water before dying.

The script's final shot is an extended low-angle one (from the dead Larry's point of view) with various characters huddled around Larry, whose face (we're told) is contorted and fiendish. Maleva hands Gwen a sprig of wolfbane and instructs her to touch Larry with it—his heart, his cheeks, his lips, his eyes. "Look! He's smiling!" Gwen exults through her tears as the wolfbane blocks out the camera, the music rises to a majestic hymn and the script ends.

In another early script, it's Sir John who slays Larry with a silver bullet just as he's about to attack Ankers. The film's superior, revised ending in which Larry is killed by the same weapon that dispatched Bela is more thrilling and even lends a poetic touch to the mayhem.

Both scripts contain a fully-detailed account of the famous deleted bear scene, which has failed to surface as of this writing but which is probably still in the vaults of Universal. At the gypsy festival, Larry, Gwen and Frank come upon a gypsy (played by Kurt Katch) with a trained bear, and Frank goads Larry into accepting the gypsy's challenge to wrestle with the beast. Talbot confronts the bear, who backs off in fear. Taking a boxer's stance, Larry grows intense and animal-like as he pummels the animal to the ground. Gwen stops him. Regaining his composure, Larry walks off as the stunned Frank remarks about how Larry "looked like a wolf" during the bout. As described in the screenplay, this is a strong, almost cruel scene that is perhaps better off deleted from all *Wolf Man* prints. Seeing it, though, after all these years would be a treat for horror buffs.

Ten years later, Siodmak, apparently fresh out of material, plundered the script of *The Wolf Man* to little effect in *Bride of the Gorilla,* which he wrote and directed for Jack Broder's Realart Pictures. In this far lesser work, Siodmak returns to the idea of an unseen menace (in this case, a man who imagines himself to be a gorilla), and includes a thinly disguised Maleva counterpart and a wolfbane-like plant bearing a name approximating the pentagram; the film even features Chaney in the cast. Once again, Siodmak had to bow to the wishes of the producers: near the end of the film there's a single nonsubjective shot of the rampaging gorilla. "They forced me to do that—sometimes you can't fight 'em," Siodmak alibis.

Is *The Wolf Man* the definitive werewolf film? It's a debatable question, though the picture may have the edge over its competitors. *WereWolf of London,* a strong but trifle clumsy warm-up act, isn't quite in the same league. The rarely-screened 20th Century–Fox *The Undying Monster* (1942) is well-regarded for its artful sets and photography and its arresting opening and closing scenes, but the rest of the picture is talky and uneventful; like Columbia's *The Return of the Vampire* (1943), it owes a considerable debt to Universal, with plenty of Sherlock Holmes-style sleuthing and even an imitation Hans J. Salter score. Once regarded as a prime example of American International sleaze, *I Was a Teenage Werewolf* (1957) has won a considerable following. To its credit, the film has a few intense horror episodes and excellent camerawork by Oscar-winner Joseph LaShelle, but overall its newfound respectability is bewildering. Admirers of Hammer's *The Curse of the Werewolf* (1961) point out its intelligent handling of the werewolf legend; far less impressive is its deadend script, indifferent acting and ponderous pacing.

The '80s updated the werewolf oeuvre with two spirited efforts, *An American Werewolf in London* and *The Howling,* both released in 1981. These films have flashes of wit and boast state-of-the-art transformation effects, but are out of the running as definitive werewolf movies. *Wolfen* (also 1981), made of sterner stuff, depicts an American Indian wolf cult operating in the South Bronx. Hard as it tries, *Wolfen* can be written off as a well-intentioned misfire.

One can pick and choose favorites from this batch, but there's little doubt that all of these films (with the exception of *WereWolf of London*) were influenced to a greater or lesser degree by *The Wolf Man;* it catapulted the werewolf legend into the popular culture. *The Wolf Man* lacks the richness of style found in the best of Whale, Freund and Ulmer; it's a well-crafted journeyman film at best. But it makes a powerful appeal to our imaginations. The tragic story of Lawrence Talbot is basic yet compelling, and so classically structured it almost transcends its often unexceptional execution. Critics may be reluctant to include the film on the list of definitive horror classics, but its popularity and influence demand its inclusion.

The Mad Doctor of Market Street (1942)

Released February 27, 1942. 61 minutes. *Directed by* Joseph H. Lewis. *Associate Producer:* Paul Malvern. *Original Screenplay by* Al Martin. *Director of Photography:* Jerome Ash. *Art Director:* Jack Otterson. *Associate Art Director:* Ralph M. DeLacy. *Film Editor:* Ralph Dixon. *Musical Director:* Hans J. Salter. *Set Decorator:* Russell A. Gausman. *Sound Supervisor:* Bernard B. Brown. *Technician:* Jess Moulin. *Gowns by* Vera West.

Una Merkel (Margaret Wentworth), Lionel Atwill (Dr. Ralph Benson/Mr. Graham), Nat Pendleton (Red Hogan), Claire Dodd (Patricia Wentworth), Hardie Albright (R.B. [William] Saunders), Richard Davies (Jim), Anne Nagel (Mrs. Saunders), John Eldredge (Dwight), Noble Johnson (Elon), Al Kikume (Kalo), Milton Kibbee (Hadley), Ray Mala (Barab), Rosina Galli (Tanao), Byron Shores (Crandall), Tani Marsh, Tavia [Billy] Bunkley (Tahitian Dancers), Boyd Davis (Ship's Captain), Alan Bridge (First Mate), Charlotte Treadway (Dowager), Clara Blore (Stout Lady), Claire Whitney, Vangie Beilby (Spinsters), Charles Sherlock (Radio Engineer), Eric Lonsdale, Douglas Gordon (Radio Operators), Guy Kingsford, Barry Bernard (Pilots), Paul Parry (Ship's Officer), Bess Flowers (Dance Extra), Tom Steele (Policeman).

This Paul Malvern production was conceived as Universal was preparing a slate of South Sea Island pictures, which had become popular since the success of John Ford's *The Hurricane* (1937). Noting that sarong queen Dorothy Lamour was reigning profitably on the Paramount lot with pictures like *Beyond the Blue Horizon,* Universal countered with such exotic potboilers as *Moonlight in Hawaii* and George Waggner's *South of Tahiti* (both 1941)

Apart from its tropical island setting, *The Mad Doctor of Market Street* is little more than a formula mad scientist movie. It has been sarcastically compared to the 1942 Abbott and Costello romp, *Pardon My Sarong,* which featured a similar performance by Lionel Atwill as well as the same bogus South Sea island sets. The original script by Al Martin was entitled *Terror of the South Seas,* but by the time the cameras rolled in July, 1941, the tag was slightly modified to *Terror of the Islands.* A real penny-pincher, shooting was completed in under three weeks with a cast composed of studio contract players and low-salaried pick-ups. *The Mad Doctor of Market Street* is a foolish but occasionally entertaining little time-killer that was used as a curtain-raiser for *The Wolf Man* during its initial playdates.

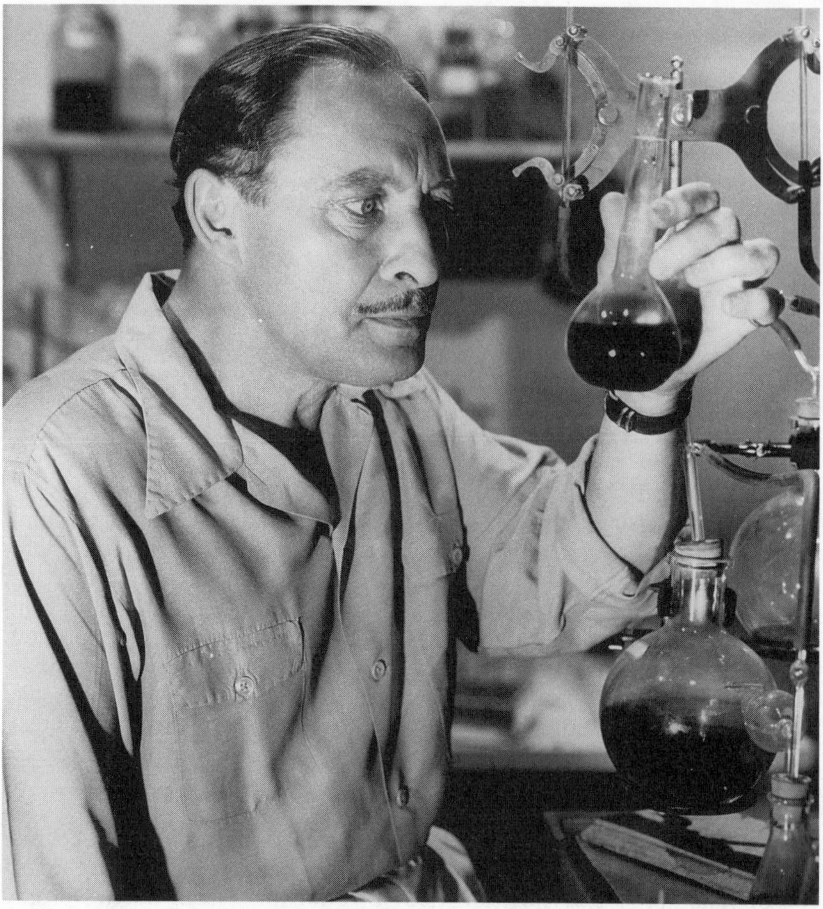

Lionel Atwill always gave an audience its money's worth even in a mediocre movie like *The Mad Doctor of Market Street*. (Photo courtesy Steve Jochsberger.)

The storyline is pure hokum. Dr. Ralph Benson (Lionel Atwill), a self-proclaimed "professor of research" (he's later referred to as a chemist), enthusiastically pursues his experiments in suspended animation. Not satisfied with laboratory animals as subjects, Benson lures down-and-out R.B. Saunders (Hardie Albright) to his San Francisco office and offers him a thousand dollars to act as guinea pig in an experiment. Saunders accepts. His wife (Anne Nagel), learning of her husband's intentions, alerts the police. As a squad car approaches Benson's office, the alarmed scientist, discovering Saunders dead, makes a quick getaway.

Dubbed "the Mad Doctor of Market Street," Benson dodges a police dragnet and boards a luxury liner destined for Australia. He passed himself off as an antiques dealer named Graham. Although undercover cop Crandall

(Byron Shores) is hot on his heels, Benson has little to fear: his adversary proves so inept, he can't even identify his man upon meeting him face-to-face. Blowing his cover, Crandall announces to all within earshot that he's out to nail the fugitive scientist. In spite of his bald pate and unmistakable build, Benson easily eludes detection by shaving off his beard. He tosses the policeman overboard at the first opportunity.

A flash fire engulfs the *S.S. Paradise.* Benson, along with a handful of his fellow passengers, board a lifeboat which beaches on a nearby island. The group is promptly abducted by hostile natives and is about to be sacrificed in a ceremonial fire. Benson convinces the tribe he is the "God of Life" and proves it by reviving the comatose wife of the native chief by administering an injection of adrenalin.

Surrounded by a throng of admiring savages who spout lines like "Anything you want, you ask," Benson sets his sights on fellow castaway Patricia Wentworth (Claire Dodd). Pressuring her to consent to marriage, Benson places her beau, the ship's steward Jim (Richard Davies), in a cataleptic state. Patricia agrees and Benson grudgingly revives Jim. Dwight (John Eldredge), the ship's cowardly officer, tries to escape from the island in a stolen canoe, but gets into an underwater fight with Barab (Ray Mala). Both men drown in the struggle. The body of the islander washes up on shore and native chief Elon (Noble Johnson) threatens Benson with execution unless he can bring the dead boy back to life by sunrise.

There is genuine tension in the last scene of the film. A nerve-wracked Benson feverishly works on the body, knowing the fate that awaits him. As the morning sun peaks over the horizon, Elon orders the lighting of the ceremonial fire and Benson is put to the stake. The blaze attracts a rescue plane which picks up the remaining castaways just as the angry natives were about to close in on them.

The Mad Doctor of Market Street was directed by Joseph H. Lewis, a longtime favorite among *auteur*-minded critics with a reputation for delivering accomplished, high-powered B pictures with style and economy. His highly over-praised 1949 sleeper *Gun Crazy,* though rarely seen today, has become his calling card to respectability. Hardcore Lewis enthusiasts come down hard on *The Mad Doctor of Market Street* just as they do his 1941 Lugosi embarrassment, Monogram's *The Invisible Ghost* (both were penned by Al Martin). However, the director does hit pay dirt in a couple of scenes.

Lewis' fire on a luxury liner sequence is an exciting little montage composed mostly of stock shots and miniatures. He makes fine use of photographer Jerome Ash's atmospheric low-keyed lighting in the opening scenes and spices up the picture with some excellent, startlingly tight shots of Atwill in action. Subjective photography is used to chilling effect as Atwill meticulously prepares his victims, descending on the camera with an ether-soaked swath of cotton (a device later purloined by Erle C. Kenton for a scene in *The Ghost of Frankenstein*).

But it is Atwill who dominates the film with another over-the-top performance. As in *Man Made Monster,* Atwill goes for the jugular, unsuccessfully trying to boost the morale of his understandably reticent subjects. ("Disease,

Pseudoscientist Lionel Atwill holds islanders Noble Johnson and Rosina Galli in thrall in the hokey *The Mad Doctor of Market Street.*

the scourge of humanity, will be cast out.... Think of it, man! The span of human life will be prolonged indefinitely!") Not even such notorious latter-day hams as Vincent Price or Michael Gough could match the sadistic glee in Atwill's eye as he is turning up the juice or coaxing his latest human guinea pig into submission. Whether he is greedily sampling a native fruit basket or beaming with sexual anticipation at the suggestion of a tryst with the leading lady, Atwill could be counted on to play it to the hilt.

The only problem is that Atwill's character just isn't much of a menace. In fact, he may be one of the dimmest mad scientists this side of Hollywood and Vine. Easily hoodwinking the natives into thinking he is the "God of Life," Atwill doesn't have the wits to realize his bluff will be called the minute the first one of them actually *dies.* Atwill has unshakable confidence in his experiments in spite of his dismal track record. He just can't seem to do *any*thing right, starting with his first human subject who predictably expires on the operating table. What he lacks in achievement he makes up for in bravura, occasionally looking up from his maze of test tubes to make a ridiculous, self-serving pronouncement like, "Just as the natives worship me, so will the whole world."

The rest of the cast has a tough time competing for the audience's attention. Amazingly, Una Merkel gets top-billing in the cast, even nudging out Atwill, in a supporting role as Claire Dodd's slightly dotty, underaged aunt. The diminutive, wide-eyed actress, with her clucking, bird-like delivery, manages to rise above some extremely asinine dialogue. ("I just love the Chinese. They're so Oriental.") A natural at light comedy, Universal put her talents to good use in pictures like *Destry Rides Again* (1939) and *The Bank Dick* (1940), in which she played W.C. Fields' daughter.

On the other hand, the amateurish, painfully unfunny Nat Pendleton nearly sinks the show as the cloddish boxer. The spunky Claire Dodd, who was winding down her film career, is likable as always as the subject of Atwill's affections. Anne Nagel, near the end of her studio contract, is barely visible in the negligible role of the weepy wife of one of Atwill's casualties. The enigmatic Noble Johnson is predictably cast as Elon, the native chief, but he has more grunts—that is, lines—than usual.

The film's nominal hero, Richard Davies, does a reasonable job. The role was something of a coup for the actor, who spent most of his career at Universal playing inconsequential juvenile parts in lightweight fare. When recently asked about his part in *The Mad Doctor of Market Street,* Mr. Davies recalled little, and even less about Atwill. "He was the star of the picture and we just had a speaking acquaintance. He was a good enough actor so that his personal problems did not affect his performance. In my opinion, the picture was not as good as the picture I made with Fred Astaire called *The Sky's the Limit* [1943] for RKO." (Mr. Davies has a persuasive gift for understatement.)

A picture like *The Mad Doctor of Market Street* could be picked apart endlessly. There are those ersatz South Pacific locales, complete with a rear-projected beach and patently Caucasian extras haplessly posing as islanders. Atwill's hamming and scenarist Al Martin's risible dialogue are usually funnier than the intended humor of Merkel and Pendleton. Moreover, the film's choppy continuity gives it a slapdash, somewhat truncated look. There are gaping holes in the action as if major scenes were left on the cutting room floor or, more likely, weren't filmed at all. There are no scenes on the lifeboat, nor are there any of the castaways arriving on the island. In a single cut, the players are imprisoned by the natives; there isn't any footage of their capture, even in complete prints.

The Mad Doctor of Market Street is poorly produced, to be sure, but the viewer can reap minor dividends. Taken as a whole, there's more fun to be had than one has a right to expect, at least as long as Atwill is center stage.

The Ghost of Frankenstein (1942)

Released March 13, 1942. 67 minutes. Produced by George Waggner. *Directed by* Erle C. Kenton. *Screenplay by* W. Scott Darling. *Original Story by* Eric Taylor. *Directors of Photography:* Milton Krasner and Elwood Bredell. *Art Director:* Jack Otterson. *Associate Art Director:* Harold H. MacArthur. *Film Editor:* Ted Kent. *Musical Director:* Hans J. Salter. *Set Decorator:* Russell A. Gausman. *Sound Director:* Bernard B. Brown. *Technician:* Charles Carroll. *Assistant Director:* Charles S. Gould. *Makeup by* Jack P. Pierce. *Gowns by* Vera West.

Sir Cedric Hardwicke (Dr. Ludwig Frankenstein), Lon Chaney, Jr. (The Monster), Ralph Bellamy (Erik Ernst), Lionel Atwill (Dr. Theodor Bohmer), Bela Lugosi (Ygor), Evelyn Ankers (Elsa Frankenstein), Janet Ann Gallow (Cloestine Hussman), Barton Yarborough (Dr. Kettering), Olaf Hytten (Hussman), Doris Lloyd (Martha), Leland [Leyland] Hodgson (Chief Constable), Holmes Herbert (Magistrate), Lawrence Grant (Mayor), Brandon Hurst (Hans), Otto Hoffman, Dwight Frye (Villagers), Julius Tannen (Sektal), Lionel Belmore, Michael Mark (Councillors), Harry Cording (Frone), Dick Alexander (Vision), Ernie Stanton, George Eldredge (Constables), Jimmy Phillips (Indian), Eddie Parker (Stunts), Teddy Infuhr (Boy).

The Ghost of Frankenstein is as much a product of Universal's management of the '40s as the initial two Frankenstein films reflected the Laemmle's upscale aspirations of the '30s. The movie is consistently exciting but it is, at the same time, slick, streamlined and artless. The assembly-line mentality of the New Universal was catching up to the series and, to compound the problem, new imaginative plots were now in short supply. Sadly, *The Ghost of Frankenstein* would be the last solo appearance of the Monster.

The fourth installment of the ever-profitable Frankenstein series was a foregone conclusion. On November 13, 1941, Universal made the formal announcement and unveiled the title of their new production. A press release indicated that the major hurdle facing the project was to find a suitable replacement for Boris Karloff in the Monster role. Undaunted, the studio assured all that the search was well underway.

On November 14, the very next day, the "search" came to an end. According to a new announcement, producer George Waggner was instructed to order the same makeup that Karloff wore for the new Monster out of fear that changing his appearance would "kill the interest of Frankenstein followers." Unsurprisingly, Lon Chaney, Jr., who was toiling on the set of *The Wolf Man,* was picked as Karloff's successor and it was reported that he would presently be fitted for "wigs, greasepaint and other gadgets" by makeup man Jack Pierce.

Universal publicly admitted it was taking a box office risk by replacing Karloff, but it had no intentions of waiting a year for the actor to fulfill his stage commitments. As such, the studio was pressing for a starting date before Christmas. This announcement, of course, was bunk. Karloff was no longer under contract and hadn't even appeared in a Universal film in two years. Since then he had carved quite a niche for himself in the Broadway production of "Arsenic and Old Lace" and personally felt the Monster role was played out.

The considerably scaled-down production of the new sequel provided even less of an incentive for Karloff to return. As in *Son of Frankenstein,* the new film had its share of script problems. The first draft by Eric Taylor was a downbeat, rather unsavory affair, so W. Scott Darling, a former writer of two-reel comedies, was brought in for a rewrite. Darling adhered to the basic structure of Taylor's scenario but made significant alterations.

The final shooting script is set four years after the events of the last sequel. The ever-complaining townspeople of Frankenstein blame the Monster's "curse" for everything from a bad harvest to the town's lackluster tourist trade. They implore the Burgomaster, now given the more Americanized title of Mayor (Lawrence Grant), to grant them the right to destroy what's left of Frankenstein's castle. The Mayor reluctantly gives his consent and the mob flocks to the castle.

The villagers' attempts to detonate the structure are thwarted by Ygor (Bela Lugosi), scarcely affected by the bullets that Wolf von Frankenstein fired into him in the previous film. As the first blasts of dynamite rock the castle, Ygor flees to the catacombs below. Dumbstruck, he sees the Monster's hand extended from the now-hardened sulphur pit. Ygor frantically unearths the Monster (Lon Chaney, Jr.) from his strange tomb and the pair make their way into the woods as the last standing walls of the castle crumble.

A fierce thunderstorm releases a bolt of lightning which strikes the Monster and gives him renewed strength. Realizing that electricity is the only way that the Monster may be restored to his former strength, Ygor and his friend head for the village of Vasaria to summon the aid of Dr. Ludwig Frankenstein (Sir Cedric Hardwicke).

The second son of the outlaw scientist, Ludwig, a prominent brain surgeon, has managed to keep his family history a secret from his daughter, Elsa (Evelyn Ankers), as well as from the community. When Ygor threatens to tell all, Frankenstein grudgingly agrees to take custody of the Monster (who has been apprehended by the constabulary for killing a villager). When Frankenstein arrives at the courthouse to examine the Monster, he goes berserk and escapes into the countryside with Ygor at his side.

That night, Ygor and the Monster make their way back to Ludwig's estate. The Monster crashes through the laboratory, kills Frankenstein's assistant Dr. Kettering (Barton Yarborough), and attempts to carry off Elsa. Ludwig manages to subdue Ygor and the Monster with an anesthetizing gas pumped in through the ventilator ducts. Determined to destroy the Monster by dissecting him piece by piece, Ludwig seeks the aid of his associate Dr. Bohmer

Stunning poster art for *The Ghost of Frankenstein,* the film that introduced Lon Chaney, Jr., in the role Boris Karloff made famous.

(Lionel Atwill). Bohmer balks, suggesting that such an act amounts to murder. Ludwig himself has second thoughts; while preparing his instruments, the "ghost" of his father, Henry Frankenstein, dissuades him from carrying out the operation and suggests instead that the surgeon replace the demented brain of the Monster with a sound one. Realizing he has a perfect specimen in the dead body of Kettering, Frankenstein becomes obsessed with restoring the Monster to his full power.

The crafty Ygor prevails upon Dr. Bohmer to trick Frankenstein into using *his* brain for the transplant. Bohmer, who has been discredited by the medical profession for a past experiment that had gone awry, seizes this opportunity to regain his standing and consents. But the Monster has his own ideas. He steals into the village and abducts Cloestine (Janet Ann Gallow), a schoolgirl who has befriended him. He brings the child back to the laboratory with the notion of using *her* brain for the operation. Ludwig intervenes, takes the child away, and prepares the Monster for surgery. The operation proceeds with Ludwig unknowingly placing Ygor's brain into the skull of the Monster.

The townspeople, meanwhile, have become frustrated with the constabulary's inability to find the Monster and the missing Cloestine. Certain that Frankenstein is responsible, they storm the estate. Elsa's fiancé, town prosecutor Erik Ernst (Ralph Bellamy), alerts Ludwig of the brewing crisis. Frankenstein admits that he has been harboring the Monster and has, in effect, rehabilitated him by giving the brain of the kindly Kettering. To prove his point, he unveils the "new" Monster, only to to discover Bohmer's treachery. Speaking in Ygor's crackling voice, the Monster revels in his power but soon finds himself going blind (the result of Ygor and the Monster's incompatible blood types). As the villagers descend upon the sanatorium, the Monster flings Bohmer into an electrical panel which sends a lethal charge through his body. Groping in the dark, the Monster topples a rack of chemicals to the floor, touching off an inferno. Ludwig and the Monster perish in the flames as Elsa and Erik flee to safety.

W. Scott Darling's screenplay departed from Eric Taylor's original story in several respects. Taylor's intention was to reprise the Wolf von Frankenstein character from *Son of Frankenstein,* presumably with Rathbone in mind. In the revised draft, Wolf has been driven into exile after his encounter with the Monster (this is hardly consistent with the upbeat ending of the last sequel). Taylor also brought back Wolf's wife (rechristened Elayne), and even invented a sister for her. (It is she who is murdered when the Monster charges into the house.) The character of Dr. Kettering wasn't created until later. Darling used the sister's name (Martha) for Frankenstein's housekeeper, played by Doris Lloyd.

More significantly, Theodor Bohmer, portrayed by Lionel Atwill, was an altered version of Taylor's Theodor character. In the initial script he was a typical horror film hunchback; he and the disfigured Ygor share a natural kinship. Theodor is later responsible for the climactic "brain switch" after the Monster accidently crushes Ygor to death. Little Cloestine's father, a victim of the Monster, was intended to be the brain donor before Theodor intervened.

Taylor obviously immersed himself in the earlier Frankenstein films to come up with a pool of ideas: the Monster's bond with children, the cliche of the villagers storming the castle, and of course the Monster's fiery death were borrowed by Darling. The most striking aspect of the Taylor script which wasn't retained in the rewrite was the powerful influence of Tod Browning's outlaw classic *Freaks* (1932). Taylor took pains to duplicate the strange kinship of the carnival freaks as Ygor and Theodor attempt to organize the village cripples into an army to take over the town with the Monster as their appointed leader. This unpleasant and ludicrous diversion was closer in spirit

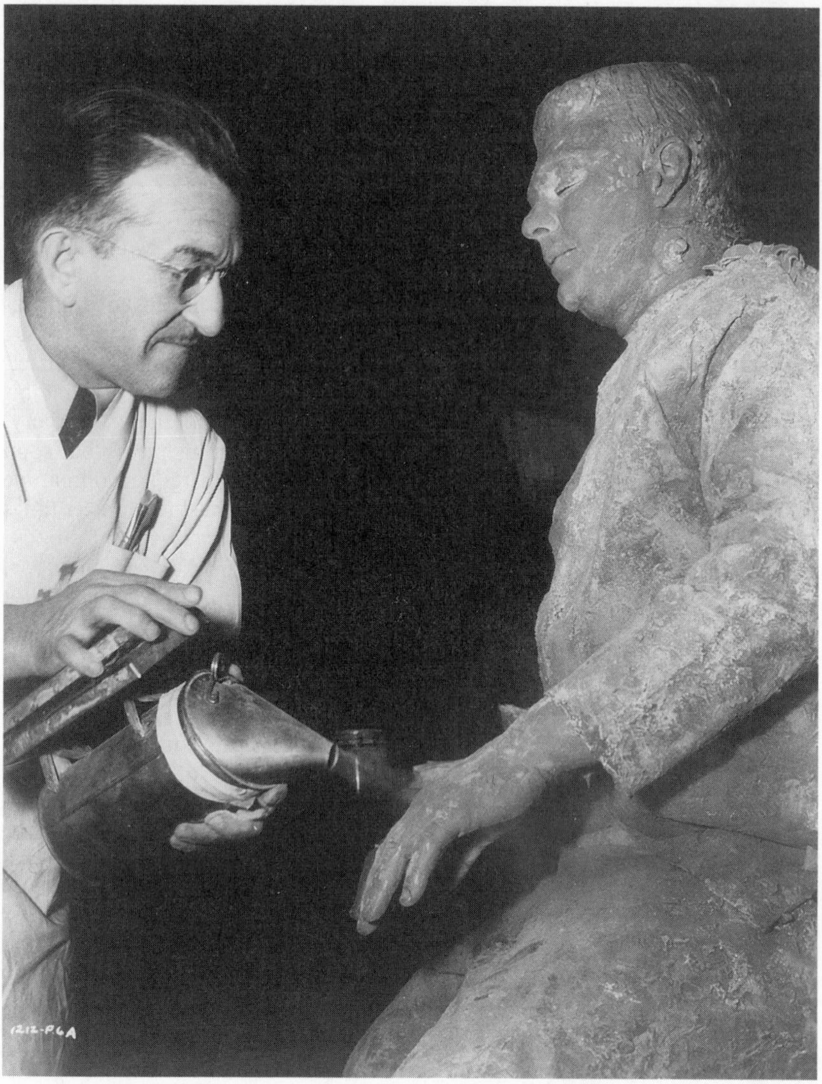

Jack Pierce conducts another makeup session with Lon Chaney, Jr., for *The Ghost of Frankenstein.*

to pre–Hays Code excesses of the '30s than it was to the comparatively bland tastes of the war years.

Darling's script is uneven but he generally does a good job of molding Taylor's quirky storyline into a more commercially viable package. There isn't quite as much memorable dialogue as in the previous films in the series, nor are the characters as sharply etched. But the script certainly doesn't lack interest. Unfortunately, Curt Siodmak's nagging influence is felt in Darling's and Taylor's drafts. Taylor's reuse of the brain transplant gimmick from *Black Friday,* a favorite Siodmak theme, hastened the series' descent into pulp. The forthcoming *House of Frankenstein* worked the brain transplant angle to new heights of absurdity as a maddeningly indecisive Boris Karloff (playing a Frankenstein-like scientist) can't make up his mind which brain he wants to pop into the poor Monster's head.

Having the Monster harbor Ygor's brain could have been a witty and novel way of wrapping up the entire series. But as Universal expected to get a lot more mileage out of their most popular horror character, the ending only served to confuse the Monster's identity in future sequels. It seemed to confuse the scriptwriters, too, since there is no mention of Ygor's brain for the rest of the series (save for the excised scenes from *Frankenstein Meets the Wolf Man*). By the time Glenn Strange got around to putting on the greasepaint, no one seemed to care. Having Lugosi dub Chaney's lines in Ygor's raspy voice is initially chilling, but the absurdity of the situation sinks in fast. It would have been to the film's advantage had Darling done a bit of research on the ill-effects of mixing incompatible blood-types before coming up with a lot of nonsense about the mismatched blood "not feeding the sensory nerves" of the Monster, thus causing his blindness.

The supernatural visitation of Henry Frankenstein (the "ghost" of the film's title) is too fanciful a plot device for the realistic, pseudoscientific tone of the rest of the movie. Darling assumes, of course, that *anything* goes in a Frankenstein film and doesn't bother with explanations. The episode is ambiguous enough that the whole thing could have been a figment of Ludwig's mind. The unflappable Hardwicke hardly turns a hair and the entire matter is conveniently dropped by the next scene. (Hardwicke himself plays the apparition, sans toupee.)

A few notes about W. Scott Darling: born in Toronto, he was educated in Scotland and came stateside to accept writing positions on various newspapers and magazines. He landed his first job in Hollywood in 1918 as a writer and later became scenario editor for the Christie studios (Mack Sennett's leading competition). By the '40s, Darling was writing for the majors, including Warner Bros., where he wrote a shameless Invisible Man parody called *The Body Disappears* (1941). He dabbled in other genres, especially mysteries and melodramas, often as a collaborator. His credits include Robert Siodmak's notorious *Cobra Woman* (1944), *Sherlock Holmes and the Secret Weapon,* at least one of the Roland Winters Charlie Chan pictures, and even a couple of Karloff's low-rent Mr. Wong frolics.

Darling's return to comedy was inglorious. In fact, he almost singlehandedly finished off the careers of Laurel and Hardy, having penned the once great comedy team's last four features. Even die-hard Stan and Ollie fans concede that *Jitterbugs, The Dancing Masters* (both 1943), *The Big Noise* (1944) and *The Bullfighters* (1945) are low-grade embarrassments.

Where *The Ghost of Frankenstein* scores impressively is its splendid cast. Bela Lugosi's encore performance as a somewhat better-groomed Ygor (at least by Ygor's standards) is welcome, and he has a spate of first-rate scenes (his coercion of Hardwicke in the latter's study is a potent reminder of how good an actor Lugosi can be). The actor also rates high marks in the scene where he conspires with Atwill in regards to the brain transplantation. For once, Lugosi's slow theatrical delivery pays off and he manages to undercut the silliness of the business at hand ("We would rule the state, and even the *whole country*!").

Lionel Atwill deceptively underplays his role, almost as though he's saving his energies for the bravura climax. Atwill is never given the opportunity to go full-throttle, but he quietly indulges in his familiar facial gyrations as the Monster overpowers Hardwicke in the finale. A "regular" in the series, Atwill would soon be relegated to minor roles; his Dr. Bohmer ranks as one of the actor's most underrated horror film performances. Bitterly serving as Frankenstein's underling, Bohmer's one last grasp for power results in his own undoing. The ill-fated doctor remains a bungler to the last.

Compared to the histrionics of Colin Clive and Basil Rathbone, Sir Cedric Hardwicke's Ludwig Frankenstein is staid indeed though his performance has a quiet intensity. Hardwicke's film work never reached the heights of his celebrated theatrical career. Always an accomplished actor, his recessive style invariably limited him to the supporting ranks. Hardwicke once complained to an interviewer that his title, which he claimed carried no social distinction in his homeland, typecast him as a stuffed shirt in Hollywood. He made many films but his talents were often wasted in mediocre material. In his twilight years, Hardwicke was plagued by poor health and a declining career. A poor manager of money by his own admission, Sir Cedric Hardwicke was forced to live off the charity of his actor friends and died as he was about to enter a New Jersey actors home.

Just as he would later demonstrate in his Mummy roles, Lon Chaney believed that all there was to playing a monster was to endure Jack Pierce's torturous makeup sessions. Karloff's interpretation of the Monster had little influence on his performance and he inherited precious little of his father's legendary gift for mime. Whether he's befriending the little village girl or carting around the corpse of Frankenstein's freshly-murdered assistant, Chaney's stone-like expression remains fixed throughout. His apathetic attitude wasn't helped by the violent allergic reaction he suffered from his facial makeup.

Of little help, too, was director Erle C. Kenton. An efficient technician, he stumbled into a horror career after making *Island of Lost Souls* (1933). Otherwise, this former Mack Sennett director and Keystone Cop was best suited for baggy-pants comedy. Kenton handles the action scenes in *The Ghost of Frankenstein* with confidence, particularly the tense rooftop episode with the Monster and the little girl, as well as the various confrontations with the incensed villagers. The Kenton formula was to keep the film moving along, leaving characterization in the hands of the cast. This may have worked for seasoned pros like Hardwicke and Atwill, but the unimaginative Chaney needed strong direction to be effective. Even the camaraderie between the Monster and Ygor lacks the chemistry of the previous film with Karloff in the lead.

Ralph Bellamy and Evelyn Ankers (like Chaney, pickups from *The Wolf Man*) prove themselves reliable performers in the romantic leads. Michael

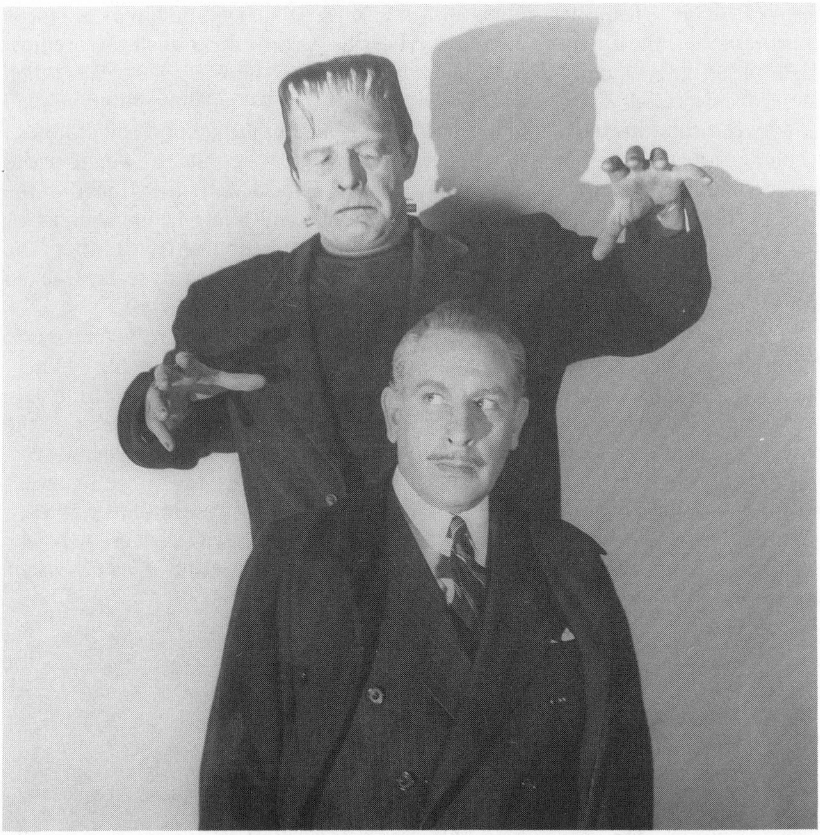

A dark secret from the family's past haunts Ludwig Frankenstein: Lon Chaney (top) and Sir Cedric Hardwicke in a publicity still from *The Ghost of Frankenstein.*

Mark and Lionel Belmore, the two burghers who met death at the hands of the Monster in *Son of Frankenstein,* make a surprise comeback in virtually the same roles. (Curiously, the *surviving* burghers are nowhere to be found!) The studio wouldn't admit to a casting blunder, explaining that it was company policy to rehire as many of the players in the Frankenstein series as possible in order to maintain a sense of continuity from film to film.

The Ghost of Frankenstein's programmer status does little to detract from the visuals (Universal's B films always looked richer than comparably budgeted pictures by such competitors as RKO and Columbia). There is excellent camerawork by Milton Krasner and Elwood Bredell, and cunning use of high- and low-angled shots to exploit the Monster's towering dimensions.

Hans J. Salter serves up a compelling orchestral Sturm und Drang, providing Universal's B film producers with an abundance of horrific musical cues that would be tapped well into the next decade. (It's a little disconcerting to hear Ygor's melancholic horn piped into the soundtrack of *Weird Woman* a few years later). Vera West's fashions for Evelyn Ankers would have been more acceptable had the film been set in Beverly Hills. One of the industry's foremost fashion designers, and a fixture at Universal since the early '30s, West died under tragic and mysterious circumstances in June, 1947. Her nightgown-clad body was found in the swimming pool of her North Hollywood ranch house; a suicide note read, "The fortune teller told me there was only one way to avoid the blackmail I've paid for 23 years—Death." (The 23 years mentioned in the note carried her back to a time when she was 24 and living in the East.) Our research could uncover no follow-up stories; apparently neither the blackmailer nor West's overly pessimistic fortune-teller was ever tracked down.

The Ghost of Frankenstein is a polished work, but hardly an artistic triumph. Though intended as a vehicle for up-and-coming horror star Chaney, the picture only showcased the actor's staggering limitations. The film is rife with minor blemishes and inconsistencies, as if someone was asleep at the wheel. But Universal had little reason to grouse. The flaws were easily overshadowed by producer George Waggner's knack for packaging attractive, well-mounted horror shows which unfailingly turned a profit. The studio wanted a slick film with plenty of action and that's exactly what was delivered. It was enough to keep the kids satisfied, but for grown-up kids, *The Ghost of Frankenstein* is another step down for a once-great series.

Mystery of Marie Roget (1942)

Released April 3, 1942. Reissued by Realart as *Phantom of Paris.* 60 minutes. *Associate Producer:* Paul Malvern. *Directed by* Philip Rosen. *Screenplay by* Michel Jacoby. *Based on the short story "The Mystery of Marie Roget" by* Edgar Allan Poe. *Director of Photography:* Elwood Bredell. *Art Directors:* Jack Otterson & Richard H. Riedel. *Film Editor:* Milton Carruth. *Musical Director:* Hans J. Salter. *Sound Director:* Bernard B. Brown. *Technician:* Robert Pritchard. *Gowns by* Vera West. *Set Decorator:* Russell A. Gausman. *Songs:* Everett Carter & Milton Rosen.

Patric Knowles (Dr. Paul Dupin), Maria Montez (Marie Roget), Maria Ouspenskaya (Mme. Cecile Roget), John Litel (Henri Beauvais), Edward Norris (Marcel Vigneaux), Lloyd Corrigan (Prefect of Police Gobelin), Nell O'Day (Camille Roget), Frank Reicher (Magistrate), Clyde Fillmore (Mons. De Luc), Paul E. Burns (Gardener), Norma Drury (Mme. De Luc), Charles Middleton (Zoo Curator), Bill Ruhl, John Maxwell, Paul Bryar (Detectives), Reed Hadley (Naval Officer), Paul Dubov (Pierre [News Vendor]), Joe Bernard, Frank O'Connor (Men), Ray Bailey (Gendarme), Charles Wagenheim, Lester Dorr (Subordinates to Prefect), Alphonse Martell (Vegetable Cart Driver), Francis Sayles, Jimmie Lucas (Parisians), Beatrice Roberts (Wife on Street), Caroline Cooke (Woman).

Mystery of Marie Roget is another instance of a slick Universal mystery dressed up in ersatz "chiller" trappings to attract the horror trade. "Who is the Phantom Mangler of Paris?" demanded the poster, falsely suggesting something of a Gallic Jack the Ripper angle which the picture itself scarcely delivers. But the Edgar Allan Poe name attached to the original story and a few gratuitously gruesome touches within the film gave the studio press boys all the ammunition they required to promote it as a full-blooded thriller. *Marie Roget* is brisk and entertaining, but it isn't horror and it isn't even good mystery.

The famous horror author's 1842 "The Mystery of Marie Roget" was a follow-up to his earlier (1841) work "The Murders in the Rue Morgue." A continuation of the exploits of the celebrated amateur detective C. Auguste Dupin, "Marie Roget" was based on the real-life murder of a young New York girl, Mary Cecilia Rogers, whose body had been found floating in the Hudson River near Weehawken, New Jersey. The Poe story mirrored the particulars of the Roget case exactly, changing only the names of the principals, the locale and a few additional minor points. Poe transposed the scene of the crime to Paris, centering his story on Dupin and his ruminations on the murder of Marie Roget, counter-girl at a perfumery in the Palais Hotel.

Poe's "The Mystery of Marie Roget" was a lugubrious and long-winded account, with the garrulous Dupin merely scrutinizing newspaper descriptions of the atrocity and drawing various conclusions without conducting an inquiry of his own. (Poe, like Dupin, never investigated personally nor did he visit the murder scene.) It is interesting to note, however, that the confessions of two individuals, made subsequent to the 1842 publication of "Marie Roget," confirmed the conclusion that Poe arrived at in his story as well as *all* of the chief hypothetical details by which his conclusion was reached.

In adapting Poe's 100-year-old story to the screen, scenarist Michel Jacoby updated the story to 1889 (to allow for a scene involving diving equipment) and changed the profession of Marie Roget from shopgirl to musical comedy star to better suit the talents of up-and-coming Universal attraction Maria Montez. Montez receives star billing in the film's opening credits but in the closing castlist she is listed second, below Patric Knowles (as Dr. Dupin). Jacoby also beefed up the insubstantial original tale, adding a veritable Poe-pourri of extra story elements and the usual B-film gallery of red herrings required to muddy the plot waters for the redoubtable Dupin.

The story opens in Paris, at the height of public commotion over the unexplained disappearance of Comédie Française star Marie Roget. Henri Beauvais (John Litel), a friend of the Roget family, is in the office of Police Prefect Gobelin (Lloyd Corrigan) haranguing the diminutive detective, when news of the discovery of a woman's body in the Seine arrives. Accompanied by Paul Dupin (Patric Knowles), the department's chief medical officer, Gobelin and Beauvais hasten to the waterfront to examine the corpse. Although the dead woman's face has been torn to a pulp, the distressed Beauvais identifies the body as that of Marie Roget.

Gobelin and Beauvais appear at the home of Marie's imperious grandmother Madame Cecile Roget (Maria Ouspenskaya) and are about to break the grim news to the old woman when Marie (Maria Montez) sweeps into the room. When Gobelin asks her about her mysterious behavior, Marie high-handedly dresses him down and Beauvais asks the inspector to leave the house.

Camille (Nell O'Day), Marie's sister, becomes engaged to Marcel Vigneaux (Edward Norris), a young man attached to the Ministry of Naval Affairs. Secretly Marie and Marcel are lovers plotting to murder Camille (she is about to come of age and receive her late grandfather's million-and-a-half franc fortune). Mme. Roget overhears Marie and Marcel planning to kill Camille at an upcoming soirée and sends for Dupin. Without divulging what she has overheard, Mme. Roget offers him 50,000 francs to act as Camille's bodyguard at the party. Dupin resists the offer until Camille enters the room, at which point the suddenly-smitten scientist-sleuth graciously accepts the position. In a surprising twist, it's Marie, not Camille, who disappears from the party. Like the unfortunate mystery girl of the opening reel, her body is later dredged out of the river, face horribly mangled.

After another reel or two of mystery-laden exposition, Vigneaux confesses to the murder of Marie, claiming to have killed her to protect Camille. Dupin, convinced that Vigneaux is banking on a verdict of justifiable homicide, imposes on Gobelin to drop the charges until they can prove premeditation on Vigneaux's part. The discovery of the identity of the initial mutilation-murder victim—Vigneaux's first wife—provides the evidence which Dupin needs. He and Gobelin race to the Roget home just as Vigneaux is attacking Camille. A running gunfight across the Paris rooftops ensues, and Vigneaux is shot and killed.

A galloping pace and an appealing roster of players help *Mystery of Marie Roget* over the hurdles and overall the 60-minute film sizes up as one of Universal's more attractive B mystery-adventures of the '40s. As a horror thriller, however, the film comes up distressingly short. All the Poe story provided the film were the title, the Paris setting, Gallicized character names and the basic premise of a woman's body being fished out of the drink. Otherwise writer Jacoby was on his own to embellish the thin story to the best of his abilities. Jacoby adds the mutilated-face angle, and leads audiences to believe that the women may have been mauled by Mme. Roget's pet leopard. (As in the later Universal film *The Scarlet Claw,* a garden weeder was actually used to commit the crimes.)

The horror highpoint of the film is a moderately effective sequence where a Phantom-like cloaked figure (Dupin, as it turns out) slips into the Rue Morgue by night to steal the brain of Marie Roget. (The scene is clearly patterned after one in Warners' 1933 *Mystery of the Wax Museum,* in which burn-faced Lionel Atwill raids the New York City morgue to filch a cadaver.) Late in the film, Vigneaux wears similar black raiment during his attempt on Camille's life and in the subsequent rooftop chase. These half-hearted horrific touches add nicely to the atmosphere of gaslit gloom, but they were probably inadequate compensation for paying customers rightfully expecting a whole-hog horror show.

Patric Knowles' Dupin is a far cry from the analytical bookworm of Poe's stories and from Leon Ames' affected and excitable medical student of the '32 *Murders in the Rue Morgue.* The Dupin of *Mystery of Marie Roget* is a glib yet basically serious-minded young chemist attached to the Paris police force; Knowles brings his usual genial charm to the role, and wrings a good bit of dry humor out of the dialogue. Jacoby's script also bestows upon Dupin a modest measure of fame (he has become something of a household name throughout Paris for unraveling the Rue Morgue mystery), although the inordinate emphasis placed on this long-past triumph leaves us with the impression that he's accomplished little or nothing since.

Knowles' interplay with Lloyd Corrigan (as the Prefect of Police) is a highlight of the film, with Knowles' nimble analytical mind always keeping him several steps ahead of the unimaginative inspector. The two men make a good screen team, and Universal's failure to follow up with a series seems regrettable. (Knowles tells us that he would have been delighted to star in a string of Dupin films.) Edward Norris, John Litel and Nell O'Day are functional in costarring roles, while a particularly colorful roundup of familiar faces (including Frank Reicher, Charles Middleton and Reed Hadley) bring up the rear in minor supporting assignments.

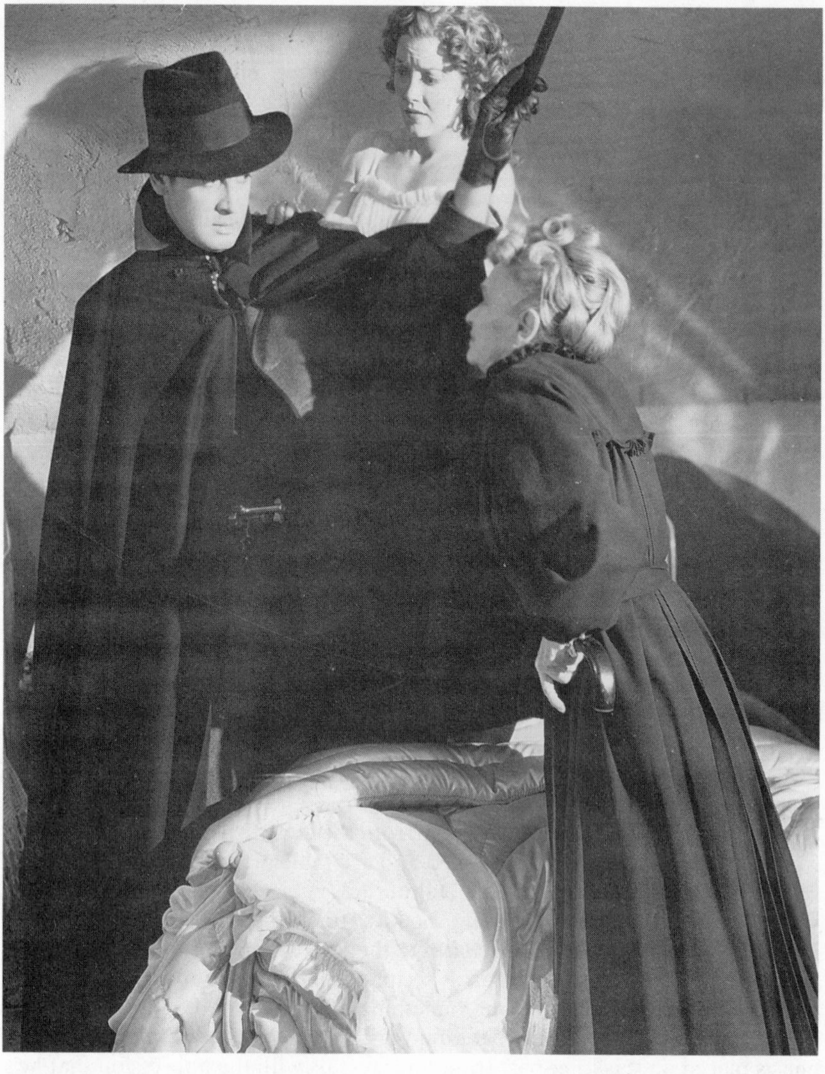

Nell O'Day and Maria Ouspenskaya are no match for caped murderer Edward Norris in the disappointing climax of *Mystery of Marie Roget*.

Up-and-coming "camp" star Maria Montez gives her usual sadly-lacking performance as the doomed Marie: the character is dead before the movie is half over, and her top-billed status is entirely undeserved. Her one song, "Mama Dit Moi," is mouthed by Montez but actually sung by off-camera vocalist Dorothy Triden.

"Maria Montez was quite new to films at the time," reminisces Nell O'Day, who played Camille in the film.

> She was from an affluent Spanish family—at one time her father had been Spain's ambassador to France. I never learned how or why she came to the U.S. and signed a contract with Universal.
>
> She was not popular with the staff and crew because she thought of them almost as servants. She treated the dressers and other people from the wardrobe department as though they were maids! I tried to tactfully tell her that *all* the people working on films were members of a guild or union, that the U.S. was somewhat different from many other countries. But she was intelligent and charming, and we got on very well. She told me I was a *real* professional, probably because I had played in the New York theater. She said more than once that she didn't want to be an actress, "I want to be a *pair-sone-ality*." She was very effective in the films she played in—beautiful and original.

"Everybody says Maria was a bitch, but I loved her," moons Peter Coe.

> She was temperamental, but we were great pals. She was a firm believer in astrology, and she wouldn't do anything without consulting Carroll Righter, who writes for the *L.A. Times*. One day on *Gypsy Wildcat* [1944] we had about six hundred horsemen, gypsy villagers and so on all set to be photographed in one spectacular shot which would eventually move into a closeup of just Maria and me. We rehearsed it until about eleven o'clock, and then the director Roy William Neill said, "Okay, let's shoot." Maria snapped, "*No*." Roy said, "What do you mean, *no?* Come on, we rehearsed it, everything is set, let's shoot the thing!" She said, "No. I do not look good."
>
> Roy was puzzled. "What the hell do you mean, you don't look good? Maria, you look beautiful, you are the most beautiful woman in Hollywood, in the world! Come on, let's take the god-damned shot!" Maria said, "No. No. No," and started to cry—there went the fucking makeup and everything! Roy said, "Why not?", and she said, "My astrologer told me I will not look good until one o'clock in the afternoon!"

Maria died young, but probably not young enough for some, in 1951.

Mystery of Marie Roget was one of three Universal films to employ the talents of Maria Ouspenskaya during her short but memorable stint as a Hollywood character actress. Ouspenskaya had hopes of becoming a coloratura singer in her native Russia before turning her attention to the theater. As a stock company player she toured the Russian provinces and later fell in with the method actors of Stanislavsky's Moscow Art Theater in 1911. She appeared in scores of stageplays and in a half-dozen silent Russian films before making her American stage debut in the mid-1920s. Remaining in America, she continued to work in the theater and founded her own acting school in 1929. Ouspenskaya made her American film debut in 1936's *Dodsworth* (reprising her stage role) and was Oscar-nominated for her performance, although she lost out to another screen newcomer, Gale Sondergaard, who won the Best Supporting Actress award for *Anthony Adverse*.

Dodsworth was the first of 20 Hollywood film roles for the 90-pound Ouspenskaya, who went back and forth between prestige pictures (*Conquest, Love Affair, Waterloo Bridge, Kings Row*) and bill-paying B's (*Judge Hardy and Son, Tarzan and the Amazons,* Republic's *Wyoming*) for the next 13 years. Ouspenskaya is not used to good advantage in *Marie Roget:* as Mme. Roget she alternates between annoyingly cagey and annoyingly cranky, and her infirm appearance and mannerisms quickly rule her out as a suspect. Her role as Maleva the gypsy in Universal's *The Wolf Man* and *Frankenstein Meets the Wolf Man* served the actress far better, and it's with the Maleva character that Ouspenskaya is now most frequently identified. Ouspenskaya fell asleep with a lit cigarette in late November 1949, and died from the burns and a subsequent stroke three days later, at age 73. Nell O'Day reminisces,

> Madame Ouspenskaya was a *real* actress—she had been acting and teaching all her long life. She and I had those scenes with Lisa, the leopard, on the hearth rug beside us. I think we were the only people on the set who were not nervous about that. I was asked more than once if I was nervous, and I quite truthfully said that I *liked* all animals—they could see that I was not afraid. Madame Ouspenskaya appeared so tiny and vulnerable in her wheelchair, the entire crew looked worried. After all, Lisa *was* a real leopard! The assistant cameraman came to the edge of the set and said quietly, "Madame, are you afraid?"
>
> In her deep contralto voice, Maria Ouspenskaya replied in a fashion that settled the entire question: "I am not afraid of *any-sing*!"

Mystery of Marie Roget is a polished B production, achieving an expensive look through the liberal use of handsome standing sets. Lighting and camerawork combine to create a convincing 19th century ambience, while director Philip Rosen keeps his players moving and talking at a fast clip. Rosen had helmed some major productions during the silent era, but spent most of his talkie career heading up minor cheapies for Poverty Row studios like Chesterfield, Liberty, Invincible, Mascot and (especially) Monogram. His other horror credits include *Spooks Run Wild* (1941) with Lugosi and *Return of the Ape Man* ('44) with Lugosi and Carradine.

Marie Roget's fast pace helps to camouflage several serious holes in the plot. It's never explained why Vigneaux murders Marie, nor why he disfigures her face before dumping her body in the river. Although it's understandable that he should mutilate the face of the first victim (his wife), the fact that he indulges in this sadistic excess a second time with Marie seems particularly ill-advised, and would serve only to eventually link him with the earlier murder. (Curiously, Dupin initially fails to connect Vigneaux with the first killing despite the identical *modus operandi.*) Vigneaux's curious plan to win over a jury (he feels that if he claims to have murdered Marie in order to protect Camille, he will be acquitted) seems similarly wrongheaded; here again, his senseless mutilation of Marie's face would obviously work very strongly against him and surely *lose* for him the sympathy of any jury. The fact that Dupin is able to ascertain Marie's criminal nature through an examination of her brain is a quaint but preposterous notion which probably fooled no one even in the less-sophisticated 1940s.

Marie Roget also breaks the cardinal rule of whodunits by failing to adequately obscure the identity of the killer. There are too few suspects, and several of the characters who *do* fall under suspicion in Dupin's eyes are not worthy of consideration. The four prime suspects in Marie's death are Camille, Mme. Roget, Beauvais and Vigneaux. Dupin *sees* Camille conversing with friends at the party scant seconds after Marie's dying scream is heard, and yet he stubbornly persists in including her name on his list of suspects. There's a scene where Mme. Roget, completely alone and unobserved, is walking with difficulty despite the use of *two* canes; this clearly eliminates Madame. Already the list has been reduced to just two candidates, and one of them (Vigneaux) is a young blackguard who was cheerfully plotting to kill Camille at the beginning of the picture. No film of this sort would allow a character to plan such a dastardly crime and escape retribution. To remove the last vestige of doubt and suspense, we get to see the "mystery" killer in the same room with *all three* of the other "suspects" minutes before his identity is exposed!

Mystery of Marie Roget is not a horror film, despite Universal's campaign to palm it off as such, and it tips its hand far too soon to cut muster as a solid whodunit. But judged strictly for what it does deliver – 60 minutes of adventuresome sleuthing, flavored with mystery and mild horror embellishments – it's a prime example of Universal's B-unit working at peak efficiency.

The Strange Case of Doctor Rx (1942)

Released April 17, 1942. 66 minutes. *Directed by* William Nigh. *Associate Producer:* Jack Bernhard. *Original Screenplay by* Clarence Upson Young. *Director of Photography:* Elwood Bredell. *Art Director:* Jack Otterson. *Associate Art Director:* Martin Obzina. *Film Editor:* Bernard W. Burton. *Musical Director:* Hans J. Salter. *Set Decorator:* Russell A. Gausman. *Sound Director:* Bernard B. Brown. *Technician:* Charles Carroll. *Gowns by* Vera West.

Patric Knowles (Jerry Church), Lionel Atwill (Dr. Fish), Anne Gwynne (Kit Logan Church), Samuel S. Hinds (Dudley Crispin), Mona Barrie (Eileen Crispin), Shemp Howard (Sergeant Sweeney), Paul Cavanagh (John Crispin), Edmund MacDonald (Captain Bill Hurd), Mantan Moreland (Horatio B. Fitzwashington), John Gallaudet (Ernie Paul), William Gould (District Attorney Nason), Leland [Leyland] Hodgson (Thomas), Mary Gordon (Mrs. Scott), Jan Wiley (Lily), Boyd Davis (Police Commissioner), Gary Breckner (Radio Announcer), Matty Fain (Tony Zarini), Eddy Chandler (Policeman), Ray "Crash" Corrigan (Bongo), Victor Zimmerman (Kirk), Harry Harvey (Night Club Manager), Selmer Jackson (Judge), Paul Bryar (Bailiff), Joe Recht (First Newsboy), Drew Demarest (Club Waiter), Leonard Sues (Second Newsboy), Jack Kennedy, Jack C. Smith (Policemen).

The Strange Case of Doctor Rx is a movie with an identity problem: it can't make up its mind whether it is a detective mystery or a horror film. It has all the basic ingredients of your standard B mystery – flip private eyes, hard-boiled dames, the usual sideline comic relief, and enough red herrings for two pictures. But, being a Universal picture, its producers couldn't resist tossing in some misplaced horror effects for good measure. There's a megacriminal who polishes off his adversaries with poisoned darts, a captive ape anxiously awaiting a brain transplant, and the threat of a terror so great it turns men's hair white from fright. And it has Lionel Atwill creeping around the corners of the plot looking sinister in thick-lensed glasses, but doing very little else. Even the ad campaign was deliberately aimed at the shock trade.

Clocking in at a little over an hour, *The Strange Case of Doctor Rx* is too inconsequential to be considered anything more than a minor miscalculation. It's far-fetched and preposterous, but not in the affable way *The Mummy's Hand* and *Man Made Monster* are. The whole affair strikes a ludicrous pose. We get the impression that no one, from the actors to those behind the cameras, believed in it for a minute.

The Strange Case of Doctor Rx went before the cameras on October 6, 1941. Jack Bernhard, who had done a competent job mounting *Man Made Monster* the year before, was put in charge of production and William Nigh was assigned to direct. Nigh had helmed all of Karloff's Mr. Wong mysteries at Monogram, as well as the star's tepid 1940 chiller, *The Ape*.

Originally entitled *Dr. RX,* the film underwent a title change in short order, possibly so it wouldn't be confused with the 1932 Warner Bros. classic, *Doctor X*. Bernhard signed Patric Knowles and Anne Gwynne as leads and once again secured the services of Lionel Atwill for the part of Dr. Fish, the film's reddest herring. His insultingly brief role amounted to little more than a cameo, wasting his wonderful facility for screen mayhem.

As the picture opens, the police are investigating the fifth in a series of strange murders in which the victims, all previously acquitted of various murder charges, are struck down by an unknown avenger who calls himself Dr. Rx. Captain Bill Hurd of Homicide (Edmund MacDonald) tries to enlist the aid of his close friend and former partner, Jerry Church (Patric Knowles), now engaged as a private investigator. Church turns Hurd down cold . . . he has decided to quit the racket once and for all and join his family's bond business ("Did you say *blonde* business?" interjects Hurd).

Church is summoned to the Long Island estate of wealthy criminal lawyer Dudley Crispin (Samuel S. Hinds). Crispin had defended three of the murdered men in court, and is upset by his understandable shortage of clients as of late.

Church's on again–off again fiancée, Kit Logan (Anne Gwynne), a mystery writer-*cum*-amateur sleuth, reappears after a long absence, and immediately takes charge of Jerry's affairs. After a quickie marriage (tossed in, no doubt, to appease the Breen watchdogs), Kit uses her influence to get Jerry to drop the case. (Dr. Rx has just claimed his sixth victim, right in the middle of a crowded courtroom.) Kit's fears are compounded after she visits the home of a former detective who has become a jibbering, white-haired idiot following a face-to-face encounter with the crazed medico (all of this beautiful exposition only increases our displeasure with the disappointments to come).

After much ado, Jerry finally agrees to his wife's demands. But, before the newlyweds can hop a train to Boston, Church is kidnapped by a gang of thugs led by Ernie Paul (John Gallaudet). Ernie is irate because the police have tagged him Suspect #1 for the last Rx murder. He forces Jerry to resume his investigation and exonerate him . . . or else.

Later, Jerry and his black valet, Horatio (Mantan Moreland), are abducted by a cowled stranger, Dr. Rx himself. Knocked unconscious, Church awakens to find himself strapped to an operating table opposite a restless caged ape (stuntman/actor/Hollywood ape impersonator Ray Corrigan). Dr. Rx, his identity concealed behind a surgical smock and hood, details the motive behind his bizarre crime. "For every crime there is a punishment. Men who sin much pay a just penalty." And then, in his best bedside manner, he adds, "You see in Bongo—he is very stupid but he will be very smart. And you will be, well, not so smart. In other words, I am going to transfer your brains. . . ."

The good doctor attaches the ape's chain to Jerry's table, then watches with grim satisfaction as Bongo inches the helpless detective closer to him.

Ray "Crash" Corrigan in the monkey suit menaces Anne Gwynne in this publicity still for what was really a standard whodunit—*The Strange Case of Doctor Rx.*

Church blacks out. The next morning, the police discover Church and Horatio wandering aimlessly around the waterfront, their hair turned dead white.

The Police Commissioner (Boyd Davis) gathers everyone connected with the case around the unconscious detective's hospital bed. Dr. Fish (Lionel Atwill), a stranger who has been seen following Jerry around town, is called forward to give medical testimony. He turns to Crispin and requests the use of his pen. Visibly shaken, the lawyer removes the pen from his pocket, points it towards his chest, then drops dead. Church leaps out of his bed (dropping his phony white hairpiece) but he is too late to stop the suicide.

Later, Jerry and Doc Fish (who, we learn, had been working with Church all along) explain the foggy details of the case to the bewildered Hurd. "The man had two phobias," Fish says. "Number one, he was an egomaniac with a desire to mesmerize a jury and get his client acquitted. Number two, he wanted to punish the criminal himself." Crispin's instrument of murder was a pen that projected poisonous darts, which left no trace on the victim's body. Jerry noticed the strange-looking pen amongst Dr. Rx's lab instruments. Another tipoff was the manner in which the lawyer signed his name . . . Dudley CRispin. The "R" matched the letter in the Rx murder notes that had been tagged on each victim's corpse.

With a more coherent script, a plausible denouement, and less ham-fisted humor by Mantan Moreland and Shemp Howard, *The Strange Case of Doctor Rx* might have amounted to something more than just a barely passable time-killer. The germ of a good idea is there, but Clarence Upson Young disinfects it by overloading his script with irritating detours and extraneous details.

The screenplay's horror elements are, to put it charitably, patently absurd. Poison dart-throwing pens have never numbered amongst Hollywood's more credible murder weapons. (The 1939 *The House of Fear* featured a similar gizmo; so did the 1943 serial *The Adventures of Smilin' Jack*.) The poison that Crispin used "strangled" the victim after it entered the bloodstream. Granted, this method proved to be successful but wouldn't it have been more practical for the deranged advocate to eliminate his foes in a dozen more convenient ways? It also seems highly unlikely that Crispin would go to such outlandish lengths to silence savvy investigators when a simple bullet in the brain would have been just as effective (not to mention saving him the cost of maintaining Kenneth Strickfaden's electrical apparatus and a live gorilla!). Casting the venerable Samuel S. Hinds as the "surprise" villain was a smart move though it's doubtful the actor actually played Dr. Rx in the abduction and laboratory sequences.

Patric Knowles and Anne Gwynne turn in their usual amiable performances as the comfortably laid-back detective and his inquisitive wife (their friends call the bickering pair the "Battling Churches"). Knowles, Gwynne and costar Edmund MacDonald have such a good chemistry going here it's quite probable that with better scripts and directors, a Jerry Church mystery-thriller series might have caught on.

Knowles, who had been on an Army furlough when he made *The Strange Case of Doctor Rx,* had the kind of easy-does-it, unassuming charm that made him perfectly suited as the second lead or the hero's best friend. A former member of Dublin's Abbey Players, he was under contract at Warner Bros., RKO, Republic, Paramount, and of course Universal (where he enjoyed working despite the fact he was once suspended by the studio after they refused to allow him to do a Broadway play). Knowles confirmed a recent claim made by Anne Gwynne that a good share of the dialogue in *The Strange Case of Doctor Rx* was improvised by the actors who were forced to work with an incomplete script.

"Yes! We all contributed," Knowles recalls. "Working with Anne was a great joy. Lionel Atwill and I shared dirty stories! I retired fifteen years ago. Nowadays some people ask me, 'Didn't you use to be Patric Knowles?' They nearly always add, 'Never got the girl, did you?'!"

In the tradition of the period's great detective series, Clarence Upson Young abuses that frequently misused ingredient known as "comedy relief." Black comic Mantan Moreland is made the butt of the kind of racist humor so prevalent at this time. His valet/servant/gofer Horatio is presumably so dense, he's forced to resort to "thought association" tricks in order to keep track of his menial duties. ("Airport . . . airplane . . . clouds . . . birds . . . nest . . . eggs . . . BREAKFAST!") This good-natured degradation has an unpleasant, rather sinister pay-off: poor Horatio suffers the fate intended for Church. Cackling like a madman, his hair turned white from fright, Moreland has the dubious honor of closing the film before the final credits flash across the screen.

Slickly made, nominally entertaining, but erratic and absurd, *The Strange Case of Doctor Rx* is a lesser light in Universal's galaxy of horror.

Invisible Agent (1942)

Released July 31, 1942. 79 minutes. A Frank Lloyd Production. *Directed by* Edwin L. Marin. *Associate Producer:* George Waggner. *Screenplay by* Curt Siodmak. *Suggested by the novel* ***The Invisible Man*** *by* H.G. Wells. *Director of Photography:* Les White. *Special Photographic Effects:* John P. Fulton. *Film Editor:* Edward Curtiss. *Art Director:* Jack Otterson. *Associate Art Director:* Robert Boyle. *Assistant Director:* Vernon Keays. *Musical Director:* Hans J. Salter. *Set Decorator:* Russell A. Gausman. *Associate Set Decorator:* Edward R. Robinson. *Director of Sound:* Bernard B. Brown. *Technician:* William Hedgcock. *Gowns by* Vera West.

Ilona Massey (Maria Sorenson/Maria Goodrich), Jon Hall (Frank Raymond/Frank Griffin), Peter Lorre (Baron Ikito), Sir Cedric Hardwicke (Conrad Stauffer), J. Edward Bromberg (Karl Heiser), Albert Basserman (Arnold Schmidt). John Litel (John Gardiner), Holmes Herbert (Sir Alfred Spencer), Keye Luke (Surgeon), Philip Van Zandt (Nazi S.S. Man), Matt Willis (Nazi Assassin), Mabel Colcord (Maid), John Holland (Spencer's Secretary), Marty Faust (Killer), Alberto Morin (Free Frenchman), Wolfgang Zilzer (von Porten), Ferdinand Munier (Bartender), Eddie Dunn, Hans Schumm (S.S. Men), John Burton (RAF Flier), Lee Tung-Foo (General Chin Lee), Milburn Stone (German Sergeant), Michael Visaroff (Verichen), Walter Tetley (Newsboy), Pat West (German Taxi Driver), Leslie Denison (British Radio Operator), William Ruhl, Otto Reichow (Gestapo Agents), Pat McVey (German), Wally Scott, Bobby Hale (English Tommies), Charles Flynn, Phil Warren, Paul Bryar, John Merton (German Soldiers), Lee Shumway (Brigadier General), Henry Zynder (Colonel Kelenski), Ferdinand Schumann-Heink (German Telephone Operator), Victor Zimmerman, Bill Pagan, Henry Guttman (Storm Troopers), Lane Chandler, Duke York, Donald Curtis (German Sentries), Charles Regan (Ordinance Car Driver), Sven Hugo-Borg (German Captain), James Craven (Ship's Radio Man), Eddie Parker (Stunts).

By 1942, Hollywood was swept into the war in earnest with each studio pitching in to boost morale at home with a spate of slick propaganda pieces. Overnight, the cynicism of the '30s was replaced by the flag-waving of the '40s. Poverty Row outfits began to inject war-related themes into their action pictures and it wasn't long before horror and propaganda merged into an uncomfortable hybrid. The result was a subgenre of wartime horror flicks. These dubious exercises in patriotism thrived at Monogram where such clinkers as *King of the Zombies* (1941), *Black Dragons* (1942) and *Revenge of the Zombies* (1943) established the formula of a mad scientist who moonlights for the Third

Reich. A bit of war talk was ineffectually shoehorned into PRC's *The Mad Monster* (1942), featuring George Zucco as a batty doctor working for *our* side who tries to convince his peers that the only way to win the war is to breed an army of werewolves! Even Warner Bros. got into the act with a borderline horror opus, *The Gorilla Man* (1943), and the atmospheric *The Mysterious Doctor* (1943), which had a Nazi agent stirring up trouble by disguising himself as a headless ghost.

On the whole, these features were a pretty poor lot but Universal's contribution to the subgenre was a cut above average. The studio had been grinding out a raft of espionage movies, each approximately 60 minutes in length, bearing titles like *Madame Spy, Unseen Enemy* and *Destination Unknown.* When the suggestion of a film about an invisible commando battling the Nazis on their own turf emerged, Universal decided to pull all stops and play it up as an A feature.

Announced as *The Invisible Spy* early in 1942, the picture was released under the slightly modified title *Invisible Agent.* Frank Lloyd and Jack Skirball, the team responsible for Alfred Hitchcock's *Saboteur,* one of the studio's few prestige releases that year, were the picture's original producers. But Skirball dropped out of the project and George Waggner was assigned the title associate producer.

The Scottish-born Lloyd was a big-time director with a decidedly elusive style. Although a polished craftsman, most of his films are best remembered for the contributions of others. He won an Oscar in 1933 for *Cavalcade,* a straightforward adaptation of a hit Noel Coward play. *Mutiny on the Bounty* (1935) is noted for the flinty chemistry of Charles Laughton and Clark Gable, and *If I Were King* (1938) for Preston Sturges' witty dialogue. Lloyd, if nothing else, had to his credit an unflinching eye for talent and uncommonly good taste until this inexplicable lapse. In 1942, he produced a couple of Universal's more ambitious features, including the John Wayne–Marlene Dietrich vehicle *The Spoilers.* How his participation in a follow-up to *The Invisible Woman* came about is anyone's guess.

Invisible Agent may seem like a respectable effort after the series had sunk to the level of silly burlesque in *The Invisible Woman.* The most gimmicky of the Universal horror characters, the Invisible Man was becoming less of a menace with each passing film. His transition to an athletic, all–American hero befuddling the Axis forces would make sense only to a studio on the brink of turning Sherlock Holmes into a Nazi hunter. It's the kind of material that could never rise above the level of pulp and one wonders why the studio inflated it to the upper brackets. The production's elevated status at least gave it the benefits of a strong cast and good production values. Best of all, *Invisible Agent* is a fast-moving and entertaining package. To its credit, the film got the series back on the right track again with a reasonably serious presentation.

The Griffin family has taken up residence in America where the infamous scientist's grandson (Jon Hall) runs a modest Manhattan print shop under an assumed name. The first scene is a good one. Four suspicious-looking men enter the shop on the premise of conducting routine business. A confrontation ensues as one of the men produces a pistol, informing Griffin he is aware of

World War II made its presence felt on the horror genre in such films as *Invisible Agent*.

his true identity. The gentleman is Conrad Stauffer (Sir Cedric Hardwicke), a top dog in Hitler's S.S. (The film has a curious aversion to awarding ranks to its military characters, but Stauffer appears to be a general.) Stauffer explains that he and his Japanese companion, Baron Ikito (Peter Lorre), are seeking Griffin's invisibility formula and are prepared to use force to obtain it. Griffin barely avoids having his fingers lopped off in a paper cropper by Stauffer's strong-arm men and manages to escape with the secret formula still in his grasp.

His cover blown, Griffin is implored by government officials to turn the formula over to the Pentagon, but he refuses. With the bombing of Pearl Harbor, Griffin finally agrees to release the formula on the condition that the drug only be used by himself. Reluctantly given the go-ahead, he is parachuted over the German lines after being inoculated with the formula.

The now-transparent Griffin locates his contact, carpenter Arnold Schmidt (Albert Basserman), who reveals that Frank's mission is to obtain a list of Japanese spies operating in the United States, now in the possession of Stauffer. Griffin dashes off to the home of Maria Sorenson (Ilona Massey), a British spy posing as a German agent and Stauffer's paramour. (The number of coincidences in the film amount to an impressive total.)

With Stauffer away on government business, Maria entertains his immediate subordinate Karl Heiser (J. Edward Bromberg), who makes no secret his affections for Maria. Griffin, who has been imbibing Heiser's champagne, takes advantage of his invisibility to harass the Nazi. Stauffer unexpectedly turns up and, sensing disloyalty, orders Heiser arrested.

Hoping to pinch the prized list of Japanese spies, Griffin arrives at

Stauffer's office only to find the German officer ready and waiting for him. Frank outfoxes his adversaries, steals the list and heads for Schmidt's shop to have the invaluable information sent to England.

Griffin's next stop is Heiser's prison cell, where he forces the condemned ex-officer to reveal the date of Germany's planned attack on New York. Heiser confesses that the attack is scheduled for that very night and in return is sprung from the jail. Unaware that Schmidt has been arrested by the S.S., Frank steals into the shop and is captured by Baron Ikito, who ensnares him in a net lined with razor-sharp fishhooks. Frank and Maria are whisked away to the Japanese embassy, which is soon overrun with Stauffer's men. Griffin and the girl escape in the melee as Stauffer and Ikito clash. The Japanese stabs Stauffer to death, then, realizing the depth of his failure to net Griffin, commits hara-kiri.

Making their way to the airfield, Griffin and Maria commandeer one of the bombers earmarked for the New York air raid. After taking off and dropping a full load of bombs on the airfield below, they make their way to England; on the ground below, Heiser is cut down by Stauffer's assassins. In a romantic wrap-up, Griffin is restored to visibility and is reunited with Maria.

H.G. Wells was officially credited as the inspiration for this film, but the real *auteur* of *Invisible Agent* is scenarist Curt Siodmak. A real-life fugitive of Hitler's regime, Siodmak gleefully made the Nazis the butt of ridicule, and at least one reviewer at the time questioned the wisdom of underestimating this very real German threat. Except for the formidable Stauffer, the Nazis come off as hapless buffoons almost worthy of the Keystone Cops. The comic low-point of the script had Griffin planting his foot into the seat of Hitler's pants in a scene that was mercifully excised from all release prints. According to the pressbook, the episode was cut after a ban of scenes making enemy dictators the target of personal attacks was invoked. Siodmak does write some sharp dialogue and the picture's many anti-Nazi diatribes are clearly his own sentiments, especially Griffin's goading of Heiser in his own prison cell. ("I pity the devil when you boys start arriving in bunches.")

Surprisingly, Griffin proves on many occasions to be a less-than-ideal hero. An amateur spy, he isn't particularly resourceful and is downright boorish in his groundless suspicion of Maria's loyalty. Indeed, he seems more interested in stomping on toes, kicking ass and pulling chairs from underneath ever-fumbling Nazi underlings than in getting down to the serious business of undercover work. This lightweight, comic-book air almost does the picture in. Of little help, too, is an insipid ending in which Maria, clad in a fur, is carried off by the invisible Griffin amid a rabble of dumbstruck German soldiers.

It is up to the heavies, Sir Cedric Hardwicke and Peter Lorre, to give *Invisible Agent* its cutting edge; their fine, controlled underplaying is the backbone of the picture. It was Lorre's only appearance in a Universal horror movie and it's a welcome one, even though he's playing what amounts to a sinister Mr. Moto. Lionel Atwill was originally announced in the cast, possibly in Hardwicke's part, although Lorre's role as the insidious Ikito can't be ruled out either. (It's pretty tough to imagine Atwill flooring Hardwicke with an expertly executed judo flip as Lorre does in the climax.) Universal wasn't averse

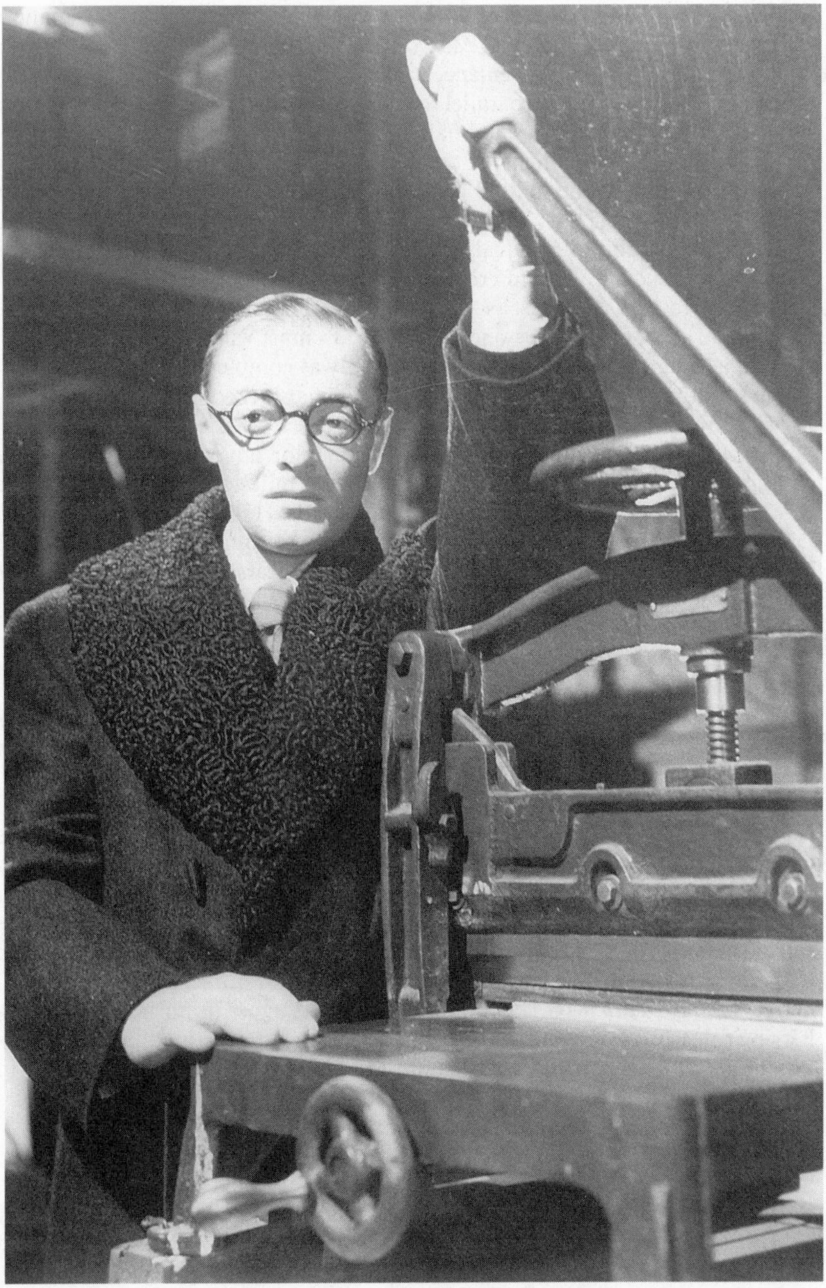

Manicure, anyone? Peter Lorre turns a paper cropper into an instrument of persuasion in *Invisible Agent*. (Photo courtesy Steve Jochsberger.)

to casting Atwill as an Oriental, assigning him in a role as an overfed Japanese saboteur in the serial *Junior G-Men of the Air* (1942).

A partnership of convenience, Hardwicke and Lorre's alliance is an uneasy one at best, roughly parallel to actual German-Japanese relations at the time. At every opportunity, Siodmak depicts them as cut-throats eagerly plotting against each other whenever the other's back is turned, with their feigned politeness hinting at the mutual contempt lurking beneath the surface. After the pair clash in their last, lethal confrontation, the camera pans to their dead bodies, making a bitter political statement. Siodmak belatedly abandoned his tongue-in-cheek attitude and created the strongest scene in the picture.

Ilona Massey is well cast as Maria and Jon Hall is adequate in the title role. Hall would soon prove to be one of Universal's most valuable players. The second film under his contract, *Invisible Agent* was completed a few weeks prior to the shooting of *Arabian Nights,* the movie that kicked off his teaming with Maria Montez. An association that lasted four years and encompassed a half-dozen movies, their gloriously garish Technicolor adventures were popular escapist fare in their day and are still considered milestones of camp by those who have the endurance to sit through them. Hall was set to join the Diplomatic Corps before being spotted by a talent scout, and later claimed he became an actor mostly for the money. Like most stars who built their careers on how well they looked in a bathing suit, Hall was hardly a major talent but proved to be a likable if somewhat wooden leading man.

Hungarian-born stage actor J. Edward Bromberg was signed in the early '40s by Universal where he easily won supporting roles as Europeans. Plump, oily and unattractive, Bromberg offered little appeal and compounded his dearth of charm with excessive mugging. His performance as Heiser is even more taxing than usual.

Invisible Agent was directed with efficiency but little style by Edwin L. Marin, a prolific Hollywood hack of the Lew Landers school whose career was checkered with missed opportunities. In 1933, he directed Reginald Owen as a pre–Basil Rathbone Sherlock Holmes in a one-shot programmer best remembered as a curiosity, *A Study in Scarlet.* Marin's version of *A Christmas Carol* (1938) for MGM reaffirms the classic status of the popular Alastair Sim remake. Horror fans' grudge against Marin goes as far back as his directorial debut in *The Death Kiss* (1933), which wasted Lugosi in an innocuous red-herring role while he was still in his prime. There is little distinction in his direction of *Invisible Agent,* though he pulls the film off with verve and polish. In his typical inattention to detail, all of Marin's supposedly German bit players have gratingly different accents.

John P. Fulton's Oscar-nominated special effects weren't quite up to par. Scuttling the usual bandages-and-goggles look established in previous pictures, Fulton materializes Hall in a bathrobe, sunglasses and a heavy application of cold cream. The effect is less than awe-inspiring and rather carelessly concocted since Hall's mouth and teeth are inexplicably visible. Hall's image is frequently silhouetted in a few of his transparent appearances (a glitch which rarely occurred in the earlier films), suggesting that Fulton was probably rushed more than usual.

Invisible Agent is a maddeningly uneven film. One is swept along by its enthusiasm and pacing and some occasional powerful passages. But the picture is built on a silly premise and there are juvenile digressions to spare. It certainly does no great service to H.G. Wells. Chalk it up as a "guilty pleasure," but not an inconsiderable one.

Sherlock Holmes and the Voice of Terror (1942)

Released September 18, 1942. 65 minutes. *Directed by* John Rawlins. *Associate Producer:* Howard Benedict. *Screenplay by* Lynn Riggs & John Bright. *Adaptation by* Robert D. Andrews. *Based on the story "The Last Bow" by* Sir Arthur Conan Doyle. *Director of Photography:* Elwood Bredell. *Art Director:* Jack Otterson. *Associate Art Director:* Martin Obzina. *Film Editor:* Russell Schoengarth. *Music Director:* Charles Previn. *Music by* Frank Skinner. *Set Decorators:* Russell A. Gausman & Edward R. Robinson. *Sound Director:* Bernard B. Brown. *Technician:* Robert Pritchard. *Technical Advisor:* Tom McKnight. *Gowns by* Vera West.

Basil Rathbone (Sherlock Holmes), Nigel Bruce (Dr. John H. Watson), Evelyn Ankers (Kitty), Reginald Denny (Sir Evan Barham), Thomas Gomez (R.F. Meade), Henry Daniell (Anthony Lloyd), Montagu Love (General Jerome Lawford), Hillary Brooke (Jill Grandis), Mary Gordon (Mrs. Hudson), Arthur Blake (Crosbie), Leland [Leyland] Hodgson (Captain Roland Shore), Olaf Hytten (Admiral Sir John Prentiss), Harry Stubbs (Taxi Driver), Harry Cording (Camberwell), Robert O. Davis [Rudolph Anders] (Schieler), Donald Stuart (Grady), Leslie Denison (London Bobby), Robert Barron (Gavin), Alec Harford (Grimes), John Rogers (Duggan), Charles Jordan (Man), Herbert Evans (Smithson), John Wilde (Heinrich), Arthur Stenning (English Officer), George Sherwood (London Cab Driver), Edgar Barrier (The Voice of Terror).

The late 1930s and early '40s were the true heyday of the detective film in Hollywood when almost every studio begat at least one series based on a popular fictional detective. Cheap and popular entertainments, the genre thrived at second tier and Poverty Row outfits as well as at the B units of the major studios. For years, Universal was producing a bumper crop of mysteries but their entry into the detective series sweepstakes had been a long time in coming. (Preston Foster's recurring Inspector Crane character in a couple of the Crime Club pictures can be safely discounted as a series.)

Sir Arthur Conan Doyle's master detective certainly had the makings of a stylish series. Several screen versions of the enduring character had already been attempted, climaxed by 20th Century–Fox's spectacularly successful pair of Holmes features (both released in 1939). By any standard, *The Hound of the Baskervilles* and *The Adventures of Sherlock Holmes* were top drawer productions, marked by good casts, fine sets and competent direction. Which is the

Basil Rathbone in *Sherlock Holmes and the Voice of Terror*

better of the two is a debatable question. *Adventures* is probably more immediately gratifying, while *Hound,* a bit of a letdown at first, improves with each viewing.

Adventures features an intriguing story and fine performances by Ida Lupino and George Zucco (at his all-time best as Professor Moriarty). *Hound,* unfolding on the craggy, fog-swept moors, offers the fine company of Lionel Atwill and John Carradine in supporting roles and boasts one of Conan Doyle's most compelling, well-calculated plots. Both films share the sure-footed sleuthing of Basil Rathbone and Nigel Bruce as Holmes and Watson.

The team was a popular success, but critical reservations persist to this day. Basil Rathbone brought a commanding stage presence to the role and continues to be almost universally regarded as the ideal Holmes. Dr. Watson, as written by Conan Doyle, was unflappable, studious and nobody's fool, and there was little contrast in the humorless, somewhat stuffy duo, at least in the opinion of the story department. To the chagrin of the critics, Watson was transformed into something of a buffoon, especially as played by the jolly, blustery Bruce. Resultantly, the latent feelings of condescension Holmes always had for his devoted sidekick came out in full force. Many critics were appalled but the audiences loved it. Rathbone himself went so far as to say that the fan's attraction to Sherlock Holmes begins with Watson.

Curiously, 20th Century–Fox spurned the possibility of a series and the rights to Conan Doyle's stories remained with the author's trustees. Universal initiated negotiations in early 1942 and a contract was reached calling for $300,000 to be paid to Conan Doyle's estate. The contract stipulated that the studio would hold the screen rights to the Sherlock Holmes character for a seven-year period, as well as the rights to 21 of the author's short stories.

Universal promptly secured the services of Rathbone and Bruce, who were cementing their identification with the roles by starring in a Sherlock Holmes radio program. With all of the legal hurdles cleared, the studio turned the series over to Howard Benedict, the newly hired associate producer, recently recruited from RKO–Radio Pictures.

With the exception of MGM's swank Thin Man pictures, Hollywood's detective movie series was almost always relegated to second features. Universal didn't intend to break the mold. The Sherlock Holmes movies were given adequate budgets and less hectic production schedules than the usual 12-day cheapies, but Universal wasn't about to match 20th Century's princely expenditure on the detective. Fortunately, Universal's standing sets, even if they were becoming increasingly familiar, could be counted on to give the pictures a richness which transcended their budgets.

The studio came very close to fudging the entire enterprise in their extraordinary decision to update the Holmes character and place him in a contemporary setting, leading the heroic fight against the Axis. It wasn't a totally unexpected move. Costume and period pictures wre rapidly going out of fashion in the harsh reality of the early war years. At other studios, private eyes such as Charlie Chan, Ellery Queen et al. were feeling the effects of the war by matching wits with spies and enemy agents. The gaslit sets, horse-drawn cabs and foggy cobblestone London streets so closely associated with Sherlock Holmes were gone, and were replaced by a *milieu* befitting of espionage and intrigue.

The ink had barely dried on Universal's contract with the Conan Doyle estate when the studio plunged into production of the series' opener. Filming commenced on May 5, 1942, under the working title *Sherlock Holmes Saves London.* In what would become a standard practice, a tentative title was assigned each picture, only to be changed well before its release. In this case, *Sherlock Holmes and the Voice of Terror* was finally chosen as the official title.

The film begins with a battering montage of images. A cruel, strident voice, identifying itself as the Voice of Terror (Edgar Barrier), interrupts British radio transmissions, painstakingly describing acts of terror and mayhem committed in the name of the Third Reich. Dams are blown up, munitions factories and supplies are destroyed, and government emissaries are slain as the Voice promises even further disasters.

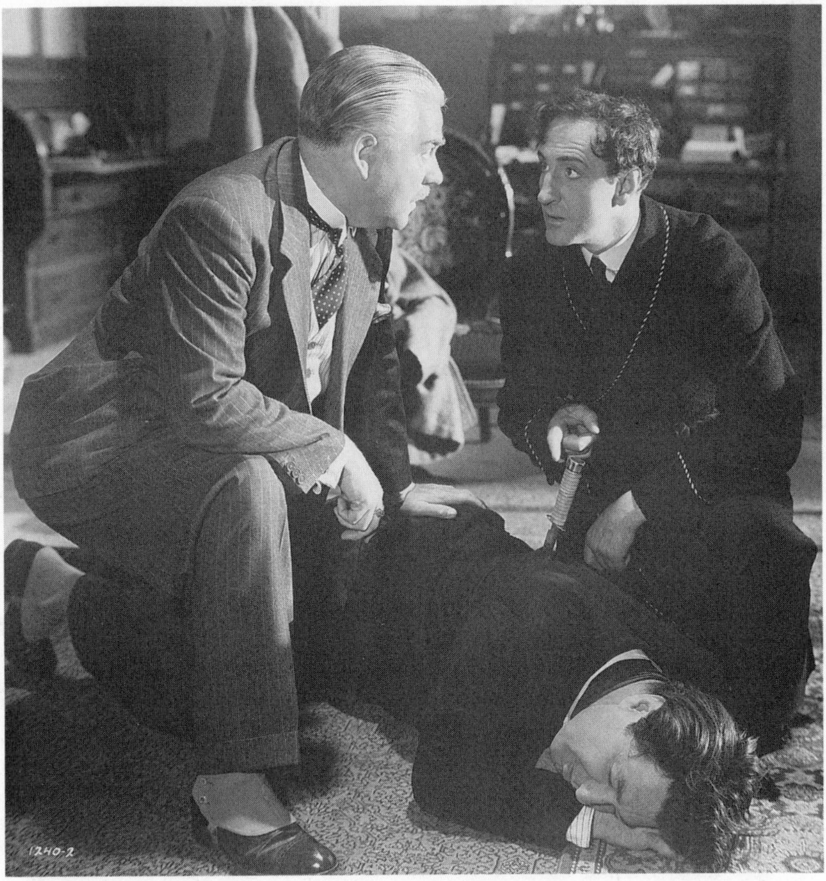

Nigel Bruce and Basil Rathbone ponder the meaning of Robert Barron's last words in *Sherlock Holmes and the Voice of Terror.*

As it is obvious that the Voice is privy to highly classified information, Sir Evan Barham (Reginald Denny) of the Intelligence Inner Council calls upon Sherlock Holmes and Dr. Watson (Rathbone and Bruce) to investigate, despite the heated objections of his colleagues. Later that evening, Gavin (Robert Barron), one of Holmes' operatives, crashes into the detective's flat with a dagger buried in his back. He utters only one word, "Christopher," before dying. The urgency of the message compels Holmes and Watson to enlist the aid of Gavin's wife, Kitty (Evelyn Ankers), a barmaid at a seedy waterfront pub, to learn the meaning of her late husband's message. Kitty responds by sending her cronies out into the night to solve the riddle.

Kitty comes through and tips off the detective that Gavin was referring to Christopher Docks. Holmes, Watson and Anthony Lloyd (Henry Daniell) of the Inner Council arrive at the site and uncover a nest of enemy spies led by

Meade (Thomas Gomez), who holds them at gunpoint. Kitty's gang intervenes and rescues the trio but Meade manages to escape in a speedboat.

Doing a bit of undercover work on her own, Kitty manages to locate Meade and promptly becomes his mistress while discreetly advising Holmes of his activities. In the meantime, the Voice of Terror haunts the airwaves again, announcing that a German air strike against England's north shore will take place the following night. Barham orders an alert to counter the attack. But Holmes is skeptical; he feels that the Voice is bluffing, and that it's the *south* shore that will be attacked.

Inducing the Inner Council to accompany him to the south shore the next evening, Holmes and his forces round up Meade and a band of German soldiers, hiding out in a crumbling cathedral (the old Castle Dracula set, slightly modified). Holmes, in his most grandiose manner, announces to the stunned members of the Council that the Voice of Terror is none other than Sir Evan Barham! The minister, it turns out, is actually a member of the German Secret Police, posing as Barham for the last 20 years after the real Barham was executed while a prisoner of war. Holmes discloses that the Council was deliberately misinformed; the RAF's defense planes are fully prepared to meet the German attack on the south coast.

Taking advantage of everyone's understandable confusion, Meade draws a pistol and murders Kitty for betraying him. He is machine-gunned to death while attempting an escape. Saluting Kitty's unswerving patriotism, the humbled Council assures Holmes that her sacrifice will not be forgotten.

Sherlock Holmes and the Voice of Terror may be only a B film, but it at least has lofty aspirations. By enlisting Holmes to safeguard national security, Universal somehow thought they were elevating the master detective to the position of a war hero. By making Holmes' adversary the entire German military machine, the studio congratulated itself on its timeliness and contribution to the war effort. The film is a bald-face rallying cry for its audience to unite in the defense of democracy. Patriotic speeches abound. The Nazis spew out their ruthless plan for world domination. The whole charade is a defensible piece of propaganda and even an entertaining movie, but why all this flag-waving was crammed into a Sherlock Holmes feature in the first place may be the most baffling mystery of all. Despite its virtues, *Sherlock Holmes and the Voice of Terror* is neither fish nor fowl and remains today a most unfocused effort.

At least Holmes' entrance is true to form. The skeptical stuffed shirts who comprise the Inner Council are treated to an incredible display of deductive reasoning. Deep footprints in the carpet tellingly indicate one member's heated disapproval of Holmes' invitation to join the group. Holmes calculates that Barham had just arrived from his country estate by noting the particular variety of clay on his boots. It's reassuring that this updated version of the detective isn't much different from his Victorian counterpart, even if his modernized wardrobe is a bit disconcerting.

The first item to go when Holmes was updated to the 1940s was his famous double-visored hunting cap. The script rather wittily handles the problem as the detective is about to charge out of his Baker Street flat hot on the trail of a fresh lead. Instinctively picking up the familiar cap, he is stopped cold by

Watson who sternly reminds him, "Ah-ah! You promised!" Obligingly, Holmes selects an up-to-date, turned-down fedora.

One feels less at home with the heavy-handed political drumbeating. Penetrating the dingiest of waterfront dives, Holmes almost hypnotically initiates Kitty into patriotic service. She responds with an off-the-cuff, too-eloquent political sermon of her own and instantly recruits a pubfull of drifters and barflies into Holmes' underground army. Later, Meade, too, sounds off with a speech rich in heavy-handed symbolism. He recalls a boyhood dream in which he's dressed in armor and trampling ruthlessly over the swarming masses. "What if this were no dream?" he ponders aloud; "what if it were prophecy?"

The speeches are earnestly written, solemnly delivered, and even moving at times. Yet one wishes Holmes were back at Baskerville Hall. *Sherlock Holmes and the Voice of Terror* is a movie with a message; since it's for a good cause, the message is delivered with little humor and even less subtlety.

There's little fault in the acting. With the exception of Thomas Gomez, who plays Meade with intensity, the performers are mostly stout Britons of the old school. Many have complained that Henry Daniell is wasted as the non-villainous but icy Anthony Lloyd, but it's always a pleasure to watch this fine actor in *anything;* he has certainly fared worse in his career. Essaying the role of the plucky Cockney bairmaid, Evelyn Ankers enjoys a change of pace from her usual slightly stuffy heroine roles and gets a chance to do some real acting. (Ankers' performance recalls her role as a down-to-earth English working girl in the 1941 B *Burma Convoy.*) The reliable Reginald Denny is in fine form as the surprise heavy. Edgar Barrier puts on a German accent for his off-camera role as the insidious "Voice of Terror." Making her Sherlock Holmes film debut, Hillary Brooke replaced Marjorie Lord in the inconsequential part of chauffeur Jill Grandis.

Sherlock Holmes and the Voice of Terror is the only Universal Holmes film *not* directed by the talented Roy William Neill but contract director John Rawlins does a polished job. Visually, the film is a distant cousin of the others in the series, mostly because of Rawlins' fondness for long, intimate close-ups. At least he keeps bubble-headed Nigel Bruce in check. Sir Arthur Conan Doyle's "The Last Bow" was supposedly the inspiration for the Lynn Riggs–John Bright screenplay, but except for cribbing a few lines of dialogue, there is little resemblance. Universal claimed that Conan Doyle's son thought that upgrading Sherlock Holmes was a great idea, and publicized the fact that he regarded the picture as the best filmization of his father's work to date. Several critics thought otherwise.

Overlooking the studio's misdirected approach to the character, *Sherlock Holmes and the Voice of Terror* can be enjoyed as a better than passable diversion. Universal sent the film out in many theaters with the raucous, very funny *Pardon My Sarong* with Abbott and Costello, inadvertently burying the political platitudes of the Holmes picture in a welter of broadly-played bellylaughs. A more inappropriate cofeature couldn't be imagined. It all seems like a strange way to treat the world's most beloved detective.

The Mummy's Tomb (1942)

Released October 23, 1942. 60 minutes. *Directed by* Harold Young. *Associate Producer:* Ben Pivar. *Screenplay by* Griffin Jay & Henry Sucher. *Original Story by* Neil P. Varnick. *Director of Photography:* George Robinson. *Art Director:* Jack Otterson. *Associate Art Director:* Ralph M. DeLacy. *Film Editor:* Milton Carruth. *Musical Director:* Hans J. Salter. *Sound Director:* Bernard B. Brown. *Technician:* William Schwartz. *Set Decorator:* Russell A. Gausman. *Associate Set Decorator:* Andrew J. Gilmore. *Assistant Director:* Charles S. Gould. *Makeup by* Jack P. Pierce. *Gowns by* Vera West.

Lon Chaney (Kharis), Dick Foran (Professor Stephen A. Banning), John Hubbard (Dr. John Banning), Elyse Knox (Isobel Evans), Wallace Ford (Babe Hanson), Turhan Bey (Mehemet Bey), George Zucco (Andoheb), Mary Gordon (Jane Banning), Cliff Clark (Sheriff), Virginia Brissac (Ella Evans), Paul E. Burns (Jim), Frank Reicher (Professor Matthew Norman), Eddy C. Waller (Chemist), Frank Darien (Old Man), Harry Cording (Vic), Myra McKinney (Vic's Wife), John Rogers (Steward), Otto Hoffman (Caretaker), Emmett Vogan (Coroner), Fern Emmett (Laura), Janet Shaw (Girl), Dick Hogan (Boy), Bill Ruhl (Nick), Guy Usher (Doctor), Pat McVey (Jake Lovell), Jack Arnold (Reporter), Glenn Strange (Farmer), Rex Lease (Al), Grace Cunard (Farmer's Wife), Lew Kelly (Bartender), Charles Marsh (Man), Walter Byron (Searcher), Eddie Parker (Stand-In for Chaney).

The joviality which marked the finale of *The Mummy's Hand* was, in retrospect, premature indeed. Released only two years after its predecessor, but picking up the plot 30 years later, *The Mummy's Tomb* brought back some of the cast members of the first film. It turns out to be a bleak reunion as the Mummy, now played by Lon Chaney, comes back with a vengeance, stalking down our favorite players in one of Universal's nastiest sequels.

Lon had renewed his contract in February, 1942, and already his horror vehicles were slipping in quality. Unlike the Laemmles, who nurtured Boris Karloff's horror career with literate scripts and generally accomplished directors, the current management was primarily interested in getting Chaney into as many monster makeups as possible. The care and talent that was lavished upon *The Wolf Man* is sorely lacking in *The Mummy's Tomb*.

As with the other films in the post–Karloff Mummy series, this movie gets by as entertainment for hardcore Universal enthusiasts by its cozy familiarity alone. All of the bromides, from the changing of the guard in the opening Egyptian scenes to the ritualistic brewing of the tana leaves, are here but these are dubious charms for the uninitiated. Praise for the later Mummy sequels is, unsurprisingly, rare in film books, although they are affectionately regarded by buffs willing to overlook their glaring shortcomings. The ever meticulous and detail-conscious Jack Pierce, at least, provided Chaney with a modified makeup taking into account Kharis' fiery demise in *The Mummy's Hand*. He's not only charred black, but he has also suffered the loss of all his right hand fingers as well as his right eye.

George Zucco returns in the role of Andoheb, now one of the old guard of high priests of Karnak, who apparently has inherited Eduardo Ciannelli's job of doling out thankless tasks to new recruits. Mehemet Bey (Turhan Bey) pulls the plum assignment of transporting Kharis (Lon Chaney), alive but dormant, to America. Setting up shop in a gloomy cemetery in Mapleton, Massachusetts, Bey is ordered to periodically unleash the Mummy to polish off the members of the accursed Banning expedition. (It is never explained how Zucco occupied his time during the ensuing decades, or why he has waited so long to wreak vengeance. The hail of bullets fired into him by Wallace Ford, he tepidly explains, merely "shattered my arm.")

Stephen Banning (Dick Foran), virile hero of the 1940 film, is now a lovable old codger who entertains his dinner guests by challenging them to checkers and recounting his adventures in Egypt (thus giving the writers a chance to recap the plot of *The Mummy's Hand* via some well-chosen excerpts). Banning and Babe Hanson (Wallace Ford) are the sole survivors of the now-famous expedition; the camera pans to a framed portrait of Peggy Moran, artlessly and unflatteringly touched up with pencilled-in wrinkles and hints of gray.

Bey administers the sacred tana fluid and restores Kharis to life. Slinking through the forest, the Mummy arrives at the Banning estate and chokes the life out of Stephen, leaving a streak of grayish mold on his throat. When his sister Jane (Mary Gordon) falls victim to the Mummy soon after, it's apparent the whole Banning family has been marked for death. Babe Hanson arrives on the scene and insists the Mummy is back in business. (The writers, in their inattention to detail, failed to note that his name was Babe *Jenson* in the first film.) His claims are shrugged off by the local sheriff (Cliff Clark), who sticks to his theory the killings are the work of a maniac. Undeterred, Babe tips off the murderer's identity to the press, but is soon silenced by the vengeful Kharis.

Impressed by the mounting death toll, Banning's son John (John Hubbard) reckons that the mysterious Egyptian caretaker at the local cemetery is the likeliest suspect, but before he can investigate, his pretty fiancée, Isobel Evans (Elyse Knox), is carried off by the bandaged baddie. Bey is shot down in a confrontation with the sheriff and his posse, who track down Kharis to the Banning estate. In a spectacularly staged climax (by far the most elaborate scene in the movie), the house is set afire and Kharis perishes in the flames.

Of all of Universal's classic monsters, the Mummy was the least well-served by the studio in the '40s. The Kharis films were cheaply made and usually assigned to second-string directors. Harold Young, who directed this one, was a former editor who, in the '30s, went to England to work under Alexander Korda. His most prestigious credit was *The Scarlet Pimpernel* (1934) with Leslie Howard and Merle Oberon. His subsequent Hollywood career consisted of an uninterrupted string of virtually forgotten B programmers. In *The Mummy's Tomb,* he shows little flair with actors but does rise to the occasion in the fiery climax.

Unlike *The Mummy's Hand,* the film scrupulously avoids comedy relief and dutifully gets down to the serious business of reviving Kharis with the required measure of tana fluid. What *The Mummy's Tomb* lacks in humor it more than makes up for in pacing, with Kharis' nocturnal prowlings yielding a surprising number of victims. Yet, one misses the high-spirited amiability of the previous picture, not to mention the remarkable artistry of the Karloff original. It's a bit sad that the Karl Freund's classic, one of the subtlest and poetic of the '30s thrillers, should spawn such formulaic and superficial sequels.

Freund's *The Mummy* wielded an almost hypnotic power and had little regard for pace. In the Kharis series (and *The Mummy's Tomb* is probably the worst offender), Freund's priorities are reversed. There's a pointed emphasis on speed and efficiency at the expense of character development and atmosphere. Kharis is an unfeeling and mechanical killing machine. His victims are primarily defenseless seniors, making the murders seem even more coldblooded. Not even Mary Gordon, later cast as dear old Mrs. Hudson in the Sherlock Holmes films, is spared. In fact, *The Mummy's Tomb* would be rather grim viewing if it weren't for the homogenized flatness of Young's direction.

The screenplay is remarkably unimaginative. Writers Griffin Jay and Henry Sucher seem hard pressed to dream up bits of business for their tired assemblage of stock characters. The same situations are rehashed with little attempt at variation. Each murder scene is predictably followed by a bombardment of newspaper headlines redundantly recounting the facts, punctuated by the thunderous accompaniment of Hans J. Salter's brass section. In an incongruous reference to the war, John Hubbard receives a letter of notification from the draft board, which is also gleefully met with the same musical blitz. (Couldn't Salter have occasionally provided a *different* piece? It becomes comical after awhile.) One of these headlines raises the question, "Has Witchcraft Been Revived in New England?" Another announces, "Ace Newsmen of Country Here to Cover Mystery," but little comes of this except a shot or two of these "crime specialists," in various stages of insobriety, chattering away at the local watering hole.

The Mummy's Tomb is so perfunctory, so small scale in ambition and execution, it seemed destined for the bottom-of-the-bill slot. Yet Universal, who was playing up Chaney big at the time, offered it as a main attraction, heading a double bill with Ford Beebe's worthier *Night Monster.* To the actor's irritation, the studio dropped the "Junior" from his name, thereafter billing him as "Lon Chaney."

The cast is a mostly colorless bunch, especially John Hubbard as the nominal leading man. Elyse Knox is a fetchingly beautiful ingenue of almost unbearable wholesomeness whose role as the bland heroine was well within her range. Dick Foran and Wallace Ford, who haplessly do their best to look like graying, distinguished types, merely look silly. Turhan Bey looks right at home with his fez and priestly garb, but otherwise doesn't summon up much conviction.

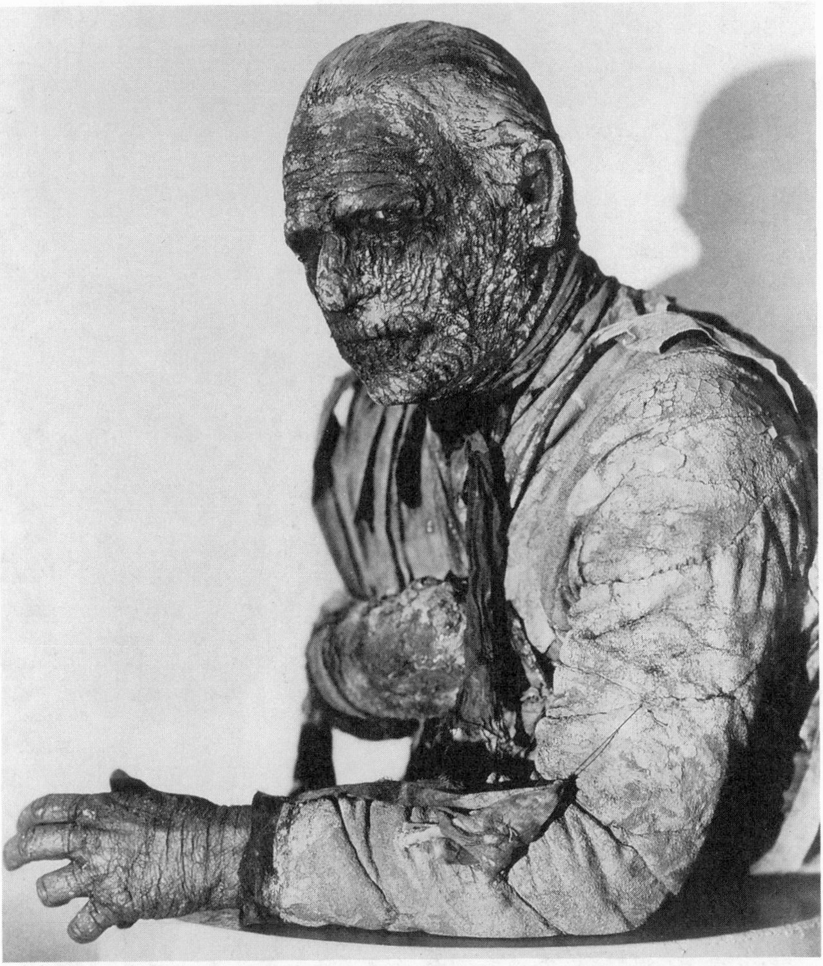

Lon Chaney in *The Mummy's Tomb.* Jack Pierce's revised makeup reflects the fiery fate Kharis suffered in the previous Mummy film.

Born in Vienna in 1922 as Turhan Selahettin Schultavey, Bey's early years can best be described as "comfortable" (his mother's family owned large glass factories and, allegedly, a film studio in Czechoslovakia while his father was the Turkish military attaché in Austria). Bey arrived in Hollywood with his mother and grandmother and a letter of introduction from a lawyer-friend of Arthur Lubin. Recalls Lubin:

> When he arrived, Bey had little spit curls that the Turkish people had in those days. He really was something! Ernie Westmore was the makeup man at Universal at the time and we cut all of this out. We restyled his hair and made a test of him. The women were *crazy* about him.

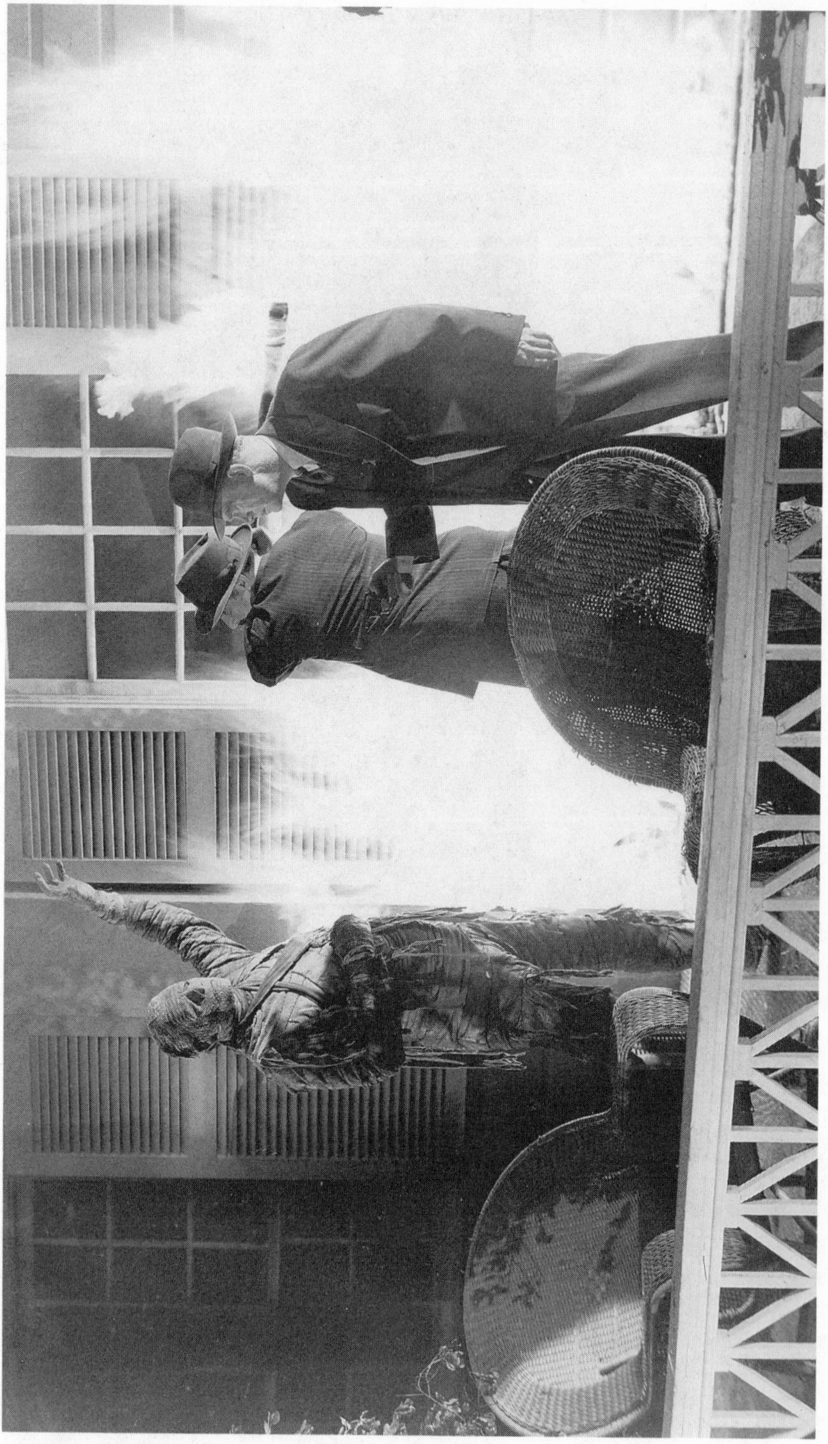

Knowing little English, Bey was sent by Lubin to the Ben Bard School of Speech. Warner Bros. offered him a screen test after seeing him play a suave young heavy in one of Bard's plays, and debuted him in a small part in *Footsteps in the Dark* (1941) with Errol Flynn. Lubin showed the young man's screen test to Universal and Bey was signed on as a contract player.

At first, the studio cast him as a minor heavy in programmers like *Burma Convoy* (1941), *Bombay Clipper* and *Unseen Enemy* (both 1942), but Bey soon graduated to playing second leads in Maria Montez's Technicolored turkeys. In a surprising move, Bey was loaned out to MGM, and was cast as a Chinese (!) opposite Katharine Hepburn in 1944's *Dragon Seed.* Bey's greatest successes were offscreen as he became known as Hollywood's most celebrated, and busiest, heartthrob; to this day many an aging actress (including Lana Turner) still swoons at the mention of his name.

Bey's brand of smarmy screen romanticism quickly became passé. In no time, he was soon back to starring in black-and-white quickies for second-rate studios. Usually dismissed as another of the '40s "camp" actors, the exotic star occasionally gave a good performance; one of his best was as a phony medium in Eagle Lion's *The Amazing Mr. X* (a.k.a. *The Spiritualist,* 1948). Bey's fading looks and bald pate finished off what remained of his career and he left Hollywood for good. Bey now lives in Vienna where he works as a free-lance photographer for soft-porn magazines, including *Penthouse.* He occasionally grants interviews and was recently asked to name his favorite picture. Bey responded, rather astonishingly, "I liked *The Mummy's Tomb.*"

Lon Chaney's debut assignment as the Mummy was merely a contractual obligation which he understandably found arduous and unfulfilling. Wrapped in yards of gauze, Chaney slouched through the part with little shading of character or nuance, apparently to the satisfaction of producer Ben Pivar, who failed to see the monster as anything more than a one-dimensional bogeyman. For an illustration of how this part should be played, catch Christopher Lee's subtly chivalrous Kharis in Hammer's 1959 Technicolor remake of *The Mummy.* An adroit, handsome compendium of the entire Universal series, this film is so derivative that even the character names are cribbed from the first three Mummy movies. Lee so effectively employs mime and a deep, soulful gaze that, by the time he disappears into a slimy green bog, one senses an eerie unspoken pathos reminiscent of Karloff's Monster.

The rest of the characters in *The Mummy's Tomb* consist of a tiresome array of skeptical sheriffs and dumb-looking sidekicks. These hick types would become the Mummy's unlikely sparring partners for the rest of the series and therein lies the fatal error in judgment from which the Mummy films never recovered. The monster's relocation to America may have been a necessary ploy to inject variety into the increasingly hackneyed plots, but the idea of a mummy slinking through the back alleys of New England was so ludicrously inappropriate, it engendered little fright or intrigue. Removed from the

A spectacular climax capped the otherwise tepid potboiler *The Mummy's Tomb.* Here, Lon Chaney battles it out with an unidentified extra and (at right) Cliff Clark. (Photo courtesy Steve Jochsberger.)

mystical trappings of Egypt, the Mummy seemed more of an anachronism than a monster, more of a curiosity than a threat. The hopelessly banal dialogue spouted by the country bumpkins in this film and *The Mummy's Ghost* only demystified the most enigmatic and balefully romantic of all of Universal's classic monsters. Poor Kharis deserved a better fate!

Night Monster (1942)

Released October 23, 1942. 73 minutes. *Associate Producer:* Donald H. Brown. *Produced and Directed by* Ford Beebe. *Original Screenplay by* Clarence Upson Young. *Director of Photography:* Charles Van Enger. *Art Directors:* Jack Otterson & Richard H. Riedel. *Film Editor:* Milton Carruth. *Sound Director:* Bernard B. Brown. *Technician:* Robert Pritchard. *Musical Director:* Hans J. Salter. *Gowns by* Vera West. *Set Decorators:* Russell A. Gausman & Andrew J. Gilmore.

Bela Lugosi (Rolf), Lionel Atwill (Dr. King), Leif Erikson [Erickson] (Laurie), Irene Hervey (Dr. Lynn Harper), Ralph Morgan (Kurt Ingston), Don Porter (Dick Baldwin), Nils Asther (Agor Singh), Fay Helm (Margaret Ingston), Frank Reicher (Dr. Timmons), Doris Lloyd (Sarah Judd), Francis Pierlot (Dr. Phipps), Robert Homans (Cap Beggs), Janet Shaw (Millie Carson), Eddy Waller (Jeb Harmon), Cyril Delevanti (Torque).

One of the most macabre horror characters of the 1940s stalks the halls and grounds of a gloomy country estate in *Night Monster,* an original and imaginative low-budget horror whodunit. This lively mix of mystery, mysticism and monster menace boasts a well-mounted eerieness, a striking and unusual plot, a handsome cast and capable direction by Ford Beebe, one of the abler—and least recognized—horror craftsmen on the Universal payroll. Relegated to the bottom of a double-bill with *The Mummy's Tomb, Night Monster* stands a full head-and-shoulders over its mechanical cofeature, and clearly sizes up as one of Universal's better B's from the wartime era.

Long before Yogism became the province of TV entrepreneurs and girls in impossible sitting positions, the ancient science enjoyed nearly 2,000 years of reasonable respectability. An orthodox system of Indian philosophy, it's an eight-stage process with the purpose of establishing identity of consciousness with the object of concentration. The age-old practice still held plenty of intrigue for '40s audiences, and writer Clarence Upson Young uses it as the hub around which his *Night Monster* screenplay rotates.

Young's plot revolves specifically around mantra yoga, involving sound vibration and prayer. (Believers in Hindu mysticism teach that the world evolved from the essence of sound, through the diversity and intricacy of vibration and utterance.) *Night Monster*'s resident yogi, Nils Asther, uses the ancient secret practice to materialize objects which he has mystically transported from faroff places. This astounding achievement is reduced to mere parlor trickery, however, measured against the more ambitious stunt of magically restoring the limbs of a twisted paraplegic lusting for revenge against the physicians who failed him. The premise, and the film built around it, are both outrageously bizarre and implausible, and it requires the best efforts of both cast and crew to put the weird story over.

In the foyer of the desolate Ingston Towers estate, Margaret Ingston (Fay Helm) catches housekeeper Sarah Judd (Doris Lloyd) in the act of sopping up bloodstains from a carpet. Margaret's not sure if she's nuts or if everybody else in the house is, and to solve this riddle she has sent for a woman psychiatrist, Dr. Lynn Harper. Judd angrily tells Margaret that Kurt Ingston, Margaret's crippled and reclusive brother, has sent for his own personal physicians, who are due to arrive shortly. After the two exit, Millie the maid (Janet Shaw), who has been eavesdropping, phones the local sheriff to apprise him of mysterious goings-on. Rolf the butler (Bela Lugosi) disconnects her and insists on knowing what gossip the girl is planning to spread, but his interrogation is interrupted by the appearance of Laurie the chauffeur (Leif Erickson), who "rescues" the girl from the suddenly aggressive Rolf. Millie quits.

Laurie drives to the railroad depot to pick up the newly-arrived Dr.'s King (Lionel Atwill), Timmons (Frank Reicher) and Phipps (Francis Pierlot), the physicians who attended Kurt Ingston in his major illness. Timmons is guilt-ridden about Ingston's disability but the pompous King is unconcerned and the dotty Phipps prattles on and on about glands.

In town, Millie tries to inveigle one of the townsmen, Jeb Harmon (Eddy Waller), to drive her to the Towers so that she can collect her belongings. Harmon is reluctant because of the Towers' proximity to Pollard Slough, the fog-bound marsh where a local physician was recently strangled by a killer so horrible that in his presence the frogs stop croaking. Millie gets her way, Harmon drives her in his horse-drawn buggy to the Towers at nightfall and waits at the main gate as the girl walks up to the house. Minutes later gatekeeper Torque (Cyril Delevanti) relays the false phone message that Millie has decided to spend the night, and Harmon departs.

When the croaking of the frogs abruptly ceases, the frightened Harmon whips his horse into a gallop, racing down the lonely road past psychiatrist Lynn Harper (Irene Hervey) and her disabled car. Millie has just begun the long walk back to town when a sinister something attacks the girl in the fog. Lynn hears Millie's scream and dimly spots the killer through the mists. She flags down a car which, conveniently, is headed for Ingston Towers. The driver is Dick Baldwin (Don Porter), a mystery writer and friend of Kurt Ingston.

Lynn and Dick arrive at the Towers where Kurt Ingston (Ralph Morgan) greets the newcomers. After dinner, Agor Singh (Nils Asther) lectures on a new healing process. Much the same way that a lobster can regenerate a new claw, man can grow new tissues at will through an understanding of the nature of cosmic substance, Singh declares. To demonstrate, Singh goes into a deep trance and the assembled party watches in astonishment as a genuflecting skeleton materializes in the room. In the ensuing commotion, Singh is startled back to consciousness and the skeleton vanishes. Curiously, blood which had dripped from the skeleton's hands fails to disappear from the library rug.

Investigating Millie's murder, local lawman Cap Beggs (Robert Homans) arrives and begins to question the occupants of the house, but his inquiry is

Don Porter (foreground) encounters the strangler of Pollard Slough (Ralph Morgan) in the tense finale of *Night Monster*.

interrupted by the discovery of the dead body of Dr. King. Like the others, King has been strangled but not wounded and a small pool of blood is nearby.

From this point on *Night Monster* is in a great hurry to kill off as many characters as possible in the remaining running time. Dr. Timmons is murdered in his room by the "night monster" (seen only in shadow). Laurie tells Dr. Phipps that he (Phipps) will certainly be next, and agrees to smuggle him out of the house to safety that night. But the killer strikes first, stalking the terrified Phipps in a striking subjective shot. Another trail of blood leads to the body of Laurie, hung in a closet.

Wisely deciding to clear out, Dick and Lynn are confronted by an angry Miss Judd, who feels they know too much and must remain. Margaret subdues Judd in a tussle as Dick and Lynn flee. The unbalanced Margaret knows that

Miss Judd has been a silent accomplice to the killer, and decides to burn the house. To Judd's horror, Margaret sets fire to the drapes and the two women die in the conflagration.

Outside, Dick and Lynn have just left the grounds when the frogs become silent and the two become aware of an unearthly pursuer. Crossing a rotted footbridge, Lynn's foot becomes wedged in a break and Dick is forced to engage in a hand-to-hand struggle with the killer—a fully ambulatory Kurt Ingston. Ingston chokes Dick into unconsciousness and is advancing toward Lynn when a shot rings out and Ingston topples over dead. Agor Singh, who fired the fatal shot, appears on the scene together with Beggs, and the four watch in amazement as Ingston's limbs vanish before their eyes. Singh explains that he had taught Ingston the secrets of matter materialization so that he could restore himself to normalcy, but the warped mind of Ingston planned only to use the mystical process to wreak vengeance on his doctors. Ingston Towers, now a blazing inferno, burns to the ground.

Night Monster has become something of a notorious film among many horror fans, who grouse about the fact that Lugosi and Atwill play such minor roles and complain about the far-out plot. It's not an easy film to defend: its detractors are right on both counts, and that seems to leave little room for argument. But for the more open-minded fan there's still plenty to recommend in *Night Monster*. Ford Beebe's direction catches just the right feel of mystery and suspense, and while the plot can perhaps be described as improbable at best, the unusual aspects of the story place the picture a rung above many of the completely standardized and formulized B Universal chillers that many fans probably like better. There's genuine atmosphere in the scenes on the marsh, and in general a creepy aura surrounding the whole production that too many other Universal films seem to miss. Despite the modest budget, the usual short (11-day) shoot and a confined setting (we hardly get beyond the house or grounds), *Night Monster* delivers the goods far more effectively than many of its costlier and better-known contemporaries.

The acting in *Night Monster* is on the whole better than that found in the usual Universal meller, and this goes a long way toward creating the mood of the picture. Irene Hervey and Don Porter give good, realistic performances, and the always-dependable Fay Helm delivers another strong portrayal as the neurotic Margaret. There's plenty of the usual loud, confrontational acting scenes in the film, but they're nicely offset by scenes of quiet tension enacted in hushed tones. *Night Monster* boasts a certain amount of this type of underplaying, and there's a quietly compelling, true-to-life quality about some of these scenes that makes the situations seem more realistic.

Where the picture falls down is in its whodunit aspects. The script goes to a great deal of trouble to divert the finger of suspicion from Ralph Morgan, without any success. Although the character's paraplegic condition would instantly remove him from consideration in any conventional movie, audiences know that in a horror film, anything goes, and that some explanation for Morgan's nocturnal perambulations will eventually be forthcoming.

A flaw oddly common to Universal's horror whodunits is that there aren't enough suspects, and ordinary logic quickly points to the inevitable killer. The only victims are Morgan's doctors and the servants who have betrayed him; there isn't any attempt to establish a motive for people like Lugosi, Nils Asther or Leif Erickson. The women in the picture never become suspects, and the string of murders begins before the three doctors arrive. The pools of blood found near the bodies are also a tip-off that paranormal forces are coming into play, and once again Ralph Morgan is the only suspect who would require "supernatural" assistance to dispose of these people.

Morgan, too, works hard to convince audiences of his innocence. In his first scene Morgan appears a benign and personable host. He engages in glib repartee with Irene Hervey and Don Porter, and hardly seems the misshapen creature discussed in dialogue. It's only later that Morgan begins to project a certain sly drollness and we detect the character's cryptic qualities and a cold, imperious streak.

Just as Ingston-the-man hardly lives up to his "misshapen creature" image, Ingston-the-monster fails to come up to the descriptions laid on him throughout the film. After hearing about the horrible, twisted fiend of Pollard Slough for an hour-plus, it comes as a letdown to see that it's Morgan with one eyebrow raised and nostrils flared. (Perhaps, like Henry Hull and the latter-day Chaney, Jr., Morgan disliked being unrecognizable beneath heavy makeup: in the 1935 cheapie *Condemned to Live,* he had played a ghoulish vampire-type, again *sans* the expected cosmetic embellishments.) In a nice touch that almost compensates for this disappointment, Morgan's legs and feet are hair-covered, with animal-like toes reminiscent of the Wolf Man.

Kurt Ingston ranks with some of the most careless and casual killers in horror history. Despite his perfect alibi, almost everyone in the film has an inkling that he is the killer: the maid has her suspicions, Miss Judd and Agor Singh are in on it, Laurie and Rolf seem to know more than they should, and both Margaret and Lynn spot him in the act but inexplicably keep the knowledge to themselves. In moving to kill Dr. Phipps he stalks the halls of his own over-populated house, in danger of being seen by passers-by, even though the house is conveniently honeycombed with secret passageways which would save him the risk and inconvenience.

Morgan is also at the center of one of the film's oddest and most memorable scenes. Convinced that Morgan is only pretending to be paralyzed, Don Porter and Robert Homans confront him in his bedroom as he lies beneath the blankets. Morgan listens politely to their accusations and then quietly asks them to pull back the blanket. Porter complies, revealing pajama-clad legs that end abruptly (above the knee) in stumps. Morgan then reaches across with his right hand and draws a mechanical left arm out of the sleeve of his nightshirt. It's a bizarre, disquieting and almost distasteful little vignette, and it boggles the mind that the Breen Office, constantly inveighing against excessive gruesomeness, should allow Morgan to casually dismantle himself in this fashion (particularly during the touchy World War II era).

Supporting performances are also capably handled by such players as Leif Erickson, Nils Asther and Doris Lloyd. Swedish-born Asther, a silent screen heartthrob whose type went out of style after the advent of sound, became a solid character actor whose one-time star status gave added dignity to B pictures like *Night Monster.* As the enigmatic yogi, the type of role that many actors (you know who) probably might have invested with a lot of mysterioso and ham, Asther gives a relaxed, assured and wholly competent performance which considerably enhances the film. Burly Leif Erickson is an imposing physical presence as the lecherous Laurie, and there's some welcome humor in some of his wry one-liners. Doris Lloyd tries to make like *Rebecca*'s Mrs. Danvers as the housekeeper, and while there are no real acting opportunities for the British actress in the film her familiar frozen face adds to the gloom. Pretty Janet Shaw (who replaced Elyse Knox as Millie the maid) is a sassy cheesecake-type and Cyril Delevanti, director Beebe's real-life father-in-law, plays the sinister gatekeeper.

Night Monster marked Bela Lugosi's next-to-last appearance in a Universal picture. For the second and last time, Lugosi is top-billed in a Universal film, but despite his impressive billing he has little to do: his scenes are few, and nothing he does affects the plot. Early scenes give the impression that Lugosi's Rolf the butler may be in on the villainy, but once the film shifts into gear Lugosi begins to vanish into the background. There's also an attempt to play Lugosi for laughs: Rolf's timid side shows through when the killer begins to strike within the house, and from then on he becomes a milquetoast character. This is a refreshing change, one supposes, from the familiarly cold and supercilious butler Lugosi started out playing, but the actor cannot play comedy, and what should have been a stereotypical role becomes yet another demeaning one. The picture doesn't even bother to let us know if he survives the fiery finish.

Lugosi's in the film strictly for name value, as is Lionel Atwill, who plays Dr. King. Atwill makes the most of his limited screen time, turning in a typically overdone performance as the puffed-up, self-satisfied medico. Atwill is particularly amusing in his scenes of exasperation with Dr. Phipps, the gland-happy physician played by Francis Pierlot. The part probably wasn't written with Atwill (or any name actor) in mind: Dr. King is the first of the three doctors to be killed, and the only one whose murder takes place completely offscreen.

It's also unflattering but true that *Night Monster* probably works better with Lugosi and Atwill confined to minor parts. On the whole there's a slightly more naturalistic acting style on display in the picture, and the broad, full-of-hot-air performances that Lugosi and (especially) Atwill give during their limited screen time aren't in tune with the type of acting that's going on around them. Similarly out of style is Robert Homans as the country constable, a peevish hick-type who detracts from the picture.

Don Porter recently reminisced:

> *Night Monster* was great fun for me, one of the reasons being I'd been nuts about Irene Hervey for years. I was just getting started and to work with Irene and some of these people that I had been seeing was a thrill. The big thing I remember about *Night Monster* was the reading of the line, "It's *blood*!" [in the skeleton scene]. It's a hokey thing to do [*laughs*], but things like that have to be played dead seriously, so we had to stifle our amusement and do our best!

Many viewers belly-ache that *Night Monster* wastes the talents of Lugosi and Lionel Atwill, but the more realistic horror film fan (a breed in short supply) will appreciate that it's a refreshing switch to have nonhorror actors playing the leads in the occasional film, with the Lugosis and Atwills spicing up the proceedings in more modest roles. During their lifetimes many horror film actors complained about the way that Hollywood had permanently pigeonholed them, and indignant fans (particularly Lugosi's) pretended to agree, or perhaps thought that they did indeed agree, with their views on the unfairness of typecasting. But oft-times it's tough to find a horror film fan who really gives a hoot about the nonhorror films their favorite actors made. Probably most every horror film fan has repeatedly seen Karloff's lousy performance in the lousy *Voodoo Island* (1957); but how many of them have seen, or care to see, his fine performance in the fine *The House of Rothschild* (1934)? What's even more notable is when people become upset over horror or mystery films (like *Night Monster*) in which their stars turn out only to be red herrings, and don't play the monsters; not only don't these fans want to see their heroes in nonhorror *films,* they don't even want to see them playing nonhorror *parts!*

One of the more memorable supporting performances in *Night Monster* comes from reliable Frank Reicher. Although Reicher's scenes are few and his dialogue is limited, the actor works to convey a sense of unease as the mild-mannered Dr. Timmons. Timmons visits Ingston Towers with a premonition of foreboding: his is the only character that appreciates the horror of the fate that has befallen Ingston, and Timmons remains almost visibly edgy throughout most of his scenes. Reicher's palpable agitation contrasts nicely with the smug, arrogant assurance of Atwill, and adds subtly to the eerie atmosphere of the film.

Like many character actors of that era, Reicher could be relied upon to contribute effectively to any film. A native of Germany, he was educated in Berlin, Wiesbaden and Hamburg, during which time he learned the English language. He was active on the German stage before he emigrated to the United States in 1899 and began to work on Broadway. In 1914 Cecil B. DeMille lured Reicher West to appear in films, but he returned to Broadway two years later, resuming his stage acting career and joining the New York Theatre Guild as a director.

Reicher went back to Hollywood again in 1926 as an actor, director and dialogue director, racking up scores of motion picture credits before his apparent retirement in 1951. His other Universal genre credits include *Life Returns, The Great Impersonation, The Invisible Ray, Night Key, Mystery of Marie Roget, The Mummy's Tomb* and *Ghost,* and *House of Frankenstein,* while at other studios the big-nosed, baggy-eyed actor added to that list titles like *The Return of the Terror* (1934), *Dr. Cyclops* (1940), *The Face Behind the Mask* (1941), *The Canterville Ghost* (1944) and *Superman and the Mole-Men* (1951), which may have been his last film. Fantasy film fans remember him best, however, for his portrayal of Captain Englehorn in the classic *King Kong* and the sequel *The Son of Kong* (both 1933). The pioneer film actor died in Playa del Rey, California, in 1964 at the age of 89.

From a technical standpoint *Night Monster* is a handsome film, with a far more polished look than bigger, "better" Universal B titles. Superbly shaded camerawork gives a uniquely cold, sinister look to the imposing but familiar sets (also seen in the same year's *The Ghost of Frankenstein*). Hans J. Salter's music—and, often, the lack of it—also contributes to the eerieness. There are also a few striking "bridges" in the film, like a shot of the skeleton's blood on the library rug dissolving to a blood splotch near Janet Shaw's body on the marsh, and another clever moment when black smoke from Fay Helm's blazing drapes cuts to a shot of prowling fog out of which Irene Hervey and Don Porter appear. Shot as *House of Mystery,* the film was completed on July 18, 1942, and reached theaters just over three months later.

Just as Western director Lambert Hillyer made the most out of *Dracula's Daughter* and *The Invisible Ray* during the Laemmle era, former serial ace Beebe appears to have lavished as much care and imagination on *Night Monster* as time and budget allowed (*Night Monster* was Beebe's first feature after his promotion from the Universal chapterplays). Universal rightly recognized Beebe's *Night Monster* as an impressive thriller, and promptly assigned him to the post of producer on *Son of Dracula* on the basis of his work.

Sherlock Holmes and the Secret Weapon (1942)

Released December, 1942. 68 minutes. *Directed by* Roy William Neill. *Associate Producer:* Howard Benedict. *Screenplay by* Edward T. Lowe, W. Scott Darling & Edmund L. Hartmann. *Adaptation by* W. Scott Darling & Edward T. Lowe. *Based on the story "The Adventure of the Dancing Men" by* Sir Arthur Conan Doyle. *Director of Photography:* Les White. *Art Director:* Jack Otterson. *Associate Art Director:* Martin Obzina. *Film Editor:* Otto Ludwig. *Musical Director:* Charles Previn. *Music:* Frank Skinner. *Set Decorator:* Russell A. Gausman. *Associate Set Decorator:* Edward R. Robinson. *Sound Director:* Bernard B. Brown. *Technician:* Paul Neal. *Technical Advisor:* Tom McKnight. *Gowns by* Vera West.

Basil Rathbone (Sherlock Holmes), Nigel Bruce (Dr. John H. Watson), Lionel Atwill (Professor Moriarity), Kaaren Verne (Charlotte Eberli), Dennis Hoey (Inspector Lestrade), William Post, Jr. (Dr. Franz Tobel), Mary Gordon (Mrs. Hudson), Henry Victor (Prof. Frederick Hoffner), Paul Fix (Mueller), Robert O. Davis [Rudolph Anders] (Braun), Holmes Herbert (Sir Reginald Bailey), Harry Cording (Jack Brady), Harold DeBecker (Peg Leg), Philip Van Zandt (Man), Paul Bryar (Waiter), Guy Kingsford (London Bobby), George Eldredge (Policeman), Vicki Campbell (Aviatrix), Gerard Cavin (Scotland Yard Man), Harry Woods (Kurt), George Burr MacAnnan (Gottfried), James Craven, Leland [Leyland] Hodgson (R.A.F. Officers), Michael Mark (George), Leslie Denison, John Burton (Men).

Universal wasted little time getting their second Sherlock Holmes film off the ground. *Sherlock Holmes and the Secret Weapon,* filmed almost back-to-back with *Sherlock Holmes and the Voice of Terror,* continued the exploits of the master detective in war-torn England. The cameras rolled on June 21, 1942, under the working title *Sherlock Holmes Fights Back.*

Roy William Neill took over the directorial reins from John Rawlins with satisfactory results; it was a position he would hold for the entire run of the series. Neill was born Roland de Gostrie in Dublin Harbor on a ship commanded by his father. After a stint as a war correspondent, he answered the lure of the theater, toured in stock companies, and became a stage manager with David Belasco for ten years. Neill drifted into motion picture work in England and upon coming to Hollywood became a contract director at the Columbia B unit in the '30s; the excellent Boris Karloff vehicle *The Black Room*

Universal revived Sherlock Holmes only to turn him into a modern-day Nazi hunter in films like *Sherlock Holmes and the Secret Weapon.*

(1935) ranks as his best-known Columbia credit. Director Edward Bernds, who worked with Neill as a sound man during his Columbia days, remembers:

> In appearance, Neill was dark, had jet black hair and plenty of it. Roy's speech was that of an educated Irishman, somewhat British-sounding, but with just a hint of the Irish lilt or brogue. Roy had some fingers missing on one hand, I'm sure it was his right hand.
>
> Some of the crew called him "Rocking Chair" Neill. The prop man had to have a rocking chair on the set for him when he directed. Eventually, they fixed up a director's chair with rockers, with a big canvas pocket hanging onto one arm of the chair to hold the director's script.

Neill's career at Universal was launched in 1942 with *Eyes of the Underworld,* a minor Richard Dix crime meller. The studio promoted the picture as a shocker, emphasizing the publicity tag line "Lon Chaney in His Most Fearsome Role!" and featuring lurid poster art of the actor in ghoulish gray tints. It was a typical tease; disgruntled horror fans found Chaney wasted in a conventional thug part, and a pretty small one at that.

Neill, affectionately called "Mousey" by his coworkers, was the ideal choice as director of the Holmes series with his sure eye for atmosphere and his crisp, straightforward style. He worked well with modest budgets and conveyed a convincingly British tone. The director's work on the series proved so satisfactory, Universal was reluctant to diversify his assignments; he finally got out of the Holmes rut with *Black Angel* (1946), a stylish *film noir* with Peter

Lorre, and the far more routine Maria Montez–Jon Hall action flick *Gypsy Wildcat* (1944).

The studio story department set "The Adventure of the Dancing Men" as the next of Conan Doyle's tales to be transposed to the screen, although little of the story survived Edward T. Lowe and W. Scott Darling's adaptation. Much to the annoyance of purists, the picture was virtually a cat-and-mouse game between Holmes and Professor Moriarity, vying for custody of a scientist.

In the original story, Holmes is summoned to the aid of a well-to-do country squire whose young American wife is driven to near madness upon receiving a series of anonymous messages bearing only random stick figures. Holmes deduces that the figures, actually pencil drawings resembling dancing men, are an alphabet substitution code. In an unlikely wrap-up, Holmes reveals the culprit to be a Chicago mobster who used to be the wife's sweetheart.

A far cry from Conan Doyle, *Sherlock Holmes and the Secret Weapon* forges a familiar cloak-and-dagger atmosphere from the first frame. The movie opens in Zurich as Sherlock Holmes (Basil Rathbone) engineers a plan to keep Dr. Franz Tobel (William Post, Jr.) out of the hands of the German agents who are hot on his trail. Tobel has invented a revolutionary bomb site of uncanny accuracy which he intends to offer to England for her defenses.

Holmes smuggles the scientist into London. It isn't long before Tobel is abducted by Professor Moriarity (Lionel Atwill), who plans to strike a deal with Germany for the secret weapon. Taking precautions, Tobel has divided up the bomb site into three separate components which he has entrusted to various scientists. As a further safeguard, Tobel has inscribed the names and addresses of the three men in a memo, written in code, using stick figures of dancing men. Working against time, both Holmes and Moriarity deduce that it's an alphabet substitution code. Moriarity manages to decode the names of the first two scientists, whom he orders killed after taking the fragment of the weapon in their possession.

In a dead heat with Holmes to decode the third name, Moriarity discovers it has been coded in *reverse*. Paying a call on the scientist, the Professor finds instead a heavily disguised Holmes. The sleuth has beaten his adversary to the punch. Realizing he can no longer offer the bomb site to Germany, Moriarity decides to sell Tobel himself, but first he must eliminate Holmes. Stalling for time, the detective suggests his own method of execution: being bound to an operating table and slowly drained of blood. Moriarity happily obliges, but before Holmes lapses into unconsciousness, Watson (Nigel Bruce) and Inspector Lestrade (Dennis Hoey) burst on the scene with a team of agents. Tobel is rescued and Moriarity, fleeing through a secret passageway booby-trapped by Holmes, plunges to his death.

In its day, the jingoism of *Sherlock Holmes and the Voice of Terror* may have been fitting, but for today's audiences, the very different *Sherlock Holmes and the Secret Weapon* comes closer to the mark. Roy William Neill seemed resigned to the film's B status and delivered an unpretentious, workmanlike programmer. (It was the second time a Holmes thriller served as a warm-up act for an Abbott and Costello comedy, this time *It Ain't Hay*.) Nationalistic sentiment was confined to a single patriotic tribute to the Empire, stirringly read by

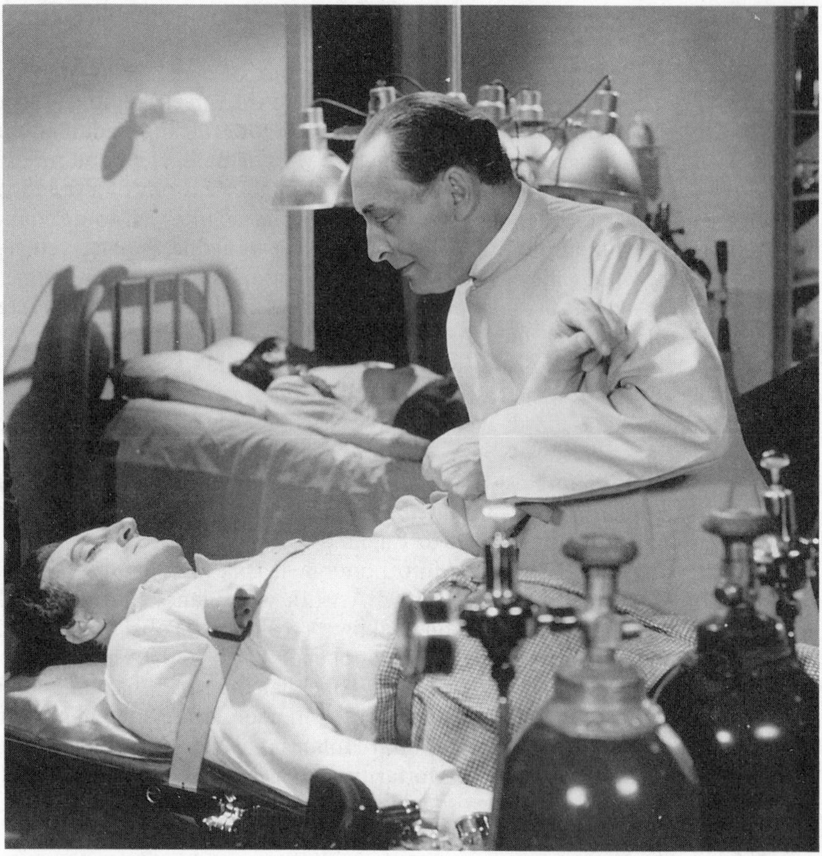

Savoring his momentary victory, Moriarity (Lionel Atwill) drains Holmes (Basil Rathbone) of his life's blood in the climax of *Sherlock Holmes and the Secret Weapon.*

Rathbone in the coda, but the bulk of the film concentrates on the business at hand, scoring high marks for pacing and audience involvement.

Last seen hurtling to his death from London Tower in 20th Century–Fox's *The Adventures of Sherlock Holmes* (1939), Professor Moriarity makes a comeback, graduating from master criminal to wholesaler of government secrets. It's a reasonable updating of the character and Lionel Atwill, George Zucco's successor in the role, is at his scene-stealing best. Shaved of his familiar moustache, his eyebrows peculiarly sloped upwards, a slightly unrecognizable Atwill bristles with corruption.

The repetition of the Sherlock Holmes roles had not yet taken its toll on Rathbone, who gives one of his most incisive performances in the series. Rathbone and Atwill were a good match over the years and in this, their final teaming, the stars are in top form, delivering the ripe dialogue flawlessly.

Cozily perched on Moriarity's overstuffed sofa, the rivals hurl salvoes at each other with deadly accuracy. Moriarity even scores points in the series' sole reference to Holmes' opium addiction ("The needle to the last, eh, Holmes?" chides Moriarity at the detective's suggestion of being bled to death with a syringe). It's a delightful scene, well worth waiting for.

The rest of the case is barely noticeable. The one exception is Dennis Hoey, making his series debut as Inspector Lestrade. The befuddled representative of Scotland Yard, Lestrade can be depended upon to be at least two steps behind Holmes, and possibly even one step behind the bumbling Dr. Watson. The role became more substantial as the series progressed and Hoey played it with endearing comic flair. Kaaren Verne, then the wife of Peter Lorre, is serviceable in the female lead, but William Post, Jr., as Dr. Tobel is a resounding dud. Reading his lines with elocutionary precision, his performance is hollow and lifeless. Chris Steinbrunner and Norman Michaels, authors of the useful and entertaining *The Films of Sherlock Holmes,* insist that Henry Daniell pops up in an unbilled cameo as a Scotland Yard agent in the last reel; however a close inspection of the film doesn't bear this out.

There are minor gaps in credibility, particularly Holmes' almost instantaneous breaking of Tobel's code (that is, until he gets to that stubborn final name). Even in Conan Doyle's original story, the detective wasn't quite that sharp or quick. It's all in the interest of pacing, of course. Holmes offhandedly explains that a previous case had him tackling a similar code, as he effortlessly assigns the correct letter to each of those pesky little ciphers.

Holmes' security measures for the highly vulnerable Tobel are so flimsy, his abduction by Moriarity is almost deserved. More than his predecessor John Rawlins, Neill encouraged the comic improvisations of Nigel Bruce. Well-known for blustery, buffoonish characterizations, Bruce, who was said to have taken a nip now and then on the set, willingly obliged. While some of the actor's babbling is funny, it wasn't long before he slipped into caricature. Holmes courts disaster by assigning Watson to act as Tobel's bodyguard, fully aware that Nazi agents are lurking in every corner. Fortunately, the Nazis prove to be even more inept than Watson after the good doctor falls asleep on the job.

One of the handful of series titles that has slipped into the public domain, *Sherlock Holmes and the Secret Weapon* has fallen victim to the recent colorization craze. The results are surprisingly better than average, and an improvement over the poor-contrast, third-generation-dupe prints that frequently make the rounds on local stations and cable. Even so, a crisp, original black-and-white print remains the best way to enjoy the picture.

The spirited dialogue often transcends the comic book storyline and director Neill refuses to let the pace flag, getting plenty of help from Rathbone and Atwill. For all its swagger, it's not in the same league as those shadowy, ominous miniclassics *The Scarlet Claw* and *The Pearl of Death,* although *Sherlock Holmes and the Secret Weapon* is probably the best of the cloak-and-dagger Holmes adventures.

Frankenstein Meets the Wolf Man (1943)

Released March 5, 1943. 72 minutes. *Produced by* George Waggner. *Directed by* Roy William Neill. *Original Screenplay by* Curt Siodmak. *Director of Photography:* George Robinson. *Art Director:* John B. Goodman. *Associate Art Director:* Martin Obzina. *Director of Sound:* Bernard B. Brown. *Technician:* William Fox. *Set Decorator:* Russell A. Gausman. *Associate:* Edward R. Robinson. *Film Editor:* Edward Curtiss. *Gowns by* Vera West. *Musical Director:* Hans J. Salter. *Makeup Artist:* Jack P. Pierce. *Assistant Director:* Melville Shyer. *Special Photographic Effects:* John P. Fulton.

Lon Chaney (Lawrence Stewart Talbot, the Wolf Man), Ilona Massey (Baroness Elsa Frankenstein), Patric Knowles (Dr. Frank Mannering), Lionel Atwill (Mayor), Bela Lugosi (The Frankenstein Monster), Maria Ouspenskaya (Maleva), Dennis Hoey (Police Inspector Owen), Don Barclay (Franzec), Rex Evans (Vazec), Dwight Frye (Rudi, the Tailor), Harry Stubbs (Guno), Beatrice Roberts (Varja), Adia Kuznetzoff (Singer), Torben Meyer (Erno), Doris Lloyd (Nurse), Jeff Corey (Grave-Digger), David Clyde (Police Sergeant), Tom Stevenson (Grave Robber), Cyril Delevanti (Freddy Jolly [Grave Robber]), Martha MacVicar [Vickers] (Margareta), Charles Irwin (Constable), Eddie Parker, Gil Perkins (Stunts).

"Never make a joke in the studio," warns writer Curt Siodmak.

> I was sitting down at the Universal commissary having lunch with George Waggner and I said, "George, why don't we make a picture *Frankenstein Wolfs the Meat Man* —er, *Meets the Wolf Man*?" He didn't laugh. This was during wartime; I wanted to buy an automobile and I needed a new writing job so I would be able to afford it. George would see me every day and ask me if I had bought the car yet. I said, "George, can I get a job?" He said, "Sure, you'll get a job, buy the car." Well, the day finally came when I had to pay for the car. George asked me that day, "Did you buy the car?" and I said, "Yes, I bought it." George said, "Good! Your new assignment is *Frankenstein Wolfs the Meat Man*—er, *Meets the Wolf Man!* I'll give you two hours to accept!"

There may be just a whiff of apocrypha in Siodmak's priceless anecdote, but the end result remains *Frankenstein Meets the Wolf Man* and the dawn of what would come to be known as the Universal monster rally. While Val Lewton and his coterie at RKO continued to titillate audiences with the unseen, Universal began to redouble their efforts in the opposite direction, assembling all-star monster casts in *Frankenstein Meets the Wolf Man* (two monsters), *House of Frankenstein* (five) and *House of Dracula* (four).

It took a good deal of imagination (and a little cheating) to bring together the Monster and the Wolf Man in a single picture. *The Wolf Man* was set in the present day (1941), but this sequel, which takes place four years later, is set in the much earlier era of the Frankenstein series. But *Frankenstein Meets the Wolf Man* was not designed to stand up to this sort of smart-alecky scrutiny. Probably almost no one noticed or cared about details like this when the film was released; by this point Universal had begun tailoring most of their pictures to the younger set anyway.

The idea of combining monsters in one picture was the shot in the arm these series (especially the Frankensteins) needed at this late date. These ghoulfests are often blamed for the decline and demise of the classic Dracula and Frankenstein series, but by the mid–40s they were on their last legs anyway. The monster rally films are far closer to juvenilia and kitsch than they are to art, but they're slick and enjoyable, and a welcome opportunity for many of the best-loved horror stars to congregate together in a single picture. *Frankenstein Meets the Wolf Man* went into production in October, 1942, with George Waggner producing and Roy William Neill directing.

Graverobbers (Cyril Delevanti and Tom Stevenson) break into the Talbot family vault in Llanwelly Cemetery with plans to steal a valuable ring from the dead Larry Talbot (Lon Chaney). The men find Talbot's body in perfect condition despite the passage of years; the corpse is covered with a blanket of wolfsbane sprigs. As the full moon shines through a crypt window, Talbot's Wolf Man side is restored to life. He kills one of the would-be defilers while the other flees in blind terror. Quitting his tomb, the Wolf Man prowls the countryside and eventually ends up in nearby Cardiff, where (as Talbot) he collapses on a deserted side street.

Hospitalized, a greatly agitated Talbot tells attending physician Frank Mannering (Patric Knowles) and Police Inspector Owen (Dennis Hoey) about his lupine alter ego, a story the two men are quick to dismiss. That night's full moon triggers a transformation, and the Wolf Man leaves the hospital and kills a bobby. (As in *The Wolf Man,* the werewolf apparently dresses before going out, even to the point of tucking in his shirttails!)

Talbot, desperate, searches Europe for Maleva (Maria Ouspenskaya), mother of the werewolf whose bite cursed him. Maleva is sympathetic to his plight, and promises to guard and protect him. Convinced that Dr Frankenstein can end his existence, Maleva sets out with Talbot in a horse-drawn cart for the Bohemian Alps and the little town of Vasaria.

The pair receive a chilly welcome in Vasaria, and are disheartened to hear that Dr. Frankenstein, along with the Frankenstein Monster, perished in a fire at the Doctor's sanitarium. (The *Ghost of Frankenstein* sanitarium and the burned-out castle seen in this film look nothing alike.) There's a full moon that night, and the Wolf Man kills a young girl (Martha Vickers). A mob of angry townspeople chase the Wolf Man into the darkened ruins of Frankenstein's sanitarium, where the beast plummets through a hole in the floor and into an underground ice cave. Later, as Talbot, he explores the frosty catacomb and discovers the body of the Monster (Bela Lugosi) embedded in a wall of ice. Talbot frees the Monster and asks it for Dr. Frankenstein's diary, which

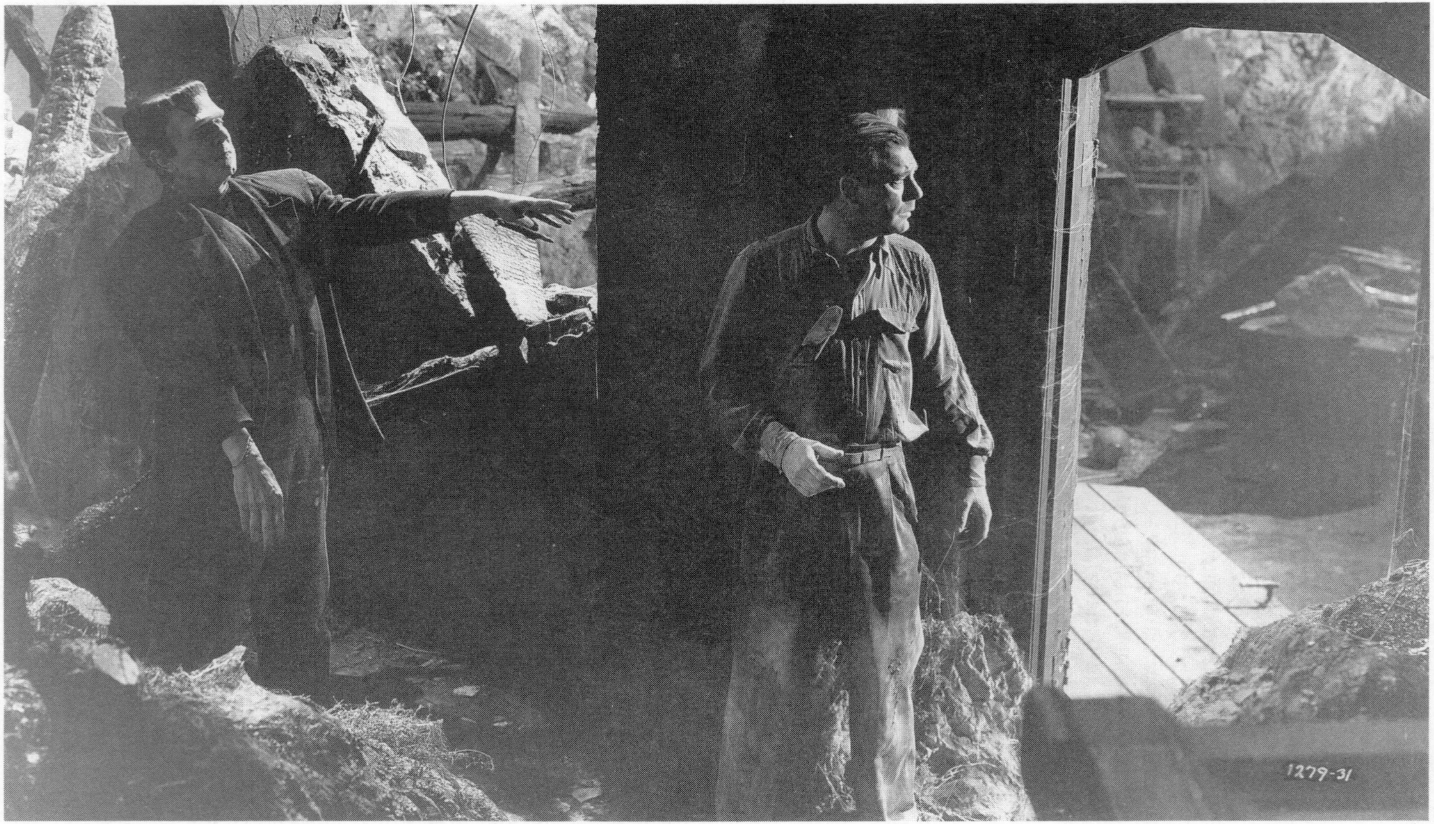
1279-31

contains the secrets of life and (more importantly for Talbot) death. The Monster leads Talbot to the hiding place of the diary, but the book is not there.

Sartorially splendid in Dr. Frankenstein's clothes (Lon Chaney and Cedric Hardwicke wear the same size?), Talbot poses as "Taylor," a potential buyer for the ruined castle, in order to make the acquaintance of Elsa (Ilona Massey), Dr. Frankenstein's lovely daughter. Grimly he admits he wants only to locate Dr. Frankenstein's diary, but Elsa refuses to help him. The mayor (Lionel Atwill) invites both Elsa and "Taylor" to be guests of honor at Vasaria's Festival of the New Wine that evening.

That night, the Festival is in full swing when Dr. Mannering unexpectedly arrives on the scene and corners Talbot. Mannering has followed Talbot across Europe via newspaper accounts of the Wolf Man murders, and is determined to see him institutionalized. The Monster blunders into town and creates a panic before Talbot is able to round up his new friend and flee in a wagon.

United in their desire to help Talbot escape his curse and to destroy the Monster, Mannering and Elsa make their way to the castle and convince Talbot of their good intentions. Elsa produces her father's diary and turns it over to Mannering, who decides that he can repair the charred electrical equipment in Frankenstein's old lab and use it to drain the life energies from both Talbot and the Monster.

Mannering puts the laboratory back into working order and prepares for the ultimate experiment with both Talbot and the Monster strapped to adjacent operating tables. But in an uncharacteristic moment of mad doctor-style zeal he decides that he must see the Frankenstein Monster at its full power, which he accomplishes by reversing the polarity (or some damn thing). Ungrateful for his new lease on life, the Monster menaces Mannering and Elsa just as the full moon begins to rise and Talbot undergoes his familiar change.

"The fight of the Titans" commences: as Mannering and Elsa flee the castle, the Monster and the Wolf Man engage in an exciting brawl complete with furious strangleholds, spectacular tackles and flying lab equipment. By a well-timed coincidence, the father (Rex Evans) of the young girl killed by the Wolf Man blows up a nearby dam in order to destroy the Frankenstein castle and the monsters within. Still locked in their life-and-death struggle, the Monster and the Wolf Man are swept away in the raging torrent.

Poor Bela Lugosi. In 1931, he had haughtily turned up his nose at the notion of playing the Monster in the original *Frankenstein* and inadvertently created a monster of his own in the person of Boris Karloff, who quickly and easily outpaced Lugosi as the screen's premier bogeyman. (One idly wonders how the stuck-up Lugosi and the imperious cold-fish James Whale would have gotten along on that picture anyway.) Hollywood in general and Universal in particular were never overly kind to Lugosi in the years following that tragic blunder, and by late 1942, when *Frankenstein Meets the Wolf Man* was filmed, the actor was in no position to turn down the Monster role, or any other.

In keeping with the finale of *The Ghost of Frankenstein,* in which the brain

Bela Lugosi (as the Monster) and Lon Chaney search the burned ruins of Frankenstein's sanitarium in *Frankenstein Meets the Wolf Man.*

of Ygor is transplanted into the head of the Monster, the script of *Frankenstein Meets the Wolf Man* called for a nearly-blind Monster that still spoke, and still nurtured Ygor's mad plans to subjugate the world. Three scenes of dialogue for the Monster were shot.

The first is the longest and most elaborate; it's set right after the Monster's rescue from the ice wall. The Monster and Talbot are sitting in the catacomb, where the Monster is warming his hands over a small fire. The Monster bemoans the loss of his sight and strength, and tells the story of how he came to be trapped in the ice, conscious for years, unable to move. The unholy pair now make their way back up into Dr. Frankenstein's old lab, ravaged by fire and festooned with cobwebs, where the Monster brags about his immortal body.

"Dr. Frankenstein created this body to be immortal! His son gave me a new brain, a clever brain. I shall use it for the benefit of the miserable people who inhabit the world, cheating each other, killing each other, without a thought but their own petty gain. I will rule the world!" (A curious *faux pas* for the brain-happy Siodmak: the Monster talks as though his old brain and Ygor's newly-installed brain were both at work in his head.) Interested not in life but in death, Talbot eagerly asks the Monster for Frankenstein's diary; the Monster leads him into Frankenstein's study, but the book cannot be located.

More Monster dialogue follows the scene of the Monster's unexpected Vasaria visit. Propped up with pillows in the castle study, the Monster explains that he had come into town because he feared that Talbot had deserted him. "I was afraid you'd left me—I thought you'd found that diary—and run away," the Monster mopes; Talbot calls him dumb. Later in the scene, after Dr. Mannering has arrived, the Monster belly-aches about his lousy eyesight. The third and final scene is set once again in the study, with the Monster (clad in a white operating gown) sitting motionless "like a Tibetan god" while Talbot paces the floor in anticipation of the coming, climactic experiment. The Monster brags that his strength will soon be renewed, then rises and tells Talbot, "Then I shall see again—and be fit to rule the world!"

The inevitable happened only a few short weeks later, when the *Frankenstein Meets the Wolf Man* production staff gathered in a studio screening room to view the finished product. The film worked well until Lugosi's Monster first opened his mouth, and the sheer ludicrousness of a talkative monster finally struck the picturemakers. The screening turned into a shambles, with the little audience nearly convulsed with laughter over Lugosi's performance.

"Lugosi couldn't talk!" Curt Siodmak explains. "They had left the dialogue I wrote for the Monster in the picture when they shot it, but with Lugosi it sounded so Hungarian funny that they had to take it out!" Take it out they did; producer George Waggner, suddenly running scared, ordered all of the Monster's dialogue scenes removed from the film, not realizing (or not caring) that every reference to the Monster's near-blindness was being deleted as well.

The effect on Lugosi's already shaky performance was disastrous. Poor Bela gropes and pokes and lurches around in a ridiculous fashion, moves his lips without speaking and looks for all the world like Fred Gwynne's Herman Munster in a state of perpetual agitation; at one point during the climactic fight

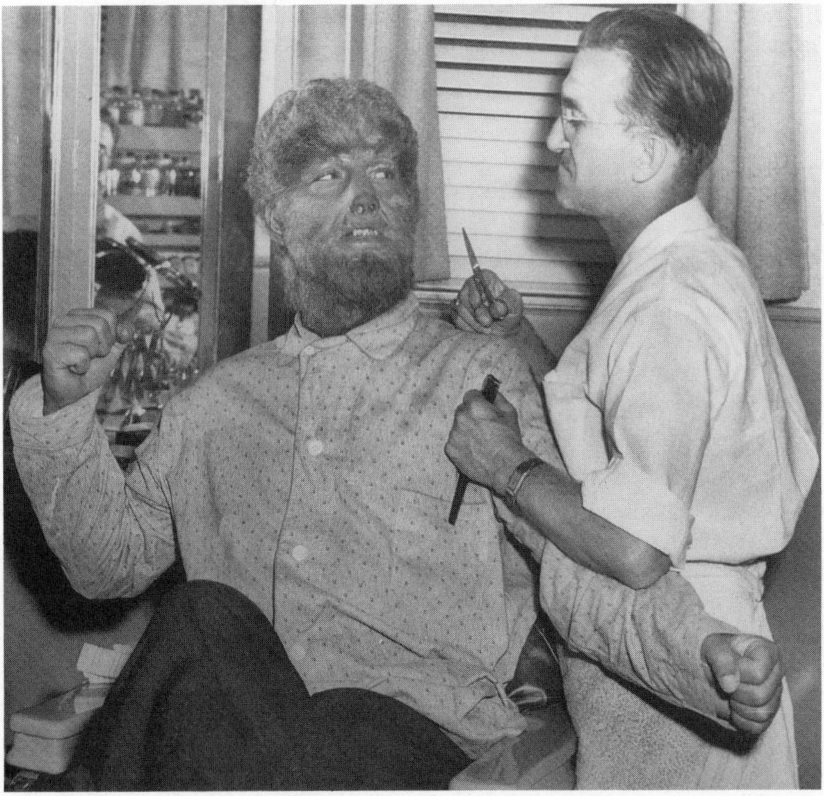

"Just a little off the top" says Lon Chaney to Jack Pierce in this behind-the-scenes shot from *Frankenstein Meets the Wolf Man.*

Lugosi spreads his arms as though he expects to turn into a bat. (It's sad and ironic that the frail Lugosi should play the Monster in this action-filled film whereas the next actor to play the Monster, burly Western tough guy Glenn Strange, hardly ever gets up off his rear!) This was Lugosi's final film for Universal.

It seems odd, in retrospect, that no one seemed to realize the effect the Monster's dialogue scenes would have; aside from being funny, these scenes quite obviously would have slowed the action and weakened the film's suspense. Siodmak admits that he wrote in at least one intentionally humorous line (responding to Talbot's claim that he turns into a wolf, the Monster frowns, "Are you kidding?"), but this bit is not much less risible than most of the other Talbot–Monster exchanges.

Edward Bernds, sound man on many a Roy William Neill Columbia B film, offers what may be an explanation as to why the director failed to recognize the comic potential of these dialogue scenes. Bernds remembers Neill as a man with "absolutely no sense of humor. I'm pretty sure that at Columbia he never directed a comedy, and if he did or if he had pictures perhaps with some lighter moments, I'm sure the humor got to the screen without much help from him."

In a Neill picture called *Wall Street* (1929), Ralph Ince plays a ruthless tycoon whose manipulations are ruining a number of other Wall Street characters. One of them comes to Ince in his office, pleading for mercy: if Ince doesn't back off, doesn't give him a break, he will be bankrupt and he will kill himself. Ince tells him to get lost. Cut to the outer office. The man dashes through, over to a window and out he goes. Ince hears the commotion, comes out of his office and looks down out of the window. Ed Bernds was on the set:

> At this point, Ince said to his secretary, "And I said he didn't have the guts!" Well, there was an absolute spontaneous roar of laughter from the crew—it just hit everybody at once. And Neill was bewildered, he wanted to know what the hell it was all about. The gruesome incongruity of looking down at a man with his insides splattered on the sidewalk, it caused what I guess would be called a black humor laugh. Yet, Neill just couldn't seem to comprehend why it got that crazy, ghoulish laugh.

On a later Neill film, 1935's *Mills of the Gods,* Bernds' wisecracking assistant kiddingly redubbed the picture *Oh, God, the Mills Brothers.* "Not funny, you might say, and maybe you're right, but it tickled the crew and a lot of people started calling it by that title. And Roy Neill, a nice man, no sense of humor, couldn't fathom why the cast and crew was getting the title of his film wrong!"

Contributing in large part to the success and popularity of *Frankenstein Meets the Wolf Man* is Lon Chaney's portrayal. Chaney gives a pent-up performance that is as good or (arguably) better than the one he gave in *The Wolf Man.* The role this time is less demanding, with Talbot fully aware of his werewolf side from his first scene.

Chaney now seems more seasoned, more at ease with the character he was later proud to call his "baby." Chaney dominates the film: forlorn but no longer whiny, desperate but not as panic-stricken, he brings some new dimensions to the melancholy Larry Talbot and evokes yet-greater sympathy as he searches vainly for the secret of death. *Frankenstein Meets the Wolf Man* also boasts some of the best Wolf Man scenes from any of the character's five movies: the opening scene in the crypt, his vicious attack on the Cardiff bobby, the posse scene in Vasaria and ultimately the roof-raising brawl with Lugosi's Frankenstein Monster.

Ilona Massey and Patric Knowles make for better-than-adequate leads. Massey, a former Metro star, brings a touch of class to the picture; occasionally her rolling r's and halting delivery get to be a bit much, but for the most part Massey fills the bill nicely (perhaps better than Evelyn Ankers), and she's an eye-opening treat in her long blond braids and lowcut nightgown.

Patric Knowles, as polished and professional a young leading man as ever drew a Universal paycheck, also acquits himself well, although his character wears perhaps a few too many different "hats" in the course of the film's 72 minutes (first he's a humble pill-pusher in a little Welsh town, then he turns amateur detective, then bloodhound, and finally electrical engineer and "mad" scientist). It seems fitting that Knowles' character—the first non-Frankenstein to revive the Monster – should have the first name of Frank, an alias later used by the mad doctors in such films as *Frankenstein's Daughter, The Revenge of Frankenstein* (both, 1958), and others.

Good character support is provided by Lionel Atwill, Maria Ouspenskaya and Dennis Hoey. Atwill, in his third of five Frankenstein films, plays a minor role as the unnamed mayor of Vasaria. While the script calls for a fairly serious portrayal, Atwill brings a few self-spoofing touches to the role, and plays the part very much in the pompous, sputtery style of a Nigel Bruce. A messy sex scandal that threatened to ruin Atwill's career was perhaps at its height at this time; on October 15, 1942, just a few days into production on *Frankenstein Meets the Wolf Man,* Atwill was sentenced to five years' probation for perjury. Bred in England, the Toast of Broadway, Atwill was now just another Hollywood crumb, and for a while it looked as though *Frankenstein Meets the Wolf Man* might be his final film.

Maria Ouspenskaya is her usual self, treating a minor role in a juvenile movie with the same dignity and sincerity she brought to A studios' A pictures. Annoyingly, the film neglects to let viewers know whether or not Ouspenskaya's Maleva survives the climactic castle destruction; asked by these writers whether Ouspenskaya lived or died at the end of the film, Curt Siodmak laughs: "She died in the meantime!" Dennis Hoey plays his role of Inspector Owen in a too-familiar fashion; it's as though Hoey's Inspector Lestrade has committed the ultimate blunder, and wandered into the wrong film!

Just as *Frankenstein Meets the Wolf Man* was the final Universal film for Bela Lugosi, it was also the last studio credit for his one-time Renfield, Dwight Frye, who died several months after its release. Plugging away day and night (by day as an actor, by night as a tool designer in a Los Angeles aircraft plant), Frye succumbed to a heart attack in November, 1943, his dream of breaking with his screen image of a drooling graveyard rat unrealized. (The script describes Frye's character in this film as a blushing newlywed; it's he, not the mayor, who dances with Elsa at the Festival.)

Future Warners star Martha Vickers, who has a bit as the girl killed (off-camera) by the Wolf Man, makes her film debut here under her real name, Martha MacVicar. Stuntman Eddie Parker is easily recognizable under Monster makeup doubling for Lugosi throughout the film, although in the Pier Six finale, Parker doubles for Chaney as the Wolf Man while Aussie stuntman Gil Perkins takes over for Lugosi. Moose, Chaney's dog since the days of *The Wolf Man*, turns up in a gypsy camp scene; this might be Moose's last film as well. Moose was road-killed on the backlot during the shooting of *Cobra Woman* (1944).

Many minor changes were made in Siodmak's script (titled *Wolf-Man Meets Frankenstein*) before cameras rolled. In the original script, the graverobbers who find Talbot's body in a state of perfect preservation notice that his fingernails had grown quite long in death. (Explaining the undecayed condition of Talbot's corpse, one graverobber nervously sputters, "The air in here – it's kept him like that!") At the hospital, when Dr. Harley (Dr. Mannering's name in this draft) and Inspector Owen examine Talbot's clothes for clues, they find them rotten and moldy as though they had been buried for years; Talbot's shirt falls apart at a touch "as if it were woven of spider's thread." Maleva is initially unsympathetic to Talbot when he appears at her camp, firmly telling him, "Go away! And don't cross my path again!" before she takes pity on the suffering lycanthrope. Pursued by a mob after the murder of Margareta, the Wolf Man hurls rocks and even a crumbling wall downhill onto the heads of the villagers. And in the finale, just before the monsters clash, it's the Wolf Man who first breaks free from his bonds and menaces Harley and Elsa, and the Monster who comes to the rescue.

Of the three monster rally films, *Frankenstein Meets the Wolf Man* is easily the best. Taking a break from the Sherlock Holmes series, the talented Roy William Neill puts forth what seems a sincere effort, injecting some mood and style into a film whose baldly exploitative title and premise set it down as routine even before a frame of film was exposed. Unlike director Erle C. Kenton, who was more of a ringmaster than a craftsman on the two *House* pictures, Neill puts his familiar stamp on the film. It's atmospheric, almost *noir*ish in spots, and is enhanced by good performances as well as some excellent technical credits.

Camerawork by George Robinson is particularly good. The film opens with an ambitious shot of the windswept Llanwelly Cemetery; Robinson's camera fixes first on the graveyard sign, glides over a high wall taking in the bleak landscape, focuses on the approaching graverobbers and accompanies them up to the door of the Talbot crypt. While there are few of the curious, striking camera compositions that crop up in *The Ghost of Frankenstein,* Robinson's cinematography remains a plus factor throughout, helping to endow the picture with some handsome pictorial values. The sets, miniatures and special effects are also high quality.

The Festival of the New Wine sequence is a pleasant interlude that breaks up the atmosphere of grimness and gives the picture a nice splash of color and pageantry. Adia Kuznetzoff, a toothy, big-eyed Russian baritone, makes the most of his minor role as the Festival singer, belting out "Faro-La, Faro-Li" (lyrics by Siodmak!) and adding appreciably to the Oktoberfest, oom-pah-pah "feel" of the film. Unfortunately, the singer's lyric "May they live e-*ter*-nally!", directed at Talbot, has the old Abbott and Costello "Niagara Falls" effect on the poor lycanthrope, prompting a silly outburst that's more embarrassing than it is dramatic.

Critical reaction to *Frankenstein Meets the Wolf Man* was generally lukewarm, with many writers treating the film as a joke, which was perhaps to be expected. Its reputation hasn't improved much in the years since its release, although fair-minded fans tend to treat the film more favorably than most. *Frankenstein Meets the Wolf Man* is a far better film than its audience required; what should have been only an exploitative horror film with its accent on monsters and action is also a well-crafted production with fine attention to detail. The film boasts the best-ever Wolf Man scenes and gives us one last real look at the Monster before he becomes a lowly prop in the *House* films. Even if this is the film that led the classic series permanently astray, it does so in handsome style. There are atmospheric as well as action highlights, a "game" cast and, of course, that terrific last-reel donnybrook, all combining to place

Frankenstein Meets the Wolf Man on a rickety pedestal as a milestone in monster movie history.

Frankenstein Meets the Wolf Man is certainly not on a par with any of the Frankenstein films of the '30s, nor is it even in a league with the original *The Wolf Man*. But a brisk pace, a plot filled with incident and Roy William Neill's artistry place it a cut above all of the other '40s sequels.

Sherlock Holmes in Washington (1943)

Released April 30, 1943. 71 minutes. *Directed by* Roy William Neill. *Associate Producer:* Howard Benedict. *Screenplay by* Bertram Millhauser & Lynn Riggs. *Original Story by* Bertram Millhauser. *Based on the characters created by* Sir Arthur Conan Doyle. *Director of Photography:* Les White. *Film Editor:* Otto Ludwig. *Art Director:* Jack Otterson. *Associate Art Director:* Martin Obzina. *Music by* Frank Skinner. *Musical Director:* Charles Previn. *Set Decorator:* Russell A. Gausman. *Associate Set Decorator:* Edward R. Robinson. *Sound Director:* Bernard B. Brown. *Technician:* James Masterson. *Technical Adviser:* Tom McKnight. *Gowns by* Vera West.

Basil Rathbone (Sherlock Holmes), Nigel Bruce (Dr. John H. Watson), Marjorie Lord (Nancy Partridge), John Archer (Lieut. Peter Merriam), Gavin Muir (Bart Lang), Edmund MacDonald (Detective Lieut. Grogan), Don Terry (Howe), Bradley Page (Cady), Holmes Herbert (Mr. Ahrens), Thurston Hall (Senator Henry Babcock), Gilbert Emery (Sir Henry Marchmont), Ian Wolfe (Clerk), Mary Forbes (Beryl Pettibone), Gerald Hamer (John Grayson/Alfred Pettibone), John Burton* (Army Inspector), Regina Wallace (Mrs. Bryce Partridge), Mary Gordon (Mrs. Hudson), Margaret Seddon (Miss Pringle), Alice Fleming (Mrs. Jellison), Clarence Muse (George), Leland [Leyland] Hodgson (Airport Official), Evelyn Cooke (Girlfriend), Charles Marsh, Gene O'Donnell (Reporters), Eddie Coke (Steward), Alexander Lockwood (Reporter), Paul Scott (Army Major), Irving Mitchell (Laboratory Assistant), Leslie Denison (Bomber Pilot), Jason Robards, Sr. (Doorman), Phil Warren (Young Officer), Lee Shumway (Army Major), Tom Martin (Waiter), Caroline Cooke (Mrs. Ruxton), Kernan Cripps (Hotel Porter), John Burton* (Commentator, "Voice of London"). [**Either the same actor or two different players with the same name.*]

On the road to becoming England's most illustrious freedom fighter (an image Sir Arthur Conan Doyle couldn't possibly have anticipated), Sherlock Holmes fought against enemy forces on American soil in *Sherlock Holmes in Washington* (original title: *Sherlock Holmes in U.S.A.*), produced at Universal City in the fall of 1942. The first Holmes entry not directly inspired by one of Conan Doyle's stories, *Sherlock Holmes in Washington* doesn't fare well with aficionados. It hasn't the verve or the color of *Sherlock Holmes and the Voice of Terror* or *Sherlock Holmes and the Secret Weapon,* nor does it boast the macabre elements that made *The Scarlet Claw* and *The Pearl of Death* so memorable. Nevertheless, the film succeeds on its own modest terms.

Marking the series debut of screenwriter Bertram Millhauser (he cowrote the script with Lynn Riggs, who had, in turn, coauthored the script of *Sherlock Holmes and the Voice of Terror* with John Bright), *Sherlock Holmes in Washington* benefits greatly from solid characterizations, an interest-holding tale couched in smart dialogue, and snappy direction by the adroit Roy William Neill.

Unlike the more highly regarded entries in the series, *Sherlock Holmes in Washington* conspicuously lacks the kind of high voltage scenes that make us want to stand up and cheer. Instead, the film is filled with little moments, inventive bits of business which, while they may not quicken the pulse, work effectively on a less audacious level. Its slow tempo and low-keyed excitement notwithstanding, *Sherlock Holmes in Washington* is still an enjoyable caper, undeserving of the *non grata* treatment it usually receives.

A secret government document of "great international importance" (that's the only clue we are given regarding its contents throughout the picture) is (presumably) entrusted to ace British diplomat Sir Henry Marchmont (Gilbert Emery) on its journey to Washington, D.C. A gang of Axis agents led by William Easter (Henry Daniell) follows the diplomat to New York, and then aboard the Washington Express.

Easter rifles through Sir Henry's baggage and concludes he is only a decoy employed by the British to throw the desperate agents off the scent. The real courier is Alfred Pettibone (Gerald Hamer), alias John Grayson, a meek senior clerk working undercover for the British Secret Service. Pettibone had the foresight to transfer the bulky document to a minuscule piece of microfilm, and then glued it inside the cover of an ordinary American matchbook folder. Minutes before he is seized by Easter's men, Pettibone passes the matchbook to socialite Nancy Partridge (Marjorie Lord), who leaves the train unaware she is carrying a "time bomb."

Back in London, Sherlock Holmes (Basil Rathbone) and Dr. Watson (Nigel Bruce) receive an urgent visit from Mr. Ahrens (Holmes Herbert) of the Home Office. Pettibone has undoubtedly been kidnapped and, chances are, the document is now in the hands of enemy agents. With all due haste, Holmes and Watson are whisked off on their first trip to America.

A grim discovery awaits the Britons immediately upon their arrival: a trunk containing Pettibone's corpse. Holmes is convinced that the agents haven't yet recovered the document (which he has already deduced has been transferred to microfilm). Although the Washington police have made a thorough search of the club car in which Pettibone was abducted, Holmes conducts his own investigation. He quickly deduces the identity of Pettibone's unwitting accomplice, Nancy Partridge.

The scene shifts to a festive afternoon reception celebrating Nancy's forthcoming marriage to Lieut. Peter Merriam (John Archer). Disguised as caterers, Easter's men, Cady and Howe (Bradley Page and Don Terry), separate Nancy and Peter from their guests. Merriam is knocked out cold and Nancy is anesthetized, wrapped up in a carpet, and carried off in full view of the celebrants (the "traveling" matchbook has fortuitously found its way back to Nancy's handbag again).

Based on a minute investigation of the foreign scrapings that clung to the blanket used to wrap Pettibone's body, Holmes concludes the spy ring operates out of an antique shop. Impersonating an eccentric collector, Holmes wrangles his way into the office of the shop's proprietor, the respected Richard Stanley (George Zucco). The detective's guise doesn't fool Stanley, nor does Stanley's veneer of reputability throw Holmes. He recognizes him to be none other than Heinrich Hinkle, ex-secret agent of the German Kaiser, now head of the most insidious international spy ring in existence.

Searching through the contents of Nancy's purse, Stanley comes across the matchbook and, unaware of the treasure it conceals, blithely uses it to light his pipe. Holmes taunts his adversary, who has obviously come to a dead end in his quest for the document, with the remark, "The man who has it doesn't know he has it." Throwing Stanley off course, Holmes suggests the possibility that the document might have been transferred to microfilm and hidden behind something as minute as a postage stamp.

Confident he now knows the whereabouts of the document, Stanley is about to murder Holmes and Nancy when the police, alerted by Watson, converge on the shop and round up Easter and his cohorts. Stanley escapes the raid by disappearing through a secret passageway hidden behind an Egyptian sarcophagus. He heads straight for the home of Senator Henry Babcock (Thurston Hall), whom Pettibone had given a stamped envelope bearing his mailing address on the train ride to Washington. But he is too late: Holmes has beaten him there. Holding the men at gunpoint, Stanley is about to flee with the envelope when the police nab him. Unable to resist the temptation to mortify his opponent, Holmes sets the envelope on fire. Removing a bit of microfilm from the matchbook folder, he reminds the livid master spy of the clue he threw his way earlier—the man who had the document *didn't know he had it!*

Sherlock Holmes in Washington was not Bertram Millhauser's first encounter with Conan Doyle's legendary detective. In 1932, the New York-born stenographer-turned-writer penned the screenplay for the Fox release *Sherlock Holmes,* inspired by the Conan Doyle short stories and the William Gillette play. Millhauser distinguished himself as one of Universal's most literate writers, specializing in motion pictures with British backgrounds (he scripted a total of five Holmes adventures for the studio). Gaining his early cinematic experience writing Pearl White serials, Millhauser came to Hollywood in the '20s as a writer-producer for Cecil B. DeMille, then worked as an associate producer for such studios as Radio, Fox and RKO. Tough-edged urban dramas of the kind that built Warner Bros.' reputation kept the writer busy. These included *The Life of Jimmy Dolan* (1933), which Millhauser adapted from his own play, *Jimmy the Gent* (1934), *They Made Me a Criminal* (1939) with John Garfield, Claude Rains and the Dead End Kids, and *The Big Shot* (1942), a lesser Bogart gangster outing.

Finely-etched characterizations and pungent dialogue were Millhauser's strong suits. With the exception of *The Pearl of Death,* probably his best work, the writer's genre pictures (*Sherlock Holmes Faces Death, The Spider Woman, The Woman in Green, The Invisible Man's Revenge* and the suspense drama

The Suspect) suffer from flaccid plotting. Although *Sherlock Holmes in Washington* doesn't pack a wallop, it does maintain a direct course, builds tension, and doesn't get preoccupied with tangential plot lines.

Neill and the screenwriters have taken a tongue-in-cheek approach to the deadly serious business of tracking down missing top security documents. One could accuse them of aping Alfred Hitchcock in one of his more mischievous moods. The document is, after all, nothing more than one of the master's beloved "MacGuffins" (i.e., an object of great desirability—usually a secret code, a weapon, or a valuable formula—which sets the plot in motion but gradually takes a back seat in terms of relevance to the characters and their adventures). The suspenseful cat-and-mouse scene played out in the club car also recalls Hitchcock. As in *The Lady Vanishes,* the car is inhabited by colorful character types, all of whom are blissfully unaware of the tense drama unfolding around them.

Ironically, the document constantly ends up in the palms of its pursuers. "You have a document I *must* have," Zucco says with grim determination to Marjorie Lord as he holds the matchbook between his fingers. Having deduced the document has been transferred to microfilm, Holmes points up the absurdity of the chase with the line, "A big country, Watson, and a small match folder."

A dour side to the detective's personality is revealed this time out. Unlike Watson, who revels in such Americanisms as chewing gum, ice cream sodas and the Sunday comics, Holmes is unfazed by his first trip to the States and is totally preoccupied with the business at hand. Sitting stone-faced in the back seat of the car en route to the hotel, he spouts an obligatory "most impressive" and "magnificent" as Detective Lieut. Grogan (Edmund MacDonald) points out such landmarks as the Lincoln Memorial and the Capitol Building.

Later, Holmes ruffles the detective's feathers when he authoritatively directs the investigation of an essential piece of evidence. Realizing he's hit a nerve, Holmes softens his approach with an apologetic, "I sometimes forget the more modern scientific methods *so particularly effective* here in America." Naturally, the remarkable sleuth uncovers evidence (some of it quite extraordinary) that the Washington police lab never dreamed existed.

But most unpleasant of all is Holmes' condescending treatment of Watson, a habit he retained for the rest of the series. He snaps at the old man as if to an unloved spouse. On more than one occasion, Holmes makes a fool of the doctor in front of strangers. While his brilliance as an investigator is beyond reproach, this offensive new character trait hardly endears us to Holmes the man.

Rathbone's climactic confrontation with Zucco harkens back to their battle of wits in the superior *The Adventures of Sherlock Holmes* (1939). It's always a pleasure to see these old pros play off each other, even though their scenes together in this film lack the fire of their earlier encounter, and are a notch below the verbal fencing match Rathbone and Lionel Atwill waged in *Sherlock Holmes and the Secret Weapon.* Rathbone's impression of a prissy antique connoisseur who questions the authenticity of Zucco's wares ("Ming for T'ang, indeed!") is a joy.

Zucco is up to his old tricks. He's rigged a Moorish chest with a deadly booby trap, a bow and arrow device which is set to fire the second the lid is opened. Searching the office for clues, Rathbone curiously fiddles with the lid as Zucco stands by with studied calm. Sensing something foul is afoot, he places a vase before the chest, stands off to the side and opens the lid. The vase is demolished. ("The Moors were an incredibly inventive people, weren't they?" he chides Zucco.) The serial-like rescue of Rathbone and Lord by the police a moment before Zucco pulls the trigger on them is, to put it bluntly, unbelievable.

In the supporting cast, Marjorie Lord (in a role the studio originally announced for Evelyn Ankers) is fine as the debutante suddenly thrust into a world of international intrigue. She and love interest John Archer eventually married and had a daughter, the lovely film actress Anne Archer. Again, Henry Daniell is slighted in an insignificant role not worthy of his gifts. With *The Woman in Green,* his *third* Sherlock Holmes caper, the actor was finally given the opportunity to share the spotlight with Rathbone. Gerald Hamer makes his series debut as the ill-fated Alfred Pettibone, while Clarence Muse, the prolific black actor whose dry wit enhanced dozens of Hollywood features (he was one of the few bright spots in the dismal 1941 Lugosi meller *Invisible Ghost*), makes the most of his small role as George, the keen-eyed porter.

Rounding out Bertram Millhauser's screenwriting career is a mixed bag of melodramas and action pictures including *The Web* (1947), *Walk a Crooked Mile* (1948) and *Tokyo Joe* (1949). He branched off into television in the '50s and worked as a story editor on two popular series, "Jim Bowie" and "The Lone Ranger." The erudite screenwriter, who put Doyle's hero through some of his most intriguing adventures and introduced two of the macabre cinema's beloved menaces, the Spider Woman and the Creeper, died of a heart attack at the age of 66 on December 1, 1958.

Captive Wild Woman (1943)

Released June 4, 1943. 60 minutes. *Directed by* Edward Dmytryk. *Associate Producer:* Ben Pivar. *Screenplay by* Griffin Jay & Henry Sucher. *Original Story by* Ted Fithian, Neil P. Varnick & Maurice Pivar. *Director of Photography:* George Robinson. *Assistant Director:* Melville Shyer. *Film Editor:* Milton Carruth. *Art Directors:* John B. Goodman & Ralph M. DeLacy. *Musical Director:* Hans J. Salter. *Set Decorators:* Russell A. Gausman & Ira S. Webb. *Sound Director:* Bernard B. Brown. *Technician:* William Hedgcock. *Makeup by* Jack P. Pierce. *Gowns by* Vera West.

John Carradine (Dr. Sigmund Walters), Evelyn Ankers (Beth Colman), Milburn Stone (Fred Mason), Lloyd Corrigan (John Whipple), Martha MacVicar [Vickers] (Dorothy Colman), Vince Barnett (Curley Barret), Fay Helm (Miss Strand), Paul Fix (Gruen), Ray "Crash" Corrigan (Cheela), Ed Peil, Sr. (Jake), Ray Walker (Ringmaster), Gus Glassmire (Coroner), Fern Emmett (Spinster), William Gould (Sheriff), Grant Withers (Vet), Joey Ray (Attendant), Frank Mitchell (Handler), Anthony Warde (Tony), Harry Holman (Clerk), Alexander Gill (Waiter), Charles McAvoy (cop), Virginia Engels (Trapeze Artist), Joel Goodkind (Small Boy), Turhan Bey (Closing Narration). And introducing Acquanetta as Paula Dupree.

Universal's most erotic offspring of ungodly scientific experimentation – a woman fashioned from the body of an ape through the injection of sex hormones – was the creation of writers Ted Fithian, Neil P. Varnick and Maurice Pivar. Christened Paula Dupree, the exotic menace was the center attraction of a three picture miniseries started by Ben Pivar. The best of the trio, *Captive Wild Woman,* is a brisk action-melodrama for the juvenile trade which made little attempt to underplay the sensationalistic aspects of its unappetizing premise.

The concept of scientifically transforming animals into humans (and vice versa) was hardly new. Charles Laughton created a nightmarish menagerie of manimals (including an alluring Panther Woman [Kathleen Burke], an ancestor of Paula Dupree) in Paramount's vivid adaptation of H.G. Wells' *The Island of Dr. Moreau, Island of Lost Souls* (1933). The previous year, Bela Lugosi vainly attempted to establish a link between man and beast in Universal's own *Murders in the Rue Morgue.* Stuart Heisler's *The Monster and the Girl,* released by Paramount in 1941, featured a vengeful ape with the mind of an executed murderer, while Monogram's 1943 *The Ape Man* had Poor Bela strutting around a cheap Poverty Row lab in a hilarious half-man/half-ape get-up. It was 20th Century–Fox's *Dr. Renault's Secret,* released a year before

Captive Wild Woman, that came closest to the Universal thriller in concept. In this minor but surprisingly well-mounted B, George Zucco transforms an ape that he had acquired on a jungle expedition into a pathetic imbecile (sympathetically played by J. Carrol Naish).

Less thoughtful but a lot more provocative than the Fox picture, *Captive Wild Woman* wears better with today's audiences. The angle of creating a *female* hybrid brought to the film an element of sensuality missing from the staid *Dr. Renault's Secret.*

A Canadian-born film editor turned director, Edward Dmytryk does an efficient job, keeping the story moving at a fast clip. After several years of working in B programmers (including the chilling Karloff vehicle *The Devil Commands* for Columbia), Dmytryk struck pay dirt with *Hitler's Children* (RKO, 1943). He made *Captive Wild Woman* while on a loan-out from RKO, then returned to the studio and established himself as a first-rank talent via pictures like *Tender Comrade* (1943), *Murder, My Sweet* (1944) and *Crossfire* (1947). The McCarthy witch hunts forced Dmytryk to seek temporary employment in Britain, but he returned to Hollywood in the early '50s and directed such critically acclaimed or commercially successful pictures as *The Caine Mutiny* (1954), *Soldier of Fortune* (1955), *Raintree County* (1957), *The Young Lions* (1958) and *The Carpetbaggers* (1964).

More than two years before its release, Universal announced its intentions to produce *Captive Wild Woman* in *The Hollywood Reporter.* August 8, 1941, was the designated starting date, yet the studio was still undecided as to who should play their newest horror creation, "The Wild Woman." Two distinctly different concepts of this character appeared in preview ads planted in the trade paper: a July 29 ad featured a furiously leering female, while a second ad showed an exotic woman, knife in hand, running through the jungle (suggesting a *Jungle Girl* or *Tiger Woman*-like character). Neither even hinted at the half-woman/half-ape hybrid that eventually surfaced from studio story conferences.

Although January 2, 1942, was designated as the release date of the new George Waggner production, *Captive Wild Woman* didn't go into production until December 10, 1942, nearly a year-and-a-half after it was first announced. By then, Waggner had dropped out of the project and horror picture "specialist" Ben Pivar had taken over. Shooting picked up again after the Christmas holidays and post-production work began at the start of the new year. Universal held up the release of *Captive Wild Woman* until June, 1943, qualifying it as an exciting summer attraction for the kids.

Griffin Jay and Henry Sucher's screenplay shifts effortlessly between laboratory and Big Top. Ace wild animal trainer Fred Mason (Milburn Stone) returns to the States after an African expedition with a cargo of killer cats and a remarkably genial ape named Cheela (Ray Corrigan in his customary gorilla skin). The animal attracts the fancy of renowned endocrinologist Dr. Sigmund Walters (John Carradine), who has been treating the ailing sister of Fred's fiancée, Beth Colman (Evelyn Ankers). Walters is a pioneer in his field. He has succeeded in changing the sex and breed of lower animals through glandular transplants and has performed miracles of surgery on deformed humans. But the doctor's scientific aspirations have a dark side.

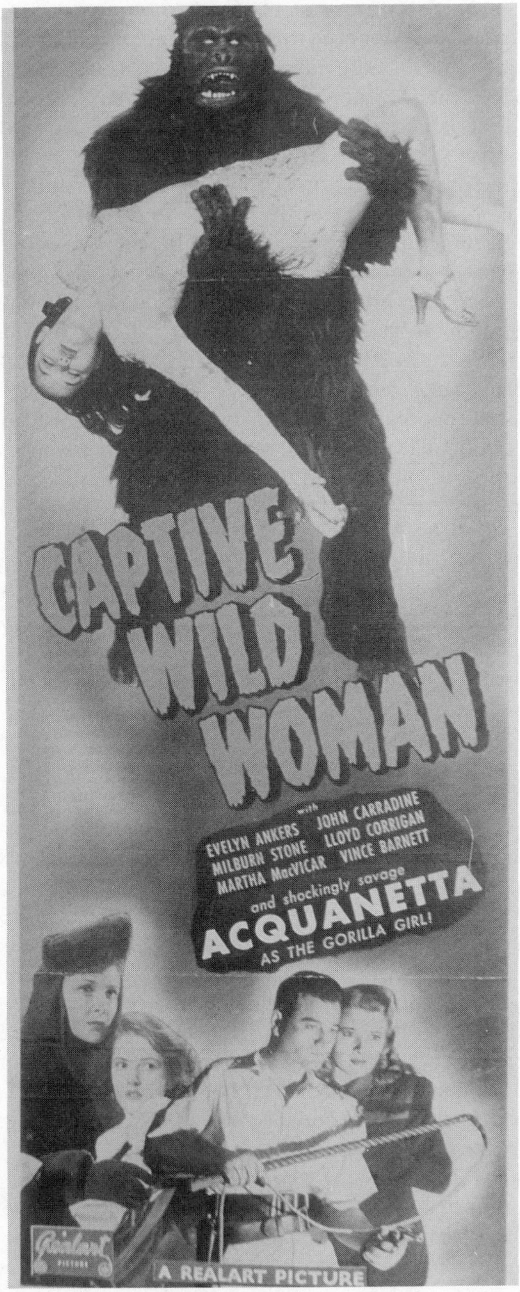

Acquanetta, the "Venezuelan Volcano," made her official screen debut in *Captive Wild Woman*.

In the basement laboratory of his Crestview Sanatorium, Walters is attempting to create a superior race through the biological interpolation of man and beast (an idea purportedly advanced by the Nazis at this time). The doctor's jittery nurse, Miss Strand (Fay Helm, giving another convincing performance), offers that old cliche that Walters mustn't "tamper with things no man or woman should ever touch." Naturally, he turns a deaf ear to her entreaties.

Drawing off sufficient amounts of excessive sex hormones from Dorothy Colman (Martha MacVicar), and injecting the fluid into Cheela (whom he has nabbed), Walters hopes to create an entirely different species of life. To achieve mental stability in his creation, he sacrifices the life of the rebellious nurse and transplants her cerebrum into Cheela's shaggy noggin. The repugnant clinical details of this bloody procedure are merely suggested through a neat montage of operating room actions. Our first glimpse of the newborn Paula Dupree (Acquanetta) is eerily underscored by Hans J. Salter's awe-inspiring musical cue. George Robinson focuses his camera on Acquanetta's vacant stare as Fay Helm's earlier dialogue ("What will you have? A human form with animal instincts!") is looped on the soundtrack.

Walters escorts Paula to Fred's circus performance, where she is introduced to her (Cheela's) former mentor. She is immediately attracted to the animal trainer while bearing a jealous grudge against Beth. The sexual ramifications of this romantic "triangle" are discreetly side-stepped. It would take a writer like Edward D. Wood, Jr. (1958's *The Bride and the Beast*) to realize the kinkier aspects of such a situation!

Paula saves Fred's life when he is knocked unconscious during a rehearsal and almost attacked by a lion. Her influence over the jungle beasts is uncanny. Ecstatic over this discovery, Fred hires Paula as his assistant; she quickly becomes the rage of the circus world.

But Paula's seething passions take a toll on her physical appearance. Her glands trigger an excessive amount of animal secretions, causing the girl to degenerate into a clawed, hirsute creature (one of Jack Pierce's most brilliant yet least heralded guises). Paula makes an attempt on Beth's life but resorts to wringing the neck of an innocent bystander (Fern Emmett) instead. Later, Beth confides to Fred that she suspects the dark stranger who entered her bedroom that night was Paula, and even suggests a link between Paula and Cheela. Fred quickly dismisses her admittedly hare-brained theory.

When Paula reverts back to Cheela completely, Walters prepares Dorothy for further surgery. Beth, who has just arrived at the sanatorium, is elected to sacrifice her cerebrum this time out. But before the procedure can begin, Beth unleashes the furious Cheela from her cage. She stomps through the lab after Walters and crushes the lunatic to death.

Fred, meanwhile, has his own problems. He loses control of a cageful of mixed cats during a bellowing storm. Sensing her master's danger, Cheela beats it to the circus grounds and carries the mauled trainer out of the arena. Her good intentions are mistaken by an overzealous cop and Cheela is shot to death.

John Carradine is *Captive Wild Woman*'s greatest asset. Unlike Lionel Atwill or George Zucco, Carradine performs the part of the crazed scientist

Paula Dupree (played by Acquanetta) reverts to her simian origins in this series of shots from *Captive Wild Woman*.

without a trace of his usual ham. Dedicated beyond reason toward "advancing" the cause of science, Carradine raises nary an eyebrow when he's forced to sacrifice his nurse of 13 years to the cause. His character's icy demeanor is first established in a scene where he placidly stands by as Cheela chokes the life out of his hired man, Paul Fix. *Captive Wild Woman* was Carradine's first starring role in a Universal horror film; in a sense, the film was primarily responsible for changing the course of the talented actor's motion picture career.

A healthy portion of *Captive Wild Woman*'s running time is devoted to the derring-do exploits of Milburn Stone in the circus ring. What might have been a pleasant diversion from the story's horror elements becomes more of an irritation as virtually all of the animal footage used in the film was lifted from the 1933 Universal production *The Big Cage* featuring Clyde Beatty. (Beatty is acknowledged by the producers for his "cooperation and inimitable talent" in the picture's title credits, but all the world-class animal trainer did was to give the okay for Universal to use snippets of his *Big Cage* performance in their new film.)

Editor Milton Carruth had his work cut out for him in mating the stock footage with live action shots. The results are generally satisfactory, although it's easy to spot Beatty filling in for Stone, despite their physical similarities. (Film historian Michael Fitzgerald noted recently that Universal never gave Stone a big star build-up due to his below-average height, and usually shuffled him around in second lead parts, small featured roles, and even voice-overs! The only reason he was given such a prominent role in *Captive Wild Woman* was his resemblance to Beatty.) In the long run, this blatant misrepresentation works against *Captive Wild Woman;* it's difficult to muster much enthusiasm over action scenes originally staged for another film with an entirely different storyline. Even more insulting are shots of advancing jungle cats printed in reverse to give the impression of the animals in retreat. (A university audience howled over this *un*special effect at a recent revival of the film.)

Proclaimed the "Venezuelan Volcano" by her friend William Randolph Hearst, Acquanetta's real origins were decidedly less exotic. "My mother was Arapaho, and I was born on the Arapaho Reservation in Wyoming," Acquanetta reveals. "I was given away to my father when I was approximately three years old. He took me to Pennsylvania and gave me to his then-wife. And I grew up in Norristown, Pennsylvania, where I went to school."

After graduating high school, Acquanetta went to New York and became a John Powers model, and lived at the Barbizon Women's Hotel.

> Louis Sobol and Walter Winchell and all the scribes were writing about me. When they found out that I was an Indian in New York, they said, "Oh, nobody cares about Indians." But Roosevelt was President, and the big South American Hands Across the Border policy was on. It was almost like "Pygmalion"—they fabricated for me this story that I came from Venezuela. And I looked the part—I was dark and exotic, and I wore these big scarfs and a big gardenia, three quarter length flowered skirts, collars and capes and those kinds of things!

On her way to South America to perform at the Copacabana, Acquanetta made a stop-over in Hollywood and ended up at the Beverly Hills Hotel.

> We went out to the Macambo—the head of MGM was there, the head of Warner Bros., Dan Kelly from Universal Studios and Walter Wanger. He was the one that really went ape over me. He tried to get me for *Arabian Nights* (1942), but unfortunately they had already signed Maria Montez. That started the big so-called "feud" between the two of us.

Although she was given a small speaking role as one of the harem girls in *Arabian Nights,* and was introduced in *Rhythm of the Islands* (1943) in a fairly good part, Universal insisted on "introducing" Acquanetta to film audiences all over again in *Captive Wild Woman.*

> I know that they were testing various actresses at the studio; I think Yvonne de Carlo was one under consideration. They were always threatening me with her, and again, like with Maria Montez, she got the big Technicolors. I think she was tested for *Captive Wild Woman,* but I'm not absolutely certain. But in any event I tested, and they said I was perfect for the role.

As with Rondo Hatton, a novelty personality in his own right, Acquanetta was far more effective in movies like *Captive Wild Woman* where she wasn't called upon to recite dialogue. Without uttering a word, the olive-skinned beauty conveyed a raw, primitive sensuality that made her the ideal Paula Dupree.

> There was no preparation on my part, but I sat sometimes for two and a half hours being made up by a makeup artist. I think I had more emotional feeling, being made up for that, than anything that I ever did, because it was exhausting. Edward Dmytryk and I had great rapport—we dated briefly. I thought he was tremendous. Eddie gave me more freedom, I think, than other directors. I've always felt that I was never "me" in movies—do you know there was never a film where I was allowed to smile?
>
> John Carradine was great—he was always acting, you know! Even when we were off the set, there was John being John! Milburn Stone was a gentleman, a real nice person, and Evelyn Ankers, too. Evelyn and I were never really close, like close girlfriends, but that could have been partly because of me. I was somewhat withdrawn.

The ultimate Saturday-afternoon-at-the-Bijou crowd-pleaser, *Captive Wild Woman* is 60 minutes of chills, thrills and good old-fashioned B-movie entertainment. Neither of its sequels—the pseudo-stylistic *Jungle Woman* and the prosaic *The Jungle Captive*—came close to capturing the *chutzpah* of this camp classic.

Phantom of the Opera (1943)

Released August 27, 1943. 92 minutes. Filmed in Technicolor. *Produced by* George Waggner. *Directed by* Arthur Lubin. *Executive Producer:* Jack Gross. *Screenplay by* Eric Taylor & (Dr.) Samuel Hoffenstein. *Adaptation by* John Jacoby. *Based on the composition* ***The Phantom of the Opera*** *by* Gaston Leroux. *Directors of Photography:* Hal Mohr & W. Howard Greene. *Technicolor Color Director:* Natalie Kalmus. *Art Directors:* John B. Goodman & Alexander Golitzen. *Film Editor:* Russell Schoengarth. *Assistant Director:* Charles Gould. *Set Decorators:* Russell A. Gausman & Ira S. Webb. *Dialogue Director:* Joan Hathaway. *Sound Director:* Bernard B. Brown. *Technician:* Joe Lapis. *Musical Score & Direction:* Edward Ward. *Opera Sequences Staged by* William Von Wymetal & Lester Horton. *Choral Director:* William Tyroler. *Orchestrations by* Harold Zweifel & Arthur Schutt. *Makeup by* Jack P. Pierce. *Hair Stylist:* Emily Moore. *Costumes by* Vera West.

Nelson Eddy (Anatole Garron), Susanna Foster (Christine DuBois), Claude Rains (Erique Claudin/The Phantom), Edgar Barrier (Inspector Raoul Daubert), Leo Carrillo (Signor Ferretti), Jane Farrar (Madame Biancarolli), J. Edward Bromberg (Amiot), Fritz Feld (Lecours), Frank Puglia (Villeneuve), Steven Geray (Vercheres), Barbara Everest (Christine's Aunt), Hume Cronyn (Gerard), Fritz Leiber (Franz Liszt), Nicki Andre (Madame Lorenzi), Gladys Blake (Jeanne), Elvira Curci (Yvette), Hans Herbert (Marcel), Kate Lawson (Landlady), Miles Mander (M. Pleyel), Rosina Galli (Celeste), Walter Stahl (Dr. Le Fort), Paul Marion (Desjardines), Tudor Williams, Tony Marlow (*Marta* Singers), Beatrice Roberts (Nurse), Marek Windheim (Renfrit), Muni Seroff, Dick Bartell, Jim Mitchell, Wheaton Chambers (Reporters), Belle Mitchell (Ferretti's Maid), Ernest Golm (Office Manager), Renee Carson (Georgette), Lane Chandler, Stan Blystone (Officers), Cyril Delevanti (Bookkeeper), John Walsh (Office Boy), Alphonse Martell (Policeman), Edward Clark (Usher), William Desmond, Hank Mann (Stagehands).

The hottest ticket on Broadway during the time this book was compiled wasn't for a new Neil Simon comedy nor a star-studded Las Vegas–style revue. The show that has theater audiences clamoring for seats and ticket scalpers doing big business is the latest adaptation of a French novel written over 75 years ago, an opulent, old-fashioned Grand Guignol melodrama filled with pageantry and spectacle. Its protagonist is one of the most darkly romantic figures ever to step out of literature, make the transition to motion pictures and, finally, steal the hearts of women (and men) in the theaters of London and New York City: the Phantom of the Opera.

Gaston Leroux's macabre, sensuously enigmatic character catapulted to cinematic immortality in the person of the brilliant Lon Chaney in Universal's opulent 1925 silent film hit. Six remakes (and free adaptations) surfaced over the decades before Leroux's creation won a new generation of fans via the phenomenally successful Andrew Lloyd Webber stageplay of the late 1980s.

Chaney's original *The Phantom of the Opera* has never been equalled by any of its successors for unadulterated chills and suspense. Archaic devices and weak supporting performances notwithstanding (Mary Philbin is especially unconvincing), the film is still a compelling, thrilling work, aided immeasurably by the flamboyance of Rupert Julian's direction. Universal flirted with the idea of remaking *Phantom* in the last months of the Laemmle regime; Charles Rogers planned a full-scale production with Anatole Litvak earmarked as director almost immediately after he took over the front office in 1936. 'Tis a pity such a remake wasn't attempted at the height of the '30s horror cycle when Whale, Ulmer, Freund and Florey were in bloom. By the time the studio got around to remaking *Phantom,* they adjusted their priorities and switched the accent from horror and mystery to music and romance. The 1925 *Phantom* and its 1943 remake are, at best, distant cousins.

Preparations for the lavish Technicolor remake of *Phantom of the Opera* began in November, 1941. Instead of concentrating its efforts on securing the ideal actor to portray the title role, Universal was more concerned with getting Deanna Durbin, one of their most bankable talents, to sign her name on the dotted line. Henry Koster, the songstress's "good luck" director, was elected to do the new production, indicating low and clear that the lighter elements of the story would take precedence over the melodramatic ones.

Much to Universal's dismay, La Durbin was in no mood to star opposite a phantom, or anybody else, for that matter. She had been conducting a one-woman strike against the film company that piloted her on the road to stardom with pictures like *One Hundred Men and a Girl* (1937) and *First Love* (1939). What's more, she didn't relish the idea of singing in a duet. With Durbin permanently out of the picture, Koster likewise withdrew his services, leaving the door wide open for Arthur Lubin.

Golden-voiced Susanna Foster, an attractive 18-year-old Paramount contract player, won the part originally created by Mary Philbin, that of the inexperienced young understudy who becomes an overnight sensation at the Paris Opera House. Miss Foster recently recalled:

> There was a man named Charles Spears who was in the publicity department. He went to Universal and worked in the casting area in an executive position. When they were looking for someone for *Phantom,* he suggested me. I met Arthur Lubin by accident at a mutual friend's home and he became interested in me because I sang. Eddie Ward remembered me from MGM.... So when I went out for the audition for [*Phantom* producer] George Waggner, they right away wanted me. BOOM! That was it.

As further proof of Universal's desire to downplay the production's horror angle, handsome blonde baritone Nelson Eddy, the romantic lead, was given

Pageantry, music and the glories of Technicolor diluted the fearsome aspects of "the screen's classic of terror!"—*Phantom of the Opera.*

top billing in the cast. (A December, 1942, *Hollywood Reporter* piece indicated that Jon Hall was pencilled in as the male lead but Arthur Lubin denies any knowledge of this.) The personable Eddy, who had just completed his final picture with Jeanette MacDonald, his singing partner of eight box office smashes for MGM, balked at having his hair dyed brown. "Don't forget, Nelson," Lubin told him, "if it doesn't look good on you, we can always wash it out."

Casting the title role was no problem for Arthur Lubin:

> Claude Rains was my only choice, and he was wonderful. He was a very difficult actor, very precise. He wanted to be *correct.* Weeks before we photographed his scenes, he practiced the piano and the violin. He was really perfect. And he was very difficult to direct. But he *was* worth listening to; most of his suggestions were very valuable. I would say to him, "Well, Claude, I don't agree with you, but we'll shoot it your way, then we'll shoot it my way and see." He forgot that the director in those days had the final cut!

Phantom of the Opera finally began production on Thursday, January 21, 1943—14 months after its first announcement. By the time the picture was in the can, Universal had pumped over $1,750,000 into it. Fortunately, the Opera House set from the Chaney version had been well maintained through the years (it had originally cost the studio $500,000 to construct plus an additional $100,000 for sound-proofing), thus saving Universal a huge sum by not having to construct a new one. (The then current wartime restrictions on set building would have had a negative effect on the new structure.) All that was left for acclaimed art director Alexander Golitzen to do was to have the set repainted and regilded and strung with fresh new curtains. The gigantic crystal chandelier used in the Chaney version was actually dropped and splintered during the filming of that famous scene. For the remake, Universal purchased Czech crystal and had the glittering fragments duplicated in a local glass factory. Twenty-thousand pieces were used in constructing the new 11′ × 14′ lighting fixture. Because of a "no waste" policy, it was dropped on a wire to prevent damage. The chandelier was then carefully taken apart and the pieces scattered. After completing the elaborate shot, the glass fragments were reassembled and stored for future use.

Phantom of the Opera is set in Paris in the 1860s. Erique Claudin (Claude Rains), a violinist with the Paris Opera House for 20 years, suffers a mental breakdown after he's discharged on account of an arthritic condition that has adversely affected his performance. Claudin has spent his last nickel advancing the singing career of operatic understudy Christine DuBois (Susanna Foster). Christine has no idea the shy, reclusive Claudin is her benefactor. Except for exchanging an occasional pleasantry, they are virtual strangers to each other.

In desperate need of money, Claudin drops in on the music publishing house of M. Pleyel (Miles Mander), with whom he has left his crowning achievement, a piano concerto, for eventual publication. Mistakenly believing his work has been stolen, Claudin flies into an insane rage and strangles the publisher. In retribution, Pleyel's assistant (Renee Carson) throws a tray of chemicals into Claudin's face, sending the violinist rushing out into the street screaming in agony. Pursued by the police, he takes refuge in the sewers.

Months later, the Paris Opera House is haunted by the presence of an uninvited guest. His petty thefts drive the Opera's directors, Amiot (J. Edward Bromberg) and Lecours (Fritz Feld), to distraction. Christine has also felt the stranger's presence on occasion, but his influence on her has always been a positive one.

When the tempestuous Madame Biancarolli (Jane Farrar, niece of opera great Geraldine Farrar) suddenly and mysteriously falls ill on the eve of an important performance, Christine takes her place and is an overnight success. Suspecting she has been drugged, Biancarolli charges Anatole Garron (Nelson Eddy), the Opera's star baritone and Christine's admirer, with attempted murder. The crafty prima donna promises to withdraw the charge providing that the understudy go back to the chorus permanently.

The next night, after a performance, Biancarolli discovers the Opera House phantom hiding in her dressing room. It is Claudin, dressed in a flowing cape and hat, his face hidden behind a stage mask. He warns the singer against standing in the way of Christine's success. When she defies him, the Phantom murders her and also slays her maid (Elvira Curci).

Hoping to draw Claudin out into the open, Amiot and Lecours stage a fabulous new opera. They refuse to heed the caped terrorist's warnings and cast Madame Lorenzi (Nicki Andre) opposite Anatole. Midway through the performance, the ticked-off Phantom severs the chain supporting the massive chandelier, sending it hurtling down onto the helpless audience.

In the ensuing melee, Claudin spirits Christine away and takes her deep into the bowels of the theater to his hideaway in the connecting sewer. Learning that his sweetheart has been kidnapped, Anatole prevails upon Franz Liszt (Fritz Leiber) to play a passage from Claudin's belatedly heralded piano concerto in the hope of attracting his attention. Anatole and his rival for Christine's affections, Inspector Raoul Daubert (Edgar Barrier), trace the sound of Claudin's piano through the sewers. Catching her kidnapper off-guard, Christine tears off his mask, revealing hideous scars left by the chemicals. Anatole and Raoul rescue her before the crumbling sewer wall gives way. Claudin is buried under tons of rubble.

Phantom of the Opera concludes with Christine becoming the rage of all Paris. Though she is heartened by her success, Christine is haunted by memories of the kindly Claudin, whom she believes played an important part in her past life.

Sumptuously produced on a scale that does justice to its grand story, and brilliantly photographed in luminous color, *Phantom of the Opera* is a treat for the eye as well as the ear. It's a full-blown musical extravaganza, outclassing anything Universal had yet produced under their current regime. Yet despite its considerable cost and impressive display of technical virtuosity—lavishly staged operatic presentations, elaborate crane shots sweeping over the stage and theater (packed 350 strong with extras), Alexander Golitzen's fine recreation of the famous sewers of Paris—the picture fails to impress in the writing, directing and performance departments. *Phantom of the Opera* is essentially a B movie with A accoutrements. While George Waggner, Arthur Lubin and coscenarist Eric Taylor were capable of turning out impressive work in average studio productions, a film on the scale of *Phantom of the Opera* deserved the collaborative efforts of the cream of Hollywood's talent.

By restructuring the plot of the Leroux novel and the Chaney version, a great deal of the story's dramatic tension and intrigue is lost. In the 1925 film, the Phantom's identity is shrouded in mystery for the first few reels, heightening the suspense and horror. Rupert Julian plunges head-first into the action with little fuss or time-consuming exposition. The more we learn about Chaney's Erik, the more of an enigma he becomes. (An intertitle card informs us he was born during France's Boulevard Massacre, was self-educated in music and the Black Arts, and spent time on Devil's Island.) Erik's grotesqueness, we assume, is the result of a genetic catastrophe, a misspent youth, or as the poet might conclude, a life deprived of love and human compassion. Chaney summons up all his resources and etches a characterization that's as movingly sympathetic as it is chilling. In spite of his ugliness, Chaney's Phantom is a romanticized tragic figure in the classic tradition of "Beauty and the Beast."

Opting for realism over sensationalism, George Waggner ordered a "rational Phantom," driven by motivations audiences could readily accept. It's a mystery why writers Eric Taylor and Samuel Hoffenstein clouded the storyline by giving Erique Claudin's obsession for Christine an ambiguous air. Is the girl his daughter, as most of the evidence indicates, or is she the object of affection of a much older man? ("They never could make up their minds during the whole making of the picture," Susanna Foster comments.)

Had Universal included a key scene in the film as planned, this issue would have never crept up. Early in the story, during one of Claudin's mental lapses, he hears the voice of a child singing the French nursery rhyme "Au Claire de la Lune." Susanna Foster made such a recording when she was five years old. Waggner sent for the record and discovered that after years of playing, the sound had developed a rather eerie quality which would have made it even more appropriate in the context of the story. In the end the idea was scrapped.

The Phantom's makeup also stirred controversy. Rains didn't want to play the part with his face completely covered, so it was decided that he'd wear a half-mask. "He thought that his image as a leading man would be hurt," Arthur Lubin recalls. "He didn't want to follow in the footsteps of Lon Chaney."

Susanna Foster adds, "We had been in the war for just over a year and they were worried about boys coming back with terrible injuries on their faces. So they decided not to make a fantastically horrible makeup."

The highlight of the Chaney film, the Phantom's unmasking, lacks impact here, occurring too late in the story. Jack Pierce's compromised makeup design consists of ragged scar tissue on the right side of Rains' face. According to publicity, this highly anticipated scene was shot on a closed set under rigid studio security. The final results hardly warranted all of the fuss.

Claude Rains is conspicuously miscast as the Phantom. Although he's appropriate enough in the early scenes, the actor's age and unimposing physique work against the dynamic image of the caped mystery man. As if Rains' physical shortcomings weren't enough, the writers conceived his character as an unsympathetic milquetoast. He's shy and awkward with Christine, gets bullied by his landlady, hardly defends himself when the conductor of the Paris

Taking a well-deserved horror break from the musical excesses of *Phantom of the Opera,* Claude Rains pays Jane Farrar an unwelcome visit.

Opera bounces him, and stands meekly by as Pleyel and his publishing house personnel shove him about like a piece of baggage (all of this occurs within the film's first 20 minutes). When Claudin finally decides to take a stand, he makes a fatal blunder: murdering Pleyel because he *mistakenly* thought the man had stolen his concerto!

Charles Laughton was among those considered for the role of Enrique Claudin; so was Broderick Crawford, of all people. Lon Chaney wanted nothing more than to inherit his father's most famous role but Universal felt he was unsuitable (he was). Typically the childish Chaney stewed over it for years.

Susanna Foster had no qualms whatsoever with Claude Rains: "I thought Rains was wonderful. He was a little reserved but he had that vicious little twinkle in his eye that was so cute. You got back so much working with him."

Music plays a vital role in the plot of *Phantom of the Opera.* A press release stated that because of the international crisis at the time the film was made, obtaining copyright releases and performing rights to legitimate operas would have proven difficult, so adaptations were devised. (This compromise no doubt invited the scorn of opera purists.) The production does feature one *true* opera segment, the third act of Von Flotow's *Marta* which opened the film.

George Waggner prided himself on his musical prowess, having enjoyed some success as a composer and a librettist. He furnished the librettos to Edward Ward's adaptations, a lovely French opera based on themes by Chopin and a fiery, impressively staged Russian opera utilizing Tchaikovsky's "Fourth Symphony." Universal enlisted the services of expert William Von Wymetal to authenticate the operatic selections, while William Tyroler (earlier an adviser on the Chaney version) maintained the integrity of the choral passages.

The leitmotif of the score, a beautiful refrain written by Ward and passed off in the picture as a French folk song, becomes the basis of the Phantom's piano concerto. Titled "Lullaby of the Bells," the composition was released as an arrangement for piano by the Robbins Music Company while the movie was in its first run.

The performances in *Phantom of the Opera* range from the modest (Foster) to the theatrical (Rains, Edgar Barrier and J. Edward Bromberg, Fritz Feld and Steven Geray in their amusing comic interplay as keepers of the Paris Opera House). Nelson Eddy's talents as a singer compensate for the occasional stiffness of his performance. (It's mildly depressing to see the youthful Susanna courted by such overripe suitors as Eddy and Barrier!) Frank Puglia, Miles Mander and the distinguished looking Fritz Leiber (made up to resemble Franz Liszt) do good work in minor roles. If you pay close attention, you may catch sight of Hume Cronyn in the thankless part of a gendarme.

A winner at the box office, *Phantom of the Opera* also had the distinction of netting five nominations in the 1944 Oscar sweepstakes: Alexander Golitzen for Best Color Art Direction, Hal Mohr and W. Howard Greene for Best Color Photography, Russell A. Gausman and Ira S. Webb for Best Set Decoration, Bernard B. Brown for Best Sound Recording and Edward Ward for Best Scoring of a Musical Picture. Golitzen, Mohr, Greene, Gausman and Webb walked away with Oscar tucked under their arms that night.

Leroux's celebrated Opera House Haunter sustained a number of wildly diverse resurrections over the past four decades. Hammer's lavish 1962 version with Herbert Lom owes more to the 1943 than the 1925 production for its inspiration. A Latin-style Phantom-of-sorts makes an appearance in Mexico's *Santo contra el Estrangulador* (1966). Masquerading as Edgar Allan Poe, AIP's *Murders in the Rue Morgue* (1971) is a blatant *Phantom* rip-off with Herbert Lom starring as a disfigured killer, terrorizing a theater. The 1974 rock opera *Phantom of the Paradise,* directed by a budding Brian De Palma, features a zonked-out rock musician (William Finley) who loses it all after he's been double-crossed. Maximilian Schell menaced Jane Seymour in a 1983 television movie version of the undying classic. Even Jimmy Cagney donned the hideous guise in a poor recreation of the unmasking scene in *Man of a Thousand Faces* (1957), Universal-International's grossly fictionalized account of the life of Lon Chaney. Capitalizing on the Phantom's comeback, 21st Century has released a screen adaptation starring the popular Robert Englund (*Nightmare on Elm Street*'s Freddy Krueger), to be followed by yet another remake, courtesy of Warners, set in 1940 France.

Sherlock Holmes Faces Death (1943)

Released September 17, 1943. 68 minutes. *Produced & Directed by* Roy William Neill. *Screenplay by* Bertram Millhauser. *Based on the story "The Musgrave Ritual" by* Sir Arthur Conan Doyle. *Director of Photography:* Charles Van Enger. *Art Directors:* John B. Goodman & Harold H. MacArthur. *Film Editor:* Fred R. Feitshans, Jr. *Set Decorators:* Russell A. Gausman & Edward R. Robinson. *Musical Director:* Hans J. Salter. *Sound Director:* Bernard B. Brown. *Technician:* Paul Neal. *Lightning Effects:* Kenneth Strickfaden. *Gowns by* Vera West.

Basil Rathbone (Sherlock Holmes), Nigel Bruce (Dr. John H. Watson), Dennis Hoey (Inspector Lestrade), Arthur Margetson (Dr. Bob Sexton), Hillary Brooke (Sally Musgrave), Halliwell Hobbes (Alfred Brunton), Milburn Stone (Capt. Pat Vickery), Gavin Muir (Phillip Musgrave), Frederic Worlock (Geoffrey Musgrave), Olaf Hytten (Capt. MacIntosh), Gerald Hamer (Maj. Langford), Vernon Downing (Lieut. Clavering), Minna Phillips (Mrs. Howells), Mary Gordon (Mrs. Hudson), Heather Wilde (Jenny), Harold De Becker (Pub Proprietor), Norma Varden (Gracie), Joan Blair (Nora), Charles Coleman, Dick Rush (Constables), Eric Snowden, Peter Lawford (Sailors), Martin Ashe (Slinking Figure).

In *Sherlock Holmes Faces Death,* Universal transported Conan Doyle's immortal sleuth back to the classic trappings of the original stories. Although the plot's time frame is still Britain at the height of World War II, politics takes a back seat to good old-fashioned murder mystery. Gone are the scheming Axis agents, complex enemy codes and eleventh hour spy bashes of the first three films of the series. Instead, a cunning killer lurking about a ghost-infested manor challenges the detective's remarkable powers of deductive reasoning.

Bertram Millhauser wrote an original screenplay using Conan Doyle's "The Musgrave Ritual" merely as his inspiration. In the story, aristocrat Reginald Musgrave enlists Holmes' aid after his butler, Brunton, mysteriously disappears following his dismissal for insubordination. It seems the family retainer was something of a lech. His latest conquest, Rachel Howells, a maid at Musgrave's estate, has also disappeared without leaving a trace.

Holmes makes a careful study of an old family document, the Musgrave Ritual, which Musgrave found in Brunton's possession. On the surface, the ritual is a meaningless collection of odd verses. Holmes deduces that its vague references to locations in and around Hurlstone, the old family manor, point the way to something of great value.

Launching an investigation, the detective discovers Brunton's corpse, hunched over a chest containing a "battered and shapeless diadem"—the ancient crown of the Kings of England. Evidently Brunton broke the secret code in the Musgrave Ritual and, with Rachel's help, discovered the chest in a hiding spot. Rachel's fury proved greater than her greed. She murdered Brunton for having rejected her and then fled the country, possibly for America.

In Millhauser's script, Hurlstone is turned into a haven for convalescing military officers by the Musgraves. Despite their altruistic gesture, only Sally (Hillary Brooke) appears to exhibit any compassion. Her brothers, Geoffrey (Frederic Worlock) and Phillip (Gavin Muir), are scheming, disagreeable men. The older Geoffrey heartily disapproves of his sister's affections for recuperating American pilot Pat Vickery (Milburn Stone), which, in a picture of this sort, is a sure bet that Geoffrey's fate is sealed.

Soon both he and Phillip are found dead with tiny puncture wounds in back of their heads. The supremely inept Inspector Lestrade (Dennis Hoey) and his Scotland Yard men arrive on the scene and immediately puts the cuffs on the least likely but most highly motivated suspect, Captain Vickery. But thanks to the shrewd detective work of Sherlock Holmes (Basil Rathbone), who has come to Hurlstone on the suggestion of Dr. Watson (Nigel Bruce) to "aid" Lestrade, suspicion is shifted from Vickery to Alfred Brunton (Halliwell Hobbes), the butler. The character of Brunton has metamorphosed from the middle-aged Lothario of the Conan Doyle piece to an alcoholic old man with a penchant for spouting verse.

In one of the film's showiest set pieces, Sally recites the Musgrave Ritual before the entire household during a furious storm (the pointless duty has been passed down to her after her brothers' deaths). It comes as no great surprise when a bolt of lightning (courtesy of Kenneth Strickfaden) crashes through the window at the height of the recital and demolishes a suit of armor.

In keeping with Conan Doyle's tale, Holmes learns that the ritual itself is the key to solving the murder mystery. Realizing the tiled floor of the Main Hall has the appearance of a giant chessboard, the cagey detective maneuvers each member of the household around the giant "board" as though they were chessmen according to the directions in the litany. This novel invention is Millhauser's; Conan Doyle's story contains no such scene.

An ancient wine cellar, reached via a maze of secret passageways, is discovered under the Main Hall. Brunton's body is found lying on the floor of a burial chamber beneath the cellar. Falling back on a timeworn ruse, Holmes discloses that Brunton scrawled a message in his own blood before expiring. But before it can be deciphered, the message must be treated with chemicals.

Giving everyone the impression he's gone into town to collect the chemicals, Holmes stations himself in the crypt and awaits the inevitable arrival of the guilty party. It is Watson's associate, Dr. Bob Sexton (Arthur Margetson). (Once again we have a case where the culprit is revealed to be a

Watson (*top;* Nigel Bruce) and Holmes (Basil Rathbone) discover the corpse of the butler Brunton (Halliwell Hobbes) in a crypt in the bowels of Hurlstone in *Sherlock Holmes Faces Death.* (The set is from *Dracula.*)

chum of the dear doctor—a sad commentary on the company he keeps!) The treasure alluded to in the ritual is not a king's crown but a forgotten land grant entitling the Musgraves to thousands of acres of local countryside. Sexton discovered the secret, murdered the two brothers and incriminated Vickery. With him out of the way, the scheming doctor planned to woo Sally, who stood in line to inherit the riches. Brunton witnessed Phillip's killing, proved to be an uncooperative accessory and was eliminated.

Having foolishly spilled out his guts to the trapped detective, Dr. Sexton pulls the trigger but finds the gun has been loaded with blanks. Lestrade and his men converge on the crypt and take Sexton away, but not before he sarcastically compliments Holmes on his prowess (as many of the detective's beaten opponents do as a gesture of "good sportsmanship").

Arthur Margetson's Dr. Sexton proves himself to be one of the sleuth's most colorless adversaries. He contributes so little to the plot that when Holmes unmasks him as the killer, our reaction is understandably mild. Sexton's confident boast that he'll win Sally's affections after Vickery is out of the picture is a great conceit even for an egomaniac like him; Sally doesn't give the mild-mannered doctor a second glance throughout the whole film.

As the first Sherlock Holmes film to feature the master detective in a Gothic setting since Fox's 1939 *The Hound of the Baskervilles,* it's a pity *Sherlock Holmes Faces Death* is such a disappointment. All of the right elements have been mixed into the brew for a first-rate whodunit but the final result is tasteless. Roy William Neill's adeptness at sustaining mood-provoking atmosphere was proven in Columbia's fine 1935 Karloff vehicle, *The Black Room,* and *Sherlock Holmes Faces Death* demonstrates he hadn't lost his touch. From the first sequence (a gossipy pub proprietor speaks of the evil Musgraves in hushed tones as the camera takes in the shadowy candlelit corridors of the windswept manor) to the closing reels set in Hurlstone's burial crypt, an aura of gloom and despair is evoked, aided in no small measure by the fine low-keyed camerawork of Charles Van Enger.

But in the chills and suspense department, the film comes up distressingly short. The problem lies in Millhauser's rather eccentric script. It's talky and lethargic. Though the mystery is unravelled in a painstakingly methodical manner, there just isn't enough red meat in the story upon which to feast. The murders of the Musgrave brothers (both of whom richly deserved their grisly demise if only for being so obnoxious) are committed off-camera, thus spoiling the potential for some sorely needed suspense.

Red herrings lurk around every corner. The most obvious are three convalescing officers all suffering from combat fatigue—one is a compulsive knitter, another is shell-shocked, and the third stutters. This peculiar trio, conceived by Millhauser to muddy the waters of the murder investigation, is too dotty to be taken seriously as suspects. They impart a self-conscious theatricality that rings false. A bell tower that sounds 13 chimes as a warning of impending doom doesn't win the screenwriter any accolades for plausibility or originality.

The recent promotion of Howard Benedict to the status of executive producer of the series prompted the studio brass to elevate Roy William Neill into the vacant associate producer's post. Neill utilized two of the studio's impressive standing sets when shooting commenced on April 12, 1943—the familiar European set (better known as Vasaria in the Frankenstein films) and the bleak burial crypt set originally used in *Dracula.*

Once again, we find Holmes in the same churlish mood as we last saw him. When Watson remarks that even a child could make a particular observation, Holmes says sarcastically, "Not *your* child, Watson." He is uncharacteristically abrupt to a hysterical Sally and downright rude to drunken old Brunton. Holmes *is* impressed by Sally's unselfish decision to destroy the land grant rather than take away the homes of thousands of farmers and villagers. "There's a new spirit abroad in the land. The old days of grab and greed are on their way out," the naively optimistic detective says with confidence.

The supporting cast boasts a number of players (Dennis Hoey, Hillary Brooke, Gavin Muir, Frederic Worlock, Olaf Hytten, Gerald Hamer, Vernon Downing and Mary Gordon) whose frequent appearances in the Holmes films qualified them as members of a rapidly growing repertory company. Hillary Brooke, who made her series bow in the first entry *Sherlock Holmes and the Voice of Terror* as a chauffeur, and three years later made a fine impression as Professor Moriarity's seductive accomplice, *The Woman in Green,* is uncharacteristically demonstrative as Sally (she even verges on hysteria at one point). The aloof, regal-mannered blonde was the kind of actress Alfred Hitchcock felt best personified cool, calculating sexuality on the screen. (She had a small, insignificant role in Hitchcock's 1956 remake of *The Man Who Knew Too Much.*)

In describing her character to Matthew Boulton in *The Woman in Green* ("a very handsome woman, not born to the purple, but giving an excellent imitation"), Rathbone accurately appraises the actress herself. An icon of sophistication in B pictures of the '40s and '50s, Hillary Brooke affected an impression of British gentility, when in reality she hailed from Long Island (her real name is Beatrice Peterson).

"Working at Universal at the time that the Sherlock Holmes pics were made was delightful," Hillary recalls.

> The Holmes pics made so much money that we were more or less on our own. Nigel Bruce became a dear friend and Basil was a darling. We both loved animals and ice cream. When we were not working we would get ice cream cones and stroll to the back of the lot to see and visit with the animals. Roy Neill was a dear person. Very easy to work with and very kind.

Veteran British stage and screen actor Halliwell Hobbes, the gentleman's gentleman in scores of Hollywood films, plays yet another butler in *Sherlock Holmes Faces Death* though this time his role has more shading than usual. Hobbes' Alf Brunton knows where all the Musgrave family skeletons are hidden and he's not talking, even though the grave responsibility has driven him to drink. ("Some were murderers and some worse, but they all knew how to keep a secret and so do I.")

Sherlock Holmes' welcome return to the Gothic milieu was regrettably brief. In his next caper, *The Spider Woman,* the great sleuth is once again firmly entrenched in intrigues of a more contemporary nature. *Sherlock Holmes Faces Death* is an opportunity wasted, a middling mystery saddled by a lame script that simmers when it should sizzle.

Flesh and Fantasy (1943)

Released October 29, 1943. 94 minutes. *Produced by* Charles Boyer & Julien Duvivier. *Directed by* Julien Duvivier. *Screenplay by* Ernest Pascal, (Dr.) Samuel Hoffenstein & Ellis St. Joseph. *Based on stories by* Laslo Vadnay, Oscar Wilde & Ellis St. Joseph. *Director of Photography:* Paul Ivano & Stanley Cortez. *Camera Operators:* William Dodds, Len Powers & Carl Webster. *Art Directors:* John B. Goodman, Richard H. Riedel & Robert Boyle. *Film Editor:* Arthur Hilton. *Music by* Alexander Tansman. *Musical Director:* Charles Previn. *Assistant Directors:* Joseph A. McDonough, Seward Webb & Phil Bowles. *Set Decorators:* Russell A. Gausman & Edward R. Robinson. *Dialogue Director:* Don Brodie. *Sound Director:* Bernard B. Brown. *Technicians:* Joe Lapis, Bill Fox & Jack Bolger. *Properties:* Leigh Carson & Robert Laszlo. *Makeup by* Jack P. Pierce. *Miss Stanwyck's Gowns by* Edith Head. *Gowns by* Vera West.

Framing Scenes: Robert Benchley (Doakes), David Hoffman (Davis). *Episode One:* Betty Field (Henrietta), Robert Cummings (Michael), Edgar Barrier (Stranger), Marjorie Lord (Justine), Charles Halton (Old Proprietor), Lane Chandler (Satan), Gil Patrick (Death), Paul Bryar, George Lewis (Harlequins), Clinton Rosemond (Old Negro), Jacqueline Dalya (Angel), Peter Lawford (Pierrot), Eddie Acuff (Policeman), Sandra Morgan, Phil Warren, Carl Vernell (Neighbors). *Episode Two:* Edward G. Robinson (Marshall Tyler), Thomas Mitchell (Septimus Podgers), Anna Lee (Rowena), Dame May Whitty (Lady Pamela Hardwick), C. Aubrey Smith (Dean of Norwalk), Ian Wolfe (Librarian), Mary Forbes (Lady Thomas), Doris Lloyd (Mrs. Roger Carrington), Heather Thatcher (Lady Flora), Edward Fielding (Sir Thomas), Bruce Lester, Geoffrey Steele (Party Guests), Leland [Leyland] Hodgson (Bobby), Olaf Hytten (Pharmacist), Harry Stubbs (Desk Clerk), Sailor Vincent, George Suzanne, Carey Loftin (Stunts), Jack Gardner, Harold De Becker, Anita Bolster, Constance Purdy, Laurence Grossmith, Ferdinand Munier, Anne Shoemaker, Paul Scott, Pat O'Hara. *Episode Three:* Charles Boyer (Paul Gaspar), Barbara Stanwyck (Joan Stanley), Charles Winninger (King Lamarr), Clarence Muse (Jeff), June Lang (Angel), Grace McDonald (Equestrienne), Joseph Crehan, Arthur Loft, Lee Phelps (Detectives), James Craven (Radio Announcer), Frank Mitchell, Lane Chandler (Acrobats), Jerry Maren, Jannette Fern (Midgets), Marcel Dalio, Frank Arnold (Clowns), Mary Ann Hyde (Gaspar's Assistant), Nedra Sandra, Beatrice Barrett, Marian Novikova, Yvette Bentley, Anita Venge, Marion de Sydow (Circus Girls), Con Colleano (Wirewalker Double for Boyer), Jack Gardner (Gunman), Eddie Kaul, John Burton, William Gould, Ted Jacques, Bob Scheerer, Charles Sherlock, Nolan Leary, Silvay Chaldicott, Eddie Coke.

The acclaimed director of such stylish '30s French films as *Le Golem, Pépé Le Moko,* and *La Fin de Jour,* Julien Duvivier leaned towards the omnibus style of storytelling during his wartime sabbatical in Hollywood. *Tales of Manhattan,* released by 20th Century–Fox in 1942, is a five-episode amalgam of stories threaded together by a single theme: the profound effect a dress tailcoat has on the lives of its wide range of owners. Sporting a top-notch cast (Charles Boyer, Rita Hayworth, Henry Fonda, Ginger Rogers, Charles Laughton, Edward G. Robinson and Paul Robeson), Duvivier's production garnered respectable reviews, encouraging the Gallic *auteur* to attempt a second such project with the supernatural as its central theme, *Flesh and Fantasy.*

Forming a coproduction partnership with his friend Charles Boyer, Duvivier sealed a deal with Universal in the spring of 1942. Barbara Stanwyck and Edward G. Robinson were signed up at $50,000 apiece. Boyer agreed to play a major role in the film aside from his coproducing duties for a flat $125,000. In the course of the production's erratic shooting schedule (lasting a little over a year), such popular players as Betty Field, Thomas Mitchell, Robert Cummings, Gloria Jean and Alan Curtis were added to the cast. Though the player roster didn't have the status of *Tales of Manhattan*'s it came close. (Other actors that Universal sought for the film included Adolphe Menjou, Deanna Durbin, Charles Laughton and, believe it or not, Greta Garbo.)

Algonquin Round Table wit Robert Benchley (a sparkling addition to any movie) was enlisted to play a comedic role in *Flesh and Fantasy*'s delightful framing scenes. As Mr. Doakes, a jittery businessman, Benchley confides the details of a disturbing dream and a recent experience with a fortune-teller to impish bookworm Mr. Davis (David Hoffman), whom he meets in the library of the Gentleman's Club. With the fervor of a salesman, Davis sets out to teach Doakes a moral lesson. He reads him three fanciful tales about ordinary people caught up in extraordinary circumstances who ultimately learn that man is the master of his own fate, and that by believing in ourselves, we may attain inner peace.

Flesh and Fantasy is cinematic story-telling at its best. Stylish, witty and urbane, it just falls short of being a minor classic. Duvivier's European influence and subtle touch are ever-present. He has a powerful, rich visual sense. Characters are artfully positioned within the frame. There's an abundance of striking close-ups and spirited montages. Bizarre camera angles impart a surreal, dream-like quality. Evocative sound effects aid in establishing a palpable, otherworldly mood. *Flesh and Fantasy* is the creation of a master filmmaker who uses the vocabulary of the cinema with expertise and assurance.

Collaborators Ernest Pascal, Samuel Hoffenstein and Ellis St. Joseph (who also authored one of the tales upon which the screenplay is based) have written a polished, generally sophisticated script containing a trio of morality plays. Though each story has a built-in message (the more worldly viewer may resent their naîveté), the accent is squarely on fanciful entertainment.

Originally, *Flesh and Fantasy* contained a fourth vignette. Costarring Alan Curtis and Gloria Jean, it told the story of an unregenerate hoodlum and a blind girl with spiritual powers whose encounter in a pastoral never-neverland ends in tragedy. While the completed movie was being edited, Universal determined it ran 35 minutes over what they considered acceptable theater running time. The episodes were already pared down to the point where any further revisions were impossible. Following the example of 20th Century–Fox (who deleted a vignette starring W.C. Fields from *Tales of Manhattan*), Universal pulled the Curtis-Jean episode out of *Flesh and Fantasy.* A year later, the vignette was placed back in production and expanded into a full-length feature, released in December, 1944, as *Destiny.*

The second episode of *Flesh and Fantasy,* an indictment against prognostication, was the first to go before the cameras. (It was shot over a three-week period, from July 21 to August 11, 1942.) Based on Oscar Wilde's "Lord Arthur Saville's Crime," this vignette ranks as the best in the trilogy. Edward G. Robinson, Thomas Mitchell, and a fine supporting cast complement the story's sardonic wit and rich black humor.

Robinson plays Marshall Tyler, an American lawyer visiting London. Attending a frivolous social hosted by his friend, Lady Pamela Hardwick (Dame May Whitty), the incredulous Tyler agrees to have his palm read by Septimus Podgers (Thomas Mitchell), a renowned palm-reader and forecaster. (Podgers' uncanny abilities are dramatically proven when he predicts the reappearance of Roger Carrington, who was presumably killed while on an expedition in Antarctica. In typical Hollywood fashion, an announcement heralding the explorer's rescue is heard over the radio just minutes after the seer had predicted his return!)

Examining Tyler's palm, Podgers suddenly grows somber. Later, he reveals to the lawyer what he had seen. "You are going to kill someone, Mr. Tyler." Dismissing the prediction as utter nonsense, Tyler attempts to put it out of his mind, but to no avail. Haunted by portentous images, he struggles with the dark side of his conscience (amusingly depicted as a leering, wicked version of himself), who reminds Tyler that he cannot escape his destiny.

Tyler finally succumbs to this unrelieved pressure and selects Lady Pam as his victim. He presents her with a charming seventeenth-century box containing a piece of poison-laced chocolate, then goes into hiding to await news of her passing. Much to his chagrin, Tyler learns the dowager has indeed died, but from *natural* causes!

Now more desperate than ever, Tyler attempts to set up the garrulous Dean of Norwalk (C. Aubrey Smith) as his next victim, but the scheme backfires when the clergyman guesses his intentions. Rushing out into the night, Tyler providentially encounters Podgers strolling across London Bridge (the old *Phantom of the Opera* set). Fearing for his life, the forecaster unconvincingly disclaims his prediction, but it is too late. The madman strangles him and dumps his body into the Thames. Spotted by two bobbies, Tyler escapes to the grounds of the Lamarr Circus, but is quickly captured. As the police take him away, the lawyer insists that he was forced to commit murder by an uncontrollable force within himself. Acrobatic star Paul Gaspar (Charles Boyer) witnesses the tragic scene; his presence leads us effortlessly into the next episode.

As ever, the Breen watchdogs kept a keen eye on the Universal production. The Code dictated that so-called predictions of future events from palm-reading, dreams, etc., must be handled in such a way that only evil results; a

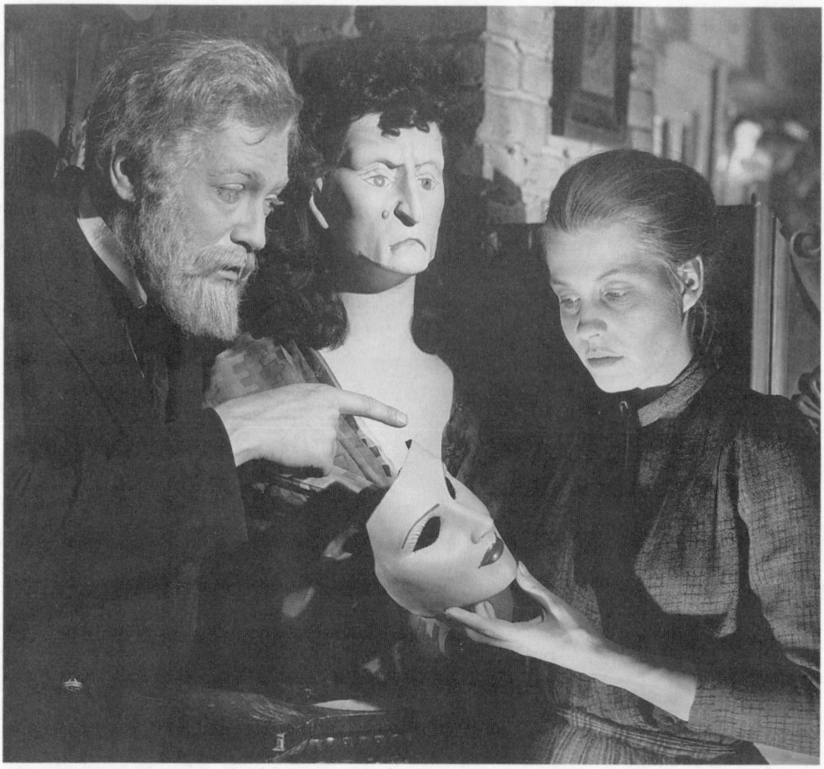

The Mardi Gras episode offered the most poetic moments in the three-part *Flesh and Fantasy*. Here, Edgar Barrier offers Betty Field a chance for a new life. (Photo courtesy Steve Jochsberger.)

person is really in control of his own destiny. To quell any apprehensions, Duvivier and Boyer met with Breen officials to reassure them the edict would be followed.

Edward G. Robinson, as always, is a joy to watch. His pompous Yankee lawyer regards the act of murder as a mere inconvenience—something to be done with immediately so he may resume his daily activities. With all the painstaking care he takes to set up Dame May Whitty, we almost feel sorry for the man when Providence intervenes and cheats him of his victim. Robinson's increased paranoia is skillfully suggested via weird montages and clever camera effects, as his mocking "other self" unexpectedly pops up in mirrors, eyeglass lenses, etc.

Anna Lee, Robinson's costar in this episode, recently recalled working with Duvivier: "It was a little odd working with him, as all his directions were in French and had to be translated by somebody else. I remember wearing a lovely green and silver gown which I took with me overseas when I was entertaining the troops—and it was stolen by the Arabs!"

On August 26, Duvivier began production on *Flesh and Fantasy*'s most elaborate episode, a sentimental, romantic vignette costarring Barbara Stanwyck and the oh-so-debonair Boyer as a pair of lovers whose meeting and ultimate separation were predestined. The screen adaptation of Laslo Vadnay's story is strong on mood (there's an aura of impending doom in the air), but it lacks the acerbic wit and sense of the unreal imparted by the other vignettes. The slim metaphysical element (predicting the future through dreams) is diluted by the schmaltzy trappings of a Hollywoodish soap opera. By comparison, it is the weakest episode in the package.

Billed as the Drunken Gentleman of the Tight Rope (a silly concept), Paul Gaspar is haunted by a recurring nightmare in which he imagines himself plummeting to the ground while performing his specialty act. The dream has an interesting sidelight: Gaspar envisions an attractive woman, wearing a pair of curious earrings, sitting in the audience, screaming in horror as he falls to earth.

Taking a rest cure, Gaspar is awestruck when he recognizes his "dream lady" amongst the passengers on board a transatlantic ship en route to New York. She is Joan Stanley (Barbara Stanwyck), a recluse with a dark secret. Joan pooh-poohs Paul's suggestion that they have met before, but starts taking him seriously when he describes in detail the pair of earrings she was wearing in his dream (two bejewelled lyres). She suggests Gaspar avoid her ("I might bring you bad luck") but Paul isn't dissuaded. When a fellow passenger addresses the young woman as Miss Templeton, Gaspar becomes even more fascinated.

During the course of the voyage, the couple fall in love. In an eerily portentous dream sequence, filled with distorted images and exaggerated sound effects, Paul "witnesses" Joan's arrest after the ship arrives in New York harbor.

His confidence restored, Paul plans on performing his act on opening night. At his request, Joan dons the earrings and sits in the audience. The performance is a success. But before Joan can reach Paul, she is stopped by a pair of detectives. Weary of fleeing the law and her jewel thief confederates, Joan had alerted the police of her whereabouts, scheduling her own date with destiny. In the tearful finis, she reveals all to the knowing Gaspar. She walks off with the policemen, just as Paul had dreamed she would.

It took Duvivier nearly three weeks to complete this episode. He suddenly fell ill in early September, causing the production to close down for two days. Henry Koster was called in on September 4 to fill in for the ailing Frenchman when he couldn't return to work. Another day was lost on account of the Labor Day holiday. Filming was finally completed on Tuesday, September 15 (or September 21, according to a second source). But nearly a month later, Boyer and Stanwyck were called back to the studio for retakes after flaws were discovered while the episode was being edited.

The Stanwyck/Boyer story's languid pacing is somewhat alleviated by the colorful circus/shipboard backgrounds. Duvivier takes advantage of these settings and creates some stunning visuals. Most of the aerial feats were performed by Con Colleano (of the world-famous family of high-wire walkers); the rest were shot on a process stage. Acquanetta was slated to appear as equestrienne Grace McDonald's assistant, but had to bow out on account of illness.

Cinematographer Stanley Cortez had a reputation in Hollywood as a perfectionist (which also meant he was painstakingly slow in his methods). He started shooting *Flesh and Fantasy,* but left after a few weeks following a disagreement with Duvivier. The director hired fellow countryman Paul Ivano to finish the film. Their chats (in French) drove Stanwyck to distraction. Ivano finally won Barbara's respect by taking the trouble to insure that the actress wouldn't be injured in the execution of a particularly dangerous crane shot.

Shortly after the Thanksgiving recess, Duvivier and Company began production on what was to become the surplus Alan Curtis/Gloria Jean vignette. The director pushed his cast and crew right up until late afternoon on Christmas Eve (a rare practice in Hollywood). Special effects men Willis R. Cook and John P. Fulton performed their intricate tasks after the holiday recess, bringing the project into its sixth month of production.

Just days before Duvivier began work on the final episode, a modern Cinderella story, Universal decided to retitle their film *For All We Know,* a tag more suggestive of a wistful love story than a surreal fantasy. But on August 24, 1943 (a week after the last scene was shot), the studio had a change of heart and restored the picture's original, appropriate title.

On a temporary loanout from her home studio, Paramount, Betty Field shared top billing with Robert Cummings, on leave while serving in the Civil Air Patrol's antisubmarine force. A precursor of the 1959 French-Portuguese classic *Black Orpheus,* this enchanting fairy tale is the purest example of fantasy in the film; there's even an old-fashioned moral at the end. The action takes place in the last hours of Mardi Gras, that magical time when the yearly celebration is at its most frenzied, when carnival masks are discarded to reveal the true identities of the revelers. Duvivier wisely positioned this moody adaptation of Ellis St. Joseph's story at the head of the others in the final cut. It captures the spirit of *Flesh and Fantasy* best, and puts the audience into a receptive mood to "accept" the paranormal elements of the forthcoming playlets.

Plain, unappealing Henrietta (Field), a New Orleans dressmaker, is an embittered shell of a woman. Friendless and loveless, she is attracted to Michael (Cummings), a disillusioned law student who is about to chuck it all and become a stoker on a departing freighter. Contemplating suicide, Henrietta is approached by a bearded old man (Edgar Barrier, in a role considered for Walter Huston) who dissuades her from leaping into the murky river. "Something miraculous might occur to change your whole life!" he tells her.

The stranger escorts Henrietta to a closed costume shop, and implores her to choose a desirable mask and costume. "For a few hours, it is still possible for you to be beautiful!" He makes her promise to return the mask before the hour of midnight.

Bedecked in the alluring disguise, Henrietta melts into the throng of cavorting celebrators. Michael "rescues" her from a would-be admirer and the couple settle into a cafe. Putting her desires and self-interests in check, Henrietta builds Michael's confidence, convincing him to believe in *himself.* She at last learns the true meaning of love: giving of oneself and expecting nothing in return.

The clock strikes 12. The time has come for everyone to unmask. Henrietta rushes back to the shop with Michael in close pursuit. She cannot bear for him to see her as she really is. "I know your face is beautiful because you are," Michael says reassuringly. Removing the disguise, Henrietta is ecstatic as she sees her features have changed to resemble those of the mask. By being selfless, Henrietta has altered her own visage of selfishness and envy. As she and Michael depart from the shop, the camera focuses on the mask of the bearded old stranger on display in the window.

With a sharp eye for the beautiful and the grotesque, Julien Duvivier has created an extraordinary tableaux of haunting images resembling an orgiastic feast before the coming of the Apocalypse. Enigmatic faces are reflected in sparkling pools. Rockets and firecrackers light up the night sky. Swirling clouds of confetti choke the air. A bizarre group of curiosity seekers including a pair of harlequins, Satan, Death, and an angel, looking as though they had stepped out of the pages of Dante, philosophize around the body of a drowned man (Alan Curtis' ill-fated hoodlum from the unused episode). It is within this surreal landscape that Henrietta and Michael seek out their destinies and find future happiness.

Duvivier shot the episode between the 8th and 24th of March, 1943, utilizing Sound Stage 12 for the exterior river bank and the old *Phantom of the Opera* set. Robert Cummings and the underrated Betty Field marked their second screen teaming as lovers (Warners' 1941 *Kings Row* was the first). Never very convincing in heavy, dramatic roles, Cummings' baby-face looks and unimposing presence were more suited to homespun comedy. Alfred Hitchcock resented his casting as the man-on-the-run in *Saboteur* (1942), but he was forced to use him on account of the actor's contractual obligations.

On August 18, 1943, after more than a year in on-and-off production, *Flesh and Fantasy* wrapped following a day's shooting of the Benchley framing scenes. (Lenore Aubert and Milburn Stone tested for small roles in these scenes, which were written out of the script.)

Universal set aside a sum of $250,000, the largest of any feature attraction in the studio's recent history, to promote *Flesh and Fantasy*. Released on October 29, 1943, the film wasn't an unqualified critical success. (*The Hollywood Reporter* ran a compendium of reviews—some of them unfavorable—in their November 22 edition.) A French language version was prepared for overseas in the spring of 1944, followed by a Spanish-language edition that summer.

Duvivier remained in Hollywood for the duration of the war, directing his long-time star Jean Gabin in 1944's *The Imposter*. Traveling to Great Britain in 1948, he directed Vivien Leigh and Ralph Richardson in an adaptation of Tolstoy's *Anna Karenina* before returning to France. Over the next two decades, the celebrated filmmaker directed a variety of French and French-Italian coproductions including *Don Camillo* (1952) with Fernandel, *The Man in the Raincoat* (1957; also starring Fernandel), *Marie Octobre* (1959), *La Chambre Ardente* (*The Burning Court*; 1962), an occult thriller, set in a castle in Germany's Black Forest, which combines elements of mystery, witchcraft and the supernatural, *Chair de Poule* (1963) and *Diaboliquement Vôtre* (1967). An automobile crash claimed Duvivier's life that same year.

Son of Dracula (1943)

Released November 5, 1943. 78 minutes. *Produced by* Ford Beebe. *Directed by* Robert Siodmak. *Associate Producer:* Donald H. Brown. *Executive Producer:* Jack Gross. *Screenplay by* Eric Taylor. *Original Story by* Curt Siodmak. *Director of Photography:* George Robinson. *Film Editor:* Saul A. Goodkind. *Art Directors:* John B. Goodman & Martin Obzina. *Musical Director:* Hans J. Salter. *Set Decorators:* Russell A. Gausman & Edward R. Robinson. *Assistant Director:* Melville Shyer. *Sound Director:* Bernard B. Brown. *Technician:* Charles Carroll. *Special Effects by* John P. Fulton. *Makeup by* Jack P. Pierce. *Gowns by* Vera West.

Lon Chaney (Count Anthony Alucard/Count Dracula), Louise Allbritton (Katherine Caldwell), Robert Paige (Frank Stanley), Evelyn Ankers (Claire Caldwell), Frank Craven (Dr. Harry Brewster), J. Edward Bromberg (Professor Lazlo), Samuel S. Hinds (Judge Simmons), Adeline de Walt Reynolds (Queen Zimba), George Irving (Colonel Caldwell), Etta McDaniel (Sarah), Patrick Moriarity (Sheriff Dawes), Walter Sande (Matt), Cyril Delevanti (Dr. Peters), Joan Blair (Mrs. Land), Charles Bates (Tommy Land), Jess Lee Brooks (Steven), Sam McDaniel (Andy), Charles Moore (Mathew), Emmett Smith (Servant), Robert Dudley (Jonathan Kirby), Jack Rockwell (Deputy Sheriff), George Meeker (Party Guest), Ben Erway, Robert Hill.

The horror market of the '40s was as dependable as it was indiscriminate; Universal learned that bad horror films did about as well as good ones. As long as the film had a monster, a pretty girl, a fast-moving and reasonably comprehensible storyline and stayed within budget, profits were almost assured. Thanks to a lucky collaboration of talent, *Son of Dracula* emerged as one of the best Universal horror pictures of the decade, but to a studio that grew increasingly indifferent to the quality of their programmers, it was just another shocker, a notch above its cofeature *The Mad Ghoul.*

George Waggner was originally set to produce the film, but was sidetracked by Universal's lavish remake of *Phantom of the Opera.* He was replaced by serial ace Ford Beebe who landed the assignment on the strength of his impressive *Night Monster.* Curt Siodmak was commissioned to write a script in May, 1942. The studio kept the writer busy with a glut of horror assignments, but he wasn't getting any richer. He recently remarked:

> I never got a raise at Universal, never. "You get a raise outside, *then* we pay you more," they told me. Basically I never pushed it because, this may sound silly, money doesn't mean as much to me as an objective in life. I'm a writer,

and to write the right things is more important than getting a lot of dough for it.

But things were looking up for Siodmak at the time. *Adventure Magazine* was set to publish the writer's eagerly anticipated *Donovan's Brain,* for which several studios were already bidding. In the end, it was Republic (*The Lady and the Monster,* 1944) that got the screen rights to the novel.

Universal's choice of a director spelled trouble for the writer: his brother, Robert. Born in Memphis in 1900, Robert was taken to Europe by his parents when he was only a year old. He had some early experience as an actor, writer, film cutter and assistant director, and collaborated with future Hollywood émigrés Edgar G. Ulmer, Billy Wilder, Fred Zinnemann and brother Curt on the ground-breaking documentary *Menschen am Sonntag* (1929). Made for $5,000, the film gave these artists their first taste of recognition. Siodmak soon joined Germany's prestigious Ufa Studios and cemented his reputation with *The Tempest* (1931) featuring Emil Jannings. Hitler's rise to power compelled Siodmak to flee to France where he scored a success directing the acclaimed musical *La Crise Est Finie* (1934). Just one day prior to the Nazi occupation of France, Siodmak fled to America.

Siodmak's impressive European credentials meant nothing in Hollywood and he soon found himself, like Joe May, faced with the impossible task of trying to rebuild his reputation on second-rate pictures at Paramount, Republic and Fox. Brother Curt reflected:

> They forced him to do this shot and that shot. Robert didn't want to do it. One day an assistant said to him, "I thought you were such a big director! Why don't you fight to do it your way?" Robert said, "Because this is Paramount shit, this is not a Siodmak picture!" So they fired him.

It was at Universal where his career eventually took off with a remarkable streak of highly-stylized thrillers: *Phantom Lady, Christmas Holiday, The Suspect* (all 1944) and *Uncle Harry* (a.k.a. *The Strange Affair of Uncle Harry,* 1945). Previously, the director bided his time with the Maria Montez–Jon Hall kitsch classic *Cobra Woman* (1944), which was preceded by his first Universal assignment, *Son of Dracula.* An option for a term deal was injected into Siodmak's contract so there was pressure on the director to make good fast.

The first thing he did was to have his brother Curt thrown off the picture. (Eric Taylor wrote the screenplay. The Siodmaks would never make another movie together.)

> We had a sibling rivalry. When we were in Germany, Robert had a magazine and when I wrote for it, I had to change my name. He only wanted one Siodmak around. This lasted seventy-one years, until he died.

The second follow-up to *Dracula* had been a long time coming. Universal enthusiastically churned out Frankenstein, Mummy and Invisible Man pictures, but was hesitant about the Bram Stoker character, even though the original film was one of their biggest grossers. The natural choice for the lead, Bela Lugosi, inspired little confidence. Even the financially-strapped Laemmle regime paid Lugosi off handsomely rather than have him appear in *Dracula's Daughter.* The Hungarian was beyond consideration for *Son of Dracula,*

The wallflower Count Dracula (Lon Chaney) spies on Louise Allbritton and Robert Paige dancing in *Son of Dracula*.

which was slated as a vehicle for Lon Chaney. The fact that Lon was grossly miscast as the charismatic count mattered little. He was now identified with horror roles and was judged "good enough." This was, after all, just another run-of-the-mill horror picture. It was quite a blow for the chronically unemployed Lugosi, who had been impatiently waiting in the wings for Universal's inevitable resurrection of Dracula, only to lose the part to a younger rival. His grudge against Chaney would last for years. (According to Reginald

LeBorg, Lugosi was still stewing over *Son of Dracula* when he costarred with Chaney in *The Black Sleep* in 1956.) Robert Siodmak, too, probably would have preferred Lugosi for the part. At one point during production, the soused Chaney sneaked up behind the director and smashed a vase over his bald head! (Chaney was not very fond of "foreigners.")

The embittered Lugosi ended up with a consolation prize—playing a Dracula-like vampire in Columbia's *The Return of the Vampire* (1943), a shameless Universal imitation if ever there was one. There were even hopes for a follow-up with Lugosi's Armand Tesla character, but the studio had second thoughts and the proposed sequel (*Bride of the Vampire*) was reworked as a werewolf film, *Cry of the Werewolf* (1944), a resounding dud.

Shooting on *Son of Dracula* commenced on January 8, 1943. Exactly one week later, the production hit a major snag: Alan Curtis, the film's heroic lead, was replaced because of the knee injury he has sustained while shooting a segment of *Flesh and Fantasy* (which eventually wound up as the full-length feature *Destiny*). Robert Paige, one of Universal's few reasonably rugged leading men still out of uniform, became Curtis' hastily-chosen replacement.

Unlike *Dracula* and *Dracula's Daughter,* which strike rich, supernatural moods immediately, *Son of Dracula,* set in modern-day America, carefully paces itself. The first scene, suggesting anything but horror, takes place in a bustling, sun-drenched train station somewhere in the Southlands. After a perfunctory establishing shot, the film cuts to two men, Frank Stanley (Robert Paige) and Dr. Harry Brewster (Frank Craven), impatiently awaiting the arrival of Count Alucard, a nobleman from Central Europe, who has been invited to Dark Oaks, the plantation home of Stanley's fiancée Katherine Caldwell (Louise Allbritton). When the Count doesn't appear, the pair leave.

Katherine's reception party proceeds despite the absence of the guest of honor. The festivities are cut short when Katherine's father Colonel Caldwell (George Irving) is found in his bed, dead from shock. Count Alucard (Lon Chaney) makes a belated arrival. When the suspicious Dr. Brewster notices the name Alucard is actually Dracula spelled backwards, he implores Katherine's sister Claire (Evelyn Ankers) to leave the plantation, and consults Professor Lazlo (J. Edward Bromberg), an authority on the occult.

Leery of Alucard's motives, and jealous over his attentions to Katherine, Frank shadows Alucard and his hostess. Confronting the pair, Frank is appalled to learn Kay and the Count were just married. Frank and Alucard clash. Frank empties his revolver into the Count but the bullets pass through his body and kill Katherine.

The next morning, Frank confesses his crime to Sheriff Dawes (Patrick Moriarity). Brewster is quick to intervene, insisting that he spoke to Kay hours *after* the alleged murder took place. Combing the grounds of the plantation, the Sheriff discovers Kay's body in the family crypt and promptly books Frank on a charge of murder.

Barely escaping being charged as an accessory, Brewster fills Lazlo in on the case. Convinced Alucard is a descendant of Count Dracula, the professor theorizes that Kay deliberately courted the vampire in order to attain eternal life, and is now plotting to initiate Frank into the ranks of the undead.

Meanwhile, the bat-form of Kay appears in Frank's prison cell and draws off a small quantity of blood while he sleeps. Kay rematerializes, awakens Frank and reveals to him her fantastic scheme. Escaping from jail, he heads for the hiding place of Dracula's coffin, camouflaged in the underbrush of a swamp drainage tunnel. Frank sets fire to the coffin and is about to make his getaway when the Count appears. The enraged vampire desperately attempts to extinguish the flames but is caught in the rays of the new day's sun and perishes.

Frank makes his way to Dark Oaks, keeping his promise to Kay to meet her in the attic nursery. Finding her body lying in a casket, he gently places his ring on her finger. Moments later, Brewster, Lazlo and Sheriff Dawes arrive to find Frank calmly standing by as the fire he set engulfs Kay's body, freeing her soul forever.

Long overdue for serious reappraisal, *Son of Dracula* is usually lumped together with the rest of the Universal horror pictures of the '40s, despite the fact it towers over most of the period's other sequels. The film has garnered little of the respectability that surrounds *Dracula's Daughter,* a favorite of critics who overstress its erotic underpinnings rather than its merits. Even hardcore vampire film devotees who tend to rhapsodize over Christopher Lee's overathletic Dracula of the '60s consider *Son of Dracula* a low-rent effort (as if the latter Hammer Dracula pictures were anything but crass, repetitious bores). *Son of Dracula* isn't a classic, but it's an unusually intelligent horror film, buoyed by excellent visuals and sturdy characterizations. Its major flaws are an uneven script and the lamentable miscasting of the two lead characters.

Transmigrating the Count to America imparts to the film a crisp, modernized look, though it is a pity Universal didn't attempt one last truly Gothic vampire bash with Dracula as a *solo* menace. (The often disguised *Tower of London* set could have provided the vampire with handsome accommodations indeed.) Cameraman George Robinson, again proving himself to be a master at conveying atmosphere, makes the most of the story's Deep South setting, eerily nestling the imposing Count in the shadows of looming plantations and murky swamplands. Except for the occasional appearance of fawning, badly stereotyped black servants, the picture forsakes its supposed Dixie settings and nary a Southern drawl is heard. In fact, most of the characters behave more like blue-blooded New Englanders than members of the well-heeled Southern gentry. Otherwise, Robert Siodmak shows a real feel for small town life, and was possibly influenced by Alfred Hitchcock's American Gothic classic *Shadow of a Doubt* (1943), which Universal had just released as production on *Son of Dracula* got underway. (The makers of 1958's *The Return of Dracula* readily admit that they were influenced by the Hitchcock film.)

Son of Dracula divides itself between brightly lit daytime scenes of incredulous lawmen and no-nonsense country doctors embroiled in a headlong encounter with the supernatural, and the shadowy, twilight world of Dracula. It's in these latter episodes that Siodmak puts his Expressionist training to work. Eric Taylor's screenplay is altogether too talky, especially in the last half, but the horror scenes are first rate and, at times, genuinely frightening. The stylistic highlight, and the most inventive moment, has Dracula's casket

A match made in Hades: Louise Allbritton and Lon Chaney in Robert Siodmak's stylish *Son of Dracula*.

ingeniously emerging from a misty bog, the Count materializing in a wisp of vapor, then commandeering the float-like coffin to land. It's an almost poetic touch that perfectly paves the way for the more visceral shocks to come.

The powerfully built but somewhat chubby Chaney cuts a more imposing physical presence than Lugosi. He is particularly effective in his confrontation scene with Robert Paige. Subduing Paige in a vise-like grip and tossing him effortlessly aside, Chaney foreshadows Christopher Lee's superenergized interpretation of the character. Chaney's piercing, death-like stare as Paige bolts from the room is haunting.

Another fine, understated shock comes a bit later when Frank Craven, investigating Paige's story, arrives at the gloomy plantation. After Chaney ushers Craven into the master bedroom, the film cuts to a long shot of the obviously vampiric Allbritton, her face a dead white, elegantly attired, smiling sardonically. Minus musical punctuation, it is a quietly disturbing moment.

Eric Taylor provides *Son of Dracula* with a gallery of offbeat, interesting characters. The coldblooded Katherine Caldwell is so ruthless, she not only conspires to draw her unwitting beau into the ranks of the undead, she also plots to do away with her sister and family friend Dr. Brewster, and callously marks her own father for death. An unconventional movie heroine to say the least, the character is a vivid one, deserving of a better performance than Allbritton can provide. The part was a change of pace for the Universal contractee, invariably cast in light roles in such films as *Who Done It?* (1942) with Abbott and Costello and 1945's *San Diego, I Love You.* A jet-black wig was fitted over her natural blonde hair but it required more than a new look to bring the role off. An obviously uncomfortable Allbritton struggles for an elusive, mysterious effect but she summons little of the dark sensuality that the role demands. The late Robert Paige told Michael Fitzgerald that the actress was quite upset during shooting, frequently retiring to her dressing room in tears between setups. This situation undoubtedly didn't help her performance. An admittedly tough part to cast; Patricia Morison or Hillary Brooke might have vested the role with more credibility.

The Frank Stanley character is also a refreshing break from the run-of-the-mill horror movie hero. Vulnerable to the punishing turns of the plot, Robert Paige starts off a bit humorless and straitlaced, but is reduced to a frazzled wreck midway through the film, and, by the final reel, is left a broken man. The actor's underrated performance is probably the best in the film.

Paige, who worked in movies in the mid–1930s under the name David Carlyle, came to Universal after a stint at Paramount. "I made four screen tests at Universal studios and was kicked out every time. I kept coming back until they couldn't stand the sight of me," he revealed in an interview.

Paige became a familiar leading man in the '40s; the studio claimed *Son of Dracula* was his first dramatic role (it wasn't). When Universal decided to groom him as a musical star, teaming him with Jane Frazee, the studio claimed it was his first *major* role. Paige's acting career sputtered out in the '50s. He was seen as a graying, heavy-set romantic lead in the senile *Abbott and Costello Go to Mars* (1953), and shortly afterward became a game show emcee and a newscaster. Years later, he insisted he missed out on the big time because of Universal's refusal to loan him out to other studios in what, he claimed, were star-making roles.

Lon Chaney's performance as Dracula, as expected, comes up short. Lacking the aristocratic bearing that Lugosi and later John Carradine easily lent to the role, Chaney is stiff and strained, his delivery graceless. Jack Pierce added a whisper of gray to Chaney's dark brown hair and encased the actor in a cadaverous, pale blue facial makeup, but the effect is lost whenever Chaney reads a line. He trudges through the part earnestly, but, alas, delivers another failed performance.

Frank Craven comes off best in the supporting cast. A former playwright and librettist, Craven is best remembered as the Narrator in the film and stage versions of Thornton Wilder's *Our Town*. The epitome of homespun American charm, he is ideally cast as Dr. Brewster. J. Edward Bromberg is tolerable as Professor Lazlo (high praise for him). Pierce slavishly duplicated Edward Van Sloan's makeup design, from the close-cropped white hairpiece to the owl-like spectacles. Applied to Bromberg's full features, he looks like a bloated, comically overfed Van Helsing, a pale copy of the original. Evelyn Ankers' supporting performance as Allbritton's sister is a nice bonus.

For all its merits, *Son of Dracula* remains an under-appreciated film; it would take a reassessment of Robert Siodmak's considerable talent to bring its merits to light. (His best known films, *The Spiral Staircase* and *The Killers* [both 1946] are considered as much producer's films as director's films.) Horror fans may be reluctant to embrace Chaney's uncharismatic count, the intrusive presence of Patrick Moriarity's hick policeman, and the excessive verbiage of the script. Craven and Bromberg's exchanges, painstakingly detailing the now familiar vampire legend, slow the film down considerably and are old hat. Yet despite these shortcomings, *Son of Dracula* is unfailingly intelligent, its characters uncompromised. It deserves high marks for trying.

The Mad Ghoul (1943)

Released November 12, 1943. 65 minutes. *Directed by* James Hogan. *Associate Producer:* Ben Pivar. *Screenplay by* Brenda Weisberg & Paul Gangelin. *Original Story by* Hans Kraly. *Director of Photography:* Milton Krasner. *Film Editor:* Milton Carruth. *Art Directors:* John B. Goodman & Martin Obzina. *Musical Director:* Hans J. Salter. *Songs: "All for Love," Adapted from "Minuet in G" by* Milton Rosen, *Lyrics by* Everett Carter; *"Our Love Will Live," From the Concerto by* Tchaikovsky, *Lyrics by* Everett Carter; *"I Dreamt I Dwelt in Marble Halls," From the Operetta* **The Bohemian Girl,** Music by M.W. Balfe. *Set Decorators:* Russell A. Gausman & Andrew J. Gilmore. *Sound Director:* Bernard B. Brown. *Technician:* Jess Moulin. *Makeup by* Jack P. Pierce. *Gowns by* Vera West.

David Bruce (Ted Allison), Evelyn Ankers (Isabel Lewis), George Zucco (Dr. Alfred Morris), Turhan Bey (Eric Iverson), Robert Armstrong (Ken McClure), Milburn Stone (Sergeant Macklin), Rose Hobart (Della Elliott), Charles McGraw (Detective Garrity), Andrew Tombes (Mr. Eagan), Addison Richards (Gavigan), Gus Glassmire (Caretaker), Gene O'Donnell (Radio Announcer), Isabelle Lamal (Maid), Lew Kelly, Bill Ruhl (Stagehands), Hans Herbert (Attendant), Bess Flowers (Woman in Audience), Cyril Ring (Man in Audience), Lillian Cornell (Vocalist for Evelyn Ankers).

Like Lionel Atwill, George Zucco approached most of his horror movie roles with his tongue planted firmly in his cheek. To this cultured stage actor, breathing life into such poorly written parts as the wacko scientist in PRC's *The Mad Monster* (1942) and the white witch doctor in Monogram's *Voodoo Man* (1944) must have been the height of indignation. *The Mad Ghoul* provided Zucco with yet another mad scientist role, but this time the stock character was conceived with more sensitivity and shading than usual. Zucco himself must have felt the part worthwhile as he performs it with atypical restraint and perception.

The Mad Ghoul is that rarity, a successful Universal horror film that didn't spawn a series. Designed to support *Son of Dracula* on an all-horror double bill, *The Mad Ghoul* deserves more credit than it's usually given. It's a slick, competently done B with a new twist on the old body-snatching theme: instead of stealing a whole corpse, this fiend is only interested in the deceased's heart.

His career as a purveyor of shock fests on the rise, Ben Pivar put *The Mystery of the Mad Ghoul* on the drawing board in February, 1943. Brenda Weisberg and Paul Gangelin contributed a solid script based on a story penned by Hans Kraly (the recipient of the 1928/29 Academy Award for Best

Screenplay for *The Patriot;* he was also nominated for the 1937 Deanna Durbin musicomedy *One Hundred Men and a Girl*).

Studio contract player David Bruce suddenly found himself cast as a walking corpse, a far cry from the pleasant young man roles that dominated his career. Born Marden (some sources say Andrew) McBroom on January 6, 1914, in Kankakee, Illinois, Bruce was groomed for stardom at Warner Bros. in the late '30s and early '40s. He landed small parts in 17 of their productions including *A Dispatch from Reuters, The Sea Hawk* (both 1940), *The Sea Wolf* as well as the second-rate comedy thrillers *The Smiling Ghost* and *The Body Disappears* (all 1941). When the United States entered the war, Bruce joined the Navy Air Service School at St. Mary's. The Air Service understandably discharged him when he showed a tendency to lose consciousness during pull-outs!

Chosen to direct the thriller was James Hogan, who had joined the studio in April after a seven-year stint at Paramount. Around the time he made *The Mad Ghoul,* Hogan directed *The Strange Death of Adolf Hitler,* then completed the script for the Montez-Hall costumer *Gypsy Wildcat.* Poor health forced him to withdraw as the film's director. The 52-year-old filmmaker died of a heart attack on November 4, 1943, just one week before *The Mad Ghoul* went into national release.

After years of research, Dr. Alfred Morris (George Zucco) recreates an insidious poison gas which the ancient Mayans used in their religious rites. The gas has a diabolical power, causing a "state of death in life." Exposed to the vapors, a sacrificial victim would slip into a living dead state. Morris determines that the Mayan ritual of removing the hearts from living men was performed not to appease their gods but to restore life to the gassed victims. His goal is to discover a method of reversing the action of the gas.

Morris enlists the aid of prize student Ted Allison (David Bruce). Using a combination of crystals and ancient herbs, Morris gasses a monkey only to revive it using heart fluid taken from another animal.

That evening, Ted and his fiancée, concert singer Isabel Lewis (Evelyn Ankers), drop in on Dr. Morris for a nightcap. Isabel is about to embark on a long-awaited multiple city tour yet seems uncharacteristically disturbed. Morris guesses the problem immediately: "You're no longer in love with Ted." For some reason known only to him, the aging intellectual now draws the conclusion that the attractive young woman has fallen in love with *him!* "It's only natural that you should turn to an older man," Morris coos solicitously. "Someone who knows the book of life, and can teach you to read it." This is all quite preposterous. Isabel is understandably oblivious to the doctor's attentions, mistaking his kindliness for fatherly concern. As their acquaintance has always been casual, Morris has absolutely nothing upon which to base his conclusion. He's just a cockeyed optimist with lascivious designs on a woman young enough to be his daughter.

Ted is easy prey for the trap Morris sets for him. Falling under the influence of the vapor, the surgeon becomes an emaciated automaton.

Jack Pierce didn't have much to go on when he created David Bruce's makeup: "All they told me was that they wanted Bruce to look like a reasonably fresh cadaver. I said, 'How fresh?' They said a couple or three weeks buried. This was not much to go on but I did my best. They seemed satisfied."

The late actor described his ordeal in Pierce's makeup chair in an interview he granted *Famous Monsters* shortly before his death.

> My makeup was green and it made my hair look red for some reason – bright red. They tinted me green and combed my hair over my eyes and for the later thing they put the false skin on, which was absolute murder. I wore it for only three days and the third time I took it off my skin was bleeding because you had to peel the makeup off. They put on spirit gum and then a layer of cotton and then another layer of spirit gum so this created an entirely false face on top of mine. Then they'd wrinkle it up and the wrinkles would stay in, you know.

The guise closely resembled Karloff's Imhotep makeup in *The Mummy.*

Pierce's makeup design is subtly effective. In the first stage of transformation, the actor appears pale, wizened and fish-eyed. But as the degenerative effect of the gas reaches an advanced stage, his features become parchment-like, resembling a corpse in an accelerated state of decomposition.

Now Ted's master, Morris plants in Ted's subconscious the fact that Isabel no longer wants him. Handing Ted a scalpel, Morris escorts him to the town cemetery, where the zombie despoils the grave of a recently interred businessman. He performs a cardiectomy on the corpse whose heart substance is used by Morris to bring the student out of the terminal state.

When the doctor's "miracle monkey" has a sudden relapse, Morris realizes the possible consequences of his act. An emotional confrontation with Isabel takes its toll on Ted's fragile condition. Once again, he reverts back into a zombified state. This time, his rendezvous in the local cemetery has tragic results. Morris is forced to kill a snoopy caretaker who stumbles upon the pair unearthing a grave. The old man's heart becomes the antidote to restore Ted to normalcy.

Unable to hide her secret any longer, Isabel confesses to a mortified Dr. Morris that she is indeed in love with another man – her handsome accompanist, Eric Iverson (Turhan Bey). Now saddled with *two* rivals, the desperate doctor drives Ted into having another seizure, and orders him to make arrangements to meet Eric later that night.

At the stroke of midnight, Ted, loaded pistol in hand, silently approaches Iverson as he paces the deserted alley behind the concert hall. Hans J. Salter's pounding score builds to a crescendo as Ted's menacing shadow closes in on his friend. But before the Ghoul can press the trigger, Isabel arrives on the scene and upsets his preprogrammed command with a piercing scream. Unseen, Ted escapes to Morris' waiting car.

Acting on a hot tip provided by a colleague, ace reporter Ken McClure (Robert Armstrong) has a hunch there's a connection between the Ghoul atrocities and Isabel's concert appearances. Planting a phony obit in the local paper of the town in which the singer is next scheduled to appear, McClure sets a trap for the killer: he stations himself inside a coffin and waits patiently for the Ghoul's arrival. But McClure makes a fatal blunder. Covering Morris with his gun, the reporter fails to notice Ted creeping up on him from behind. The

Top: **David Bruce (right) made a favorable impression in his first and only horror picture. Here he takes orders from his sinister mentor George Zucco.** ***Bottom:*** **Evelyn Ankers has a tough time choosing between prospective suitors David Bruce and George Zucco, in this posed shot from** ***The Mad Ghoul.***

pair overtake the clever but careless reporter and use his heart for the procedure.

Convinced McClure's hunch was on-target, Police Sergeant Macklin (Milburn Stone) and Detective Garrity (Charles McGraw) pay Isabel a visit on the night of her last concert appearance. They suspect Eric might be their man. Aghast at their accusations, Isabel confides in Ted. Her tearful admission of love for Eric and her denial of the police's suspicions put everything in perspective for Ted. "What am I? Alive or dead? Man or beast? What have you done to me!" the anguished student beseeches his mentor.

Planning a devilish revenge, Ted writes a suicide note, prepares a mixture of the deadly gas, and lures Morris into the lab. Suddenly seized by the effects of the gas, Ted becomes Morris' blindly obedient slave once again. The doctor hands his victim a revolver and order hims to kill Eric, then himself.

To his horror, Morris realizes that he, too, has been exposed. Seizing the surgeon's scalpel, he implores Ted to help him, but it is too late. His initial command has already been programmed in the zombie's mind. Ted blunders onto the stage as Isabel is in mid-performance and aims the gun at Iverson. Before he can shoot, the Ghoul is cut down by Sergeant Macklin's bullets.

In a grimly ironic postscript, Morris, his features distorted, attempts to dig up a grave to obtain heart substance for himself, but collapses and dies, scalpel in hand.

There's no shortage of carnage, either visualized or implied, in *The Mad Ghoul,* yet the film manages to stay within the guidelines of accepted standards for the period it was made. Considering its morbid preoccupation with death (cemeteries, funeral parlors, blood sacrifices, desecration of the dead and murder), cowriters Weisberg and Gangelin did a commendable job in appeasing those watchdogs of the Production Code, the Breen Office. They've managed to soft-pedal yet not render sterile the story's abundant indelicacies. Hogan is simpatico with their efforts: during the potentially graphic murder/mutilation scenes, the director fixes the camera's gaze on Bruce's deadpan face, discreetly cutting away from the bloodbath.

The stifling restrictions of the Breen Office no doubt influenced the writers to tone down the love interest element as well. Ankers spends almost the entire film in a guilt-ridden pout over her betrayal of Bruce. Bey's attitude is more moderate and realistic. Although he's not pleased he has "stolen" his best friend's girl, the suave accompanist isn't about to let this peccadillo impede romance. By the time the last reel unwinds, Ankers has suffered enough and deserves vindication, while Bey comes away from the tragedy smelling like a rose. None but the most jaded of viewers is bound to hold the couple in contempt, even as they stand over Bruce's bullet-riddled body.

Saddled with a title that must have kept sophisticated moviegoers away in droves, and promoted by Universal with all of the usual shock-it-to-'em campaign gimmicks, *The Mad Ghoul* nonetheless ranked as one of the studio's more mature thrillers. Once again, an innocent person's life is destroyed by the renegade experiments of an over-zealous scientist. Along with his desire to prove his theories to a doubting world, the medico often has an ulterior motive (more often than not, to avenge himself on his oppressors, but occasionally to gain financial reward or the love of a woman). Universal had exploited this horror movie cliche only recently in *Captive Wild Woman,* and before that in *Black Friday* and *Man Made Monster,* to name just a few.

The first two reels of *The Mad Ghoul* are of necessity slow and talky: the background is revealed regarding Zucco's experiments and the multisided romantic dilemma. Once this is accomplished, the picture travels a steady course, handling its shock sequences with grim enthusiasm. The inclusion of Robert Armstrong's comic reporter-*cum*-investigator is a jarring note, but it isn't long before even he becomes grist for the gore mill. (Armstrong's unbridled enthusiasm and show-bizzy tactics bring back warm memories of Kong-stalking Carl Denham.) James Hogan does a competent, craftsman-like job of directing and elicits good performances from the sturdy cast. The director draws a maximum amount of suspense out of the major shock sequences and pulls off a couple of particularly arresting bits (i.e., the Ghoul walking directly into the camera, blocking out the lens; Bruce, standing behind Armstrong, holding the scalpel inches away from his neck, as the camera lights cast an effectively menacing gleam on its smooth surface), but he fails to generate enough high voltage suspense when the Ghoul staggers across the old *Phantom of the Opera* stage and points the pistol at Eric in front of the panic-stricken audience.

George Zucco and David Bruce take top honors in the acting department. Zucco tempers his stock villain mad scientist with an affecting vulnerability. Discovering the antidote is effective only temporarily, he earnestly warns Bruce of this dire situation without spilling the beans about what he has done. ("Ted, we've got to find a permanent cure!") Later, learning that the "other man" in Ankers' life isn't he but Turhan Bey, Zucco says with touching remorse, "We see what we want to see most of the time, Isabel. Even I, a scientist, have such moments of weakness."

David Bruce is the ideal victim, a naive child-man who is blissfully unaware of the deceptions in operation around him. He is appropriately void of emotion as the Ghoul, and seems to operate on automatic pilot while in this condition. His state of mental oblivion is especially chilling at those times when he's committing heinous acts.

Bruce's career at Universal was an uneventful one. Lacking the rugged look, the actor was relegated to unimpressive parts in such film as *Calling Dr. Death, Christmas Holiday* (both 1944), *Lady on a Train* and *Salome, Where She Danced* (both 1945). As the years wore on, Bruce got bigger roles in cheap exploitation potboilers for outfits like Eagle-Lion, Monogram, Lippert and Howco-International. Following a regular role as the head of the house in television's "Beulah," Bruce retired from acting and went into business. His show business comeback 20 years later was short-lived: he succumbed to a heart attack on May 3, 1976.

Evelyn Ankers lends beauty, charm and intelligence to the role of Isabel. At first, Universal planned to have the actress-singer record the classic pieces in her own voice, but the idea was scrapped at the the last moment. Library recordings of Lillian Cornell were ineffectively substituted. There was little Turhan Bey could do with the colorless role of Eric, Ankers' lover, but to act suave and Continental, yet remain sympathetic. The supporting cast is headed up by old reliables like Robert Armstrong, Rose Hobart, Addison Richards and a wryly amusing Andrew Tombes as an overzealous funeral director.

Boasting a macabre tale generously plied with gruesome effects, unusually good performances and deft writing and direction, *The Mad Ghoul* is several cuts above the average grindhouse quickie released by the likes of Columbia, Monogram and PRC.

Calling Dr. Death (1943)

Released December 17, 1943. 63 minutes. An Inner Sanctum Mystery, produced by arrangement with Simon and Schuster, Inc., Publishers. *Directed by* Reginald LeBorg. *Associate Producer:* Ben Pivar. *Original Screenplay by* Edward Dein. *Director of Photography:* Virgil Miller. *Special Photography:* John P. Fulton. *Film Editor:* Norman A. Cerf. *Art Directors:* John B. Goodman & Ralph M. DeLacy. *Set Decorators:* Russell A. Gausman & Andrew J. Gilmore. *Musical Director:* Paul Sawtell. *Sound Director:* Bernard B. Brown. *Technician:* William Hedgcock. *Gowns by* Vera West.

Lon Chaney (Dr. Mark Steele), Patricia Morison (Stella Madden), J. Carrol Naish (Inspector Gregg), Ramsay Ames (Maria Steele), David Bruce (Robert Duval), Fay Helm (Mrs. Duval), Holmes Herbert (Bryant), Alec Craig (Bill), Isabel Jewell* (Peggy Morton, Night Club Singer), Mary Hale (Marion), Fred Gierman (Father), Lisa Golm (Mother), George Eldredge (District Attorney), Charles Wagenheim (Coroner), John Elliott (Priest), David Hoffman (Inner Sanctum), Norman Rainey (Governor), Rex Lease, Paul Phillips (Detectives), Frank Marlowe (Newspaper Reporter), Keith Ferguson (Telephone Operator), Charles Moore (Prisoner), Earle Hodgins (Bartender), Perc Launders, Jack Rockwell (Detectives), Robert Hill (Judge), Jack C. Smith, Al Ferguson (Guards), Kernan Cripps (Officer). [**Does not appear in the final print.*]

> This is the Inner Sanctum . . . A strange, fantastic world, controlled by a mass of living, pulsating flesh . . . the mind! It destroys . . . distorts . . . creates monsters . . . commits *murder!* Yes, even you, without knowing, can commit *murder!* —David Hoffman, Master of the Inner Sanctum

Reaping the financial rewards of Hollywood's second great horror cycle, Universal turned to popular literature for a fresh source of filmable material. In June, 1943, the studio struck a deal with Simon and Schuster, Inc., publishers of the popular Inner Sanctum mysteries, obtaining the screen rights to the Inner Sanctum name (though, curiously, not the pulps nor the Inner Sanctum radio plays themselves) for a brand new series of murder mysteries starring their hottest horror property, Lon Chaney.

By installing Ben Pivar as the series' guiding mentor, Universal inadvertently revealed their modest ambitions towards the project immediately. Instead of pulling all the financial stops and producing a slate of classy little B's (or minor A's) with first-rate talent, the cost-conscious studio heads decided (once again) to take the safe route. The result is a half-dozen feebly conceived melodramas with little to recommend beyond their camp qualities and the morose spectacle of seeing the badly miscast Chaney struggle his way through roles that were beyond his depth.

Having grown disenchanted with the way Universal was shuffling him from one uncomfortable monster guise to another, Chaney had hoped that the Inner Sanctum films would provide the diversity he craved. Evidently, Universal still hadn't grasped the fact that this was an actor of limited talent and appeal, who simply did not fit the mode of the archetypical Inner Sanctum hero: the suave mustachioed professional man who is all the rage with the ladies.

Searching for a suitable property as the kickoff entry of the series, Pivar purchased an original screenplay penned by freelancer Edward Dein, entitled *Calling Dr. Death.* A former bit player who turned to writing and later to directing, Dein was proficient at writing whodunits; at various times, he wrote for RKO's Falcon series and worked on Columbia's Lone Wolf and Boston Blackie pictures. More importantly, Dein was a part-time member of Val Lewton's RKO production unit, contributing to the screenplay of *Cat People* (1942) and writing the script for *The Leopard Man* (1943), although sole screen credit was given to novice Ardel Wray. (Dein's other genre credits include the Faustian Columbia shocker *The Soul of a Monster,* 1944, Universal-International's preposterous horror Western *Curse of the Undead,* 1959, and that same studio's 1960 release, *The Leech Woman.)*

In a 1984 interview, the late writer-director recalled his brief career at Universal, where he wrote the screenplays for *Jungle Woman* and the 1946 *The Cat Creeps:* "I recall having a job at Universal as a reader for a few weeks, which was another horror story. We called this the Snake Pit. In those days, we were not considered to be prolific writers; we were hacks."

At the outset, Pivar planned to produce two Inner Sanctum mysteries a year, each featuring Chaney and Gale Sondergaard in starring roles. Reginald LeBorg, who had done an admirable job directing *The Mummy's Ghost,* was selected by Pivar to direct *Calling Dr. Death.* "Pivar had confidence in me because I was a fighter who tried to get better and better material. Pivar was sometimes afraid that I would go over budget, but whenever he saw that I *was* on budget, he didn't worry anymore—he stayed in his office and played gin rummy."

Calling Dr. Death went into production on October 25, 1943, and was completed within twenty days. Just a few days prior to the start of filming, Gale Sondergaard was dropped from the cast. Her role was substantially rewritten and given to Patricia Morison. Despite the studio's original intent, Gale would never appear in an Inner Sanctum meller.

Chaney portrays eminent neurologist Dr. Mark Steele, whose professional success is eclipsed by a miserable home life: Steele's beautiful but unfaithful wife Maria (Ramsay Ames) refuses to grant him a divorce. He confides his problems to his adoring nurse, Stella Madden (Patricia Morison); although they're evidently attracted to one another, the rules of propriety insist that they keep their desires in check.

Distraught over Maria's behavior, Steele suffers a mental blackout. When he awakens, it's Monday morning. The doctor finds himself seated behind his

David Hoffman introduced the "Inner Sanctum" mysteries in an eerie prologue, backed by suitably spooky organ music.

office desk, unshaven and disheveled. Two detectives (Rex Lease and Paul Phillips) of the "Dragnet" school of interrogation inform the understandably confused Steele that his wife has been found brutally murdered.

Steele's trepidations concerning his own innocence are fueled by the suspicious Inspector Gregg (J. Carrol Naish). ("You're big game, doctor. Makes the chase interesting.") Relieved when the police arrest Maria's last paramour, businessman Robert Duval (David Bruce), for her murder, Steele's nagging doubts about himself return after he speaks with Duval's crippled wife (Fay Helm). Stella's vain attempts to prove Mark's innocence only muddy the waters further.

On the eve of Duval's execution, the desperate doctor places Stella in a deep hypnotic trance. In a surrealistic flashback, Stella's "subconscious voice" betrays her: she confesses to having murdered Maria and implicating Duval in the crime. Gregg arrives at the office in time to hear her statement and places her under arrest.

Calling Dr. Death set the standard for the other films in the Inner Sanctum series by introducing several intriguing devices and recurrent plot motifs. With the exception of *Pillow of Death* (the final entry), each picture is prefaced by a brief sequence in which a wizened seer (David Hoffman), staring out of a crystal ball, forewarns the audience (à la "The Twilight Zone") that it's about to enter the realm where even the most innocent amongst else is capable of committing murder. In all but two pictures, an innocent man (always Chaney) is accused of committing or instigating one or more murders. He may find himself at odds with the evidence presented and may even doubt his own innocence. After several reels of self-flagellation, Chaney learns he has been duped by a jealous lover, best friend or ambitious business associate into *believing* he was responsible for the crime(s).

Another recurrent device peculiar to the Inner Sanctum mysteries is the "stream of consciousness" voice-over. Effective at times, laughably intrusive at others, this gimmick might have been better received had it been used more judiciously. Edward Dein maintained he incorporated these dialogues into his script for *Calling Dr. Death* at Chaney's behest: "Lon Chaney, Jr., begged me to put the dialogue on the soundtrack because it was too technical, and although he played a doctor in it, he just couldn't say the words."

Reginald LeBorg insists that Ben Pivar was as much the reason for Dein's using this gimmick as Chaney, and for not very complimentary reasons: "We had to do a little bit of simplification, that's true, but I think it was not only Chaney but also Pivar. Pivar was very, very crude, not very intelligent, and he couldn't read very well."

Calling Dr. Death's tediously paced story is somewhat enlivened by LeBorg's impressive stylistic touches. Contemplating mayhem, Chaney quietly advances on his sleeping wife, only to be interrupted by the sudden screech of a cockatoo. Emphasizing Ramsay Ames' devious nature, Virgil Miller's camera zooms into a tight close-up of the woman's cruel eyes in an oil portrait. Patricia Morison's climactic hypnosis-induced confession is highlighted by distorted camera angles and eerie sound effects. One of the film's unique sequences has the camera standing in for Chaney as he visits the scene of Ames' murder: LeBorg explains,

> I had the camera *become* Lon Chaney, with everybody else looking *into* the camera. That was one sequence in the whole film which I thought was a novelty at that time. It was so fresh and new that when Robert Montgomery saw *Calling Dr. Death,* he made a whole picture this way [*Lady in the Lake,* 1946], and it was a *flop.* For one sequence that was all right, but it couldn't sustain an entire film.

Nearly all the characters Chaney portrays in the Inner Sanctum mysteries are undeserving of our sympathies because they're so weak and naive. In *Calling Dr. Death,* Dr. Mark Steele and his nurse Stella are drawn towards one another, yet neither is capable of expressing any gesture more passionate than an occasional peck on the cheek or pat on the shoulder. This reticence (obviously encouraged by the Breen bluenoses) is all the more absurd in light of the fact that Stella committed *coldblooded murder* in an effort to win the doctor for herself.

Patricia Morison and J. Carrol Naish head a particularly strong supporting cast. Morison, a one-time contender for Paramount stardom, was often cast as a lethal lady or "other woman" in '40s B's. Her cool, deliberate emoting in *Calling Dr. Death* gives every indication she's less than innocent. Morison's

Lon Chaney uses hypnosis to draw a confession of murder out of Patricia Morison, in the "Inner Sanctum" *Calling Dr. Death.*

unsettling confidence is especially effective in the confession flashback wherein she beats Ramsay Ames to death with a fire poker, then disfigures the corpse's face with acid. Though shown only in shadows (a favorite device of LeBorg's), the scene's dramatic power comes across undiminished. Naish's persistent policeman, given to turning up at the oddest moments, stalks Chaney with the zeal of a predatory cat. (Naish has a similar role in William Castle's Columbia thriller *The Whistler,* 1944, playing a hit man "shadowing" Richard Dix, plotting to scare him to death by staying on his heels.) His subtle underplaying and confidence contrasts with Lon's awkwardness. In a 1944 interview, Naish denied that *Calling Dr. Death* is a "horror" picture: "That's what a lot of people call it, though . . . it's strictly a psychological study in crime."

Edward Dein proudly recalled a compliment paid to him by one of the screen's finest character actors: "J. Carrol Naish read the script and thought it was one of the best examples of screenplay writing he had ever read, which was a great compliment coming from this wonderful actor. He wanted me to direct it, but Universal preferred Reggie LeBorg."

Fresh from his memorable performance in *The Mad Ghoul,* David Bruce arouses compassion as the wrongly accused Duval. Bruce replaced George Dolenz in the part after shooting began; Dolenz was forced to forfeit the part on account of a studio cross-scheduling error. Fay Helm once again demonstrates her talents at playing distraught females, and invests her brief part with sensitivity and dignity. Ramsay Ames, on the other hand, is pathetically amateurish as Chaney's fulsome mate. (Ames was proof that all the looks in the world couldn't *really* compensate for a woeful lack of talent.)

New York stage actor David Hoffman does the honors of introducing the Inner Sanctum mystery to audiences in the series' eerie preface. The diminutive thespian fulfilled a similar function in *Flesh and Fantasy* and, three years later, played the part of the ill-fated lawyer in Warners' *The Beast with Five Fingers.* Although Isabel Jewell is given official billing, her performance as a night club singer didn't survive the final cut.

Universal's Inner Sanctum mysteries are unanimously regarded by buffs and film historians as a missed cinematic opportunity. (Television had its own series of Inner Sanctum mysteries in 1952, narrated by Paul McGrath.) Had the studio lavished more care on these productions in terms of writing, directing and performing, the series might have attained the quality standards set by a similar series of B mystery thrillers, the Columbia Whistler films. Defeated by slipshod production values and the apathetic efforts of its creative team, they are but a footnote in Universal's legacy of chillers.

The Spider Woman (1944)

Released January 21, 1944. 61 minutes. *Produced and Directed by* Roy William Neill. *Screenplay by* Bertram Millhauser. *Based on a story by* Sir Arthur Conan Doyle. *Director of Photography:* Charles Van Enger. *Art Directors:* John B. Goodman & Martin Obzina. *Film Editor:* William Austin. *Set Decorators:* Russell A. Gausman & Edward R. Robinson. *Musical Director:* Hans J. Salter. *Sound Director:* Bernard B. Brown. *Technician:* Paul Neal. *Gowns by* Vera West.

Basil Rathbone (Sherlock Holmes), Nigel Bruce (Dr. John H. Watson), Gale Sondergaard (Adrea Spedding), Dennis Hoey (Inspector Lestrade), Vernon Downing (Norman Locke), Alec Craig (Radlik), Arthur Hohl (Adam Gilflower), Mary Gordon (Mrs. Hudson), Teddy Infuhr (Larry), Stanley Logan (Robert [Colonel]), Lydia Bilbrook (Susan [Colonel's Wife]), Donald Stuart (Artie), John Burton (Announcer), Belle Mitchell (Fortune Teller), Harry Cording (Fred Garvin), John Roche (Croupier), John Rogers (Clerk), George Kirby, Jimmy Aubrey (News Vendors), Marie de Becker, Sylvia Andrews (Charwomen), Angelo Rossitto (Pygmy), Arthur Stenning (Plainclothesman), Frank Benson (Attendant), Gene Stutenroth [Roth] (Taylor), Wilson Benge (Clerk).

Sherlock Holmes' fifth Universal visitation was a brief one, turning in a gag appearance in the Olsen and Johnson free-for-all, *Crazy House* (1943). It's a typically disjointed opus for the stuck-on-overdrive comedy team, but of minor interest. For one thing, it was actually set on the Universal backlot, which the comedy team turns upside down on the pretense of shooting a musical. Recruiting just about every contract player on hand (Lon Chaney, Andy Devine, Leo Carrillo and Shemp Howard are among the familiar faces), the picture contains several guest shots, including Rathbone and Bruce in their Holmes and Watson garb. It was a sly piece of self-promotion, giving the two Britons the welcomed opportunity to poke fun at themselves in their well-established roles.

The bit was actually shot during a break in shooting on the upcoming adventure tentatively titled *Sherlock Holmes in Peril* but soon to be rechristened *The Spider Woman.* It was Holmes' first of several entanglements with various *femme fatales* and possibly the best. Redeeming himself after the lackluster *Sherlock Holmes Faces Death,* Bertram Millhauser wrote a lively, original script with only a suggestion of the Conan Doyle story "The Adventure of the Dying Detective."

In an attention-grabbing opening, the dim figure of a man crashes through a high window and plunges to the street below. It is the latest in a rash of "pajama suicides" that has gripped London. Noting that none of the victims left suicide notes, Sherlock Holmes (Basil Rathbone) is convinced of foul play. Hoping to lure the killer (whom he suspects is a woman) out into the open, Holmes fakes his own death while vacationing in Scotland.

When it turns out that all of the victims were known gamblers, Holmes goes undercover, disguises himself as an Indian diplomat, and heads for London's posh gambling parlors. In short order, he befriends the glamorous Adrea Spedding (Gale Sondergaard); she consoles the "Indian" who claims to have lost his fortune. She persuades him to cash in his insurance policy, making her the beneficiary. Holmes is now certain he has found the culprit, but Spedding catches on to the detective's game.

Holmes learns that Spedding is using a deadly breed of spiders to do her dirty work, a species so poisonous its venom drives victims to self-destruction. When tiny footprints are found at the crime scene, Holmes deduces that Spedding is using a child to deliver the spiders to her victims.

Holmes and Dr. Watson (Nigel Bruce) pay a call on a well-known entomologist whom the sleuth suspects is supplying Spedding with her lethal pets, but finds the scientist murdered in his study. Rifling through the dead man's notes, Holmes finds proof that the Spider Woman's accomplice is not a child but an African pygmy whose immunity to the deadly venom makes him a likely candidate to transport the spiders.

Playing a hunch, the detective locates Spedding's hideout, the back room of a bustling carnival shooting stand, and finds himself entrapped by the Spider Woman and her gang. Propping the bound-and-gagged detective behind a shooting stand mock-up of Hitler, Adrea and her cohorts watch from the sidelines as Holmes is nearly shot by an unsuspecting Watson, idly trying his hand at target practice. The detective manages to free himself and delivers Spedding and company into the hands of Scotland Yard.

Spinning a compelling web of intrigue, *The Spider Woman* emerges as one of the better Sherlock Holmes adventures. The Gothic but overly genteel atmosphere of *Sherlock Holmes Faces Death* palls in comparison to this less stylized but more compelling yarn which quickly thrusts the viewer into the mystery. As the gruesome details of the "pajama suicides" come to light, a disturbing underbelly of corruption sets in that the film never quite shakes off. Yet *The Spider Woman* walks a thin line between campiness and well-calculated suspense.

It's typical of the series that no one in the film is quite who they appear to be. Holmes and his adversaries continually try to outdo one another by affecting different disguises and enlisting a procession of imposters; Holmes astounds Watson with his "resurrection" from the dead by enacting the role of an insolent postman. But his disguise as a suave Indian diplomat can't deceive the cunning Adrea Spedding.

The Spider Woman responds in kind, trying to throw the detective off track, by arriving at his Baker Street flat with her "nephew" (Teddy Infuhr). An apparent mute, the odd, scrawny youngster makes an uneasy impression,

Nigel Bruce, Dennis Hoey and Basil Rathbone flank Gale Sondergaard in a corny publicity pose for *The Spider Woman.*

curiously swatting flies and moving about with sudden jerks. Easily hoodwinking Holmes into believing he is the child who's been planting the spiders on her victims, Spedding casually exits, leaving behind a cache of poison gas powder to do its work.

The ensuing air of mistrust provides Watson with one of his funnier blunders. Holmes arranges a consultation with a noted scientist. When a coarsely-bearded stranger in dark glasses arrives at the doorstep, Watson is convinced it's the detective buried under another disguise. Prodding his caller into a corner with a blast of ridicule, the doctor is about to yank the befuddled scientist's whiskers when Holmes saunters onto the scene and sternly rebukes his red-faced friend.

The highlight of *The Spider Woman* is the malignant presence of Gale Sondergaard in the title role. Described by Holmes as a "female Moriarity," the detective more than meets his match in the Dragon Lady of screen terror. Sondergaard is a delight, gloating and chewing up the scenery, her cold, fixed smile exuding poison with ever frame. It's more or less a standard performance for the actress, who enjoyed a reputation as one of America's leading character players.

At her scene-stealing best, Sondergaard puts on a grand show, but despite several Academy Award nominations, one suspects there's a bit less to Gale than meets the eye. Whether playing snooty aristocrats or glum housekeepers, her performances are stamped with an icy theatricality which became ripe for parody in Bob Hope and Abbott and Costello comedies. It was a role in which the actress excelled; she could never be accused of slumming. Sondergaard displayed the same earnestness in such prestige fare as *Anthony Adverse* (1936) and *The Mark of Zorro* (1940) as she did in Saturday matinee potboilers like *The Black Cat* and *Gypsy Wildcat* (1944).

The Spider Woman, at least, afforded Sondergaard with a worthwhile vehicle. She makes the most of every scene. The critics were receptive and showered the actress with notices even better than Rathbone's. Realizing they really had something, Universal signed Sondergaard to a long-term contract before *The Spider Woman* wrapped in May, 1943.

Sondergaard's cat-and-mouse game with Rathbone is a delectable display of one-upsmanship which occasionally spills over into camp. Sizing up Raghni Singh (Holmes' undercover moniker) as a possible victim, Spedding turns to her epicene partner-in-crime Norman Locke (Vernon Downing) and inquires, "What do they do in India, Norman?" "Ride elephants," he sarcastically replies. In the next scene, Adrea, who has obviously boned up on Eastern culture, gallantly tries to evoke the spirit of "Mother India" for her tea-time companion (Holmes in disguise). Draped in an Indian sari, emerging from a mist of burning incense, she's a startlingly incongruous sight as Holmes discreetly pulls rental company labels from her bogus Asian decorations.

The sparring match delivers a neat payoff a few scenes later. Angling for a sample of his adversary's fingerprints, "Singh" entices Adrea with a silver cigarette case. After she eagerly snatches up her new trinket, he abruptly takes it back, promising to have it personally inscribed. In their next encounter, at Baker Street, Holmes returns the case which bears not Adrea's monogram, but a striking etching of a black widow spider.

The Spider Woman works up a considerable head of steam as the final pieces of the puzzle fall into place, only to stop dead in its tracks in a disappointing, washed-up climax. Her wits seemingly failing her, Spedding's plans to dispatch Holmes in an amusement park shooting gallery is a singularly clumsy and contrived method of murder. The film resorts to old-hat suspense gimmicks as Watson (Holmes' would-be executioner) fumbles every opportunity to hit his target. Spedding bows out in style at least. In our last glimpse of her, she is cozying up to Inspector Lestrade with thoughts of escape obviously looming in her mind.

With such overpowering leads as Rathbone and Sondergaard, the supporting players fade into the woodwork. Vernon Downing, who twitched his way through *Sherlock Holmes Faces Death* as a shell-shocked soldier, is outclassed as Spedding's accomplice. Nigel Bruce and Dennis Hoey share some quietly touching scenes reminiscing about the supposedly-dead detective. The enigmatic pygmy turns out to be nothing more than a black-faced Angelo Rossitto, one of the busiest midgets in Hollywood.

Roy William Neill's direction is spare and efficient, with an evident focus on pacing. Universal used *The Spider Woman* as bottom-of-the-bill fodder, pairing it with the lavish and heavily promoted *Ali Baba and the Forty Thieves,* another of the studio's overstuffed Technicolor vulgarities. Sherlock Holmes' touch of class was a welcome addition to the program—especially with Gale Sondergaard doing the menacing.

Weird Woman (1944)

Released April 14, 1944. 63 minutes. An Inner Sanctum Mystery, produced by arrangement with Simon and Schuster, Inc., Publishers. *Directed by* Reginald LeBorg. *Associate Producer:* Oliver Drake. *Executive Producer:* Ben Pivar. *Screenplay by* Brenda Weisberg. *Based on the novel* ***Conjure Wife*** *by* Fritz Leiber, Jr. *Adaptation by* W. Scott Darling. *Director of Photography:* Virgil Miller. *Special Photography:* John P. Fulton. *Assistant Director:* William Tummel. *Film Editor:* Milton Carruth. *Musical Director:* Paul Sawtell. *Art Directors:* John B. Goodman & Richard H. Riedel. *Set Decorators:* Russell A. Gausman & Andrew J. Gilmore. *Sound Director:* Bernard B. Brown. *Technician:* William Hedgcock. *Gowns by* Vera West.

Lon Chaney (Professor Norman Reed), Anne Gwynne (Paula Clayton Reed), Evelyn Ankers (Ilona Carr), Ralph Morgan (Professor Millard Sawtelle), Elisabeth Risdon (Grace Gunnison), Lois Collier (Margaret Mercer), Elizabeth Russell (Evelyn Sawtelle), Harry Hayden (Professor Septimus Carr), Phil Brown (David Jennings), Jackie Lou [Kay] Harding, William Hudson (Students), Hanna Kaapa (Laraua), Chuck Hamilton (Carpenter), David Hoffman (Inner Sanctum), Milburn Stone (Voice of Radio Announcer).

> I believe that voodoo merely is the untutored savage's realization of the power of auto-suggestion. —Lon Chaney, quoted in publicity for *Weird Woman*

The second installment of the Inner Sanctum series, *Weird Woman* is regarded with contempt by those who hold the Fritz Leiber novel upon which it was based (*Conjure Wife)* and the second screen adaptation (*Burn, Witch, Burn*) in high esteem. But for those willing to place their critical faculties in reserve, and approach the movie with their tongue firmly planted in their cheek, *Weird Woman* is an absolute joy, outclassing the other films in the series for its sheer audaciousness alone. Brenda Weisberg's mildly hysterical screenplay has all the veracity of a Carol Burnett skit and is almost as funny.

Once again, Chaney is laughably miscast as a broody intellectual. One of his legion of female admirers in this film describes him as a "mental giant," though he's incapable of solving the slightest social disorder. Lon gets fine support from an uncharacteristically venomous Evelyn Ankers as the proverbial "woman scorned"; Anne Gwynne, who's quite excellent as Chaney's neurotic island bride; Lois Collier and Phil Brown as a pair of naive romantics; and RKO's Empress of Menace Elizabeth Russell, cutting a striking figure (as always) in the role of a vindictive widow. This canny combination of lampoonish writing and spirited performances makes *Weird Woman* a high camp classic.

Just weeks after Universal closed their deal with Simon and Schuster, the studio picked the Leiber novel as its next screen adaptation. The voodoo-witchcraft theme of *Conjure Wife* was made-to-order for a film studio whose stock-in-trade was scaring the wits out of audiences. However, the novel's strong supernatural angle was inevitably compromised in W. Scott Darling's treatment, with the plot's malevolent incidents being blamed on a vengeful woman acting out of jealousy, and not the machinations of a modern-day sorceress.

By the time shooting was completed on *Calling Dr. Death,* Universal had a change of heart and decided to follow up their first Inner Sanctum mystery with *The Frozen Ghost* instead of *Conjure Wife (Weird Woman*'s original title). This decision was short-lived; *Ghost* had seven more months of labor pains before its multiauthored script was deemed suitable for filming. And by then, it followed yet *another* Inner Sanctum release, *Dead Man's Eyes.*

By early December, 1943, Universal began production in earnest on *Weird Woman.* (A trade paper write-up at the time revealed that the studio had established a precedent by hiring a publicist whose sole function was to coin catchy titles, "to insure the most effective way of publicizing each film.")

Having done such an efficient job directing *Calling Dr. Death,* Reginald LeBorg was "rewarded" with the job of directing *Weird Woman.* The charming octagenarian offers this insight on what it was like working on a typical B at Universal:

> I got the script on a Friday and was told to start shooting a week from Monday. So I had to read it over the weekend and then come in and prepare. That was the norm at Universal. Sometimes you'd get two or three weeks in between, if they had no script, but sometimes they had to rush these things out. Of course, me being a hard worker and a fast worker, they gave me the *dirt.* When they had something they wanted done fast, they rushed me in.

LeBorg admits he didn't even have the time to study the Leiber novel.

Just prior to the December 6 shooting date, Anne Gwynne was chosen to portray Paula, probably the most demanding role of her career, thus sparing her the indignity of appearing in yet another of the studio's featherweight farces (*Hi, Good Lookin'*). Lois Collier, a pretty newcomer from radio, and Phil Brown, an actor and occasional dialogue director at Universal, landed key roles. Brown's Hollywood career came to a screeching halt during the McCarthy era. Settling in England, the young man picked up a few directing and acting assignments (most notably, Edward Dmytryk's 1949 suspense-melodrama *The Hidden Room*). In 1977, a grayer, plumper Phil Brown popped up as Luke Skywalker's (Mark Hamill) uncle in *Star Wars.*

Monroe College sociology professor Norman Reed (Lon Chaney) has his hands full. Instead of celebrating the success of his new book *Superstition Versus Reason and Fact,* and looking forward to the day when he'll most assuredly win his department's chairmanship, Reed nervously paces the floor of his study, chain-smoking, and staring questioningly into the grotesque faces of the native ceremonial masks he's collected while exploring the South Seas. It was on one of those lush tropical islands Reed met his childlike bride Paula (Anne Gwynne), the source of all his troubles. The daughter of American

Top: Fritz Leiber, Jr.'s thrice-filmed novel _Conjure Wife_ first reached the screen as the Inner Sanctum mystery _Weird Woman. Bottom:_ Evelyn Ankers, Universal's Queen of Screamers, matches wits with Elizabeth Russell, RKO's Houri of Horror, in _Weird Woman._

missionaries, Paula was raised by Laraua (Hanna Kaapa), the high priestess of Kauna-Ana-Ana, who taught the impressionable girl to put her faith in voodoo gods and follow her people's superstitions.

Norman struggles valiantly to free his wife of these strange rituals. He gets little support from his old flame, librarian Ilona Carr (Evelyn Ankers). When Norman rebuffs her generous offer of a little extramarital monkey business, Ilona, not one to take rejection lying down, sets out to poison the minds of the gullible against the unhappy couple. She tells everyone within earshot that Paula is a "witch wife" and has been using her magical powers to insure Norman's recent success. Ilona finds a ready audience in Evelyn Sawtelle (Elizabeth Russell); her hen-pecked husband Millard (Ralph Morgan) is Norman's only rival for the coveted chairmanship. With Evelyn safely in tow, Ilona works on Margaret Mercer (Lois Collier), a starry-eyed minx who regards Professor Reed with the kind of adoration usually reserved for rock stars. ("He's the most brilliant man on the campus!" she swoons.) Banking on the insecurities of Margaret's Dobie Gillis-like boyfriend David Jennings (Phil Brown), Ilona lasciviously suggests that there's something going on between Reed and Margaret.

But Ilona's biggest coup is the discovery of an obscure but brilliant thesis that was filched by Millard Sawtelle to form the basis for his new book. Pretending to be the professor's ally, Ilona misinforms the timorous old man that Reed plans on using this information as a means of getting him to withdraw from the chairmanship race.

Fed up with Paula's nightly prowlings, Norman follows her to a local cemetery. Aghast, he watches her light a ceremonial candle, don a headpiece, and perform a rite over an effigy of Ilona. Unable to bear it, Norman interrupts the ceremony and destroys his wife's collection of tourist-trap voodoo paraphernalia. The "circle of immunity" she has created to protect herself and Norman from the forces of evil has been destroyed.

It isn't long before the couple are beset with all manner of tragedy. Sawtelle commits suicide; Evelyn accuses Norman of "murder." Reed is forced to discharge Margaret as his student secretary after she makes a play for him; as a consequence, word spreads around the campus that he's a philanderer. Paula is tormented by an anonymous caller who plays a voodoo death chant over the phone. An insanely jealous David makes two attempts on Norman's life. The second one ends in tragedy: David's gun goes off in a struggle with the professor and he's killed. Norman is jailed and released on bail pending a court case. Understandably, Norman himself begins to believe maybe there's something to Paula's babblings about protective medallions and circles of immunity. Life hasn't exactly been a bed of roses since he destroyed her collection of artifacts.

Reed finally gets to the bottom of this mess when Evelyn admits it was Ilona who had warned Millard of impending disaster and that it was she who filled Margaret and David's minds with false notions. Realizing the only way he can clear himself of the murder charge is through Ilona's confession, Reed hatches a plan and enlists Evelyn's cooperation.

Late that night, Evelyn summons Ilona to her home and pretends to be shaken up over a dream she's just had. "Millard came and stood over me.... He said, 'I am dead because a woman lied. *A woman lied*!'" The widow produces a hideous effigy which, she claims, represents the woman who lied. Unless this woman confesses (in 13 days, one minute after midnight), she will be choked to death.

The ruse works. Ilona rushes from Evelyn's home in hysterics. In a wonderful series of quick cuts, we see glimpses of Ilona over the next two weeks, slowly going out of her mind. On the night of the appointed hour, the hagridden librarian storms into Evelyn's house and demands the effigy. As the clock strikes the hour of midnight, Ilona hysterically blurts out a confession. Surprise! Norman, Paula and Margaret emerge from the next room and confront her. "You tricked me!" Ilona cries, and dashes for an open window. Racing across a garden catwalk, she slips through the slats and is choked to death by the entwining vines ... just as Evelyn's dream predicted she would.

While it may not be 100 percent faithful to its source, *Burn, Witch, Burn* is the definitive version of the Leiber novel. Although Charles Beaumont and Richard Matheson received a screenplay credit, it was George Baxt who reconstructed and polished their script, which was deemed "unfilmable" by the producers. (Like Reginald LeBorg, Baxt didn't read the Leiber novel either!) One of the most thoughtful thrillers of the skeptic-turned-believer school, *Burn, Witch, Burn* is, essentially, an allegorical conflict between the powers of reason and superstition, or rationality and irrationality. *Weird Woman* has no such pretensions. In true Inner Sanctum tradition, the movie sidesteps being a full-blooded fantasy chiller and merely uses the supernatural elements of Leiber's work to set up a standard melodrama. *Weird Woman*'s approach is heavy-handed, resulting in the viewer's enjoying more titters than thrills. But its lunacy is contagious as the plot takes on the dimensions of a comic opera with crisis upon crisis piling up on Chaney's doorstep.

Structurally, *Weird Woman* suffers from episodic pacing. The opening scenes of Gwynne arriving at home in the middle of the night from a secret rendezvous as Chaney, alone in his study, tries to make sense of his new wife's puzzling behavior, create an instant mood of mystery and intrigue. Following a campy flashback scene, set on Paula's superstition-ridden isle (replete with all the usual phony trappings typical of the Hollywood sarong epic), the pace is temporarily stalled by a series of talky exposition episodes. However, once Gwynne's medallion is destroyed in the fire, the plot shifts into high gear again.

Seldom have so many neurotic characters been crammed into one picture. It's amazing how easily this presumably well-educated bunch fall prey to Ilona's schemes. Only wise, sardonic Grace (nicely played by Elisabeth Risdon) displays any semblance of rationality. Surprisingly, Evelyn Ankers didn't relish the challenge of portraying a miscreant for a change. LeBorg recalls,

> Evelyn Ankers was a very sweet girl and a very good actress, but she *wasn't* very happy about her part. She was a very good friend of Anne Gwynne's, and she had to play Gwynne's enemy, to torment her. When Ankers had a scene with Gwynne that was rather macabre, she *couldn't* do it very well because she loved Gwynne so much; she *couldn't* be mean to her. I gave her a few pointers, and after three or four takes, she did it very well.

The two actresses remained friends right up until Ankers' death. In fact, Gwynne acted as Evelyn's character witness when the actress obtained her United States citizenship in August of 1946.

One player who didn't have qualms about playing evil roles (in moderation, that is) was Elizabeth Russell. The statuesque ash blonde (christened the Houri of Horror by *The Hollywood Reporter*) got the showy part of Evelyn Sawtelle through her agent, E.A. Dupont. Russell enjoyed a lucrative career as a top New York fashion model for John Robert Powers and fostered no ambitions toward becoming an actress. She submitted to a screen test in 1936 and was signed up to a long-term contract with Paramount. After reappearing in a trio of undistinguished programmers, Russell returned to modeling after the studio dropped her option.

Her friend ZaSu Pitts convinced Russell to give the picture business another whirl and that she did, appearing in two of ZaSu's comedies. This led to her first horror film appearance as Bela Lugosi's remarkably preserved 80-year-old wife in Monogram's riotous *The Corpse Vanishes* (1942). Then came *Cat People* and a long and fruitful association with Val Lewton. The producer's superb *The Curse of the Cat People* is Elizabeth's finest hour. Jokingly calling herself "a female Bela Lugosi in a constant zombic state," Russell has no regrets concerning the brevity of her acting career ("I made a lot of mistakes because I wasn't aware of the opportunities involved").

In 1980, the Fritz Leiber classic underwent a third screen adaptation, a TV-moveish feature called *Witches' Brew*. In this uncomfortable melding of light comedy and suspense/horror, the obnoxious Richard Benjamin is cast as the hapless professor saddled with an oddball wife (Teri Garr). Lana Turner has a featured role as a smug, devious doyenne of an informal coven of surburban witches. Codirected by Richard Shorr and Herbert L. Strock, *Witches' Brew* follows the general plotline of *Burn, Witch, Burn,* right down to Benjamin's professor being pursued by a winged, demonic creature. (Leiber isn't given a word of credit!) Garr's method of winning her husband the psychology seat (by smearing his bare back and belly with bat guano, cat urine and lamb's blood and leaving him out on the front lawn overnight) is indicative of this film's sense of humor.

The Scarlet Claw (1944)

Released May 26, 1944. 74 minutes. *Produced & Directed by* Roy William Neill. *Screenplay by* Edmund L. Hartmann & Roy William Neill. *Original Story by* Paul Gangelin & Brenda Weisberg. *Based on the characters created by* Sir Arthur Conan Doyle. *Director of Photography:* George Robinson. *Art Director:* John B. Goodman. *Associate Art Director:* Ralph M. DeLacy. *Musical Director:* Paul Sawtell. *Film Editor:* Paul Landres. *Special Photography:* John P. Fulton. *Set Decorators:* Russell A. Gausman & Ira S. Webb. *Sound Director:* Bernard B. Brown. *Technician:* Robert Pritchard. *Dialogue Director:* Stacey Keach. *Assistant Director:* Melville Shyer. *Camera Operator:* Eddie Cohen. *Properties:* Henry Gundstrom.

Basil Rathbone (Sherlock Holmes), Nigel Bruce (Dr. John H. Watson), Gerald Hamer (Potts/Jack Tanner/Alastair Ramson), Paul Cavanagh (Lord William Penrose), Arthur Hohl (Emile Journet), Miles Mander (Judge Brisson), Kay Harding (Marie Journet), David Clyde (Sergeant Thompson), Ian Wolfe (Drake), Victoria Horne (Nora), George Kirby (Father Pierre), Harry Allen (Taylor), Frank O'Connor (Cab Driver), Olaf Hytten (Hotel Clerk), Gertrude Astor (Lady Penrose), Tony Travers (Musician), Charles Francis (Sir John), Norbert Muller (Page Boy), Al Ferguson (Attendant), Eric Wilton (Night Clerk), Peter [Pietro] Sosso (Trent), Clyde Fillmore (Inspector), Charles Knight (Inspector Assistant), Gil Perkins, Charles Morton (Stunts/Doubles), William Allen.

As Universal's horror line was quickly eroding with one rehashed plot after another, the Sherlock Holmes series was, conversely, reaching its peak. With all references to the war abandoned, the studio embarked on the detective's darkest, grimmest—and bloodiest—adventure.

The Scarlet Claw is, hands down, the perennial favorite of the Universal Holmes pictures, although most Conan Doyle buffs still rate the film a notch below the two 20th Century–Fox features which inspired the series. *The Scarlet Claw* is, first and foremost, a mystery, yet the film can pretty well stand on its own as a genuine horror movie, arguably the best that Universal released in 1944.

Pictorially, this back-to-basics feature harkens to *The Hound of the Baskervilles* with a plot set on the foggy marshlands (the Canadian wilderness substitutes for the north of England). Much of *The Scarlet Claw*'s success is attributable to Roy William Neill. The director's uncanny ability for creating a rich, horrific atmosphere hadn't been tapped since the opening scene of *Frankenstein Meets the Wolf Man.* He found the ideal cameraman in George

Robinson, whose fine work was the saving grace of the '40s Frankenstein romps (*The Scarlet Claw* was his only Holmes film). It was the first time Neill received official writing credit on the series, sharing billing with Edmund L. Hartmann. (Tom McKnight, the technical advisor on the early Holmes pictures, also worked uncredited on the script.)

The screenplay of *The Scarlet Claw* is, in the final analysis, serviceable but unexceptional; the film's real merit lies in its brooding sense of evil and madness. The plot maintains interest by offering a spate of reliable horror bromides: a legendary monster on the prowl, a psychopath with the unique ability to master any disguise, and huddled throngs of superstitious townsfolk who fearfully retreat to the village inn. Wrenching every ounce of atmosphere from this catalogue of cliches, Neill produced one of the two minor classics of the series. (Inspiration was running high; the second, *The Pearl of Death,* was released a mere four months after *The Scarlet Claw.*) Routinely conceived as just another assignment for an original Holmes story, the task went to contract writers Paul Gangelin and Brenda Weisberg. The third film of the series in the 1943–1944 production year, the project got underway under the title *Sherlock Holmes Versus Moriarity.* Gangelin and Weisberg strayed far from their original concept and the arch-criminal was eliminated from the plot altogether. The script was completely rewritten by Hartmann and Neill and blandly retitled *Sherlock Holmes in Canada* (it was destined to be changed to *The Scarlet Claw* by the first day of shooting, January 12, 1944). Director Neill overshot his 16-day schedule three days, bringing the picture in on February 3. He took advantage of nearby Nagana Rocks, a reasonable substitute for the Canadian marshlands, at least with the artificial fog machines operating at full capacity. Additional exterior shooting was done on the European Street, which was rendered unrecognizable by Robinson's dark, moody photography.

The Scarlet Claw gets right down to business with the eerie pealing of a church bell on the misty moors of La Morte Rouge, a small hamlet nestled on the outskirts of Quebec. The patrons of the local inn, run by Emile Journet (Arthur Hohl), fear that the bells are a harbinger of doom. The local farmers report that their sheep have been found dead with their necks cut, and a glowing "phantom" has been seen stalking the marshlands. Father Pierre (George Kirby) induces the postman, Potts (Gerald Hamer), to drive him out to the village church to investigate. There, clutching the bell-pull, is the body of Lady Penrose (Gertrude Astor), her throat slashed.

Sherlock Holmes (Basil Rathbone) and Dr. Watson (Nigel Bruce), in Quebec to address the Royal Canadian Occult Society, receive an urgent letter written by Lady Penrose shortly before her death. Fearing for her life, she implored the pair to come to her aid.

Holmes and Watson arrive at the village and waste little time formulating a list of suspects: Journet the innkeeper; Judge Brisson (Miles Mander), the retired, wheelchair-bound magistrate whose paralysis the detective discovers to be a hoax; and Lord William Penrose (Paul Cavanagh), the husband of the slain woman, who seems more than willing to pin the crime on supernatural forces.

As the sightings of the legendary monster of the moors begin to mount,

Seaman Jack Tanner is one several disguises assumed by crazed killer Alastair Ramson in *The Scarlet Claw.* Left to right: Gerald Hamer ("Tanner"), Basil Rathbone, Nigel Bruce, David Clyde.

Holmes embarks on a search of his own. He is followed by a figure glowing with luminescence. When the creature leaves behind a fragment of "skin" on the thorny underbrush, Holmes discovers it is merely a cotton wrap treated with phosphorescent paint. As he suspected, a human agent is at work.

Focusing his investigation on Lady Penrose's past, Holmes uncovers evidence that she was a former actress who years before witnessed the murder of one of her colleagues by another actor, the psychopathic Alastair Ramson. The detective is convinced that Ramson, who was believed to be killed in a prison break, is the marsh killer. Learning that Judge Brisson passed sentence on Ramson, and that Journet was a former prison guard where the murderer was incarcerated, Holmes suspects that they, too, are marked for death.

The detective dashes to Brisson's home but it is too late. The jurist has been slain by the madman, disguised as the housekeeper. When Journet's daughter Marie (Kay Harding) is found with her throat slashed, Holmes implores the innkeeper to help him trap the murderer. Using himself as bait, Holmes, disguised as Journet, walks along the lonely trail through the foggy marshlands. Potts, concealing a blood-stained garden weeder, suddenly appears on the path. A struggle ensues and Holmes reveals his true identity. Ramson/Potts attempts to escape but finds himself hemmed in by the local police and villagers. He spots Journet in the group and wrestles him to the ground. The innkeeper slays his daughter's murderer with the man's own instrument of death. *The Scarlet Claw* concludes with Holmes reciting some choice lines from a recent Churchill speech as he and Watson head for home.

The Scarlet Claw suffers from occasional flaws and gaps in logic. From the outset, Ramson's intended victims (Lady Penrose, Journet and Judge Brisson) all confess to an unshakable premonition of death. While this ploy fuels the oppressive mood of the movie, the script offers little justification for this state of mind so early in the story. Why Ramson's roster of victims, all of vastly different backgrounds and social positions, should all settle in a singularly remote and dreary backwater town, is a little too convenient to be believed.

Rathbone's authoritative playing can't disguise the fact that we're watching the master detective at his bungling worst. Ramson outfoxes Holmes at every turn, and has little difficulty dispatching practically all of his intended victims right under the detective's hooked nose. Holmes can't even prevent the female lead from being killed off, an unconventional, if not downright shocking development for this kind of film. Confronted by a gun-toting Ramson, Holmes manages to save his own skin when the ever-klutzy Watson creates a diversion by plummeting down a flight of stairs at the crucial moment. Not even the sleuth's celebrated powers of deduction serve him well enough to catch the killer. When his investigation hits a dead end, Holmes simply dresses up as the next likely victim, and patiently waits to be pounced upon by the guilty party. The climax of *The Scarlet Claw,* too, is somewhat anticlimactic, as the murderer turns out to be a character so minor and incidental to the plot, most viewers have a tough time trying to identify him.

Yet these are relatively minor flaws in an overall impressive thriller. Though the script occasionally falters, Neill's crack direction passes muster, especially in the horrific moments. Holmes' confrontation with the monster of the moors yields some suspense. Another fine creation of special effects ace John P. Fulton, the luminous specter is an eerie sight, darting across the foggy marshlands between knotted trees.

Also memorable is Neill's staging of the murder of Judge Brisson. Paul Sawtell's funereal strings serve as an appropriate background as the "housekeeper" methodically draws each window shade before creeping up behind the unsuspecting magistrate. (The real housekeeper, played by Victoria Horne, is trussed up and locked in a closet.) Neill cuts to a shock close-up of the dimly-lit "housekeeper" (Ramson in drag), menacingly clutching the talon-like garden weeder, ready to attack. It's a truly terrifying moment, worthy of Hitchcock.

One of the few survivors in the cast of *The Scarlet Claw,* Horne offers her recollections of making the film:

> The Sherlock Holmes pictures were a joy to do. It was like working in a stock company: all the actors knew each other and worked so well together. Mr. Hamer and I both shared that darkly lighted scene. I remember admiring the great strength of Basil Rathbone when he lifted me from the floor of the closet easily.

The Scarlet Claw is, predictably, top-heavy with red herrings, all smoothly played by a familiar cast of Holmes regulars. Paul Cavanagh is the icy Lord Penrose, seemingly hellbent on keeping his wife's murder unsolved. The excellent Miles Mander is the judge who fakes his own paralysis, Arthur Hohl is the grim Journet, and Ian Wolfe plays a slightly batty family retainer. Least adequate is the inexperienced Kay (formerly Jackie Lou) Harding as the doomed Marie Journet, whose bogus French accent is as awkward as her acting.

As the demented but ingenious murderer, Gerald Hamer spents most of his time affecting various disguises. The little-known British actor found himself on the list of suspects in many a Holmes thriller, including *Sherlock Holmes Faces Death, Pursuit to Algiers* and *Terror by Night.* He was also the ill-fated spy in *Sherlock Holmes in Washington.* Finally getting his chance to play an all-out heavy, Hamer enacts his climactic unmasking scene with beady-eyed savvy. Until then, his role as a slightly tipsy mailman is an innocuous one.

The plot of *The Scarlet Claw* is dimly reminiscent of MGM's *London by Night* (1937) a lightweight whodunit starring George Murphy and Virginia Field. *London by Night*'s killer (Leo G. Carroll) also adopts a long series of disguises, and (perhaps *too* coincidentally) both films include a whistling postman carrying the same tune ("British Grenadiers").

The Scarlet Claw was strong enough to springboard Roy William Neill out of the Sherlock Holmes series into the mainstream, but Universal was content to keep him where he was. Neill had surpassed himself, but his enthusiasm and inspiration for the series could not, and did not, last its entire run. Film critic Andrew Sarris once described Roy William Neill as "a minor stylist," and that's about as close as he came to making a mark for himself in Hollywood; in most circles he's still an unknown director. *The Scarlet Claw* not only proved that the Sherlock Holmes series could, on occasion, produce a really class thriller, but that Roy William Neill was another misused Hollywood talent.

The Invisible Man's Revenge (1944)

Released June 9, 1944. 77 minutes. *Produced & Directed by* Ford Beebe. *Executive Producer:* Howard Benedict. *Suggested by the novel* ***The Invisible Man*** *by* H.G. Wells. *Original Screenplay by* Bertram Millhauser. *Director of Photography:* Milton Krasner. *Special Photographic Effects:* John P. Fulton. *Film Editor:* Saul A. Goodkind. *Camera Operator:* Maury Gertsman. *Assistant Director:* Fred Frank. *Musical Score & Direction:* Hans J. Salter. *Art Directors:* John B. Goodman & Harold H. MacArthur. *Set Decorators:* Russell A. Gausman & Andrew J. Gilmore. *Sound Director:* Bernard B. Brown. *Technician:* William Hedgcock. *Property Master:* Eddie Keyes. *Gowns by* Vera West.

Jon Hall (Robert Griffin), Leon Errol (Herbert Higgins), John Carradine (Dr. Peter Drury), Alan Curtis (Mark Foster), Evelyn Ankers (Julie Herrick), Gale Sondergaard (Lady Irene Herrick), Lester Matthews (Sir Jasper Herrick), Halliwell Hobbes (Cleghorn), Leland [Leyland] Hodgson (Sir Frederick Travers), Ian Wolfe (Jim Feeney), Billy Bevan (Police Sergeant), Doris Lloyd (Maud), Cyril Delevanti (Malty Bill), Skelton Knaggs (Alf Parry), Olaf Hytten (Grey), Leonard Carey (Constable), Yorke Sherwood (Yarrow), Tom P. Dillon (Towle), Guy Kingsford (Bill), Jim Aubrey (Wedderburn), Arthur Gould-Porter (Meadows), Lillian Bronson (Norma), Janna DeLoos (Nellie), Beatrice Roberts.

Universal's final entry in the overworked Invisible Man series has a nice little macabre touch that prevents the formula from lapsing into total unconsciousness. Just as blood had been the antidote that returned Vincent Price back to a state of visibility in the last moments of *The Invisible Man Returns,* that precious fluid performs a similar service in Ford Beebe's *The Invisible Man's Revenge.* Only the invisible protagonist here happens to be a homicidal maniac who doesn't blanch at the prospect of draining men dry in order to obtain it.

As was his custom, Beebe invested his horror films at Universal with exceptionally strong values and solid casts, but, in the case of *The Invisible Man's Revenge,* the producer-director failed to overcome the malaise that affects all late bloomers. Once-startling camera tricks—a cigarette puffing away in midair, a talking headless body, everyday household objects darting about the room with a life of their own—fail to arouse the same sense of wonder as they had only a few years before.

In shaping up his "original" screenplay, Bertram Millhauser tossed out a few of the plot contrivances established in the earlier films of the series. Following the example set by *The Invisible Woman* and *Invisible Agent,* Millhauser eliminated any reference to monocane (or duocane), thus cancelling out the Invisible One's facility for total madness in the grip of the insidious drug. Instead, the screenwriter created in the story's antihero, Robert Griffin (absolutely no relation to the Griffins of previous entries), a made-to-order psychopath who doesn't require the degenerative effects of serum to corrupt his personality. Griffin harbors none of the lofty pretenses of his invisible predecessors. He cares nothing about advancing scientific progress, isn't seeking vindication for a crime he didn't commit, nor is he interested in using his newly acquired powers to promote world peace. At first, Griffin isn't even tempted by the real possibility of world domination. His only (rather trivial) goal is to avenge himself on the titled British family whom he mistakenly believes has done him wrong.

When Universal first announced its plans on June 10, 1943, to produce another Invisible Man sequel, it had hopes of obtaining the services of Claude Rains in the starring part. (It seems highly unlikely that the British actor would have accepted such a role at this stage of his film career.) When this arrangement failed, the studio drafted Jon Hall to play the part. Since his first appearance as an *heroic* transparent man, Hall had become firmly entrenched in Universal's vacuous Maria Montez miniepics, so portraying a *homicidal* invisible man was a real change of pace. Surprisingly, the nominally talented star invests the part of "Rob" Griffin with melodramatic zest.

Harboring a persecution complex, Griffin escapes from the psychopathic ward of a Capetown asylum (a newspaper clipping informs us that he's left behind a trail of murder and mayhem). Griffin pays a surprise visit on his former friends and business partners, Sir Jasper Herrick (Lester Matthews) and his wife Irene (Gale Sondergaard). The lunatic accuses the couple of trying to murder him while the trio was on an African safari in search of a diamond field in Tanganyika five years before. Although the Herricks are innocent, the ambiguous tone of Millhauser's dialogue in the stormy confrontation scene suggests otherwise. Matthews is the epitome of the pampered English aristocrat who lives comfortably off the fruits of his ancestor's labors. In her aloof, coolly sophisticated manner, Sondergaard can't help but exude wickedness, regardless of the innocent nature of her character. A line like "Don't worry, Rob, you'll get all that's coming to you" carries a malevolent charge when spoken by the marvelously malicious Gale.

Cast out by the Herricks, the fugitive seeks shelter in the home of a reclusive scientist, Dr. Peter Drury (John Carradine in a delightfully fruity performance). Introducing Griffin to his transparent menagerie, a parrot named Methuselah and a shepherd called Brutus, the eccentric Drury cackles, "In this house, you've got to believe what you *can't* see!"

Drury explains that after years of tireless research, he has developed a formula capable of rendering any living creature invisible. Unlike Carradine's coldblooded Dr. Walters in *Captive Wild Woman,* Drury is just a harmless crackpot whose burning goal is to take his place with such immortals as

Halliwell Hobbes, Alan Curtis and Evelyn Ankers confront the transparent protagonist of *The Invisible Man's Revenge.*

Copernicus, Faraday, Darwin and the rest of the crew. By endowing a hardened criminal with the powers of invisibility, Drury proves his brilliance is outmeasured by his lack of common sense.

The Invisible Man's Revenge contains few of the elaborate effects which distinguished the earlier Wells adaptations. As in *Invisible Agent,* several effects sequences (particularly those shots of Jon Hall walking around sans head and hands) have a careless, slapdash quality. Still, John P. Fulton pulls off a few startlingly effective tricks: a beautifully composed shot of Hall dashing down a corridor as his hands and face rapidly fade from sight, a chilling bit wherein the actor dips his hand into an aquarium and dabs water on his face, creating a ghostly visage that frightens Sondergaard into hysterics, and the always-fascinating effect wherein the Invisible Man removes his goggles, thus allowing the audience to see clear through to the inside-back of his gauze-wrapped head.

An undeveloped element of the story deals with Griffin's passion for the Herricks' daughter, Julie (Evelyn Ankers). Though he has never encountered her in the flesh, Griffin falls in love with the willowy girl strictly on the basis of seeing her picture (shades of Otto Preminger's *Laura*). Realizing he doesn't stand a ghost of a chance of winning Julie away from her present beau, newspaperman Mark Foster (Alan Curtis), in his present translucent state, the determined suitor returns to Drury's lab and demands to be changed back to normal once again.

At this point in the story, Millhauser's most interesting deviation from the Wells classic, the "vampire" gimmick, is introduced. Drury informs the recalcitrant guinea pig that the only way in which he may attain a *temporary* state of visibility is through a complete transfusion of blood from another person. How he's supposed to store all of this excess fluid in his body is a trifling matter the script doesn't attempt to answer (individual blood types are seldom a matter of great concern to movie monsters, either). When Drury foils Griffin's plot to trick Mark Foster into becoming his unwilling donor, the Invisible Man knocks the scientist out cold and drains him dry. Griffin sets the house ablaze and beats a path to the Herrick estate as Drury's now-visible dog Brutus trails him in hot pursuit.

Using an assumed name, Griffin worms his way into Julie's good graces and, during dinner, is in the midst of giving one of those repetitious power trip speeches about how wonderful it must be to be invisible when he slowly begins to fade away. The film's exciting climax takes place in the wine cellar where Griffin has successfully lured Mark, beaten him unconscious, and prepared him for a massive blood donation. Midway through the procedure, Drury's dog claws his way into the wine cellar, attacks Griffin, and mauls him to death.

Prior to the first day of shooting on *The Invisible Man's Revenge,* Universal's attorneys struck a deal with H.G. Wells for the rights to make two more Invisible Man sequels between July, 1943, and October, 1951, remunerating the author with a sum of $7,500. In a letter dated December 14, 1943, the Breen Office notified Maurice Pivar that Bertram Millhauser's screenplay needed the usual amount of revisions, including a hold on all excessive gruesomeness, deletion of the offensive word "shyster," and one or two changes in dialogue (Julie's line "He says the chambermaids are so obliging" was deemed unacceptable).

Production on *The Invisible Man's Revenge* began on January 10, 1944, and continued for five weeks and three days, wrapping in mid–February with John P. Fulton taking over to complete the special effects sequences. Pollard Lake on the Universal backlot was used in some of the outdoor shots with the exterior of the Hacienda set doubling for the Herrick estate, Shortlands. Sound Stage 17 became the Herrick wine cellar and saw extra duty when Fulton's effects crew took over on February 17.

Character player/second lead Edgar Barrier was lined up for a key role in *The Invisible Man's Revenge* (probably that of Sir Jasper), but bowed out on January 6, four days before the start of production. Barrier, who had important roles in *Cobra Woman* and *Phantom of the Opera,* had grown disenchanted with the kind of roles the studio was offering him and requested an amicable discharge. On a happier note, Universal retained the services of five-year-old German Shepherd Grey Shadow, great-grandson of the silent-picture canine luminary Strongheart.

Unquestionably, the weakest aspect of *The Invisible Man's Revenge* is comic relief Leon Errol's village shoemender-turned–petty blackmailer. As Hall's cohort, Errol offers some mild amusement but his role consumes too much screen time and detracts from the horror element. (Millhauser very likely modeled this character on the tramp Marvel from the H.G. Wells novel.)

Errol's Herbert Higgins is reminiscent of the Cowardly Lion, bold and daring on the outside but a shivering heap underneath. The comic's seemingly endless dart-throwing match at the Running Nag Inn (with an invisible Griffin piloting the darts to the bullseye) stops the plot's action dead in its tracks. A vaudeville and Broadway headliner for over 40 years, Australian-born Leon Errol broke into films in 1924 and achieved modest fame as the star of countless two-reel comedies and a running part as Lord Epping at RKO's Mexican Spitfire series with Lupe Velez. He died in 1951 at the age of 70.

While it's hardly in the same league as *The Invisible Man* nor even *The Invisible Man Returns, The Invisible Man's Revenge* is a distinct improvement over Universal's previous bastardizations of the H.G. Wells character, *The Invisible Woman* and *Invisible Agent.* (*The Hollywood Reporter* labeled the film "one of the best and most entertaining of the series.") Valid performances, smart dialogue and a high calibre B look give this Ford Beebe production that touch of class which many of its contemporaries lacked.

Jungle Woman (1944)

Released July 7, 1944. 60 minutes. *Directed by* Reginald LeBorg. *Associate Producer:* Will Cowan. *Executive Producer:* Ben Pivar. *Screenplay by* Bernard L. Schubert, Henry Sucher & Edward Dein. *Original Story by* Henry Sucher. *Director of Photography:* Jack Mackenzie. *Musical Director:* Paul Sawtell. *Art Directors:* John B. Goodman & Abraham Grossman. *Film Editor:* Ray Snyder. *Set Decorators:* Russell A. Gausman & Edward R. Robinson. *Dialogue Director:* Emory Horger. *Director of Sound:* Bernard B. Brown. *Technician:* Jess Moulin. *Makeup by* Jack P. Pierce. *Assistant Director:* Melville Shyer. *Camera Operator:* Dick Towers. *Special Effects:* Red Guthrie. *Properties:* Dan Fish. *Gowns by* Vera West.

Evelyn Ankers (Beth Mason), J. Carrol Naish (Dr. Carl Fletcher), Acquanetta (Paula Dupree), Samuel S. Hinds (Coroner), Lois Collier (Joan Fletcher), Milburn Stone (Fred Mason), Douglass Dumbrille (District Attorney), Richard Davis (Bob Whitney), Edward M. Hyans, Jr. (Willie), Christian Rub (George), Pierre Watkin (Dr. Meredith), Nana Bryant (Miss Gray), Alec Craig (Caretaker), Richard Powers (Joe), Heinie Conklin, Nolan Leary, Charles Marsh, Edward Clark, Diane Carroll, Beatrice Roberts (Members of the Jury), Wilson Benge (Court Stenographer), Kernan Cripps (Policeman), Julie London* (Girl). [**Does not appear in the final print.*]

"Aw-w-w, it's a *gyp*!" —Edward M. Hyans, Jr., in *Jungle Woman*

The Universal horror mill was in full bloom in 1944, churning out thrillers at a furious rate. But a close look at the studio's output indicates that creativity was dwindling fast. In spite of a burgeoning stockpile of horror and melodramatic properties Universal was readying for production, 1944 was a sequel-heavy year. Even the pricy Technicolor bauble *The Climax* was merely a warmed-over serving of *Phantom of the Opera*. The dubious decision to attempt a sequel to the undistinguished albeit swiftly-paced *Captive Wild Woman* suggests a less-than-discriminating story department on the verge of desperation.

Announced as *Jungle Queen* in early 1944, it was the first dramatic credit of Will Cowan, a Scottish-born producer who used to be a song-and-dance man. After a string of musical shorts with titles like *South Sea Rhythms* and *Dancing on the Stars* (both 1943), Cowan found himself, like his colleague Ben Pivar, impersonally grinding out a score of second-grade shockers straight off the studio assembly line. The crucial difference was that Cowan's credits were a cut *below* Pivar's unexceptional potboilers.

The title of Cowan's first horror outing was soon changed to the modest

Jungle Girl during contract negotiations, and decisively retitled *Jungle Woman* after shooting had commenced on February 14, 1944. J. Carrol Naish, who had barely enough time to recover from a thankless mad scientist role in the PRC fiasco *The Monster Maker,* was cast as John Carradine's benevolent successor. The versatile character actor was slumming between Academy Award-nominated performances in *Sahara* (1943) and *A Medal for Benny* (1945). This latest indignity had, at least, a mercifully brief shooting schedule. Milburn Stone and Evelyn Ankers, both still under contract, slid back into their old roles as did Acquanetta, whose frail talents were now challenged by a considerably beefed-up part as Paula, the Ape Woman.

In the opening scene, a dim figure of a man is seen prowling the wooded grounds of a private sanatorium at night. Photographed in shadow, what appears to be a creature, half-woman and half-ape, charges out of the shrubbery. The two clash and a violent struggle ensues. The snarling, clawing creature appears to have the upper hand when the man reaches into his pocket, produces a hypodermic needle and plunges it into his adversary's body. Within seconds, the beast falls to the ground, apparently dead.

Having revealed its most exciting sequence, *Jungle Woman* quickly descends into unrelieved tedium. After the inevitable flash of newspaper headlines, we are thrust into the "drama." The District Attorney (Douglass Dumbrille at his smarmy worst) suggests that Dr. Fletcher (J. Carrol Naish), the fellow with the syringe, be held for the murder of Paula Dupree. Feeling that his story is too fantastic to be taken seriously, Fletcher withholds the facts but is coaxed by the coroner (Samuel S. Hinds) into revealing all that he knows.

Fletcher recalls attending a performance of the Whipple Circus on the night that the ape Cheela saved animal trainer Fred Mason (Milburn Stone) from being mauled to death by a cat. (The film neatly segues into the finale of *Captive Wild Woman,* supplemented by new footage of Naish nestled in the bleachers among a popcorn-munching crowd.) After a trigger-happy cop shoots Cheela dead, Fletcher secures permission to bring the ape's carcass to his laboratory for experimentation.

Fletcher detects a mild heartbeat and successfully nurses the creature back to health (Universal economized by conveying the incident verbally via a dull courtroom scene, thus saving the rental costs of an ape suit). So obsessed does the doctor become with his furry pet, he runs out and purchases Dr. Walter's old sanatorium just so that he may have access to the late medico's notes. Cheela escapes from the laboratory off-camera (another bit of economizing). Later, Fletcher's dim-witted houseboy Willie (Edward M. Hyans, Jr.) drags a sultry brunette out of the bushes. Fletcher diagnoses the strange girl (Acquanetta) is suffering from shock and seems to have super-human strength.

Snapping out of her trance, the girl identifies herself as Paula Dupree and immediately sets her sights on Bob Whitney (Richard Davis), the naive fiancé of Fletcher's daughter Joan (Lois Collier). When Bob and Joan take a moonlit canoe ride, an unseen creature topples their boat and tries to drown Joan. Later, Joan sees a strange, animal-like face staring through her bedroom window. When Willie's mangled body is found on the grounds of the sanatorium,

Fletcher, now well-versed in Walters' work, correctly concludes that Paula and Cheela are one and the same. Armed with a syringe containing a knockout drug, Fletcher follows Paula into the forest. She emerges as the Ape Woman and attacks him. He plunges the needle into her body, accidentally killing her with an overdose.

Back in court, the D.A. scoffs at Fletcher's story and insists that an examination of Paula's body be made. The coroner's idea of a medical examination is to troop the entire jury over to the city morgue. (Were they planning to stick around for the autopsy, too?) The jurors are shocked to discover Paula's body in its hideous half-ape state. Fletcher is cleared of the murder charge and, flanked by Joan and Bob, leaves the grim scene. The film fades with a Lewtonesque closing quotation: "The evil man has wrought shall in the end destroy itself."

An obscure little film, *Jungle Woman* strangely eluded the various horror television packages for years. It finally surfaced in the late '60s but screenings were rare as local stations were dropping black-and-white B features from their schedules.

The movie's inaccessibility is hardly a major loss; in fact, it's really no loss at all. *Jungle Woman* is one of the worst Universal horror films ever. Produced on a minuscule budget, it looks every bit as shoddy and threadbare as anything Monogram or PRC ever churned out. Amazingly, Universal released it as a headline attraction, sharing the bill with the far worthier *The Mummy's Ghost*. On every conceivable level, *Jungle Woman* delivered less than it promised, even down to its lurid poster art featuring a cheesecake pose of Acquanetta clad in a low-cut leopard skin. Not only doesn't Acquanetta wear any such costume in the movie, she never ventures a single foot into a jungle.

A mere 60 minutes long, *Jungle Woman* is a contrived farrago of unseen terrors and old filmclips. Its narrative is easily divided into two distinct segments, the first, a garbled recapping of *Captive Wild Woman,* and the second, a foolish and uneventful continuation of the tale. *Jungle Woman* begins and ends at a coroner's inquest with all of the action unreeling in a clumsy flashback format. If it sounds confusing, wait until you see it. To make matters even more taxing, there are flashbacks *within* flashbacks. All of this expended energy for a lame horror story about an ape who transforms herself into a girl and then back again. *Jungle Woman* is a miscalculation from start to finish.

Although only ten minutes' worth of footage from *Captive Wild Woman* is used, it seems endless, especially with all those mismatched animal shots from Clyde Beatty's *The Big Cage.* (Beatty is again given token credit in the titles.) With the added reaction shots of J. Carrol Naish cut into the climactic moments of *Captive Wild Woman,* the viewer is actually watching footage from *three* different movies! Film editor Ray Snyder didn't even bother to correct the cutting room foibles of the first Ape Woman film. At one point, Milburn Stone peers into a cage and sees himself (actually Beatty) battling the ferocious cats. The next shot has Stone just about to enter the cage. This hopeless clutter of film does little to clarify the muddled storyline and, unless one has seen *Captive Wild Woman,* its sequel is all but incomprehensible.

Jungle Woman's "let's-get-it-over-with" attitude creeps into every phase of

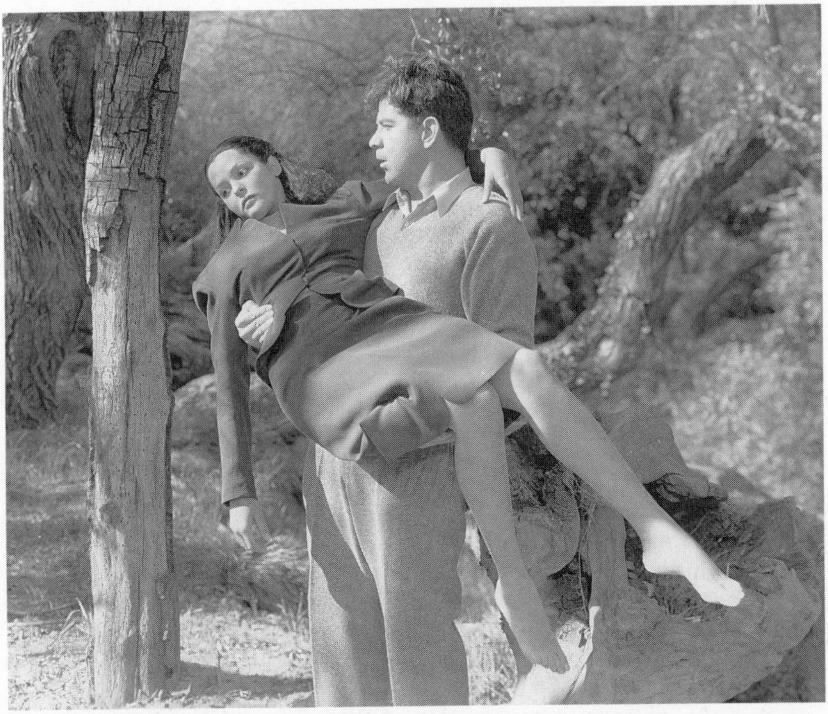

Acquanetta and Edward M. Hyans, Jr., in *Jungle Woman,* the bottom rung of the Universal horror cycle.

the production. In a 1984 interview, the late Edward Dein, who cowrote the script, barely recalled any of the low-budget features he worked on, including this one.

> I don't remember much about *Jungle Woman,* but the economy . . . was commonplace. We always used old sets from other films. These jungle pictures and horror films were exploitable, so we did them. Sixty minutes was about right for a B film because they were used as filler, like a newsreel.

Jungle Woman's director Reginald LeBorg has little regard for the film:

> I think we made it in one week. Most of these pictures were done in ten days, and this one was practically done in seven. It was an atrocious script, and a silly idea anyway. But again, I was under contract. If I had refused it, I would have been suspended without pay, and I wouldn't have gotten *anything* good anymore. You had to play ball with the front office.

Studio records indicate that LeBorg is in error in regard to the film's schedule. Amazingly, *Jungle Woman* took a full 12 days to shoot, utilizing such familiar studio locations as the Shelby Home and Pollard Lake.

In a desperate attempt to upgrade the script and inject some ingenuity into Universal's overworked horror formula, LeBorg resolved to turn *Jungle*

Woman into a Lewtonesque exercise, stressing atmosphere rather than physical terror. Dein, who wrote Lewton's *The Leopard Man* (1943) and worked uncredited on *Cat People* (1942), was apparently attuned to LeBorg's idea. As a result, Paula is not seen in her bestial stage until the "shock" finale. LeBorg explains,

> I think that was the only way to make the script palatable. I tried that especially because I think you have suspense that way. If you'd seen the Ape Woman immediately, you wouldn't care about it anymore. The story was so bad, I felt I had to do *something*. If I gave it away in the first reel, I would have no more picture.

The gimmick was a dreadful mistake. LeBorg's attempt to capture Lewton's tone failed miserably. The famous scene in *Cat People* of Simone Simon stalking Jane Randolph down a dimly-lit city street is recreated with Lois Collier being pursued through the forest by Acquanetta, who assumes a preposterous Frankenstein-like stance. The results are laughable. Since the scene of the Ape Woman stealing into Evelyn Ankers' bedroom in *Captive Wild Woman* is used in the flashbacks, LeBorg's insistence on *not* showing the monster until the wrap-up makes little sense.

Though a tad on the verbose side, Lewton's pictures worked because they had a logical buildup of suspense, well-developed characters and literate dialogue. The Ape Woman is the only thing that *Jungle Woman* has going for it and, taking that away, all that remains is a lot of dull actors talking to each other (and the audience) to death.

And the dialogue! After learning of Paula's monstrous nature, Collier warns boyfriend Richard Davis, "She's no ordinary girl! She's a horrible creature!" To which our insipid hero dumbly replies, "She isn't *that* bad!" Milburn Stone suggests to Naish that Cheela the Ape (whom he describes as "the smartest and most affectionate creature I ever took out of the jungle") was, according to the natives, a human being transformed into an animal by black magic. Naish, supposedly a redoubtable scientist, nods and says, "Yes. There have been many efforts made in that direction." (He was undoubtedly referring to the mad scientist antics of 20th Century-Fox's *Dr. Renault's Secret,* 1942, wherein George Zucco transforms a simian into *Naish*!)

No one in the cast makes much of an impression, from the leading players down to the mannequin-like extras who comprise the jury (notice their ho-hum response when the Ape Woman is finally revealed to them at the morgue). Evelyn Ankers' walk-on undeservedly earned her top billing; she reads her few lines with little conviction. J. Carrol Naish is just *burdened* with dialogue, all of it of gaseous quality which he seems unable to surmount. A frequent visitor to the horror genre, Naish excelled in reasonably well-written roles such as the inspector in *Calling Dr. Death* and Daniel the hunchback in *House of Frankenstein.* Here he's a forlorn-looking simpleton whose performance is as bad as Acquanetta's. Instead of hamming it up in the style of Atwill or Carradine, or playing it in a throw-away, tongue-and-cheek fashion, Naish sleepwalks through the part.

As the juvenile lead, Lois Collier alternates between swooning over the stars in a romantic haze or screaming her head off at the slightest provocation. Richard Davis, not to be confused with Richard DaviEs of *The Mad Doctor of Market Street,* had only a brief acting career and it's easy to see why.

Acquanetta is a charming and gracious woman, but her stiff, unprofessional acting cannot be whitewashed or ignored. Although effective at playing Paula as a mute in *Captive Wild Woman,* the decision to supply her with the faculty of speech in *Jungle Woman* was the wrong one. Even the sobs she utters after she's romantically spurned by Davis were obviously dubbed in by another actress. Acquanetta recently said about the film,

> I just did *Jungle Woman* because I was assigned to it. But once I accepted it, I did it to the best of my ability. It made money because Acquanetta was in it. I came to realize that I was the property, not the film. That why I left Universal. I felt that I was being used.
>
> J. Carrol Naish helped me more than any actor or actress that I ever worked with. I thought he was a fabulous actor, one of the greatest. I think he accepted *Jungle Woman* in order to work with me. He always had visions of the two of us working together in something fabulous. I had met him at Universal prior to *Jungle Woman,* and we became friends; he was like a mentor.

On the subject of why she left Universal:

> I went to Mexico at the instigation of the President, Mr. Roosevelt, as one of the emissaries from Hollywood. I made lots of contacts with some of the producers, and they wanted me to come to Mexico and do films. When I came back, I asked for a release from my contract. Universal never forgave me for that. They had this Jungle Woman series on the boards. They tried desperately to find someone else, and in fact they did get a girl who did *one* film [Vicky Lane in *The Jungle Captive*] and it bombed, and that was the end of that.

The authors of this book were invited by LeBorg to his North Hollywood home to chat about his Universal days, and were treated to a double-bill of his horror films on video. The amiable director had generally pleasant memories of the first film we screened, *Weird Woman,* recognizing its qualities and acknowledging its weaknesses. *Jungle Woman* brought a different reaction altogether. As the movie progressed, LeBorg griped about the flatness of Jack Mackenzie's photography and the poor dialogue of the script. But it was Acquanetta's playing that really set him on edge. Her first pathetic lines, "Hello, my name is Paula," brought a disparaging reaction. It wasn't long before LeBorg was mimicking her wooden delivery with deadly accuracy. Over forty years later, Acquanetta's thoroughly amateurish playing is still an open wound.

The strategy of not showing the Ape Woman in all her bestial glory put the brakes on *Jungle Woman*'s potential for thrills and excitement. The screenplay is padded with dead, talking-head scenes (like Acquanetta consulting another physician after a confrontation with Naish, and endless palaver about her mental state). Determined to sustain the boredom, Collier works herself into a jealous snit when she suspects that her dullard boyfriend is two-timing her with Acquanetta. Here's a film that seems to congratulate itself on going nowhere.

Jungle Woman fails miserably in its feeble attempts at being an atmospheric, stylish thriller of the Val Lewton school; it's far too unexciting to compare favorably with Universal's standard horror fare. While admittedly a juvenile potboiler, *Captive Wild Woman* is at least enthusiastically acted and has the crisp, spirited direction of young firebrand Edward Dmytryk to its credit. *Jungle Woman* is just a glum, boring misfire.

The Mummy's Ghost (1944)

Released July 7, 1944. 60 minutes. *Associate Producer:* Ben Pivar. *Executive Producer:* Joseph Gershenson. *Directed by* Reginald LeBorg. *Screenplay by* Griffin Jay, Henry Sucher & Brenda Weisberg. *Original Story by* Griffin Jay & Henry Sucher. *Director of Photography:* William Sickner. *Art Directors:* John B. Goodman & Abraham Grossman. *Film Editor:* Saul A. Goodkind. *Musical Director:* Hans J. Salter. *Sound Director:* Bernard B. Brown. *Technician:* Jess Moulin. *Set Decorators:* Russell A. Gausman & L.R. Smith. *Assistant Director:* Melville Shyer. *Makeup by* Jack P. Pierce. *Gowns by* Vera West.

Lon Chaney, Jr. (Kharis), John Carradine (Yousef Bey), Robert Lowery (Tom Hervey), Ramsay Ames (Amina Mansouri), Barton MacLane (Police Insp. Walgreen), George Zucco (High Priest), Frank Reicher (Professor Matthew Norman), Harry Shannon (Sheriff Elwood), Emmett Vogan (Coroner), Lester Sharpe (Dr. Ayad), Claire Whitney (Ella Norman), Oscar O'Shea (Night Watchman), Jack C. Smith, Jack Rockwell (Deputies), Carl Vernell (Student), Stephen Barclay (Harrison), Dorothy Vaughan (Ada Blade), Mira McKinney (Martha Evans), Bess Flowers, Caroline Cooke (Townswomen), Eddy Waller (Ben Evans), Fay Holderness (Woman), Ivan Triesault (Guide), Anthony Warde (Detective), Peter [Pietro] Sosso (Priest), Martha MacVicar [Vickers] (Girl Student), Voice of David Bruce (Radio Actor).

Shambling stiffly out of the silent world of out-of-work movie monsters, Kharis the Mummy reappears to once again terrorize the townsfolk of sleepy Mapleton in *The Mummy's Ghost,* third installment in Universal's continuing Kharis saga. Arguably the best of the three sequels to *The Mummy's Hand,* this newest series entry reintroduces the theme of reincarnation, a plot wrinkle unused since the long-gone days of Karl Freund's evergreen 1932 *The Mummy.* This new angle, coupled with okay production values and capable handling on the part of first-time horror director Reginald LeBorg, help to compensate for the film's frequent lapses, and overall *The Mummy's Ghost* ranks as one of the more satisfying sequels to emerge from Universal's '40s film factory.

Evidently Isis, Osiris, Set and Mr. Big himself, Amon-Ra, aren't the hardnoses that the previous Mummy films had depicted them: after 3700 years, the "forbidden love" of Kharis and Ananka suddenly appears to be sanctioned by these ancient deities of Egypt, and now it has become the will of the gods to reunite Kharis with his "beloved princess." Although this approach does not fit in at all with events in the previous Mummy pictures, it enables screenwriters Griffin Jay, Henry Sucher and Brenda Weisberg to develop their scenario along new and different lines. The vengeful and unstoppable Kharis is now portrayed in a slightly different light, and although his murderous tendencies are not curbed (the Mummy adds four more to his list of victims) we begin to recognize his undying love for the Princess and to contemplate his noble sacrifice. It's this added element of pathos that sets *The Mummy's Ghost* apart from and above the other Kharis films.

Director Reginald LeBorg began his film career as an extra in mid–30s pictures at Paramount and MGM before moving up the Hollywood ladder. He staged the opera sequences for a number of early musicals, worked on second units for Metro, Goldwyn and Selznick and eventually wound up grinding out band shorts for Universal.

> The first feature I made at Universal was an overgrown short musical, *She's for Me* [1943]; it had no stars in it, just their stock players. I was *supposed* to get a comedy afterwards, because I had some comedy in *She's for Me* and Universal liked it very much. Ben Pivar, an associate producer at Universal, had a director assigned to *The Mummy's Ghost*—I don't know who the man was—but I think he had an accident or something, and they had nobody there right then to take his place. Pivar seemed to like me and he said, "How 'bout reading the script?"

The Mummy's Ghost went before William Sickner's cameras on August 23, 1943, with Acquanetta in the costarring role of Amina Mansouri; production hit an unexpected snag that very morning when according to LeBorg the actress suffered a fainting spell and collapsed, striking her head. Unconscious for half an hour, she was taken to the Universal dispensary with a slight concussion while producer Pivar pulled actress Ramsay Ames from Universal's bullpen of curvy contract actresses to take over the role. Acquanetta recalls the incident differently:

> We had scabs on the set. We had a scene where I had to fall, and these scabs had put real rocks down on the path. They were supposed to have papier-mâché rocks but they didn't—these scabs painted real rocks white. I fell and struck my head, and that's all I remember. I woke up in the hospital. I have the effects of that to this day; I struck my arm, too, when I fell, and when I had my second son, my elbow swelled up like a ball. They said that was still from that accident because it crushed a little bone in my elbow.

The film opens in Egypt as Yousef Bey (John Carradine), a religious fanatic in the Andoheb/Mehemet Bey tradition, is arriving at the Temple of Arkam (formerly Karnak). The High Priest (George Zucco), well recovered from his death at the beginning of *The Mummy's Tomb,* instinctively goes into his now-tired *schtick,* recounting for Bey the ancient tale of Kharis. In mid-story the scene switches to a classroom in Mapleton, where Prof. Norman (Frank Reicher), noted Egyptologist, is relating the same narrative to a group of college students. After class, student Tom Hervey (Robert Lowery) meets his girlfriend, Egyptian exchange student Amina (Ramsay Ames). When Tom brings up Prof. Norman's lecture, Amina becomes unnerved and upset. Any mention of Egypt agitates the girl, and holding a book on the subject nearly causes her to swoon. (One shudders to think what she must have been like when she actually *lived* there!)

Far from their native Egypt, Kharis (Lon Chaney) and Ananka (Ramsay Ames) do it the American way—under the boardwalk, in *The Mummy's Ghost*.

That night, at Prof. Norman's home, the antiquarian is brewing tana leaves in a ceremonial lamp. Kharis, lurking in the nearby woods, senses his activities and heads for the scientist's house. As the Mummy shuffles past Amina's home, the girl goes into a trance and begins to follow Kharis at a distance. In what is easily the film's best scene, Kharis arrives at Norman's house, limping across the lawn and up to the door of the library. Sensing his presence, Norman turns and sees the Mummy framed in the entranceway. Norman rises from his chair and staggers backward in shock and disbelief as Kharis lurches into the room. The camera now alternates between subjective shots of Norman, backing away in abject terror, and of the Mummy, his face livid with hate, strangling arm extended. Kharis pins the startled scientist against a wall, chokes him to death and quaffs the steaming tana fluid. Ananka, sleepwalking onto the scene, falls unconscious at the sight of the departing Mummy.

The next morning, Sheriff Elwood (Harry Shannon) and his men begin their investigation. Even though the mold on Norman's throat indicates the return of Kharis, the Sheriff wrongly believes that Amina is holding back some clue. (Amina has also developed an unseemly streak of white in her hair—clumsily spotlighted in a grainy optical close-up—which no one comments upon or tries to explain away.) Yousef Bey arrives in Mapleton, locates the Mummy and declares that his mission is to reunite the ill-starred lovers. The pair invade New York's Scripps Museum at night to steal the body of Ananka, but the bandaged corpse vanishes before their astonished eyes when Kharis reaches into the sarcophagus. Grasping the significance of this newest development, Bey announces that Ananka's soul has entered another form, and that their task now is to find that reincarnation.

Returning to their hideout in an elevated mining shack outside Mapleton, Bey and Kharis pray for a sign that will lead them to the reincarnation of Ananka. A gust of wind blows open a shuttered window and an unearthly shaft of light appears. Guided by the light, Kharis trudges to Amina's home, abducts the unconscious girl and carries her to the shack. Yousef suddenly develops a case of the hots, ogling the curvaceous coed while his "inner voice" commands him to forsake his mission and take Amina for himself. Succumbing to temptation, Bey is about to touch a mixture of immortalizing tana fluid to her lips when Kharis, perceiving his treachery, knocks him out a window to his death far below. (According to the pressbook, the Mummy and Bey "argue.") The Mummy carries Amina into the nearby swamp just as Tom and a mob of townsmen converge on the area. With the mob at his heels, Kharis retreats into a pool and becomes mired in quicksand. Tom sees that Amina has mystically turned into a withered hag. He turns away in revulsion as Kharis and his reincarnated princess are swallowed by the swamp.

What bolsters *The Mummy's Ghost* are the new reincarnation slant, effective Lon Chaney and John Carradine performances, and some well-staged Mummy murder scenes. For the first and only time, Chaney brings some color to his Mummy role: in the scene at the Scripps Museum, where Kharis reaches out with trembling hand to touch the cheek of Ananka, and in a scene at the mining shack where the monster lowers his head praying for guidance from the gods, we see a side of Kharis never before portrayed. (The fourth and final

Kharis film, *The Mummy's Curse,* is an extension of *The Mummy's Ghost* with Chaney once again on the trail of his reincarnated sweetheart, but in that final series entry he returns to the mindless wind-up Mummy of *Hand* and *Tomb.*)

When a United Press reporter dropped in on the set of *The Mummy's Ghost* to get a story, Chaney was indulging in his second favorite pastime: bellyaching. Kharis was the actor's least favorite horror role, and not without justification. For *The Mummy's Ghost* Chaney was tightly bound in hundreds of yards of dirty gauze tape which was then soaked with a specially conceived liquid to give the appearance of age. On his hands he wore rubber gloves (with warts) and over his head was fixed a rubber mask with holes for mouth, nose and one eye. After strenuous takes the 6′4″, 220-pound Chaney would be partially unwrapped and allowed to sit in the shade for a few minutes before being wrapped up once again.

"I sweat and I can't wipe it away. I itch and I can't scratch," a steam-cooked Chaney groused to the U.P. reporter as makeup men sprinkled him with fuller's earth. Chaney also told the writer that movie audiences were nuts for spending their money to see Mummy films.

Reginald LeBorg recalls that he baited Chaney a bit, hinting at the likelihood of the actor's playing a dapper gentleman-type role in their next joint picture. What LeBorg apparently didn't know was that a little bit of Chaney went a long, *long* way. In shooting the scene where the Mummy strangles Prof. Norman, Chaney seized actor Frank Reicher's throat "and squeezed so forcefully that Reicher nearly fainted," LeBorg remembers. "Reicher was an old man, and frail, and Chaney got carried away. Reicher cried out, 'He nearly killed me! He took my breath away!'" There is evidence of this in the film itself: in the few frames where Reicher's face is visible as Chaney chokes him, the pinched expression on the older actor's face looks uncomfortably real. In the Scripps Museum scene, LeBorg intended to have the Mummy shatter a plate glass window, but when cast and crew converged on the museum set it was found that the breakaway glass had not yet been installed. Not wishing to hold up production, LeBorg told Chaney that the window glass was still real and to forget the idea of crashing through it. But when cameras rolled Chaney went ahead and recklessly shattered the glass. "I wanted to show you that I had the courage," the actor later told LeBorg as he nursed a gashed hand.

LeBorg's direction makes the most of scenes like these and other more modest highlights. Despite a few minor *faux pas* (a clumsy and obvious bit where a black cat crosses Amina's path; the silly scene where Yousef Bey is taunted by his inner voice) and an excess of extraneous passages, *The Mummy's Ghost* is easily the director's best horror film, possibly his best film overall. LeBorg also takes credit for the unusual downbeat finale (Amina ages hideously before sinking into the swamp), although he admits without prompting that he was inspired by the climax of Frank Capra's 1937 classic *Lost Horizon.*

"We discussed the finale with Pivar and I said, 'Why not let Amina sink with the Mummy? Why should there always be a happy ending?' Somebody else said, 'No, we might make a sequel.' I told him, 'The Mummy is *always* coming up—Ananka doesn't have to!'"

The ecstasy Kharis (Lon Chaney) feels at finding the mummy of his beloved Ananka is shortlived when he discovers her soul has entered another form, in *The Mummy's Ghost,* costarring John Carradine.

LeBorg's handling of *The Mummy's Ghost* rises above the level of the sloppy script turned in by scenarists Jay, Sucher and Weisberg. Apparently these screenwriters saw little purpose in building upon the groundwork laid by the earlier Kharis films, and decided to branch off on tangents of their own. Admittedly, the series was in dire need of rejuvenation; *The Mummy's Tomb,* while fast-paced, was filled with repetitive episodes, and all members of the Banning expedition were now dead. Without an added twist the Kharis saga clearly had nowhere to go. The new "live-and-let-live" attitude of the imperious Egyptian gods—hard-asses for thousands of years, now frustrated matchmakers—furnished the avenue that the series required. But the gods' sudden change of heart is not explained, nor can we fathom the reason for their apparent unconcern over the similar fates of thousands of other mummies in museums throughout the world. After listening through two pictures about the "dread horror" of Set and the "mighty power" of Amon-Ra, it comes as a letdown to discover that the whole gang of them can't filch one measly mummy out of the Scripps Museum without calling out the reserves.

Obviously Jay, Sucher and Weisberg felt that audiences would not remember the series' fine points from one picture to the next. It's also clear that they felt that in pictures of this sort, anything weird could happen, with or without benefit of explanation, and many of their careless plot machinations defy analysis. Where has the Mummy been hiding out since the Banning house fire, and why isn't he even slightly burned? Who fed him the tana fluid which gave him the life and movement to trudge to Prof. Norman's house? Why is Amina upset by references to Egypt *before* the spirit of Ananka enters her body? What causes Ananka's corpse to vanish? Why do the gods go out of their way to make Kharis' mission more difficult? Why does Amina suddenly age at the end? Since when are there mining shacks and quicksand in Massachusetts? Some of these may seem like petty or pedantic quibbles, but even within the realm of fantasy films, where bizarre events are commonplace, there should at least be a passing effort to maintain continuity and to establish a pattern of cause and effect. There are more loose ends in the *Mummy's Ghost* script than there are in Kharis' rotten wrappings.

Slipshod writing of this same sort also results in making Robert Lowery's Tom Hervey the most disagreeable "hero" of any Universal horror film. Although Hervey has the patience of a saint with the hypochondriac Amina, the character apparently feels compelled to take his frustrations out on others. He dresses down a fellow student who points out that Amina is Egyptian, and later barks angrily at the roommate who brings him the news of Professor Norman's murder. Rushing to Norman's house he nearly gets into a shoving match with some poor deputy and also antagonizes the Sheriff. While all able-bodied men are being urged to help in the search for the Mummy, he goes out on a date with Amina. A farmer tells Hervey that he tripped and fell while on patrol, but instead of expressing sympathy Hervey tells him to beat it.

The problem is compounded by the fact that Lowery is already too old to convincingly play a college student. A Kansas City, Missouri, native and a direct descendant of Abraham Lincoln, Lowery got his start as a singer with orchestras and as an actor in little theater groups. Shortly after making his film debut in 1936's *Come and Get It,* he was placed under contract by 20th Century–Fox, where he played many bit roles while being groomed in the Fox studio training school. Lowery's early publicity made much of his supposed resemblance to Clark Gable, but Lowery didn't even remotely resemble Gable until he was much older and *both* actors had lost their looks. Lowery played a succession of seedy villains in a number of 1950s B films, and eventually ended up in rock-bottom '60s fare like *When the Girls Take Over, Zebra in the Kitchen* and the awful *The Undertaker and His Pals.* His other horror film credits include Monogram's *Revenge of the Zombies* (1943) and Universal's *House of Horrors* (1946), in which he once again played a curiously bilious and belligerent "hero." He died at his Hollywood apartment in 1971, at age 57.

Ramsay Ames is similarly ineffectual as the mopey Amina. A former rumba band leader in Miami and Chicago and a singer at New York's Stork Club, the 24-year-old contract player (née Ramsay Philips) is equally handicapped by slapdash screenwriting: in every scene she comes across as a whining, worrying wet blanket, and we never get any hint of what Lowery sees in her. Barton MacLane seems aloof and slightly disinterested as the Manhattan police inspector who turns up in mid-picture to assist in the Mummy manhunt;

after years of playing nasties in Warner Bros. crime films, the actor is now completely unacceptable in the role of a policeman. Nearly all of his scenes are extraneous, and exist only to pad the picture out to its 60-minute running time. George Zucco is almost completely unrecognizable beneath Jack P. Pierce makeup as the quavering High Priest, and adds really nothing to the picture.

Unquestionably an asset to the film is the performance of John Carradine as the swarthy Yousef Bey. Carradine brings his customary blend of cold authority and commanding screen presence—as well as the usual slice of ham—to his role of the newest Mummy mentor. Although Carradine would appear to be *under*-acting in several scenes, the blustery stage actor in him comes through at other points, resulting in a slightly uneven but entertaining performance. Chaney's Kharis puts an end to Carradine's hot-and-cold acting with a neck-breaking karate blow. LeBorg agrees that Carradine hammed it up as the High Priest,

> . . . but considering the character he played it wasn't too much of a fault. There were no heavies in that picture other than him—Chaney was no heavy, playing that poor mummy—so we had to have somebody to fill that slot. Carradine's voice was sonorous and excellent, much better than the average actor's, so I let him go on. In a picture like that you *can* be a little hammy—it was usually kids and teenagers that went to see that kind of a picture.

It's sad and maybe a little scary that after a 60-year career which largely centered on horror films, Carradine's best starring or costarring *genre* credits might be four of the films he did for Universal. These enjoyable but basically mediocre titles—*The Mummy's Ghost, Captive Wild Woman, House of Frankenstein* and *House of Dracula*—probably represent his best work in the field. (Carradine gave a a particularly restrained and sensible performance as the tormented strangler in director Edgar Ulmer's 1944 *Bluebeard,* a stylish cheapie which falls just short of being a horror film.)

Despite its shortcomings, *The Mummy's Ghost* shapes up as one of Universal's better B's from this era of decline. By imbuing Kharis with some tragic qualities, new dimensions were added to the spavined series, and the road for a final sequel, 1944's *The Mummy's Curse,* was neatly paved.

Ghost Catchers (1944)

Released June 16, 1944. 67 minutes. *Written and Produced by* Edmund L. Hartmann. *Directed by* Eddie Cline. *Based on the story "High Spirits" by* Milt Gross & Eddie Cline. *Director of Photography:* Charles Van Enger. *Musical Director:* Edward Ward. *Musical Numbers Devised & Staged by* Louis DePron. *Songs:* "Blue Candlelight," "Three Cheers for the Customer," "Quoth the Raven" (*by* Paul F. Webster & Harry Revel), "I'm Old Enough to Dream" (*by* Everett Carter & Edward Ward). *Art Directors:* John B. Goodman & Richard H. Riedel. *Director of Sound:* Bernard B. Brown. *Technician:* Joe Lapis. *Set Decorators:* Russell A. Gausman & Andrew J. Gilmore. *Film Editor:* Arthur Hilton. *Gowns by* Vera West. *Assistant Director:* Howard Christie. *Special Photography:* John P. Fulton.

Ole Olsen (Himself), Chic Johnson (Himself), Gloria Jean (Melinda Marshall), Martha O'Driscoll (Susanna Marshall), Leo Carrillo (Jerry), Andy Devine (Horsehead), Lon Chaney (Bear), Kirby Grant (Clay Edwards), Walter Catlett (Colonel Marshall), Ella Mae Morse (Virginia Bennett), Morton Downey (Himself), Henry Armetta (Signatelli), Walter Kingsford (Chambers), Tom Dugan (Brick-Layer), Edgar Dearing (Police Sergeant), Ralph Peters, Wee Willie Davis, Frank Mitchell, Sammy Stein, Tor Johnson (Mugs), Mel Torme (Drum Player), Leonard Sues (Trumpet Player), Al Mirkin, Harry Monty (Midgets), Mary Louise Houk, Marie E. Wagner, Cornelia Bona, Miriam R. Lickert (Four Harpists), Christine Forsyth (Tired Blonde), Armando & Lita (Specialty), Barbara Blain, Bill Alcorn, Genevieve Grazis, John Duncan, Venia Archer, Johnny Archer, Betty Story, Don L. Gallaher, June Williams, Jerry Warren, Jean Davis, Bobby Scheerer, Bill Raymond, Joy Vahl, Betty Marie, Tim Taylor, Sheila Roberts, Gil Dennis, Patty Lacey, Nancy Marlowe, Jack Arkin, Jean Marlowe, Mike Termini, Lennie Smith, Marion Musso, Nickie Reed, Alice Scott, Barbara Hall, Mike Musso, Walter Lee Doerr, Laurie Sherman (Jitterbugs), Jack Norton (Wilbur Duffington), Larry Steers (Man), Ken Brocker, Perc Launders (Cops), Bess Flowers (Woman), Forrest Taylor (Passerby), Alec Craig (Diggs), Edward Earle (Ticket Seller), Buddy Wilkerson (Man), Cy Ring (Man in Tuxedo), Carey Harrison (Man), Billy Curtis (Midget), Lee Bennett (Man), Isabelle LaMal (Woman), Belle Mitchell (Mrs. Signatelli), Robin Raymond (Gag Specialty), Kay Harding, Joe Kirk, Irene Thomas (Bits).

At a time when the War Production Board was exhorting the Hollywood studios to conserve in all phases of production, *Ghost Catchers* represents a flagrant waste of 67 minutes of film stock. The film is just another noisy

Universal attempt to wring laughter and box office bucks out of a combination of low comedy and haunted house hijinks—but the film fails on every count.

At the head of the cast, and the root of the problem, are Ole Olsen and Chic Johnson, vaudeville buffoons who teamed in 1914 and enjoyed a long career on stage, in radio and (sporadically) in Hollywood films. Olsen and Johnson were never a hit with the critics, but their bizarre antics caught the fancy of audiences, especially in the sticks, and the two men remained a team with never a thought of splitting, right up until Johnson's death in '62.

It's hard to knock a comedy team that collaborated successfully for almost half a century, starred in one of Broadway's longest-running shows ("Hellzapoppin'") and still retains a small following of comedy fans today. But to the uninitiated viewer who innocently stumbles upon a mindless pile of debris like *Ghost Catchers,* the Olsen and Johnson schtick is painful and pathetic. Their forte was wild sight gags, hoary jokes and puns and what film historian Leonard Maltin lovingly calls "a flair for the ridiculous that has never been duplicated." Time, however, has passed Olsen and Johnson by: there's no longer any humor in stumpy, middle-aged loudmouths in women's clothes or zoot suits, no pleasure left in the dreamworld plots left over from their surrealistic vaudeville pastiches. Fans of Olsen and Johnson complain about the big band musical numbers and mundane romantic subplots which bog down their pictures, but these added plot elements represent a welcome respite from O & J's high-volume antics, their prehistoric gags and their obnoxious predilection for howling at each other's jokes. Universal lost interest in these two after their fourth film for the studio (1945's *See My Lawyer*) and sent them packing. Like the Ritz Brothers, who walked out on Universal the year before, Olsen and Johnson never worked in pictures again.

Colonel Marshall (Walter Catlett), a pauper still posing as the moneyed Southern gentleman he once was, brings his daughters Melinda (Gloria Jean) and Susanna (Martha O'Driscoll) to New York to make their Carnegie Hall concert debut. The trio move into a Manhattan brownstone, but Chambers (Walter Kingsford), the lawyer who leases them the property, and Diggs (Alec Craig), the cleaning man, fail to mention that it's haunted. Strange nocturnal noises awaken the Marshalls, and Susanna runs next door to find help. The neighboring house, unfortunately for her (and for us), is the Olsen and Johnson nightclub, a three-ring madhouse. Susanna is seized by headwaiter Jerry (Leo Carrillo) and other stooges, strapped into an "electric chair" and forced to watch the "fun": acrobats flinging themselves around, Olsen throwing knives at Johnson (who's in drag), the chefs marching around like a parade, and songstress Virginia Bennett (Ella Mae Morse) belting out "Three Cheers for the Customer." Susanna has departed (through a trap door) before O & J realize that the girl may have been in real trouble, and the pair hurries next door to investigate. Grateful for company—even Olsen and Johnson's—the Marshalls offer to put them up for the night, and Ole and Chic retire to their room. They are undressed by invisible hands and spun like tops by a supernatural force which now dresses them in pajamas; neither one of them realizes that anything unusual is happening until they're both in bed, at which point they sit up and scream. Tee-hee.

Colonel Marshall wants to break the lease and move out but Chambers insists that they live up to their signed agreement. Chambers reveals that the ghost is that of Wilbur Duffiington, a millionaire who plummeted from a third-story window during a turn-of-the-century New Year's Eve bash; Wilbur haunts the house because he never got to enjoy his own party. Olsen and Johnson hope to satisfy and exorcise Wilbur's ghost by throwing a new party with Wilbur as the guest of honor. The festivities degenerate into the usual Olsen and Johnson brawl with raucous music and jitterbugs dancing up and down the stairs and through the entire house. Toting a white flag, the invisible Wilbur pinches Melinda's behind and leaves. Ho, ho, ho.

Susanna is sweet on bandleader Clay Edwards (Kirby Grant), but bitchy Virginia is also mildly attached to him and doesn't want to let go. Even though the house has been exorcised, Melina and the Colonel are seized and abducted in a mysterious fashion, and Susanna finds the body of the cleaning man in a closet. Olsen and Johnson investigate and find a bizarre assortment of idiots overrunning the house: midgets dressed as Santa Claus, a guy wearing a horse costume (Andy Devine), another one dressed as a bear (Lon Chaney), and a motley collection of gangster-types. It turns out that there's a secret cellar full of valuable pre–Prohibition era liquor, and these crooks have dressed up in their Halloween best in order to scare off the Marshalls and steal the hootch. Olsen and Johnson are temporarily mistaken for gangsters and ordered to pitch in and help move the stuff out, but eventually the real gangsters catch on and a chase ensues. Olsen (or Johnson, who gives a damn?) puts on Devine's horsehead and pretends he's dead while the other jerk bemoans the demise of his horse; the assembled gangsters become weepy as they watch this scene in solemn silence. O & J are almost able to get away using this ruse, but one of the brighter gangsters finally catches on ("Wait a minute—he ain't no horse!"). Ha ha ha.

Chic and Ole are caught and walled up, "Cask of Amontillado"–style, together with Melinda and the Colonel. Luckily the ghost of Wilbur (Jack Norton) appears and gives them the idea to break through a wall into the basement of their own next-door nightclub. Johnson (or Olsen, who gives a damn?) just happens to have a pick, an ax and a jackhammer on his person, and they use the tools to escape. After a series of chases and brawls, the gangsters are apprehended along with their secret leader, who turns out to be Jerry, the headwaiter. The Melinda-Susanna Carnegie Hall concert is cancelled because only one ticket was sold, so they put on their show at the O & J nightclub and are a hit.

Olsen and Johnson buffs give *Ghost Catchers* high marks; Leonard Maltin, who is clearly a fan, wrote that it comes closer to O & J's original conception of insane humor than any of their other films. But even the most open-minded newcomer to the film will probably have trouble finding the qualities that made the comedians such favorites on the vaudeville circuit and in corny movies. The two men don't have a "funny" or even a distinctive look to them, there's never any attempt at characterization, and their material is older than they are themselves.

The free-wheeling, anything-goes atmosphere doesn't help any, since bad jokes and insulting sight gags don't improve with extra volume or with speedier delivery. And the surreal touches which Olsen and Johnson brought to their Universal films aren't offbeat enough to be humorous: it's stupid, not inspired, when the men walk through an exploding wall into crooked lawyer Walter Kingsford's office, or when they start pulling pickaxes and jackhammers out of their pockets. There's no rhyme or reason in any of the Olsen and Johnson shenanigans, and like all the rest, *Ghost Catchers* just deteriorates into self-indulgent slapstick tomfoolery.

"They weren't funny," smirks Reginald LeBorg, who worked as a second-unit director on the first Universal O & J outing, *Hellzapoppin'* (1941). "They were not as good as Abbott and Costello, they were not even as good as the Bowery Boys—at least the Bowery Boys had some élan, and there was some characterization! These guys were like the Three Stooges, they were just stupid."

As poor as *Ghost Catchers* is in the comedy department, it falls even flatter in the area of thrills-and-chills. The film is slightly unique in that the ghost is a real one (haunted house comedies usually wind up with the supernatural menaces explained away), but this ghost is one of the least interesting spooks ever to turn up in a motion picture. The spirt of Wilbur Duffington, a silly playboy with a passion for plum brandy and soft-shoe dancing, he remains invisible nearly all of the time; about all he ever does is pinch Gloria Jean's derrière and leave senseless messages on the walls. Simple special effects (floating props) indicate the apparition's unseen presence throughout most of the film, although toward the end he does make a brief appearance in the person of Jack Norton, the repellent one-note actor who made a sorry career out of playing drunks. Wilbur is never a threat, just a nuisance; the film's one killing is committed by the "gangster-ghosts," and it takes place off-screen.

A good supporting cast is squandered. Gloria Jean and Martha O'Driscoll are pleasant and easy on the eyes, and up-and-coming Kirby Grant, who plays the romantic interest, is agreeable but has nothing to do in the film. Andy Devine and Lon Chaney are utterly wasted (Chaney plays his small role straight, despite the ignominy of a bear costume, while Devine plays his usual dolt). Leo Carrillo, who is seen as Olsen and Johnson's headwaiter, doesn't get much more than a minute's worth of footage in the entire film; you don't suspect that he's the mystery killer because you've forgotten that he's even in the picture! In his "monster" scenes Carrillo wears a mask which is either a duplicate of the Chaney Kharis mask or which is indeed an actual Kharis mask, cut up for the occasion. Tor Johnson, kitschy horror star of '50s low-budgeters, has a bit part as one of the mugs, Mel Torme is a drum player in the nightclub orchestra and Kay Harding, a Universal starlet-in-the-making, also has a bit part. Morton Downey, father of television's acerbic talk-show ringmaster, is an attraction at the O & J nightclub, singing in a distressingly high voice.

The late Jerry Warren, later the producer/director of such schlocky films as *The Incredible Petrified World* (1960) and *The Wild World of Batwoman* (1966), also appears very briefly in *Ghost Catchers,* as one of the jitterbugs. . . or does he? When we interviewed Warren in 1984, he was touchy on the subject of his age; he wanted us to believe that he was 21 years old in the mid–50s when he turned out his first picture, *Man Beast*. But he made the mistake of telling us that he started out in the business as a bit player "a short time" prior to that. We had spotted the name Jerry Warren on a *Ghost Catchers* castlist, and we asked him if that was him. "Was that at Universal?" he asked; we told him it was. "Olsen and Johnson, right?"; right. "I danced in that, didn't I?"; "Yeah, you played a jitterbug." "Right, right! Say, what year was that?"; we told him it was 1944. The year seemed to stun him; he shook his head and told us with a straight face, "Then, no, that couldn't have been me." The interview moved ahead, but after that it was tough for *us* to keep a straight face.

Diana Barrymore was originally pencilled in for the role of Susanna, but she felt it was beneath the dignity of a Barrymore to appear in a burlesque like *Ghost Catchers* and refused the role. This killed her Universal contract, and the studio probably couldn't have been happier: the effects of alcohol were already showing up so badly on the 23-year-old actress' face that even makeup failed to hide it.

The only mildly interesting moment in the film comes early on, as Olsen and Johnson are preparing for bed in the haunted brownstone. Olsen asks, "Remember Abbott and Costel*la* [sic] in *Hold That Ghost*? The whole thing turned out to be gangsters." Their clothes are being yanked off them by the unseen Wilbur as they talk casually about the earlier A & C film and how preposterous it was; when the famous "moving candle" routine is mentioned, their candle begins to slide back and forth across a table. The scene isn't good, and it certainly isn't funny, but hearing Olsen and Johnson talk about Abbott and Costello does make for an unusual in-joke moment that sticks in the mind after everything else about *Ghost Catchers* has faded from memory. (The same cartoon is run behind the opening credits of both *Hold That Ghost* and *Ghost Catchers*.)

Ghost Catchers began shooting (under the title *High Spirits*) on February 22, 1944, and wrapped up at the end of March. There are no evidences of this extravagant 32-day shooting schedule in the film itself; from a production or technical standpoint it looks no better than the 10-day Universals from this same period. (According to Universal expert Michael Fitzgerald, several musical numbers were filmed and later cut from the picture, which would at least partially explain the longish shooting schedule.) At 67 minutes it's no longer than the average Universal quickie, although director Eddie Cline, a former Keystone Cop whose best directing days were behind him, manages at least to make it seem longer.

Ghost Catchers has always been an idiot's delight for the dyed-in-the-wool Olsen and Johnson aficionados, but for the horror fan looking for some haunted house fun, there isn't a laugh or a thrill in the whole unpalatable affair.

The Pearl of Death (1944)

Released September 22, 1944. 68 minutes. *Produced and Directed by* Roy William Neill. *Screenplay by* Bertram Millhauser. *Based on the short story "The Adventure of the Six Napoleons" by* Sir Arthur Conan Doyle. *Director of Photography:* Virgil Miller. *Musical Director:* Paul Sawtell. *Art Directors:* John B. Goodman & Martin Obzina. *Director of Sound:* Bernard B. Brown. *Technician:* Joe Lapis. *Set Decorations:* Russell A. Gausman & Edward R. Robinson. *Film Editor:* Ray Snyder. *Gowns by* Vera West. *Dialogue Director:* Ray Kessler.

Basil Rathbone (Sherlock Holmes), Nigel Bruce (Dr. John H. Watson), Dennis Hoey (Inspector Lestrade), Evelyn Ankers (Naomi Drake), Miles Mander (Giles Conover), Ian Wolfe (Amos Hodder), Charles Francis (Francis Digby), Holmes Herbert (James Goodram), Richard Nugent (Bates), Mary Gordon (Mrs. Hudson), Rondo Hatton (The Hoxton Creeper), J. Welsh Austin (Sgt. Bleeker), Connie Leon (Ellen Carey), Charles Knight (Bearded Man), Al Ferguson, Colin Kelly (Guards), Audrey Manners (Teacher), Billy Bevan (Constable), Lillian Bronson (Housekeeper), Leslie Denison (Constable Murdock), John Merkyl (Dr. Julian Boncourt), Harry Cording (George Gelder), Eric Wilton (Chauffeur), Harold DeBecker (Boss), Arthur Mulliner (Thomas Sandeford), Wilson Benge, Arthur Stenning (Stewards), Leland [Leyland] Hodgson (Customs Officer), Diana Beresford (Bit Woman).

While the quality of Universal's horror films was deteriorating, the studio's Sherlock Holmes series enjoyed its best year in 1944. The May release of *The Scarlet Claw* marked the high point for the popular and profitable series, but September's *The Pearl of Death* follows close behind; in fact, some Holmes buffs prefer *Pearl* to *Scarlet*. Howard Benedict, executive producer of the series, rates *Pearl* as his personal favorite, and the *Hollywood Reporter* reviewer called it "an easy topper" for the group.

The film opens aboard the boat to Dover. James Goodram (Holmes Herbert), a museum agent entrusted with the task of delivering the Borgia Pearl (value: £50,000) to the Royal Regent Museum, is lured out of his stateroom with the false news of an urgent message. Nefarious Naomi Drake (Evelyn Ankers) seizes the opportunity to break into the stateroom and steal the pearl, which she conceals inside a camera. Fearing that customs agents in Dover will discover the hidden gem, she dupes an elderly clergyman into carrying the camera ashore for her, and retrieves it from him later. Naomi presents the camera to her boss, international criminal Giles Conover (Miles Mander), who opens it and discovers only a note. The clergyman was Sherlock Holmes in disguise, and the note informs Conover that the pearl has been safely recovered by the famous detective.

The Borgia Pearl is placed on display in the Royal Museum, but Holmes fears for its safety with Conover on the loose. Museum curator Digby (Charles Francis) smugly explains that the pearl cannot be removed from its case without triggering alarm bells and activating steel shutters that would trap the would-be thief, but Holmes (Basil Rathbone) perceives a flaw in museum security: he secretly cuts off the electricity, demonstrating that the pearl can be stolen. Conover, disguised as a workman, has overheard the conversation, filches the pearl from its deactivated case and escapes through a window. Conover is apprehended after a chase, but the master criminal no longer has the jewel. Conover is released for lack of evidence. Holmes is nearly discredited for his unwitting part in the affair, and determines to retrieve the Borgia Pearl.

A series of broken-back murders begins, with each victim found dead in their home amidst a litter of smashed plaster and china; since Conover's right-hand man in murder has always been the spine-snapping Hoxton Creeper, Holmes is convinced that the killings are tied in with the theft of the pearl. The bodies pile up as Holmes continues his investigation; Conover even makes two attempts on Holmes' life.

Through an examination of shattered bric-a-brac taken from all the murder houses, Holmes eventually deduces that the object common to all the killings is a plaster bust of Napoleon; further inquiry leads him to the manufacturer, whose workshop is near the Royal Museum. Holmes figures out that, during his flight from the Museum, Conover dashed into the plasterer's shop and inserted the pearl into one of six still-wet plaster Napoleons; Conover and the Creeper are now tracking down the people who bought the busts in order to find the one that houses the pearl. (The extra breakage conceals the true object of their search.) At the art shop of Amos Hodder (Ian Wolfe), Holmes learns the address of Dr. Boncourt, the sixth and final customer; Naomi, who has infiltrated the shop, also finds this information and passes it along to Conover before Holmes spots and apprehends her.

Conover and the Creeper (Rondo Hatton) drive to Boncourt's and break in, but Holmes has beaten them there and disguised himself as the physician. Conover gets the upper hand in a struggle with Holmes, and holds him at gunpoint while the Creeper searches the house for the bust. In a voice loud enough to be overheard by the Creeper, quick-thinking Holmes tells Conover that Naomi has been arrested and will be hanged; the Creeper, who worships the girl, goes berserk and kills Conover. Holmes is then forced to shoot and kill the monster. As Lestrade and his men arrive at the scene, Holmes smashes open the last of the six Napoleons and finds the Borgia Pearl safely inside.

The Pearl of Death is a model example of the B Sherlock Holmes unit working at peak efficiency. Bertram Millhauser's screenplay (loosely based on Conan Doyle's "The Adventure of the Six Napoleons") is an ingenious blend of mystery and horror, and director Roy William Neill succeeds in extracting the full measure of suspense from Millhauser's work. Rathbone and Bruce are also in top form, perhaps at their best, in this film, with excellent support from Miles Mander, Evelyn Ankers and series regular Dennis Hoey.

The Hoxton Creeper (Rondo Hatton) puts the squeeze on Giles Conover (Miles Mander) in the suspenseful climax of *The Pearl of Death*.

Failing to fall prey to the usual movie cliches, Giles Conover comes across as a unique and offbeat Holmes antagonist: seedy and perverse, he's a criminal with none of the silky charm or Machiavellian cunning that generally mark the Baker Street detective's big-brained arch-nemeses. The only problem with Conover is that Holmes gives him perhaps too big a buildup. In an early dialogue scene, Holmes tells Watson that Conover "pervades England like a plague. No one had heard of him. That's what puts him on the pinnacle in the records of crime." Later he adds, "If I could free society of this sinister creature, I should feel that my own career had reached its summit."

But none of Conover's superior qualities are really on display in *The Pearl of Death;* he operates like a small-timer with aspirations toward grandeur. He takes on menial jobs that a Moriarity would leave to confederates, needs Holmes' unwitting help to steal the pearl, and never sees the easy way to do anything (he has Naomi take a job in an art shop so that she can break two Napoleons he should have just walked in and bought).

But it's Conover's foibles, and his sordid side, that make him an interesting, lifelike villain. Between the unsavory dialogue descriptions and Miles Mander's fine performance, we get the distinct impression that *The Pearl of Death* scarcely scratches the surface of this slippery sadist. (Instead of making time with lovely Naomi, who looks to be more than willing, he chooses instead to taunt her with news of the Creeper, whose company he seems to prefer; this unhealthy situation brings all sorts of new possibilities to mind!) Mander was probably a sweetheart of a guy in real life but he's got that seedy, debauched look that probably lost him a lot of babysitting jobs in his day.

Miles Mander actually led the sort of colorful life that sounds like a Hollywood publicist's wacky concoction: New Zealand sheep rancher, auto racer, pioneer aviator, novelist and playwright, prizefight promoter, radio news commentator, owner of British movie studios, film actor, writer and director. The son of an affluent varnish manufacturer in Staffordshire, England, Mander had a knack for getting kicked out of school and a genius for going broke. Early on, the young and wealthy Mander pursued his horse racing and auto racing enthusiasms (in 1910 he set the Monte Carlo–Nice racing record and reached the finals for the Prix at Paris) before losing all his money and joining the Army. Later on he formed several of his own motion picture firms but they all eventually collapsed despite the fact that he turned out the most successful of all British silent films, 1928's *The First Born,* which he produced, directed, acted in and cowrote (based on his own novel and play!).

Mander had also produced a number of talking short features in 1925, and is credited with discovering screen stars Merle Oberon and Madeleine Carroll. Apart from the films he wrote, produced or directed, and apart from the Swedish, German, Danish, Italian and French films in which he appeared in the late '20s, he also turns up in British pictures like Hitchcock's *The Pleasure Garden* (1926) and *Murder* (1930), as well as *The Private Life of Henry VIII* (1933). After campaigning unsuccessfully for a seat in Parliament in 1934, he gravitated to Hollywood where he played a long string of character parts in costume pictures and historical epics. Dead in Hollywood of a heart ailment in February, 1946, the 57-year-old actor left a will that read in part, "I wish to take this last opportunity to express my gratitude to the American people and their Government for permitting me to spend the last years of my life in their marvelous country, enjoying the American way of life."

Rathbone and Bruce are in rare form in *The Pearl of Death,* thanks to a good, dramatic story that puts Holmes' reputation in danger. Implicated by the London press in the Borgia Pearl theft, Rathbone's Holmes seems more harried and intense, and takes out quite a bit of his frustration on poor Lestrade; it's an interesting bit of character development, seeing Holmes with a new, frazzled attitude now that it's *his* ass that's in the sling. Nigel Bruce is also somewhat more serious and generally helpful in this entry, although there are of course the expected comedy relief moments for the bumbling Watson. (Rathbone pulled down $20,000 for appearing in *Pearl,* Bruce $12,000.) Dennis Hoey gets a bigger than usual part, and enjoys several of the film's funnier bits.

As usual, disguises and false identities play a large part in *Pearl,* with Rathbone, Mander and Evelyn Ankers donning a variety of facial makeups and silly outfits. Rathbone's tend to be transparent this time around: the series had reached a point where, whenever a new character concealed his face from the camera, a savvy audience knew immediately that it had to be Holmes in disguise. Holmes' impersonation of a clergyman on the Dover boat is particularly ineffective. The character keeps his face in darkness, skulks mysteriously about and speaks in a dubbed voice; he looks more like The Shadow than a clergyman, and we know instantly that there's something fishy about this guy. Mander fares somewhat better impersonating a museum workman and an elderly, nearsighted visitor to Holmes' Baker Street digs. Ankers spends so much of her screen time imitating others (a tourist, a dishwasher, a match girl, a prim shop clerk) that we really never get to see her as Naomi Drake.

Making his Universal horror film debut in *The Pearl of Death* is Rondo Hatton, the real-life victim of acromegaly, playing Mander's strong-arm man. Universal saw horror movie star potential in Hatton, but apparently not enough to give him the sort of buildup he really needed. Hatton was not a Titan of Terror, like Karloff or Lugosi, or a Master of Menace like Chaney, Jr.; he wasn't even on a level with Elizabeth Russell, the Houri of Horror, or Acquanetta, the Venezuelan Volcano. A lowly Glutton of Glands, Hatton remained a minor-league player, added to the Universal lineup at the bottom of the horror cycle's final inning. As a starring or featured actor he went to bat four times for the studio after his introduction in *The Pearl of Death,* and went down swinging every time. Hatton was a formidable physical presence, and in the right vehicle, like *Pearl,* he could be an imposing asset to the picture. Universal felt that Hatton would catch the public's fancy, and plug-ugly roles for the one-time bit player were written into desultory pictures like *The Jungle Captive* and *The Spider Woman Strikes Back.* It might not have been dignified work but at least it eventually paid well: Hatton's paychecks grew, from the $408.35 he raked in for his work on *Pearl* to the $3,500 he earned for starring in 1946's *The Brute Man* (he was that film's highest-salaried player).

Suspense builds nicely around Hatton's Creeper character in *The Pearl of Death.* Early dialogue references to the back-breaking killer whet our curiosity ("A monster... with the chest of a buffalo and the arms of a gorilla"); later we get short glimpses of the Creeper in silhouette or in shadow. Swaying side-to-side in an apelike fashion, the character seems more monstrous than human; there's no mention of his facial deformity at all, making the first close-up of Hatton (in Boncourt's foyer, at the very end of the film) a genuine eye-opener. The Breen Office recommended that Holmes only shoot the Creeper once, but a unique and terrifying menace like Hatton deserved more than just a single bullet; ignoring the censors' mandate, Holmes plugs him three times. The Breen Office additionally suggested the removal of a scene of Evelyn Ankers (as the dishwasher) kicking her boss in the groin after he has slapped her.

Composer Paul Sawtell wrote one of his very best film scores for *The Pearl of Death;* the score is at its most effective in the last scene, mounting to a chilling crescendo as the Creeper stalks an uncharacteristically panicked Holmes. Other technical credits are on an equally high level, particularly Virgil Miller's cinematography and Ray Snyder's tight, crisp editing.

Wrapping up two days over its three-week schedule (April 11–May 1, 1944), *The Pearl of Death* is a gem of a B mystery. Roy William Neill's direction is strong on pace, and he makes the most of a script that mixes up a good balance of action, humor and low-key horror atmosphere. Almost *noir*ish in spots, the film boasts three colorful villains for the price of one and provides a fine debut vehicle for Rondo Hatton's Creeper character. Suspense-filled and excitingly mounted, *The Pearl of Death* is at or near the apex of Universal's Sherlock Holmes series.

The Climax (1944)

Released October 20, 1944. 86 minutes. Filmed in Technicolor. *Executive Producer:* Joseph Gershenson. *Produced & Directed by* George Waggner. *Screenplay by* Curt Siodmak & Lynn Starling. *Adapted by* Curt Siodmak *from the play by* Edward J. Locke. *Directors of Photography:* Hal Mohr & W. Howard Greene. *Technicolor Color Director:* Natalie Kalmus. *Associate:* William Fritzsche. *Musical Score & Direction:* Edward Ward. *Librettos:* George Waggner. *Operettas Staged by* Lester Horton. *Vocal Direction:* William Tyroler. *Orchestration:* Harold Zweifel. *Art Directors:* John B. Goodman & Alexander Golitzen. *Director of Sound:* Bernard B. Brown. *Technician:* William Fox. *Set Decorators:* Russell A. Gausman & Ira S. Webb. *Film Editor:* Russell Schoengarth. *Dialogue Director:* Gene Lewis. *Makeup by* Jack P. Pierce. *Costumes by* Vera West. *Assistant Directors:* Charles S. Gould & Harry O. Jones. *Special Effects:* John P. Fulton.

Boris Karloff (Dr. Fredrick Hohner), Susanna Foster (Angela Klatt), Turhan Bey (Franz Munzer), Gale Sondergaard (Luise), Thomas Gomez (Count Seebruck), June Vincent (Marcellina), George Dolenz (Amato Roselli), Ludwig Stossel (Carl Bauman), Jane Farrar (Jarmila Vadek), Erno Verebes (Brunn), Lotte Stein (Mama Hinzl), Scotty Beckett (King), William Edmunds (Leon), Maxwell Hayes (King's Aide), Dorothy Lawrence (Miss Metzger), Cyril Delevanti (Sweeper), Rex Lease, George Eldredge (Reporters), Roy Darmour (Secretary), Polly Bailey (Cleaning Woman), Ernie Adams (Old Man), Genevieve Bell (Dowager), Francis Ford (Man), Grace Cunard, Maurice Costello, William Desmond, Stuart Holmes, Eddie Polo, Jack Richardson, Ann Cornwall, Harry Mayo, Gertrude Astor, Helen Gibson, Fred Curtis, Homer Dickerson, Barry Regan (Bits).

With *Phantom of the Opera* cleaning up at box offices nationwide and well on its way to becoming one of Universal's top grossers, it was inevitable that the studio would plan a sequel. In August, 1943, while *Phantom* was still in general release, Universal announced its intention to film a *Phantom* follow-up which would be the most expensive picture on their 1943–4 schedule. The new film would team Nelson Eddy and Susanna Foster under the supervision of *Phantom* producer George Waggner.

By November, however, Universal's plans had been overhauled. *The Climax* would no longer be a sequel to *Phantom* (even though it would reunite Waggner, Foster and now *Phantom* director Arthur Lubin) but would be based on the 1909 Edward Locke play "The Climax." (Why the *Phantom* sequel had the title of the Locke play practically from the first day of planning is not clear;

perhaps the initial idea was to shoehorn the Phantom character into Locke's story.) Locke's play, previously filmed by Universal in 1930, underwent a change in setting, with the story now taking place in an opera house in 1870s Vienna. At this point George Waggner had hopes of adding Claude Rains to his cast, but ultimately it was Boris Karloff who took the top spot. More reverses lay ahead: in January, 1944, a last-minute change in starting dates caused Arthur Lubin to be diverted to another project, and producer Waggner now took on the added responsibilities of director.

Scheduled for a 47-day shoot, *The Climax* commenced on Friday, January 28, with three days' preproduction activity on the Phantom Stage and on Stages 14 and 21; cameras rolled for the first time on Tuesday, February 1 on the Phantom Stage. At 11:10 on the evening of April 1, at the end of a long 14-hour day for players Foster and Turhan Bey, production wrapped up on *The Climax,* which had run six days over schedule. A dour Arthur Lubin remembers the project well: "It was the picture that finished off George Waggner's career."

Somber Dr. Fredrick Hohner (Boris Karloff), resident physician at the Royal Theatre, carries a dark secret. Ten years before, Hohner strangled his sweetheart, young opera star Marcellina (June Vincent), because her voice and the success of her starring vehicle "The Magic Voice" had come between them. In an upstairs room of his palatial home, Hohner has built a shrine around the embalmed body of his former love.

Music student Angela Klatt (Susanna Foster) and her fiancé Franz Munzer (Turhan Bey) are rehearsing "The Magic Voice" in the Royal Theatre's music library when Angela's golden voice is overheard by Hohner and Count Seebruck (Thomas Gomez), the theatre impresario. Hohner is outraged that Angela should give voice to this "sacred" music, but Seebruck is impressed by her talent and offers her a singing role in the theatre's current production. Angela is a smash and Seebruck now plans to revive "The Magic Voice" as a vehicle for the pretty newcomer.

The mad Hohner is determined to thwart Seebruck's plan. He lures Angela to his home under false pretenses, then hypnotizes the girl and plants in her mind the notion that she will never again wish to sing. Hohner also makes her a present of an atomizer which will remind the girl, even in her posthypnotic state, of his control.

Count Seebruck gathers members of the press at the Royal Theatre to announce his plans for Angela. When Angela attempts to sing an aria for the assembled party, she is helpless but to obey the subconscious command Hohner planted in her mind: her voice breaks and the mystified girl rushes to her dressing room in tears. Plans for the revival of "The Magic Voice" progress but Seebruck now intends to star Jarmila (Jane Farrar), a bitchy prima donna, in the production.

Hohner insists that Angela requires professional care and convinces the girl to stay in his home, where the hypnosis treatments secretly continue. Hohner's housekeeper Luise (Gale Sondergaard), once a maid and friend to Marcellina, works for Hohner because she is convinced that someday she will find evidence that links him to Marcellina's "disappearance." (You would think

SUSANNA
FOSTER
Sensation of "Phantom of the Opera"!
TURHAN
BEY
Romantic Hit of "Dragon Seed"!
BORIS
KARLOFF
Great star of "Arsenic and Old Lace"!
The Screen's Classic of Suspense!
the CLIMAX
IN TECHNICOLOR!
with
GALE SONDERGAARD
JUNE VINCENT THOMAS GOMEZ
GEORGE DOLENZ JANE FARRAR

Universal sought to repeat the box office success of *Phantom of the Opera* with a dull, over-produced melodrama that many critics redubbed *The Anticlimax*. Notice Karloff's ignominious third billing.

that, after ten years of working under Hohner's roof with this in mind, she should have found the shrine by now!) Luise tricks Hohner into leaving the house, which gives Franz an opening to rush in and carry Angela off to safety.

Franz feels that if Angela has an opportunity to sing "The Magic Voice" in front of a live audience, she will be cured of her mysterious malady. Seebruck balks at the notion, but Franz and his uncle Carl (Ludwig Stossel) are able to convince the country's boy-king (Scotty Beckett) to command a performance. On opening night, Angela is apprehensive about the coming performance until Franz smashes the atomizer, which releases the girl from Hohner's spell. Hohner abducts Angela and spirits her away to his house, where he is preparing to slit her vocal cords when Franz and Carl arrive on the scene; Franz rushes her back to the theatre while Carl holds Hohner at gunpoint. Angela appears on stage and, after a false start, finds her voice and her confidence once again.

Back at Hohner's, the mad sawbones clubs Carl and rushes upstairs to the shrine just as police arrive at the house. Hohner accidentally knocks over a flaming brazier which sets fire to the room's curtains, and Hohner perishes in flames.

It's difficult, in dissecting a

hopeless muddle of a picture like *The Climax,* to figure out just where to start. *The Climax* is some poor fool of a Hollywood executive's idea of a work of art with its gaslit sets, gaudy costumes, stiff acting and long stretches of pseudoclassical music. Clearly George Waggner's intent was to create a plushy, "artful" costume melodrama with an added accent on classy operatic themes. Actually, it is only a case of costume jewelry posing as the real thing. It comes no closer to art than a 60-minute horse opera.

The Climax has all of the weaknesses and none of the virtues of *Phantom of the Opera.* Here again, as in *Phantom,* the horror elements which ought to be the main thrust of the film are subordinated. The plot pivots around a young soprano and her boyfriend while the menace is reduced to a secondary character. Splashy, protracted musical interludes break up the picture and dilute the suspense. Nearly everything that could possibly be wrong with this sort of picture afflicts *The Climax,* seemingly beyond the laws of chance.

The film's "horrific" moments, few in number, are appallingly tame. Dr. Hohner sweeps Marcellina off her feet and strangles her (offscreen, with one hand) in a matter of only a few seconds; never once does the gloomy expression on his face change. His frequent references to the dead diva are tiresome, and he begins to sound like a broken record. Ominous musical chords greet every appearance of the dreaded atomizer, but the effect is comical. Hohner's "attack" on Luise is especially badly written and staged. The woman calls him a murderer, promising to call the police, but foolishly stands her ground as he advances menacingly toward her; her face takes on a look of mild surprise when he reaches out and squeezes her throat.

Probably intended as the horror highlights of the film are the short scenes set in Hohner's shrine to Marcellina (called the Blue Beard Room in a set construction memo). Here in a canopied bed lies the embalmed (stuffed?) body of Marcellina, untouched by decay despite the passage of years; there's just a hint of necrophilia here, although no objections were raised by the Breen Office puritans. Breen did object (in a letter dated January 4, 1944) to an early script's implication that Hohner commits suicide by throwing himself upon Marcellina's burning bier, and Universal accepted his suggestion that Hohner attempt to escape before collapsing onto the bed. (The fiery finish is a lazy copout, although one disgruntled critic pointed out that the scene illuminates a movie theater nicely and permits a smart viewer to leave ahead of the crowd!)

The musical score is as undistinguished as the film's half-hearted horror highlights. George Waggner and his frequent collaborator Edward Ward worked with a variety of popular themes based on Chopin and Schubert, adding their own original lyrics and operatic arrangements. The result is not grand opera but low-grade operetta, with silly lyrics, foolish costumes and garish, highly-colored sets.

Karloff gives the sort of cool, distant performance which makes it clear that he considered the film beneath him. Although the actor's fans don't care to admit it, it's fairly obvious from watching films like *The Climax, House of Frankenstein, Voodoo Island* (1957), *Frankenstein 1970* (1958), etc., that Karloff had adopted a take-the-money-and-run policy when it came to lesser assignments, and brought to these potboilers none of the enthusiasm or on-screen professionalism he now saved for "better" projects. Edward Bernds, who worked as a sound man on some of Karloff's early starring vehicles at Columbia, got a firsthand look at "both" Karloffs:

> Because of Karloff's standing, [director] Roy William Neill had a pretty decent budget and schedule on *The Black Room* [1935], and Roy took real pains with the picture. He didn't have to work long hours to meet a quickie schedule and I believe the film turned out well. I had the feeling that Neill and Karloff had a lot of respect for one another, and Karloff seemed well-satisfied with the film and his performance in it. That certainly wasn't true of some other films he made for Columbia with other directors. Karloff on them was more aloof and seemed a lot less happy with the material.

Karloff plumbs new depths of detachment in *The Climax,* turning in a grim, poker-faced portrayal which is less disappointing than irritating. Susanna Foster has no fond memories of her condescending costar.

> Boris Karloff was ice cold, and I never had any kind of a relationship with him. On *Phantom,* Claude Rains was reserved but he had that little vicious twinkle, so cute—you could understand why he had four wives! He and I had a friendship that was kind of quiet. I loved him and I loved working with him. Working with Karloff was like working with a slab of ice.

The Climax might have played far better had Karloff sought to create some sympathy for his character; while Dr. Hohner had few of the tragic qualities of Claude Rains' Phantom, there were still opportunities to present Hohner as something other than a one-dimensional baddie. But Karloff plays it deadpan: cold and stolid, Dr. Hohner is just a stuffy, selfish creep, seeking to ruin Angela's life and career because of a baseless fetish.

Hohner is a reverse Svengali in his efforts to keep Angela from singing, but this backwards premise isn't sufficiently dramatic to keep the picture alive. Horror had also taken a backseat to music in *Phantom of the Opera,* but at least that film had a certain number of highlights: the acid-throwing attack, scenes set in the sewers and catacombs, several murders, the falling chandelier and the climactic unmasking. The closest thing to a highpoint in *The Climax* are the scenes of Susanna Foster finding herself unable to sing, an unsatisfying, uncinematic device. Had *The Climax* been made without a horror star like Karloff in the lead, it's doubtful that it would even have been promoted as a horror film, and it probably wouldn't have made this book at all.

Curiously, the cost for this tepid, tired-blood script ran up to a staggering total. A $650 a week writer, Curt Siodmak worked on the project for nearly 20 weeks, raking in $12,891.65. Lynn Starling, whose list of credits otherwise leans heavily toward comedies (including the 1939 *The Cat and the Canary*), worked four-and-a-half weeks at a weekly rate of $1,250. Dialogue director Gene Lewis, who worked on the script as well, earned another $700-plus for his writing contribution while stenos and miscellaneous were paid over $1,200. The total script cost amounted to $20,500.

Lovely Susanna Foster gives a good performance, easily the best in the picture. While the studio's nightingale-in-residence allows that Universal did talk about making a sequel to *Phantom of the Opera,* she maintains that no real plans for a sequel were ever laid.

Boris Karloff shows off the gloomy puss he wears through all 86 minutes of *The Climax*. It's the man next to him who ought to look unhappy: *The Climax* kiboshed producer George Waggner's career at Universal.

> They just took me and Karloff and Turhan Bey and did *The Climax,* which was a kind of sequel. I loved working with Turhan, the color was beautiful and I loved working with Hal Mohr, the cameraman. I enjoyed it very much. What I didn't like were those hypnosis scenes—I was sick for days after watching that damned hypnosis gizmo winding around. Nauseating! They kept going back, shot after shot. And the title *The Climax* was terrible—it should have been called *The Magic Voice.*

Remembering producer/director George Waggner, Foster recalls both good times and bad.

> George Waggner was a very stoic, stiff-upper-lip kind of person—he hid his emotions. I was always very good about being on time, but I came back late from lunch one day on *Frisco Sal* [1945] and he bawled me out unmercifully. He broke me up completely, and I cried one whole afternoon—they couldn't work the whole day! I didn't do it on purpose, I just couldn't believe that George would do a thing like that.

Another time that Waggner disappointed Foster was the day he discharged her musical director-friend Edward Ward.

> George fired Eddie from the lot because of drinking and I felt just everything went for me because Eddie and I just bloomed together. That just killed me.

And I thought, how could George, after all of those years of being associated with Eddie, cut him off like that? I didn't care if Eddie did sometimes come in shaking, he still did his job.

George Waggner was like a soldier and his idea was to discipline you. And I meant a lot to George; he told me that recently, just before he passed away. He said, "I'll never forget you coming down the stairs in *Phantom.*" He was a warm-hearted man, basically, but he had this military thing about him.

Waggner was back to Universal B's after the *Climax* debacle. He directed only seven films after leaving Universal – *The Gunfighters* (1947), *The Fighting Kentuckian* (1949) and *Operation Pacific* (1951), both with John Wayne, *Destination 60,000, Pawnee* (both 1957), and *Fury River* and *Mission of Danger* (both 1959) – although he also worked extensively in television, where he whimsically billed himself george waGGner. He died at the Motion Picture Home in 1984.

Every other performance in *The Climax* is disappointing. Turhan Bey, badly miscast, plays the fool as Franz, the film's juvenile lead. Nervously watching Foster make her stage debut, Bey absent-mindedly eats his program, sings along from the audience and applauds with paper hanging out of his mouth; during a later appearance, he claps long and loud after everyone else has stopped. (Bey had just returned from a loanout to MGM, where he made his one major film, *Dragon Seed,* 1944, with Katharine Hepburn.) All of the "humor" in *The Climax* is equally forced, from the bickering of rival opera stars George Dolenz and Jane Farrar to the frumpy hijinks of Ludwig Stossel and the cutesy posturing of boy-king Scotty Beckett. Thomas Gomez doesn't fit the role of the opera manager and Gale Sondergaard is her customarily saturnine self as Karloff's housekeeper. Maria Ouspenskaya met with George Waggner on the fourth day of shooting to discuss a role in the film (probably the part of Mama Hinzl, played by Lotte Stein), but obviously came away empty-handed.

The Climax was the first color film for Karloff, who worked on the picture from February 1 to March 29. The actor had signed a two-picture, $60,000 contract with Universal, with two-thirds of his salary earmarked for *The Climax* and the remaining third designated for a second picture-to-come (*House of Frankenstein*). Susanna Foster was paid $13,000, Turhan Bey $7,000, George Dolenz $6,000.

"It was not a great picture as far as I was concerned," says Susanna Foster, in a textbook example of understatement. An unpalatable blend of period romance, hoary drama, deep-dyed villainy and tenth-rate operetta, *The Climax* has the added embarrassment of a stench of failed pretension. Evening clothes, a cape and a silk hat do not make a class act out of a bored Karloff, a Radio City Music Hall extravaganza doesn't pass for opera and an unimaginative reverse-twist on the Trilby theme can't sustain 86 minutes of silly pomposity. A disappointment and a flop, *The Climax* sizes up as one of Universal's most dismal thrillers.

Dead Man's Eyes (1944)

Released November 10, 1944. 64 minutes. An Inner Sanctum Mystery, produced by arrangement with Simon & Schuster, Inc., Publishers. *Directed by* Reginald LeBorg. *Associate Producer:* Will Cowan. *Executive Producer:* Ben Pivar. *Original Screenplay by* Dwight V. Babcock. *Director of Photography:* Paul Ivano. *Film Editor:* Milton Carruth. *Musical Director:* Paul Sawtell. *Art Directors:* John B. Goodman & Martin Obzina. *Dialogue Directors:* Stacey Keach & Phil Brown. *Set Decorators:* Russell A. Gausman & Leigh Smith. *Special Photography:* John P. Fulton. *Sound Director:* Bernard B. Brown. *Technician:* William Hedgcock. *Assistant Director:* Seward Webb. *Camera Operator:* William Dodds. *Properties:* Ernie Smith. *Gowns by* Vera West.

Lon Chaney (Dave Stuart), Jean Parker (Heather Hayden), Paul Kelly (Dr. Alan Bittaker), Acquanetta (Tanya Czoraki), Thomas Gomez (Police Captain Drury), Jonathan Hale (Dr. Samuel Welles), George Meeker (Nick Phillips), Edward Fielding (Stanley "Dad" Hayden), Eddie Dunn (Policeman Moriarity), Pierre Watkin (Attorney), Beatrice Roberts, Gwen Kenyon (Nurses), John Elliott (Trevers), Rex Lease (Taxi Driver), Allen Fox (Waiter), Leslie O'Pace (Headwaiter), David Hoffman (Inner Sanctum), Gil Perkins (Stunts).

The first two chapters of the Inner Sanctum series were passable diversions at best, but any hope that these films would tap into its rich, stylistic possibilities were gone by the third go-round. *Dead Man's Eyes* is a languid and uninspired effort. Reginald LeBorg reluctantly returned to the director's chair, itching for a change of pace and better assignments: "The Inner Sanctum pictures made a lot of money. They only cost $125,000 to $150,000 each. That was the trouble. I was good with these. I couldn't get any better."

LeBorg, who admitted to liking stories that had some basis in medical fact, was attracted to the Dwight V. Babcock script. The bare storyline of *Dead Man's Eyes,* in fact, has the makings of an intriguing, well-structured thriller: A blind man is accused of killing his benefactor to obtain his eyes for a corneal transplant. When his sight is restored, he fakes blindness in order to ensnare the guilty party. Unfortunately, the plot is poorly executed in a thuddingly unimaginative screenplay, but it was "good enough" by the deteriorating standards of the series.

The final script of *Dead Man's Eyes* was in need of a complete overhaul in order for its potential to be realized, but, alas, only a slight fine-tuning was ordered before the film went into production. It was neither the banality of the dialogue nor the flatness of the characters that necessitated the last minute changes; only the prolonged scenes of cloddish Lon Chaney, drowning his miseries in booze, were altered in order to satisfy the ever-vigilant Breen Office. Executive producer Ben Pivar gave his assurances that the offensive scenes would be kept to a minimum in order to uphold public standards. It was also agreed that a scene in which Chaney flushes his eyes with acid would not be overly gruesome and would stay within the boundaries of good taste.

Dead Man's Eyes was afforded the usual shoestring budget and quickie 12-day schedule, with contract players Chaney and Acquanetta commanding the top salaries in the cast: $10,000 and $4,000, respectively. Supporting actor Paul Kelly walked off with $2,750 for his labors, even nuzzling out leading lady Jean Parker, who was only paid $2,500. Directors came considerably cheaper, with a $1,500 paycheck earmarked for Mr. LeBorg.

On March 14, 1944, Chaney, Acquanetta and Parker gathered on Stage 20 for the first shot (appropriately, the first scene in the film). Art directors John B. Goodman and Martin Obzina transformed the set into a reasonable representation of an artist's studio. The plush, often-used Hacienda set was used for the palatial digs of heiress Jean Parker in several key scenes.

David Stuart (Lon Chaney), a promising but not-much-in-demand artist, is about to call it a day. He is confident that when his latest work, an oil canvas of a fiery gypsy dancer, is completed, he'll at least be able to call his own shots in the art world. It might even earn him enough to continue indulging his rich fiancée Heather Hayden (Jean Parker) in the furs to which she's become accustomed. But a freak accident cuts the artist's plans short. When his model, sultry Tanya Czoraki (Acquanetta), inadvertently rearranges the contents of his work shelf, Dave grabs a bottle of acetic acid, thinking it's only eyewash. Gripped by pain and shock, the artist desperately calls for an ambulance as the room is plunged in darkness.

Heather responds to the emergency call at the hospital flanked by her father, Stanley "Dad" Hayden (Edward Fielding) and former beau, Nick Phillips (George Meeker). Eye specialist Dr. Sam Welles (Jonathan Hale) confirms that Dave's condition is permanent. Offering Dave a glimmer of hope, the good doctor discloses that grafting the corneas from an undamaged pair of eyes might restore his sight completely.

Dave's adjustment to his new life is clumsy and filled with bitterness. His career in a shambles, he spends most of his days in an alcoholic haze. "Dad" Hayden arrives to console his future son-in-law and breaks the news that he has made legal arrangements to "will" his eyes to Dave. Stuart rejects the offer and the pair clash over Tanya's culpability for the accident.

Dave arrives at Hayden's estate to made amends only to find the old man's bludgeoned body lying on the floor of his study. Heather breaks in on the scene and accuses Dave of the crime. Captain Drury (Thomas Gomez) of Homicide investigates but postpones putting the cuffs on Dave until he can get more evidence.

In spite of Dave's status as a murder suspect, the corneal transplant proceeds on schedule. The graft apparently doesn't take, leaving the artist as blind as before. Back at his studio, Dave shows Tanya a tiny threaded nail he found

Acquanetta comes face-to-face with the assassin in *Dead Man's Eyes,* third of the "Inner Sanctum" mysteries.

at the murder scene. When she reacts suspiciously, the artist is convinced she knows the identity of the murderer. The next day, Tanya is found clubbed to death.

An urgent calls brings Tanya's beau, psychiatrist Alan Bittaker (Paul Kelly), to Dave's apartment. Accusing him point-blank of being the murderer, Dave shows him that the tiny nail fits perfectly into the silver top of Bittaker's walking stick (it became dislodged during the attack on Hayden). The old man's fate was sealed when Bittaker realized that winning Tanya's affections hinged on Dave's recovery (she was in love with Stuart and blamed herself for his blindness). When Tanya recognized the nail was missing from Alan's cane, the psychiatrist was forced to eliminate her, too. Bittaker is about to club Dave, but the artist foils him. Dave reveals he feigned blindness after the operation in order to trap the murderer. Drury arrives on the scene and takes Bittaker into custody.

Lacking the minor stylistic flourishes of *Calling Dr. Death* and the endearing campiness of *Weird Woman, Dead Man's Eyes* pretty much sets the standard for the increasingly drab Inner Sanctum series. Even within the limited confines of the grade B Hollywood whodunit, most of the remaining offerings were sterile, plodding exercises.

Dead Man's Eyes falls flat on almost every level. As a mystery, it's inept and predictable, with virtually every turn of the plot telegraphed long before it transpires on the screen. Starting with the murder of "Dad" Hayden, the ensuing plot complications become increasingly obvious. We are to assume that the murder weapon, "the well-known blunt instrument," is Dave's walking stick, but Bittaker's own cane is a dead giveaway, especially since he dutifully totes the thing around with him in every scene.

The narrow field of suspects doesn't leave much room for speculation. The calculating Tanya is knocked off well before the finale. Nick Phillips, Heather's simpering bore of a suitor, has red herring written all over him and is almost beneath consideration. Stuart earnestly pursues the only shred of physical evidence found on the crime scene. This leaves only Bittaker, although the script is hard-pressed to contrive the feeblest of motives for such a coldblooded murder, nor can it furnish even a cobweb of intrigue for seasoned mystery addicts. The entire focus of the mystery falls squarely on a tiny threaded tack that Stuart found near the body (no mean feat for a blind man). The tack is far too trifling a plot contrivance for even a 64-minute mystery.

The "surprise" revelation that Stuart was faking blindness in the last half of the movie is given away long before the climax. He virtually flaunts his restored sight, dabbling with his paint brushes and easel yet tapping all over the place with his walking stick even when he *isn't* being observed by other characters. Writer Dwight V. Babcock, unsure whether he wanted to give the game away completely, seems to want it both ways.

The characters are a singularly dreary lot, but the somnambulistic acting provides the movie with a few unintended chuckles. The whole cast is convinced that Dave's fairly dreadful canvas of Tanya, which isn't even a very good likeness, will skyrocket the fledgling artist to fame. One look at the painting calls *everyone's* eyesight into question. The dialogue attributes enigmatic qualities to Tanya, which she clearly does not possess. "There's something primitive and passionate about her. She intrigues me!" admits a swooning Bittaker as the camera cuts to the girl's pained expression of indifference. Stuart, no stranger to inconsistency himself, entertains his rich girlfriend in ritzy nightspots, unmindful that he's supposed to be a struggling artist.

Jean Parker, one of the classiest and most likable of the B leading ladies, shines as Heather ("Jean Parker was excellent. She was very chic and amiable," recalls Reginald LeBorg). Lon Chaney's tortured artist act quickly becomes tiresome and Thomas Gomez lays it on a bit thick, as usual, as the undeterred policeman. The same goes for Paul Kelly, a mildly unattractive actor who was the subject of one of Hollywood's most spectacular murder trials of the '30s. He unfailingly won the admiration of his colleagues, who were inclined to overstate his talents, possibly out of sympathy; even LeBorg praises his performance in the film lavishly. (Years later, Kelly would cop a Tony Award for Best Actor, amazingly beating out Marlon Brando who was in the running for his milestone performance in "A Streetcar Named Desire.") Acquanetta once again proves she's no volcano, Venezuelan or otherwise, and gives her customary drab performance.

I got along with Lon Chaney beautifully. He was a good friend [Acquanetta told us]. I finally had some dramatic scenes, but they still would not allow me to "come out." Everything was kind of capped; they wanted me to hold it to a low key. Emotions inside that were building, I had to hold down. [Were you happy with your performance?] *Pleased,* let's say. When you're new and never had the experience, as they call it, the directors are in charge. And they like that because they project themselves through you. Reginald LeBorg was a gentleman—with the accent on the *gentle.* My views were simply that, whatever I was given, I did my best. But acting wasn't something that was so meaningful to me that I would give up something else *for* that. That's why I walked away.

LeBorg tried valiantly to bring a bit of style to the material. He recalls,

I did one shot that was never done before. Simultaneously, I did two close-ups. I had two cameras on the stage, one on each actor. I thought it was better acting; they could talk to each other, and they didn't have somebody behind the camera. I wanted to see photographically what it would look like if they lit it this way, and it came out beautifully.

Nevertheless, *Dead Man's Eyes* leaves few viewers impressed. LeBorg recalls his frustrations with the front office in delivering a better product.

Acquanetta was doing a scene and she was terrible and I wanted to rewrite it. Ben Pivar wanted to know of any changes. I changed it so it would be easier for her to act it. I called him from the stage and said, "Ben, I want to rewrite this," and he said, "Don't rewrite! Don't rewrite!" So I said, "Let's talk it over first." He said, "I'm busy. Do it as it is and we can see it in the rushes and then see what is no good."

Annoyed, LeBorg sent his second assistant director to see what Pivar was doing that was so important that he couldn't come on the set for a few moments. The assistant presently returned with his report: "He's playing gin rummy!"

LeBorg finally got fed up with his assignments at Universal and what he considered to be factory-like conditions. He got a worthwhile opportunity in *Destiny* and found a comedy script to his liking, the well-regarded but rarely seen *San Diego, I Love You* (1945) with Jon Hall and Louise Allbritton. LeBorg considers both of these films to be his personal favorites, but it wasn't enough to keep him happy. He was released from his studio contract, at his own request, in February, 1945. It was a decision the director would later regret in light of the studio merger with International Pictures and their commitment to upscale entertainment. Even as a freelance director LeBorg couldn't escape the grind of B picturemaking and found himself directing Joe Palooka and Bowery Boys quickies. Ironically, Reginald LeBorg's best-remembered movies were released by the studio from which he tried so hard to break away.

Murder in the Blue Room (1944)

Released December 1, 1944. 61 minutes. *Associate Producer:* Frank Gross. *Directed by* Leslie Goodwins. *Screenplay by* I.A.L. Diamond & Stanley Davis. *Based on the short story "Secret of the Blue Room" by* Erich Philippi. *Director of Photography:* George Robinson. *Musical Director:* Sam Freed, Jr. *Art Directors:* John B. Goodman & Harold H. MacArthur. *Director of Sound:* Bernard B. Brown. *Technician:* Charles Carroll. *Set Decorators:* Russell A. Gausman & Edward R. Robinson. *Film Editor:* Charles Maynard. *Dance Director:* Carlos Romero. *Gowns by* Vera West. *Dialogue Director:* Howard Banks. *Special Photography:* John P. Fulton. *Songs: "The Boogie Woogie Boogie Man" (by* Milton Rosen & Everett Carter), *"A-Do-Dee-Doo-Doo" (by* Lew Porter, F.J. Tableporter & Ted Erdody), *"One Starry Night" (by* Dave Franklin & Don George). *Assistant Directors:* Fred Frank & Mort Singer, Jr. *Camera Operator:* Eddie Cohen. *Assistant Cameraman:* Phil Lathrop.

Anne Gwynne (Nan Kirkland), Donald Cook (Steve Randall), John Litel (Frank Baldridge), Grace McDonald (Peggy), Betty Kean (Betty), June Preisser (Jerry), Regis Toomey (Police Insp. McDonald), Nella Walker (Linda Baldridge), Andrew Tombes (Dr. Carroll), Ian Wolfe (Edwards), Emmett Vogan (Hannagan), Bill MacWilliams [Williams] (Larry Dearden), Frank Marlowe (Curtin), Grace Hayle (Dowager), Alice Draper (Maid), Milton Parsons (Driver), Jack Gardner (Booking Agent), Victoria Horne (Maid), Robert Cherry (Ghost).

This third filmization of the Erich Philippi short story "Secret of the Blue Room" is a silly but watchable 61 minutes of B comedy, mystery and music. It doesn't come near the quality of the original *Secret of the Blue Room* (a picture that seems to improve with every insipid remake), but neither is it an insufferable stiff like the first Americanized rehash, *The Missing Guest*. *Murder in the Blue Room* falls prey to many of the problems that plagued *Guest*—the mystery isn't mysterious and the comedy isn't funny—but at least *Guest*'s obnoxious tone is left behind. *Murder* has new problems all its own, but it also has a better cast, a lighter approach and, best of all, a shorter running time.

An old country house, rumored to be haunted since the death of owner Sam Kirkland in the mysterious Blue Room, is reopened after 20 years by Kirkland's widow Linda (Nella Walker), her new husband Frank Baldridge (John Litel), and Linda's daughter (by her first marriage) Nan (Anne Gwynne). Determined to dispel the rumors of ghosts, the Baldridges throw a housewarming party complete with an orchestra and dancing. Larry Dearden (Bill Williams), one of Nan's most ardent admirers, proposes to her as they dance, but she declines; she likes but doesn't love him. Nan later asks another one of the guests, debonair mystery writer Steve Randall (Donald Cook), to use his talents to solve the mystery of the Blue Room. Despite the gay atmosphere, a sudden blackout and a piano that plays "Moonlight Sonata" by itself get the guests to wondering whether ghosts still occupy the house. The Three Jazzybelles (Grace McDonald, Betty Kean, June Preisser), entertainer friends of Nan's, do one of their dancing/singing numbers, which is a hit. As the girls are leaving, they are accosted by a nerdy-looking ghost in a derby who asks for a match.

Larry, who has been invited to spend the night, announces his intention to sleep in the Blue Room, to dispel once and for all the rumors that the chamber is haunted. Baldridge raises objections but Larry persists. In the morning the room is found empty and Larry is presumed to have fallen out of a window into the raging sea far below.

Inspector McDonald (Regis Toomey) and his men begin their investigation. The Jazzybelles are brought back to the house to answer questions, and end up being detained there by the suspicious McDonald. The dizzy dolls want out so badly that they determine to solve the case themselves.

Steve Randall becomes convinced that Sam Kirkland's murder and Larry Dearden's disappearance are somehow linked; the only people involved in both cases are Frank Baldridge, the family physician Dr. Carroll (Andrew Tombes) and the butler, Edwards (Ian Wolfe). In a too-long comedy relief sequence, the Jazzybelles truss up Edwards and grill him before lapsing into a singing/dancing rendition of the spooky novelty number, "The Boogie Woogie Boogie Man." Somewhere along the line the comic ghost turns up again and scares one of the girls.

Steve decides to spend a night in the Blue Room; he vanishes mysteriously, although Larry's dead body is now found in the room. Dr. Carroll tells Nan that Larry was her half-brother; Sam Kirkland had had an extramarital affair with a woman who became Larry's mother. The Jazzybelles find the gun which killed Larry, and Frank Baldridge, the gun's owner, is arrested.

Acting mighty suspicious, Dr. Carroll opens a panel leading into a secret passageway and steps inside. An unseen figure, gun in hand, is already in the passageway, and a gunfight between the two men ensues; Carroll is hit. McDonald arrives on the scene and finds that Steve Randall, no worse for wear from his Blue Room experience, has done the shooting as well as cracked the case. Steve explains that Dr. Carroll had found out about Sam Kirkland's little fling and threatened him with blackmail; Kirkland balked and Carroll killed him in the Blue Room. When Larry found out that Kirkland was his dad, he eventually put the facts together and began to suspect Carroll, so *he* had to go, too.

During his night in the Blue Room, Steve had found an entrance to the secret passage where Larry's body was hidden; he placed the corpse in the Blue Room where it could be found so that the killer would know that he (Steve) was on to him. Dr. Carroll, dying, congratulates Steve on his fine detective work. Romance blooms between Steve and Nan, and the comedy ghost scares the Jazzybelles one last time as the curtain closes.

Murder in the Blue Room was originally written with resident Universal clowns the Ritz Brothers slated for the comedy relief roles. (Probably a rescreening of *The Missing Guest,* in which Billy Wayne and George Cooper do a nauseatingly accurate Ritz Brothers imitation, gave some studio exec the notion.) But the Ritzes apparently had become disenchanted with Universal's quickie schedules and hour-long B's, and left the studio after completing the misleadingly-titled *Never a Dull Moment* (1943); they began to work the nightclub circuit and later television, and never made another film.

The departure of the Brothers Ritz prompted some rethinking, and a decision to spotlight a trio of female bumblers was made. According to Universal expert Michael Fitzgerald, not a single change was made in the existing script; actress Betty Kean told him that the script used in shooting still called for the Ritzes, and that she read the dialogue ascribed in her script to "Harry" (Ritz). At least a few small modifications had to have been made (for one thing, the name of the trio was changed to The Three Jazzybelles from The Mad Hatters), and the story cost ultimately ran up to a total of $3,200. I.A.L. Diamond, later the writer of such Billy Wilder hits as *Some Like It Hot* (1959), *The Apartment* (1960), *One, Two, Three* (1961) and *Kiss Me, Stupid* (1964), pocketed $2,400 while cowriter Stanley Davis, stenos and miscellaneous walked off with the rest.

With or without the Ritz Brothers, *Murder in the Blue Room* is an innocuous, thoroughly unexceptional B; there's more emphasis on the humor and the musical numbers than on the event promised in its title. The story of the Blue Room itself had held center stage in *Secret* but was slightly subordinated in *The Missing Guest;* here it gets buried almost completely by silly comedy scenes, dance numbers and acrobatic routines. The original *Blue Room* story also underwent some more modifications, some for the better, others for the worse. The reporter character played by Paul Kelly in *The Missing Guest* is wisely dumped, with a clever mystery writer taking his place. "Vic" and "Jake," the comic goons in *Guest,* are replaced by the Jazzybelles, whose roles are expanded. And Larry, the poor bastard, is no longer a killer but a victim while Dr. Carroll extends his homicidal streak.

No one in the cast seems affected by the tragic goings-on in the house. Anne Gwynne, here nearing the end of her Universal tenure, wrings her hands and frets most prettily, but never conveys any real sense of anxiety. Donald Cook looks upon the whole business as an interesting challenge while John Litel regards it as a nuisance; McDonald, Kean and Preisser, playing the type of scared characters that only exist in movies, use the spook-talk as an excuse to make their corny jokes. The trio also does some fancy dancing and lets loose with several songs during the course of the film's 61 minutes, although it's Martha Tilton's rendition of "One Starry Night" (mouthed by Anne Gwynne in the opening scene) that comes off as the best number in the film.

A viewer attracted to the film by its mystery angles is bound to feel cheated, as there's not even the slightest attempt to build atmosphere. Contrary to the title of the classic James Whale film, the Baldridge mansion ought to be called the New Bright House; the place is relatively small and modern, overcrowded with family, friends, police and servants, and you never get the impression that anything scary or supernatural could go on here. A ghost does show up several times, but in keeping with the ridiculous tone of the film he's a comedy ghost. Played by Robert Cherry, he's a white-faced clod in a sheet, wearing a derby; he has his very own cutesy-funny musical motifs, and all he does whenever he comes on is to frighten one (or more) of the Jazzybelles. The process of elimination indicates that this would have to be the ghost of Sam Kirkland, who is the only person known to have died in the house, but it's difficult to believe that this pasty-faced goon of a ghost could be Anne Gwynne's father. Of course we're not supposed to make that assumption: he's just another zany character in a movie that's already brimming with inane lowjinks.

The Breen Office offered up its usual comments and objections, recommending restraint in the gruesomeness and horror angles and insisting that, in the climactic secret passage gunfight, Dr. Carroll fire first. Breen also objected to the speech in which Dr. Carroll implies that Larry was an illegitimate child. Breen suggested a change in the dialogue and even turned screenwriter, proposing a convoluted line ("Your father was secretly married to Larry's mother before he married your mother") to use in its place. Associate producer Frank Gross stuck to his guns, however, and in a discussion with a Mr. Metzger of the Breen Office, Gross pointed out that the identical situation and dialogue had been passed by the censors for *The Missing Guest*. Apparently deciding that two wrongs make a right, the Breen Office okayed the speech but continued to insist on great restraint in the romantic scenes between Nan and Larry (shades of incest!).

Interestingly, in mid–March, 1944, when this film was made, every film that was being shot at Universal was horror, horror-related or science fiction-related: *Murder in the Blue Room, The Climax, Ghost Catchers, Dead Man's Eyes* and the serial *The Great Alaskan Mystery* (see the serial appendix at the back of this book). Even at a horror-happy studio like Universal this situation had to have been unique, and it says a lot for Universal's confidence in the genre and their continuing perception of themselves as leaders in that field. It's just too bad that none of these films is really much good.

Director Leslie Goodwins, who finished the film on schedule March 22, 1944, was paid $2,000. Star salaries included $6,500 for Donald Cook, $3,000 for Anne Gwynne and $3,500 for Grace McDonald; these Universal contractees fared better than outside talent like Betty Kean and June Preisser, who earned $1,875 apiece for their two-and-a-half weeks' work. An early wardrobe estimate also indicates that several of the smaller parts were reassigned: this memo lists Samuel S. Hinds as Dr. Carroll, Andrew Tombes as the inspector and Edward Gargan as Curtin. While *Murder in the Blue Room* was in production, Universal announced that associate producer Gross' next assignment would be another musical "chiller," this one called *Night Life.* The resultant film, retitled *Night Club Girl* (1944), was a musical comedy with Vivian Austin and Edward Norris, well beyond the scope of this book despite the initial false alarm.

Despite the film's silly excesses, *Murder in the Blue Room* is still a fun film for fans who enjoy this type of escapism. McDonald, Kean and Preisser are talented dancers who put on a good show, Gwynne and Cook make a handsome couple, veteran players like John Litel, Regis Toomey, Andrew Tombes and Ian Wolfe have good parts and the sturdy old *Blue Room* story gets its last airing. And when the going does begin to get rough, all one has to do is to remind one's self how much worse the picture would have been with the Ritz Brothers, and suddenly it's not so bad anymore.

Destiny (1944)

Released December 22, 1944. 65 minutes. *Directed by* Reginald LeBorg (& Julien Duvivier). *Associate Producer:* Roy William Neill. *Executive Producer:* Howard Benedict. *Screenplay by* Roy Chanslor & Ernest Pascal. *Story Idea by* Jean Levy-Straus. *Director of Photography:* George Robinson & Paul Ivano. *Camera Operators:* Fleet Southcott & Walter Strenge. *Film Editor:* Paul Landres. *Music by* Frank Skinner & Alexandre (Alexander) Tansman. *Song, "Only Those Who Listen to a Dream" by* Paul Webster. *Art Directors:* John B. Goodman, Abraham Grossman & Richard H. Riedel. *Set Decorators:* Russell A. Gausman & Victor A. Gangelin. *Assistant Director:* Seward Webb. *Director of Sound:* Bernard B. Brown. *Technician:* William Hedgcock. *Sound Mixer:* Joe Lapis. *Gowns by* Vera West.

Gloria Jean (Jane Broderick), Alan Curtis (Cliff Banks), Frank Craven (Clem Broderick), Grace McDonald (Betty), Vivian Austin (Phyllis), Frank Fenton (Sam Baker), Minna Gombell (Marie), Selmer Jackson (Warden), Lew Wood (Prison Guard), Robert Homans (Grogan), Perc Launders (Sergeant), Harry Strang (Sgt. Bronson), Lane Chandler (Patrolman), Billy Wayne (Bartender), Gayne Whitman (Radio Announcer), Frank Hagney, Edgar Dearing, Bill Hale, Dale Van Sickel (Motorcycle Cops), Erville Alderson* (Man), Dorothy Vaughan (Maggie), Bill O'Brien (Waiter), Bob Reeves (Cop), Ken Terrell, Bud Wolfe (Radio Patrolmen), Carey Loftin, Frosty Royce, Johnny Daheim (Stunts), Kate McKenna, Teddy Infuhr*, Edgar Barrier*, Bob Pepper, Lois Schoonover, Reba King, Tom Steele, Helen Thurston. [**Does not appear in the final print.*]

A delicate, sentimental fantasy-drama, stylistically enhanced by expressive visuals, *Destiny* was derived from the unused fourth episode of the whimsical Julien Duvivier omnibus *Flesh and Fantasy.* Padded out to 65 minutes, *Destiny* is a misfire but an interesting one, encapsulating the faults and strengths of its parent film. Ernest Pascal's scenario, a hard luck tale about a two-time loser who's steered off his destructive course by an afflicted girl with extraordinary capabilities, is preachy and laden with bromides. As in *Flesh and Fantasy,* we're willing to overlook the banal story and concentrate instead on the arresting techniques of the French director and his cinematographer, Paul Ivano. Both men were responsible for the movie's most arresting set piece, the supernaturally-induced storm.

By the time Universal decided what it wanted to do with the surplus vignette from *Flesh and Fantasy,* nearly a year had gone by since that film's release. Roy Chanslor was hired to compose a new screenplay, building upon

Pascal's original material. Reginald LeBorg was selected to direct, Alan Curtis was contracted to appear in the new scenes and a small cast of players was assembled. LeBorg soon learned that more was required of him than he thought: "I took over for Roy William Neill as associate producer, but he still got the title. There was no producer. I had to make all the producing decisions."

Both Julien Duvivier and Charles Boyer relinquished all rights to their work for a settlement of $25,000 apiece. First called *Faith,* then retitled *The Fugitive* while the picture was still in the works, it was finally released as *Destiny,* that often-applied but heretofore never used monicker of many a Universal production. *Destiny* began around August 30, 1944, and wrapped a day over the 12-day schedule.

Destiny gets off to an exciting start with a rousing car chase, courtesy of Duvivier. Pursued by the cops, bank robber Sam Baker (Frank Fenton) and his stooge Cliff Banks (Alan Curtis) take off on separate paths and disappear into the hills. Chanslor's expanded script provides some interesting insights into Curtis' character. Through his chance encounters with various strangers (most of them female), we witness his dramatic catharsis.

An attractive librarian named Betty (well-played by hoofer Grace McDonald) is taken into the fugitive's confidence after she picks him up on the roadside. The popular tune, "I'll See You in My Dreams," heard over the car radio, sets off a series of flashbacks. It seems that Cliff was an okay guy until he hitched up with Phyllis (Vivian Austin), an alluring torch singer, and her shifty pal, Sam Baker. Thanks to Baker, Cliff is involved in an armed robbery and is sent to San Quentin for three years.

The sorry details surrounding Cliff's downfall unfold further when he encounters Marie (Minna Gombell), a hardbitten but seemingly compassionate café woman. In a second series of flashbacks, we learn that Cliff's recent run-in with the law came as a result of yet *another* association with the trouble-maker Baker. Marie proves to be treacherous; she alerts the cops to Cliff's whereabouts in the hopes of collecting the reward. He just barely gets away.

After this point, Duvivier's footage dominates the remainder of the film. Cliff arrives in Paradise Valley, an idyllic community whose inhabitants are so trusting of one another they never bother to bolt their doors. Stopping at a roadhouse, the weary young man meets Clem Broderick (Frank Craven) and his daughter Jane (Gloria Jean). Blind since birth, Jane has developed amazing extrasensory powers: she's in complete accord with the natural elements and the valley's wildlife, and has had some success as a dowser (a person capable of locating hidden water sources with a divining rod).

But for all her powers, Jane is unable to see through the scheming stranger. Embittered by the hard blows life has dealt him, Cliff has become immune to the faith and generosity of others, and coldbloodedly plots to take control of the Broderick farm. He accompanies Clem into the woods on the pretext of disposing of a bear. Minutes later, two shots ring out. Cliff returns home alone. Forcing himself on the terrified Jane, Cliff is attacked by her faithful dog. Summoning up her unearthly powers, Jane conjures up a raging storm.

In a *tour de force* display of special effects and riveting camerawork, Cliff pursues Jane through the forest to the swollen river. All the forces of nature ally themselves with their blind compatriot. Branches of trees strike out, blocking Cliff's path. Reaching the dock, Jane attempts to untie the rowboat but Cliff intervenes. He plunges into the river, is swept away by the current and drowns.

On this bleak, pessimistic note, the Duvivier-directed playlet came to a close. (A neat "bridge" connecting this story to the Betty Field–Robert Cummings Mardi Gras episode had the costumed revelers discovering Curtis' body on the river bank.) Settling for a contrived, uplifting finis, Chanslor dismissed the murder/drowning incidents as a dream (or perhaps a premonition of Cliff's destiny). Not only is the youth redeemed by saving Clem's life following a skirmish with the bear, but all criminal charges against him are dropped after the pesky Sam Baker exonerates him.

Back in November, 1942, Duvivier trotted his *Flesh and Fantasy* company up to Angelus Crest and other popular locales to shoot exterior scenes. The troupe labored through December, took time off for a Christmas recess, then resumed production, finally wrapping on January 26, 1943. Willis R. Cook's special effects department constructed a whirlpool in the studio tank for the uncomfortably-realistic storm sequence. Though confined to a water depth of three-and-a-half feet, the current proved powerful enough to capsize a ten-foot-long rowboat. Another intriguing effect devised by Cook's crew was a field of 1200 wildflowers that magically bowed to Gloria Jean as she strolled amongst them. A piece in *The Hollywood Reporter* revealed that the stunt was accomplished by having 12 men operate a piano-like keyboard which controlled the hundreds of flowers by means of invisible thread. However, only a modest-size bed of flowers turned up in the final cut, leading one to assume that the stunt was reduced in scope just before shooting, or that Universal's rabid press boys got carried away again with exaggeration.

Today, *Destiny* walks a narrow line between fanciful drama and unintentional parody. (One shudders at the thought of the beating this naive little picture would receive at a revival screening attended by a typical modern-day audience of smartass hipsters and jaded intellectuals.) The messages preached in *Destiny*—have faith in your fellow man, practice good will toward others—are delivered with enthusiasm as though they're novel concepts. The film draws a distinct contrast between the corrupt inhumanity of urban life and the euphoric, at-peace-with-oneself serenity of Paradise Valley. To his credit, Duvivier imbues these segments with a hauntingly surreal and otherworldly quality, capturing the feel and texture of a vintage French film.

While the Duvivier/Pascal vignette presents Cliff Banks as an incorrigible good-for-nothing, richly deserving of the watery fate that awaits him, the LeBorg/Chanslor footage characterizes the man in an entirely different light: a basically decent, naive fellow caught up in a spiralling set of circumstances over which he has little control. The Cliff Banks of *Destiny* is ripe for redemption; the Cliff Banks of *Flesh and Fantasy,* on the other hand, is headed on a collision course with the devil.

Some of this vulnerability is lost in Alan Curtis' stilted performance. Ruggedly handsome but stoic and inflexible, Curtis, who achieved minor celebrity as a B picture lead through the '40s, brought an air of icy detachment to his screen performances. (He died at a youthful 43 in 1953.) "You had to get friendly with him, then he was very nice. But he was a little arrogant...," Reginald LeBorg remembers. Curtis was brought into the cast of *Flesh and Fantasy* as a replacement for Warner Bros. brat-packer John Garfield. Evidently unhappy with his loan-out to Universal, Garfield withdrew his services on *Flesh and Fantasy* and was suspended by Jack Warner.

Gloria Jean is excellent as the angelic Jane, a role that required an unaffected naturalness and sensitivity for it to work. The young soprano, groomed by Universal to fill Deanna Durbin's shoes whenever that high-priced songbird stepped out of line, gives a flawless rendition of the blind girl who "sees" more deeply than her sighted comrades.

Had *Destiny* wound up as a vignette in *Flesh and Fantasy,* it would have stood on a par with the equally enchanting (and similarly ingenuous) Mardi Gras episode. Both are the stuff of which fairy tales are made.

House of Frankenstein (1944)

Released December 15, 1944. 70 minutes. *Directed by* Erle C. Kenton. *Produced by* Paul Malvern. *Executive Producer:* Joseph Gershenson. *Screenplay by* Edward T. Lowe. *Based on a story by* Curt Siodmak. *Director of Photography:* George Robinson. *Camera Operator:* Eddie Cohen. *Special Photography:* John P. Fulton. *Film Editor:* Philip Cahn. *Special Effects:* Carl Elmendorf. *Assistant Director:* William Tummel. *Art Directors:* John B. Goodman & Martin Obzina. *Musical Director:* Hans J. Salter. *Set Decorators:* Russell A. Gausman & Andrew J. Gilmore. *Sound Director:* Bernard B. Brown. *Technician:* William Hedgcock. *Properties:* Eddie Keys. *Makeup by* Jack P. Pierce. *Gowns by* Vera West.

Boris Karloff (Dr. Gustav Niemann), Lon Chaney (Lawrence Stewart Talbot, the Wolf Man), John Carradine (Count Dracula), J. Carrol Naish (Daniel), Anne Gwynne (Rita Hussman), Peter Coe (Carl Hussman), Lionel Atwill (Inspector Arnz), George Zucco (Professor Bruno Lampini), Elena Verdugo (Ilonka), Sig Ruman (Burgomaster Hussman), William Edmunds (Fejos), Charles Miller (Toberman), Julius Tannen (Hertz), Philip Van Zandt (Inspector Muller), Hans Herbert (Meier), Dick Dickinson (Born), George Lynn (Gerlach), Michael Mark (Frederick Strauss), Olaf Hytten (Hoffman), Frank Reicher (Ullman), Brandon Hurst (Dr. Geissler), Glenn Strange (The Monster), Belle Mitchell (Urla), Eddie Cobb (Driver), Charles Wagenheim (Prison Guard), Gino Corrado (Man at Horror Show), Joe Kirk (Schwartz), Gil Perkins, Carey Loftin, Billy Jones (Stunts), George Plues, Babe De Freest.

Val Lewton could have his artsy camera angles, ominous silhouettes and psychologically-induced chills. Universal had *monsters* and made no apologies about flaunting the best of them in the 1944 horror spectacular *House of Frankenstein.* The enthusiastic box office reaction to *Frankenstein Meets the Wolf Man* was proof enough to the big thinkers in the Front Office that monsters were more potent in numbers. With plotlines rapidly deteriorating and gimmicks growing stale, Universal hoped that quantity would compensate for lack of quality. With the exceptions of the Mummy and the Invisible Man, the studio's major league horrors were destined to cohabit with one another for the remainder of the '40s horror cycle.

House of Frankenstein had a rather tentative genesis. On June 7, 1943, *The Hollywood Reporter* announced that Universal was developing a new shocker entitled *Chamber of Horrors* with an all-star cast of ghouls including the Invisible Man, the Mad Ghoul, the Mummy, and "other assorted monsters." George Waggner was named as the ringleader of this three-ring circus of horrors. The cast read like a Who's Who of cinemacabre: Karloff, Chaney, Lugosi, Lorre, Rains, Zucco, Atwill, Hull and . . . James Barton (?!). *Chamber of Horrors* never saw the light of day. (This same trade paper also noted that Karloff, Lugosi and Lorre had been assigned leading roles in an RKO farce called *Star Strangled Rhythm* with Boris and Bela portraying movie actors whose bodies are taken over by the bogey-men characters they played on the screen. An even more outrageous *Hollywood Reporter* "scoop" was the October 13, 1943, announcement that RKO had just handed over to Val Lewton a property entitled *They Creep by Night,* boasting a cast of characters that included Dracula, the Monster, the Invisible Man, Cat People, plus a variety of werewolves and zombies.)

Preparations for *The Devil's Brood* (the shooting title of *House of Frankenstein*) began in August, 1943, although it wasn't until February of 1944 that the cast was assembled. Paul Malvern took charge of the production, assigning prominent roles to Boris Karloff (fulfilling the second half of his two-picture deal with Universal and receiving $20,000 for his efforts), Lon Chaney (paid a flat $10,000 for his third appearance as the Wolf Man), John Carradine and J. Carrol Naish (paid $7,000 apiece). Lionel Atwill and George Zucco were paid $1,750 and $1,500 respectively for their "cameo" appearances while Glenn Strange picked up an easy $500 for his nominal efforts as the Monster.

Curt Siodmak, who is given a story credit on *House of Frankenstein,* is decidedly terse on the subject of this particular film: "The idea was to put all the horror characters into one picture. I only wrote the story. I didn't write the script. I never saw the picture."

The task of writing a screenplay melding together so many different plotlines and personal dramas required a magician, not a studio hack. Edward T. Lowe, whose only previous horror credit was the 1933 Majestic quickie *The Vampire Bat,* accepted the challenge. Bearing the generic title *Destiny,* Lowe's completed script was subjected to the scrutiny of the Breen Office, who passed it under the condition that a cap was put on undue gruesomeness, emphatic religious references, suggestive gypsy dance gyrations, etc.

A $354,000 budget plus a generous 30-day shooting schedule was arranged. Initial shooting began on Tuesday, April 4, 1944, on the old *Green Hell* and *Pittsburgh* sets, now doing duty as a medieval prison and an underground tunnel, respectively. Art directors John B. Goodman and Martin Obzina took full advantage of leftover sets from *Gung Ho!* and *Tower of London* in designing the production while extensive outdoor shooting was done on the studio's spacious backlot. Director Erle C. Kenton and his company contended with inclement weather while filming the flavorsome gypsy came scenes on the grounds of the Shelby Home and a campfire scene at Nagana Rocks. Kenton's schedule called for the early Dracula sequences to be shot last. John Carradine, Anne Gwynne and Peter Coe had to report to work one hour earlier than usual to make up for the time lost in transporting them to Sherwood Forest near Malibu, a spot frequently used by film studios for pastoral location shoots. With the final scenes in the can, the production came to a close on Monday, May 8.

Gypsy girl Elena Verdugo learns the hard way that being in love with a werewolf (Lon Chaney) is a risky proposition in this climactic scene from *House of Frankenstein.*

In August, Universal announced in the Hollywood trades that the title of their monster fest had been changed from *The Devil's Brood* to the more bankable *House of Frankenstein.* (The studio had long since forgotten Laemmle Junior's 1932 edict discouraging multiple title changes which, he believed, translated into a loss of valuable publicity dollars.) In teaming the feature with *The Mummy's Curse* for nationwide distribution, Universal racked up outstanding box office grosses while at the same time painting a glum portrait of the decline and fall of its once-great monster series.

The episodic story of *House of Frankenstein* begins in the slimy dungeons of Neustadt Prison. Serving a long sentence for following in the blood-stained footsteps of the renegade scientist Frankenstein, Dr. Gustav Niemann (Boris Karloff) is driven by two obsessions: to secure Frankenstein's journals so that he may perfect his own experiments in brain transplantations, and to gain vengeance on the three men who sent him to Neustadt 15 years before. Daniel (J. Carrol Naish), his hunchbacked cellmate, promises the doctor his allegiance in return for a "perfect body" once the records have been secured.

In an expertly executed, thrillingly scored sequence, a lightning bolt demolishes the cellblock. Escaping into the storm, Niemann and Daniel are given shelter by the bombastic Professor Bruno Lampini (played with *savoir-faire* by George Zucco). The proprietor of a traveling "Chamber of Horrors," Lampini boasts of the most prized item in his grisly collection: the skeleton of Count Dracula. Having conveniently rattled off a résumé of the vampire's powers and foibles, Lampini is choked to death by the hunchback.

Disguised as the late showman, Niemann travels to the village of Burgomaster Hussman (Sig Ruman), one of his nemeses. Withdrawing the stake from the skeleton's ribs, Niemann watches in amazement as flesh and blood (and clothing) take form again. Count Dracula (John Carradine) has returned to life. (When *House of Frankenstein* was aired on a Philly horror show in the late '70s, guest star Carradine claimed that it was his idea to have the Count "gasp" as life returned to his skeletal remains.)

Using the pseudonym of Baron Latos, Dracula charms his way into the Hussman household. In one of the film's finest moments, the vampire changes himself into a bat, hypnotizes Hussman and, in a nightmarish silhouette, feeds on his throat. He spirits away the old man's granddaughter Rita (Anne Gwynne) in his coach, and is followed in hot pursuit by her husband Carl (Peter Coe) and Inspector Arnz (Lionel Atwill) and his gendarmes. The vampire's horses bolt, spilling the coach and its occupants down an embankment. Racing up the side of a hill, Dracula is cut down in his tracks by the first rays of dawn. Resembling a huge prostrate bat, his caped arms like black wings, the vampire struggles to lift open the lid of his coffin (conveniently dropped off by Niemann). By the time his pursuers arrive on the scene, the Count has been reduced to a skeleton again. Kenton directs the sequence with dramatic intensity and is given strong support by Hans J. Salter's surging score.

Arriving on the outskirts of the village of Frankenstein, Niemann and Daniel make preparations to penetrate the flooded Frankenstein ruins (inexplicably, the site of Ludwig's burnt-out sanatorium has been changed from Vasaria [now called *Visaria*] to his hometown). Visiting a gypsy camp, Daniel saves a young dancer from being fatally thrashed. In the film's most touching moment, the hunchback shyly romances the girl, Ilonka (Elena Verdugo), as she recuperates in the berth beneath the coach driver's seat. She can only see the man's kindly face. Her gratitude towards her knight is tinged with sexual curiosity and she playfully invites him to come closer. In a moment worthy of Victor Hugo, the hunchback stands triumphantly over the girl, only to see her shrink in disgust at his physical grotesqueness. Filled with compassion, Ilonka assures Daniel of her friendship.

Penetrating the ruins, Niemann and Daniel discover the frozen bodies of the Monster (Glenn Strange) and Lawrence Talbot, the Wolf Man (Lon Chaney). A roaring fire frees the two monsters from the ice tomb. Talbot emerges from it all unscathed but the Monster suffers internal damage and requires medical attention. Banking on Niemann's promise that the doctor will free him of his affliction, Talbot furnishes him with Frankenstein's secret records.

The bizarre party heads for Niemann's boarded-up old castle in Visaria. Edward T. Lowe seems to have taken his inspiration from *The Wizard of Oz* at this point, with Niemann aping the Great and Glorious Oz, promising new brains and or bodies to his followers once they reach their destination. Predictably, Ilonka falls in love with Talbot. After two lifetimes worth of suffering, the doom-ladened man is immune to emotion, but he doesn't discourage her attentions. Daniel understandably takes offense at Talbot's ill-timed intrusion and a triangle-of-sorts develops between the trio.

Reopening his lab, Niemann becomes immediately immersed in nursing the Monster back to health. Late that night, the doctor and Daniel steal into town and kidnap Niemann's last two persecutors, Ullman (Frank Reicher) and Strauss (Michael Mark). The brain transplant subplot that made *The Ghost of Frankenstein* so ridiculous was a minor distraction in comparison to the wholesale organ switching that goes on here. For starters, Niemann plans to transplant the Monster's brain into Ullman's skull and give Strauss the brain of Talbot (thus passing on the curse of the werewolf onto his foe). Niemann ignores Daniel's plea for Talbot's body. "Talbot's body is the perfect home for the Monster's brain!" he insists. Of course, that would make *two* brains in *one* skull (Ullman's and Talbot's), a minor detail evidently overlooked by Lowe. Also, no mention is made of what the ambitious scientist plans to do with the "leftovers"—Ullman's brainless body and Strauss' bodyless brain!

In a jealous fit, Daniel spills the beans about Talbot to Ilonka. She determines to free the man she loves from his unspeakable torment. Armed with a revolver containing the required silver bullets, Ilonka stands outside Talbot's bedroom window. She raises her hand to fire but cannot bring herself to pull the trigger. In a beautifully executed transformation scene, Talbot becomes a snarling werewolf. He attacks Ilonka and murders her but not before she fires two bullets into his body.

The grief-stricken hunchback has had his fill of Niemann's treachery. He seizes the doctor by the throat and snaps his spine. The Monster, infused with renewed strength, sends Daniel hurtling through the skylight to his death. In a scene fraught with irony, the Monster picks up the half-dead Niemann and cradles him in his arms. It's a precious moment in horror film history: the originator of the role and his final successor locked in a poignant embrace.

Bearing flaming torches, the irate villagers storm the castle and chase the pair into the adjoining marshes. As the brush around them is set ablaze, the terrified Monster and his benefactor are driven back into a quicksand bog. Within moments, they are swallowed up by the slime.

One of the horror screen's finest Draculas—John Carradine in *House of Frankenstein*. (Photo courtesy Steve Jochsberger.)

High-keyed, aggressive and shrewdly calculated, *House of Frankenstein* is horror filmmaking at its slick, superficial best. The abundance of thrills are logged in with clockwork precision. Cherished cliches are dusted off and polished to a shine. That the whole picture tastes of yesterday's leftovers is besides the point and in this instance, almost forgivable.

What isn't quite so forgivable is the shameful manner in which the Monster is shunted aside as though he were an inconsequential bit player.

Since *Son of Frankenstein,* the Monster played second fiddle to Frankenstein's sons, Ygor, Larry Talbot, and in *House of Frankenstein,* a cast full of competing menaces. While the Frankenstein legacy fuels the plot of this film, the Monster *per se* is in and of itself negligible.

The late Glenn Strange, a great big teddy bear of a man, very graciously credited Boris Karloff for taking the time and energy to coach him in the fine art of Monster playing. Sadly, precious little of Karloff's guiding influence comes through in Strange's performance. The lion's share of the blame rests on the shoulders of Kenton and Lowe, whose concept of the creature is an imbecilic brute, acting on pure animal instinct. What Glenn Strange's portrayal lacks in characterization, it makes up for in sheer physical presence. The actor's stark features and imposing physique give the part an added dimension of strength and gruesomeness (his is a Monster that's truly frightening to behold). The actor brought these same physical qualities to his "werewolf" character in PRC's vapid *The Mad Monster* in 1942.

Although he could never be accused of being a stylist in the strict sense of the word, Erle C. Kenton was nevertheless an efficient house director. *House of Frankenstein,* like his earlier series entry *The Ghost of Frankenstein,* demonstrates the director's flair for breathless action and thrill sequences. The storm-swept jail break, Dracula's pursuit and ultimate destruction, and the fiery climax (in which five leading characters are killed off in rapid succession) are trenchantly realized. Kenton also had a knack for composing vivid images: the subjective shot of Naish lurching forth to strangle Zucco, the vampire bat dining on Sig Ruman's jugular, Elena Verdugo's brutal flogging (discreetly blocked off by extras standing in the foreground), Chaney's first werewolf transformation in the film, and Naish's strangling of Karloff, visualized as giant shadows cast against the laboratory wall, to name just a few. The collaborative efforts of musical director Hans J. Salter, Paul Dessau and the tireless Charles Previn underscore these memorable images and give the picture a dramatic aural richness; happily, most of the music was written specifically for *House of Frankenstein* and is not the usual collection of oft-heard musical cues dating back to 1938.

On the verge of beginning his happy association with Val Lewton, Karloff gives the impression of marking time in this film. His performance is in the same mode as the one he contributed in *The Climax*—stolid and detached, with an occasional touch of condescending hamminess. No doubt, it aggravated Karloff to see just how much his beloved Monster had degenerated in 13 years. That he himself was a party to this sacrilege must have been doubly painful for him. In any event, the character of Dr. Niemann is so unsympathetic and one-dimensional, even a heartfelt reading wouldn't have alleviated the taint of the familiar here.

Although Lon Chaney's gloom-and-despair schtick was quickly reaching the point of parody by now, the actor does infuse the qualities of sincerity and dignity in his performance. Providing Talbot with a gypsy love interest, however brief, is a bittersweet touch, particularly in light of the fact it was a gypsy who passed the curse of the lycanthrope onto him.

John Carradine has gotten a well-deserved share of applause for his stylish performance as Count Dracula over the years. There are those of us who prefer Carradine's enactment to Lugosi's, though the eccentric Shakespearean lacks those elements of loneliness and tragic resignation that Bela brought to the part. (Supposedly, Lugosi was considered for the Dracula role in *House of Frankenstein* but was forced to bow out on account of other commitments.) Carradine's Count is the devil incarnate – seductive, ruthless, unconscionable. His subtle underplaying and impeccable appearance give the character a genuine air of distinction.

"Do it real, do it honestly, and don't worry about being big." That was the credo J. Carrol Naish followed throughout the course of his wonderful screen career. The Irish-American actor whose stock in trade was impersonating all manner of humanity – from Latins and Orientals to blacks and Hindus – had a reputation for studying his stage and movie roles meticulously, using real life subjects whenever he could find them. According to studio publicity, the diligent Naish discovered a hunchback derelict living in a poverty-stricken area of Los Angeles and observed the man's mannerisms in preparation for his role in *House of Frankenstein.*

"It's interesting . . . to put yourself into the character of this psychopathic deformity," he told a reporter who was visiting the set in late April, 1944. "It [the costume] doesn't fit too well, but it takes five-and-a-half hours to get into this makeup. I have to get up at half past two so I can get here on time."

Naish's performance in *House of Frankenstein* is unquestionably his best work in the horror genre. In the film's early reels, Daniel is personified as a homicidal misfit and a puppet of the nefarious Niemann, just another single-sided stock horror film character. With the introduction of Ilonka (a barely disguised imitation of Esmeralda), the hunchback's loneliness and overwhelming desire for love surfaces. By giving Daniel a vulnerable disposition, Lowe puts us squarely in his corner in spite of the fact he's left behind more broken bodies than any other character in the film.

Heading up the supporting cast is an impressive lineup of seasoned troupers and talented second leads. Frank Reicher, Michael Mark, Brandon Hurst, William Edmunds, Sig Ruman, and of course Lionel Atwill and George Zucco add a sweet, nostalgic "old home week" flavor to the film. Topped with a curly black wig, vivacious Elena Verdugo acts up a storm as the ill-fated Ilonka though Anne Gwynne seems a bit out of place as the saucy American bride who's swept off her feet by the flirtatious vampire. (Disillusioned with the kind of roles Universal was assigning her, Gwynne asked for and got a release from her contract following her work in this film.)

Anne Gwynne wasn't the only contract player in the film dissatisfied with the way Universal had managed their career. Yugoslavian-born actor Peter Coe abandoned a budding career on the Broadway stage at the behest of the studio with the promise he'd be groomed as the next Charles Boyer. No sooner did Universal feature him as the second male lead in the Technicolored Maria Montez-Jon Hall spectacle *Gypsy Wildcat* (1944) than they lost interest in their romantic young star, offering him mediocre roles in routine programmers. Coe responded favorably to the studio's offer to costar him as Anne Gwynne's husband in *House of Frankenstein* because it gave him the opportunity to perform opposite Karloff and Chaney. Recalling his memories of making *House of Frankenstein,* the genial Coe painted a less-than-flattering portrait of costar John Carradine:

> In my first encounter with John Carradine, we had a scene where he's dressed up in tails and hat and is on a coach. My wife Annie Gwynne and I are walking at night. And he stops by, and in his very Shakespearean way says [Coe impersonates the ham-fisted actor], "I beg your pardon, but if you happen to be going my way, I'll be delighted to give you a lift." I said to myself, "*Jesus Christ! What did I get myself into*!" So he went *up* and I went *down.* I underplayed it. He looked so ridiculous when they saw it the next day in the rushes, they had to reshoot it. So I told John, "Are you going to be on the level with me or am I going to pull the same shit? Don't try to fuck with me!" He liked that, and we became good friends afterward.

It was with Chaney, Jr., that Coe struck up a lasting friendship.

> I met him when we did *The Mummy's Curse,* and we really became friends. He had a ranch up in the northern part of California, the pheasant season had just opened and we went hunting. We were so drunk—I mean *drunk*—it's a wonder we didn't shoot each *other*! We had a case of booze as we drove up to his ranch—a seven or eight hour drive—and we drank like crazy. Lon was a good drinker, an excellent drinker. We got to the ranch about 9:00 at night at we had to get up early, about two or three in the morning, to go hunting. Lon shook me and woke me up, and in his hand he was holding a glass. I thought to myself, "Oh, tomato juice or orange juice, how wonderful!" I took a sip and choked—it was straight booze! *That* was an eye-opener!
>
> We did a horrible thing on this trip. We were in the rice fields up north, it was about 10:00 in the morning and the sun was shining on us, when all of a sudden, *boom,* it was dark. We looked up and there was a flock, a whole *sky* of Canadian geese. They landed in the rice field, and Lon said, "We're gonna get some geese, baby!" So we crawled on our bellies holding our rifles, just like in the Army—we got up close and started firing, *pow pow pow pow pow pow.* Lon turned around to leave—"Come with me, run!" he said. I asked, "What about the geese?" and he said, "Tonight!" I asked, "Why?" and he held up a single finger: "*One goose* per hunter!" We had killed 47! We had to come back at night with a truck and load it up!

With its top flight cast, thrill-packed narrative and pyrotechnic display of special effects, *House of Frankenstein* would have been a more fitting final tribute to Universal's fabled monster series than the low-keyed *House of Dracula,* the film it directly inspired.

The Mummy's Curse (1944)

Released December 22, 1944. 62 minutes. *Directed by* Leslie Goodwins. *Associate Producer:* Oliver Drake. *Executive Producer:* Ben Pivar. *Screenplay by* Bernard L. Schubert. *Original Story and Adaptation:* Leon Abrams, Dwight V. Babcock, Bernard L. Schubert & T.H. Richmond. *Director of Photography:* Virgil Miller. *Camera Operator:* William Dodds. *Special Photographic Effects:* John P. Fulton. *Film Editor:* Fred R. Feitshans, Jr. *Assistant Director:* Mack Wright. *Art Directors:* John B.Goodman & Martin Obzina. *Musical Director:* Paul Sawtell. *Song, "Hey, You," Music by* Oliver Drake, *Lyrics by* Frank Orth. *Set Decorators:* Russell A. Gausman & Victor A. Gangelin. *Sound Director:* Bernard B. Brown. *Technician:* Robert Pritchard. *Properties:* Ernie Smith & Eddie Case. *Makeup by* Jack P. Pierce. *Gowns by* Vera West.

Lon Chaney (Kharis), Peter Coe (Dr. Ilzor Zandaab), Virginia Christine (Princess Ananka), Kay Harding (Betty Walsh), Dennis Moore (Dr. James Halsey), Martin Kosleck (Ragheb), Kurt Katch (Cajun Joe), Addison Richards (Pat Walsh), Holmes Herbert (Dr. Cooper), Charles Stevens (Achilles), William Farnum (Michael), Napoleon Simpson (Goobie), Ann Codee (Tante Berthe), Herbert Heywood (Hill), Nina Bara (Cajun Girl), Eddie Abdo (Pierre), Tony Santoro (Ulysses), Eddie Parker, Bob Pepper (Lon Chaney's Doubles), Carey Loftin, Teddy Mangean (Stunts), Heenan Elliott, Al Ferguson, Budd Buster.

The last chapter of a long-running horror series rarely offers anything fresh for aficionados to feast on. Generally it's a tired rehash of all the tried-and-true elements that have worked before. While *The Mummy's Curse* doesn't break any new ground in regards to plot, it does offer a few pleasant surprises—a welcome shift in locale, a strong performance by Virginia Christine, the most beautifully executed sequence in the entire series, plus lots of eagerly anticipated Mummy murders (in fact, more than in any of the other series entries).

The marshy grave that consumed Kharis and his reincarnated lover Princess Ananka in *The Mummy's Ghost* was just a temporary resting place for the indefatigable pair. Even before the LeBorg film was released, Universal announced plans (in early spring, 1944) to produce a fourth sequel, *The Mummy's Return.* It could be produced quickly, at nominal cost, and be released in time to support the studio's all-star horror spectacular, *House of Frankenstein* (then called *The Devil's Brood*) on a double bill.

Ben Pivar assigned Leslie Goodwins to the task of directing his new chiller, retitled *The Mummy's Curse,* a week before it went into production on July 26, 1944. Twelve days were allotted to get this quickie in the can. Goodwins took full advantage of standing sets and backlot locations. The *Tower of London* set stood in as the lower level of the monastery where Kharis is brought back to life. The Singapore Street (used in many a lusty action programmer) served as the rear entrance to Tante Berthe's cafe. Bernard L. Schubert's script called for extensive outdoor location work. Such familiar locales as the *Gung Ho!* jungle, Lubin Lake and Pollard Lake did extra duty for the eerie swamp shots.

On August 8, after hours of toiling in the stifling mid-summer heat, the production drew to a close. There still remained, however, additional pages of script to be shot, most of which centered around the picture's most elaborate sequence, the rebirth of Ananka from the mire. After careful consideration, the producers decided to shoot this scene straight and eliminate the complicated camera effects originally called for. Apparently, the higher-ups feared Virginia Christine's health would be in jeopardy from the prolonged effects of the makeup she wore and the conditions under which the scene would be shot. In short, Universal didn't want a lawsuit on their hands.

The Mummy's Curse exploits further the intriguing reincarnated love theme introduced in *The Mummy's Ghost.* Instead of picking up the story where it left off, in the Mapleton marshes, Schubert changed the setting to the Louisiana bayous, land of the dreaded *loup garou,* forsaken by all but the superstitious Cajuns. Twenty-five years after the disappearance of Kharis and Ananka in the swamplands (which, by rights, would set this story in 1969!), a team of excavators, commissioned by the U.S. government to drain the marshes, unwittingly uncovers the mummies. Two representatives from the Scripps Museum, Dr. James Halsey (Dennis Moore) and Dr. Ilzor Zandaab (Peter Coe), arrive on the scene. Zandaab, an Egyptian, has recruited Ragheb (Martin Kosleck), one of the workmen, to assist him in his sacred mission: to recover the mummies and return them to their rightful tombs in Egypt.

Under cover of night, Zandaab and Ragheb (referred to in an early stage of the film's production by their Egyptian names, Ismail and Abbas, respectively) sneak away to an abandoned monastery at the edge of the swamp. There, Zandaab initiates his new recruit into the Royal Den of High Priests. (Those old clips from *The Mummy* and *The Mummy's Hand* are trotted out once again to refresh our memories of Kharis' and Ananka's forbidden tryst.) Kharis (Lon Chaney) is brought back to live with tana brew and, after permanently silencing the sacristan (William Farnum), sets out to claim his bride.

In what ranks as one of the most arresting sequences of '40s cinemacabre, the withered Princess Ananka (Virginia Christine) emerges from her swamp tomb. One clawing, parchment-skinned hand breaks the slimy surface, then the other. A sphinx-like face, encrusted with mud, follows. Moments later, a woman painfully struggles to her feet. She draws strength from the rays of the late afternoon sun. (Later, at Halsey's camp, Ananka turns to the sun again for sustenance.) The age-old princess slips into a pond and steps out in all her 20th century glory (coiffured black tresses and mascara-lined brows).

Lon Chaney, director Leslie Goodwins and Virginia Christine take a breather during the shooting of *The Mummy's Curse.*

Ananka is discovered wandering aimlessly through the swamp like a sleepwalker. She is taken to Halsey's campsite. The archaeologist is astonished by her knowledge of the ancient Egyptians. Zandaab is even more impressed. Returning to the monastery, he commands a visibly weary Kharis to track her down.

This quest results in a string of murders. Two of them are particularly well-staged. Cafe singer Tante Berthe (Ann Codee) is strangled to death by Kharis as a jaunty Cajun folksong is heard from the next room. In another, Virgil Miller's camera stands directly behind Cajun Joe (Kurt Katch) as he vainly pumps bullets into the indestructible fiend.

Haunted by feelings that she is being dragged back to a world of which she has only fleeting recollections, Ananka confides her fears to Dr. Cooper (Holmes Herbert), who is understandably confused. Kharis suddenly bursts into the tent. Ananka escapes from his clutches once again. Cooper is not so lucky.

Ananka's luck finally runs out. Kharis takes her to the monastery where a triumphant Zandaab feeds her tana brew. Ragheb, meanwhile, has grown tired of the chaste life of a disciple of Amon-Ra, and lures Betty Walsh (Kay Harding), niece of the swamp project manager, to the secret hideaway. Zandaab is furious. "The vultures will pick the flesh from your bones when Kharis learns of your treachery!" he threatens. The unrepentant laborer plants a dagger in the priest's back. Enraged over the murder of his mentor, the Mummy corners Ragheb in a cell and literally brings the house down trying to reach him. Both are buried under tons of rubble. Halsey and his party arrive and discover the mummified remains of the strange young woman they had sheltered.

Suffering from a plodding, repetitive script (the movie is essentially one prolonged chase), *The Mummy's Curse* redeems itself with a generous share of cheap thrills. It lacks the polish of the previous Kharis pictures, but this works to its advantage. The plot wastes little time in getting down to the grisly business at hand. We are gratefully spared those ponderous police investigation scenes that dragged down the previous two sequels. And, unlike *The Mummy's Hand,* it has minimal comedy relief.

Probably no one was happier than Chaney that Universal dumped the Mummy series after this film. He hated the role with a passion and goes through the familiar paces with little heart. Virtually none of his tortured character's centuries-old passions are conveyed in the screenplay or Chaney's performance. For years, it was rumored that Chaney never played the part of Kharis in this film or any of the other sequels, that only his name was used for publicity purposes. Writer-turned-director Joe Dante was the first to hatch this theory in a 1962 edition of *Famous Monsters;* William K. Everson seconded it years later in his book, *More Classics of the Horror Film.* Although the horror star had various stand-ins and stunt doubles (Edwin Parker and Bob Pepper, to name two) during the shooting of these pictures, the fact that he did indeed don the wrappings is attested by Reginald LeBorg, Elyse Knox, Peter Coe, Martin Kosleck, Virginia Christine and a backlog of studio production reports.

Chaney walked off with an easy $8,000 for his uninspired performance. Peter Coe came in second with $3,500, followed by Martin Kosleck ($1,200) and Dennis Moore ($1,000). Second female lead Kay Harding received a total of $750 for her services, while seventh-billed Kurt Katch made that same figure on a per week basis. Considering she was third-billed, gave the best performance in the picture, and endured immeasurable discomfort during shooting, Virginia Christine ended up with the poorest salary—a total of $541.67 for a bit over two weeks' work (that comes out to $250 per week!). Even Napoleon Simpson ($500 per week) and Charles Stevens ($525 total for a week and a half service) fared better. Christine improved her purse when she received an extra $250 to cover the intervening time between completion of her role and her recall for shooting the arduous rebirth-of-Ananka scene. A few intriguing budget tidbits: Tom Tyler received a $60 check for the use of his clips from *The Mummy's Hand;* a $100 salary allowance was reserved for a narrator (this part was scrapped); the producers paid one dollar each for the songs "Hey, You" and "Monsieur Le Good for Nothin'" (the latter was not recorded); and, most fascinating of all, the mummy suit set Universal back $100.

Although she has made hundreds of motion picture and television appearances, Virginia Christine is most frequently recognized as "Mrs. Olson," the amiable Swedish woman of the now-defunct Folger's Coffee commercials. (It is a part she essayed for 21 years!) Born in Iowa, the actress came to Hollywood as an accomplished pianist. There, she met and married the enormously talented Fritz Feld. "Fritzie," as he is affectionately called by his friends and family, took charge of his young wife's career. She received critical recognition when she appeared on the Los Angeles stage in a 1942 revival of

Virginia Christine as the mummified Princess Ananka in *The Mummy's Curse,* another example of Jack Pierce's makeup wizardry.

Ibsen's "Hedda Gabler." Fox and Warner Bros. offered Virginia short-term contracts. She chose Warners. Her stay there was not particularly lucrative, but she has warm memories of working with Errol Flynn in *Edge of Darkness* (1943).

The lovely actress signed up with Universal, and was cast as Lionel Atwill's partner-in-crime in the 1944 western serial, *Raiders of Ghost City.* ("He was a wonderfully pompous old ham. I kind of stood in awe of him. We got along very nicely, but he was the kind of man that you would call 'Mr. Atwill.' He was this wonderful matinee idol-type ham.") *The Mummy's Curse* marked the horror film debut of the 27-year-old blonde actress. Her performance as the tormented Ananka is the finest of the entire Kharis series. With great humor, Christine recalls her bizarre experience shooting the resurrection scene:

> I had to be okayed by Jack Pierce in order to get the part. He elevated himself to the position of top monster maker in the business. He was an arrogant man, but we got along beautifully. He said my cheekbones were fine, so I got the part.
>
> We shot the film, and then came the last day of shooting when I change from a mummy to a lovely Egyptian princess. All through the picture, Jack kept coming on the set, saying, "I'm using something new on you, Virginia. It's going to be terrific. *Don't worry,* it won't hurt your skin." I was very young and "It won't hurt your skin" began to ring in my ears. I was a basket case the night before shooting. So, "Fritzie" called Jack on the phone late that night and said, "Jack, what are you going to put on Virginia's face? She's as nervous as a cat!" Jack laughed and said, "Oh, it's nothing—it's a Denver mudpack!"

I was there at four or five in the morning, and sat in the makeup chair for five-and-one-half hours. He started with pieces of cotton dipped in witch hazel to fill in all the youthful lines. Then, he lined it with an orange stick to make the wrinkles. That had to be dried. And then came the Denver mudpack, and that had to be dried. He worked a little patch at a time. Unfortunately, we made a mistake in wardrobe because we left the arms bare, which meant that the arms had to be done, too, and the hands . . . every place the skin was exposed. It was a tedious, long process. And, of course, the natural thing happened . . . I had to go to the bathroom. The body makeup lady was Jack's wife. She took me in like a baby because if I spoiled the hands we'd have to start all over again as they would crack. It was hardened now. I couldn't smile, I couldn't laugh. I couldn't talk. And I got the giggles in the john. It was so ridiculous! We got through that and I got hungry. I would have stolen for food. And so they spoiled the lips a bit and got me a malted milk.

After the full session, they put me in a cart and took me out to the back lot. Very carefully, they dug a hole, my height, right in the dirt. For any big star, they would have sifted the sand and done it on the stage, and had it *cleaned.* They laid me down in the thing and covered me with burnt cork which photographs like dirt. They turned the hose on so the dried cork got wet and looked like the earth around it. I laid there with this much of me exposed and thought, "Oh, God, how many creepy, crawly things are in this with me?!" And just before they shot, they covered my face. So I emerged—and you have to do a little acting along with this . . . and how do you act like a mummy? They had built steps in this murky, ugly, swampy, greenish lake. I'm supposed to take two or three steps . . . I took one look and said, "I can't do it, I simply can't do it." And then you psyche yourself up and say, "You wanted to be an actress, *do it!* This time tomorrow, it'll be over." Ingrid Bergman was shooting on an adjacent stage. They all heard about this episode that was being shot, and everybody came out to watch the sequence. We got through it in only one take.

Les Goodwins was one of the sweetest guys on earth. He didn't help *at all.* He could get a picture finished on time, was good-natured, but you never really got any direction from him. You were pretty much on your own in those films. Ben Pivar was very good to me all through the years. I played in several of his films. I never regretted making *The Mummy's Curse.*

As Virginia's film career escalated, so did her fantastic film credits. She appeared briefly but memorably in *House of Horrors* (1946) and *Invasion of the Body Snatchers* (1956), as well as *Billy the Kid Versus Dracula* (1966) and television's *Daughter of the Mind* (1969). Valued as one of Hollywood's "dependables" by producers like Stanley Kramer (who cast her in a number of his major productions), Virginia came within a hair's-breadth of achieving stardom when she was a leading contender for the Pat Kroll role opposite Ronald Colman in the 1947 Universal-International melodrama, *A Double Life*—but lost to Shelley Winters.

The supporting cast of *The Mummy's Curse* includes Kay (formerly Jackie Lou) Harding and Dennis Moore as the nominal romantic leads. Moore had previously portrayed the whiskered, bespectacled professor who commits a series of "vampire killings" for which stage magician Bela Lugosi is blamed in Monogram's 1941 East Side Kids farce. *Spooks Run Wild.* Peter Coe's Ilzor Zandaab proves himself to be Arkhon's staunchest disciple. Unlike his

Perhaps the most striking scene of the Kharis series: Virginia Christine emerges from the swamplands in *The Mummy's Curse.*

predecessors Zucco, Bey and Carradine, Coe zealously sticks to his game plan and doesn't succumb to weaknesses of the flesh. That transgression is committed by acolyte Martin Kosleck, who literally oozes treachery with every grimace. Coe overacts his part. He's as inscrutable and coolly aloof as Turhan Bey was in the same role, but he lacks Bey's assurance and his velvety delivery.

Coe recalls one particular incident during shooting which tested his mettle as a professional. He was in the midst of a lunch break interview with columnist Hedda Hopper, when an assistant director informed him he'd have to prepare for an extra scene the company planned on shooting within the hour. "I looked at the script—thirteen pages of soliloquy—solid dialogue. Nobody would believe it but I did it in one take! The whole crew stood up and cheered."

Coe paints a different picture of Lon Chaney than many of his coworkers did during this phase of his career. Aging silent picture star William Farnum was cast as the sacristan, the Mummy's first victim. Apparently, Farnum had problems remembering his few lines and caused Leslie Goodwins a lot of grief. "He was a friend of Chaney's father—a big star. Both Chaney and I said, 'Lee—get him a star's chair, otherwise we're going to walk off the set.' Chaney didn't have to do that for the old man."

According to Coe, Chaney never showed any discontent playing Kharis under such oppressive conditions. After the picture was completed, the two actors became drinking buddies and went geese and pheasant hunting a few days before Peter's induction into the service. Years later, the two lived a short distance from each other.

Both Virginia Christine and Martin Kosleck recall Chaney was almost constantly fortified during the filming of *The Mummy's Curse.* Christine recalls:

> They had this old shrine built at Universal, and the steps leading up to it were kind of worn. Chaney got into that mummy suit – he was a *very* big guy. Evelyn Ankers had played the leading lady before that, in other monster movies opposite Lon. She was big and tall, and heavy, so Chaney had a canvas strap that went around the back of his neck and then attached to her waist, so that his arms wouldn't have to support her whole weight. I inherited that. Chaney had to carry me up these steps – all uneven surfaces. Lon was weaving a little bit and I had to play limp. And I'm *attached* to this big guy, so there's no way to get loose if *he* falls. Thank God Les Goodwins said, "Hold it a second!" and he got a stand-in to go into the mummy suit.

Lon Chaney retired his tattered mummy outfit after making *The Mummy's Curse,* never dreaming he would reprise the role twice more in the future. In the 1959 Mexican film *La Casa del Terror* (*The House of Terror*), Chaney plays a mummy who also turns out to be a werewolf. (This poor film was finally released in the United States in 1965 under the title *Face of the Screaming Werewolf.*) And in 1963, the Mummy was one of three great horror characters (the other two were the Hunchback and the Wolf Man) Chaney recreated for the all-star "Route 66" Halloween special entitled "Lizard's Leg and Owlet's Wing."

The crumbling, 3000-year-old Kharis returned to the screen ten years after the release of *The Mummy's Curse* to face perhaps his greatest challenge – upstaging a sadly aging and painfully unfunny comedy team in *Abbott and Costello Meet the Mummy.* The screenwriters have inexplicably changed his monicker to *Klaris,* but it doesn't really matter – it's still our favorite Mummy, portrayed this time by Eddie Parker, who stalks about some interesting Egyptian temple sets looking more like a bandaged Creature from the Black Lagoon.

In 1959, Hammer did the Mummy a good turn when they revived the ancient menace for a lavish Technicolor update. *The Mummy,* one of the British horror house's most handsome remakes, presents a Kharis that was a good deal more than just a slavish killing machine. Alas, the sequels/spinoffs this film spawned (*The Curse of the Mummy's Tomb, Blood from the Mummy's Tomb*) were among the worst horror films Hammer ever produced. Colorless and grim, they were the antithesis of the brashly absurd, maddeningly repetitious, but immensely enjoyable Universal romps of the Fabulous Forties.

The House of Fear (1945)

Released March 16, 1945. 69 minutes. *Produced and Directed by* Roy William Neill. *Screenplay by* Roy Chanslor. *Based on the story "The Five Orange Pips" by* Sir Arthur Conan Doyle. *Director of Photography:* Virgil Miller. *Camera Operator:* Edward Cohen. *Musical Director:* Paul Sawtell. *Art Directors:* John B. Goodman & Eugene Lourie. *Director of Sound:* Bernard B. Brown. *Technician:* William Hedgcock. *Set Decorators:* Russell A. Gausman & Edward R. Robinson. *Film Editor:* Saul A. Goodkind. *Dialogue Director:* Ray Kessler. *Assistant Directors:* Melville Shyer & Mort Singer, Jr.

Basil Rathbone (Sherlock Holmes), Nigel Bruce (Dr. John H. Watson), Aubrey Mather (Bruce Alastair), Dennis Hoey (Inspector Lestrade), Paul Cavanagh (Dr. Simon Merrivale), Holmes Herbert (Alan Cosgrave), Harry Cording (Capt. John Simpson), Sally Shepherd (Mrs. Monteith), Gavin Muir (Mr. Chalmers), Florette Hillier (Alison MacGregor), David Clyde (Alec MacGregor), Wilson Benge (Guy Davies), Leslie Denison (Sgt. Bleeker), Alec Craig (Angus), Dick Alexander (Ralph King), Cyril Delevanti (Stanley Rayburn).

Another attempt to remove the Universal Sherlock Holmes character from his Baker Street haunts and from the World War II setting, *The House of Fear* is a moderately interesting but mostly unmemorable mystery/thriller. Like other films in the series (*Sherlock Holmes Faces Death, The Scarlet Claw*), *House of Fear* tries to give the impression that it's set in the earlier era of the original Conan Doyle stories: automobiles and other 20th century conveniences are seldom if ever seen, and no references to the current state of world politics are made. Compared to the other films in this Holmes subgenre, *The House of Fear* falls harmlessly in the middle: it's not the ponderous stiff that *Faces Death* is, nor has it got the chills or action of *The Scarlet Claw. The House of Fear* is in no danger of ever being called anyone's favorite Holmes picture, but it features a sufficient number of minor plusses to stand safely above the detective's notoriously flaccid film adventures.

The House of Fear has as its basis the Conan Doyle story "The Five Orange Pips," a pointless and unsatisfying Holmes adventure. In this original story, young John Openshaw appears out of a fierce London rainstorm and lays out his story to Holmes. Openshaw explains that his uncle, Col. Openshaw, a quick-tempered man who was once a slaveowner in Florida, returned to England a few years after the Civil War and settled down to a reclusive life on a Sussex estate. One day the uncle received a letter containing orange pips (seeds); scrawled upon the inner flap of the envelope were the letters K.K.K.

The uncle took the letter as a death threat, burned some of his papers, and soon after died a mysterious death which was ruled a suicide. Some months later, Openshaw continues, his own father received a similar envelope containing orange pips along with a letter that demanded the uncle's papers (the letter-writer doesn't know that the uncle burned them); a few days later, the father died, "accidentally." And now young Openshaw reveals that he, too, has received the dreaded letter. Holmes promises to investigate and, after sending Openshaw on his way, deduces that the letters are from the Ku Klux Klan; obviously the Colonel, a former member, was in possession of incriminating documents. But before Holmes can act, word reaches him of John Openshaw's "accidental" death. Holmes vows to bring the killers to justice, but the bark upon which the Klansmen had sailed is lost at sea.

Screenwriter Roy Chanslor (later the author of such well-known Western novels as *Johnny Guitar* and *Cat Ballou*) apparently found little to work with in the Conan Doyle story, and went about adding his own plot elements. Chanslor's script pivots around a private club which is being killed off one by one, each victim receiving shortly in advance of his disappearance and death an envelope containing orange pips. Under the working title *The Murder Club,* the film was shot in May, 1944 ("wrapping" three days over schedule on the 31st of the month), with exteriors photographed at Nagana Rocks and on the Hacienda lawn. The all-purpose *Green Hell* set is seen as a cellar at the conclusion.

The film opens with a series of flashbacks. A dulcet-voiced narrator introduces us to the Good Comrades, an unusual seven-member club headquartered in Drearcliff House, a centuried castle-like mansion perched on a seaside cliff in Scotland. The club members enjoy a laugh when one of them, Ralph King (Dick Alexander), receives a letter containing seven orange pips; King is killed in a fiery car crash shortly thereafter. There's no laughter when Stanley Rayburn (Cyril Delevanti) receives six orange pips; his mangled body is later dragged out of the sea. Both deaths conform to the gruesome legend of Drearcliff House, where "no man ever goes whole to his grave."

The narrator of these flashbacks is Mr. Chalmers (Gavin Muir), an insurance underwriter who is telling the story to Holmes and Watson. Chalmers considers the deaths suspicious in that the Good Comrades have set themselves up as a tontine (with the death of each beneficiary, the insurance money is divided among the survivors). Intrigued, Holmes accepts the case.

Holmes and Watson journey to Scotland, arriving just in time to receive news of the death of a third member, who was incinerated. The four remaining Good Comrades are Bruce Alastair (Aubrey Mather), Dr. Simon Merrivale (Paul Cavanagh), Alan Cosgrave (Holmes Herbert) and John Simpson (Harry Cording). Holmes and Watson move into desolate Drearcliff House and begin their investigation. Cosgrave is the next to receive orange pips (four), and despite police protection from the newly-arrived Inspector Lestrade (Dennis Hoey), he disappears; his blown-to-bits body is found in the ruins of a dynamite shed. Simpson finds three pips in his envelope and pretty soon there's nothing left of him but a torso. MacGregor (David Clyde), a tobacconist in the nearby village, sends a note which indicates that he has stumbled upon a clue, but before Holmes can get to the man, he's shot by the Drearcliff killer.

A shortage of action and an easily-seen-through mystery cripple the eighth Sherlock Holmes opus, *The House of Fear*.

Acting on a hunch, Holmes has Watson exhume MacGregor's coffin shortly after his funeral: the coffin is empty. This confirms some unspecified suspicion of Holmes' and he rushes back to Drearcliff House, where the body of Dr. Merrivale has just been found, crushed to a jelly by a fallen boulder. Lestrade places the last surviving Good Comrade, Alastair, under arrest. Watson discovers a clue, but before he can bring it to Holmes' attention he vanishes mysteriously. Holmes and Lestrade discover a hidden passage that leads to a secret room; in it, the two men find the six supposedly-dead Good Comrades. To collect money from the insurance company, the men had faked their own deaths using the stolen and mutilated corpses of recently-buried villagers, and framed Alastair. Alastair is cleared and Watson is rescued as Lestrade places the men under arrest for the murder of MacGregor.

Although a synopsis of *The House of Fear* may suggest a fast-paced, action-packed mystery, it's actually a slow-moving and overly talkative film. Despite the high death rate, none of this mayhem occurs on-screen: the murders cannot be depicted since they really do not occur. All the viewer is left with is repetitive episodes of victims receiving the orange pips and disappearing, quickly followed by scenes of Holmes discovering a body. This device has already begun to wear thin before the opening flashback sequence has concluded, and it becomes exceedingly tiresome later when it represents the only activity in the film.

Director Roy William Neill tries to get around this intrinsic flaw by creating old-dark-house atmosphere in the ancient Scottish castle, but without action to liven up the proceedings the film drags. There are no deep-dyed villains to chew scenery nor any outstanding performers in the supporting cast. The mystery outlined in the film is a bewildering one at first, but toward the end the killers' plans become obvious. The screenplay also halts abruptly once in a too-long comedy relief scene where Nigel Bruce searches the house during a violent rainstorm and skittishly engages in a one-sided gunfight with suits of armor and moving shadows.

Despite the dreary ambience, *The House of Fear* still rests notches above some of the other Holmes films. Rathbone's performance seems to lack its customary zip at times, but for the most part both he and Bruce are in good form. Dennis Hoey gets more than his accustomed share of the footage as Lestrade, and for once Hoey comes off funnier and livelier than Bruce does. A dinner-table scene where Hoey becomes apoplectic upon receiving a hand-delivered letter (it's just a note, but he thinks the envelope contains orange pips) is particularly amusing, and far brighter than anything Nigel Bruce gets to do in the picture.

The balance of the cast is colorless. Aubrey Mather, on loanout from Fox, is fey and phlegmatic as Alastair, and begins to grate on the nerves after a point, while Paul Cavanagh is too smooth and convivial to be effective in his role as the primary red herring. Holmes Herbert and Harry Cording have substantial roles, and it's good to see these veteran supporting players finally getting an opportunity to play bigger and better than usual parts. Sally Shepherd, as a solemn housekeeper, adds yet more gloom to a film that was gloomy enough already.

Collaborating with Universal vet John B. Goodman on the film's art direction was Eugene Lourie, the celebrated Russian-born set designer of *Grand Illusion/The Rules of the Game/Limelight* fame. Additionally contributing to the film's desired atmosphere of spooky weirdness is Virgil Miller's cinematography, with its frequent use of odd (and often distracting) "tilted" shots.

By and large *The House of Fear* is a substandard Sherlock Holmes exploit which offers very little besides the usual Rathbone-Bruce-Hoey acting chemistry. But for a legion of mystery fans this is adequate compensation for a 69 minute investment, and like most of the rest of the Universal-Holmes series, the film remains a late-night television favorite.

That's the Spirit (1945)

Released June 1, 1945. 87 minutes. *Original Screenplay Written & Produced by* Michael Fessier and Ernest Pagano. *Directed by* Charles Lamont. *Director of Photography:* Charles Van Enger. *Musical Score and Direction:* Hans J. Salter. *Art Directors:* John B. Goodman & Richard H. Riedel. *Dance Ensembles Staged by* Carlos Romero. *Numbers for Peggy Ryan and Johnny Coy Staged by* Louis De Pron. *Songs: "No Matter Where You Are," "Evenin' Star"* (Jack Brooks & Hans J. Salter), *"Fella with a Flute," "Oh, Oh, Oh"* (Sidney Miller & Inez James), *"Nola"* (Felix Arndt), *"How Come You Do Me Like You Do?"* (Roy Bergere, Gene Austin), *"Baby, Won't You Please Come Home?"* (Clarence Williams, Charles Warfield), *"Bugle Call Rag"* (J. Hubert Blake, Carey Morgan), *"Ja-Da"* (Bob Carleton), *"Do You Ever Think of Me?"* (Earl Burnett, John Cooper, Harry D. Kerr). *Director of Sound:* Bernard B. Brown. *Technician:* Charles Carroll. *Set Decorations:* Russell A. Gausman & Andrew J. Gilmore. *Film Editor:* Fred R. Feitshans, Jr. *Gowns:* Vera West. *Dialogue Director:* Monty Collins. *Assistant Director:* William Tummel. *Special Photography:* John P. Fulton.

Jack Oakie (Steve Gogarty), Peggy Ryan (Sheila Gogarty), June Vincent (Libby Cawthorne Gogarty), Gene Lockhart (Jasper Cawthorne), Johnny Coy (Martin Wilde, Jr.), Andy Devine (Martin Wilde), Arthur Treacher (Masters), Irene Ryan (Bilson), Buster Keaton (L.M.), Victoria Horne (Patience), Edith Barrett (Abigail Cawthorne), Rex Story (Specialty), Karen Randle (Dark Lady), Harry Tyler, Billy Newell (Detectives), Jack Roper (Ticket Taker), Virginia Brissac (Miss Preble), Charles Sullivan, Sid Troy (Men), Monty Collins (Bellhop), Jack Shutta, Fred Kelsey (Detectives), Dorothy Christy (Nurse), Eddie Dunn, Ed Gargan (Policemen), Mary Forbes (Woman), Mabel Forrest, Genevieve Bell, Herbert Evans, Lloyd Ingram, Nelson McDowell (Guests), Wheaton Chambers (Doctor), Herbert Heywood (Doorman), Bobby Barber (Butcher), Lou Wood (Assistant Dance Director), Brooks Benedict (Assistant Stage Manager), Mary McLeod, Gloria Marlen (Secretary), Teddy Infuhr (Page Boy), Eddie Cutler, Charles Teske (Dance Specialty), Jerry Maren, Billy Curtis (Specialty Midgets).

This is a pesky title: It's a musical comedy that revolves around a ghost, so it has to be included in the book, but it's about as suitable as *The Mummy's Curse* would be in a book on musicals. Let's make it short and sweet.

Jasper Cawthorne (Gene Lockhart) is a turn-of-the-century New York banker/bluenose who unrelentingly imposes his prudish will upon his long-suffering wife Abigail (Edith Barrett) and daughter Libby (June Vincent); he is unforgiving when Libby woos and weds an oafish vaudeville hoofer, Steve Gogarty (Jack Oakie). Libby is dangerously near death as her baby is born and Steve wishes aloud that if anything is to happen, it will happen to him; the Dark Lady, a distaff Grim Reaper, overhears him as she's heading into the hospital's maternity ward and claims Steve instead.

In Heaven, Steve is convinced that stuffed-shirt Cawthorne will continue to dominate the unhappy family and asks for a chance to return to Earth and set things right. After an 18-year probationary period he is permitted to make the journey, materializing again on this side of the veil as a spirit invisible and inaudible to everyone except his now-grown daughter Sheila (Peggy Ryan) and, of course, the audience. Sheila has showbiz in her blood and wants to become a singer/dancer in a show but Cawthorne has put his aristocratic foot down.

Acting with her mother's consent, Sheila joins the production anyway, but Cawthorne buys up all of showman Andy Devine's I.O.U.'s and forces him to can her. Using a magic flute whose music brings out the kid in people, Steve brings about a showdown in which Cawthorne is soundly told off by his family and even by members of the household staff. Cawthorne begins to see the error in his willful ways and cheerfully becomes a partner in the show instead. Sheila and her leading man (Johnny Coy) dance their way into each other's hearts while Steve, now joined by the spirit of Libby (who has died), returns to Heaven.

That's the Spirit is a minor entry in the heavenly-comedy sweepstakes that began with *Here Comes Mr. Jordan* in 1941. That successful Columbia film was followed by pictures like *Heaven Can Wait* (1943), *A Guy Named Joe* (1943), *The Horn Blows at Midnight* (1945), *Stairway to Heaven* (1946), *Down to Earth* (1947) and, best and most famous of all, *It's a Wonderful Life* (1946). *That's the Spirit* is the least-known title on this formidable list, and deservedly so: it's an unimaginative little picture that merely latched onto what was then a money-making formula and tailored it to the talents of teenage singer-dancer Peggy Ryan. It's not a bad film, but the spirit of fun is quickly and measurably outpaced by the overwhelming sense of déjà vu.

There are a few neat touches in the film, and it benefits appreciably from the efforts of special effects ace John P. Fulton. (Oakie's ghost is a forerunner of science-fiction's *4D Man* in his ability to walk through walls; there's even a surprising and ambitious bit where Oakie walks across a busy street as cars and trucks run through him.)

It's also unusual, and a little creepy, to see Death embodied in the film: actress Karen Randle plays the Dark Lady, a silent wraith who turns up several times during the proceedings. She first appears early on, as newlywed Oakie carries June Vincent over a threshold, tripping as he enters. The two end up in a heap and are about to clinch when they see the raven-tressed, white-faced Dark Lady framed in the doorway; she regards them dispassionately for a few seconds before quietly moving away. Her unexpected appearance, and the eerie organ chord that accompanies it, are enough to raise a few goosebumps, which is more than Universal's straight horror films were doing at this point. This female harbinger of death turns up again at the hospital, as June Vincent is in danger of dying in childbirth, and toward the end of the film she boards a train behind Vincent and Gene Lockhart. (The audience—or at least *this* audience—assumes that Scrooge Lockhart is going to get his comeuppance, but it's Vincent who soon dies, paving the way for the happy ending where she joins Oakie on his return trip to Heaven.)

Curiously, nearly every review of *That's the Spirit* (even ones written today) claims that Oakie returns to Earth to straighten out a misunderstanding with his wife. This does figure into the plot in a minor way, but it's really for his daughter's sake that Oakie makes the trip. It's strange how mistakes like this get repeated in review after review, and it doesn't speak well for critics who are obviously giving their opinions of movies they haven't seen. Speaking of mistakes, some of the songs heard in *That's the Spirit* were written years after the film's 1916 setting; the dancing and some of the clothes are also too new for the period. But somehow it seems petty to pick at things like this in a movie about a ghost with a magic flute; once you've swallowed that premise, you might as well let it roll over you.

A good cast meets the minor demands of the picture. Beefy Jack Oakie is especially appealing and likable as the title ghost, and there's even some pathos in a scene where he moons over his grieving wife, who can neither see him nor hear his heartfelt words. Peggy Ryan and screen newcomer Johnny Coy do an okay job of filling their singing/dancing/acting juvenile roles, while pros June Vincent, Gene Lockhart and Andy Devine go through their paces almost effortlessly. (Lockhart is at the center of the film's funniest scene: at a dreary little dinner party he is singing "Evenin' Star" in his usual solemn fashion until Jack Oakie's flute works its magic: soon Lockhart is belting out the oldtime song in swing fashion and his superannuated guests are raising the roof with their jukin' and jivin'.) Arthur Treacher, as a disdainful butler, has no screen presence, and it's easy to understand why no one remembers him as anything other than Merv Griffin's flunky or as the Fish and Chips man. (How many Arthur Treacher movies can *you* name?) Irene Ryan, Granny to television's "Beverly Hillbillies," is a rubber-faced maid constantly alarmed by the sound of ghost Oakie's squeaky shoes.

Victoria Horne, later real-life's Mrs. Jack Oakie, plays Patience, a snooty, insufferable relative, in the film. Oakie died in 1978 but his dedicated wife has devoted herself to keeping his memory alive:

> *That's the Spirit* was the happiest picture to make. The entire cast looked forward to the entrance of Jack every day, he brought the most contagious happiness with him. On the last day of shooting Gene Lockhart presented my husband with a poem he wrote honoring him, and two of the lines are now engraved on Jack's plaque at Forest Lawn: "In a simple double-take, thou hast more than voice e'er spake."

Wifely devotion notwithstanding, the biggest name in *That's the Spirit* is, of course, Buster Keaton, that most brilliant of all silent screen comedians. Keaton's comedies are landmarks of the pre-talkie era, but by 1933 good fortune was no longer smiling upon the Great Stoneface: talking pictures, alcohol and a series of marital mishaps had reduced the once-great funnyman to a has-been relegated to the Hollywood hinterlands. In the mid '40s he made two appearances in Universal pictures (*San Diego, I Love You* and *That's the*

Spirit), probably through his friendship with Ernest Pagano, who cowrote and coproduced both pictures. Keaton has little more than a cameo in *That's the Spirit* as L.M., head of Heaven's complaint department: he wears his characteristic porkpie hat (a nice touch) and plays, for the first and only time in his entire talkie career, a character who is sensible and articulate rather than his usual idiot. Keaton seemed on the verge of regaining some of his lost popularity when the Dark Lady carted *him* off in 1966.

Partially Heaven-set but scarcely heavensent, *That's the Spirit* is a poor cousin to the bigger, better celestial fantasies of the 1940s. According to Michael Fitzgerald, it's the favorite picture of both Peggy Ryan and June Vincent, and there certainly is some airy, nostalgic fun to be had, but a fan drawn to the film by its supernatural aspects is bound to find it disappointingly derivative.

The Frozen Ghost (1945)

Released June 29, 1945. 61 minutes. An Inner Sanctum Mystery, produced by arrangement with Simon and Schuster, Inc., Publishers. *Directed by* Harold Young. *Associate Producer:* Will Cowan. *Executive Producer:* Ben Pivar. *Screenplay by* Bernard L. Schubert & Luci Ward. *Adaptation by* Henry Sucher. *Original Story by* Harrison Carter & Henry Sucher. *Director of Photography:* Paul Ivano. *Musical Director:* Hans J. Salter. *Art Directors:* John B. Goodman & Abraham Grossman. *Sound Supervisor:* Bernard B. Brown. *Technician:* William Hedgcock. *Set Decorators:* Russell A. Gausman & Ray L. Jeffers. *Film Editor:* Fred R. Feitshans, Jr. *Dialogue Director:* Edward Dein. *Assistant Director:* Fred Frank. *Camera Operator:* William Dodds. *Property Master:* William Nunley. *Gowns by* Vera West.

Lon Chaney (Alex Gregor), Evelyn Ankers (Maura Daniel), Milburn Stone (George Keene), Douglass Dumbrille (Police Inspector Brandt), Martin Kosleck (Rudi Poldan/Dr. Feldon), Elena Verdugo (Nina Coudreau), Tala Birell (Valerie Monet), Arthur Hohl (Skeptic), Leland [Leyland] Hodgson (Doctor), Pauline Drake (Girlfriend), Bobby Barber (Fat Man), Polly Bailey (Gray-Haired Woman), Jan Bryant (Bobby-Sox Girl), Charles Jordan (Second Reporter), Dennis Moore (Announcer), William Haade (Cop), Jan Jacobson (Organist), Eddie Bruce (Audience Member), Bud Wolfe (Cab Driver), Eddie Acuff (Reporter), David Hoffman (Inner Sanctum), Ken Terrell (Double for Martin Kosleck), June Davies, Norma Holm (Stand-ins).

The fourth Inner Sanctum entry, *The Frozen Ghost,* was apparently conceived with little confidence. A couple of versions of the script were circulating around Universal's story department for some time. Reginald LeBorg intended to shoot the film back-to-back with the series opener *Calling Dr. Death* in 1943, but the production was postponed.

Filming on *The Frozen Ghost* finally got underway on June 19, 1944, on a 12-day schedule. Though it officially wrapped on July 1, *The Frozen Ghost* wasn't released until a year later (it ended up heading a dismal all-horror double bill with *The Jungle Captive*).

LeBorg's departure from the series had caused a rift between him and Lon Chaney. "At the beginning Chaney thought I would be his *pal,* and when after three Inner Sanctums I wanted to do a musical—a Deanna Durbin picture or something—he said to me, 'You traitor! We were supposed to do big things together!' I told him, 'We'll get together again, don't worry!'" LeBorg and Chaney finally *did* get together again—12 years later on the set of *The Black Sleep.*

Harold Young, director of *The Mummy's Tomb,* took over the reins from LeBorg, but he didn't have the know-how to turn the rickety script into a cohesive thriller. There's a touch of style in the film's first scene as stage hypnotist Alex Gregor (Lon Chaney), who performs under the monicker Gregor the Great, places his assistant Maura Daniel (Evelyn Ankers) in a trance during a live radio broadcast. Branded a fake by a drunken skeptic (Arthur Hohl), Gregor invites the abusive heckler on stage, and is in the process of placing him in a trance when the man keels over and dies. Although a heart attack is listed as the cause of death, Gregor insists he's a murderer for subconsciously "willing" the man's demise.

Despondent, Gregor breaks off his engagement to Maura, gives up the act and takes a job at friend Valerie Monet's (Tala Birell) wax museum. The jealous Monet mistakes Alex's casual friendship with her niece Nina (Elena Verdugo) for romance and she bitterly confronts the hypnotist. Gregor blacks out, only to discover when he recovers that Valerie has mysteriously disappeared. Police Inspector Brandt (Douglass Dumbrille) investigates but cannot find the body; the eternal pessimist, Gregor is once again convinced he is responsible. This time the police start taking him seriously.

Unbeknownst to Gregor, there's a conspiracy afoot between the hypnotist's business manager, George Keene (Milburn Stone), and Rudi Poldan (Martin Kosleck), a disgraced plastic surgeon who works in Valerie's museum as a sculptor. Hoping to drive the hypnotist insane in order to gain control of his estate, the pair have put Monet into a state of suspended animation. But Rudi botches the job and Monet dies as a result of his negligence.

When Nina learns what has been going on, Rudi overpowers and drugs her. In a desperate attempt to unravel the mystery, Gregor places Maura into a state of deep hypnosis in order to unleash her psychic powers. Maura points an accusing finger at George, who is quickly nabbed by Bryant. Gregor and Maura rush down to the wax museum's furnace room and find Rudi is about to plunge Nina into the flames. Scuffling with Gregor, Rudi loses his footing and suffers the fiery fate intended for the girl.

The Inner Sanctum films alternated between standard whodunits (*Calling Dr. Death, Dead Man's Eyes*) and pseudosupernatural melodramas (*Weird Woman*). With *The Frozen Ghost,* the pendulum happily swings back to the latter. Once again, the series bungles a genuinely promising concept. Presumably operating under the theory that four hacks are better than one, a quartet of writers received the story credit for this fiasco (and that's not including Maurice Tombragel, whose contribution went uncredited). It's too bad that none of these chefs provided this bleak little number with anything resembling a plot. For the record, this is the only Inner Sanctum picture where all of the supernatural twists are *not* logically explained away in the last reel, even though it only turns out to be be a mild case of extrasensory perception. *The Frozen Ghost* is Universal's only attempt at a horror film set in a wax museum, a favorite stomping ground of screen terror and mayhem since the 1933 Warner Bros. classic *Mystery of the Wax Museum.* But the setting is a mere backdrop for the "action" and art directors John B. Goodman and Abraham Grossman's efforts are only perfunctory, even for this bargain basement offering.

The idea of a mentalist who uses his psychic powers to kill hasn't been used often despite a spate of "hypnosis" melodramas from *The Cabinet of Dr. Caligari* (1919) to *Calling Dr. Death* (Universal's earlier *The Love Captive,* 1934, involving murder by hypnosis, falls short of being a horror film). Cinematographer Paul Ivano pulls off some interesting effects in *The Frozen Ghost*, especially in Chaney's psychic bludgeoning of Tala Birell. Ivano tries to pump as much atmosphere as he can into this uneventful story with plenty of low-key lighting but results are more dismal than frightening.

Unbelievable as it may seem, the Inner Sanctum pictures were real moneymakers in their time. Dirt-cheap budgets, the popularity of the Simon and Schuster novels and the renowned radio show had a positive effect on the profit margin. Universal wasn't anxious to vary the formula so the same bromides turn up in film after film: the best friend of the hero ends up being the heavy, a procession of attractive females mystifyingly vie for Chaney's affections, and a persevering detective with a talent for barking up the wrong tree heads up the dead-end investigation. The stylistic hallmark of the series, yards of stream-of-consciousness dialogue slopping up the soundtrack, is played against Paul Sawtell's endlessly recycled, radio-style spook music. (Sawtell moved on to Columbia's B unit where his Inner Sanctum musical cues got a second lease on life in several of Bill Castle's *Whistler* mysteries.) For good measure, *The Frozen Ghost* adds a knife-throwing plastic surgeon and an unconvincing bit about suspended animation. With all of this mayhem, one would expect a fast-moving hour. Instead, it's just a hodgepodge of ingredients served up as an indigestible stew.

The Frozen Ghost is slovenly to the point of ridiculousness. Disguised as a wax figure, the "missing" body of Tala Birell is plainly visible to all but the on-screen characters, who blithely walk right by it in their search. The motive fueling the conspiracy is to get Chaney's fortune, leaving the viewer to wonder just how much loot even a *good* stage hypnotist is likely to acquire. It's also stubbornly unclear how business manager Milburn Stone intends to make any profit by railroading his meal ticket into the nuthouse.

The title is as desultory as anything in the film. Surely a marketable *and* appropriate title could have been conceived. So depressingly little effort went into *The Frozen Ghost,* its lack of suspense is almost a foregone conclusion. The writers didn't even bother to come up with a climactic twist in revealing the culprits. Instead, Stone and Kosleck's guilt is matter-of-factly divulged in a dull dialogue exchange long before the wrap-up.

As in *Dead Man's Eyes,* Chaney again is a whimpering, unsympathetic lead. Falling apart at the first obstacle, his Gregor the Great (a misnomer if there ever was one) hasn't the wit to see through the motives of those closest to him. Again, one wonders what all of these females see in Gregor: "He's very special—in fact, he's *wonderful*!" gasps Nina. His allure is all the more mystifying since Chaney plays the mesmerist in a slightly-deranged fashion. Nagging all within earshot with his own misplaced guilt, Chaney's self-flagellation routine quickly becomes a bore.

Pregnant at the time of filming, Evelyn Ankers' disinterested performance is forgivable, especially considering the quality of the script. Milburn Stone is

Top: **Gregor the Great (Lon Chaney) probes the dark recesses of his assistant's (Evelyn Ankers) mind; *bottom:* Patrolman William Haade catches Lon Chaney on one of his somnambulistic strolls—from *The Frozen Ghost,* an Inner Sanctum mystery.**

rather amiable as the villain. He is, in fact, more appealing than our tiresome hero. The supporting players, including Tala Birell, Douglass Dumbrille and Elena Verdugo, are good enough, but the *real* star of *The Frozen Ghost* is Martin Kosleck as the mad Rudi.

Kosleck came onto the set of *The Frozen Ghost* fresh from a nine-week personal appearance tour promoting Paramount's *The Hitler Gang* (1944). Universal was intent on grooming Kosleck as a new horror star; the script of *The Frozen Ghost* even had him talking to his waxworks, an obvious reference to Lionel Atwill in *Mystery of the Wax Museum.* "I liked Universal studios because I had wonderful parts," he comments. "I had my own dressing room on the lot and I felt very, very important. It wasn't a factory then."

Tala Birell, however, was far less pleased. She received her theatrical training on the Viennese stage where she, like Kosleck, worked under Max Reinhardt. The blonde actress signed a long-term contract with Carl Laemmle, Jr., in the '30s, and was promoted as another Garbo or Dietrich. Her hopes for a major career were quickly dashed and it wasn't long before Birell ended up playing supporting roles in program quickies. (Horror fans might remember her being chased by J. Carrol Naish's ape in PRC's *The Monster Maker,* 1944.)

Kosleck recalls participating in a particularly grim scene in *The Frozen Ghost.* "Tala Birell was shot dead or something, and I had to pull her out of the room. She was put on rollers and she just said, 'God! Can you imagine what we would have thought in Berlin!'"

Universal was delighted with Kosleck's work and exercised their option on his contract, slating him to appear in two additional films with Chaney. The pair were reunited for only a single feature, *The Mummy's Curse,* and then never worked together again. Kosleck admits to having shed few tears over their premature parting, and found his frequently inebriated costar difficult and unpleasant. (Though released later, *The Frozen Ghost* was shot two months before the Mummy film.) "The director [Harold Young] apparently liked me and I had a lot of close-ups. Chaney always came in and said, 'That's enough.' He *hated* me and I returned it. He was the star and he just wanted me out of the way."

Chaney regarded the Inner Sanctum series as *his* starring vehicles, and wasn't pleased when Kosleck got better notices than he for *The Frozen Ghost.* By the time the pair got together on *The Mummy's Curse,* an all-out feud was brewing. Chaney particularly relished stalking the diminutive Kosleck in the climactic moments of that film. Says Kosleck, "He enjoyed that thoroughly! I remember it well, I was pushed around. Why they had him as a star is beyond me. He was roaring drunk!"

Except for an occasional kind word for Martin Kosleck, the critical verdict on *The Frozen Ghost* was hostile. In an uncharacteristically venomous mood, *The Hollywood Reporter* ribbed Universal by publishing the choicest barbs from a sampling of scathing reviews. Not accustomed to courting favor with the highbrows, especially for their programmers, Universal undauntedly put another Inner Sanctum project on the drawing boards.

The Frozen Ghost was the last film Evelyn Ankers made under her Universal contract. Her marriage to actor Richard Denning was an enduring one, and her subsequent pictures like *Queen of Burlesque* (1946) and *The Texan Meets Calamity Jane* (1950) were forgettable. In the '60s, she and her husband relocated to Hawaii, where Denning enjoyed a recurring role as the governor on television's "Hawaii Five-O." In 1980, after the long-running series was finally terminated, Denning remarked, "Evelyn and I are looking forward to the '80s as a new era—'retirement and pensions.' We hope it beats working."

But this "new era" of bliss was not to be. Evelyn developed cancer shortly afterwards, but bravely determined to win her battle with the dreaded disease. By 1985 she seemed well on her way to a remarkable recovery. She had regained all lost weight, walked three miles a day, and felt and looked terrific; she frequently wrote to her Hollywood friends from her Maui home, emphasizing that she was once again on the road to good health. The inevitable finally occurred on August 28, 1985, when the veteran actress succumbed in her home. (She and Gale Sondergaard died only days apart.) Evelyn Ankers' beauty, talent and dignity will be long remembered.

The Jungle Captive (1945)

Released June 29, 1945. Rereleased as *Wild Jungle Captive*. 63 minutes. *Associate Producer:* Morgan B. Cox. *Executive Producer:* Ben Pivar. *Directed by* Harold Young. *Screenplay by* M. Coates Webster & Dwight V. Babcock. *Director of Photography:* Maury Gertsman. *Musical Director:* Paul Sawtell. *Art Directors:* John B. Goodman & Robert Clatworthy. *Director of Sound:* Bernard B. Brown. *Technician:* Robert Pritchard. *Set Decorators:* Russell A. Gausman & Andrew J. Gilmore. *Film Editor:* Fred R. Feitshans, Jr. *Assistant Directors:* Howard Christie, Harry Jones & Charles S. Gould. *Dialogue Director:* Willard Holland. *Camera Operator:* Harold Smith. *Assistant Cameraman:* Phil Lathrop. *Key Grip:* Fred Buckley. *Costumes by* Vera West.

Otto Kruger (Mr. Stendahl), Vicky Lane (Paula Dupree, the Ape Woman), Amelita Ward (Ann Forrester), Phil Brown (Don Young), Jerome Cowan (Police Insp. W.L. Harrigan), Rondo Hatton (Moloch), Eddie Acuff (Bill), Ernie Adams (Jim), Charles Wagenheim (Fred), Eddy Chandler (Motorcycle Cop), Jack Overman (Detective), Billy Murphy (Johnny), Pat Gleason (Tom), Bob Pepper (Policeman), Dale Van Sickel (Double for Rondo Hatton), Billy Jones, Walter Tetley.* [**Does not appear in the final print.*]

The third installment of a series that was good for only one, *The Jungle Captive* is a sad pastiche of everything that had come before in Universal's pallid Ape Woman series. The film is a grab-bag of horror movie cliches, bleak and unexciting, dirt-poor in production values, exasperating in its repetitious scenes and obvious padding. It hasn't got the mind-deadening, jaw-dropping effect of *Jungle Woman* (the ultimate in junky Universal horror), although common sense and logical plot progression are in short supply this time around as well. Petty in concept and minor in execution, *The Jungle Captive* is a fittingly drab and peremptory finish to Universal's Paula Dupree trilogy.

The Jungle Captive is one of those pictures where a better story went on behind the camera than anything that happened out in front. Betty Bryant was originally signed to play the heroine, but this unheard-of actress apparently had some funny ideas about how the picture business worked. On August 30, 1944, one day before production began, she appeared in the office of associate producer Morgan B. Cox and informed him that she didn't know whether she could find a babysitter to stay with her two-year-old child on certain nights she was scheduled to work. On the first day of shooting she was unprepared, and on the second day she arrived 40 minutes late, just in time for a reprimand from director Harold Young.

To quiet the actress' maternal apprehensions, Bryant's physician was summoned. (In the great and continuing tradition of editorial cowardice, we shall refer to him only as Dr. R.) In private, Dr. R. emphatically told Cox that there was nothing about motion pictures or motion picture people that he could admire. According to Dr. R., all the men in the movie business were concerned primarily with "making" any and all women in any way connected with the industry. Bryant was drawn into the argument and Dr. R. nearly succeeded in creating a scene.

Over the next several days this embarrassing situation continued, with Dr. R. hanging around the set, creating disturbances, recklessly careening around the darkened lot in his car and, in the words of Cox (in a 16-page 9/12/44 memo), "acting more like a thwarted lover than a reputable doctor." Cox concluded in his memo that Bryant, slightly ill throughout much of this ordeal and genuinely apologetic for the entire situation, was a victim of circumstances over which she had little control. Of course the boom was inevitably lowered on the hapless actress, and she was bumped. Amelita Ward replaced her in the picture, which ran two days over schedule ("wrapping" on September 16) probably as the result of the turmoil created by the mysterious Dr. R.

The film opens at the Medical Building, in a typically big but (as ever) unnamed major city. Stendahl (Otto Kruger), a biochemist, is conducting a revolutionary experiment, using electric current and blood transfusions to revive the heart of a dead rabbit (shades of *Life Returns*). To the delight and amazement of his young assistants Ann (Amelita Ward) and Don (Phil Brown), the operation is an unqualified success.

The scene switches to the city morgue, where deformed bruiser Moloch (Rondo Hatton) appears out of the night with a note of release for the body of Paula the Ape Woman. When the morgue attendant (Charles Wagenheim) becomes suspicious, Moloch attacks him from behind, choking him to death. Stealing a morgue wagon, he transports the body of the Ape Woman out onto a desolate stretch of highway where he now places the cadaver in his own car and sends the wagon hurtling off a cliff. Moloch drives on, arriving at last at his destination, a lonely country house on nearby Old Orchard Road.

A surgical smock found near the wreckage of the wagon brings Inspector Harrigan (Jerome Cowan) of the Homicide Squad to Stendahl's offices. The glib policeman determines from laundry marks that the smock once belonged to Don, and he questions the young intern casually before leaving.

Stendahl asks Ann to accompany him on an errand, and the pair end up at the Old Orchard Road house. It was Stendahl who masterminded the theft of the Ape Woman's body, and now with Ann in his clutches he can use the girl's blood in his efforts to restore life to the Ape Woman. As Stendahl siphons off her blood Ann hovers dangerously near death, prompting a sympathetic reaction from Moloch.

The Ape Woman returns to life, and Stendahl realizes that he must now engineer her metamorphosis back into a woman if he hopes to claim that he has restored life to a human. Moloch is dispatched to steal the records of Dr. Walters (*Captive Wild Woman*) from Dr. Fletcher (*Jungle Woman*); in a later dialogue exchange we learn that Moloch killed Dr. Fletcher during the robbery.

Now using Ann's glandular secretions, Stendahl is able to change the Ape Woman into the beautiful Paula (Vicky Lane). But Paula's brain has somehow been damaged, and she has only the instincts of an animal. Stendahl plans to transplant Ann's brain into Paula's head.

Paula escapes from the house and strays into the nearby woods. Moloch, panicked by her disappearance, drives to the Medical Building to notify Stendahl, and gets into an argument with Don. Don notices that Moloch is wearing a fraternity pin which he had given to Ann, and trails Moloch as he returns to the country house. Stendahl and Moloch get the drop on Don, and he becomes a bound and helpless spectator as Stendahl prepares to operate on the Ape Woman. When Don tells Moloch that Stendahl is planning to remove Ann's brain, the giant brute becomes enraged and Stendahl is forced to shoot him to death. The Ape woman decides to add to the confusion, rising from the operating table and throttling the startled scientist. The Ape Woman is menacingly advancing on the unconscious Ann when Inspector Harrigan and his men, led to the house by a clue found in Stendahl's office, burst in and shoot her down.

If *The Jungle Captive* serves only one purpose, it's as a catalogue of time-tested horror film ingredients. They're all here: the mad doctor, scientific laboratories, life-restoring experiments, a dumb-brute assistant, a monster, Jekyll-and-Hyde transformations, the young hero, the swooning ingenue and every other convention which has hounded the genre from Day One. Screenwriters M. Coates Webster and Dwight V. Babcock blithely wallow in cliches, almost as though they're afraid to miss one. Of course nearly every such horror thriller falls back on some of these basics, but *The Jungle Captive* seems an almost conscious effort to cram all of these dreary chestnuts into a 63-minute running time. Tellingly, even the name of the film is cribbed from words in the earlier series titles; we've all heard of pinching pennies, but pinching *words* surely represents the ultimate in economizing. Had the series lasted longer, further installments would no doubt have been called *Captive Woman, Wild Captive, Wild Woman* and *Woman Captive,* at which point it could have gone no further without the expenditure of another word. (This amazing practice extended even to *The Jungle Captive*'s rerelease title, *Wild Jungle Captive*.)

With the type of lazy disregard which was by now *de rigueur* for Universal writers, Webster and Babcock made no effort to add to or improve on the Ape Woman mythos. The Ape Woman gets the sort of treatment heretofore reserved for the latter-day Frankenstein's Monster: she remains comatose and helpless throughout most of the picture, while the human members of the cast gobble up the running time with their petty comings and goings. There isn't enough plot here for an hour television show, but the picture compensates for this with mindless padding and scenes that go nowhere. We get our first taste of this in the opening scene, as a shiftless nerd of a delivery boy flirts glibly with Amelita Ward; later we're treated to not one, not two, but *three* foiled escape attempts (two by the Ape Woman and one by Don) which add nothing to the picture but extra minutes. After seeing Rondo Hatton steal the Ape Woman's body, we have to sit through scenes of Inspector Harrigan trying to pin the crime on Don. After witnessing the Ape Woman's first escape, we get to watch

Hatton search the empty house for her. The time wasted here could much more wisely have been spent reminding audiences just exactly who Dr. Walters, Miss Strand (*Captive Wild Woman*) and Dr. Fletcher (*Jungle Woman*) were, rather than simply dropping their names and smugly assuming that viewers had seen and remembered the earlier movies.

Adhering to the dictates of the party-poopers at the Breen Office, Paula remains demurely clothed throughout the film: as the Ape Woman she wears what looks like a surgical gown, and as Paula she's clad in a low-cut print dress that Stendahl and Moloch must have enjoyed putting on her. The Ape Woman's makeup here is slightly different from that in the earlier films, and an improvement. It's sleeker and more bestial-looking, and for the first and only time in the series the Ape Woman has a dangerous, almost frightening look about her. But this modified makeup is squandered in a picture where she lies around dead much of the time and is allowed only two mild tantrums.

The acting never rises above the script. It's always good to see an old pro like Otto Kruger in action, but he's generally better than he is in *The Jungle Captive.* Kruger's mad scientist is an arrogantly cold fish; he turns in the same self-consciously villainous performance he gives in Hitchcock's *Saboteur* (1942). Kruger is also saddled with the kind of mad-doctor dialogue that drips with mildew: lines about the unimportance of a single life in the furtherance of science, a mini-tirade against the doctors who laughed at his theories, and so on. Amelita Ward, who plays Ann, really only acts in a few scenes, spending most of the movie snoozing uncomfortably on a hard lab table; it's amusing that a sick girl (Betty Bryant) was bounced from the picture and a healthy girl (Ward) replaced her in the role of a sick girl. The acting skills of former MGM contractee Vicky Lane (Mrs. Tom Neal), who plays Paula and the Ape Woman, also go untested since (like Acquanetta in the original *Captive Wild Woman*) she isn't permitted a single word of dialogue. Other cast members wading through the dullness include Phil Brown, who plays a too-boyish, ineffectual "hero," and Jerome Cowan, a smilin' fool of a police detective.

The Jungle Captive also marked the second appearance of Rondo Hatton in a Universal horror film. The grim, imposing actor who caught the fancy of '40s audiences in *The Pearl of Death* is seen again as a homicidal henchman, but with one major renovation: in *The Jungle Captive,* he gets dialogue. And the whole Hatton mystique so artfully built up in the earlier Sherlock Holmes film is instantly and permanently lost. Even roles as rudimentary as Moloch are completely beyond Hatton's depth; he's incapable of delivering even the simplest lines with conviction. You doubt that he's really aware of what's going on around him and sometimes you wonder if he understands what he's saying himself. He was back to mute roles by the time *The Spider Woman Strikes Back* went into production, but the damage had been done; audiences now knew that the poor soul was more sap than menace. (In their review of *The Jungle Captive, The Los Angeles Times* wrote, "Rondo Hatton drew only giggles from the audience kids.") Hatton was probably the farthest thing from an actor that was ever maneuvered in front of a movie camera, but here again the real-life story eclipses his negligible on-screen accomplishments.

An only child, Hatton was born in 1894 in Hagerstown, Maryland, and

PAWN OF A MAD MONSTER
Ravishing beauty transformed into raging beast... loving to kill!
JUNGLE CAPTIVE
with OTTO KRUGER
Amelita Ward Phil Brown
Jerome Cowan
and VICKY LANE
as the Ape Woman
RONDO HATTON
as Moloch, the Brute
UNIVERSAL

Acquanetta's sudden departure from Universal sounded the death knell for the Ape Woman series. Vicky Lane tried unsuccessfully to fill her shoes in 1945's *The Jungle Captive.*

grew up in Hagerstown and in Tampa, Florida, where he attended Hillsborough High School. Photos of a youthful Hatton (published in *Midnight Marquee* #37) depict a lean, big-eared but good-looking teenager; the accompanying text (written by latter-day exploitation director Fred Olen Ray) indicates that Hatton at that time was a hit with the girls as well as an all-around high school athlete. Joining the National Guard, Hatton wound up in World

War I France, where he was exposed to German poison gas in a battle near Paris. As a result, he contracted the rare metabolic disorder acromegaly. As all fans of *Tarantula* (1955) already know, it's a disfiguring disease that manifests itself gradually: facial features become exaggerated, feet and hands are enlarged, the skin thickens and many internal organs are also enlarged. The ailment is also characterized by excessive body odor, an unpleasant side effect which we can only hope Hatton (and his costars!) were spared.

Returning to Florida, Hatton found work as a writer for Tampa newspapers; his first marriage went to pot because his acromegalic condition was worsening. Visiting the set of the Florida-made film *Hell's Harbor* (1930), Hatton was offered the part of a burly saloon proprietor by director Henry King. Years later, when Hatton and his second wife relocated to Hollywood, Rondo looked up the director and got another movie bit part, as a henchman in King's 1938 *In Old Chicago.* Hatton played similarly small parts in numerous films during this late '30s to early '40s period, including *Alexander's Ragtime Band, The Hunchback of Notre Dame, Chad Hanna* (Henry King again), *The Moon and Sixpence* (as a leper), *The Ox-Bow Incident* and more. His appearance in *The Pearl of Death* led to a string of appearances in Universal horror films and even to a short-lived series of his very own, as the simple-minded Creeper. Hatton was paid a flat $1,250 for his work in *The Jungle Captive,* a distinct improvement over the $408.35 he pulled in for his week-and-a-day's work on *Pearl,* and fatter paychecks lay ahead as Universal continued to groom him for bush-league stardom.

Hatton was no doubt pleased with his belated "star" status, but one has to wonder what crossed his mind whenever his real-life looks were cruelly commented upon in these films. Sensitivity toward the unfortunate actor is at a record low in *The Jungle Captive,* in a scene where Otto Kruger becomes annoyed with Hatton for showing sympathy toward Amelita Ward. "No offense, Moloch, but with that face you're not exactly a Casanova, you know," Kruger deadpans, then adds insult to injury by indicating the dead body of the Ape Woman and suggesting, "*This* is more in your line!" You'd think that Hatton would have balked at this dialogue, if not to preserve his own dignity, then for the sake of his current wife. ("Universal was starring him and exploiting him, which was sort of too bad," recalls Hatton's *Brute Man* costar Jane Adams.)

Stendahl's not only insensitive, he's also pretty mixed up. There's no explanation as to why he needs the body of the Ape Woman for his life-restoring experiment; using this freak as an experimental subject would only tend to cheapen and sensationalize his work. And since Moloch killed the morgue attendant to get the body, you'd think that the Ape Woman would be the *last* person he'd want to present to the scientific community.

Using the Ape Woman's body also entails a maddening multistep process for poor Stendahl. First he has to steal the body and return it to life. To transform her into Paula, he needs to steal Dr. Walters' records, which prompts a second murder. Now, since Paula's brain is damaged, he has to crack open Ann's skull and use her brain. So even if he could somehow miraculously sidestep the issue of the two murders (placing all the blame on Moloch, perhaps), the new Paula would have the brain of Ann and publicly charge Stendahl with *her* mutilation and murder! Stendahl could have avoided all this unnecessary to-do simply by restoring life to some poor dead slob who could really use it, but this common-sense approach never occurs to him. Stendahl's the Rube Goldberg of Universal mad scientists; despite his standing as an endocrine researcher, an electrolytic researcher and a clinical pathologist, not once in the film does anyone extend him the courtesy of calling him "Doctor."

There's also some unintentional humor when Stendahl decides that he must remove Ann's brain and place it in the head of Paula. Clearly the man has never before performed any such operation, so he sends Moloch to steal Dr. Walters' papers. The instructions are typewritten on a single index card, and using this as a guide, first-time surgeon Stendahl expects to successfully transplant the girl's brain. (The card, seen in a split-second closeup, reads in part, "A light mallet should be employed and the chisel should be held with the point directed to the nose, so that a slip would not enter either the eye or the brain.") This incredibly ridiculous scene, with Stendahl approaching the operation with the hopeful enthusiasm of an amateur chef or a home handyman, pretty well encapsulates the hopeless naîveté of the entire picture.

Economy was the order of the day once again, with recognizable stock footage from earlier Universal films turning up throughout the picture. The shot of the Ape Woman in the morgue drawer is an optically-darkened clip from the climax of *Jungle Woman,* while a shot of the Ape Woman's hand transforming (seen twice) is lifted from *Captive Wild Woman.* Additionally, the morgue wagon which crashes in flames is actually Dr. Kemp's car from *The Invisible Man.*

At the end of *The Jungle Captive* Phil Brown uses the same tactic that Basil Rathbone did at the end of *The Pearl of Death,* employing psychology to turn Hatton against his master. (And again, as in *Pearl,* the empty-handed Hatton is stupid enough to boldly stalk a man with a gun—with the same disastrous results.) The later Hatton film *House of Horrors* had the same denouement and *The Brute Man,* with a slight variation, tried it a fourth time. Universal's screenwriters were clearly at the end of their frayed rope.

Seemingly stretched out even for its 63-minute length, *The Jungle Captive* remains a tawdry, almost mean-spirited little time-waster which does no more than foist onto audiences themes done countless times in the past. Quality-wise, it falls into the wide gulf between *Captive Wild Woman* and *Jungle Woman:* it's not nearly as slick or as entertaining as *Captive,* nor is it the blatantly awful mess that *Jungle* is. But both of these earlier films have a leg up on *The Jungle Captive* in that they were done with some semblance of style; even *Jungle Woman* rates a small nod for its misplaced and wrong-headed attempts at originality. *The Jungle Captive* is a dashed-off assembly-line job exploiting all of the overused ingredients of the commonplace horror action film. Slack and depressing, it represents a most welcome end to a most unwelcome series.

The Woman in Green (1945)

Released July 27, 1945. 68 minutes. *Produced & Directed by* Roy William Neill. *Original Screenplay by* Bertram Millhauser. *Based on the characters created by* Sir Arthur Conan Doyle. *Director of Photography:* Virgil Miller. *Musical Director:* Mark Levant. *Art Directors:* John B. Goodman & Martin Obzina. *Set Decorations:* Russell A. Gausman & Ted Von Hemert. *Film Editor:* Edward Curtiss. *Special Photography:* John P. Fulton. *Sound Director:* Bernard B. Brown. *Technician:* Glenn E. Anderson. *Dialogue Director:* Raymond Kessler. *Assistant Director:* Melville Shyer. *Production Manager:* Charles Stallings. *Camera Operator:* Ross Hoffman. *Special Effects:* Chris Guthrie. *Property Master:* Willard Nunley. *Gowns by* Vera West.

Basil Rathbone (Sherlock Holmes), Nigel Bruce (Dr. John H. Watson), Hillary Brooke (Lydia Marlowe), Henry Daniell (Professor Moriarity), Frederic Worlock (Dr. Onslow), Paul Cavanagh (Sir George Fenwick), Mary Gordon (Mrs. Hudson), Matthew Boulton (Inspector Gregson), Tom Bryson (Corporal Williams), Eve Amber (Maude Fenwick), Sally Shepherd (Crandon), Percival Vivian (Dr. Simnell), Harold DeBecker (Shabby Man), Olaf Hytten (Norris), Tommy Hughes (Newsman), Kay Harding (Victim), Maurice Marks (Basil Rathbone's Stand-In), Captain George Hill (Nigel Bruce's Stand-In), Leslie Denison (Bar Man), John Burton (Waring), Violet Seaton (Mowbray), Arthur Stenning (Porter), Norman Ainslee (Electrician), Tony Ellis (Carter), Ivo Henderson, Colin Hunter (Constables), Boyd Irwin (Short Tempered Officer), Alec Hartford (Commissioner).

The popular and ever-profitable Sherlock Holmes series had reached its third year of production, proving to be one of the studio's smartest investments. On December 23, 1944, Universal exercised its option on the rights to the Sir Arthur Conan Doyle short stories, again dealing directly with the late author's son, Dennis P.S. Conan Doyle. The studio hyped up the occasion by announcing it was upgrading the series, increasing the budgets to "top proportions" and regarding each story as a "separate and individual production."

Seasoned readers of trade journals and press releases saw through this sham. The Holmes films were dependable moneymakers, and to tamper with the formula would be folly. Unsurprisingly, the budgets remained fixed and so did the series' status as supporting features. Not only didn't the films improve, but a general air of tiredness began to manifest itself; clearly, Roy William Neill's Holmes unit was running low on inspiration. After reaching the pinnacle with *The Scarlet Claw* and *The Pearl of Death,* the series was in a slump despite a promising new script by Bertram Millhauser entitled *Invitation to Death.*

Loosely derived from "The Empty House" and "The Dying Detective," Millhauser's screenplay pitted Holmes against the seemingly indestructible Professor Moriarity for one final confrontation. Giving up the espionage business for grimmer pursuits, Moriarity engineers a bizarre blackmail/murder plot using hypnotism and a cool blonde seductress to lure wealthy dupes. With the casting of that iciest of actors Henry Daniell as the arch-criminal, the picture had all the earmarks of a compelling mystery.

The Breen Office saw things differently. Millhauser's script, submitted on December 21, 1944, was deemed in flagrant violation of the Production Code. The shocking, brutal depiction of the murders and mutilations of eight- and nine-year-old girls would have been much too strong for wartime audiences weaned on Andy Hardy. Alarmed that the film would "lower the moral sensibilities of the audience" and might even influence the weak-minded to imitate the crimes it depicted, the purity squad judged the script unacceptable.

Millhauser hammered out a revised script and not only was it approved, but it inspired a letter of congratulations for the "excellent manner in which the revisions were made." The major change in the new draft involved upping the age of the victims from elementary school age to about 20 years old. Satisfied that the addition of a dozen or so years on victims' ages would uphold public morality, the production was given the go-ahead, barring other minor adjustments. Among the other deleted offenses were Moriarity's disguise as a Church of England minister, a nude silhouette of the leading lady in the shower and a reference to hypnotism as a "holy science."

With all the bugs finally ironed out of the script, pre-production got underway. Series veteran Hillary Brooke was signed on January 6, 1945, landing one of her juiciest screen roles as Moriarity's sultry accomplice. Exactly one week later, shooting began on the production which was retitled *The Woman in Green*. Neill brought the shooting to a close on February 5.

The Woman in Green begins with the dreary narrative of Scotland Yard Inspector Gregson (Matthew Boulton), recalling the case of a series of ghastly crimes dubbed the "Finger Murders," in which the victims, all young girls, had a single finger hacked off their dead bodies. When a full scale investigation fails to turn up a lead, Sherlock Holmes (Basil Rathbone) and Dr. Watson (Nigel Bruce) are consulted. Holmes discounts the widely accepted theory that a maniac is responsible, believing a cold, calculating intelligence is at work.

Maude Fenwick (Eve Amber) pays the detective an urgent call at his Baker Street digs after making a gruesome discovery: the severed finger of a young girl, apparently belonging to the most recent murder victim. Miss Fenwick confesses that she witnessed her father, the eminent Sir George Fenwick (Paul Cavanagh), burying the body part under cover of night.

Holmes, Watson and Gregson pay a call on Fenwick, only to find him dead from a bullet wound. Holmes insists that Fenwick was murdered for learning the secret behind the crimes, and further deduces that the scheme is a blackmail ploy hatched by none other than Professor Moriarity (Henry Daniell). Holmes' investigation points to a female accomplice, the beautiful Lydia Marlowe (Hillary Brooke), who judiciously selected Fenwick as their foil. After being romanced by Lydia, Fenwick was placed in a hypnotic trance and was duped into believing he has committed murder (the severed finger was planted on his person). Confronting Fenwick with this incriminating evidence, Moriarity demanded a sizable payment in return for his silence.

An assassination attempt is made on Holmes' life. When the culprit turns out to be a discharged soldier (Tom Bryson) acting under hypnotic suggestion, the detective is positive his theory is correct. Lured to the Mesmer Club, a social gathering of hypnotists, Holmes strikes up a conversation with Lydia. She entices Holmes to her penthouse apartment where he is placed under hypnosis on Moriarity's orders. Moriarity commands his rival to walk across a narrow ledge. But before he can give the order to jump, Watson, Gregson and a detail of policemen burst onto the scene. As Moriarity and Lydia are being led away in cuffs, Holmes confesses that he was shamming hypnosis all along. Moriarity attempts to leap across to the next ledge but loses his balance and falls to his death.

The Woman in Green is a medium grade Holmes adventure, falling squarely in the middle on the quality scale. The film is ripe with possibilities, not many of which are fully realized. Working with far less promising ingredients, *The Pearl of Death* yielded more consistent and satisfying results. Apparently the sheer repetition of the series was getting the best of Neill and Rathbone. *The Woman in Green* lacks the crispness of the Holmes adventures released only a year before.

The plot is a strong one. Never before has such oft-used Holmes adjectives as "cold-blooded," "insidious" and "diabolical" rang with more conviction. As the dialogue suggests, the "Finger Murders" are about the closest Holmes gets to confronting a Jack the Ripper-type killer at Universal, even though the culprit turns out to be Moriarity up to his usual tricks. Neill's usually sure-footed direction is slack this go-around, and even wanting in style. Virgil Miller's camerawork, which enhanced *The House of Fear* (1945), is surprisingly dull and flat here but John P. Fulton perks up the visuals with some hallucinatory process shots in the hypnosis scenes, framing the reflected images of the players in Lydia's trance-inducing whirlpool.

Millhauser's screenplay is stronger in concept than it is in execution. There are holes in the plot that Neill couldn't quite fill (he worked without credit on many of the Holmes scripts). Four murders had been already committed before the trap is set for Fenwick, yet he is only implicated in the most recent crime. Was Fenwick the only blackmail victim? There's no indication that Moriarity ensnared other victims in his scheme, so why did he butcher four girls needlessly? And why must the professor resort to hypnotizing an unwitting soldier to kill Holmes when he already has a veritable army of assassins and henchmen on his payroll?

The screenplay not only fails to stand up to scrutiny but at times is just plain lazy. (One can almost hear the audience groan in disbelief when Holmes reveals he has substituted Lydia's sedative with an anesthetizing drug in order to fake hypnosis in the finale.) The early reels, however, are most involving as Holmes gradually uncovers the details of Moriarity's scheme. The suggestion of a cloaked, crazed murderer stalking the back alleys of London is enough to keep anticipation running high. Even the hypnosis angle, though tired stuff even by 1945, keeps the film moving along at an agreeable pace, at least until the last quarter.

As usual, Watson's comedy scenes are more irritating than funny, especially during a demonstration of hypnotism at the Mesmer Club. When the doctor denounces all subjects of hypnosis as being "weak-minded morons," we know it won't be long before he falls under the mesmerist's spell. The original script had the doctor dropping his trousers upon the order of the hypnotist (Frederic Worlock), but the scene was toned down to appease the ludicrously puritanical standards of the Production Code. It's a crude, gratuitous attempt at humor that the film doesn't need. Watson's character had become so insultingly stupid that when Holmes teasingly reveals Moriarity's intended murder victim as "a fellow named Watson; a medical man I believe," the befuddled physician absent-mindedly responds with, "I never heard of him!" before doing an astonished double take.

Even more inexcusable is a tired, unimaginative ending in which Scotland Yard nabs the culprits at the instant Holmes is about to meet his death at the hands of Moriarity. Lydia, deserving a more colorful exit, is whisked away without so much as a parting line of dialogue, while Moriarity, not profiting from past mistakes, again demonstrates a talent for falling from high places. *The Woman in Green* marks the third time that he plummets to his death (at least he makes good his promise never to stand upon the gallows!).

Henry Daniell and Hillary Brooke, the two stand-outs in the cast, more than make up for the film's deficiencies. "I enjoyed playing the *femme fatale*," Miss Brooke remarked recently. "As a matter of fact I enjoyed playing any part but because I was tall and blond I worked with a great many comedians. It was great fun and I did have a marvelous time." Brooke's veneer of elegant, aristocratic sensuality never betrays the cruel ruthlessness of her personality. Moriarity is even more reptilian in Daniell's hands. The two make a formidable, if frosty, pair, he the mastermind lurking behind the scenes, she the alluring and highly visible bait. In Rathbone's autobiography *In and Out of Character* the actor credits his old friend Daniell as being "masterful" in the role. "There are other Moriaritys but none so delectably dangerous as that of Henry Daniell." Unfortunately, the surly Englishman is let down by Millhauser's script, which fails to come up with a single memorable line of dialogue. Holmes and Moriarity's sterile, business-like exchanges pall in comparison to the two characters' electric confrontations in *Sherlock Holmes and the Secret Weapon.*

Daniell's film career seemed doomed from the outset by his rigid, unyielding demeanor (ironically, in his younger days, Daniell frequently complained to interviewers of his resentment towards being typecast as a juvenile). He always delivered crisp, dependable performances in even the most perfunctory of roles (for instance, *Sherlock Holmes in Washington* and 1942's *Nightmare*). Despite his magnetic presence and flawless diction, Hollywood was hard pressed to cast him in worthwhile roles befitting his rather narrow range. *Camille* (1936), *The Great Dictator* (194]) and *The Body Snatcher* (1945) showed him to excellent advantage, but such roles were rare. Daniell's stylish villainy insured him of a busy career right up until his death in 1963, but his contempt for Tinsel Town wasn't entirely justified; he simply had neither the stature nor the flexibility of a Claude Rains or Cedric Hardwicke.

The rest of the cast is uneven. Series regular Paul Cavanagh comes off well as Sir George Fenwick, the bland Eve Amber plays his daughter, and Frederic Worlock is his usual curmudgeonly self as the hypnotist. Bit player Matthew Boulton, graduating to the supporting ranks, is an ineffectual Inspector Gregson, while second-stringer Kay Harding takes a step backward in her career in a thankless nonspeaking role. Last seen in a major part in *The Scarlet Claw,* most of Harding's screen time is spent immobile on a morgue slab as one of Moriarity's victims. The once razor-sharp Rathbone walks through his role, in contrast to the indefatigable (if occasionally idiotic) Nigel Bruce.

With a bit of development and a lot more panache, *The Woman in Green* might have been among the best Sherlock Holmes thrillers. Had it been made two or three pictures earlier in the cycle, it probably would have been. Despite the presence of a pair of first-rate villains, all involved seemed to be operating below capacity. Even the score, patched together from earlier pictures by musical director Mark Levant, seems tired and indifferent. Though it has its moments, *The Woman in Green* was further proof the series was crying out for new blood.

Strange Confession (1945)

Released October 5, 1945. 62 minutes. Rereleased as *The Missing Head.* An Inner Sanctum Mystery, produced by arrangement with Simon and Schuster, Inc., Publishers. *Produced by* Ben Pivar. *Directed by* John Hoffman. *Screenplay by* M. Coates Webster. *Based on the play "The Man Who Reclaimed His Head" by* Jean Bart [Marie Antoinette Sarlabous]. *Director of Photography:* Maury Gertsman. *Musical Director:* Frank Skinner. *Art Directors:* John B. Goodman & Abraham Grossman. *Director of Sound:* Bernard B. Brown. *Technician:* Jess Moulin. *Set Decorations:* Russell A. Gausman & Andrew J. Gilmore. *Film Editor:* Russell Schoengarth. *Gowns by* Vera West. *Dialogue Director:* Willard Holland. *Assistant Directors:* Seward Webb & Harry Jones. *Camera Operator:* John Martin.

Lon Chaney (Jeff Carter), Brenda Joyce (Mary Carter), J. Carrol Naish (Roger Graham), Milburn Stone (Stevens), Lloyd Bridges (Dave Curtis), Addison Richards (Dr. Williams), Mary Gordon (Mrs. O'Connor), George Chandler (Harper), Gregory Muradian (Tommy Carter), Wilton Graff (Brandon), Francis McDonald (Jose Hernandez), Jack Norton (Jack [Boarder]), Christian Rub (Mr. Moore), Leland [Leyland] Hodgson (Jason [Graham's Butler]), Ian Wolfe (Frederick [Brandon's Butler]), Wheaton Chambers (Mr. Reed), Edward Mahler (Tommy as an Infant), Carl Vernell (Chemistry Student), Beatrice Roberts (Miss Rodgers), Jack Perrin (Patrolman), William Desmond (Bit Vendor/Dock Extra), Arthur Thalasso (Dock Extra), Charles Jordan (Boarder), Jody Gilbert (Mrs. Todd), David Hoffman (Inner Sanctum), Eric Mayne, Ella Ethridge, Jack Davidson, James Carlisle, Brod O'Farrel, Tony Santoro, Carlyle Blackwell, Jr., Lois Austin, Ann Lawrence, Dorothy Reisner, Gene Garrick, Sam Woolfe.

The penultimate entry in the Inner Sanctum sweepstakes, *Strange Confession* has little in common with the other films in the series. It's a well done little domestic tragedy, with none of the phony supernatural overtones that mark most of the rest of the Inner Sanctum films. A refreshing change-of-pace, it might arguably be the best of the six-film series.

As a church bell chimes midnight, Jeff Carter (Lon Chaney) roams the dark streets of New York carrying a large valise. Seemingly in a daze, Jeff makes his way to the residence of prominent attorney Brandon (Wilton Graff), who dimly remembers former classmate Jeff as a chemistry whiz. The unbalanced Jeff opens the valise and shows the horrified Brandon what's inside (a disembodied head) before telling the lawyer his incredible story.

In flashback, we see Jeff and his wife Mary (Brenda Joyce) enjoying a spartan Christmas dinner in their cheap boarding house apartment. Jeff is a brilliant chemist who cares nothing about money; to him it's more important to help suffering humanity, so he lets his boss Roger Graham (J. Carrol Naish) have all the credit and the monetary rewards his discoveries garner while he himself lives in near poverty. Graham, a Grade-A heel, takes every advantage of Jeff, but he presses his luck when he insists on marketing an untested drug. Jeff and Graham argue and Jeff tenders his resignation. ("Well, that's gratitude for you," Graham sulks.) Graham blackballs Jeff, who ends up working as a pharmacist in a small drugstore.

Finding that he can't get along without Jeff, Graham appears at the Carter home and offers him his old job back at his own terms. Jeff stubbornly turns him down but Mary, who has overheard the conversation, justifiably berates her husband after Graham has gone: she's tired of counting pennies to preserve his stupid integrity. Jeff sees the light and agrees to take Graham up on his offer.

Now a top-salaried chemist, Jeff works to develop a drug called Zymurgine, a powder to be used in the treatment of colds, influenza and pneumonia. He tells Graham that he needs a mold from a certain South American plant in order to perfect the formula; this sits well with Graham, who's got his eye on Mary. Jeff and his assistant Dave (Lloyd Bridges) are sent south of the border to continue their work while Graham platonically wines and dines Mary.

When an influenza epidemic hits New York, Graham takes advantage of the situation, manufacturing and marketing Zymurgine using one of Jeff's unproven, discarded formulae. Jeff, who has no knowledge of what's going on back home, perfects the stuff in South America and sends Graham the formula, but Graham already has the untested Zymurgine in production and doesn't care to start over again. Tommy (Gregory Muradian), the Carters' little boy, develops influenza and Mary gives him store-bought Zymurgine, which doesn't help. Tommy buys the farm.

Carrying a grudge and a gun, Mary calls on Graham intending to kill him for marketing a drug which she now knows to be useless. Graham easily disarms her just as Jeff appears in the doorway. Newly returned from South America and apprised of Tommy's death, Jeff has gone temporarily insane. Snatching a handy bolo-knife from a wall display, he attacks Graham and hacks off his head.

The flashbacks at an end, we return to Jeff and lawyer Brandon just as Mary and the cops arrive. Brandon is sympathetic to Jeff's plight, and consoles Mary with a promise to defend him in court as the police place Jeff in custody.

Strange Confession is a remake of Universal's 1934 *The Man Who Reclaimed His Head,* the pseudohistorical melodrama that starred Claude Rains, Joan Bennett and Lionel Atwill. Modernization of the story and a shift in locale were required in tailoring the property to the talents of Lon Chaney and to the Inner Sanctum mode, and screenwriter M. Coates Webster responded with a workable if slightly simplistic update. (The mind boggles at the thought of a faithful remake of *Reclaimed* with Chaney as the impassioned political writer.)

Cast against type (as usual), Lon Chaney does a creditable job in *Strange*

***Strange Confession*, a remake of 1934's *The Man Who Reclaimed His Head*, was the least typical, and most sober, of the "Inner Sanctum" series.**

Confession. Like most of his other Inner Sanctum protagonists, Chaney's Jeff Carter is a sensitive genius with the puffy face and body of an out-of-shape bouncer, but this time Chaney nearly pulls it off. For once, things tend to go his way throughout much of the picture, and we are spared Chaney's overdone exhibitions of anxiety and emotion as well as the silly "stream-of-consciousness" voiceovers that became the series' trademark. Chaney's performance does not come up to Claude Rains', although Rains had the distinct natural advantage of being the type for the role (Rains comes off like a dreamy-eyed innocent, Chaney like Simple Simon). There are some scenes which don't play well, like Chaney's "Leave It to Beaver"–style exchanges with his son, but for the most part he handles the role convincingly. Outside of his portrayal of Larry Talbot, this may well be his best work in a Universal picture.

Unfortunately, one scene which doesn't come off is the opener, potentially the most memorable and dramatic in the film. In *The Man Who Reclaimed His Head* Rains seems convincingly unbalanced as he appears at the lawyer's home; Chaney just seems like a simpleton, and when he rambles on and on about the strange things that can happen in a brilliant mind, you start to wonder whose mind he can be talking about. (In both films Rains and Chaney are supposed to be temporarily insane at this point, although it's interesting that, after committing their murders, both men still have enough savvy to immediately go out and find a good mouthpiece!) In *Reclaimed*, there was a certain logic in the way Rains convinced himself that Lionel Atwill had stolen his mind, a certain justice in the way in which he took it back. In a streamlined, modernized B like *Strange Confession,* however, the decapitation of J. Carrol Naish seems ghoulish and poorly motivated. Although Chaney spouts the same sort of dialogue that Rains did ("Why, it's just like he'd taken my head – my mind and brain, and used it. . . !"), his climactic attack on Naish is a self-indulgent bit of butchery that no amount of spook talk could justify.

Supporting performers are competent but unremarkable. Brenda Joyce is adequate as Chaney's wife and J. Carrol Naish also does well as the heel, although Naish's character is perhaps a bit too oily and obvious; it's difficult to believe that even a sucker like Chaney could fail to spot Naish for the pint-sized snake-in-the-grass he clearly is. Lloyd Bridges is amiable and amusing as Chaney's assistant, and it's fun to see a future television star bringing up the rear in an Inner Sanctum cheapie. On the debit side, Milburn Stone plays his role of Naish's righthand man like he thinks this is a gangster picture and Naish is Mr. Big. Gregory Muradian is cutesy as Chaney's son and (like all kids) all he does is slow the movie down.

Strange Confession benefits from its Inner Sanctum status for the simple reason that one quickly learns to approach the Inner Sanctum films with low expectations. Inner Sanctums tend to be ponderous and overblown: farout programmers filled with silly dramatics, built around an inadequate actor (Chaney) always unsuited to his role. Done in the style of a more conventional B, *Strange Confession* is a welcome variation from the series norm. Although he plays a ninny, Chaney is still effective in this slightly more down-to-earth role, and the film works well without the absurd embellishments (voiceover narration, weird organ chords, "supernatural" plot turns) that the series relied so heavily upon. *Strange Confession* is sober without being heavy, dramatic without becoming exaggerated. It's not as much fun as a film like *Weird Woman,* which has a few legitimate highpoints and reaches some inspired heights of lunacy, but it's a more respectable film overall.

The oddest pressbook item this time around described how a lavish dinner scene was dropped from the *Strange Confession* script at Chaney's insistence. Dispatches from Nice, France, had told of riots breaking out when a large plate of caviar was shown on screen during a recent showing of an American film; Chaney supposedly feared that a big display of food might offend his Gallic admirers. This silly little story is probably just another pack of pressbook lies, although there is a good, true story to be told as long as we're on the subject of Chaney and chow. Chaney apparently was haunted by the specter of poverty, and could not put out of his mind the days when he and his wife Patsy were struggling and had no money for food. In a 1943 news item he described how,

> When I got some money, I bought me hundreds of cans and some apparatus for using them. I've canned foods of all kinds. I've gone out in the ocean and caught tuna fish and canned them. I've shot game and canned it. It makes me feel better to see all that food, because a fellow never can tell how long his luck's going to run in the movies.

Chaney's fear of hunger persisted; a fishing and hunting pal of Chaney's used to tell the story that, between Los Angeles and Chaney's ranch in San Diego, the actor had several freezer-lockers full of frozen food.

Strange Confession went into production on February 1, 1945, shooting on Universal's New England Street, the New York Street and on a *Gung Ho!* set. It was the first directorial stint for John Hoffman, a former montage technician who had worked on such films as *Boom Town* (1940), *Cover Girl* (1944) and *A Song to Remember* (1945). The film wrapped up on February 14, five days over schedule, and the next Inner Sanctum, *Pillow of Death,* was hustled into production only a few days later, as if there were people out there waiting for these things. Over at Columbia a series of films based on the "I Love a Mystery" radio program had just gotten underway, and perhaps Universal was anxious to crank out as many Inner Sanctums as possible before the combined efforts of the two studios created a glut on the market.

Although reissued by Realart in 1953 (as *The Missing Head*), *Strange Confession* was never part of television's famous "Shock" package, has yet to make its video debut and apparently has never made a reappearance at any revival house; it's one of the toughest Universals to track down. The story that goes around is that Universal made the decision to remake *The Man Who Reclaimed His Head* without rechecking their contract with Jean Bart, who wrote the original play. The contract allowed for only one version of the play to be filmed, and Universal had inadvertently stepped outside their legal rights in making *Strange Confession* at all. Consequently, *Strange Confession* has been caught in a legal tangle ever since. If this is the case, the film may never again see the light of day: there isn't a lot of profit to be made off this little drama in this day and age, and it probably wouldn't be worth anybody's while to try and cut through all the red tape. And this is unfortunate, since *Strange Confession* is the one half-decent film in an otherwise lugubrious series.

Pursuit to Algiers (1945)

Released October 26, 1945. 65 minutes. *Produced & Directed by* Roy William Neill. *Executive Producer:* Howard Benedict. *Original Screenplay by* Leonard Lee. *Based on the characters created by* Sir Arthur Conan Doyle. *Director of Photography:* Paul Ivano. *Film Editor:* Saul A. Goodkind. *Musical Director:* Edgar Fairchild. *Art Directors:* John B. Goodman & Martin Obzina. *Director of Sound:* Bernard B. Brown. *Technician:* Robert Pritchard. *Set Decorators:* Russell A. Gausman & Ralph Sylos. *Director of Makeup:* Jack P. Pierce. *Dialogue Director:* Raymond Kessler. *Assistant Director:* Seward Webb. *Gowns by* Vera West.

Basil Rathbone (Sherlock Holmes), Nigel Bruce (Dr. John H. Watson), Marjorie Riordan (Sheila Woodbury), Rosalind Ivan (Agatha Dunham), Morton Lowry (Sanford), Leslie Vincent (Nikolas), Martin Kosleck (Mirko), Rex Evans (Gregor), John Abbott (Jodri), Gerald Hamer (Kingston), Wee Willie Davis (Gubec), Frederic Worlock (Prime Minister), Gregory Gaye (Ravez), Wilson Benge (Clergyman), Sven Hugo Borg (Johansson), Dorothy Kellogg (Fuzzy-Looking Woman), Tom P. Dillon (Restaurant Proprietor), Olaf Hytten (Stimson), Alan Edminston (Furtive Man), James Craven (Customer), Ashley Cowan (Steward), George Leigh (Reginald Dene), James Carlisle, Sayre Dearing (Aides).

Hollywood treated few of its aging detectives gracefully. *Pursuit to Algiers,* the tenth but not the last of the Sherlock Holmes adventures, proved that the series was on its last legs. A depressingly unambitious programmer, it not only pits the detective against unworthy adversaries, but also relegates him to the thankless duty of serving as bodyguard to a visiting monarch. A hangdog air hovers over the whole production. It is probably the weakest film in the series.

The set-up of the story is more intriguing than the plot itself. Contemplating a holiday in Scotland, Holmes and Watson (Basil Rathbone and Nigel Bruce) saunter down a foggy London lane when they are accosted by a couple of seemingly innocuous passersby. One plants a newspaper on Holmes, insisting that he dropped it. Another draws the pair into a dingy fish and chips bar. Stepping into the pub, Holmes becomes aware that he is being pitched a series of clues by the waiters as well as the diners; the newspaper and menu, he notes, are rife with leads. The detective deduces that he is being directed to a particular address and dashes out to find the clandestine meeting place.

After this attention-grabbing opening, *Pursuit to Algiers* promptly falls apart. The entire charade was cooked up by the ministers of a tiny European democracy whose monarch was recently killed in a motor accident (actually a well-disguised assassination plot). The heir to the throne, the young Prince Stephen, who is vacationing in England, now faces a similar fate, possibly while en route to his homeland. Over Watson's protests, Holmes agrees to escort the newly-installed monarch as far as Algiers.

A snag in the plans forces Holmes to proceed with the Prince on a two-passenger plane while Watson reluctantly agrees to board an ocean liner to meet his companion in Algiers. Not long into the voyage, Watson hears a bulletin describing the fatal crash of Holmes' plane. Barely recovering from the blow, Watson is asked by the ship's steward Sanford (Morton Lowry) to minister to a stricken passenger. The patient is none other than Holmes, who explains that his plans to fly to Algiers were ditched for security reasons and that he and the Prince will arrive at their destination on that very ship. The detective introduces his friend to the Prince, who is traveling under the guise of the doctor's nephew, Nikolas (Leslie Vincent).

Keeping a watchful eye out for potential assassins amongst his fellow passengers, Holmes is immediately suspicious of American nightclub singer Sheila (Marjorie Riordan). The songstress takes a romantic interest in Nikolas and is visibly shaken by the detective's presence. The sharp-eyed Holmes observes that the girl is never without her music case and deduces she is carrying the recently-nabbed Duchess of Brookdale's emeralds. After a confrontation, Sheila admits she found the gems in her music case and has become an unwitting accomplice in a scheme to smuggle them out of the country. Holmes gladly takes the emeralds off her hands and promises Sheila the sizable reward.

An unscheduled stop brings three additional passengers on board: the suave, heavyset Gregor (Rex Evans) and his traveling companions, the wiry Mirko (Martin Kosleck) and a giant mute, Gubec (Wee Willie Davis). Holmes recognizes Mirko as a famous carnival knife-thrower wanted by the police. He deduces the three are on board to assassinate Prince Stephen. Mirko is outwitted by Holmes when he attempts to murder the detective in his berth. Holmes shrewdly uncovers a deadly explosion planted in a party favor meant for Nikolas.

As the ship anchors in Algiers, the trio make one final attempt on Stephen's life. Breaking into Holmes' cabin, they subdue the detective and whisk Nikolas aboard a small boat. The Prince's official reception party arrives to find Holmes bound and gagged. Holmes assures them that the culprits have been apprehended on shore, and that young Nikolas was actually a decoy. The real Prince Stephen is Sanford, disguised as the steward throughout the voyage.

Pursuit to Algiers may have been conceived as a thinking man's thriller. Leonard Lee's generally humorless, dialogue-heavy script scrupulously eschews action; the confrontations between Holmes and his adversaries are genteel and matter-of-fact and there's a climactic if undramatic twist ending. It's the kind of picture that could only be brought off with a lot of style but *Pursuit to Algiers* has virtually none to offer.

The ocean liner setting is a novelty but it's an obvious studio mock-up. Director Roy William Neill wisely avoids the flatly lit, sun-drenched ship's deck and crams as much moody night footage into *Pursuit to Algiers* as possible. A scene in which the ship passes through a fog bank gives the film a much

It's the assassins vs. Holmes and Watson in *Pursuit to Algiers:* Nigel Bruce, Leslie Vincent, Basil Rathbone, Martin Kosleck and Rex Evans.

needed visual lift, but this is all window dressing for a banal, uninteresting screenplay. Except for recovering a cache of stolen emeralds in an unrelated subplot, Holmes' investigative skills remain sadly underused. For the remainder of the screen time, he is merely a bodyguard for the Prince's decoy. The picture is a throwback to the detective's earliest adventures which pitted Holmes against foreign agents and fifth columnists, but at least then the series had much more zip. *Pursuit to Algiers* is so mannered, even the villains are rounded up off-camera.

In spite of the film's leanings toward international intrigue, all of the standard mystery movie conventions are employed to little effect, including the usual line-up of red herrings. John Abbott and Gerald Hamer skulk about conspiratorially only to be revealed as a harmless pair of archaeologists in the last reel. Marjorie Riordan's secret is unveiled halfway through the movie. Rosalind Ivan as a nosy eccentric can't be taken for anything but comedy relief. Considering the heavies are such a brazen lot—they practically conduct business out in the open—the secondary characters are little more than excess baggage. Rex Evans, the leader, could be counted on to goad Rathbone into a genial verbal sparring match after each botched assassination attempt but lacking the intended wit, their exchanges are merely tedious.

An uninspired choice to play Gregor, Evans is probably best-remembered by horror fans as the pie-eyed bartender who blew up the dam at the climax of *Frankenstein Meet the Wolf Man.* While pursuing his acting career he ran a Hollywood art gallery, probably a necessity considering his usually scanty roles. Evans' husky build and supposedly sparkling repartee suggested a bargain basement Sydney Greenstreet, especially with Martin Kosleck at his side (Kosleck lost out to Peter Lorre in the Joel Cairo role in *The Maltese Falcon*). Evans ranks with Arthur Margetson (*Sherlock Holmes Faces Death*) as the detective's most colorless foe.

Evans is easily upstaged by the dependable Kosleck, whose performance as a petulant knife-throwing psycho is the highlight of the film. Knives became the official weapon of the actor in his stint at Universal, having cut, slashed and stabbed his way through *The Frozen Ghost* and *The Mummy's Curse.* There's a delightful scene in *Pursuit to Algiers* in which Rathbone is all apologies after smashing Kosleck's wrist with a porthole cover during a foiled murder attempt. Off-camera, the actors shared a common respect and affection. Kosleck recently said,

> I *adored* Basil. He was the most wonderful guy to work with. I remember I had an interview for a part in *The Mad Doctor* [1941] and I thought I had to give an audition, but he was in the producer's office when I came in. He got up and shook my hand. He had seen me as Dr. Goebbels in my first American film [*Confessions of a Nazi Spy,* 1939] and he said, "You don't have to give an audition." And I got the part right then and there through his kindness. Working with him was just beautiful. We walked around the Paramount lot and discussed how to play scenes.
>
> We were always together on *Pursuit to Algiers.* There was a friend of mine in it who was not talented, only stuck-up [Leslie Vincent]. He got the part in the film through my influence. Basil took me aside and said, "Martin, how can you live with a person like that—a person who has *no talent*!" He's now a millionaire and lives in Hawaii.
>
> I visited with Basil and Lorre on the set of *The Comedy of Terrors* [1964]. They both tried to get me into that series, but I didn't get it.

Hardly anyone else in the *Pursuit to Algiers* cast deserves comment. Nigel Bruce's comedy antics are less intrusive than usual. Strongman Wee Willie Davis as Evans' mute henchman is barely noticeable. And, of course, Basil Rathbone's Holmes is always a pleasure, even under these less-than-ideal circumstances.

Pursuit to Algiers was announced under the title *The Fugitive.* This tag is inappropriate enough for one to suspect the script was subject to a last-minute overhaul, or possibly just cranked out after another Holmes project was ditched. Apparently, Universal or Neill regarded *Pursuit to Algiers* as a missed opportunity. *Terror by Night,* the next Sherlock Holmes chapter, is a thinly-disguised remake. The action unreeled on a Scotland-bound train with the detective guarding a fabulous jewel rather than an imperiled monarch, only the ingredients came together with splendid results. *Pursuit to Algiers* is, by comparison, an uninspired dry run.

House of Dracula (1945)

Released December 7, 1945. 67 minutes. *Executive Producer:* Joe Gershenson. *Produced by* Paul Malvern. *Directed by* Erle C. Kenton. *Original Screenplay by* Edward T. Lowe. *Story by* George Bricker & Dwight V. Babcock. *Director of Photography:* George Robinson. *Film Editor:* Russell Schoengarth. *Musical Director:* Edgar Fairchild. *Art Directors:* John B. Goodman & Martin Obzina. *Director of Sound:* Bernard B. Brown. *Technician:* Jess Moulin. *Set Decorators:* Russell A. Gausman & Arthur D. Leddy. *Gowns by* Vera West. *Makeup by* Jack P. Pierce. *Hair Stylist:* Carmen Dirigo. *Assistant Director:* Ralph Slosser. *Special Photography:* John P. Fulton.

Lon Chaney (Lawrence Stewart Talbot, the Wolf Man), John Carradine (Count Dracula), Martha O'Driscoll (Miliza Morelle), Lionel Atwill (Inspector Holtz), Onslow Stevens (Dr. Franz Edelmann), Jane Adams (Nina), Ludwig Stossel (Seigfried), Glenn Strange (The Frankenstein Monster), Skelton Knaggs (Steinmuhl), Joseph E. Bernard (Brahms), Gregory Muradian* (Johannes), Beatrice Gray* (Johannes' Mother), Fred Cordova, Carey Harrison (Gendarmes), Dick Dickinson (Villager), Walter DePalma, Arthur W. Stern, Carey Loftin (Stunts), Harry Lamont. [**Does not appear in the final print.*]

Horror characters stretched out way beyond their potential stalk the *House of Dracula* in Universal's final monster rally. The seventh installment in the Frankenstein series and the fourth entry for both Dracula and the Wolf Man, *House of Dracula* is a continuation of the silly spookfest presented in the previous year's *House of Frankenstein;* in many ways this sequel is almost a remake of the prior film. The Universal writing staff (represented here by Edward T. Lowe, George Bricker and Dwight V. Babcock) was plum out of fresh ideas, although this last episode in the studio's monster saga does feature some ingratiatingly macabre touches and a new Jekyll and Hyde–inspired character who conspires to steal the limelight from his classic colleagues.

The first hint that yet another monster rally was in the offing came in the April, 1944, Hollywood trade papers, while *House of Frankenstein* was still in production. The original announcement was that the title of this new film would be *The Wolf Man vs. Dracula,* and that Ford Beebe had been assigned to produce and direct. A script for *The Wolf Man vs. Dracula* remains an elusive item, although examination of a December 4, 1944, letter from spoilsport Joseph Breen to Universal's Maurice Pivar gives the strong impression that this script is considerably different from that of *House of Dracula;* it may in fact be different altogether. Breen's letter makes reference to the script's inclusion of folksongs, a stake being driven into a body (Dracula's?)

with accompanying "ear-splitting screams," and a scantily-clad character named Yvonne.

By February, 1945, the film was being called *House of Dracula* (a new or much-revised script obviously having been written); Beebe was still listed as producer/director of the upcoming project. But by the time the film went into production in September, producing/directing chores were divvied up between Paul Malvern and Erle C. Kenton, the men who made *House of Frankenstein.* In retrospect, it's unfortunate that Beebe didn't get a shot at *House of Dracula.* Beebe had brought a semblance of style to *Night Monster,* did a fine job as producer of *Son of Dracula,* and also fared well with *The Invisible Man's Revenge;* he might conceivably have delivered the goods on *House of Dracula,* and ended the series on a high note.

Count Dracula (John Carradine), tiring of his undead existence, pays an unexpected predawn visit on renowned surgeon Franz Edelmann (Onslow Stevens) in his castle home in seaside Visaria. Proving to Edelmann that he is a vampire by showing him his coffin, hidden in Edelmann's own basement, the Count urges the scientist to accept his case and discover a cure for the curse of vampirism.

Together with his nurses, Miliza (Martha O'Driscoll) and humpback Nina (Jane Adams), Edelmann has been cultivating a tropical plant which produces mold that can be used to soften bones, a revolutionary alternative to surgery. Edelmann sets his work aside to concentrate on Dracula's plight. Larry Talbot (Lon Chaney) arrives at the castle seeking a consultation; when Miliza explains that the doctor is occupied, Talbot becomes frantic with worry and runs out. Later that night, Edelmann receives an emergency call from Inspector Holtz (Lionel Atwill) of the Visaria police: Talbot has turned himself in, claiming to be a werewolf. As the moon shines through the window of his jail cell, Talbot undergoes the transformation, rattles the bars and then faints(!). Edelmann, a workaholic, decides to take on Talbot's case as well.

At Edelmann's castle, Talbot suffers yet another anxiety attack, leaping off a cliff and into the sea only to get washed inside a sea-level cave. Descending via bosun's chair into the cave to rescue him, Edelmann discovers not only his pessimistic patient but also the body of the Frankenstein Monster (Glenn Strange) and the skeleton of Dr. Niemann (quicksand and the long arm of coincidence has deposited them here). The Monster ends up on an operating table in Edelmann's lab.

Edelmann continues to treat Dracula, unaware that the Count has got the hots for Miliza. Now deciding to stick with being a vampire, the Count turns the (operating) tables on Edelmann during a blood transfusion: he hypnotizes Edelmann, then maliciously infuses the doctor with some of his own tainted blood. Unaware of what has transpired, Edelmann recovers in time to race to Miliza's room and ward off the hovering Dracula with a crucifix. The vampire flees to the castle basement and the sanctuary of his coffin just as the dawn breaks. Edelmann exposes Dracula to the rays of the rising sun, destroying the undead creature.

When Edelmann becomes aware of the vampiric blood in his veins, he unselfishly redoubles his efforts to cultivate more mold for the coming operation on Talbot, which he eventually performs. But that night he transforms into a gaunt, black-eyed killer who tears out the throat of his own servant Seigfried (Ludwig Stossel). Talbot sees enough to know that Edelmann is the murderer, but he naturally sympathizes with Edelmann and keeps the knowledge to himself.

Boldly stepping out into full moonlight to gauge the success of Edelmann's surgery, Talbot is elated to find that the operation has been proved a success and that his curse of werewolfry is at an end. But Edelmann has turned into the mad killer once again: he hurries to the lab, where he revives the Monster. Talbot, Miliza and Inspector Holtz arrive on the scene just as Edelmann strangles Nina and the Monster begins his usual rampage. Talbot is forced to shoot Edelmann, then topples a huge shelf of combustible chemicals onto the Monster. Talbot and Miliza flee the castle as the Monster is once again consumed by flames.

Little care or imagination went into the "new" Edward T. Lowe screenplay: basically it was a rehash of the previous *House* film. Once again Dracula is a warm-up act, dispatched much too early on. The Wolf Man vies with a mad doctor and a hunchback for audience attention throughout most of the remaining footage, and the Monster remains in a coma until he's needed as a curtain closer.

Despite the title, the house is not Dracula's although the Count certainly makes himself at home there, moving into the basement armor room, bag and baggage. As in *House of Frankenstein,* John Carradine's soft-spoken Dracula is less Continental Count than Kentucky Colonel: dignified and courtly, he has all the style and panache we hear ascribed to Lugosi's creaky portrayal. "When they asked me to play Dracula, I said yes, if you let me make him up and play him the way Bram Stoker described him—as an elderly, distinguished gentleman with a drooping mustache," Carradine told *Fangoria.* "[Universal] didn't like a big mustache, so I had to trim it and make it a very clipped, British mustache. It wasn't really in character."

Carradine's remains the best Dracula, easily outshining the ossified Lugosi as well as Christopher Lee's red-eyed acrobat. Pedants may quibble that Carradine is the wrong "type"—he does exude Southern style charm—but the fact that the actor is still able to put it over attests to his near-perfect playing of the role. Carradine brings just the right balance of sinister elegance and sexual magnetism to *House of Dracula;* he's at his best in the creepy scene where his otherworldly influence over piano-playing Martha O'Driscoll turns her rendition of "Moonlight Sonata" into a macabre, bone-chilling dirge. It's truly a pity that Carradine never had the opportunity to play Dracula in an appropriate vehicle; aside from the two *House* films, he later played the role in *Billy the Kid Versus Dracula* (1966), in which he was pitted against the young gunslinger (Chuck Courtney); *Las Vampiras* (1969), a Mexican-made, Spanish-language stinker where he was confined to a cage throughout the film; and in the R-rated *Nocturna* (1979), in which the tax man turns the Count's castle into a disco.

It's unclear how Dracula has managed to live for hundreds of years and yet be such a hopeless bungler of a vampire. In both *Dracula* and *House of Dracula* he keeps his coffin in a hiding place that's known to his enemies; it

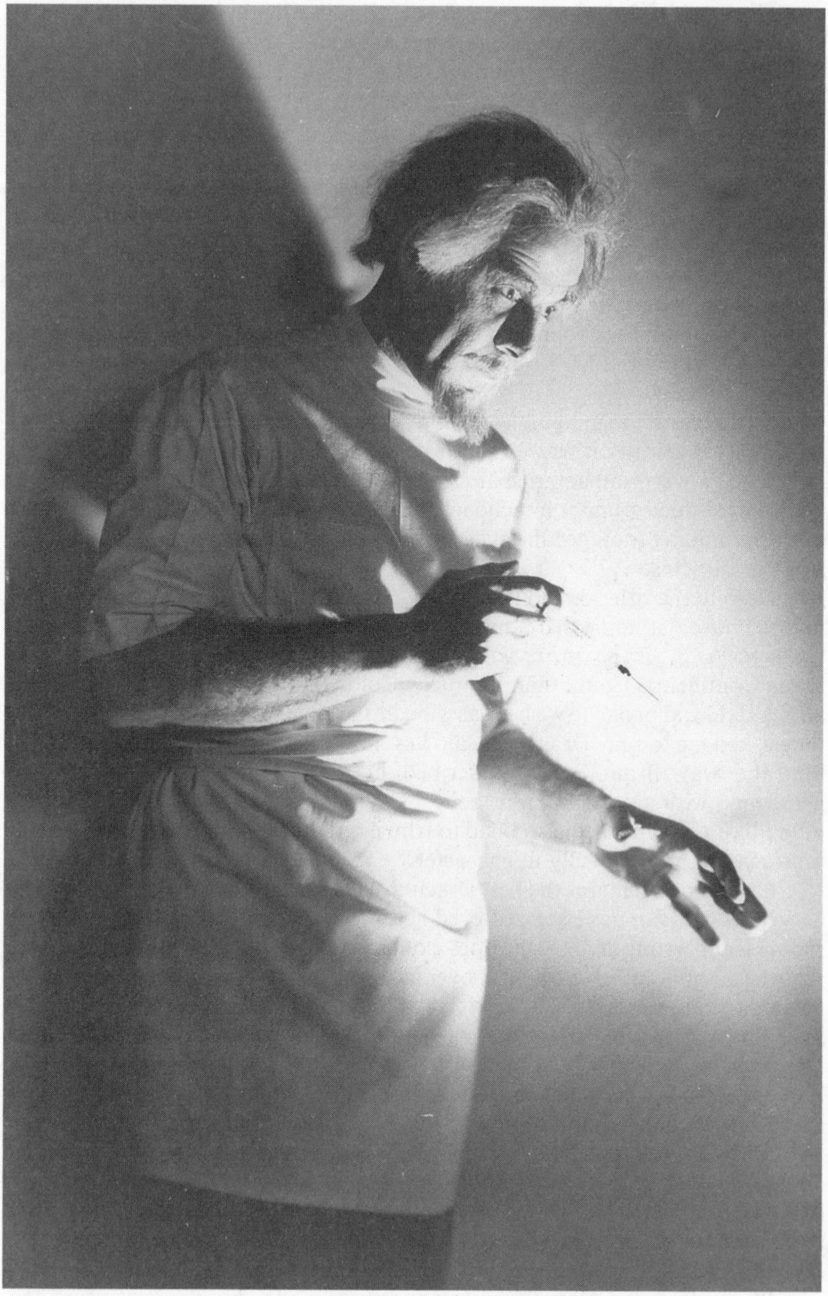

The camera catches Onslow Stevens in one of his darker moods, in *House of Dracula*. (Photo courtesy Steve Jochsberger.)

seems such a poor strategy, to antagonize people who know where you lay helpless half the day. The Count would also have been well-advised to invest a few dollars in a wristwatch: in *Dracula* as well as in both *House* films he makes his Big Move at five minutes before dawn, giving himself just enough time to incite people to chase him back to his coffin.

There are actually two "vampires" in *House of Dracula,* and for years a fuss has been made over the wrong one: there's been something of a tendency among fans to make too much of Onslow Stevens' performance as the vampiric Edelmann. There's really very little that's remarkable about it. Stevens plays the role with a striking lack of restraint, falling back on a lot of hoary horror cliches. His Hyde-inspired character does steal the show, but that's no trick considering the fact that, by the time he comes on, we've already seen the last of Dracula and the Wolf Man, and the Monster is in his usual helpless stupor. Stevens' performance is almost anachronistically broad, with the actor chewing the scenery and leering hammily; he does everything but twist the end of his mustache in Simon Legree fashion. There's some fun in Stevens' overly melodramatic delivery, but little justice in the fact that it's played up almost constantly while Carradine's portrayal of Dracula is often taken for granted.

Stevens fares better as the "normal" Edelmann, although this character's insistence on sticking labels on the monsters' maladies becomes annoying. Edelmann isolates the "peculiar parasite" in Dracula's blood that causes his vampiric condition, and also determines why Talbot changes into a werewolf. (For the record, it's because Talbot has a metabolism that's "like a steam engine without a balance wheel.") It's irritating and a little insulting to have a patronizing smart-aleck present such cut-and-dried diagnoses for our favorite monster characters. But there is a touch of sadness about Edelmann, both in the writing and in Stevens' portrayal, and overall he comes off far better than the crabbed and condescending Karloff does in *House of Frankenstein.*

Lon Chaney gives a good performance as Talbot, but by this fourth Wolf Man installment he's clearly on autopilot. Little is seen of Talbot's Wolf Man self this time around, reportedly because of a shortage of yak hair but more probably to satisfy censors who didn't want the Wolf Man killing anyone in a film where Talbot survives to the end. In a special effects blunder, Chaney is allowed to open and close his mouth in bestial fashion during his Wolf Man transformations; consequently, John P. Fulton's double exposures give the actor twin sets of upper and lower teeth. (Fulton had already resigned from Universal, returning for a brief time to complete his work on *House of Dracula*.) Glenn Strange is his usual dopey-looking "prop" Monster, laid out on an operating table throughout most of the film anticipating his mild climactic tantrum.

Leading ladies Martha O'Driscoll and Jane Adams go through their paces without creating much of an impression; there really are no acting opportunities for either actress in the film. O'Driscoll is at her best in scenes of tenderness with Chaney; there's a hint of blossoming romance between the two throughout the film. Adams is her usual simpering self, although there is some pathos in her unrequited love for Onslow Stevens. Emaciated English actor Skelton Knaggs and the fat, frumpy, Germanic Ludwig Stossel are seen as brothers, which is indicative of the kind of thinking that went into the picture.

The screenplay for *House of Dracula* is a highly derivative one, lifting scenes and ideas from many earlier films. Again, the film is in large part a remake of *House of Frankenstein,* but apart from this major influence there are other "steals" visible as well. The Carradine–Martha O'Driscoll piano scene is clearly presaged by a similar sequence in *Dracula's Daughter;* Edelmann's cat Bartholomew reacts almost hysterically to his transformation just as Henry Hull's similar looking house pet does in *WereWolf of London;* Edelmann's hallucinogenic dream, with its Freudian overtones, is copped from the MGM *Dr. Jekyll and Mr. Hyde* (1941). Also noticeable are traces of the 1931 *Dr. Jekyll and Mr. Hyde,* like a scene where "vampire" Edelmann approaches a door yet (from the other side) we now see "normal" Edelmann open it.

A September 20, 1945, draft of the script (titled, what else?, *Destiny*) includes many of the kind of script-to-screen changes that make for interesting reading. Early on there's a short scene where Edelmann examines a seven-year-old boy whose leg he has healed. (The scene was filmed, with Gregory Muradian playing the boy and Beatrice Gray as his peasant-mother. It ended up on the cutting room floor, although there's still a reference to it in the finished film.) According to the script, the "pagan" piano tune Dracula compelled Miliza to play should be heard faintly every time the vampire exerts his hypnotic influence over her. "Vampire" Edelmann's hands have webbed fingers and "vulture-like" claws. The dream sequence is longer and more elaborate, with scenes of the Monster killing Miliza and hurling villagers around like matchwood. Steinmuhl is a belligerent "braggart-extrovert" who angrily harangues the townspeople. (It's also noteworthy that the script puts an approximate date on these goings-on, describing a "period of about 1880.")

Released only a few months before the second Universal horror cycle sputtered to a close, *House of Dracula* represents one of the last Universal credits for most of the people involved. It was the final horror film for burly Lon Chaney, Universal's Master Character Creator. Chaney, whose hard drinking and boisterous hijinks won him few friends on the lot, was dropped from the studio payroll shortly after *House of Dracula* wrapped, and was forced to work as a freelancer. With horror films temporarily out of vogue, Chaney scrambled for work, taking roles in a long string of minor films before science fiction and monster pictures came back into style in the 1950s. By that time the actor's drinking problem had worsened to the point where most producers would only entrust him with the type of nonspeaking brute-man roles where the audience wouldn't know if he was drunk or sober.

By the 1950s Chaney appears also to have mellowed somewhat; most of the actors and producers for whom he worked during this later period look back fondly on the experience. Outspoken Beverly Garland, star of *The Alligator People* (1959), recalls that "Lon Chaney was fabulous, fun and easy. . . . He was a favorite person of mine." Robert Clarke (*The Black Pirates,* 1954), remembers him as "a fun-type man" and Howard W. Koch, producer of *The Black Sleep* (1956), reminisces, "He was a sweet, compassionate, wonderful man. He was great with me, and I was really crazy about him."

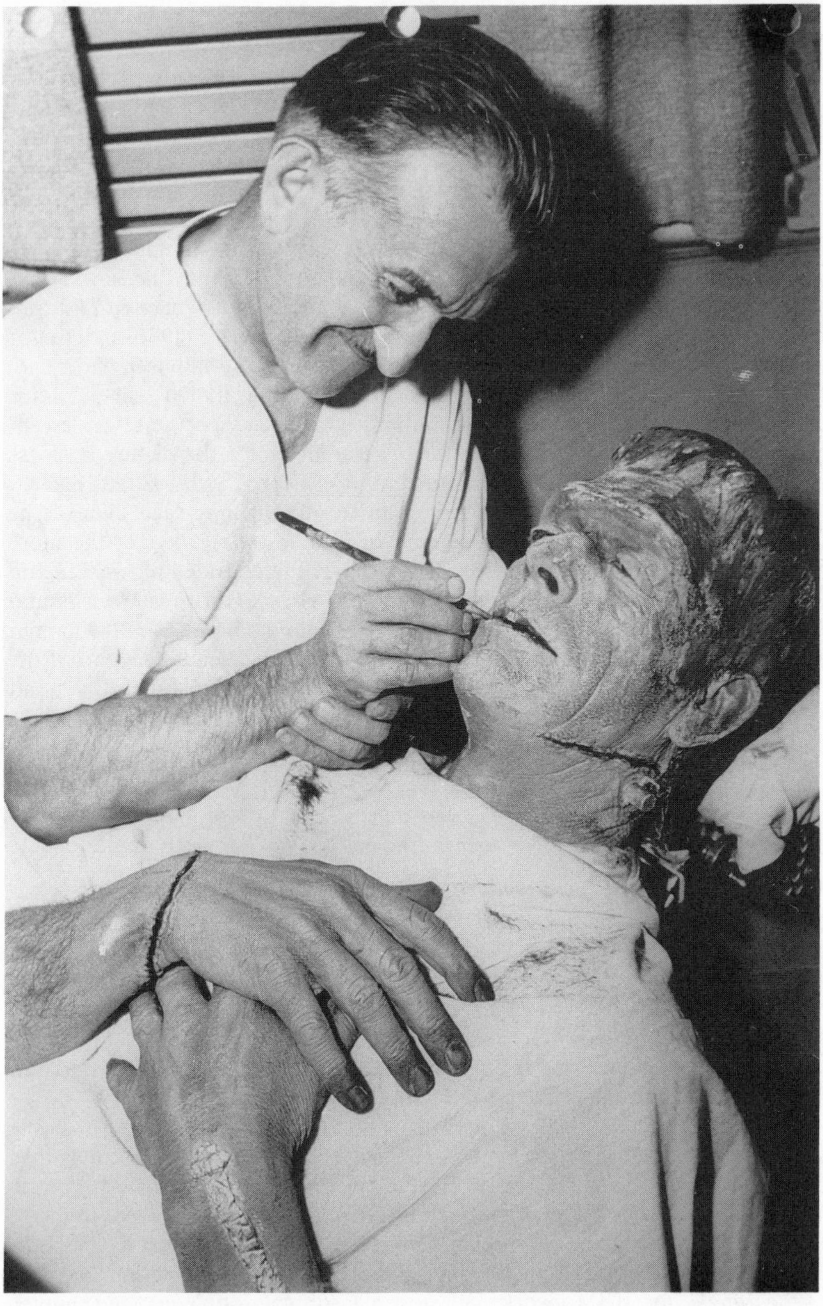

Jack Pierce applies the Frankenstein makeup for the last time – on Glenn Strange, in *House of Dracula*.

Anthony Eisley, who worked with Chaney toward the end of the actor's life in 1969's *Dracula vs. Frankenstein,* recalls, "He was very, very ill then—he would have to lie down after every take—but to talk with him and to hear his stories was just incredible. He was a wonderful, lovely, unbelievably interesting man."

Jack Pollexfen, producer/director of *Indestructible Man* (1956), laughs, "I found him intelligent, probably more so than most actors. He warned me before we started shooting, 'Don't make any changes in dialogue, or add new dialogue, after lunch!'—which he drank down rather liberally." But it was probably Gloria Talbott, star of *The Cyclops* (1957), who summed it up: "He was a darling, darling man—but drunk as a skunk!" Chaney died in 1973.

There are other sad stories connected with the cast of *House of Dracula.* Onslow Stevens, who played Dr. Edelmann, died January 5, 1977, a victim of abuse in the Van Nuys, California, nursing home where he had been under care for a heart ailment. A coroner's inquest jury ruled that the 70-year-old actor died "at the hands of another other than by accident" in the convalescent hospital. Director Erle Kenton was forced to retire from the picture business due to Parkinson's disease, which killed him on February 6, 1980, at age 83.

Diminutive tyrant Jack P. Pierce, Universal's grumpy Guardian of the Greasepaint, was dropped by the studio in 1947 to make way for the more modern methods of makeup ace Bud Westmore. Pierce ended up working on low-budget claptrap like *The Brain from Planet Arous, Teenage Monster* and *Giant from the Unknown* in the '50s, and later found a home as makeup man on television's "Mr. Ed." Frank Taylor, writing in the calendar section of the August 11, 1968, *Los Angeles Times,* bitterly describes Pierce's funeral as "a sad affair," with mourners hardly filling a solid row of pews.

> A minister who had never met Pierce was bravely trying to eulogize him, but said little more than a few prayers and some kind words. In the audience of twenty-four people, only three were makeup artists. His union brothers sent flowers but most found it inconvenient to say farewell in person.... Hollywood bid farewell by staying away.

(Pierce's nephew, actor Ted Sorel, appears in newish horror movies like *From Beyond* and *Basket Case II.*) Even Universal's familiar European Street, seen in numerous horror films dating back to the original *Frankenstein,* came to an ignominious end: in 1986, the set was gutted by a blaze which fire investigators report was set deliberately. It took firefighters nearly a half hour to control the blaze, which spread quickly because so much of the set was dry old wood and foam rubber. Universal officials estimated the damage at $2,500,000.

Saddest of all these tales is the story of Lionel Atwill, who died of bronchial cancer six months after *House of Dracula* completed production. Things had finally begun to look up again for the much put-upon British actor in the mid '40s: the sex scandal finally seemed behind him, he was newly wed to Paula Pruter, a young woman, and became the father of a baby boy (at age 60!). In February, 1946, Atwill dropped from the cast of the Universal serial *Lost City of the Jungle:* too sick to work, he was replaced by a double and the chapter play wrapped without him. Reginald LeBorg, longtime friend to Atwill, visited the ailing character star in his Palisades home.

> I saw him once when he was very sick with cancer, at the end, about a week before he died. He must have lost thirty pounds, and he was pale, and he was lying in bed. He was very bitter—he knew he was going. He wanted to live because of the son—and he loved Paula. It was very tragic because, instead of being quiet and giving up his soul, he became sore at the world.

The Maddest Doctor of Them All died April 22, 1946; *House of Dracula* was his final Universal feature credit. You can hear him hacking off-camera in one scene.

Not unexpectedly, economy rears its ugly head at several points during the movie. Footage from *Bride of Frankenstein* turns up in the dream sequence, and much of the fiery climax from *The Ghost of Frankenstein* is used in the climax as Edelmann's castle burns. The laboratory where Edelmann revives the Monster is a spartan, barn-like set, probably the cheapest mad lab in the series. And in an inexplicable *faux pas* in the film's climax, Atwill's Inspector Holtz is accompanied into the Edelmann house by two gendarmes, but by the time he walks into the lab there's only one.

There's a juvenile air about *House of Dracula.* There isn't even a hint as to how Dracula and the Wolf Man survived their respective destructions in *House of Frankenstein;* they walk into this new picture without benefit of explanation. Edelmann doesn't believe in vampires until Dracula shows him his coffin, which is all the proof the doctor needs. It's also unclear what Edelmann becomes after he's infused with the blood of Dracula: he casts no reflection in a mirror, which indicates that he's a vampire, and yet sunlight has no effect upon him. Neither nightfall nor moonlight trigger his transformations: he changes into the mad killer at the scriptwriter's whim, whenever the picture needs a dash of action. It's insulting, too, that all the monsters coincidentally converge at Dr. Edelmann's home. At least in *House of Frankenstein* Karloff's Dr. Niemann *sought out* the monsters; silly as it was, at least it made sense. In *House of Dracula* they just turn up, one after another, at Edelmann's door, giving the picture the realistic air of a "Munsters" episode.

But for all of its many failings, the film has an agreeable, low-key atmosphere as well as a number of exciting highpoints. Carradine's early scenes as Dracula are a delight, and the scene where he hypnotizes Martha O'Driscoll at the piano is a gem. There's a clever, innovative touch in the transfusion scene, with the images of Dracula and Edelmann blurring and running together while nurse Nina stands undistorted in a corner of the picture. A highlight of the film is Edelmann's murder of poor Seigfried, as well as the ensuing chase scene with the vampiric Edelmann dashing through the streets with the angry mob at his heels.

It's hard to determine where to bestow the credit for the modest saving touches in *House of Dracula;* these are, after all, the same hacks who cranked out *House of Frankenstein.* Universal released *House of Dracula* on December 7, 1945, on a double-bill with the Western *The Daltons Ride Again,* also with Lon Chaney and Martha O'Driscoll. Critics brushed it off as yet another kiddie-oriented monster opus and the three classic series, intertwined and hopelessly cheapened, came to a simultaneous end.

Pillow of Death (1945)

Released December 14, 1945. 66 minutes. An Inner Sanctum Mystery, produced by arrangement with Simon and Schuster, Inc., Publishers. *Directed by* Wallace Fox. *Produced by* Ben Pivar. *Screenplay by* George Bricker. *Original Story by* Dwight V. Babcock. *Director of Photography:* Jerome Ash. *Camera Operator:* Russ Hoffman. *Assistant Director:* Melville Shyer. *Film Editor:* Edward Curtiss. *Art Directors:* John B. Goodman & Abraham Grossman. *Set Decorators:* Russell A. Gausman & Leigh Smith. *Musical Director:* Frank Skinner. *Dialogue Director:* George Bricker. *Sound Director:* Bernard B. Brown. *Technician:* Jess Moulin. *Sound Editor:* Carl Elmendorf. *Makeup by* Jack P. Pierce. *Gowns by* Vera West.

Lon Chaney (Wayne Fletcher), Brenda Joyce (Donna Kincaid), J. Edward Bromberg (Julian Julian), Rosalind Ivan (Amelia Kincaid), Clara Blandick (Belle Kincaid), George Cleveland (Sam Kincaid), Wilton Graff (Captain McCracken), Bernard B. Thomas (Bruce Malone), J. Farrell MacDonald (Sexton), Victoria Horne (Voice of Vivian Fletcher), Fern Emmett* (Mrs. Williams), Arthur Hohl* (Mr. Williams), Harry Strang, Lee Phelps. [**Does not appear in the final print*.]

The last gasp of the dying Inner Sanctum series, *Pillow of Death* titillated postwar audiences with spiritualists, an alleged haunted house, spectral voices and murder-by-suffocation. As had been the case with most of the other films in the series, the supernatural elements of the badly-written script are counterfeit, and are exploited for the sole purpose of attracting horror fans. J. Edward Bromberg's cherubic seer is somewhat ambiguous. Although the police have made frequent uses of his gift of extrasensory perception in murder investigations, the séances he stages couldn't be phonier. The "phantom voice" of the killer's victim is written off in the end as nothing more than a guilt-inspired hallucination. All of the ingredients for a taut, even chilling melodrama are here, but *Pillow of Death* is so absurd and indifferently produced, it squanders any potential it may have had.

The stately home of wealthy Belle Kincaid (Clara Blandick) and her curmudgeon brother Sam (George Cleveland) is where most of the story's "action" takes place. Belle, a student of the occult, consults regularly with psychic investigator Julian Julian (J. Edward Bromberg) to conjure up spirits of long-dead Kincaids. When her live-in niece Donna (Brenda Joyce) takes a romantic interest in her employer, lawyer Wayne Fletcher (Lon Chaney), Belle gets in touch with Fletcher's wife, Vivian, who's also an occultist.

Wayne decides finally to ask his wife for a divorce. Returning home after a late night at the office, Fletcher is met by Captain McCracken (Wilton Graff) and Julian. Vivian has been murdered; the cause of death was asphyxiation. Julian insists Vivian contacted him *after* she died: "She was that rare individual, a natural medium for communication with the spirit world." When Wayne's alibi doesn't bear scrutiny, he is arrested, but is soon released on a writ of *habeas corpus.*

Despite Donna's objections, Belle and her cousin Amelia (Rosalind Ivan) stage a séance in an effort to reach Vivian's spirit. Wayne reluctantly attends. During the proceedings, a ghostly voice resembling Vivian's brands Fletcher as her murderer. Enraged by the accusation, Wayne discovers Bruce Malone (Bernard B. Thomas), Donna's persistent beau, hiding in the shadows, and accuses him of conspiring with Julian to frame him for murder.

Alone that night, Wayne is haunted by Vivian's voice (Victoria Horne). In a low-keyed, somberly effective scene, Jerome Ash's camera follows a semihypnotic Chaney through a cemetery and up to Vivian's crypt. When her voice fades away, Wayne goes into hysterics.

The next morning, Amelia discovers Sam's body; he has been suffocated in the same manner as Vivian Fletcher. Wayne confides to McCracken about his experience hearing Vivian's voice and a check is made of her crypt. Her body is missing.

Belle is the next to fall to the mysterious Pillow Killer. Julian comes under McCracken's suspicion when the policeman learns the seer was once a stage ventriloquist. Her mind unhinged by the murders and Julian's incarceration, Amelia traps Wayne and Donna in a closet. She is about to pump it full of gas when Julian (released for lack of evidence) intervenes and saves the couple's lives. Conducting their own investigation, the pair find Vivian's corpse in the Kincaid cellar. Bruce admits he stole the body to trick Fletcher into admitting his guilt.

Later that night, Donna hears Wayne's voice coming from her late uncle's bedroom and investigates. She is horrified to find Fletcher holding an imagined "conversation" with Vivian. "Donna can't hear me, but she knows," Vivian's disembodied voice warns Wayne. "At last she realizes that you are a psychopathic killer. Isn't it too bad that you can't have her and all that Kincaid money now that we are out of the way."

At Vivian's prompting, Wayne attempts to suffocate Donna to death with a pillow. McCracken and Bruce storm into the room and stop him. Obeying his wife's instructions, Wayne leaps out of the window to his death.

Pity the staunch souls at the Breen Office who came into daily contact with scores of wretched scripts just begging for their censorial approval. In the case of *Pillow of Death,* the Breen moralists got their bowels in an uproar over what, today, seems like nothing at all. In a January 3, 1945, letter to Universal editorial head Maurice Pivar, the Breen people emphasized their displeasure with the method of murder utilized in *Pillow of Death,* complaining that suffocation can be too easily imitated by the more impressionable viewer. Pointing out several lines of offensive dialogue ("Someone smothered her with a pillow while she dozed" and "I'll be very gentle with the pillow," among others), the Breen Office recommended the script be amended.

For once, Lon Chaney is actually guilty of the crimes he is accused of, in *Pillow of Death,* the long overdue finale to the "Inner Sanctum" series.

The adulterous relationship between Donna and Wayne also came under fire; producer Ben Pivar was instructed to "cool it" as much as possible. (One can only speculate how the board of censors reacted to such incendiary productions as *Double Indemnity* and *The Postman Always Rings Twice*!) On the other hand, Wayne's suicide was deemed "acceptable" because he was off his rocker. Pivar (Ben or Maurice, take your pick) saw to it that the script alterations were made, and, after a few more weeks of bellyaching, George Bricker's scenario was approved. The Breen officers got in one last dig, however, by reminding Universal that the killer's easily imitable *modus operandi* might spell trouble for *Pillow of Death* when the movie reached the state political censor boards.

Director Wallace Fox began shooting the first scenes of *Pillow of Death* on February 26, 1945, just two weeks after the wrapping of *Strange Confession.* Fox shot the eerie cemetery/crypt scene outside the Shelby home, while the Hacienda was used for the exterior of the Kincaid mansion. Once again, the old *Phantom of the Opera* stage was pressed into service for various interior shots. A labor strike on the lot held up production for a few days, causing *Pillow of Death* to wrap on March 13, two days beyond the allotted 12-day schedule.

Assigned to portray Chaney's ill-fated wife Vivian, Victoria Horne suffered the ultimate indignity for an actress: her performance ended up on the cutting room floor. Bricker's screenplay had called for Victoria to play host to fellow occultists Fern Emmett and Arthur Hohl in a scene that was later scrapped. The fact that the actress spent a day working closely with John P. Fulton is a good indication Victoria's Vivian also made at least one phantasmic appearance in the script.

Asked if she recalled any of her lost scenes in *Pillow of Death,* Victoria Horne recalls a quip made by her late husband, Jack Oakie, at the time the picture was released: "Mommy dear," he said, "beauty is favored in motion pictures. That's why they put the camera on Lon Chaney and used only your voice."

Tediously paced and uninspired on every level, *Pillow of Death* pretty much encapsulates the chronic ailments of the Inner Sanctum series: a fairly intriguing tale is demolished by ludicrous plotting, unbelievably bad dialogue, and aimless direction, with no effort to elevate the material above the level of Class B status. Worse yet, the films placed their most exploitable asset, Lon Chaney, at a disadvantage by putting him in roles unsuited to his persona.

With the possible exception of Chaney's nocturnal romp through the graveyard, and the surprise climax, all of the shock scenes fizzle. All three murders occur off-camera, no doubt to preserve the anonymity of the killer. (It might have been interesting to have the *camera* stalk each victim, but that would be asking too much of a hackster like Wallace Fox.) Many scenes run far too long. In a vain attempt to build suspense and drive home the point that the Kincaid manse is infested with spirits, most of the cast shuffles up to the attic to investigate some strange sounds (rattling chains, weird guffaws, etc.); presumably it's the ghost of old Uncle Joe stirring up trouble again. After an interminable stretch, the source of the disturbance is revealed as a mischievous raccoon!

Taking advantage of its honorable status as the last Inner Sanctum mystery, *Pillow of Death* dispenses with the seer-in-the-crystal-ball prologue, and doesn't bother to reinstate Chaney's "stream-of-consciousness" asides (which were previously abandoned in *Strange Confession*). For once, Chaney is actually guilty of the crimes for which he has been accused; we're not counting *Strange Confession,* as Chaney was the *victim,* driven to justifiable homicide. Wayne Fletcher murders his wife in cold blood, then slays the two Kincaids while acting on a psychopathic impulse, much as Bela Lugosi did in 1941's *Invisible Ghost.* Stilted throughout most of the movie, Chaney comes to life in the climax, assuming a childlike, or Lennie-like *Of Mice and Men* stance as the authorities (and his own conscience) close in on him.

Bricker's supporting characters are, for the most part, stagey and irritatingly eccentric. Whether he's attuning himself to metaphysical vibes or slipping into or out of psychic trance, J. Edward Bromberg's unctuous, overfed Julian is disagreeably "odd." (Nils Ashter radiated infinitely more charm and suaveté in a similar role in *Night Monster.*) Unlike the average horror film heroine, Brenda Joyce is surprisingly unsympathetic as Donna; she's spoiled and self-centered, and expresses no outward remorse over having been at least partially responsible for the destruction of a marriage. As Belle, Clara

Blandick (Auntie Em of *The Wizard of Oz*) is a dour old crone with a one-sided disposition. On the flip side is George Cleveland's Uncle Sam, a crusty, painfully cute old man whose only interest in life is appeasing his appetite (for food, that is).

But the most exasperating character of all is Bernard B. Thomas' snoopy next-door neighbor. If he isn't emerging from secret hiding places in the Kincaid house (he seems to know more about the layout of the place than the people who inhabit it), the callow youth is peering through windows, sneaking around corners, or making a general nuisance of himself. Bruce goes to any length to prove Fletcher's guilt—including stealing the corpse of the man's wife (for which he goes unpunished!). To cap it off, this noxious little worm gets the girl in the final clinch. This comes as a greater surprise than Fletcher's unmasking as the murderer! On a more positive note, there's Rosalind Ivan, walking away with the acting honors as Amelia, a poor relation from England who's reduced to serving as a domestic.

Pillow of Death predictably racked up more than its share of bad notices upon its release in December, 1945. However, it did get at least one *favorable* review (from Jack D. Grant of *The Hollywood Reporter*), several lines of which bear repeating here:

> Few screen mysteries succeed in mystifying and by smartly turning just that trick *Pillow of Death* lifts itself out of the ordinary.... This offering is one of the better Inner Sanctum mysteries and owes much to the pace and movement maintained in the direction by Wallace Fox. There are also a number of top grade performances. Lon Chaney does a thoroughly believable job.

It kinda makes you wonder if Jack saw the same picture as the rest of us.

Terror by Night (1946)

Released February 1, 1946. 60 minutes. *Produced & Directed by* Roy William Neill. *Executive Producer:* Howard Benedict. *Screenplay by* Frank Gruber. *Adapted from a story by* Sir Arthur Conan Doyle. *Director of Photography:* Maury Gertsman. *Film Editor:* Saul A. Goodkind. *Musical Director:* Milton Rosen. *Art Directors:* John B. Goodman & Abraham Grossman. *Set Decorators:* Russell A. Gausman & Carl Lawrence. *Assistant Director:* Melville Shyer. *Dialogue Director:* Raymond Kessler. *Sound Director:* Bernard B. Brown. *Technician:* Jack A. Bolger, Jr. *Makeup by* Jack P. Pierce. *Hair Stylist:* Carmen Dirigo. *Gowns by* Vera West.

Basil Rathbone (Sherlock Holmes), Nigel Bruce (Dr. John H. Watson), Alan Mowbray (Major Duncan-Bleek/Colonel Sebastian Moran), Dennis Hoey (Inspector Lestrade), Renee Godfrey (Vivian Vedder), Frederic Worlock (Professor William Kilbane), Mary Forbes (Lady Margaret Carstairs), Skelton Knaggs (Sands), Billy Bevan (Train Attendant), Geoffrey Steele (Roland Carstairs), Leland [Leyland] Hodgson (Train Conductor), Boyd Davis (Inspector McDonald), Janet Murdoch (Mrs. Shallcross), Gerald Hamer (Alfred Shallcross), Harry Cording (Mock), Bobby Wissler (Mock, Jr.), Charles Knight (Guard), Gilbert Allen (Steward), Colin Kenny (Constable), Tom Pilkington (Attendant).

The placid shipboard intrigues of *Pursuit to Algiers* paved the way for this second, superior mystery-in-motion, *Terror by Night.* Set aboard a roaring express train, this eleventh entry in the waning Sherlock Holmes series has a locale every bit as claustrophobic as its predecessor's, but it shrewdly overcomes this handicap through savvy editing, taut direction by the accomplished Roy William Neill, and a story that keeps moving. Tailored to a compact 60 minutes, *Terror by Night* is rhythmically paced and set at high speed.

The concise screenplay was written by Frank Gruber, a prolific writer of pulp fiction since 1927. Gruber's film writing credits eventually rivalled his literary output in terms of volume (Westerns and action dramas were his specialty, but his best work was the 1944 adaptation of Eric Ambler's novel, *The Mask of Dimitrios*). In *Terror by Night,* Gruber spices up a routine fabulous jewel heist with interesting touches—the murders are committed with an air pistol that shoots poisonous darts, the architect of the heist is Professor Moriarity's second-in-command, Colonel Sebastian Moran, and there's a Creeper-like henchman with a strangulation fixation. The dialogue is sharp, and there are several highly amusing vignettes dealing with peculiar passengers on board.

Sherlock Holmes (Basil Rathbone) and Dr. Watson (Nigel Bruce) are commissioned to protect one of the world's most fabulous jewels, the Star of Rhodesia, on a rail journey from London to Edinburgh. Like *The Pearl of Death,* this jewel also has a blood-stained heritage. Its current possessor, the high-hatted Lady Margaret Carstairs (Mary Forbes), has the stone taken right out from under her nose by Holmes, who craftily substitutes a phony.

Lady Margaret's son Roland (Geoffrey Steele) is found murdered in his compartment. Though there are no visible signs of foul play on the body, Holmes deduces Carstairs has been poisoned. The imposter jewel is missing from its case. Inspector Lestrade (Dennis Hoey), also on board, launches an investigation in his typically stumbling manner. With the aid of an old school chum, Major Duncan-Bleek (Alan Mowbray) of the Twelfth Indian Lancers, Watson sets out to ensnare the guilty party.

Holmes detects certain similarities between this robbery and others in his experience and determines it was perpetrated by Colonel Sebastian Moran, "the most sinister, ruthless and diabolically clever henchman of our late and unlamented friend, Professor Moriarity. His speciality was spectacular jewel robberies." Though Holmes has never met the Colonel face to face, he nearly met death at his hands on three different occasions. The Colonel takes another crack at ending the famous sleuth's life by pushing him out of a compartment door. Holmes struggles to maintain his grip on the door as his assailant (whose features are obscured by shadows) tries to dislodge him. Seconds before the roaring train disappears into a tunnel, Holmes kicks through a window and unlocks the latch. Vivid editing and dizzying camera shots of rushing landscapes give this scene a discomforting air of reality.

A stooped figure emerges from a false-bottom coffin in the baggage compartment. It is Sands (Skelton Knaggs), Moran's diminutive underling. He enters Duncan-Bleek's compartment and addresses the jovial Englishman as Colonel Moran! The pair quietly enter Lestrade's compartment and find him conveniently eyeing the real gem. Sands knocks the inspector unconscious and retrieves the precious stone, but is shot dead by Moran with the killer's own air pistol.

Inspector McDonald (Boyd Davis) of the Edinburgh Police and his men board the train and arrogantly take charge. A brief interrogation of Duncan-Bleek convinces the inspector he is indeed Moran. But before McDonald can take him into custody, Moran grabs a revolver and holds everyone at bay. Watson overpowers his "old chum" with a swift blow from behind. In the ensuing struggle in the dark, Moran is apparently bagged and dragged from the train by McDonald and his men.

Much to Watson's surprise, Moran hasn't been taken off the train after all, but lies, disarmed, in an adjoining seat. Holmes explains that McDonald and his men were imposters, summoned to rescue their leader. Lestrade surprisingly grasped the situation and, during the fight, pulled his coat over his head, tricking the phony policemen into thinking he was the Colonel. Outside on the train platform, the inspector reveals his identity and carts "McDonald" and the other members of Moran's gang off to the station house. The Star of Rhodesia, now stained with the blood of several more victims, is reclaimed.

Under the guidance of the unit's executive producer, Howard Benedict,

Terror by Night went into production in October, 1945. Tightly budgeted, the film borrowed extensively from the studio's library of stock shots of bustling train stations (including a shot used in the 1934 *The Black Cat*), speeding locomotives and barren landscapes fading into the distance. These insertions, edited into the new footage by former serial director Saul A. Goodkind, give the picture fluidity and a sense of urgency, and doubtlessly perk up what could have been a static presentation.

By no coincidence, *Terror by Night* shares some basic similarities with its immediate predecessor, *Pursuit to Algiers.* Both stories are set on modes of transportation that inspire mystery and intrigue. Deception plays an important role in both pictures (in *Terror by Night,* Holmes substitutes a fake jewel; in *Pursuit to Algiers,* a phony prince). Lastly, the villains in both films are plump, genteel Englishmen who leave the dirty work to their seedy underlings.

Red herrings play an important part in almost every Sherlock Holmes picture. In *Terror by Night,* we have an interesting lot. There's Vivian Vedder (Renee Godfrey, the wife of director Peter Godfrey), barely concealing her Cockney origins behind a veneer of respectability, who is escorting her mother's body to Scotland for burial. Holmes unmasks her as an accomplice of Colonel Moran; the coffin she brought on board has a secret compartment which concealed Sands.

The passenger list also includes a mathematics professor named William Kilbane (Frederic Worlock). Holmes recalls that Colonel Moran is known to be an aficionado of the subject, but this amounts to a false lead. Nigel Bruce and Worlock have a wonderful scene wherein the ever helpful Watson attempts to interrogate the grouchy prof, only to have the tables turned on him when the defensive Kilbane accuses *Watson* of the crime and has the bumbling medico pleading *his* innocence! Another amusing bit has Watson probing into the affairs of the mild-mannered Shallcross couple (Janet Murdoch and the dependable Gerald Hamer). When Mr. Shallcross confesses freely to having committed a theft, the triumphant Watson calls in Holmes and Lestrade, only to wither with embarrassment when the stolen item turns out to be a teapot nabbed from a tourist hotel!

Alan Mowbray delivers a smooth performance as Moriarity's trusted successor. He is quite above suspicion throughout, indulging in flightly banter with Watson, even taking a stab at solving the mystery. Once his cover is blown, he is as treacherous as any of Holmes' previous arch rivals. A veteran of hundreds of films and television shows, Mowbray essayed the part of Inspector Lestrade in the 1933 Holmes picture *A Study in Scarlet,* and had a supporting role as a Scotland Yard man unapproving of the Baker Street sleuth in the 1932 Fox film *Sherlock Holmes.*

As Colonel Moran's ill-fated henchman, Skelton Knaggs is slime personified. The emaciated English actor, a former Shakespearean mime, was a familiar face in many '40s horror films. Apart from his Universal credits, he was also seen in such pictures as *The Lodger* (1944), *The Picture of Dorian Gray* (1945), *Dick Tracy Meets Gruesome* (1947), *Master Minds* (1949) and Val Lewton's *The Ghost Ship* (1943), *Isle of the Dead* (1945) and *Bedlam* (1946). Knaggs died at a youthful age of cirrhosis of the liver in 1955.

A minor entry to be sure, *Terror by Night* combines all the right ingredients in properly measured doses and emerges as a better-than-average, late-in-the-games Holmes entry. Not only was it colorized by Hal Roach Studios in 1988, but the last sequence (in which Holmes explains how Lestrade traded places with Moran during the fight) was reedited so that Rathbone's words are heard over a reprint of the actual scene. Unethical tampering perhaps, but effectively done nonetheless.

The Spider Woman Strikes Back (1946)

Released March 22, 1946. 59 minutes. *Directed by* Arthur Lubin. *Produced by* Howard Welsch. *Original Screenplay by* Eric Taylor. *Director of Photography:* Paul Ivano. *Cameraman:* William Dodds. *Film Editor:* Ray Snyder. *Assistant Director:* Fred Frank. *Art Directors:* John B. Goodman & Abraham Grossman. *Musical Director:* Milton Rosen. *Set Decorators:* Russell A. Gausman & Ralph Warrington. *Dialogue Director:* Joan Hathaway. *Sound Director:* Bernard B. Brown. *Technician:* Robert Pritchard. *Director of Makeup:* Jack P. Pierce. *Hair Stylist:* Carmen Dirigo. *Gowns by* Vera West.

Gale Sondergaard (Zenobia Dollard), Brenda Joyce (Jean Kingsley), Kirby Grant (Hal Wentley), Milburn Stone (Commissioner Moore), Rondo Hatton (Mario), Hobart Cavanaugh (Bill Stapleton), Ruth Robinson* (Mrs. Wentley), Adda Gleason* (Martha), Lois Austin* (Jinnie Hawks), Tom Daly* (Sam Julian), Eula Guy* (Molly Corvin), Norman Leavitt (Tom), Eva Mudge, Guy Beach, Guy Wilkerson, Horace Murphy, Hans Herbert, Bill Sundholm. [**Does not appear in the final print.*]

The Spider Woman Strikes Back has attained the status of a camp classic over the years. This lurid little B boasts sinister seductress Gale Sondergaard at her deliciously wicked best, Rondo Hatton as a deafmute in cahoots with the deadly lady and a rubbery subtropical plant with papier-mâché leaves that subsists on spiders and human blood, and goes by the vampiric-sounding name Drochenema.

Actually, *The Spider Woman Strikes Back* is no worse than the average shocker released in this dismal period, the tail-end of the second great horror cycle. It's slow-paced and repetitious (giving one the impression it runs longer than its trifling 59 minutes) and the story is trite and silly, with more than its share of absurd dialogue (a few lines would have done George Bricker and M. Coates Webster proud). Still, *The Spider Woman Strikes Back* doesn't merit the scathing reactions it has gotten from the late Miss Sondergaard and director Arthur Lubin, who, up until recently, had all but forgotten he made the picture!

When Universal decided to launch a Spider Woman series in March, 1945, with Ford Beebe acting as both associate producer and director, it would have been safe to assume that the studio planned to revive the Adrea Spedding character from 1944's *The Spider Woman.* Beebe was soon relieved of this assignment; his duties as a producer were assumed by Howard Welsch while

Arthur Lubin (who happened to be in between film projects) was handed the directorial reins.

In late May, Sondergaard flew in after an eastern hospital tour to begin preparations for *The Spider Woman Strikes Back*. She ought to have saved herself the trouble, as production was delayed for over four months (possibly, script alterations were made during this period which may have had a bearing on the elimination of the Spedding character). Shooting finally began on October 1 with the Providencia Ranch and the Shelby Home, two popular backlot locations, figuring prominently in the plot's action. Following the urgings of the Breen office, Lubin minimized the picture's grislier aspects. The fiery deaths of Sondergaard and Hatton were staged so as not to suggest suicide. The final scenes were shot on October 18, three days over the standard two-week schedule.

Jean Kingsley (Brenda Joyce) arrives in the small Nevada cattle farming community of Domingo (population: a patriotic 1492) to act as companion to wealthy Zenobia Dollard (Gale Sondergaard). She is driven out to the blind woman's estate by local rancher Hal Wentley (Kirby Grant), a former beau, who can't speak highly enough of the philanthropic Zenobia. (Had we not known in advance that Zenobia is the title menace, all of this adoration would've *definitely* aroused our suspicions.)

At the candlelit Dollard home, Jean meets Zenobia's manservant Mario (Rondo Hatton), a deformed deafmute. In a well-executed shot, the blind woman enters the dimly lit parlor from the shadows. Zenobia's kindliness puts Jean at ease; she has Mario bring the tired young woman a glass of warm milk. Jean drinks it and retires for the evening.

It doesn't take long for Jean to discover that something foul is afoot. A letter arrives at the house for Betty Sanders, Zenobia's former companion, who purportedly left her on short notice to get married. When Jean sends her a letter, it is returned by the post office: Betty's whereabouts are a mystery. Jean's health takes a sudden turn. She is plagued by headaches and loss of appetite and awakens each morning drawn of strength.

The cause of Jean's problems soon becomes apparent. Zenobia has been drugging her milk and then, after she retires, withdrawing a considerable amount of blood from her veins. In her basement laboratory (the same lab set used in *WereWolf of London*), Zenobia nurses huge carnivorous plants resembling oversized Venus flytraps, with wavy tendrils and hungry blossoms. By feeding the specimens a diet of live spiders and human blood, Zenobia is able to distill from the plants an elusive poison which she has been using to poison the cattle belonging to the local ranchers.

After a child sickens and dies from drinking milk taken from the poisoned livestock, droves of panic-stricken farmers, fearing financial ruin, threaten to leave Domingo. Hal calls in Commissioner Moore (Milburn Stone) of the Agriculture Department to investigate the area for poison weeds but his efforts fail to turn up anything conclusive.

Becoming evermore suspicious of Zenobia and Mario, Jean observes the blind woman alone in the dining room and catches sight of her feeding a spider an ensnared moth. Realizing Jean knows the truth about her feigned

***The Spider Woman Strikes Back:* See the poster but skip the film.**

blindness, Zenobia plans to add the young woman's name to her list of victims.

Introducing Jean to her lethal specimens, Zenobia brags of her scheme to rid the land once belonging to the Dollard family of farmers. "The poison from Drochenema's beautiful flowers leaves no trace. Feed it, Jean, let it drink," she says, handing Jean a vial of blood. "With your own strength you've made it strong. You're going to die, Jean, like the others. But it won't be really dying, because you'll live on in this beautiful plant."

Discovering Hal and Commissioner Moore are onto her, Zenobia orders Mario to destroy all of the evidence. Within moments, the lab is transformed into a raging inferno. Mario tries to save Zenobia, who has become entangled in the plants' tendrils; both perish in the flames. Hal is able to get Jean out of the Dollard house seconds before it is levelled by explosions.

An examination of Eric Taylor's screenplay reveals additional scenes that don't appear in the final cut of *The Spider Woman Strikes Back*. That these episodes were actually filmed and not just discarded from the script prior to the start of production is evidenced by the listing of five players in the main title that don't turn up in the picture itself.

Tossing out these episodes was a good idea; most of them are thuddingly repetitive and would have slowed down the pace of an already well-padded movie. Several of these scenes feature townspeople extolling Zenobia's virtues

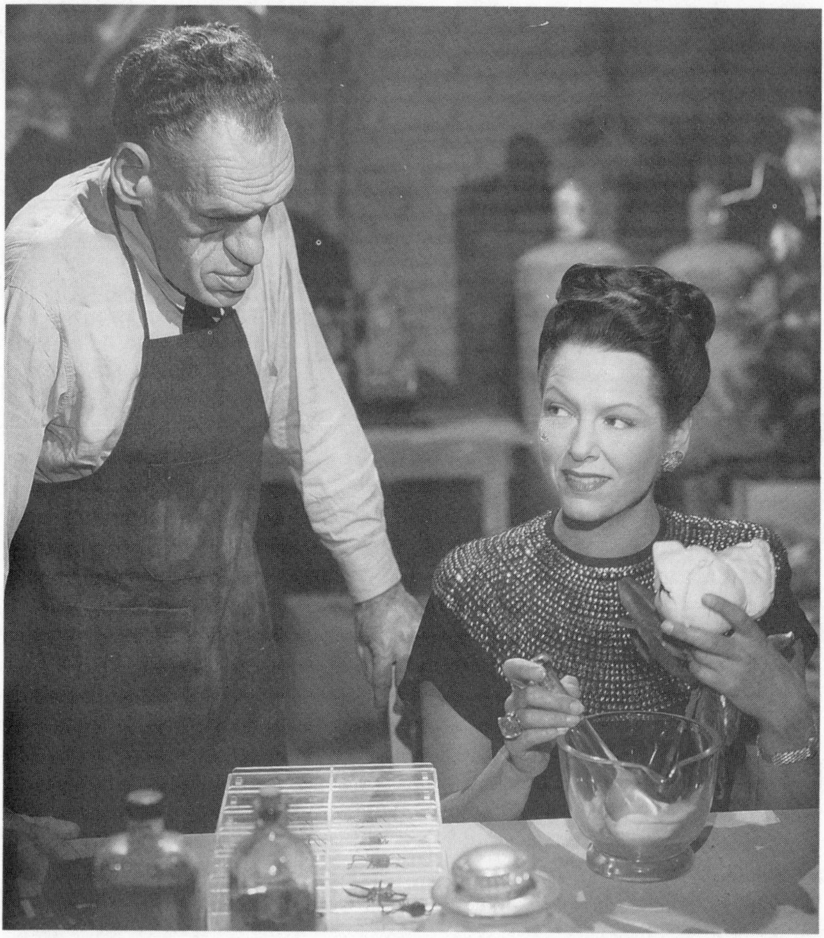

Up to little good, Gale Sondergaard flashes that familiar, sinister smile as Rondo Hatton looks on, in, lamentably, *The Spider Woman Strikes Back*.

while others concern Hal's efforts to quell Jean's suspicions toward her new employer. When a little boy dies after drinking the poisoned milk, the saintly Zenobia sends the family a check for $100 to cover funeral expenses! Jean complains to Hal about suspicious tapping sounds coming from inside her closet; he dismisses them as probably the result of a faulty ventilator. One little episode that's missing from the final cut would have *improved* the story's continuity. After Jean learns Zenobia is feigning blindness, she rushes up to her room and starts to pack. Suddenly the whole door frame of her closet moves slowly inward. Zenobia appears from out of the shadows; Jean screams and faints. When she awakens, Jean finds herself in the laboratory, held prisoner by the Spider Woman and Mario. Curiously, the film's cheery coda *does not* appear in the script (which concludes with Hal and Jean rushing away from the exploding building).

The Spider Woman Strikes Back had long been a thorn in Gale Sondergaard's side. She eventually resigned herself to the film's notoriety and her intimate association with the role with a keen sense of humor:

> They thought they would do a series starring me as the Spider Woman and it had nothing to do with the other one. Well, I almost had hysterics at one time out of just hating it so, I remember. It came out, and people still talk about it, think it's great. And I'm all right.... I've seen it, and it isn't anything to be ashamed of, but I didn't like it when I did it.

Arthur Lubin shared his thoughts about *The Spider Woman Strikes Back* recently. "That was a horrible picture. It was always a joy to have Gale Sondergaard. She was a charming, charming woman." The director added that Sondergaard had been a guest at his home in the Hollywood Hills shortly before she died in August, 1985.

A "guilty pleasure" for some, an unmitigated bore for others, *The Spider Woman Strikes Back* was further proof that Universal's pre-eminence in the business of making slick, entertaining shockers was over. The whole film has a depressing claustrophoic aura about it. The gloomy old house setting is milked dry of all its potential. There are endless shots of Brenda Joyce flitting through darkened hallways as a sullen Rondo Hatton lurches closely behind. Instead of creating suspense, these bits of business irritate us by their repetitiveness and lack of imagination.

There is only the slightest similarity between the character Sondergaard portrays in *The Spider Woman Strikes Back* and Adrea Spedding. Zenobia Dollard's kinky preoccupation with spiders is a gratuitous touch, included only to give the title some validity. On a figurative level, however, this association works: like a spider, she spins a web of deceit and destruction; she even uses poison to overcome her victims. Gale keeps a pretty tight rein on her performance and only occasionally succumbs to some good old-fashioned camping. The mere sight of the exquisitely wicked Sondergaard dropping spider snacks into the gaping blossoms of the vampire plants, her face beaming with perverted joy, is enough to warm the cockles of a horror fan's heart.

Rondo Hatton's appearance in *The Spider Woman Strikes Back* amounts to little more than window dressing. Portraying a deafmute was a change of pace for the actor (he uses "signing" to communicate with Sondergaard). But aside from poisoning cattle and making Brenda Joyce feel so insecure she's forced to undress in a closet, Hatton has little to do. (In trying to recall the actor, Lubin mistakenly referred to Hatton as a "dwarf" rather than a victim of acromegaly.)

Any proposal to extend their new Spider Woman series beyond *The Spider Woman Strikes Back* never materialized. By discarding their first conception of the character and featuring her replacement in a dull, uninspired formula thriller, Universal sabotaged what might have been an intriguing new series.

House of Horrors (1946)

Released March 29, 1946. 66 minutes. *Produced by* Ben Pivar. *Directed by* Jean Yarbrough. *Screenplay by* George Bricker. *Original Story by* Dwight V. Babcock. *Director of Photography:* Maury Gertsman. *Camera Operator:* John Martin. *Art Directors:* John B. Goodman & Abraham Grossman. *Musical Director:* Hans J. Salter. *Set Decorators:* Russell A. Gausman & Ralph Warrington. *Film Editor:* Philip Cahn. *Assistant Director:* Ralph Slosser. *Property Master:* Robert Murdock. *Sound Director:* Bernard B. Brown. *Technician:* Robert Pritchard. *Makeup by* Jack P. Pierce. *Gaffer:* John Brooks. *Gowns by* Vera West.

Robert Lowery (Steven Morrow), Virginia Grey (Joan Medford), Bill Goodwin (Police Lieutenant Larry Brooks), Martin Kosleck (Marcel DeLange), Alan Napier (F. Holmes Harmon), Howard Freeman (Hal Ormiston), Joan Fulton [Shawlee] (Stella McNally), Virginia Christine (Daisy Sutter), Byron Foulger (Mr. Samuels), Tom Quinn (Taxi Cab Driver), Jack Parker (Elevator Boy), Billy Newell (Tomlinson), Oliver Blake (Janitor), William Ruhl (Ellis), Syd Saylor (Jerry), Clifton Young, Kernan Cripps (Detectives), Terry Mason (Clarence), Stephen Wayne (Speed), Danny Jackson (Office Boy), Mary Field (Nora), Charles Wagenheim (Walter), Janet Shaw (Girl Cab Driver), Perc Launders (Smith), Ed Cushing (Rondo Hatton's Stand-in). And introducing Rondo Hatton *as the Creeper.*

> "Out of the murk of the river . . . Out of the clammy mist . . . Rises a *new* fiend of horror . . . The Creeper!" —Preview trailer for *House of Horrors*

On November 8, 1944, *The Hollywood Reporter* noted that producer Ben Pivar was in the midst of developing an entire new series of horror characters. The enterprising producer had recently been relieved of all lower budget pictures on his shooting schedule so that he could concentrate his efforts on higher bracket product. One of Pivar's planned coups was to star Rondo Hatton as that lumbering brute the Creeper in a round of top-budget movies, beginning with *House of Horrors.*

Either this bit of wishful thinking was cooked up by the boys in the publicity department or Pivar had a parting of the ways with the head honchos, for when *House of Horrors* went into production in September, 1945 (under the shooting title *Murder Mansion*), nearly a year after its initial announcement, it was given the same B budget as Pivar's other productions since he joined the organization in the late '30s. Up to the day he left Universal, Pivar never surpassed his rank as a purveyor of B picture entertainment.

Although Universal insisted via the film's main title and publicity materials it was "introducing" the Creeper to theater audiences, the fact remains that the brooding, acromegalic actor had already played the part (then called the Hoxton Creeper) in *The Pearl of Death.* In *House of Horrors,* the Creeper's monicker might have been shortened, his country of origin changed from the British Isles to America, even some of his behavioral traits modified, but he's still the same lovable Creeper, snapping victims' spines like matchsticks at the slightest provocation.

The Breen Office had more reason than ever to exercise its powers when George Bricker's shooting script crossed its desk in August, 1945. After all, *Murder Mansion* was a tale about a crazed spine-snapper who preyed on lovely young women (and cynical critics) in an avant-garde setting. No objectionable artwork would be tolerated. Excessive gruesomeness including lurid screams and "gurgling" sounds wouldn't pass muster, nor was the Creeper allowed to leer at women with sexual desire. And, for heaven's sake, that "flashily dressed blonde" strolling around the waterfront at midnight must in no way suggest a prostitute!

Kent Taylor was originally selected to play the part of police lieutenant Brooks but on the fifth day of production, before Taylor had appeared in a single frame, he was replaced by Bill Goodwin. In a curious postscript to this, Taylor in later years told interviewers that he did indeed play the role but then, dissatisfied with the picture and the way it exploited Rondo Hatton, demanded that he be taken out of the film. The original Assistant Director's Daily Reports put the lie to Taylor's cocamamie story, and Virginia Grey reconfirms this, telling us that Goodwin was the only one to play the part. In another, more mundane casting switch, Billy Newell took over the role of Detective Tomlinson from Milburn Stone.

Rondo Hatton's eerie nocturnal prowlings were shot on such familiar backlot sets as the New York Street and Waterfront Street. Fully recovered from her torturous ordeal as the mud-packed Ananka in *The Mummy's Curse,* Virginia Christine made a brief but unforgettable appearance as the shapely blond prostitute who got her back wrenched by the touchy killer. Virginia's scene was shot on gloomy Tenement Street over a two-day stretch (Saturday, September 15–Monday, September 17). She vaguely recalls her participation in the picture: "I needed the money [*laughter*]—all actors need money! It was a very short scene. They had a cat following me down the street. And in order to get the cat to follow me they put some anchovies or sardines on the back of my heel [*more laughter*]! And that's all I remember about that film—absolutely all." (Note: the nosey cat didn't survive the final cut.)

After a day of shooting odds and ends on a number of sets, director Jean Yarbrough closed down production on September 25, 1945, one day over schedule.

Rondo Hatton may have garnered audience attention as the picture's main "attraction," but *House of Horrors* is unquestionably stolen by Martin Kosleck as Marcel DeLange, a classically impoverished Greenwich Village artist whose surrealist sculptures have made him (according to one hostile critic) "the

Running low on imagination, Universal stooped to exploiting a medical misfortune, in *House of Horrors.*

laughing stock of New York's art circles." Marcel is about to drown his sorrows in the waters of the murky Hudson when he spots a limp figure crawling his way out of the drink. Studying the exhausted man's misshapened features, the artist gets an inspiration. "The perfect Neanderthal Man!" he rejoices. Before long, the ecstatic Marcel is elbows-deep in clay, creating another "deathless masterpiece." He doesn't turn a hair when he discovers his saturnine model is none other than the Creeper (Rondo Hatton), a homicidal brute whom the police believe had drowned while escaping their dragnet.

Late that night, the Creeper steals out of Marcel's studio and, for no apparent reason, murders a hooker (Virginia Christine). Police Lieutenant Larry Brooks (Bill Goodwin) recognizes the Creeper's brutal methods and comes to the conclusion the killer is still at large.

Underrated and unappreciated (at least in his own eyes), Marcel prays for the day when he can strike a blow against the critical establishment whom he believes is responsible for his lowly circumstances. Now with the Creeper in his corner, Marcel's day of vindication is at last at hand. "Soon, the whole world will recognize my genius," he muses modestly.

Soon, the city's most respected art critics are found dead behind their typewriters. (In the case of Howard Freeman's Hal Ormiston, the police find the plump columnist sprawled across his kitchen floor dressed in one of the most garish robes ever to be drafted from a studio wardrobe department.) Only Joan Medford is spared. Sporting Hedda Hopper-style hats, Virginia Grey plays the part in a style more befitting a society reporter on a big city daily. The savvy art critic lifts a rough sketch of the Creeper from Marcel's work table and takes it to her newspaper for further investigation.

Finding the sketch gone and realizing what Joan has been up to, Marcel sends the Creeper to the studio of her fiancé, hot-headed commercial artist Steven Morrow (Robert Lowery). Instead of Joan, the Creeper finds Morrow's luscious blond model, Stella (Joan Fulton). A victim of being in the wrong place at the wrong time, the poor girl meets the fate intended for Joan. (Contract player Joan Fulton eventually changed her last name to Shawlee and was pretty active in pictures of the '50s and '60s. The late actress is probably best remembered as the leader of the all-girl band which included Marilyn Monroe in 1959's *Some Like It Hot*.)

Returning to Marcel's studio, the Creeper watches from hiding as his friend and the snoopy Joan engage in a heated conversation. Marcel accuses her of betraying him. "My devoted friend is my symbol of strength, of power. Through him I shall destroy all my enemies ... including you," he brags. "Marcel, you're mad! Things like this just don't happen!" Joan exclaims. (Obviously, she hasn't seen enough B horror pics.) Joan shakes the artist's security by reminding him his signature on the Creeper's sketch puts his neck squarely in the noose. Marcel shrugs it off: he plans on telling the police he had no knowledge of his model's identity. (The chances of the police believing the Creeper knocked off Marcel's antagonists without the artist planting the idea in his head first is pretty slim.)

Understandably irked by Marcel's disloyalty, the Creeper strangles him to death and destroys the finished bust. Stalking Joan like a hungry cat, the Creeper is seconds away from adding her to his list of victims when a shot fired through the window by Lieutenant Brooks puts the maniacal killer in the hospital.

Rondo Hatton's one-gimmick screen persona had already been milked dry by the time *House of Horrors* rolled around, but that didn't stop Universal from finding further avenues to exploit at the unfortunate actor's expense. Whether or not Hatton resented this crass commercialism by a money-hungry Hollywood studio is debatable, though it might perhaps be fairer to say that Hatton exploited his own ugliness in Universal pictures. After all, no one forced him to accept work in films. After many years of movie bit parts he may even have been pleased to suddenly find himself a star of Universal attractions. Whatever his innermost feelings were, he never exposed them to his costars and always behaved like a true professional.

Whatever Hatton's traits were as a person doesn't discount the fact he was a terrible actor, incapable of mouthing even the most mundane dialogue. Photographer Maury Gertsman's use of silhouettes and low angles in capturing Hatton's grotesqueries heighten the chill factor of *House of Horrors* but even his efforts are jettisoned whenever Rondo deadpans abysmal dialogue like, "You're my friend, shake," or, "You're going to tell the police about me, huh?"

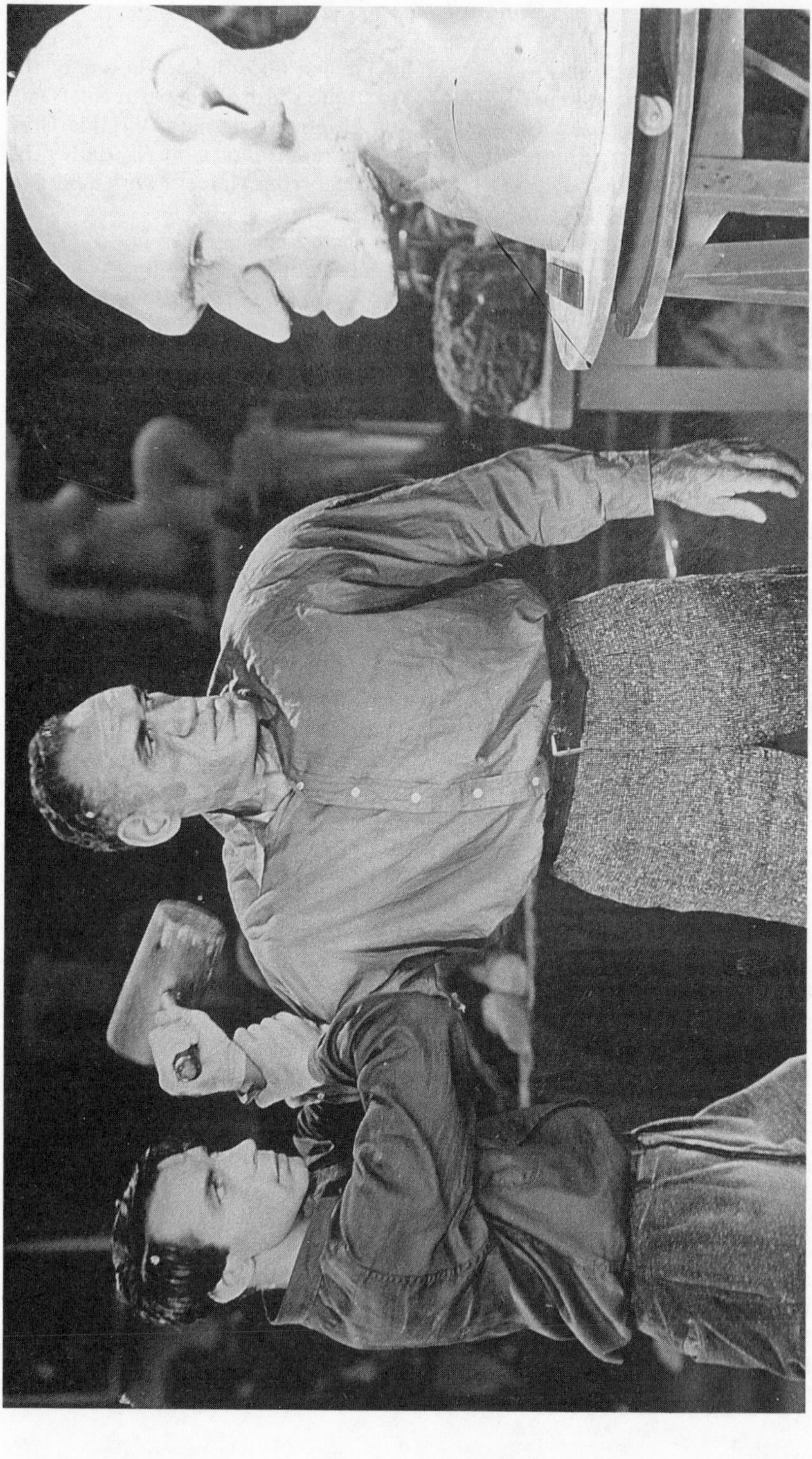

Virtually every character in the picture is a cliche: the flippant girl reporter (pardon, art critic), the wiseguy Irish detective, the dumb blond model, the rugged, All-American boyfriend whose career as a commercial artist is limited to painting calendar girls, and the starving surrealist who lives from one sale to the next. Even broader are the churlish art critics played by Alan Napier and Howard Freeman. Their critiques are little more than character assassinations that are more befitting a scandal sheet than an art column. And *no one* on the Universal payroll wrote clinker lines like George Bricker could. "I have often wondered why a man would want to snap a woman's spine is a classic example of Bricker at his inept best."

Despite all these misgivings, *House of Horrors* rates as the best shocker in this round of Universal releases. It boasts creepy, atmospheric *film-noir*ish settings, evocative camerawork and is seldom dull. For a studio hack director with only one genre credit, the 1941 Lugosi PRC laugh-fest *The Devil Bat,* Jean Yarbrough conveys a properly unhealthy mood in the scenes set in Marcel's candlelit studio, its inventory overcrowded with all sorts of aberrations in clay.

The suspenseful climax of *House of Horrors* ends with the Creeper's being wounded by a policeman's bullet. By not polishing off the murderer, Universal left the door wide open for a sequel. But instead of picking up the story where it left off, the studio decided to fill in the details of the killer's life and career by proffering a *prequel* to *House of Horrors,* the lamentable *The Brute Man.* Though its justification for the Creeper's existence and motivation to kill is inept (the Creeper was a love-scorned college student who, through his own impetuosity, caused a lab explosion that triggered the disfigurement of his face and affected his reason), *The Brute Man* does shed light on what makes this nasty killer tick.

But these belated revelations don't help first-time viewers of *House of Horrors* understand where the Creeper is coming from. Aside from some sketchy details provided by the police (he murdered at least one woman before the cops traced him to the river's edge), we know nothing about him and presume he is just some loathsome denizen of New York's violent night world. Bricker doesn't give us a clue as to his reason for committing these sordid crimes (other than an apparent lust to kill). The murder of the prostitute (which has all the earmarks of a Jack the Ripper–type killing) raises even more questions. Since there was no passion or profit motive, we can only guess that the Creeper murders innocent women because they are repulsed by him. (When Marcel brings up the death of the neighborhood hooker to his morose house guest, the Creeper's only response is, "She screamed.")

The Creeper's alliance with Marcel is a marriage of brains and brawn. Once the pair hook up, Marcel blueprints his long-dreamed-of critic bash. The Creeper is only too happy to oblige. This partnership is well illustrated in a fine moment wherein Marcel, after having read aloud a scathing critique by art critic Holmes Harmon (Alan Napier), boasts how he would love to tear Harmon

Everyone's a critic! Martin Kosleck tries to prevent Rondo Hatton from creaming his "deathless masterpiece," in *House of Horrors.*

apart. The camera pans from Marcel's violently gesticulating hands to those of the Creeper's idly kneading a mound of clay. Without uttering a word, the strangler rises from the table and stalks off into the night.

Martin Kosleck walks away with the acting honors in the film's most challenging role (and unjustly received the lowest salary of all the principals—$1,334). The slightest bit of overacting would have destroyed the credibility of the part and robbed the character of sympathy but Kosleck is right on the money from first scene to last. He is proud of his performance. ("I get more fan mail on that . . . I loved that part.") The actor was working on the Universal lot one day when he was approached by a producer (Ben Pivar most likely; Kosleck doesn't remember) and asked if he'd like to audition for a part in the man's forthcoming production. "He gave me a script to study during the lunch hour for an audition. I gave a completely memorized audition and got the part immediately."

The scene which Martin was required to read was the poignant little monologue Marcel speaks to his cat. A lifelong animal lover, Kosleck still remembers how well the scrawny little alley cat behaved in front of the camera, particularly in the scene where the animal was required to nestle close to his dead master's body.

Playing a succession of Nazi madmen and leering psychotics didn't sour Martin Kosleck's outlook on Hollywood film acting. He loved to work and considered every role a challenge. The sensitive, cultured actor spent his childhood in the idyllic forests of Pomerania in Germany. His father hailed from a proud family of Russian aristocrats whose heritage dated back to the 19th century. Though he developed a passionate interest in art, Martin's burning desire was to become an actor.

Kosleck's artistic talents paved the way for his settlement in California in 1932. His canvases won him the acclaim of the West Coast critical establishment and the Hollywood community as well (one of his early champions was Albert Einstein!). Plum roles in productions staged by the Pasadena Playhouse led to a screen test at Warners for the second lead in *Confessions of a Nazi Spy* in 1939. Francis Lederer got the part but Kosleck was awarded a featured role: Nazi propagandist Joseph Goebbels. The die was cast. For the next five decades, Martin Kosleck's name beame synonomous with the beasts spawned by the Third Reich.

Kosleck alternated his appearances in propaganda pictures with featured parts in B horror films and mystery thrillers, earning him a reputation as one of Tinsel Town's most reliable baddies. Paramount's stylish 1941 melodrama *The Mad Doctor,* a modern-day Bluebeard tale, offered Martin an exceptionally strong role as homicidal psychiatrist Basil Rathbone's parttime lover, fulltime back-stabber. Playing the part of a fascist in Universal's 13-chapter serial *The Great Alaskan Mystery* (1944) won Kosleck entry into the portals of Hollywood's nightmare factory. His performances for the studio cemented his celebrity as one of horrordom's beloved bogeymen.

Frequent television appearances, successful engagements on New York City stages, and a sprinkling of movie credits (most notoriously, the 1964 sf cheapie *The Flesh Eaters*) kept Kosleck busy (and happy) through the late

'70s. Poor health forced him into retirement long before he was ready to settle down. Though he rarely goes out in public anymore, Martin Kosleck has hardly been forgotten: he receives fan mail and requests for autographs regularly, not only from members of his own generation but from youngsters who've discovered him via television reruns.

Night in Paradise (1946)

Released May 3, 1946. 84 minutes. *Filmed in* Technicolor. *Directed by* Arthur Lubin. *Produced by* Walter Wanger. *Associate Producer:* Alexander Golitzen. *Screenplay by* Ernest Pascal. *Based on the novel* ***Peacock's Feather*** *by* George S. Hellman. *Adaptation:* Emmet Lavery. *Directors of Photography:* Hal Mohr & W. Howard Greene. *Technicolor Director:* Natalie Kalmus. *Associate:* William Fritzsche. *Special Photography:* John P. Fulton. *Art Directors:* John B. Goodman & Alexander Golitzen. *Film Editor:* Milton Carruth. *Musical Score & Director:* Frank Skinner. *Song "Night in Paradise" by* Jack Brooks & Frank Skinner. *Set Decorators:* Russell A. Gausman & Edward R. Robinson. *Assistant Director:* Fred Frank. *Dialogue Director:* Joan Hathaway. *Sound Director:* Bernard B. Brown. *Technician:* William Hedgcock. *Makeup by* Jack P. Pierce. *Costumes by* Travis Banton.

Merle Oberon (Delarai), Turhan Bey (Aesop [Jason]), Thomas Gomez (King Croesus), Gale Sondergaard (Queen Attossa), Ray Collins (Leonides), George Dolenz (Frigia Ambassador), John Litel (Archon), Ernest Truex, Jerome Cowan, Marvin Miller (Scribes), Douglass Dumbrille, Moroni Olsen, Francis McDonald (High Priests), Paul Cavanagh (Cleomenes), Richard Bailey (Lieutenant), Wee Willie Davis (Salabaar), Roseanne Murray (Marigold), Hans Herbert (Priest), Julie London, Barbara Bates, Daun Kennedy, Ruth Valmy, Karen X. Gaylord, Kathleen O'Malley, Karen Randle, Kerry Vaughn, Audrey Long (Palace Maidens), Eula Morgan, Art Miles, Al Chosis, Myrtle Ferguson, Frank Hagney (Townspeople), James Hutton (Delarai's Messenger), Juli Lynne (Song Specialty), Jean Trent (Iris), Jane Adams (Lotus), John Merton (Sailor), Don Stowell (Sentinel), Pedro de Cordoba (Magus), Harry Cording (Captain), Ann Everett, Dorothy Tuomi, Marguerite Campbell, June Frazer (Flower Girls), Colin Campbell (Goatman), Nikki Kerkes, Mercedes Mockaitis (Special Water Girls), Harland Miller (Slave), Denny Burke (Contortionist), Neal Young (Nobleman), Joe Bernard (Old Man), John Berkes, Al Ferguson, Peter [Pietro] Sosso (Beggars), Dick Alexander, Earle Ozman (Temple Guards), Rex Evans (Chef), Jack Overman (Man), Wade Crosby (Rough Man), Charles Bates, Clyde Flynn, Joel Goodkind, Jimmy Fresco, Mickey Fresco, Juan Estrada, Robert Espinosa, Louis Montoya (Boys), Kit Guard (Man in Crowd), Maxine Hoppe (Handmaiden).

This fanciful tale about the semilegendary Greek writer Aesop warrants inclusion in this book only for the fleeting appearance of Gale Sondergaard as a sorceress. Otherwise, it's a lightweight costumer that enabled Universal to strut its highbrow pretensions by luring a top Hollywood star (Merle Oberon) through its gates. *Night in Paradise* was the brainchild of Walter Wanger, the hotshot producer who had previously made films in collaboration with some of Hollywood's top directors (Ford, Hitchcock, Capra, et al.), but having fallen on hard times, settled down at Universal in 1942. *Night in Paradise* was Wanger's second attempt at bringing a Technicolor version of the George S. Hellman novel *Peacock's Feather* to the screen; the first (featuring RKO star Ann Harding) was scrapped in the mid-30s. He revived the project just as his stock at Universal was sliding—Wanger's high-budget *Salome, Where She Danced* (1945) drew disastrous notices. The cameras finally rolled on *Night in Paradise* a full decade after its inception, but the finished film languished in post-production at the studio for nearly a year. It was not released until spring, 1946.

The storyline is an obvious fabrication, occasionally cribbing a detail or two from the legend of Aesop, alleged author of scores of time-honored fables, whose very existence has been the source of speculation through the ages. (It became the fashion to credit Aesop with all manner of traditional stories and bits of folk wisdom, many of which must actually have come down from prehistoric times.)

The action is set in Lydia, circa 560 B.C. The all-powerful King Croesus (Thomas Gomez) incurs the wrath of Queen Attossa (Gale Sondergaard) when he selects Princess Delarai (Merle Oberon) of Persia as his bride. Jilted in love and bilked of a fortune in gold by the greedy Croesus, the Frigian queen appeals to the gods to double her powers of sorcery so that she may avenge this personal affront. Attossa spirits herself in disembodied form to the king's magnificent palace and taunts him mercilessly. Driven near mad, Croesus is advised by Aesop (Turhan Bey) to use reason to battle the queen's sorcery. Aesop, the former slave turned famed storyteller, has just arrived from the Isle of Samos in a shaggy, simian-looking disguise to plead the case of his freedom-loving countrymen.

Aesop develops a fascination for Delarai, who reveals herself to be a beautiful but vain and heartless creature. Enraged by the wise man's perceptive ability to bare her soul, she brands him an "insolent ape" and scoffs at his prediction that she will one day beg for his love. Leonides (Ray Collins), Croesus' schemy chamberlain, and the mocking Attossa prey on the king's jealousies to discredit Aesop.

Aesop foils a trap set by Delarai and Leonides by arriving at the bride-to-be's sleeping chamber sans disguise. Calling himself Jason, a "dear friend" of Aesop, the strapping young man sweeps Delarai off her feet. But a scar reveals Jason's true identity. "People don't accept wisdom without age," Aesop laments, and tells the Princess that his sole purpose was to humble her pride and reject her, not to fall in love with her. When Leonides and his men break into the chamber as planned, Aesop is nowhere to be found. Croesus accuses his chamberlain of betraying him and orders his execution, but withdraws the order in the nick of time.

Determined to ruin Aesop, Leonides and the High Priest (Douglass Dumbrille) convince the king that the gods want war between Lydia and Samos. Forsaking his disguise, Aesop assumes the role of Lydian ambassador and consults the oracle in the Greek temple of Delphi. He finds the high priests to be a corrupt lot whose Apollian "revelations" can be swayed with the right amounts of gold. Delarai, who has sneaked off to the ancient city to find Aesop, is discovered hiding in the temple by the high priests, who condemn the lovers to death on the cliffs overlooking the rocky shoreline. With no hope of rescue possible, the writers fall back on a trite *deus ex machina* resolution by having the couple miraculously whisked away by the benevolent Attossa right under the noses of their executioners.

A Maria Montez vehicle without Maria Montez, *Night in Paradise* is among the last of Universal's tongue-in-cheek extravaganzas of the 1940s. Overripe and meretricious, it is every bit as vulgar as any in the studio's stable of exotic big budgeters in the *Arabian Nights* school. These outings were spirited, good-natured hokum at best, but *Night in Paradise* adds a pompous, pseudoliterary veneer to the shopworn formula. The result is unsurprisingly disappointing—a talking heads epic with little verve and even less wit. Serving up a gossamer plot woven around a production of elephantine gaudiness, *Night in Paradise* is resounding proof that if there is anything worse than kitsch, it's boring kitsch.

Art director Alexander Golitzen's credit as associate producer is a tip-off to the film's visual style. *Night in Paradise* has all the earmarks of a set designer's movie. The film unreels amid the plaster mock-ups of Grecian temples and painted powderblue backdrops. Obvious, stage-bound sets are consistent with the production's artificial texture; reality rears itself suddenly via the exterior footage seen late in the film. *Night in Paradise* straddles the fence between ham-fisted burlesque and standard Hollywood costumer conventions. Writer Ernest Pascal, whose talents were well-suited for the grimly allegorical *Flesh and Fantasy,* contributes a murky, convoluted script that defies comprehension: a veritable Rubik's cube of obscure motivations, muddled characterizations and dreary palace intrigues. To make all this seem palatable, the film is steeped in jarring, modern-day dialogue, includes street-smart actors like Jerome Cowan (playing a scribe!) in its cast, and shamelessly offers a torchy, '40s-style number for good measure. Even less appealing is the tasteless, prepubescent sexual tone that passes for humor. Except for Oberon and Sondergaard, the female cast members are restricted to a procession of smiling, curvaceous handmaidens; their male counterparts are hardly more dignified, drooling and gawking at all this mammary splendor on cue.

At center stage, of course, is Turhan Bey's Aesop, who is more than a little reminiscent of Jean Marais in *Beauty and the Beast* (1946). After years of being groomed as an exotic romantic lead, he spends the better part of his screen time under the shaggy mange of Jack Pierce's unflattering makeup. Bey's brief emergence as his youthful, ever-unctuous self is anticlimactic. Spouting pearls of wisdom at every turn, Bey, Hollywood's bargain basement version of Charles Boyer, comes off looking ridiculous.

Merle Oberon's performance has all the smirky condescension of a A-player slumming in a B production (Some sources claim that Louise Allbritton was originally slated for the role.) The elegant Miss Oberon fails to bring much sympathy to a scheming, self-centered character but at least cameraman

Paul Ivano does her beauty full justice in several rapturous close-ups. Thomas Gomez gets into the spirit of the thing, playing to the rafters like a would-be Charles Laughton. Character actor Ray Collins' contribution as the corrupt chamberlain isn't far removed from his standard crooked politician roles, except that he's never performed as broadly as he does here.

Gale Sondergaard is very much in her element as the sorceress Attossa. The actress, who was once up for the Wicked Witch role eventually played by Margaret Hamilton in *The Wizard of Oz* (1939), may have regarded this assignment as an inglorious consolation prize. Her first scene, set in a windswept mountaintop lair, has the vengeful queen gleefully exhibiting her occult skills, briefly adding some badly needed mayhem to the poky plot. But Sondergaard's appearance unfortunately amounts to little more than a cameo, though her few scenes are imaginatively handled. Materializing enigmatically in a flame, or in the mirror-like surface of a wall ornament, she goads Gomez into fulfilling her own mischievous ends. John P. Fulton displays his resourcefulness on several occasions, most notably in a dazzling bit whereby Sondergaard, appearing as a reflection in a pond (à la *The Thief of Bagdad* [1940]), hands Bey a vial of poison. But such momentary diversions don't go far in relieving the tedium in this tinseled turkey of a movie.

Night in Paradise did little to bolster the career of its director, Arthur Lubin, who recently offered these vague recollections of the production.

> *Night in Paradise* was a fairy tale based on one of Aesop's fables. It was a silly story, it didn't make sense, but it was a very lavish production for Universal to make in those days. That production cost, I think, under a million dollars. Today, it would cost about five or ten million. It was a little longer than the average production for Universal, about ten weeks. I was under contract to Universal and, in those days, when a director finished a picture they assigned him immediately to something that was ready to go so they didn't lose his salary by having him sit around. Walter Wanger was the producer. I had made a previous picture for him [*Eagle Squadron,* 1942), and he liked me. It was a big picture, and I brought it in on time. And the studio said, "Well, Lubin's available. Let's put him into *Night in Paradise.*"

Night in Paradise became a bitter pill for Lubin to swallow as the film's release hastened his departure from Universal. Playing no small part in the termination of Lubin's contract was Turhan Bey, who, ironically, was given his first big break by the veteran director a few years before. Lubin recalls,

> Turhan Bey and I did not get along too well together. His rise to fame was too quick for him to handle, and he got very, very difficult. He was impossible! He didn't have me fired, but the studio didn't pick up my contract. He complained that I was giving Miss Oberon too many close-ups, and not enough to him. He was just an unknown boy when he came to Universal studios. He was sent out from my lawyers in New York to me. I was the first one to make a screen test of him. The studio signed him and his rise was fabulous, but it went to his head.

It's a sad postscript to a depressingly inept picture.

She-Wolf of London (1946)

Released May 17, 1946. 61 minutes. *Directed by* Jean Yarbrough. *Produced by* Ben Pivar. *Screenplay by* George Bricker. *Original Story by* Dwight V. Babcock. *Director of Photography:* Maury Gertsman. *Camera Operator:* John Martin. *Film Editor:* Paul Landres. *Art Directors:* Jack Otterson & Abraham Grossman. *Musical Director:* William Lava. *Set Decorators:* Russell A. Gausman & Leigh Smith. *Dialogue Director:* Raymond Kessler. *Sound Director:* Bernard B. Brown. *Technician:* Joe Lapis. *Director of Makeup:* Jack P. Pierce. *Gowns by* Vera West.

June Lockhart (Phyllis Allenby), Don Porter (Barry Lanfield), Sara Haden (Martha Winthrop), Jan Wiley (Carol Winthrop), Dennis Hoey (Inspector Pierce), Martin Kosleck (Dwight Severn), Eily Malyon (Hannah), Lloyd Corrigan (Latham), Frederic Worlock (Constable Ernie Hobbs), David Thursby, Olaf Hytten, James Finlayson, Warren Jackson (Policemen), Joan Wells* (Phyllis as a Child), William H. O'Brien (Bobby), Jimmy Aubrey (Cabby), Clara Blandick* (Mrs. McBroom). [**Does not appear in the final print.*]

She-Wolf of London is the type of thriller horror fans love to hate. It's one of those deceptive little ditties that tease us for an hour or so with tantalizing horror effects and grim atmospherics, only to come toppling down like a house of cards with the disclosure that it wasn't the forces of the supernatural that were responsible for the mayhem after all, just a greedy guardian attempting to gain control of an estate. We've seen it all before; it's an old trick that doesn't improve with age.

In the case of *She-Wolf of London,* there's absolutely no reason why George Bricker and Dwight V. Babcock couldn't have conceived the tale as a bonafide horror story rather than a predictable whodunit. They had the resources of Hollywood's premier horror factory at their disposal, yet the writers settled on a musty, old-fashioned murder melodrama that merely exploits the plot's supernatural angle. Cribbing a portion of the title from one of Universal's early horror classics only compounded the fraud.

Heralded in the trades more than a year before it went before the cameras, *She-Wolf of London* was hardly an example of the top flight fare Ben Pivar was promised after his promotion at the studio in November, 1944. Signing on *House of Horrors/The Brute Man* director Jean Yarbrough, Pivar obtained the services of June Lockhart, Don Porter, Sara Haden, Jan Wiley, Forrester Harvey and Una O'Connor. O'Connor was dropped from the cast in favor of Eily Malyon; Forrester Harvey passed away suddenly on the evening of

December 14, 1945, before any of his scenes were shot and was replaced by the jovial character actor Lloyd Corrigan.

Phyllis Allenby (June Lockhart) lives in dread of an ancient curse cast on her family by wolves. Residing with her kindly aunt, Martha Winthrop (Sara Haden) and her cousin, Carol (Jan Wiley), Phyllis is ignorant of the fact that neither woman is really her blood relative, and that the palatial home they share actually belongs to her.

When a series of violent attacks occur in a nearby park, Phyllis is convinced she is responsible. Plagued by nightmares, Phyllis awakens each morning to find her shoes muddied, her nightgown torn and her hands streaked with blood. After a young boy is found mangled to death, she becomes hysterical and goes into seclusion, breaking off her engagement to barrister Barry Lanfield (Don Porter). Barry, Martha and Carol can't make Phyllis realize that she's letting her imagination run away with her, all on account of the preposterous curse.

Latham (Lloyd Corrigan), a Scotland Yard investigator, firmly believes the attacks are being committed by a "she-wolf," and does a house-to-house check of Phyllis' neighborhood. Late that night, a veiled figure emerges from the home and

At top, the all-too human murderess of *She-Wolf of London*.

disappears into the fog-enshrouded park. Latham becomes separated from his men and comes face-to-face with the she-wolf. By the time the bobbies find him, he is bleeding to death from wounds received in the struggle.

Launching his own investigation, Barry stations himself outside Phyllis' house. He watches as Carol, a veil covering her head, emerges and disappears into the park. Minutes later, Dwight Severn (Martin Kosleck), Carol's secret sweetheart, is almost clawed to death by a cloaked figure. The next day, Barry confronts Carol with his suspicions that she is the homicidal murderer. Appalled by his accusations, Carol volunteers to accompany Barry to the police in an effort to get to the bottom of this grisly business.

Martha, meanwhile, has prepared a glass of warm milk for the distraught Phyllis. She drinks it and suddenly sinks into a semiconscious state. Beaming malevolently, Martha confesses she doctored the milk (as she had been doing all along) and is going to kill her. Realizing only too well that Phyllis' marriage to Barry will mke the young woman eligible to claim her inheritance, thus costing Martha the home she's managed for years, the scheming woman set out to implicate Phyllis in the attacks that she herself committed. Withdrawing a knife, Martha is about to plunge it into the paralyzed girl's body when Hannah (Eily Malyon), the housekeeper, intervenes. Martha pursues Hannah down a staircase but slips and plummets down the steps. The knife deeply embedded in her own bosom, Martha dies moments before Barry, Carol and the authorities arrive on the scene.

Dusting off the Hacienda set as a stand-in for the Winthrop home and terrace, and flooding an area of the Providencia Ranch with "bee smoke" to simulate a misty London Park, Yarbrough began shooting *She-Wolf of London* on December 8, wrapping up production on the 21st, three days over schedule. But the shooting of several retakes required that June Lockhart, Don Porter, Yarbrough and the technical crew work right through Christmas Eve.

> The scene in the buggy was a process shot. It took *hours;* they never got the process right. They closed the set so people couldn't get away and go to all the Christmas parties on the other sets. We damned near starved to death. We smuggled in some sandwiches and finally they got the process right. I was focused and got the words right. The director said, "Cut! Print! That's a wrap!" and before I could get out of the buggy and help June, the set was cleared . . . everybody left! The "bee smoke" that they used [in the park scenes] made it very difficult to talk. If you had a scene, they'd roll that stuff in at about ankle-height, then it would rise. Trying to do lines and keep from choking was a little difficult.

It doesn't take a detective (much less a moviegoer with half a brain) to pick out the *real* culprit in *She-Wolf of London.* Lest we tax our intelligence, George Bricker has done the work for us. Sara Haden's early revelation that she really isn't Phyllis' aunt, but an old family domestic who has been living comfortably off the girl's money, is a dead giveaway. Add to this her disclosure that she was once Phyllis' father's sweetheart and the case is solved before it's begun. (*New York Times* critic Thomas M. Pryor probably felt he wasn't ruining anyone's good time when he identified the "diabolical old crone" as the she-wolf in his review!)

For once, Martin Kosleck is on the receiving end of harm in *She-Wolf of London*. The woman in the veil is presumably Sara Haden but is more likely a stand-in.

The Allenby Curse is given rather short shrift in the release print of *She-Wolf of London*. (In England, the picture was distributed as *The Curse of the Allenbys*.) Such unanswered queries as to *why* the Allenbys were accursed in the first place might have been explained in an episode cut from the final print. Set in Allenby Hall in the late 19th century, the missing scene(s), featuring seven-year-old Joan Wells as the young Phyllis and Clara Blandick as her nanny Mrs. McBroom, would have undoubtedly shed more light on this less-than-pressing matter.

For a tightly-budgeted B, *She-Wolf of London* is well-mounted. Jean Yarbrough makes the most of his limited resources and manages some real atmosphere in the prowling wolf-woman scenes. William Lava's broody musical score, heavy on portentous strings, and Maury Gertsman's faultless photography and lighting effects contribute to the overall aura of foreboding. (Gertsman isn't above incorporating such stylistically obvious little tricks as tilted camera effects and distorted lenses to alleviate the flat narrative.)

As ever, George Bricker demonstrates his woeful deficiencies as a writer. Lloyd Corrigan's seasoned detective theorizes, on the flimsiest of evidence, that a werewolf is afoot in modern London. In a failed attempt at cheering Phyllis,

Barry rattles off several particularly graphic passages from Shakespeare's "The Merchant of Venice" with the aplomb of a thespian. Clunker lines abound: "The newspapers are full of it!" Carol gasps in regards to the latest she-wolf attack. To the drug-prostrated Phyllis, Martha comfortingly coos, "Perhaps we can arrange to have you taken care of in a private institution until you're cured."

As poor, neurotic Phyllis, June Lockhart is too mousy and whiny to generate any sympathy. The only child of acting couple Gene and Kathleen Lockhart, June had her first taste of show business when she made her Metropolitan Opera debut at the age of eight as a ballerina. Don Porter and Jan Wiley contribute mature, no-nonsense performances but Sara Haden indulges in the kind of broad, wicked witch theatrics that are more apt to draw chuckles than chills. Haden has the same problem as Gale Sondergaard. She can't help but exude malice, even when she's being nice. (The actress is best remembered for her frequent appearances as Aunt Polly in the Mickey Rooney *Andy Hardy* movies.) As Jan Wiley's lover, an impoverished artist, Martin Kosleck is laughably out-of-character. (Not only is he on the outside of the mayhem looking in, Kosleck even walks away with one of the female leads in tow!) He recalls the experience with a chuckle, regarding his part in the film as a "consolation prize" for having played so many heavies.

Curious as it may seem, *She-Wolf of London*'s insipid plotline was echoed in several other minor productions, most notably *Devil Bat's Daughter* (1946), which was reviewed by *Variety* on the same day as *She-Wolf of London!* Former Miss America Rosemary LaPlanche plays the orphaned daughter of a scientist who is reputed to have been a vampire; she's troubled by nightmares, implicated in a murder and (of course) begins to believe that *she's* a vampire. It turns out that the girl's guardian (Michael Hale) has been spiking her nightly tonic with dream-producing drugs and is guilty of perpetrating the crimes. Universal alumnus Griffin Jay penned the tepid screenplay for this PRC turkey. In the 1951 Columbia film *The Son of Dr. Jekyll,* Louis Hayward plays the hardheaded scion determined to vindicate this infamous father. He attempts to duplicate the senior Jekyll's experiments; a string of attacks suddenly disturb the once-peaceful community.

In a fiery climax, it is revealed that Hayward's guardian (Alexander Knox), who has been stealing from the estate, was responsible for the recent deaths as well as for the killings blamed on Hayward's father. In 1957, Jack Pollexfen (who cowrote the story for *The Son of Dr. Jekyll*) wrote and produced *Daughter of Dr. Jekyll,* which is practically a remake of *She-Wolf of London.* Janet Jekyll (played by Gloria Talbott in the same irritatingly despondent style as Lockhart) returns to the ancestral stomping grounds and learns from her guardian (Arthur Shields) that her father was *the* Dr. Jekyll. Distressed by this bit of unwelcome news, she sinks into depression and tries to break her engagement to stolid beau John Agar. Talbott blames herself for a shocking series of nocturnal murders, basing her suspicions on nightmares and blood-splattered nightclothes. As might be expected, Shields is behind the mystery: he has been doping Talbott's nightly glass of milk with dream-inducing drugs and then committing the murders himself (the twist here is that he actually *becomes* a werewolf-like Hyde). As ever, Shields' motive for all this mayhem is the Jekyll estate and fortune.

Sharing a twin bill with another pseudohorror film, *The Cat Creeps, She-Wolf of London* sustained its fair share of raspberries from critics and disappointed horror fans alike. Although it's by no means a good film, at least *Daughter of Dr. Jekyll* does deliver a red-blooded monster, which is more than can be said for either *She-Wolf of London* or its other half-baked derivatives.

The Cat Creeps (1946)

Released May 17, 1946. 58 minutes. *Directed by* Erle C. Kenton. *Associate Producer:* Will Cowan. *Executive Producer:* Howard Welsch. *Screenplay by* Edward Dein, Jerry Warner & (uncredited) Gertrude Walker. *Original Story:* Gerald Geraghty. *Directors of Photography:* George Robinson & (uncredited) Elwood Bredell. *Camera Operator:* Edward Coleman. *Film Editor:* Russell Schoengarth. *Art Directors:* Jack Otterson & Abraham Grossman. *Musical Director:* Paul Sawtell. *Assistant Directors:* Melville Shyer & Fritz Collings. *Set Decorators:* Russell A. Gausman & T.F. Offenbecker. *Sound Director:* Bernard B. Brown. *Technician:* William Hedgcock. *Gowns by* Vera West.

Noah Beery, Jr. (Pidge "Flash" Laurie), Lois Collier (Gay Elliot), Paul Kelly (Ken Grady), Fred Brady (Terry Nichols), Douglass Dumbrille (Tom McGalvey), Rose Hobart (Connie Palmer), Jonathan Hale (Walter Elliot), Iris Clive [Eden] (Kyra Goran), Vera Lewis (Cora Williams), William B. Davidson (James Walsh), Arthur Loft (Sampler), Jerry Jerome (Polich).

By the mid-40s the popularity of horror films was apparently waning, and nearly all of Universal's one-time competitors had begun dropping out of the race. Universal kept plugging away, maybe just out of simple force of habit, but by 1946, nearly everything that had once been *right* about the company's horror films was now depressingly, demoralizingly *wrong*. The great stars like Karloff and Lugosi were long gone, and even the second-team players like Chaney, Atwill, Zucco and Carradine were also already names out of the studio's past. The very best a 1946 audience could expect from a Universal chiller was a Gale Sondergaard or a Martin Kosleck; even Poverty Row horror films usually boasted better name stars than these. The classic Universal monsters were also on ice, girding themselves for encounters with Abbott and Costello; Rondo Hatton, a poor soul with a big head, was their one monster character of the year. The studio's horror directors and writers were no long specialists nor even journeymen, just workaday hacks who brought no élan nor even enthusiasm to their projects. The sets were still impressive, but by this point they were just hangouts for B actors mouthing clunker lines. Indeed, how much real difference is there between a cheap, dreary Universal like *The Spider Woman Strikes Back* or *The Cat Creeps* and a Monogram, PRC or Republic horror film from that same period? Horror film fans had truly been seduced and abandoned by the New Universal.

The Cat Creeps is a perfunctory assembly-line horror-whodunit emblematic of the type of below-par programmers Universal was now foisting onto horror film fans. It's a shabby, half-cooked little time-waster that

Universal promoted as a chiller on the shaky basis of its setting (a creepy mansion) and some silly spook-talk about cats. Apart from the title and the *de rigueur* old-dark-house elements, the film bears no relation to the 1930 version of *The Cat Creeps* nor to that film's antecedent, 1927's *The Cat and the Canary.*

Long-shrouded in mystery, the questionable "suicide" of Eric Goran becomes the object of scrutiny once again as the result of a letter written to the daily newspaper *The Morning Chronicle.* The letter writer, elderly crackpot Cora Williams, insists that Goran's death was a case of murder for money—$200,000—and insists that the investigation be reopened. Enclosed with the letter is a $1,000 bill which has been out of circulation since the time of Goran's death. Newshawk Terry Nichols (Fred Brady) balks at tackling the assignment because it appears that Walter Elliot, his girlfriend's father and a Senate hopeful, may be drawn into the scandal. When Nichols' corrupt bosses threaten to turn the assignment over to a notorious muck-raking reporter, Nichols reconsiders.

Nichols calls on Elliot (Jonathan Hale) to warn him that the case is being reopened. Elliot's daughter Gay (Lois Collier) can't understand why her boyfriend has accepted the job of tying her father in with murder, and tells him off. After Nichols leaves, Elliot phones his lawyer Tom McGalvey (Douglass Dumbrille) to make hasty arrangements for a visit to Mrs. Williams at her island home on lonely Key Towers.

Converging at the mainland waterfront for a midnight trip to the island are Elliot, Gay, McGalvey, McGalvey's secretary Connie Palmer (Rose Hobart) and unscrupulous private eye Ken Grady (Paul Kelly). Nichols and his friend Pidge Laurie (Noah Beery, Jr.), a news photographer, turn up at the scene (without explanation) and insist upon accompanying the group to the island. Elliot reluctantly consents.

The seven arrive at Key Towers in a striking long shot: the landing dock, the launch and its passengers in the foreground, the spooky mansion and a bright full moon looming over them in the distant background. It's an eerily atmospheric moment that shows that Universal had not lost their feel for the genre entirely. The group tramps through jungly undergrowth to the mansion and then everyone disperses in different directions. In an upstairs bedroom Mrs. Williams (Vera Lewis) is attacked by an unseen figure who is (of course) one of the seven newcomers to the island. The mystery man (woman?) also sets fire to the launch, making a return to the mainland temporarily impossible.

Mrs. Williams is not dead, but is in bad shape. There's plenty of arguing and finger pointing, Pidge is kicked in the face by the mystery assailant, and a second attempt on Mrs. Williams' life is successful. Kyra (Iris Clive), a strange young woman who claims to be Eric Goran's daughter, appears on the scene, explaining that she has been "beckoned" by the dead Mrs. Williams. This odd new character, who seems to have mystically stepped in out of *Cat People,* also insists that the spirit of Mrs. Williams now possesses her housecat. Connie, a cat hater whose nerves are fairly shot by now to begin with, faints at the implication.

Amidst a lot more spook-talk and hot air, Gay is roughed up by the mystery figure and Connie and Grady are killed by him. With the roster of

IT WILL SCARE YOU
OUT OF YOUR SKIN!
UNIVERSAL
PRESENTS
The Cat Creeps
with LOIS COLLIER FRED BRADY
PAUL KELLY NOAH BEERY, JR.
DOUGLASS DUMBRILLE ROSE HOBART
Screenplay by Edward Dein and Jerry Warner • Original Story by Gerald Geraghty

Lois Collier's broody ingenue takes on spectral dimensions not evident on screen, in this poster for *The Cat Creeps*.

suspects now reduced to just two—Elliot and McGalvey—Nichols sets a trap which closes around McGalvey. After coming out on the losing end of a fistfight with Nichols, McGalvey confesses to murders both old and new. He admits to having killed Eric Goran, a crooked lawyer, in hopes of stealing the man's $200,000 but since Goran had craftily hidden the money, McGalvey ended up with nothing. Connie and Grady learned of McGalvey's crime and bled him white with blackmail for years, so they had to go, too. In the conventional end to this conventional movie, Pidge finds the money in Mrs. Williams' birdhouse, Kyra turns out to be an actress imported by Nichols, Elliot can run for the Senate without fear of scandal, Nichols and Gay wind up in the customary clinch and the creeping cat has kittens.

The Cat Creeps went into production on January 3, 1946, with Howard Welsch and Will Cowan divvying producers' responsibilities, Erle C. Kenton directing and George Robinson acting as director of photography. (Elwood "Woody" Bredell replaced Robinson during the latter stages of production.) The film's screenplay had already been subjected to the sharp scrutiny of the bluenosed Breen Office, who offered their by-now tiresome caveats against character-choking and excessive gruesomeness. Additionally the Breen letter advised that Connie's two uses of the word "witch" be carefully pronounced ("there can be no possible confusion with the unacceptable word 'bitch'"), and that scenes of cruelty to the titular cat be scrupulously avoided. Universal complied with all of the censor's suggestions: the word "witch" was struck from Connie's dialogue, and the Assistant Director's Daily Report officially records that the cat received the same hour-long lunch privileges as the human members of the cast. Scenes of choking were also carefully avoided, although in its haste to comply with that requirement the film carelessly neglects even to tell its audience how Mrs. Williams and Connie are killed.

The Cat Creeps is filled with strange plot glitches of this sort. Although the entire picture revolves around the 15-year-old murder of one Eric Goran, we are told nothing about the man until the last minute of the picture. No one explains what Elliot's connection with Goran was, why Elliot fears the reopening of the case or how Goran, a mouthpiece for bootleggers, happened to hide $200,000 in the rooftop birdhouse of an old lady's island mansion. We learn at the end of the film that Connie has been blackmailing McGalvey for years, yet an earlier scene shows McGalvey and Connie working together in a relatively business-like and convivial office environment. The "trap" that Nichols sets for the killer is a childish and inconclusive one; caught in it McGalvey confesses to the string of murders for no reason whatsoever. What the writers of *The Cat Creeps* lacked in imagination they clearly compensated for with sloppy haste.

Probably the oddest element in the picture is the strange character played by Iris Clive. "Kyra Goran" seems to appear supernaturally on the island, full of dreary prattle about spirits and cats. Parallels with characters from Val Lewton's *Cat People* (1942) are immediately apparent: Kyra initially speaks in an unrecognizable tongue (reminiscent of Elizabeth Russell's brief *Cat People* scene) and makes obtuse references to a cat-worshipping race. Since *The Cat Creeps* was cowritten by Edward Dein, who was an uncredited collaborator on *Cat People,* it seems safe to assume that the Kyra character was part of Dein's contribution. Dein apparently was influenced by having worked with Lewton (*Jungle Woman,* another Universal that carries Dein's name, also boasts several Lewtonesque touches), but was never able to successfully apply what he learned at the RKO B-unit to Universal pictures. There was no point in keeping the Ape Woman off camera throughout *Jungle Woman,* and the introduction of the Kyra character into *The Cat Creeps* only makes a silly picture sillier yet.

Like several of the Inner Sanctums, the story of *The Cat Creeps* builds around a group of basically ordinary people in a realistic environment;

audiences just know instinctively that in this type of set-up, any "supernatural" element that crops up will eventually be exposed as ersatz. There's never any doubt that Kyra will turn out to be a simple red herring; the picture gives this away frequently by showing her conspiratorially schmoozing with Nichols, with whom she's clearly in cahoots. Yet the mature, cosmopolitan characters played by Rose Hobart, Jonathan Hale and Douglass Dumbrille appear to swallow her fantastic claims whole-hog: the cat frightens Hobart into agreeing to confess, and Dumbrille and Hale start following the fleabag around the house expecting to be led to the money. These bogus "paranormal" trimmings are unsuited to the tone of the picture, and detract from the general seriousness of the proceedings.

Apart from this one bizarre character, every other plot ingredient in *The Cat Creeps* has been pretested in scores of features: an obnoxious newsman-hero, a swooning ingenue, a gloomy old house, fleeting shadows, clutching hands and a group of bickering suspects that scatters whenever anything's about to happen. Fred Brady and company respond to screams by bounding up a staircase not *once,* not *twice* but *three* separate times (always viewed from the same prosaic camera angle); every hinge in the place gets a frequent workout. These elements were old hat before pictures began to talk yet *The Cat Creeps* trundles them out for another go-round. It's "Plot #38" for the umpteenth time, and the only concern the makers of *The Cat Creeps* had was exposing just enough film to call it a movie before dumping it onto the public.

What hurts the picture perhaps more than any other factor is the exasperating and unfunny performance of the central player, Fred Brady. Brady's Terry Nichols is a smug, condescending blowhard, a never-empty well of glib, humorless banter. Newsman-heroes have always tended to be an irritating breed in horror films, with Lee Tracy (*Doctor X*) and Wallace Ford (*The Mysterious Mr. Wong*) springing to mind as perhaps the best-known offenders, but Brady, who looks like a cross between Donald O'Connor and Howdy Doody, also rates a spot on that lamentable list. He is a bland and unappealing actor even in his rare serious moments, and it comes as no surprise that his Hollywood career was a short one. Prior to *The Cat Creeps* Brady was a radio writer and actor, and after his inauspicious movie-acting fling he became a screenwriter on pictures like *Champagne for Caesar* (1950), *Hollywood Story* (1951), *Never Wave at a WAC* (1952) and *Taxi* (1953). The character of Pidge, his shutterbug-sidekick, is equally obnoxious, but top-billed Noah Beery, Jr., is a breezier and more personable actor and he comes across far better than Brady despite their similar roles. ("Pidge" is Beery's real-life nickname.) Lois Collier gives her usual near-miss performance while Paul Kelly, Douglass Dumbrille and Jonathan Hale are their old dependable selves. Smoky, the creeping cat of the film's title, caused some minor delays by fixing its gaze on the microphone rather than its trainer (the problem was solved with catnip). Like Fred Brady, Smoky too has gone on to great obscurity.

Rose Hobart was another in the legion of talented actresses that never got a fair shake in Hollywood. A major Broadway actress of the 1920s, she came to Hollywood in 1930 to star with Charles Farrell in Fox's *Liliom.* As a Universal contract player during this early 1930s era, she costarred in a trio of the studio's films as well as working on loanout on pictures at First National and Paramount. (She was strikingly lovely and gave a good performance as Fredric March's fiancée in the classic 1931 *Dr. Jekyll and Mr. Hyde*.) Hobart divided her time between stage and infrequent screen appearances for the balance of the decade, then picked up the threads of her motion picture career in the early '40s. By now she had been reduced by Hollywood to a supporting player, and appeared in mostly routine films. Blacklisted after a brush with the House Committee on UnAmerican Activities, Hobart found that her film career was at an end, although years later she became quite active in television (including a semiregular role on the '60s nighttime soap "Peyton Place"). Still witty and well-spoken in her 80s, she now resides at the Motion Picture Country House in Woodland Hills, California. She was a lovely lady and a very good actress in her day, and it almost hurts to find her in a minor role in a piece of junk like *The Cat Creeps.*

The Cat Creeps wrapped up one day over schedule, with director Kenton pocketing a cool $5,000 for his 13 days of work. Released in the spring of 1946 on a double-bill with *She-Wolf of London,* the film garnered a tepid critical response. Box office receipts were probably not much better.

The film is an eminently forgettable one, not only for fans but even for its cast and crew. Rose Hobart remembers only that she enjoyed working with Paul Kelly, and Edward Dein, who wrote the picture, could recall nothing at all about the experience. Even today the mention of the title prompts horror buffs to think instantly of the 1930 *The Cat Creeps*—a lost film which few if any of them has ever seen!

The Cat Creeps would probably rank with Universal's worst horror films but for a few minor highlights: the spooky shot of the boat arriving at the island, the murder of Paul Kelly and the violent climactic fistfight (both Brady and Dumbrille come away from the brawl with nasty facial gashes). But a minute of worthwhile footage does not compensate for nearly an hour of tiresome gab, endless pussy-footing and repetitious old-dark-house hijinks, and overall *The Cat Creeps* represents just one more nail in the coffin of Universal horrors.

Dressed to Kill (1946)

Released June 7, 1946. 72 minutes. *Produced & Directed by* Roy William Neill. *Screenplay by* Leonard Lee. *Adapted by* Frank Gruber, *from a story by* Sir Arthur Conan Doyle. *Executive Producer:* Howard Benedict. *Director of Photography:* Maury Gertsman. *Film Editor:* Saul A. Goodkind. *Musical Director:* Milton Rosen. *Art Directors:* Jack Otterson & Martin Obzina. *Director of Sound:* Bernard B. Brown. *Technician:* Glenn E. Anderson. *Set Decorators:* Russell A. Gausman & Edward R. Robinson. *Assistant Director:* Melville Shyer. *Dialogue Director:* Raymond Kessler. *Director of Makeup:* Jack P. Pierce. *Hair Stylist:* Carmen Dirigo. *Gowns by* Vera West. *Song by* Jack Brooks.

Basil Rathbone (Sherlock Holmes), Nigel Bruce (Dr. John H. Watson), Patricia Morison (Hilda Courtney), Edmond Breon (Julian Emery), Frederic Worlock (Colonel Cavanaugh), Carl Harbord (Inspector Hopkins), Patricia Cameron (Evelyn Clifford), Tom P. Dillon (Detective Thompson), Harry Cording (Hamid), Mary Gordon (Mrs. Hudson), Topsy Glyn (Kilgour Child), Ian Wolfe (Scotland Yard Commissioner), Lillian Bronson (Tourist), Holmes Herbert (Ebenezer Crabtree), Olaf Hytten (Alfred), Leland [Leyland] Hodgson (Tour Guide), Charlie Hall (Cab Driver).

Artistically, the Sherlock Holmes series was running out of gas, but the faithful still flocked to each new adventure in spite of the repetition of plots and the formulized characters. The ever-loyal audience and the customary low budgets assured a profit for Universal who had every intention of continuing the series. But the twelfth entry, *Dressed to Kill,* was to be the last. Unsurprisingly, the film turned out to be another second-drawer outing, not without charm but certainly lacking in invention.

Julian Emery (Edmond Breon), a well-bred, country-club Londoner, pays a call on his good friend Dr. Watson (Nigel Bruce). Watson cannot fail to notice a bandaged wound on his visitor's forehead. Emery recounts how he was attacked the night before by a housebreaker who absconded with a music box from his sizable collection. The bewildered Emery points out that the crook made off with a box of only marginal value, passing up others worth a small fortune. Sherlock Holmes (Basil Rathbone) suspects that the crime was something more than just a petty theft. When Emery is found murdered in his apartment the next day, the detective initiates a full-scale investigation.

Holmes traces the stolen music box to an auction gallery and learns it was one in a set of three manufactured at Dartmoor Prison. When it turns out that the prisoner who made the boxes is serving a stretch for stealing a duplicate set of Bank of England plates from which five-pound notes are printed, Holmes deduces that the boxes contain a message to the prisoner's accomplices revealing the whereabouts of the missing plates.

The gang includes Hilda Courtney (Patricia Morison), a slinky, mink-clad brunette, the dapper Colonel Cavanaugh (Frederic Worlock), and Hamid (Harry Cording), who works double-duty as their chauffeur and assassin. The trio find themselves competing with Holmes for possession of the complete set of music boxes.

The conspirators nab the detective, shackle him to a pipe and attempt to dispatch him with carbon monoxide, but Holmes escapes in short order. Assembling the last pieces of the puzzle, Holmes concludes that the tune played by the boxes conceals a code. Assigning a letter to each note, the hiding place of the missing plates is revealed: a bookcase in the memorial home of writer Dr. Samuel Johnson. Holmes and the police catch the gang red-handed as they are about to make off with the goods, bringing the detective's last adventure to a close.

Dressed to Kill is far from an underrated picture, but its few agreeable qualities are usually glossed over by reviewers. The film is small-scale and ungimmicky; in fact, it is the most rudimentary of the last group of Sherlock Holmes thrillers. It lacks the stylish visuals of *The Woman in Green* and avoids the novelty settings of *Pursuit to Algiers* (an ocean liner) and *Terror by Night* (a Scotland-bound train). In *Dressed to Kill,* Holmes rarely strays from his old, familiar environs, picking up obscure clues from musical boxes and half-forgotten dance hall ditties. The mystery is commonplace and unspectacular, but there is a certain appeal in the film's simplicity (in many of the best Conan Doyle stories, the detective never even leaves his drawing room). The early reels promise a cozy and reassuring entertainment, but the film soon gets stuck in a rut of cliches. Indeed, *Dressed to Kill* is the most derivative of the Sherlock Holmes adventures; virtually every turn of the plot has been cribbed from a previous entry.

As in *The Pearl of Death,* Holmes and his adversaries are in a dead heat, competing for piecemeal clues concealed in *objets d'art,* all of which fall into the hands of unsuspecting collectors. As in *Sherlock Holmes and the Secret Weapon,* the detective is confounded with a seemingly unbreakable code. Hilda Courtney, like Adrea Spedding (the Spider Woman), is quite adept at using smoke bombs and poison gas against her rivals, and like so many other Holmes villains, has mastered the art of disguise. Following the example of killer Alastair Ramson (*The Scarlet Claw*), she'll get rid of a bothersome witness, in this case a little girl, by trussing her up and leaving her in a closet.

Watson is as inept as ever, but his baby talk somehow provides Holmes with the decisive clue: a mere quote of Dr. Samuel Johnson tips off the detective to the location of the stolen bank plates. The typically over-zealous Holmes outsmarts himself by falling into Courtney's clutches, but her method of disposing of him proves so clumsy and ill-conceived, the detective practically walks away from it. The whole production seems as tired as the overused *Son of Frankenstein* music cues on the soundtrack.

Patricia Morison, the perfect choice for the role of the ruthless Hilda Courtney, is a disappointing *femme fatale* thanks to a script that offers her few

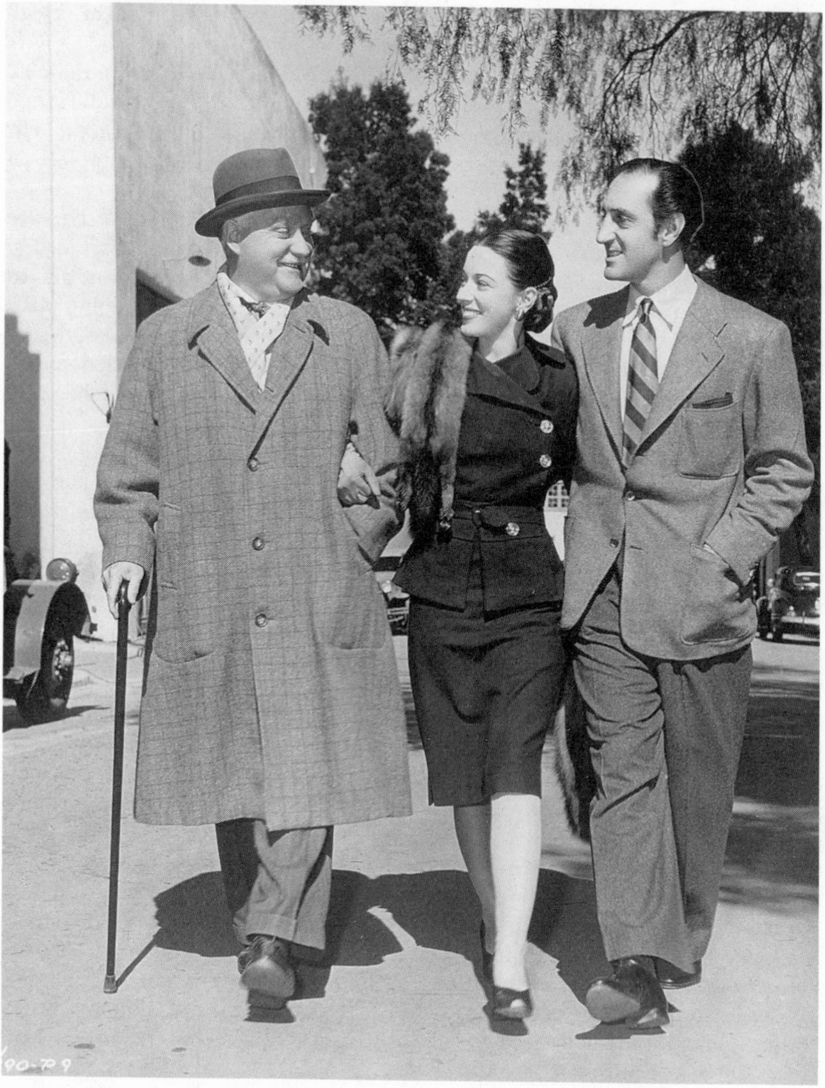

Nigel Bruce, Patricia Morison and Basil Rathbone enjoy a stroll around the Universal lot during the shooting of *Dressed to Kill*.

opportunities. When her big confrontation scene with Holmes finally arrives, she's up against some pretty limp dialogue and an understandably bored sparring partner. More impressive is her disarmingly accurate turn as a frumpy Cockney charwoman who gets the best of Holmes in a particularly witty scene. Leonard Lee's stubbornly uncinematic script probably would have worked better as one of Rathbone and Bruce's Sherlock Holmes radio plays. Director

Roy William Neill concentrates on the details of the story and creates a flavorful and authentic British ambience, reuniting many of the series semiregulars (Frederic Worlock, Olaf Hytten, Leland Hodgson, Holmes Herbert and Harry Cording) for one last fling.

Basil Rathbone's unshakable identification with Sherlock Holmes caused him much personal anguish as well as costing him some choice film roles (he lost out to George Sanders in a principal part in MGM's *The Picture of Dorian Gray*, 1945). Determined to salvage his career, the proud actor bowed out of the series, forcing it to a halt. The move irritated the studio, which owned the rights to the character for three more years. Rathbone's costar, Nigel Bruce, who rather enjoyed being so lucratively typecast, was not amused, either. It is difficult to see how the series could have sustained more entries in any case. The budgets on the Holmes pictures were being gradually cut and inspiration was dwindling fast. More importantly, Universal's upcoming merger with International Pictures sounded the death knell for the studio's B features.

Rathbone's renunciation of his most famous role caused dismay to Sherlock Holmes followers worldwide. Although he would eventually reprise the character on stage, *Dressed to Kill* marked Rathbone's last screen appearance as the detective. The picture's release hardly caused a stir and most critics seemed more interested in griping about the inappropriateness of the title. One wonders where these critics were looking when the sleek, elegantly coiffured Patricia Morison dispassionately retracted her ermine from under the body of poor old Emery (played to perfection by Edmond Breon), and then coldbloodedly walked over him. A very felicitous title, indeed, and far better than its original appellation, *Prelude to Murder*. (In England, the picture was released as *Sherlock Holmes and the Secret Code.)*

Universal's Sherlock Holmes films are a classic case of the whole of a series adding up to more than the sum of its parts. Over the long haul, these erratic but enduring movies will probably outlive Universal's well-regarded Deanna Durbin musicals, the Abbott and Costello comedies and perhaps even their horror classics.

In a cruel twist of fate, the termination of the series did not profit Roy William Neill. In October, 1946, five months after the release of of *Dressed to Kill,* the director died of a heart attack while visiting relatives in England. "I can see traces of the Roy Neill I knew in the Columbia days in the skillful composition and staging of his scenes," Edward Bernds remarked in reference to the Holmes series. "I'm glad that he had a chance to exercise some of his skill, or you can call it artistry, without Columbia's tyrannical production office goading him to speed up, to get the scheduled day's work done any way he could."

The last laugh may be on Universal, who foolishly sold off the rights to their entire Holmes series before their renewed popularity peaked, even allowing a few titles to slip into the public domain. The series is constantly revived on television and among the most popular package of B black-and-white features in circulation. The public domain titles have even been colorized.

To the surprise of no one, Sherlock Holmes not only outsmarted the critics, but the shortsighted Hollywood mavens as well.

The Time of Their Lives (1946)

Released August 16, 1946. 82 minutes. *Directed by* Charles T. Barton. *Produced by* Val Burton. *Executive Producer:* Joseph Gershenson. *Original Screenplay by* Val Burton, Walter DeLeon & Bradford Ropes. *Additional Dialogue for Abbott and Costello by* John Grant. *Director of Photography:* Charles Van Enger. *Film Editor:* Philip Cahn. *Art Directors:* John B. Goodman & Richard H. Riedel. *Musical Director:* Milton Rosen. *Special Photography:* David S. Horsley & Jerome Ash. *Assistant Director:* Seward Webb. *Camera Operator:* Harold Smith. *Sound Director:* Bernard B. Brown. *Technician:* Jack A. Bolger, Jr. *Set Decorators:* Russell A. Gausman & Ruby R. Lovitt. *Dialogue Director:* Morgan Farley. *Gowns:* Rosemary Odell. *Hairstylist:* Carmen Dirigo. *Director of Makeup:* Jack P. Pierce.

Bud Abbott (Cuthbert Greenway/Dr. Ralph Greenway), Lou Costello (Horatio Prim), Marjorie Reynolds (Melody Allen), Binnie Barnes (Mildred), John Shelton (Sheldon Gage), Gale Sondergaard (Emily), Lynne Baggett (June Prescott), Jess Barker (Tom Danbury), Robert Barrat (Major Putnam), Donald MacBride (Lieutenant Mason), Anne Gillis (Nora), William Hall (Conners), Rex Lease (Sergeant Makepeace), Selmer Jackson (Professor Dibbs), Vernon Downing (Leigh), Marjorie Eaton (Bessie), Wheaton Chambers (Guard), Myron Healy, John Crawford (Dandies), Harry Woolman (Motorcycle Rider), Kirk Alyn, Boyd Irwin, Walter Baldwin.

Well, it isn't exactly *Blithe Spirit,* but *The Times of Their Lives* is one of Abbott and Costello's best outings. The story is solid, the look and tone of the film is right, and much of the time it's funny when it wants to be.

The Time of Their Lives was shot when the boys' relationship was at one of its lowest ebbs and their basic formula was beginning to wear thin. Costello wanted to strike out on his own and try his hand at roles rich in Chaplinesque pathos, leaving Abbott in the awkward positon of being a supporting player in one of his own vehicles. In *Little Giant* (1946), the team hardly shared any scenes at all, much to the bewilderment of ardent admirers. The film was profitable but less so than the two's earlier attractions.

The Time of Their Lives continued the pattern, but it's a far more imaginative undertaking. It was the team's last feature before the studio's restructuring and the first to be directed by Charles T. Barton, who stayed on to helm over a half-dozen of the duo's pictures. Beginning his career in vaudeville and stock companies, Barton got his first movie break in two-reel comedies. He became an assistant director for William Wellman, worked on *Wings* (1927), and finally became a full-fledged director at Paramount and later Universal. He kicked off the first of the team's series of horror-comedies, *Abbott and Costello Meet Frankenstein* (1948), and carried on with the much inferior *Abbott and Costello Meet the Killer, Boris Karloff* (1949).

Abbott and Costello's movies were usually afforded leisurely production schedules (by Universal's B standards) to accommodate the boys' legendary gin rummy sessions and their apathy towards learning lines. The studio didn't seem to care as long as A&C continued to make money. *The Time of Their Lives,* which was shot under the title *The Ghost Steps Out,* had a 48-day schedule, spanning March 6 to April 30, 1946.

The bickering Bud and Lou put as much distance between themselves as they could off-camera, and even gave up their card playing. But the production was still faced with a major obstacle. According to *Bud and Lou,* the joint biography by Bob Thomas, three weeks into shooting, Costello phoned Barton with an ultimatum. Unless he switched roles with Abbott, he was off the picture. It was a ridiculous demand even if a single frame hadn't been shot, but with half the film in the can already, it was totally unreasonable. The comedian stubbornly sat it out for two weeks while the frantic company shot around him as much as possible. Finally coming to his senses, Lou returned to the set without explanation and completed the film.

The most charitable excuse was that Lou didn't know a good script when he saw one. For someone eager to develop his character, Costello could have done, and *had* done, a lot worse than *The Time of Their Lives.* The story opens during the American Revolution. Tinker Horatio Prim (Lou Costello) receives a letter of commendation from George Washington. He proudly delivers it to his girlfriend Nora (Anne Gillis), a servant girl in the house of wealthy landowner Tom Danbury (Jess Barker). Nora discovers that her master is actually a traitor to the cause, but before she can act, Danbury abducts her and hides Horatio's letter in the secret compartment of a clock. Danbury's fiancée Melody Allen (Marjorie Reynolds) and Horatio learn of Danbury's treason and set out to rescue Nora, but are pursued by American soldiers. Mistaking the pair for traitors, the troops shoot them down on the spot, dumping their bodies into a well on Danbury's estate. Major Putnam (Robert Barrat) curses their souls to be forever imprisoned on the grounds unless evidence of their innocence is uncovered.

More than 150 years later, the spirits of Horatio and Melody still haunt the grounds. By this time, Sheldon Gage (John Shelton) has rebuilt Danbury Manor, even recovering most of the original furnishings. When the ghosts get wind of this, they frantically search the house to find Washington's letter to Horatio which will free their souls. Horatio's pranks on Gage and his houseguests send them into a panic. A favorite target is Dr. Ralph Greenway (Bud Abbott), a descendant of Cuthbert Greenway, who was Danbury's butler and the ghost's rival for Nora's affections.

Sheldon's girlfriend June Prescott (Lynne Baggett) suggests holding a séance to make contact with the spirits. Emily (Gale Sondergaard) the housekeeper, who happens to be a psychic, reaches not only Horatio and

Melody, but the ghost of Tom Danbury as well. The hiding place of Washington's letter is finally revealed, but there's a hitch: the clock is now in the possession of a New York City museum. Greenway manages to steal it out of the museum but is pursued by the police. After a harrowing car chase, Washington's letter is finally found, freeing the spirits of Horatio and Melody forever.

The Time of Their Lives presented Abbott and Costello with probably the best script of their careers. The boys' "usual" featured a loose storyline upon which they could hang their familiar but expertly delivered routines, occasionally interrupted by a musical act. It was a safe, predictable format but this time around, they had a well-developed plot that afforded them few opportunities for slapsticky diversions. Veteran Abbott and Costello gagster John Grant inserted additional material into the script, but his contribution is probably limited to the slap-in-the-face antics that slow the movie down.

Much of the rest of the picture works extremely well, including some clever bits which required the expert trick work of David Horsley and Jerome Ash to bring off. Costello's ghost, still not used to walking through walls, gets stuck between rooms until he gets a helping hand from Reynolds. In another scene, Costello and Reynolds "walk through each other," swapping clothes in the process.

But the real highlight of *The Time of Their Lives* is the séance scene, which manages to be both funny and genuinely chilling at the same time. An ancient incantation recited by Sondergaard whisks the spirits into the circle. In a startling, creepy moment, Tom Danbury's spectral voice is heard speaking through Sondergaard's lips. As he did in *Abbott and Costello Meet Frankenstein,* director Barton plays the supernatural scenes straight, displaying a genuine talent for the macabre. Barton, who was under contract with the studio through most of the '40s, was never given a full-fledged horror assignment. It's rather a pity, considering directors with little affinity for the genre (Jean Yarbrough and Harold Young come immediately to mind) routinely headed up the studio's monster shows.

As Melody, Paramount loan-out Marjorie Reynolds is a fetching and spirited spirit. The snooty Binnie Barnes is out of place but does a reasonable job as the wisecracking friend of the heroine. Gale Sondergaard is impeccably typecast as the pickle-faced housekeeper, receiving more than her share of barbs. Most quotable is Barnes' line, "Haven't I seen you in *Rebecca*?" which perfectly encapsulates the Sondergaard image. Not to be outdone is Costello, doing a double-take in his first encounter with the actress: "What well did *she* come out of?!" John Shelton and Lynne Baggett are the congenial romantic leads.

The Time of Their Lives doesn't quite hold up to the conclusion; in fact, the last third doesn't seem to belong to the rest of the movie. The business of Abbott walking out of the museum with the concealed clock protruding from underneath his coat is typical movie nonsense, and the climactic car chase is second-drawer slapstick. One is left wondering how an obscure Yankee army officer ever became empowered to invoke such a potent curse. Also, Costello and Reynolds' supernatural powers seem to fluctuate from scene to scene. Supposedly, ordinary mortals cannot hear them, yet Costello "spooks" Abbott by tooting in his stethoscope. (A 1934 Universal comedy titled *Love Birds* had also featured a ghost in a brief comedy sequence.)

The Time of Their Lives has been described as an Abbott and Costello movie for people who don't like Abbott and Costello. The team's departure from their established formula is an auspicious success even if the film didn't set the box office on fire. Nor did it make much headway in courting respect from the gentry of movie critics who either ignored or dismissed it as just another juvenile romp. In their next outing, the boys went back to basics with the conventional *Buck Privates Come Home* (1947), their only sequel. While this was a far more profitable venture, *The Time of Their Lives* is deservedly remembered for presenting Abbott and Costello at their offbeat best.

The Brute Man (1946)

A Universal Picture. Released by Producers Releasing Corporation on October 1, 1946. 58 minutes. *Produced by* Ben Pivar. *Directed by* Jean Yarbrough. *Screenplay by* George Bricker & M. Coates Webster. *Original Story by* Dwight V. Babcock. *Director of Photography:* Maury Gertsman. *Film Editor:* Philip Cahn. *Art Directors:* John B. Goodman & Abraham Grossman. *Musical Director:* Hans J. Salter. *Musical Score:* Hans J. Salter & Frank Skinner. *Director of Sound:* Bernard B. Brown. *Technician:* Joe Lapis. *Set Decorations:* Russell A. Gausman & Edward R. Robinson. *Gowns by* Vera West. *Hair Stylist:* Carmen Dirigo. *Director of Makeup:* Jack P. Pierce. *Dialogue Director:* Raymond Kessler. *Assistant Directors:* Ralph Slosser & Harry Jones.

Rondo Hatton (The Creeper), Tom Neal (Clifford Scott), Jan Wiley (Virginia Rogers Scott), Jane Adams (Helen Paige), Donald MacBride (Police Capt. M.J. Donelly), Peter Whitney (Police Lt. Gates), Fred Coby (Hal Moffat), JaNelle Johnson (Joan Bemis), Beatrice Roberts (Nurse), Oscar O'Shea (Mr. Haskins), John Gallaudet, Pat McVey (Detectives), Peggy Converse (Mrs. Obringer), Joseph Crehan (Police Commissioner Salisbury), John Hamilton (Prof. Cushman), Lorin Raker (Mr. Parkington), Charles Wagenheim (Pawnbroker), Tristram Coffin (Police Lieutenant/Radio Announcer), Jack Parker (Jimmy), Jim Nolan (Police Radio Announcer), Margaret Hoffman (Mrs. Hart), Alan Foster (Jeweler), Cy Schindell, Warren Jackson (Policemen), Martin Skelly (Cab Driver), Danny Jackson (Newsboy), Rodney Bell, Perc Launders, John Roche (Men), Karen Knight, Norma Gilchrist (Women), Mary Ann Bricker (Child), Jim Clark, Joyce Stuart, Carl Anders, Gabrielle Windsor, Paula Gray, Larry Wyle (Students).

Like the Universal horror cycle itself, the careers of all the great Universal horror stars ended under unhappy circumstances. An emaciated Bela Lugosi wound up in Edward D. Wood movies; Karloff hobbled around the superheated sets of *el cheapo* Mexican productions; Lon Chaney, Jr., spent his last days, sick and bloated, working in low-budget independent films; and John Carradine kicked around at the bottom of the barrel for most of the rest of his life.

Rondo Hatton's "bogeyman" career lasted only a scant two years, but even within that short period of time he managed to adhere to what would become the classic pattern. After a "high" of *The Pearl of Death,* a fine film in which his mute character created a tremendous impression, the Glutton of Glands instantly went downhill in lesser movies like *The Jungle Captive* and *The Spider Woman Strikes Back*. But even these thoroughly inferior Universals take on a new veneer of comparative respectability measured against Hatton's final film, *The Brute Man*.

The Brute Man can be looked upon as an unofficial "prequel" to the earlier Hatton film *House of Horrors: House of Horrors* picks up where *The Brute Man* left off, with Hatton's already-notorious Creeper character returning to continue his well-publicized reign of terror. If this was indeed Universal's intention, then *The Brute Man* probably holds the distinction of being filmdom's very first prequel (*Another Part of the Forest,* the 1948 prequel to 1941's *The Little Foxes,* is generally listed as the first prequel). Reference books will continue to spotlight *Another Part of the Forest,* however, as most la-de-dah film historians tend to ignore B-films and the many "firsts" that should be chalked up to these low-budget pictures.

Hatton was signed to play (what else?) the title role in *The Brute Man* on December 5, 1944, although production did not commence until nearly a year later. By the time cameras rolled in November, 1945, Hatton had been joined in the cast by second-feature stalwart Tom Neal and leading ladies Jan Wiley and Jane Adams. Jean Yarbrough assumed directing chores, working from a screenplay that was below par even for minor screen scribes like George Bricker and M. Coates Webster.

A big-city police manhunt is on for the killer of Hampton University Professor Cushman. The killer is the Creeper (Rondo Hatton), a hulking, deformed man who walks to the suburban home of Joan Bemis (JaNelle Johnson) and watches from hiding as the socialite escorts departing guests to their car. After the guests have gone, the Creeper speaks to Joan from the shadows, identifying himself as Hal Moffat—a name Joan dimly recognizes. When he steps out into the light Joan sees his face for the first time and backs away stammering in horror. The Creeper lurches forward and strangles her.

The Creeper later finds himself hemmed in by police in a slum neighborhood. Scaling a fire escape, he breaks into the apartment of Helen Paige (Jane Adams), a piano teacher. Helen, who does not flinch at the Creeper's ugliness, accepts his story that he is being chased by a gang, and stalls the police who barge in and search her rooms. The Creeper gets away.

The next morning, at a local market, delivery boy Jimmy (Jack Parker) is listening to a radio broadcast concerning the Creeper as his boss Mr. Haskins (Oscar O'Shea) arrives. A note slid under the door during the night orders groceries delivered to 23 Waters Street, and Haskins dispatches Jimmy with the parcel. 23 Waters Street turns out to be a dilapidated storage area below the nearby waterfront pier, with the river lapping at the door; it's beyond belief that this dismal hovel would have a mailing address, but it does (and Jimmy knows right where to find it!). Jimmy spies on the Creeper from the shack next door (which *doesn't* have an address), but the Creeper catches on and kills his nosy new neighbor.

At Police Headquarters, Captain Donelly (Donald MacBride) and Lieutenant Gates (Peter Whitney) treat the Creeper's murder spree as a joke. Grudgingly investigating Jimmy's disappearance, they find the boy's body at the Waters Street "address." The Creeper takes his time making an unobserved getaway through the pilings.

A press clipping found in the shack leads Donelly to believe that the Creeper is Hal Moffat, Hampton University Class of 1930. Further investigation leads Donelly to Moffat's old classmates Cliff Scott (Tom Neal) and Virginia Rogers (Jan Wiley), now man and wife. Cliff narrates flashbacks which depict Hal Moffat (Fred Coby) as a handsome young college gridiron hero here involved in a four-pointed romantic triangle with Cliff, Virginia and the late Joan Bemis. Cliff tricked Moffat into giving a wrong answer during an exam, and the late Professor Cushman (John Hamilton) ordered the football star to remain after class. Hotheaded Hal had a fit of pique and shattered a beaker of chemicals which exploded in his face. His glands and nerves—and facial features—were affected by the chemicals, and an embittered Moffat disappeared from the University. After hearing Scott's story, Donelly is convinced that Moffat is the Creeper, that his mind has been affected by his experience and that the Scotts are next on the deformed killer's list.

Meanwhile, the Creeper's thoughts have turned to love. He kills a pawnbroker (Charles Wagenheim) and steals a pin which he presents to Helen Paige. Helen turns out to be blind, which explains a lot, but she takes a liking to her attentive new beau. She tells him that blind people are excellent judges of character, and invites the four-time murderer to drop by as often as he likes.

The picture just goes on and on, from bad to worse to worse yet. Donelly and Gates play gin rummy while the Police Commissioner (Joseph Crehan) implores them to do something about the Creeper case. Helen gives a piano lesson to a brat who's interested only in boogie-woogie. The Creeper tries to figure out a way to get Helen the money for a sight-restoring operation, the last thing in the world you'd think he would want her to have. By this point the 58-minute picture seems like it's been playing for hours.

The Creeper appears at the Scott home and demands their money, but Scott outfoxes the dimwitted killer and shoots him in the hip. The Creeper chokes Scott to death and escapes. He presents the jewels to Helen, telling her to pawn them and use the money for her operation. Helen is picked up by the police when she tries to hock the hot rocks. Donelly tells the blind girl that her boyfriend is the Creeper, knocking her stupid conceit about the judgment of blind people into the proverbial cocked hat. When the Creeper reads in the paper that Helen is cooperating with the police, his twisted mind snaps. He returns to her apartment and silently advances on the unsuspecting girl, strangling mitts extended. Suddenly Donelly, Gates and uniformed policemen burst in and wrestle the killer into submission. For helping them lay their trap, the police arrange for Helen to have her operation.

The Brute Man stands out like a black mark even on a list of Universal's *bad* films. It's a dark, morbid movie which weaves into its seamy story autobiographic details of Rondo Hatton's actual life. Hatton's character is seen in flashbacks as a handsome young football hero, which is precisely what Hatton was in real life, at the University of Florida, before acromegaly set in. Finding actors playing "themselves" is not uncommon (snobs call these "films à clef"): we have John Barrymore (*The Great Profile*), Bette Davis (*The Star*), Hedy Lamarr (*The Female Animal*), Errol Flynn (*The Sun Also Rises*), Judy Garland (*I Could Go On Singing*) and more. But incorporating elements of

Hatton's private life into the *Brute Man* story is just plain sordid, a cruel, tasteless excess which could not have been lost upon the unfortunate actor.

Hatton was by far the worst actor ever to labor in Universal horror films, and *The Brute Man* finds him at his most garrulous. Despite his newspaper background and the reminiscences of people like Martin Kosleck, who remember him as an intelligent guy, its's difficult to see this side of Hatton's personality in his performances. He speaks in a rasping monotone, slurs his lines, gropes for words and often seems on the verge of losing his train of thought entirely; at one point in *The Brute Man* he says *yes* while shaking his head *no,* a bizarre sight. ("His mentality was just—average," says Jane Adams. "He had an awful time remembering his lines.") The screenplay for *The Brute Man* must have been written at a time when Universal still held out hope for Hatton as an actor; it's hard to believe that anybody would write such a dialogue-heavy part for him after viewing his work in *House of Horrors.*

Jane Adams' performance as the naive blind girl is every bit as embarrassing and amateurish as Hatton's work in the film. It's a badly-written role that no actress could have salvaged, but Adams' dulcet singsong delivery, cloyingly sweet demeanor and vacuous stare make this "sympathetic" character almost completely unpalatable. Adams toiled in films only a few more years, apparently throwing in the towel after completing her final film, the Bowery Boys comedy *Master Minds,* in 1949.

Tom Neal was "a strong, healthy, happy-go-lucky exfootball player, exboxer who had a physique that cried for female attention and got it," reminisced Barbara Payton in her autobiography (titled *I Am Not Ashamed* and crammed with 190 pages of reasons why she ought to have been). A reliable B actor, Neal gives an adequate performance in *The Brute Man,* although he looks silly in the sloppy "middle-age" makeup foisted upon him for his role. Neal's acting career collapsed after he beat the bejesus out of actor Franchot Tone, his rival for Barbara Payton's romantic attentions; he became a landscaper, went bankrupt, shot and killed his wife and pulled down a six-year prison stretch. He died of heart failure in 1972, at the age of 58. Pert and pretty leading lady Jan Wiley, who plays Neal's wife, does an equally professional job but has very few scenes and almost nothing to do in them; it isn't surprising that today she hardly remembers being in *The Brute Man* at all.

What hurts *The Brute Man,* more than the atrocious performances of Hatton and Adams, is the unremittingly dismal atmosphere. The film is a bleak world of deformed killers, helpless victims, blind ingenues, dark tenements and squalid waterfronts. There's too heavy an emphasis on the Creeper character, and no hero: just when Tom Neal begins to shape up in the derring-do department, Hatton strangles him with scarcely a struggle. What little comedy relief there is comes from the byplay between Donald MacBride and Peter Whitney, the policemen in charge of the Creeper case. They're a couple of shiftless connivers, more concerned with protecting their cushy jobs than in catching the killer, and the film tries to milk some laughs out of this situation. But there's nothing comical about a police force that can't catch a disfigured killer who boldly walks the streets all night; it's sad, not funny, that MacBride and Whitney can't catch a fugitive so slow that he's nicknamed the Creeper.

Rondo Hatton, *The Brute Man.*

The Brute Man is set up almost like a formula television cop show, bouncing back and forth between the killer enacting his crimes and the police, several steps behind, always missing out on the action. The central portion of *The Brute Man,* where the origin of the Creeper is laid out in comic book–style flashbacks, provides temporary relief from the tedium; these scenes were shot on the thirteenth and final day of shooting, November 30, 1945. It's worth noting that the origin of Dr. Doom, archnemesis of comicdom's *Fantastic Four,* is too similar to the Creeper's to safely chalk up to coincidence.

The depiction of the police force in an unfavorable light probably explains why we never get to know where *The Brute Man* is taking place. Because *House of Horrors* was set in Manhattan it seems safe to assume that *The Brute Man* is, too, but no one in *Brute Man* ever mentions the city by name nor are the newspapers seen in the film identified as New York papers. In fact, *The Brute Man* appears very mixed-up indeed in terms of locale. There are several unmistakable indications that the film is set in a major city (the tenement scenes, the size and operation of the police force, the City Hall bureaucracy) and yet at other points we get the "feel" of a college town. Hatton walks everywhere he goes, from urban-type slums to the neatly-manicured suburban homes of his victims to the ivied walls of his old football university.

For a film that has almost nothing going for it, *The Brute Man* has a surprisingly effective opening. A police broadcaster transmits news of a killing, sparking a minimontage of careening stock-footage squad cars scouring the city's dark streets. Now, in low-key, low-angle photography, we see the dour Hatton prowling the streets, conscious of the wailing police sirens but curiously unhurried. The sound of jukebox music replaces the sirens on the soundtrack as Hatton approaches the Collegiate Cafe, a student hangout where, in striking contrast to the bleak atmosphere that's building, several dozen young people are juking and jiving to the newest swing hit. As the record ends, Hatton saunters up to the window and peers wistfully inside. But his reverie is short: one by one, every head in the cafe turns and the students gape in voiceless horror at the deformed onlooker. Hatton plods away grimly; the silent, slack-jawed students remain rooted in place. It's a great, mood-evoking opener, atmospheric and *noir*ish, but nothing else in the film even comes close to it.

At 58 minutes, *The Brute Man* clocks in as Universal's shortest horror film, although while the damn thing is unspooling it seems every bit as long as a *Son of Frankenstein* or a *Phantom of the Opera*. The film develops with painful slowness, progressing from one killing to the next without suspense or excitement. Hatton's victims are a particularly helpless bunch (an older man, a woman and a kid), and until the picture's midpoint the murders are committed seemingly without reason or provocation. The Tom Neal-narrated flashbacks furnish the Creeper with a motive, but not a valid one: the laboratory accident was no one's fault but his own, and none of his victims deserves their fate.

In a curious twist, *The Brute Man* ended up being released not by Universal but through PRC. In the face of their coming merger with International Pictures, Universal adopted a policy of no-more-B's and *The Brute Man* became a casualty of that edict. The sale of the picture to PRC came at a propitious time for that Poverty Row studio, whose schedule had lagged behind due to the organization of Eagle-Lion on the old PRC lot. By 1946 the quality of Universal's horror films had reached such a low level that there were probably viewers (and maybe even some industry insiders!) who thought that *The Brute Man* indeed *was* produced by the ignominious little studio.

Rondo Hatton shuffled off life's stage February 2, 1946, two months after the completion of *The Brute Man*. The 51-year-old actor died in Beverly Hills, felled by a heart attack brought on by his glandular condition. (From a career standpoint, Hatton probably couldn't have kicked off at a better time; with the horror cycle at an end, it's difficult to think of him as anything but unemployable in postwar Hollywood. He probably would have drifted back to playing bit or extra parts, and might have ended up with a Tor Johnson–style part or two in '50s horror cheapies.) His remains were shipped to Tampa, Florida, and planted under the auspices of the American Legion. Hatton didn't live to see either of his starring films theatrically; both *House of Horrors* and *The Brute Man* were released after his death.

Epilogue

Curt Siodmak was entirely correct when he told us that there is a parallel between time, history and horror movies:

> When we made those pictures throughout the Second World War, we couldn't show an American with a machine gun mowing down five thousand Japanese. Nobody would believe it; it wouldn't work. So we had the Gothic stories...
>
> When the war ended, the bottom fell out of the horror film business. Then, when they began testing the atom bomb, it all started again.

Three-eyed atomic mutations, gargantuan insects and radioactive amoebas were the new stars on the fantastic film scene. Vampires, werewolves and living mummies took a brief hiatus. Occasionally, when one of these old favorites staged a comeback in such films as *The Werewolf* (1956), *The Vampire* and *I Was a Teenage Werewolf* (both 1957), their *raison d'être* was rooted in science, not folklore. The atom became the ultimate monster in this new age of Hollywood horror films. Even Mary Shelley's beloved Monster felt the heat. In 1958's *Frankenstein 1970,* the lab-created human is brought to life with the aid of an atomic reactor instead of good, old-fashioned electricity. On occasion, an old film was repackaged to reflect the changing times (*Man Made Monster* became *Atomic Monster* when Realart reissued it in 1953).

Universal-International was quick to jump on the sci-fi bandwagon, too. Having released two atmospheric but dramatically anemic period horrors, *The Strange Door* (1951) and *The Black Castle* (1952), while polishing off former breadwinners like the Mummy and the Invisible Man in geriatric forays with Abbott and Costello, U-I turned its attention to more topical preoccupations. Richard Carlson stemmed an interplanetary feud in *It Came from Outer Space* (1953). A deadly *Tarantula* (1955), bigger than a two-story house, wreaked havoc on a Southwest desert town. Atomic tests thawed the ice prison that held a mammoth, million-year-old insect in *The Deadly Mantis* (1957). Towering skyscrapers of stone marched across the desert, crushing (or petrifying) everything in their path in *The Monolith Monsters* (1957). And a radioactive cloud reversed the growth processes inside the body of a suburban businessman, changing him into *The Incredible Shrinking Man* (1957).

Earlier in the decade, and at various times throughout the 1930s and 1940s, Universal reissued its vintage horror films through its own distribution channels or via Film Classics, Inc., a minor outfit whose only claim to fame was for releasing the chintzy 1948 Cinecolor dinosaur epic *Unknown Island.* When the outfit was absorbed by Eagle-Lion in January, 1950, the reissuing rights to the Universal shockers was assumed by Jack Broder's Realart Pictures, which played off the films through 1954. Over the next few years, these old favorites made sporadic appearances at occasional Saturday afternoon kiddie matinees and all-night drive-in thrill-o-ramas.

Ironically, it was Great Britain, the nation that was indirectly responsible for putting the freeze on all domestic horror film production in the mid-30s, that revived the ailing genre with an extravagant, handsomely appointed Technicolor shocker called *The Curse of Frankenstein* in 1957. Produced by Hammer Studios and released in America by Warner Bros., it had as much influence in kicking off a new cycle of horror pictures as Universal's *Dracula* had 26 years earlier. Taking full advantage of the relaxed censorial restrictions of the period, Hammer promoted the heretofore repressed sex and gore elements inherent in these films and produced a body of work that swapped subtlety and style for sheer moxey.

The year 1957 proved to be a significant one for horror buffs for yet another reason: Universal sold its first package of classic horror movies to television. Overnight, a whole new audience, many of whom had never even *heard* of Karloff and Lugosi, became addicted to these movies. Not even Screen Gems, the Columbia Pictures television subsidiary that packaged the features under the title "Shock," could have anticipated the tremendous public response that greeted these films as they began their trek across the nation's airwaves in the autumn of 1957. Sensational publicity campaigns, geared to initiate into the world of the bizarrre a television generation bred on "Father Knows Best" and "The Ed Sullivan Show," were launched in five leading markets. In 90 cities across the country, "Shock Theater" (or monickers to that effect) garnered top ratings, giving such nightly institutions as Jack Paar and "The Late Show" a run for their money. Out of this phenomenon emerged a subculture of horror show hosts, kinky farceurs hired by local stations to boost the appeal of the less attractive items in the package. Most of these jesters were fly-by-nighters, but at least one, Philadelphia's Roland (soon to become New York City's Zacherley) attracted a devoted following, branched out into the rock music field, and still turns up occasionally on television retrospectives and college campuses.

Listing 52 features, the original "Shock" catalog may surprise the uninitiated upon first glance. Incredibly, it didn't include *Bride* or *House of Frankenstein,* nor did it boast such indisputably macabre fare as *Black Friday, Captive Wild Woman, The Mummy's Curse* or *The Invisible Man's Revenge.* What it *did* contain was an inordinate number of B's that do not classify as horror films by the furthest stretch of the imagination (*Chinatown Squad, The Spy Ring, Reported Missing, Destination Unknown,* and a number of others).

This first batch of features was so well received that, a year later, Screen Gems picked up a second package of creepies and called it (what else?) "Son of Shock." This streamlined roster of 21 films contained many of the titles that should have been included in the first package, plus a select group of Columbia's own penny-dreadfuls – the Karloff Mad Scientist movies (from *The Man They Could Not Hang* to *The Boogie Man Will Get You*), *Night of Terror* with Lugosi, *Island of Doomed Men* and *The Face Behind the Mask* with Peter Lorre and, on the distaff side, Rose Hobart in *The Soul of a Monster.* (For a title breakdown of these legendary film packages, see Appendix II.)

While the Frankensteins and the Draculas will still be in circulation (presuming, of course, that the negatives remain in printable condition) for quite some time, there's a looming possibility that the minor B's will fall by the wayside within the decade. As television revivals grow increasingly scarce and 16mm screenings remain a luxury for a minority of buffs, home video must bear the burden of keeping these pictures alive. Vast libraries of cassettes containing homemade recordings of these goodies when they were televised on a regular basis are nurtured with loving care, and are supplemented by costly but superior quality prerecorded video tapes and laser discs issued by MCA. Just as the classics of the silent screen have survived through the decades thanks to the support of a legion of admirers, there will always be a dedicated corps of hardcore buffs who'll preserve their collections of Universal Horrors as time marches on.

Appendix I
Universal Serial Horrors

This is a list of every Universal sound serial that features "fantastic" film elements. Edited feature versions of some of these serials were made and distributed by Universal, but we have refrained from listing these "features" in the main section of the book. (The serial was an art form in and of itself; full-blown critiques of butchered serials seemed to serve no function that we could think of.) This appendix is intended only as a quick reference guide for readers interested in delving deeper into Universal's nonfeature SF/horror output.

The Ace of Scotland Yard (1929). Directed by Ray Taylor. Cast: Craufurd Kent, Florence Allen, Herbert Prior, Albert Priscoe, Monte Montague, Grace Cunard. Touted by Universal as the first talking serial, this sequel to the silent chapterplay *Blake of Scotland Yard* (1927) was issued in both sound and silent versions. A valuable ring is targeted by thieves in this borderline-horror mystery. 10 episodes.

Tarzan the Tiger (1929). Directed by Henry MacRae. Cast: Frank Merrill, Natalie Kingston, Lillian Worth, Al Ferguson. Based on the Edgar Rice Burroughs novel *Tarzan and the Jewels of Opar,* this profitable follow-up to the silent serial *Tarzan the Mighty* (1928) pits the Ape Man against slavetraders, jewel thieves and (more pertinently) a spell-casting queen and ugly beastmen. Issued in silent and sound editions (the "sound" version boasts only music, sound effects and a few lip-synched lines of dialogue). 15 episodes.

The Jade Box (1930). Directed by Ray Taylor. Cast: Jack Perrin, Louise Lorraine, Francis Ford, Wilbur S. Mack. Members of an Oriental cult vie with our heroes for possession of a jade box containing a vial that holds the secret of invisibility. What do you mean, you haven't seen it? Silent and sound versions. 10 episodes.

Detective Lloyd (1932). Directed by Henry MacRae. Cast: Jack Lloyd, Wallace Geoffrey, Muriel Angelus, Lewis Dayton. Detective Lloyd battles international crooks and the priests of the Temple of Amenhotep II for possession of a valuable amulet. A death ray and possibly even a ghost figure into this British serial, which is also known as *The Green Spot Mystery.* A 66-minute feature version, *Lloyd of the CID,* was also issued. 12 episodes.

The Jungle Mystery (1932). Directed by Ray Taylor. Cast: Tom Tyler, Cecilia Parker, William Desmond, Philo McCullough, Noah Beery, Jr., Sam Baker. Zungu, a half-man, half-ape creature (played by Baker), buys this

forgotten little epic a spot on our list. Lots of jungle hijinks with everybody seeking a large ivory cache; the ape-man is friendly, and helps our heroes. 12 episodes.

Phantom of the Air (1933). Directed by Ray Taylor. Cast: Tom Tyler, Gloria Shea, LeRoy Mason, Hugh Enfield, William Desmond, Walter Brennan. The MacGuffin this time around is the Contragrav, a device which overcomes the effects of gravity; villain Mason's efforts to steal it are thwarted by "The Phantom," Desmond's remote-controlled plane. 12 episodes.

Perils of Pauline (1934). Directed by Ray Taylor. Cast: Evalyn Knapp, Robert Allen, James Durkin, John Davidson, Frank Lackteen, Pat O'Malley. In Indo-China, an ivory disc engraved with the formula for a deadly gas is sought by Knapp, who's good, and Davidson, who isn't. A walking mummy, unfriendly natives and a henchman named Fang are also on hand. 12 episodes.

The Vanishing Shadow (1934). Directed by Louis Friedlander [Lew Landers]. Cast: Onslow Stevens, Ada Ince, Walter Miller, James Durkin, William Desmond. After an evil political group hounds a man to death through a smear campaign, the man's son (Stevens) vows to get revenge. His arsenal of science fiction-style weapons includes a destroying ray, a vest of invisibility and a robot. Stevens was plenty steamed at Universal for sticking him in this one. 12 episodes.

Ace Drummond (1936). Directed by Ford Beebe & Cliff Smith. Cast: John King, Jean Rogers, Noah Beery, Jr., Guy Bates Post, Arthur Loft, Lon Chaney, Jr. The archvillainous Dragon strives to thwart a globe-girdling airplane service; heroic Ace Drummond (King) strives to thwart the Dragon; atomic ray guns somehow come into play. With a character name like Ivan, Chaney has to be playing a bad guy. King swings "Give Me a Ship and a Song," no doubt a highpoint. Based on the newspaper feature by Eddie Rickenbacker. 13 episodes.

Flash Gordon (1936). Directed by Frederick Stephani. Cast: Larry "Buster" Crabbe, Jean Rogers, Charles Middleton, Priscilla Lawson, John Lipson, Richard Alexander, Frank Shannon. The best-known (but not the best) of all sci-fi serials is also the most expensive (a reported $350,000) serial ever made. Flash (Crabbe), Dale Arden (Rogers) and Dr. Zarkov (Shannon) rocket to the planet Mongo, which is on a collision course with Earth. There, in the course of 13 increasingly juvenile episodes, they encounter monkey-men, shark-men, hawk-men, a dragon-dinosaur (played by Glenn Strange), and various other misfits, all under the baleful eye of the despicable space dictator Ming the Merciless (Middleton). Includes sets and props from *Just Imagine* (1930), *The Mummy, Bride of Frankenstein* and *Dracula's Daughter.* For kids of all ages; others need not apply. An 82-minute feature, *Rocket Ship,* was fashioned; television feature-titles include *Spaceship to the Unknown, Space Soldiers* and *Atomic Rocketship.* Based on the comic strip by Alex Raymond.

Radio Patrol (1937). Directed by Ford Beebe & Cliff Smith. Cast: Grant Withers, Catherine Hughes, Mickey Rentschler, Adrian Morris. Here's a unique ploy: international crooks who want the formula for a new, flexible bulletproof glass kill the inventor and try to adopt his little son. Ought to work.

Buster Crabbe and Jean Rogers on the familiar Frankenstein watchtower set, in *Flash Gordon.*

There's hypnosis somewhere in here, too. Based on the King Features syndicate comic strip. 12 episodes.

Flash Gordon's Trip to Mars (1938). Directed by Ford Beebe & Robert Hill. Cast: Larry "Buster" Crabbe, Jean Rogers, Charles Middleton, Frank Shannon, Beatrice Roberts, Richard Alexander, Donald Kerr. Hey, who's stealing the earth's nitrogen? Flash (Crabbe), Dale (Rogers) and Zarkov (Shannon) trace the culprits to Mars, where the usual pattern of captures and escapes develops. Clay People, Tree People, a Queen of Magic (Roberts) and, of course, our old friend Ming (Middleton) provide menace. Includes a tinted sequence. Whittled-down feature versions: *Mars Attacks the World* (a 1938 theatrical release) and *Deadly Ray from Mars* (TV title). 15 episodes.

Buck Rogers (1939). Directed by Ford Beebe & Saul A. Goodkind. Cast: Larry "Buster" Crabbe, Constance Moore, Jackie Moran, Jack Mulhall, Anthony Warde, Henry Brandon. Buck (Crabbe) and his sidekick Buddy (Moran) go into suspended animation following an Arctic aircrash, reawakening 500 years later to find that the world has been taken over by Killer Kane (played by cheap-thug specialist Warde). Based on novels and a comic strip. All the accouterments of a Flash Gordon serial: spaceships, antigravity devices, ray guns, robots, ad absurdum. Feature versions: *Planet Outlaws* and *Destination Saturn*. 12 episodes.

The Phantom Creeps (1939). Directed by Ford Beebe & Saul A. Goodkind. Cast: Bela Lugosi, Robert Kent, Regis Toomey, Dorothy Arnold, Edward Van Sloan, Eddie Acuff. Boris Karloff made his last serial in 1931 but here's Poor Bela still plugging away. As the antisocial Dr. Zorka, Lugosi manufactures a divisualizer belt, a death ray, a mechanical spider and a big, dopey-looking robot; in Chapter 12 he tries to destroy the world by dropping little bombs out of a biplane. Van Sloan's a baddie, too, and Lee J. Cobb turns up in a bit. Karloff is briefly seen in a snippet from *The Invisible Ray*. Also released as a 75-minute feature. 12 episodes.

Flash Gordon Conquers the Universe (1940). Directed by Ford Beebe & Ray Taylor. Cast: Larry "Buster" Crabbe, Carol Hughes, Charles Middleton, Frank Shannon, Anne Gwynne, Roland Drew. Hey, who's sprinkling Purple Death dust on the planet Earth? Could it be Ming the Tireless (Middleton)? Flash (Crabbe), Dale (Hughes) and Zarkov (Shannon) take another one of their intergalactic jaunts to combat Ming a third and last time. Goodbye and good riddance. Three featurizations too many: *Peril from the Planet Mongo, Space Soldiers Conquer the Universe* and *Purple Death from Outer Space*. 12 episodes.

The Green Hornet (1940). Directed by Ford Beebe & Ray Taylor. Cast: Gordon Jones, Keye Luke, Anne Nagel, Wade Boteler, Philip Trent. The Hornet (Jones) and Kato (Luke), do-gooders forced to work outside the law, use their super-speed car and a gas gun in the war on crime. Anne Gwynne and Alan Ladd have small parts. Based on the popular radio serial. 13 episodes.

The Green Hornet Strikes Again (1940). Directed by Ford Beebe & John Rawlins. Cast: Warren Hull, Keye Luke, Wade Boteler, Anne Nagel, Eddie Acuff. More of the same. Hull's a better Hornet than Jones, but this is still pretty rough going; the '60s television series starring Van Williams and Bruce Lee is a lot slicker and more entertaining all around. 13 episodes.

Bela Lugosi is upstaged by a bilious robot (Bud Wolfe), in *The Phantom Creeps.*

Junior G-Men (1940). Directed by Ford Beebe & John Rawlins. Cast: Billy Halop, Huntz Hall, Gabriel Dell, Bernard Punsley, Roger Daniels, Phillip Terry. The Dead End Kids team with G-man Terry in battling the Order of the Flaming Torch, an anarchist group. Scientific innovations include deadly new high explosives, a wireless detonator and an aerial torpedo. 12 episodes.

Sea Raiders (1941). Directed by Ford Beebe & John Rawlins. Cast: Billy Halop, Huntz Hall, Gabriel Dell, Bernard Punsley, Hally Chester, William Hall, Edward Keane, Reed Hadley. The Sea Raiders, foreign agents led by Keane and Hadley, are saboteurs who run afoul of a band of pugnacious juveniles. SF ingredients include a secret time bomb device and a newfangled torpedo boat. 12 episodes.

Don Winslow of the Navy (1942). Directed by Ford Beebe & Ray Taylor. Cast: Don Terry, Walter Sande, Wade Boteler, Paul Scott, John Litel, Peter Leeds, Anne Nagel, Claire Dodd. A two-way television turns up in this story of Naval Intelligence officer Winslow (Terry) fighting to frustrate the evil plans of the Scorpion, a wily saboteur. One of Beebe's last serial assignments before his long-due promotion to features. 15 episodes.

Gang Busters (1942). Directed by Ray Taylor & Noel Smith. Cast: Kent Taylor, Irene Hervey, Ralph Morgan, Robert Armstrong, Richard Davies, Joseph Crehan. Archcrook Professor Mortis (Morgan) seemingly recruits his gang from the dead, using a death-simulating drug and an antideath treatment. A slightly ghoulish premise and an attractive cast make this one sound like more fun than it probably is. Based on the radio show. 13 episodes.

Junior G-Men of the Air (1942). Directed by Ray Taylor & Lewis D. Collins. Cast: Billy Halop, Gene Reynolds, Lionel Atwill, Frank Albertson, Richard Lane, Huntz Hall, Gabriel Dell, Turhan Bey. All the usual serial gadgetry, plus the added enticement of Atwill as the Japanese head of a sabotage ring. 13 episodes.

The Great Alaskan Mystery (1944). Directed by Ray Taylor & Lewis D. Collins. Cast: Milburn Stone, Marjorie Weaver, Edgar Kennedy, Samuel S. Hinds, Martin Kosleck, Ralph Morgan, Joseph Crehan, Harry Cording. Another great cast in a story of Americans battling fascists for Morgan's Peratron, a device capable of transmitting matter through space. Released in England as *The Great Northern Mystery*. 13 episodes.

Jungle Queen (1945). Directed by Ray Taylor & Lewis D. Collins. Cast: Edward Norris, Eddie Quillan, Douglass Dumbrille, Lois Collier, Ruth Roman, Tala Birell. While the Nazis attempt to sic an African tribe on the Allies, Americans Norris and Quillan fight to keep the peace. Lothel (Roman), the supernatural Queen of the Jungle, uses her unearthly powers to help the Yanks defeat the German agents. 13 episodes.

The Master Key (1945). Directed by Ray Taylor & Lewis D. Collins. Cast: Milburn Stone, Jan Wiley, Dennis Moore, Addison Richards, Byron Foulger. Scientist Foulger's machine, the Orotron, extracts gold from sea water and triggers the expected clashes between lawmen and Nazis. "Lash" LaRue plays Migsy. 13 episodes.

Lost City of the Jungle (1946). Directed by Ray Taylor & Lewis D. Collins. Cast: Russell Hayden, Jane Adams, Lionel Atwill, Keye Luke, Helen Bennett. Warmonger Sir Eric Hazarias (Atwill) hopes to spark World War III using Meteorium 245, a metal defense against the A-bomb. Atwill died during production, materially adding to the depressing atmosphere of an already tepid serial. 13 episodes.

The Mysterious Mr. M (1946). Directed by Lewis D. Collins & Vernon Keays. Cast: Richard Martin, Pamela Blake, Dennis Moore, Jane Randolph, Danny Morton. The villainous Mr. M uses Hypnotrene, a drug which produces a hypnotic effect, in his campaign to steal the newest submarine equipment. Universal's last serial. 13 episodes.

Appendix II
Screen Gems "Shock" Television Packages

Titles not covered in this volume are listed with their year of release and featured stars.

The Original "Shock" TV Package

Dracula
Frankenstein
Murders in the Rue Morgue
The Mummy
Secret of the Blue Room
The Invisible Man
The Black Cat (1934)
Secret of the Chateau
Mystery of Edwin Drood
The Raven
The Great Impersonation (1935)
WereWolf of London
Chinatown Squad (1935, Lyle Talbot, Valerie Hobson)
The Invisible Ray
Dracula's Daughter
Night Key
The Man Who Cried Wolf (1937, Lewis Stone, Tom Brown)
Reported Missing (1937, William Gargan, Jean Rogers)
The Spy Ring (1938, William Hall, Jane Wyman)
The Last Warning (1938, Preston Foster, Frank Jenks)
Son of Frankenstein
Mystery of the White Room (1939, Bruce Cabot, Helen Mack)
The Witness Vanishes (1939, Edmund Lowe, Wendy Barrie)
The Invisible Man Returns
Enemy Agent (1940, Richard Cromwell, Helen Vinson)
The Mummy's Hand
Man Made Monster
A Dangerous Game (1941, Richard Arlen, Andy Devine)
Horror Island
Sealed Lips (1941, William Gargan, June Clyde)
The Wolf Man

Rondo Hatton, last and least of the Universal Horrors.

The Mad Doctor of Market Street
The Strange Case of Doctor Rx
Night Monster
Mystery of Marie Roget
The Mummy's Tomb
Nightmare (1942, Brian Donlevy, Diana Barrymore)
Destination Unknown (1942, William Gargan, Irene Hervey)
Frankenstein Meets the Wolf Man
The Mad Ghoul

Son of Dracula
Calling Dr. Death
The Mummy's Ghost
Weird Woman
Dead Man's Eyes
The Frozen Ghost
Pillow of Death
House of Horrors
She-Wolf of London
The Spider Woman Strikes Back
The Cat Creeps (1946)
Danger Woman (1946, Patricia Morison, Don Porter)

The "Son of Shock" TV Package

Behind the Mask (1932, Columbia, Boris Karloff, Jack Holt)
Night of Terror (1933, Columbia, Bela Lugosi, Wallace Ford)
The Black Room (1935, Columbia, Boris Karloff, Marian Marsh)
Bride of Frankenstein
The Man Who Lived Twice (1936, Columbia, Ralph Bellamy, Marian Marsh)
The Man They Could Not Hang (1939, Columbia, Boris Karloff, Lorna Gray)
The Man with Nine Lives (1940, Columbia, Boris Karloff, Roger Pryor)
Black Friday
Before I Hang (1940, Columbia, Boris Karloff, Evelyn Keyes)
Island of Doomed Men (1940, Columbia, Peter Lorre, Robert Wilcox)
The Devil Commands (1941, Columbia, Boris Karloff, Amanda Duff)
The Face Behind the Mask (1941, Columbia, Peter Lorre, Evelyn Keyes)
The Ghost of Frankenstein
The Boogie Man Will Get You (1942, Columbia, Boris Karloff, Peter Lorre)
Captive Wild Woman
The Soul of a Monster (1944, Columbia, Rose Hobart, George Macready)
The Invisible Man's Revenge
House of Frankenstein
The Mummy's Curse
The Jungle Captive
House of Dracula

Appendix III
Universal Horror Oscars

The following Universal horror films were nominated for Academy Awards in the categories listed. Winners are shown in **bold.**

MUSIC – SCORING

Frank Skinner, *The House of the Seven Gables* (1940)
Edward Ward, *Phantom of the Opera* (1943)

CINEMATOGRAPHY

Hal Mohr, W. Howard Greene, *Phantom of the Opera* (1943)

ART/SET DIRECTION

Alexander Golitzen, John B. Goodman, Russell A. Gausman, Ira S. Webb, *Phantom of the Opera* (1943)
Alexander Golitzen, John B. Goodman, Russell A. Gausman, Ira S. Webb, *The Climax* (1944)

SPECIAL EFFECTS

John P. Fulton, Bernard B. Brown, William Hedgcock, *The Invisible Man Returns* (1940)
John P. Fulton, John Hall, *The Invisible Woman* (1940)
John P. Fulton, Bernard B. Brown, *Invisible Agent* (1942)

SOUND

Gilbert Kurland, *Bride of Frankenstein* (1935)
Bernard B. Brown, *Phantom of the Opera* (1943)

Index

Page numbers in **bold** indicate photographs.

A

B

C

D

E

G

I

M

N

Q

R

S

X

Y

Z